Personality in the Classroom

Motivating and inspiring every teacher and student

David Hodgson

Crown House Publishing Limited
www.crownhouse.co.uk
www.crownhousepublishing.com

First published by

Crown House Publishing Ltd
Crown Buildings, Bancyfelin, Carmarthen, Wales, SA33 5ND, UK
www.crownhouse.co.uk

and

Crown House Publishing Company LLC
6 Trowbridge Drive, Suite 5, Bethel, CT 06801-2858, USA
www.crownhousepublishing.com

British Library of Cataloguing-in-Publication Data
A catalogue entry for this book is available
from the British Library.

Print ISBN 978-184590741-9
ePub: ISBN 978-184590830-0
Mobi ISBN: 978-184590829-4

LCCN 2011940627

Edited by Katherine Bennett

Myers-Briggs Type Indicator® and MBTI® are registered trademarks of The MBTI Trust, Inc.

Thunks® are a registered trademark of Independent Thinking Ltd.

Printed and bound in the UK by
Gomer Press, Llandysul, Ceredigion

Foreword

What kind of student would you be in today's classroom?

To ponder this, try to recall your reactions to assignments, activities and events when you were the age of the students you now teach. Or, if you're a parent, the current age of your children. Or, if you're an administrator, the year you liked most in school. What engaged you so completely that you couldn't wait to return to class? When did you check out by daydreaming, doodling or disrupting others?

Now, with those impressions in mind, visit a few classrooms or look through a sampling of current assignments. Would you be engaged? Better yet, compare your reactions to someone you know who thinks a bit differently than you do. Are your reactions the same or are there some startling contrasts? Chances are, you learn differently.

In this book, David Hodgson masterfully guides us through the unique worlds of sixteen types of teachers and students using the framework of personality type. Jungian type, popularised through the Myers-Briggs Type Indicator® (MBTI®), is an amazing lens for understanding how the people around us are energised, gather information, make decisions, and approach life – all key elements in helping students master not just knowledge but how to learn. Readers will benefit from David's deep passion for educating students and his years of refining workshop exercises and information to make these concepts come alive for adults and students alike.

To discover how this rich theory might help you reach more students, read Chapter 1 to discover your own personality. If you start thinking, 'Oh this is just a horoscope,' choose your four letters. Turn to your type's description in Chapter 2 – and then to the opposite description. For example, if you selected ISTJ (Polar Bear) as your preferences, also read the page for ENFP (Clownfish). Can you see how different they are? Picture what you might experience if taught by a teacher with opposite preferences.

If you still aren't sure that the differences described by type are real, try one of David's great exercises in Chapter 3, with several groups if possible. Both David and I have yet to see adults who engage in these kinds of task conclude anything other than, 'Okay … type is real! My students have incredibly different needs!'

Then, immerse yourself in what David has to say with a pen or notebook or highlighter, whatever tool will help you mark what surprises you. Bring to mind a child whom you've struggled to reach or teach. Where might your personalities be the same? Where might they be different? Which of the tips found in these pages might be worth a try? This isn't about labelling a child, but rather considering new strategies that wouldn't work for a student like you but just might be the answer for someone with a very different approach to life.

I've been working with type for over twenty years, and the more research I gather, the more I'm motivated to help educators grasp these natural differences and the impact they have in the classroom. For example, my research – filming students completing the same maths tasks – shows that while the students that David refers to as Bears and Cats need pictures and manipulatives to master the big concepts of mathematics, the Birds and Sea Animals are more trustful of abstract numbers. And, while a few types love to complete multiple practice problems when mastering a new concept, others actually do *worse* the more they practice. My colleague Dario Nardi, a professor at University of California, Los Angeles, found that the brains of two types (Hodgson's Lions and Panthers) actually show more brain activity when looking out the window than when doing traditional classroom seatwork and problem sets. Their brains need action to engage! Students are truly wired differently.

When people say, 'Why can't we go back to the good old days where students simply paid attention and learned what they were taught?' I gently remind them that those days never existed. Fifty years ago, students frequently opted out of traditional schooling to pursue the trades or to start their own businesses. Now, without a diploma, those options aren't available.

Furthermore, it's no longer enough to help students master what is taught. Why? Roland Barth, founder of the Principal's Center at Harvard, points out that in the 1970s, students finished Year 12 with about 75% of the knowledge they would need for the rest of their lives. Now the estimate is 3% because knowledge constantly changes. It's imperative that we graduate students who are lifelong learners, who enjoy gaining new insights and knowledge enough to pursue it on their own.

How does type fit in? If we don't meet students' needs, we aren't supporting them in becoming the best scholars they can be. They may survive, but they won't thrive as lifelong learners. As Chapter 1 explains, the lens of type isn't about labelling or boxing students in, but rather about understanding and supporting their natural pathways for development and growth. While millions of people worldwide have been 'typed', that's different from delving deeply and applying the theory. This book makes it easy to do just that.

You might start by considering the needs of one student, as suggested above. With an older student, let them select their preferences. Then, talk about your similarities and differences. How might each of you adjust to achieve more success? Or, try one of the basic strategies, such as altering 'wait time' (described on pages 62–63). Some experts estimate that it takes at least six tries for teachers and students to get used to any new techniques, so give it time.

Choose your own way to start, but dig in with David as he provides insightful stories, tools for sorting your preferences, descriptions that articulate your own and other's approaches to school and practical ideas you can use immediately – all flowing from his deep passion to make the framework of type as useful to you as it is to the countless teachers and students he has trained. Enjoy!

Dr Jane Kise

Acknowledgements

Thank you to all the teachers and students I've worked with over the past twenty-five years who have helped me better understand type theory and human nature. We are an amazing and silly species. Having fun together under the name of Inset or training is always a pleasure and a privilege. To paraphrase an old joke: sharing the personality type model is the most fun you can have with your clothes on. A special thanks to Crown House Publishing, especially David, Caroline and Tom, and Katherine Bennett for their support in pulling this book together.

I'd also like to thank Jane Kise for her encouragement and support. She is an inspiration to me and many others in the calm, warm and clear way she advocates and champions type in the classroom and beyond.

Contents

Part 1

Chapter 1
Personality Types and Preferences

In this chapter:

- **Learn about personality type theory**

- **Discover your own personality preferences and type**

- **Find out how type theory can be used to transform education**

If we all knew this stuff we would change the world.
Janice, head teacher, South Wales

If we all knew this stuff we would change the world.
Janice, head teacher, South Wales

This is the kind of Inset feedback I like. If you're not in teaching to change the world you shouldn't be a teacher. This book is designed to help you change the world, one child at a time, by helping you better understand yourself and your students.

Let's start by understanding yourself, by identifying your preferences and strengths using the personality type model.

How would you define personality?

You may like to think about it for a minute or two. The definition of personality best suited to appreciating the type model, and therefore the definition applied in this book, is: *The underlying characteristics that make us who we are that are pretty stable over time.*

Essentially, personality is the stuff about us that doesn't change on a day-to-day basis. Mood and behaviour can change quickly. Skills can be developed over hours, weeks or years. Personality is the stuff underneath that remains relatively stable: the qualities that are similar when we're 15, 30 or 65. Examples of stable traits include impulsiveness, shyness or daydreaming. We can change our behaviour. One day we can be adventurous and the following day play safe. By developing skill we gain more flexible behaviour and this is a fantastic thing to do, as it invites us to embrace more choice and control in our lives.

So think of personality as our default position – the core essence of who we are when we look beyond the weather and our mood. This is important because if there are bits of us that are pretty constant throughout our lives they can help us understand ourselves and others better. They can guide us to wiser decisions.

Climate is like our personality. Weather is like our behaviour. Sunshine or drizzle is like our mood. Climate doesn't predict the weather each and every day. It doesn't guarantee sun or rain. But it does provide a useful overall description that informs our wardrobe choices. We know to take more t-shirts than jumpers on holiday to Jamaica due to our knowledge of climate. Similarly, personality type will not predict the behaviour of each student during each lesson but it does help teachers prepare and perform most effectively in the classroom.

Are you ready to identify your own personality preferences?

Your mission is to identify which of the following opposites are your preferences. If you access a state of benevolent scepticism you can assess your preferences quickly using the word clouds that follow on pages 112–115. If you'd like a little more detail this is provided on pages 4–11. If this still isn't enough the frequently asked questions about type on pages 18–23 are designed to reassure you (or doubting colleagues you later seek to convert to using the type model within their work). If you are already familiar with type through the Myers-Briggs Type Indicator® (MBTI®) or the many other incarnations of Carl Jung's work on personality types you can skip merrily past this section altogether.

One who knows their opponent and knows themselves will not be in danger in a hundred battles. One who does not know their opponent but knows themselves will sometimes win, sometimes lose. One who does not know their opponent and does not know themselves will be in danger in every battle.

Sun Tze, *c.*500 BC

stand out **confident** exude

limelight **E** action **outside**

assertive outgoing not quiet

movement

contribute to breadth interrupt

show

concentration reflection gentle

quiet **calm** **inside** serene

part of the crowd **I** still depth

watchful **good listener** blend in

careful

absorb take in

What are your personality preferences?

Although we can write with both hands we tend to just use one – our preference. It is the same with four chunks of personality. We could use both opposites but we don't, we mostly use just one. Of the five pairs shown here, which one is your preference, the one you tend to use most? Remember, neither is better or worse – just different.

1. From where do you gain your energy – inside or out?

E	Your Preference	I
I think out loud	☐ or ☐	I think before I speak
I generally act quickly	☐ or ☐	I generally act carefully
I'm a good talker	☐ or ☐	I'm a good listener
I prefer to stand out	☐ or ☐	I prefer to blend in
I tend to work best in groups	☐ or ☐	I tend to work best alone

On balance?
I'm more **E** ☐ or I'm more **I** ☐

At their best E's tend to be
• confident
• assertive

Famous E preferences
• Victoria Beckham
• Homer Simpson

At their best I's tend to be
• careful
• good listeners

Famous I preferences
• David Beckham
• Marge Simpson

E = External

Gain energy from people or things around them – recharge their batteries by being around people or being involved in activities.

I = Internal

Gain energy from inside themselves – recharge their batteries by spending time alone.

How to spot an **E** or **I**?

Listen to someone in a conversation. If they often interrupt they're probably **E**. If they are often interrupted they're probably **I**.

intent

facts

direct **practical** real sequences

S **grounded**

literal **step-by-step** realism

actual

remember things utility **tactical**

present

vision **future** scatterbrain

ingenious **random** **possible** global

concoct **N** original

metaphor **imaginative** **creative** **invent**

strategic

2. How do you take information in – detail/facts (S) or big picture/ideas (N)?

S	Your Preference		N
I look for the facts	□ or □	I look for possibilities	
I look for details	□ or □	I look for patterns	
I focus on what works now	□ or □	I focus on how to make it different	
I prefer applying what I've learned	□ or □	I prefer learning new things	
I tend to go step-by-step	□ or □	I tend to join in anywhere	

On balance?
I'm more **S** □ or I'm more **N** □

At their best S's tend to be	**At their best N's tend to be**
• practical	• imaginative
• realistic	• creative
• sensible	• dreamers
Famous S preferences	**Famous N preferences**
• Shrek	• Cinderella
• James Bond	• Dr Who

S = Facts

Take information in by looking at the detail. Tend to have 'their feet on the ground'. Good at thinking 'inside the box'.

N = Ideas

Take information in by looking at the big picture. Like to think about how things could be changed. Good at thinking 'outside the box'.

How to spot an **S** or **N**?

Ask someone to look out of a window and describe what they see. If they describe with details and facts they're probably **S**. If they describe by interpreting and making stories about the scene they're probably **N**.

compassion

softer **friendly** **caring** sympathise

F

passion emotion

empathy

subjective

values

feedback taken
as criticism

criticism taken
as feedback

objective

justice

T

scrutinise

harder

principles **candid** **logical** thick-skinned

analyse ethics

3. How do you decide things – with your head (T) or heart (F)?

T	Your Preference	F
I generally follow my head	☐ or ☐	I generally follow my heart
I ask 'is it the right decision?'	☐ or ☐	I ask 'how will it affect people?'
I can give and take criticism quite easily	☐ or ☐	I tend to avoid giving or receiving criticism
I tend to tell it how I see it	☐ or ☐	I tend to be careful about saying things that might upset someone
I am more likely to be called 'hard'	☐ or ☐	I'm more likely to be called 'soft'

On balance?
I'm more **T** ☐ or I'm more **F** ☐

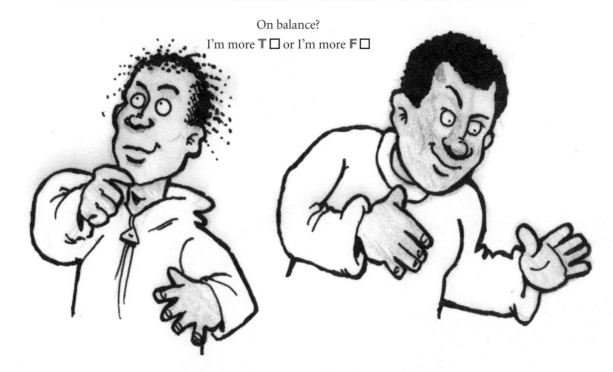

At their best **T**'s tend to be	At their best **F**'s tend to be
• logical	• friendly
• objective	• sympathetic
• honest	• caring
Famous T preferences	**Famous F preferences**
• Richard Branson	• Jonathan Ross
• Katie Price	• Cheryl Cole

T = Objective

Make decisions by doing the 'right thing' as they see it. Like fairness.

F = Subjective

Make decisions by considering how something will affect people. Like to be liked.

How to spot a **T** or **F**?

When in a conversation if someone tends to disagree with the person they're talking to a lot, they're probably **T** but if they tend to try and agree and see the other's viewpoint, they're probably **F**.

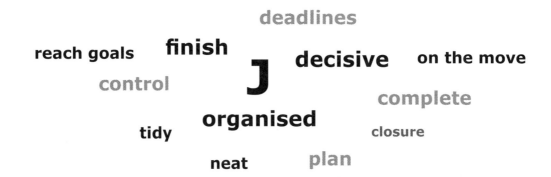

4. What's your attitude to life – spontaneous (P) or a planner (J)?

J	Your Preference			P
I like to plan and organise	☐	or	☐	I like to wonder how things will turn out
I like writing lists	☐	or	☐	I don't like writing lists
I like things tidy	☐	or	☐	I don't mind things untidy
I prefer it when I've finished a task	☐	or	☐	I prefer it when I've started a task
I usually work at a steady pace until the job is done	☐	or	☐	I often work at the last minute to get things done

On balance?
I'm more **P** ☐ or I'm more **J** ☐

At their best **J**'s tend to	At their best **P**'s tend to be
• get things done	• flexible
• be on time and on schedule	• open minded
Famous J preferences	**Famous P preferences**
• Delia Smith	• Jamie Oliver
• Will Smith	• Bridget Jones

J = Plans

J behaviour is organised and planned. Employers tend to like **J** behaviour.

P = Options

P behaviour is flexible and spontaneous.

How to spot a **J** or **P**?

Ask someone if they like to get things finished and sorted before they relax or can they relax anytime? First answer and they're probably **J**, second answer and they're probably **P**.

Your preferences:

I or E

S or N

F or T

J or P

The Perfect Teacher

If we were to create a perfect teacher to be cloned and deployed to classrooms across the land, after a kiss on the forehead from the Education Minister, what would they be like?

E

Classroom charisma – able to engage and inspire classes, visible, stimulating, commanding and orchestrating the energy of a group like a lead singer on stage at glastonbury.

I

Classroom control – able to calm a whole group or individual student quickly to create a clear focus and united purpose, able to set stretching personalised tasks and assignments for students that consolidate learning.

S

Real and relevant learning – breaks subjects and topics into discrete coherent chunks that are easily taught, assessed and evaluated.

N

Innovative and inspiring learning – brings curriculum to life using their imagination and ingenuity.

F

Encouraging and nurturing style – motivates by getting to really know their students, developing strong personal relationships using empathy.

T

Firm and fair style – motivates by setting transparent objectives and standards and interpreting these consistently and candidly. Develops student competence and confidence and maintains discipline.

J

Organised and well-planned inside and outside the classroom, completing goals to agreed deadlines.

P

Flexible and adaptable, open to new suggestions from their students and colleagues.

+

An enthusiastic and positive attitude which seeps into the classroom walls, infecting students with self-assurance and aspiration.

Does this teacher exist? Is this a perfect teacher?

Personality type theory implies that every teacher naturally possesses an innate preference for half of the above characteristics. They develop naturally with classroom experience. Great, we're all halfway to outstanding! Fortuitously, the other half can be learned and honed.

Chapter 1 guides you through all eight preferences, helping you to confirm your four natural preferences and to explore the four that can be developed through extra practice.

Sign your name twice in the boxes below, on the right with your right hand and on the left using your left hand.

Your four natural preferences (e.g. **ESTJ**) are the equivalent of your signature using your preferred hand. The opposite pairings (i.e. **INFP**) are equally useful in the classroom and life generally but are less well developed – the equivalent of your signature using your other hand. With practice we can develop skill using all eight letters. There are activities in Chapter 3 which help you develop all eight letter preferences so you can be a great teacher to all of your students. You can also share the model and activities with your students because the above outline for the perfect teacher looks pretty close to a description for the perfect student too. Together you could create the perfect classroom.

What are your top ten classroom challenges? These are the top ten suggested by teachers during the Inset sessions I deliver: (1) stress, (2) workload, (3) results, (4) behaviour, (5) lack of motivation, (6) stretching all students, (7) pushy parents, (8) chaotic home lives, (9) Michael Gove and (10) boredom.

Factors *outside* our control (e.g. the government, education policy, school leadership, Ofsted, exam results, curriculum, people – parents and colleagues) are not worth the worry. Instead, look at ways you can achieve your own objectives as a professional within the framework imposed by others. Doctors, care workers, fire-fighters (basically everybody doing a really worthwhile job) have to do this. Stress can be understood through the lens of type.

If you'd like to change the imposed framework, that will be achieved outside of the classroom – and outside of the scope of this book. Thinking about the Secretary of State for Education will not help you when you're in the classroom.

The factors you can control are *inside* the classroom (e.g. stretching all students, personalisation, students' (poor) behaviour and lack of motivation/boredom). The type framework helps teachers inside the classroom by strengthening personal relationships – the foundation of all great teaching. Personality type can at worst alleviate the top ten challenges, and at best transform and reinvigorate your classroom experience.

To remind yourself of the real reason you became a teacher think of the last time you inspired a young person. I'm hoping you can think of a recent example. If not you really do need this book.

Personality revealed?

Humans have been trying to understand what makes us tick long before psychologists joined in. However, the contribution of psychologists has been incredibly useful, especially in the past hundred years or so. Most researchers agree that personality can be broken down into separate and specific chunks that vary between individuals. There is fairly strong agreement that there are five big chunks of personality as follows:

1   **Openness:**

    The degree to which we are open-minded, abstract, divergent and global *or* grounded, traditional, convergent and specific in the way we make sense of our environment. This correlates with **S** and **N** type preferences.

2   **Conscientiousness:**

    The degree to which we crave order, self-control and conformity *or* flexibility, impulsiveness and options in our approach to life. This correlates with **J** and **P** personality type preferences.

3   **Extraversion:**

    The degree to which someone is outgoing, lively, bold and seeks to impose their thoughts and ideas on their immediate environment *or* is reserved, reticent, private and self-contained. This aspect of personality is generally easy to spot and has been one of the most studied areas of personality difference. This correlates with **E** and **I** type preferences.

4   **Agreeableness:**

    The degree to which we make decisions based on subjective *or* objective considerations is linked to **F** and **T** personality type preferences, as well as feminine and masculine roles and archetypes.

5   **Neuroticism:**

The degree to which we are anxious in response to our internal wiring (some people are tense, apprehensive 'worriers' and afraid of their own shadow while others are unperturbed and adaptive to stressors) and aroused by external events (the setting for our fight-or-flight response). Although important, this factor is not linked to type theory. For strategies on how to control this aspect of personality refer to my book *The Buzz* (2006). It is important that teachers attempt to appear low on neuroticism during lessons, despite the intense pressure that can engulf classrooms so quickly. It is unlikely that a highly strung and fretful teacher (or parent) can create a relaxed and positive learning environment suitable for fostering resilient young people. The ability to treat change as a challenge to be overcome by generating additional choices is an attitude children learn mostly by modelling (copying) the adults they encounter.

There are two different approaches used by psychologists to describe these five chunks. The *trait* approach measures chunks, usually by asking a series of questions and comparing the answers to those of large sample groups. People are then given their 'score' so they can be placed on a scale. For example, someone could be low on extraversion and high on neuroticism compared to others of the same age and gender – and then they go home and quietly worry about their feedback, especially if they also score high on the conscientiousness chunk! This approach is used in recruitment and it can be applied either benignly or ominously depending on the skill and intent of the professional clutching the test results.

The other approach is *type*. This is based on the idea that we develop an either/or preference for one type or another, as we do with our left or right hand. Although we can use both we have a definite preference. Remember, no type is better than any other type but we can all be better within our own type profile. This simple concept is at the heart of type theory and must be grasped and welcomed for the model to make sense. If not, you'll be playing the role of cynical old buffer sat at the back of my Inset grumbling behind a raised copy of your newspaper of choice and unwilling to entertain a new idea – a dangerous mindset for teachers. Treat the concept as you would a toddler learning to walk. With encouragement and practice the child will not only be walking but will soon run, jump and shimmy like a professional dancer on *Strictly*.

The nature versus nurture debate has thankfully moved on and most research confirms that both play their part in child development. How they interact is the current line of enquiry. In my experience parents offer a useful insight. Those with one child sit on the nurture side of the fence. They convince themselves their child is so lovely and gorgeous due to the extensive hours of care and support they diligently provide around the clock. Parents with more than one child are inclined to sit (exhausted) on the other side of the fence. They notice that their children are so different in personality that it can have little to do with nurture. They tend to think their children were basically born the way they are and parenting has far less to do with who they become than we'd like to believe. I'm not arguing that good parenting isn't crucial to a child's development; it is more to do with how to help children become aware of their strengths and apply these in the world for success in life rather than actually influencing underlying personality traits. Effective parents influence by living positive values such as respect, tolerance, bravery, compassion and so on, that their children will absorb and apply; they cannot mould personality traits directly and expect a healthy outcome.

Good parenting is also crucial in helping our children understand their weaknesses and how these can be overcome through the development of skills or behavioural flexibility. Good parenting provides the framework – like a climbing frame or trellis – of positive identity, values and beliefs that allow the child's personality to develop strongly and flourish around the strong structure.

This is the way nature and nurture can both play their part. Freud referred to parenting as the impossible profession. Personality type is one tool that helps both parents and their children better understand each other.

Personality in context

Over the past twenty years I've spent an increasing amount of my time in schools and colleges with teachers and other professionals learning how to apply the type model to enhance the quality of experience in the classroom, staffroom and beyond. This book, which looks at type from the viewpoint of the adult, complements *The Buzz*, which peered in through the eyes of the teenager. So welcome aboard.

At the start of the training sessions I deliver I often ask 'How do you feel right now?' I generally receive the following responses:

> *'I'm a bit cold.'*
>
> *'I'm a bit tired.'*
>
> *'I'm a little nervous about what I'm expected to contribute to this session.'*
>
> *'I'm looking forward/not looking forward to putting my own thoughts across.'*
>
> *'I'm wondering what I've done with the last thirty years of my life.'*

None of these answers are more wrong or right. They're all acceptable. But it would be nice to have a method to better understand them.

On the following page you'll see how we can structure these replies.

We function at different levels, stacked like the Russian dolls above, all equally important and valid. We mostly express ourselves and interact with the world around us at the level of behaviour. Our identity and personality are filtered through our behaviour. They may drive it but they are mostly unseen.

When we see cars whizzing past below us, when we watch from a service station bridge, we don't see the driver. We see the car and can react to it, but it is the driver who is in control. The car we see is like our behaviour and our personality is like the driver. Our skill determines the success we achieve with our behaviour.

It is worth identifying at which *logical level* a student is operating as it has an enormous impact in the classroom. If everyone is focused on their environment – because it too hot or too cold or there is noise pollution – then there is little chance of any real learning taking place. It's possible but unlikely. When the roof of your Portakabin classroom is straining under the weight of snow and you can see freezing breath trails swirling around your students like a load of forty-a-day smokers, you may need to adjust your learning outcomes. I've managed to deliver a great session in a dinner hall just after lunch with the sound of kitchen staff cackling away behind a rattling metal screen as pots and pans were being cleaned and put away. I've also delivered average sessions in state-of-the-art theatres. However, most learning will occur when teacher and students are united at the level of skill and behaviour in a way that is consistent with individuals applying their own personality strengths and identity to the skill or knowledge being developed. To foster learning we should build up, develop and praise positively the identity and personality of our students. Criticism of skill and behaviour is OK but don't 'dis' identity.

This rule applies in the staffroom as well as the classroom; criticise behaviour not personality or identity. I recently overheard a teacher sharing the following with her colleagues in the staffroom: 'They (the Head of Department) said my *lesson* wasn't good enough. I told her I was doing my best. She's never liked me or appreciated the effort I've put in over the years. It's soul-destroying.'

The teacher had been given feedback about the *lesson* she'd delivered. The assessor may have offered a suggestion as to how to improve one tiny bit of the lesson. This is feedback at the level of *behaviour*; not skill, as a lack of skill would result in recurring mistakes or problems in the classroom. Skill can be developed if the area of skill lacking is first identified and then rectified. Occasional problems in lessons are likely to be behavioural level issues, often identified with phrases such as 'Sometimes a lesson just goes off track', 'Some classes are great and others just never seem to gel for me' or 'I can teach most of my subject really well but dread such-and-such a topic because it never works'. The teacher was interpreting the feedback as an *identity* level criticism, which is hard to take because it is an assault on us as a person.

I've heard teachers make the same mistake in classrooms with comments such as: 'You're a terrible year group!' or 'You're the worst class I've had since 1983!' The mistake can be rectified by communicating at the level of *behaviour*. Behaviour is easier to influence than identity, offering students and teachers a chance to change and improve – which is surely one of the main purposes of being at school. A probation officer recently shared a potent example of businesses positively influencing behaviour. Their intervention resulted in the most impressive reduction in city centre violence at closing time ever recorded. As large groups of young people jostled and rutted for taxis at 2 a.m., lolly-pops were handed out. Young men with lollies in their mouths are immediately more quiet, calm and perhaps whisked back to warm childhood memories. Don't try this if you value your 'Healthy School' status!

Frequently asked questions about type

How should I start using this book?

Type can be utilised in many ways. Some teachers use it to better understand the relationships they have with their students and their parents as well as partners and friends; and why not, type is a tool used by marriage guidance counsellors across the globe. Here are six suggestions on how to get the best out of type and this book. These recommendations are ideally explored in the sequence suggested:

1   Audit, understand and develop own personality and teaching style (Chapters 1 and 2).
2   Audit, understand and develop student personality and classroom style (Chapters 2 and 3).
3   Learn how you and your students can develop all eight preferences (Chapter 3).
4   Use type model to enhance your leadership skills (Chapter 4).
5   Use type resources to bring the model to life in classrooms and staffrooms (Chapter 5).
6   Audit, understand and develop better relationships with individual students (Chapter 6).

Isn't this just pseudoscience/pop psychology?

Physicists use *effective theory* to make sense of incredibly complicated systems. It is a framework for modelling observable phenomena without describing in detail all underlying processes and influences. Personality type is the psychological equivalent to effective theory; it is a valuable working model which can still acknowledge deeper unseen complexity.

> *Science is what you know. Philosophy is what you don't know.*
>
> **Bertrand Russell**

Psychology is about halfway between science and philosophy.

> *Science transformed medicine around one hundred years ago, now it can transform educational practice.*
> **Royal Society, *Neuroscience: Implications for Education and Lifelong Learning***

Science has regularly been misinterpreted on its way into the classroom over the past twenty years. However, some insights can positively inform classroom practice. Specifically, the plastic brain (it has the capacity to develop throughout our lives) and education as a powerful form of cognitive enhancement are concepts to warm every teachers' and students' heart as well as brain.

> *Each person constitutes an intricate system operating at neural, cognitive, and social levels, with multiple interactions taking place between processes and levels. It is a mistake to regard biological predispositions as deterministic, their impact is probabilistic and context dependent. If biological differences are not taken into account important opportunities to optimise learning will be missed.*
> **Royal Society, *Neuroscience: Implications for Education and Lifelong Learning***

Personality is part of this intricate system.

Isn't this like astrology?

Type does divide people into groups sharing similar traits and characteristics; as does astrology. Thereafter the similarities end. Personality type is based on each person answering questions about their own preferences of behaviour to match underlying personality traits, whereas astrology is based on the random position of planets at our time of birth. There is no convincing evidence to validate astrology.

> *Astrologers can produce any old tosh and, providing it is sufficiently vague and flattering, the majority of people will tick the 'highly accurate' box.*
>
> **Richard Wiseman, *Quirkology***

The psychologist Hans Eysenck discovered that people who believe in astrology confirm the accuracy of its predictions, whereas for non-believers the astrological interpretations are bereft of accuracy. Astrology offers useful insights into the dangers of describing people types. A combination of Barnum statements (general and vague) and flattery (positive traits) can produce convincing personality descriptions. In the personality descriptions offered in this book positive traits relating to each type are stressed but negative characteristics are tactfully paraded, particularly when highlighting communication problems that can understood and minimised by the application of type theory.

Student Activity: **Profiling**

An interesting activity to introduce personality profiling to a group of students is to challenge them to write a description that is sufficiently vague and flattering for everyone in the class to agree it's a good personal fit. For example: 'You are self-critical and often tough on yourself. Other people have more faith in you than you sometimes do in yourself. You know you have potential but may not be sure how best to realise it. You've made some mistakes in the past but do know the difference between right and wrong.'

Isn't is dangerous and/or limiting to label people?

Yes. Superficially it might look like *typing* people is designed to pigeonhole or categorise but that is to misinterpret or to apply the model poorly. Type is a great way to describe and explore some of the prominent differences between individuals. Before bringing this into your classroom spend at least a term getting to understand your own type. Consider and apply type in your own life inside and outside of the classroom. Introduce changes to your practice based on individual letter pairs one at a time. Read additional books (see the Bibliography) or attend type-based courses (more information is available from www.thebuzzbook.co.uk).

When you introduce type to students adhere to the following guidelines:

1. Choice and control is with the student. They decide their preferences, not you; you explain and support. If the student does not want to reveal their thoughts/preferences do not push them. They will if and when they're ready.

2. Describe clearly to students why you're introducing type and clarify how you intend to use it. Keep it within your classroom unless other teachers share your enthusiasm for type and have positive reasons for introducing it. If you intend to share a student's type with others make this clear at the outset.

3. Make sure you explore how type enhances rather than limits self-awareness. Stress that all types are good and positive whereas some behaviour (as defined by aspects of a letter) are contextually inappropriate.

4. Stress type as a starting point not a finishing point.

Type reveals more than it limits so it is more of a mirror than a label. It is only when we see ourselves from a different perspective that we can really understand who we are.

> *What do they of England know,*
> *that of only England know.*
>
> **Rudyard Kipling**

We only know what it is to live in England (or anywhere) after we have travelled abroad. We need perspective for clarity. In the thick of it we cannot see. We only know that we like a proper cup of tea, fish fingers or *Newsnight* after we've been denied these pleasures during a fortnight in Mallorca. We have a comparison forged from a new experience. This is why people often make huge decisions following an accident. They suddenly see that their life is delicate and precious and not to be wasted. Personality type is an excellent way for us to travel, to view ourselves as we really are and also to glimpse who we might become. This is important for teachers and students because when we understand ourselves, and those around us, we become more honest, tolerant, open and kind; more human.

Isn't type a bit simplistic?

When asked to summarise the appeal of country music Dolly Parton suggested it is simply three chords and the truth. Apparently simple ideas are so often the most compelling. Framing personality around four interacting dimensions may seem rudimentary but it is remarkably accurate and robust. Understanding the model is not difficult; applying it in your life is a different matter and will last a lifetime.

Personality type theory is based on the concept that people are fundamentally different. The earliest description was offered by Hippocrates around 400 B.C. Carl Jung formalised some of these differences, specifically how we perceive the world (**S** and **N**) and how we decide to act upon these perceptions (**F** and **T**) in his book *Psychological Types* in 1920. He also identified extraversion and introversion as part of a natural difference between people that is neither better nor worse but just different. This contrasts with much psychological theory, which seeks to find, describe and treat 'bad' personality characteristics, which is at the heart of its purpose. His work was brilliantly popularised by Myers-Briggs in the 1950s and is now the most widely used personality assessment in the world. They added the Judging/Perceiving scale and created a questionnaire to help people identify their type from sixteen descriptions. This book draws upon the decades of research started by Myers-Briggs and others such as David Keirsey, Otto Kroeger, Paul Tieger and Jane Kise.

The shoe that fits one person pinches another; there is no recipe for living that suits all cases.

Carl Jung

Surely we're more than our 'type'?

Absolutely. Type explains much but not everything. The type model can positively transform relationships by helping us appreciate differences and similarities. The following statements are both true:

- We are all the same (every human shares common needs, desires and dreams – to be loved, respected, able to make a contribution).
- We are all different (there are seven billion humans and we're all unique – even identical twins differ; we all have our own exciting path to follow).

There are times when we may deny our underlying type preferences. We can all surely succumb to peer pressure or be influenced by mood, alcohol, social occasion and other factors. Jung described it as the mask of appearing different to type. At a wedding reception we are likely to behave far differently than we would at a funeral; jolly, invigorated and slightly giddy with joy at one event; sober, reticent and taciturn at the other. This doesn't undermine or obliterate our essential character. It shows us that we can override our preferences at the level of skill and behaviour, unless you're my Uncle Jason who behaves with equal debauchery at all family gatherings, with or without his false teeth.

I'm no prophet. My job is making windows where there were once walls.

Michel Foucault

French philosopher Michel Foucault summarises the best way to apply type in our lives. It is not meant to describe completely who we are and what we might become. Nor is it to be used as a weapon of power over others. It provides welcome windows in the huge wall covering our complex personalities. The light shining through these openings reveals fascinating glimpses of who we are and who we might become, and who our friends are and what they might become.

Is there a best type to be?

All types are equally valid. Each type has natural strengths and weaknesses. Some types are more likely to excel in certain situations than others. For example, traditional classroom situations are likely to be more challenging for Falcons and Panthers than other types. This prediction is based on their preference for action, variety and a willingness to challenge authority. However, these qualities can be useful in other contexts such as jobs involving advocacy and debating, but these fidgety students are the most likely to be labelled hyperactive or troublemakers. An awareness of type preference helps us understand students (and boosts student self-awareness) at a deeper level and directs us towards strategies that enhance relationships and performance rather than antagonise and negatively label students.

Can I change my type?

The theory suggests not. We do change as we age (it would be terrible if we didn't), but it is not our underlying personality preferences that alter, it is our skills, knowledge, confidence, circumstances and attitudes. There are three phases of type development. First, as children, we explore all preferences through learning and experience to gain an accurate awareness of our strengths, glimpsing what our best might be. Second, we apply these strengths and preferences in our career and relationships so we can be our best as adults. Third, we begin to develop an interest in our non-preferences (the four other letters) so we become adaptable and effective in all, or most, situations. We hopefully reach this level of maturity by the time we're parents. However, many people say we reach this stage when we're grandparents! In this book I'm proposing teachers and students consider moving through all stages together in the classroom. Now that's what I call education.

Where do the 'animals' come from?

People often forget their four type letters. I've added animal names as I thought these would be easier to remember and this has proven to be the case. Students tend to remember their own and their friends' animal type, which brings type to life in a way four abstract letters doesn't. Positive animals were chosen deliberately to avoid labelling some people as a Fox, Shark or Earwig! Occasionally a student may be disappointed with their animal but stressing the positive aspects of the actual personality traits dissipates any initial frustration and rightly focuses the student on the content rather than the label. The groups of animals also incorporate the work of David Keirsey who uses the concept of four temperaments to neatly summarise the sixteen personality types. Professionals familiar with Keirsey's work can easily apply the animal groupings to explore type and temperament.

Comparison of type descriptions

Myers-Briggs	Keirsey	Hodgson
NF	Idealists	Sea Animals
NT	Rationals	Birds
SJ	Guardians	Bears
SP	Artisans	Cats

Is education the problem or the solution?

Homer Simpson once said alcohol is the cause of and the solution to all the world's problems. At the risk of putting teachers and alcohol together, this epigram equally captures the attitude of societies across the world to education: the cause of and the solution to all of the world's problems.

This sumptuous dichotomy places education on the front pages of *The Guardian* and *Daily Mail*, fills politicians' postbags and makes some parents move house to be within the catchment area of a 'good' school. Across the world nothing is considered more important than a good education; quite right too. When do we know if we had a good education? When we (a) see the grades printed out in front of us on the results sheet, or (b) when we see a happy, confident adult member of society? Each teacher must decide (a) or (b) or (a) and (b). You may add your own (c).

The teacher is cast as both villain and hero. This book is designed to help teachers release more of their inner hero by helping them really connect with each student – the basis of teaching as the solution. Go on, you deserve it and so do your students.

Which is better for development, praise or criticism?

Neither. It is how the message is delivered that demolishes or builds a child. We need to fail before we can really excel. The best individuals and teams need to taste defeat and be chastened prior to success. This is how resilience is developed. Learning is the same. To learn we must start afresh, without preconceived ideas and theories. The journey must begin by learning about us (and type can play its part). Success and failure are interesting concepts and are regularly misrepresented.

Success is a lousy teacher. It seduces smart people into thinking they can't lose.

Bill Gates

Not quite, Bill. By applying this logic, failure must be an equally lousy teacher as it seduces not smart people into thinking they can never win. Lavishly praised and success-rich children only ever achieving 'A' grades can be in for a shock when they head off to university or leave in search of a job, unfamiliar with the real meaning of success and failure and its place in learning. Many children receiving no grades at all, because they weren't entered for any exams, never recover a belief in education or themselves.

The danger of this definition of success and failure is that it operates at the *identity* level. It brutally marries a child's worth and value to their performance in a given task or test. Wise teachers define success and failure at the level of *skill*, thus protecting student confidence and love of learning. It is better to discuss with a child what they might have learned and what they might do differently to develop their skill in a task, rather than whisk them off to the low-achievers' table plagued with existential doubt and the thought that they'll be sat at this table with the thick crayons until they're 16.

Here are some better definitions of a mistake:

> *What is a mistake? Nothing but education, nothing but the first step to something better.*
>
> **Wendell Phillips**

> *An error does not become a mistake until you refuse to correct it.*
>
> **John F. Kennedy**

There are so many new ideas and initiatives, why should I choose this one?

We need approaches, ideas and techniques that will work for us with our students. Type is a unique model to help enhance your own flexibility of performance and understand students individually. John Corrigan, founder of Group 8 Education, neatly summarises the development of educational approaches of which there have been two basic models: the *obedience model* ('Do as you're told or we'll hit you') which was replaced by those pesky hippies in the 1960s with the *conformity model* ('Work hard and you'll get a good job'). A new approach is now needed.

Business models have developed in a similar arc. The most recent business models are based on an *engagement model* – around themes of coaching, mentoring, personal development, partnership and progress. We do not persuade students by asking them to do something for us or themselves; we do so by doing asking them to do something interesting and valuable. Interesting and valuable is far closer to most teachers' definition of education than those ideas linked to the obedience and conformity models, and these new approaches have trickled into schools. Personality type fits these new approaches as snugly as a new pair of M&S pants.

Tom Sawyer was asked to whitewash a fence. He really didn't want to but his understanding of how motivation works helped him unearth a perfect solution. When his friends asked him what he was doing he excitedly declared he was buzzing because he was going to have so much fun painting the fence. Buying in to his excitement they offered to help Tom. Cleverly, he initially declined; it was his treat. Only after his friends offered to pay to join the fun did he relent. A satisfied Tom not only sat and watched other people complete the chore; he was being paid to do so. Teachers can learn much from Tom.

Which teaching methods work best?

> *We should be concerned with how we teach as we have been traditionally concerned with what we teach.*
> **John Bruer, *Schools for Thought***

Personality type can have an immense impact as a model for exploring how you teach and how you can adapt your teaching to suit all the students in your class. Recent research by Professor Steve Higgins of Durham University for the Sutton Trust, aimed at helping schools effectively spend the pupil premium, identifies three ripe areas:

1 **Effective feedback**

   Teacher providing clear, specific feedback to students, linked to defined targets (adding an additional 9 months progress per student).

2 **Meta-cognitive and self-regulation strategies**

   Teacher helps student identify the ways they learn best in specific subjects and tasks (adding an additional 8 months progress per student).

3 **Peer-tutoring/peer-assisted learning**

   Teacher introduces peer-tutoring and peer-assisted learning where students support each other (adding an extra 6 months progress per student).

These three approaches had the most positive impact in schools. Other interventions studied and considered less effective were: early intervention, one-to-one tutoring, Assessment for Learning, increased participation in sport, lower class sizes, ability grouping, uniforms and parental involvement.

Other research will reach other equally valid conclusions contradicting those reported above. The explanation is context. The only factor that really matters is the relationship between teacher and student, and student and student. If these are good any of the above factors will be positive; and if these are poor all of the above factors will have a negative impact. At a recent Inset day a PE teacher was dismissive of this research after I revealed that increased participation in sport did not have a positive impact on students. He had personal proof that it did boost confidence, attitude and friendship within the groups of children he'd worked with over the past five years. This intervention worked for him because it suited his style and strengths. It may not work for other teachers but that's not the point.

Teachers can reach more students more of the time when they better understand themselves and their students. Type theory helps transform classroom relationships and thus has a positive impact in all lessons. It is a prerequisite to techniques, not another technique. Arthur C. Clarke encapsulated the essence of teaching when he was asked if technology could one day replace teachers. His reply, 'Any teacher that could be replaced by technology should be', reminds us that the most important and irreplaceable thing going on in any classroom are human interactions. All the theories and approaches only work when these are healthy.

Why is type so good then?

Most people who discover and then apply type in their life are amazed at how useful it is. Some even become overzealous in their type appreciation and try to convert the world, convinced even their pet cat or hamster displays type preferences! One of the reasons it is such a useful model is that it allows us to view ourselves with kindness, as most of the time we're our own harshest critic. Few of us, when we stare into the bathroom mirror in the morning, think kind thoughts; it's more likely we mercilessly focus in on our flaws like Paxman tearing into a naive politician, rather than congratulate ourselves on our age-defying beauty and burgeoning wisdom.

There are moments in life when we stop pretending; moments we stop trying to be something we're not; moments when we stare into a mirror or the eyes of a loved one and say 'This is me, this is who I am.' As we bare our true self we must wait an eternal second for their reply. Repulsion and rejection or respect and rejoice. In that moment we are broken or built, crushed or connected. In a breath we live or die. In these dazzling moments we dare to see who we really are. Type and teachers are at their best when they reveal to a student their best.

> *No one is big enough to be independent of others.*
>
> **Dr William Mayo**

Type offers most when we apply the model to communication and relationships. It is used across the world to transform marriages, build teams in business, improve parenting and generate more informed career decisions. We are inextricably linked to others. We need to get along by understanding their strengths and their differences. Nowhere is this more relevant than in the classroom.

Can I use type in the staffroom?

Yes. Type is used extensively in business to develop leadership skills and build strong teams. Chapter 4 explores leadership through the lens of type. The section is also useful as an overview for leading students in the classroom based on their animal type (Bears, Cats, Sea Animals and Birds).

> *If someone goes into your house and moves the furniture around, the first thing you do is to move it all back again.*
> **Catherine Fuller and Phil Taylor, *A Toolkit of Motivational Skills***

Instead of trying to make everybody think like you it is far more effective to understand how they think, by applying the type model, and deliver your message accordingly.

Chapter 2
Personality Types in the Classroom

In this chapter:

- **Explore your personality profile**

- **Understand your natural teaching style**

- **Identify your students' personality profiles**

- **Discover what works best for you and your students**

You grow up the day you have your first laugh – at yourself.
Ethel Barrymore

There is only one corner of the universe you can be certain of improving, and that's your own self.
Aldous Huxley

Polar Bear   ISTJ

quiet

by-the-book

critical

careful   scrupulous   loyal

dependable   finisher   calm   strict

process   sensible   trustworthy

process

get things done   traditional

schedules

goal   orderly

consistent   impact

stubborn   role   steady

expert   reliable   planner

objective   practical

strong   serious   structured   plans   monitor   managerial

risk-averse   clear   purposeful   task   conscientious

systematic

Polar Bears are the most common personality type and most people know at least one Polar Bear in their family or neighbourhood. They are the Royal Family of personality type. At their best they're the most organised (to the point of obsessive-compulsive disorder) and reliable of all types. Tradition, purpose and rules are the foundation of their outlook on life. Their adult-like qualities show up early in their development and teachers can often be heard asking Polar Bears 'Where are we up to again?' Organised groups (including societies, schools and companies) benefit greatly from the reassuring reliability and structure delivered by Polar Bears. However, they are often the most maligned group/team members when their unflappable belief in their way as 'the right way' impinges upon everyone else. Flexibility, especially around people, is a necessary life lesson. If this can be learned at school teachers will be helping Polar Bears immensely in later life.

Motto: It's my way or the highway.

To be happy in the classroom I prefer to:

- Work systematically, organising my time and activities while working towards a concrete and measurable outcome.
- Apply practical skills and behaviours I've learned.
- Be assessed using fair, objective and explicit standards.
- Work in a stable, friendly but hardworking environment where everyone focuses on concrete tasks.
- Be given clear responsibility, expectations and deadlines.
- Be able to work independently.

Teaching style:

- Tried and tested methods are best.
- Structure leads to learning.
- Objective assessment methods are the most accurate.
- I'll provide clear expectations, procedures and be on top of administrative details.
- Stick to lesson plans, curriculum.

As children:

- Often intense and serious (they are trying to make sense of their world) and appear more mature than many of the adults around them!
- Often attracted to interests that require precision and skill (may prefer solitary rather than team games/hobbies).
- Learn best by doing and being shown how to do something, prefer being corrected in private.
- Tend to value routine and structure rather than surprises.

- Like to research topics in detail and become an 'expert' – allow them such opportunities.

When teaching Polar Bears:

- Respect their need for privacy, self-control and independence.
- Help them learn that things are not always black and white; especially to develop tact and sensitivity.
- Offer responsibility; ask their advice (around areas of interest).
- Share your schedule and stick to it if at all possible; they really don't respect teachers who appear unreliable or disorganised.

Team contribution:

- Offer hard work to complete tasks.
- Attention to detail and procedures.
- Able to set up and implement projects.

Achilles heel:

- Rigid, judgemental, rule-obsessed.

Polar Bear in numbers (%):

- UK/USA population: 14/12
- Primary teachers: 8
- Secondary teachers: 12
- University lecturers: 13
- Head teachers: 25
- Risk-taker as child (rank/16): 12/16[1]

[1]Allen L. Hammer and Jean M. Kummerow. (1996). *Strong and MBTI Career Development Guide* (Consulting Psychological Press).

Black Bear ESTJ

serious task clear conscientious
purposeful
analytical energy assertive action trustworthy
lively
strict loyal decisive
matter-of-fact leader
logical plans
managerial composed
process boss
realistic practical
strong finish orderly
hunger routine gregarious robust
impact procedure
direct
implementation get things done
expert bold no loose ends

Lord Sugar is probably a Black Bear. He tends to seek a mini-me Black Bear on his annual search for an Apprentice. He continually extols the virtues typical of Black Bears – direct, assertive, focused and unsentimental – to the star-struck hopefuls as they shuffle nervously on leather seats, buttocks clenching tighter when his pointed finger wafts teasingly in their direction. The format of the programme reveals potential weaknesses in Black Bears. Unfettered, the type can be too macho, aggressive and self-absorbed; but most Black Bears learn to moderate these characteristics by gaining experience and being part of balanced teams. The classroom is a great place for Black Bears to learn how to balance their natural ease in taking the lead and organising by working in teams and learning from others the benefits of genuine teamwork and cooperation. *Dragons' Den* Black Bears such as Duncan Bannatyne successfully blend their business skills and work ethic with the raw ideas and passion of the candidates; this is a template all Black Bears can apply for success inside the classroom and beyond.

Motto: I'll be the boss.

To be happy in the classroom I prefer to:

- Work systematically, organising people, time and activities while working towards known and measurable outcomes.
- Apply practical skills and behaviours I've learned.
- Assess/be assessed using fair, objective and explicit standards.
- Work in a stable, friendly but hardworking environment where everyone focuses on concrete tasks.
- Give/be given clear expectations and deadlines.
- Be able to work with and consult others when I decide to.

Teaching style:

- Tried and tested methods are best.
- Structure leads to learning.
- Objective assessment methods are the most accurate.
- I'll provide clear expectations, procedures and be on top of administrative details.
- Stick to lesson plans/curriculum.

As children:

- High energy, natural leaders.
- Practical, sensible and enjoy routine and order.
- Usually take pride in their honesty and reliability.
- Enjoy facts and like to focus on a task.
- May need to learn about tact and its value.
- Can become restless when bored – need a channel for their energy and go-for-it, problem-solving attitude.
- They prefer honest feedback to false compliments.
- Can appear to be mature from an early age.

When teaching Black Bears:

- Be direct, honest, specific, organised and logical to bring harmony (and expect it back!). If you don't have all your own facts ready a Black Bear will not only notice; they'll possibly correct you in front of the class or Ofsted inspector.
- Allow as much responsibility (within clear boundaries) for the child to flourish (it might be hard to keep up with them sometimes!).
- Help them take charge of their own lives and show people their best.
- Share your plan and stick to it if at all possible; they really don't respect teachers who appear unreliable or disorganised.

Team contribution:

- Offer hard work to complete tasks.
- Use resources economically.
- Able to set up and implement projects.

Achilles heel:

- Rigid, know-it-all, impatient.

Black Bear in numbers (%):

- UK/USA population: 11/9
- Primary teachers: 8
- Secondary teachers: 9
- University lecturers: 7
- Head teachers: 26
- Risk-taker as child (rank/16): 10/16

Teddy Bear   ESFJ

compassionate

peacemaker

kind   exuberant

enthusiastic   energy   organised   generous

down to earth   carer

completer   finisher

loyal   sympathetic   empathy

nurturing

cooperative   altruistic

gracious   benevolent

tidy

patient   order

respectful   warm   determined

team player   friendly   communicator

action   neat   considerate

sincere   smiling   caring

supportive

emotional   congenial

Teddies are the most naturally sociable of all types. Their ideal environment is a hairdressing salon, wedding reception or a zumba class. They like being with people and keeping up with everything that's going on. Their classrooms can sometimes resemble a social gathering. The Teddy teacher will usually know their students well and easily remember personal details years later. Most students will respond very well to this genuine interest on seeing them progress, though some may find the interest instrusive.

Motto: I need to feel loved.

To be happy in the classroom I prefer to:

- Be the host/hostess, listening to the contributions of all.
- Work with the group, helping each person apply their strengths to the task at hand.
- Socialise in a warm and empathetic atmosphere.
- Understand and apply rules and adhere to a clear structure.
- Be clear about what work needs to be done.

Teaching style:

- Tried and tested methods are best.
- Positive relationships underpin learning and society.
- Objective assessment methods are the most accurate.
- I'll provide clear expectations, procedures and be on top of administrative details (potentially stifling creativity).
- I'll create a positive and caring classroom environment to develop the responsible and mature citizens of the future.

As children:

- Bundles of energy and warmth; friendly and cheerful.
- Confident, sociable and like doing new things.
- Love cuddles and wear their hearts on their sleeves.
- Natural performers.
- Tend to like school as a place to make friends and enjoy parties, playing at friends' houses and family gatherings.
- Thrive when they feel liked by teachers and other adults.
- Respect and preserve traditions.
- Usually enjoy discussing opinions, values and views, especially about people.
- Can put other's feelings and needs ahead of their own.

When teaching Teddy Bears:

- Expect a lot of energy, enthusiasm (and noise).
- Give them lots of physical attention and praise.
- Encourage them to express their ideas and opinions; it's OK to disagree with people sometimes.

Team contribution:

- Building morale.
- Task completion.
- Networking and summarising.

Achilles heel:

- Guilt, oversensitive, controlling.

Teddy Bear in numbers (%):

- UK/USA population: 12/12
- Primary teachers: 14
- Secondary teachers: 10
- University lecturers: 4
- Head teachers: 5
- Risk-taker as child (rank/16): 13/16

Koala Bear   ISFJ

feelings   sincere   **conscientious**   humble

tranquil   **caring**   **tolerant**   **committed**   stable

private

responsible   **loyal**   lovely

diplomatic

thorough   **trusting**

calm   values

                                             original

determination   considerate

                                            sensitive

perceptive   **thoughtful**   reflective

specific

concentration   **friendly**   **respect**   **empathy**   **harmony**

cooperative   **quiet**   **nice**   modest   **orderly**   timid

intense   integrity   protective

good memories

Koalas are the type least likely to blow their own trumpet. In fact, they're unlikely to even pick up their trumpet let alone blow it. They are the most self-effacing of all types and need to be gently nurtured by teachers over long periods of time; they take a while to get to know and trust people. In classroom-sized groups of thirty students they're most likely to be the invisible ones. One thing in their favour is that so many teachers are Koalas – over 20% of primary and around 15% of secondary teachers. These teachers should be able to understand their students and draw out their strengths and talents. This advice applies to teachers too. Koalas are least likely to apply for promotion so they are rare as heads. Coy Koala teachers and students need to learn to blow their trumpet! If not, not only do they suffer but every other type suffers too because great ideas and contributions will be lost.

Motto: I'll get on with it quietly.

To be happy in the classroom I prefer to:

- Work logically and patiently, organising my time and activities on one thing at a time for specified results.
- Apply practical skills and behaviours I've learned.
- Be assessed using fair, objective and explicit standards.
- Work in a stable, friendly but hardworking environment focusing on accuracy and attention to detail.
- Be given clear responsibilities, expectations and deadlines.
- Be able to work independently or in small groups but have my contributions recognised and appreciated within a cooperative and caring environment.

Teaching style:

- Tried and tested methods are best.
- Positive relationships underpin learning and society.
- Objective assessment methods are the most accurate.
- Provide clear expectations, procedures and be on top of administrative details (potentially stifling creativity).
- Create a positive and caring classroom environment to develop the responsible and mature citizens of the future.

As children:

- Usually gentle, quiet, persistent, patient and careful.
- Like to watch what's going on and try it out until they feel confident that they understand.
- Enjoy routine and structure.
- Like 'personal space'.
- Like to get on with everyone, sometimes at their own expense.
- Can be drawn towards animals and nature.
- Often like to look cool and fashionable.
- Often talented in crafts, art or music.

When teaching Koala Bears:

- Combine being gentle and consistent and your student will flourish.
- Offer plenty of hands-on learning experiences (e.g. water, crafts, walks, visits).
- Offer fair and consistent rules, reward good behaviour with more responsibility. They'll feel more let down if you break promises than other types.
- Accept they are naturally reserved and quiet. They are unlikely to seek the limelight and may be reluctant to contribute in class discussions, but do not interpret this necessarily as disinterest.

Team contribution:

- Attention to detail and procedure.
- Caring and inclusive.
- Background research.

Achilles heel:

- Resentful, nit-picking, door-mat.

Koalas in numbers (%):

- UK/USA population: 13/14
- Primary teachers: 18
- Secondary teachers: 12
- University lecturers: 7
- Head teachers: 5
- Risk-taker as child (rank/16): 16/16

Lion ESFP

active empathy cooperative gentle

spontaneous craft **outgoing** artistic sympathetic

spirited **calm**

practical hedonistic optimistic

party animal

artisan

improviser **adaptable**

nurturing exciting common sense

caring **generous**

cheerful considerate

observant **gregarious**

kind warm

playful dashing

harmony **action** fun **patient** **perceptive**

friendly

high-spirited tolerant

determination peacemaker

The immortal line by the footballer George Best, 'I spent most of my money on women and booze, the rest I wasted,' encapsulates the unfettered personality preferences of the Lion. They are the most natural of types; comfortable in their bodies and the world around them. Living for and in the moment brings challenges as well as freedom to Lions. If they aren't at a party they can easily become the party. They are emotionally expressive and affectionate which tends to generate a wide circle of friends. As teachers they'll be exciting, entertaining, somewhat unpredictable and sometimes maligned. As students they'll try to make every lesson a party – a challenge in many classrooms.

Motto: Let's party!

To be happy in the classroom I prefer to:

- Have fun, variety and action, working with different groups on a range of content.
- Work in groups to discuss ideas, values and beliefs spontaneously and without conflict.
- Have few (or no) rules, schedules and structure.
- Work with others, helping each person apply their strengths to the task at hand.

Teaching style:

- Tried and tested methods are best.
- Positive relationships underpin learning and society.
- Objective assessment methods are the most accurate.
- I'll provide clear expectations but be flexible in their delivery.
- I'll create a positive and caring classroom environment to develop the responsible and mature citizens of the future.
- Emphasis on experiential learning.

As children:

- Active and energetic.
- Enjoy activities, frequently the life and soul of a party and will often create a party if there isn't one!
- Usually enjoy the natural world (puddles, swimming pools, forests).
- Life is a roller-coaster or a theme park – sensations, adventures and experiences to try out and enjoy.
- Respond well to playing and surprises.
- Lions may need to be encouraged to rest and recharge their batteries.

When teaching Lions:

- Let them explore and be their talkative and adventurous best.
- Show them how and let them try it rather than give verbal instructions.
- Their confidence often comes from learning practical new skills.
- Provide rewards that are real such as treats, money or social activities.

Team contribution:

- Hard working and all-action approach.
- Flexible and inclusive.
- Get to the point/purpose quickly.

Achilles heel:

- Impulsive, unreliable, hedonist.

Lion in numbers (%):

- UK/USA population: 8/8
- Primary teachers: 5
- Secondary teachers: 2
- University lecturers: 2
- Head teachers: 2
- Risk-taker as child (rank/16): 7/16

Panther   ESTP

realist

engaging   confident   **pragmatic**

action

tolerant   action   **achiever**   hedonistic

practical

forceful

get things done   stubborn

impact

negotiate   stylish

decisive   **improviser**

purposeful

stimulating   performer

process   do   strong

flexible   **implement**

risk-taker   variety

deliver   observer   analyser   **boisterous**

assertive   **trouble-shooter**   strict   adaptable

results-focused

Bart Simpson, Zorro and Ron Weasley fly the flag for Panthers. They live to experience life. They are at their best when moving from one adventure to the next, hedonistically absorbed in the present with little concern in planning the next activity, until they become bored with the current party. Bart Simpson typifies the cheeky, charming, attention-seeking side to their personality. At school this can quickly earn Panthers a reputation for being trouble (alongside Falcons), especially if academic pursuits do not provide sufficient fulfilment. Teachers need to help the Panther focus their considerable energy in activities that satisfy both Panther and school. They are natural deal-makers and negotiators and are therefore useful in the staffroom or classroom.

Motto: Let's enjoy this!

To be happy in the classroom I prefer to:

- Generate fun, variety and action, leading groups on a range of discussions, playing devil's advocate if necessary.
- Have minimal rules, schedules and structure.
- Improvise and innovate.
- Be the conductor, orchestrating the resources available to me.
- Generate a fast pace, strong work ethic and be bold and decisive.

Teaching style:

- Tried and tested methods are best.
- Structure leads to learning.
- Objective assessment methods are the most accurate.
- Pragmatic.
- I'll provide clear expectations, procedures and just about stay on top of administrative details.
- Emphasise experiential learning.

As children:

- Active, energetic, gregarious and sometimes fractious.
- Enjoy activities, frequently the life and soul of a party and will often create a party if there isn't one!
- Usually enjoy the natural world (puddles, swimming pools, forests).
- Life is a roller-coaster or a theme park – sensations, adventures and experiences to try out and enjoy.
- Respond well to playing and surprises.
- Panthers may need to be encouraged to rest and recharge their batteries.

When teaching Panthers:

- Let them explore and be their talkative and adventurous best.
- Show them how and let them try it rather than give verbal instructions.
- Their confidence often comes from learning practical new skills.
- Provide rewards that are real such as treats, money or social activities.

Team contribution:

- Energetic and candid.
- Get to the point/purpose quickly.
- Action orientated.

Achilles heel:

- Hedonistic, unreliable, aggressive.

Panthers in numbers (%):

- UK/USA population: 6/4
- Primary teachers: 1
- Secondary teachers: 1
- University lecturers: 1
- Head teachers: 2
- Risk-taker as child (rank/16): 3/16

Tiger   ISTP

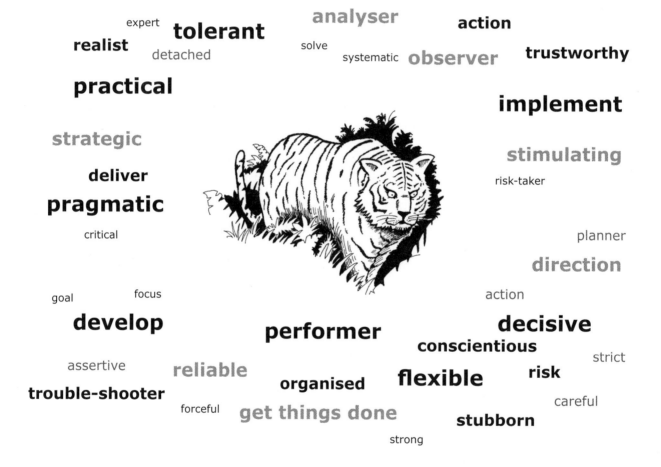

expert   **tolerant**   analyser   **action**

realist   detached   solve   **observer**   **trustworthy**

systematic

practical

implement

strategic

stimulating

deliver   risk-taker

pragmatic

critical   planner

direction

goal   focus   action

develop   **performer**   **decisive**

conscientious

assertive   **reliable**   **flexible**   risk   strict

trouble-shooter   **organised**

forceful   **get things done**   careful

stubborn

strong

The Tiger personality is the strong and silent type. They get on with the job in hand when they believe the job to be necessary and relevant. If not they're inclined to resist. Clint Eastwood and Michael Caine are representative of the Tiger personality. They are under-represented in teaching which is a pity as their no-nonsense focus on tasks, which are all part of life's journey of learning skill and competence, provides a compelling backdrop to any subject. To excel as students they need to be kept on-board by the teacher because if it comes to a shoot-out it's unlikely to end well when you're up against Clint Eastwood! The nomadic, roaming lifestyle of the cowboy reveals and mirrors much of the Tiger personality: spirited and resolute, hankering after a quest to prove their mettle.

Motto: I was born under a wandering star.

To be happy in the classroom I prefer to:

- Practise, hone and master skills in my own way.
- Apply my understanding, trouble-shoot and be given help only when I seek it (which is rare).
- Be challenged and avoid doing any stuff just to kill time.
- Avoid sentimentality.
- Work best with a minimum of rules and supervision.

Teaching style:

- Tried and tested methods are best.
- Structure leads to learning.
- Objective assessment methods are the most accurate.
- Provide clear expectations but be flexible in their delivery.
- Emphasis on experiential learning.

As children:

- Enjoy learning, especially facts that help them understand how the world works.
- Very individualistic and determined to do things their way!
- Often enjoy competitive games and toys.
- May not seek or need lots of physical attention (it doesn't mean they don't respect you).
- Will question authority and don't like being fussed over.
- Imaginative problem-solvers, enjoy testing theories and ideas (including challenging their parents!).
- Enjoy privacy and may take things apart to see how they're made.

When teaching Tigers:

- Delegate as many decisions as you can (within clear, logical boundaries).
- Can be very self-critical so describe how they can be their best in a logical way.
- Find common interests you can share to create a strong bond.

Team contribution:

- Hard working and candid.
- Willing to work independently.
- Get to the point/purpose quickly.

Achilles heel:

- Procrastinate, cynical, tough.

Tigers in numbers (%):

- UK/USA population: 5/5
- Primary teachers: 1
- Secondary teachers: 2
- University lecturers: 2
- Head teachers: 2.5
- Risk-taker as child (rank/16): 4/16

Cat   ISFP

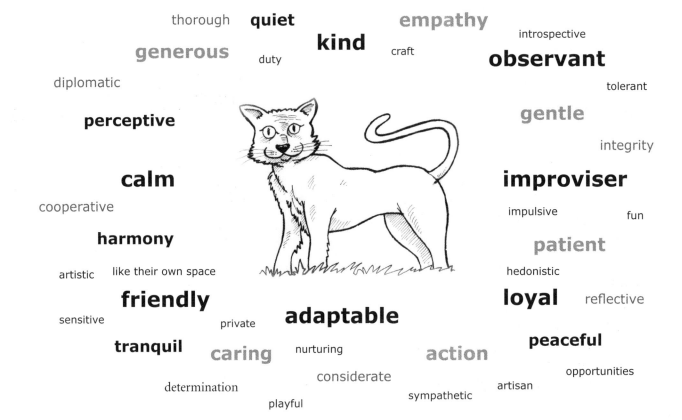

thorough   **quiet**   **empathy**   introspective

generous   duty   **kind**   craft   **observant**

diplomatic   tolerant

perceptive   **gentle**

                                          integrity

calm   **improviser**

cooperative   impulsive   fun

harmony   **patient**

artistic   like their own space   hedonistic

friendly   **loyal**   reflective

sensitive   private   **adaptable**

tranquil   **caring**   nurturing   **action**   **peaceful**

determination   considerate   artisan   opportunities

         playful   sympathetic

Cats as people are like cats as cats! They're friendly but independent, restless and impatient around routine tasks and small-talk, yet they can spend hours perfecting skills such as fishing, crafts, dance, DIY, working on vehicles, athletics, arts or music. They prefer to express themselves through their actions rather than their words. Cats are the type most likely to be uncomfortable in the classroom. They prefer to develop and apply skill whereas most of the curriculum is centred on developing and applying knowledge. Also, their thirst for action and adventure, combined with a preference for solitude, sets them at odds with much of the classroom experience, particularly in secondary school. Crafts and action are often offered more space in primary education and this is where Cats are likely to be most comfortable both as teachers and students. Cats are generally considered the kindest of all types and are attracted to outdoor work and leisure activities.

Motto: Let me explore!

To be happy in the classroom I prefer to:

- Practise, hone and master skills on practical things I believe in.
- Know what I'm supposed to do but not how to do it (I'll work that out for myself, or ask).
- Be able to see the results of my efforts.
- Be in a supportive and friendly environment.
- Work best with a minimum of rules and supervision.

Teaching style:

- Tried and tested methods are best.
- Positive relationships underpin learning and society.
- Objective assessment methods are the most accurate.
- I'll create a positive and caring classroom environment to develop the responsible and mature citizens of the future.
- I'll provide clear expectations but be flexible in their delivery.
- Emphasis on experiential learning.

As children:

- Active and energetic in a deliberate and measured style.
- Enjoy activities, frequently the life and soul of a party and will often create a party if there isn't one!
- Usually enjoy the natural world (puddles, swimming pools, forests).
- Life is a roller-coaster or a theme park – sensations, adventures and experiences to try out and enjoy.
- Respond well to playing and surprises.

When teaching Cats:

- Let them explore and reflect on their experiences.
- Show them how and let them try it rather than give verbal instructions.
- Their confidence often comes from learning practical new skills.
- Provide rewards that are real such as treats, money or social activities.

Team contribution:

- Hard working and caring.
- Willing to work independently.
- Get to the point/purpose quickly.

Achilles heel:

- Self-critical, ignore rules, withdrawn.

Cats in numbers (%):

- UK/USA population: 6/9
- Primary teachers: 5
- Secondary teachers: 2
- University lecturers: 2
- Head teachers: 2.5
- Risk-taker as child (rank/16): 9/16

Seahorse   INFJ

perceptive

unconventional

spiritual

creative   complex

deep

inspiring

calm

nurture

empathy

vision

decisive

caring

respect

salubrious

catalyst

curious

imaginative

intuitive

mystical

original

articulate

vision   feelings

introspective

values

organised

advocate

tranquil

ideas

wise

quiet

conscientious

advise

authentic

ethical

foresight

growth

insight

integrity

harmony

guide

Seahorses are rare personality types, perhaps as little as just 3% of the general population. They are over-represented as classroom teachers and at their best they will quietly nudge and nurture their students towards their full potential. They use their warmth and imagination to create a calm and invigorating class-room environment. At their worst they will be overwhelmed by confrontation and aggression. Seahorses are naturally interested in words and languages. Western culture, and in particular the utilitarian school culture imposed by consecutive governments, can marginalise the contribution of Seahorses (and their close relation in personality type, the Seal). Native American Indian culture is very close to the natural inner beliefs and values of Seahorses.

Motto: Let's think about it.

To be happy in the classroom I prefer to:

- Encounter (or create) variety and action, with time to explore and grow my own ideas, beliefs and meanings.
- Develop and use my imagination and creativity to solve problems.
- Organise my own time, short term and long term.
- Have my contributions recognised and appreciated.
- Work autonomously within a cooperative and caring environment.

Teaching style:

- Aim to develop the unique potential of all students.
- Offer choice and variety in learning to motivate and inspire students.
- Value creativity and discussion in their students.
- May neglect formal assessment and evaluation.

As children:

- Sensitive and emotional dreamers can be clingy toddlers needing a parent to reassure and support.
- Sweet and affectionate, often drawn to look after younger children around them (they can make up stories).
- Mostly easy-going and good-natured; see people as more important than rules.
- Tend to have a small circle of close friends.
- They seek self-identity as they travel through their teens, trying to work out who they are and want to be.

When teaching Seahorses:

- Encourage their creativity and understanding (through books, art, music) of what makes people tick.
- Respect their need for privacy, quiet and time to think.
- As they take criticism personally, be careful and positive.
- Help them feel understood and accepted.

Team contribution:

- Offer hard work to complete tasks.
- Imagination and vision.
- Predict impact of projects on people.

Achilles heel:

- Withdrawn, resentful, critical.

Seahorse in numbers (%):

- UK/USA population: 3/2
- Primary teachers: 5
- Secondary teachers: 6
- University lecturers: 8
- Head teachers: 2
- Risk-taker as child (rank/16): 15/16

Seal   INFP

complex

easy going

tranquil   **inimitable**

passionate   introspective   **original**   **conceptual**   integrity

immersed

dreamer   **adaptable**

reflective   **creative**

caring   **create**

intense

thoughtful   **ideas**   comfortable

deep   **quiet**

global

curious   **loyal**   patterns

respect

harmony   **genial**   **calm**   **wise**   private

idealistic   **empathy**   concentration

authentic   **conscientious**   advocate   vision

nurture   catalyst

growth

Seals are the biggest daydreamers of all personality types. They are liable not only to get lost in their thoughts but also get lost in their house, classroom and holiday – because they are the most easily distracted type. It's unsurprising that they're over-represented as writers because they easily create vivid and lucid alternative realities inside their heads. They are attracted to the mystical and magical. Terry Pratchett is a model Seal, bubbling with ideas that blur and merge reality and imagination. At their best, as teachers, they can transport students to magical places and ideas while nurturing their creative potential. At their worst, they can be the disorganised and rambling outsider caricatured by Harry Potter's Divination teacher, Professor Sybill Trelawney (played by Emma Thompson). As students they're equally likely to hero-worship or totally ignore a teacher or subject depending upon its capacity to grab hold of their imagination. Western culture, and in particular the utilitarian school culture imposed by consecutive governments, can denude the contribution of Seals (and their close relation in personality type, the Seahorse). Native American Indian culture is very close to the natural inner beliefs and values of Seals.

I was the only female sharing a flat with four blokes and I was banned from the kitchen after I accidently set fire to it a second time. My problem was I'd start something on the hob, pop into another room for something else and totally forget about the cooking, until the smell of smoke found me.

Caroline, an easily distracted Seal who, thankfully, decided against a career as a chef

Motto: Let's think about it.

To be happy in the classroom I prefer to:

- Encounter (or create) variety and action, with time to explore my own ideas, beliefs and meanings.
- To think outside the box.
- Develop and use my imagination and creativity to solve problems.
- Have few (or no) rules, schedules and structure.
- Improvise and innovate.
- Work autonomously within a cooperative and caring environment.

Teaching style:

- Aim to develop the unique potential of all students.
- Offer choice and variety in learning to motivate and inspire students.
- Value creativity and discussion in their students.
- May neglect formal assessment and evaluation.

As children:

- Sensitive and emotional dreamers can be clingy toddlers needing a parent to reassure and support.
- Sweet and affectionate, often drawn to look after younger children around them (they can make up stories).
- Mostly easy-going and good-natured; see people as more important than rules.
- Tend to play a peacemaker role in group situations.

- Tend to have a few good friends rather than many acquaintances.
- They seek self-identity as they travel through their teens, trying to work out who they are and want to be.

When teaching Seals:

- Encourage their creativity and understanding (through books, art, music) of what makes people tick.
- Respect their need for privacy, quiet and time to think.
- As they take criticism personally, be careful and positive.
- Help them feel understood and accepted.

Team contribution:

- Collaborative, bring everyone on board.
- Imagination and vision.
- Flexibility.

Achilles heel:

- Withdrawn, secretive, moody.

Seals in numbers (%):

- UK/USA population: 3/4
- Primary teachers: 5
- Secondary teachers: 6
- University lecturers: 8
- Head teachers: 1
- Risk-taker as child (rank/16): 11/16

Clownfish   ENFP

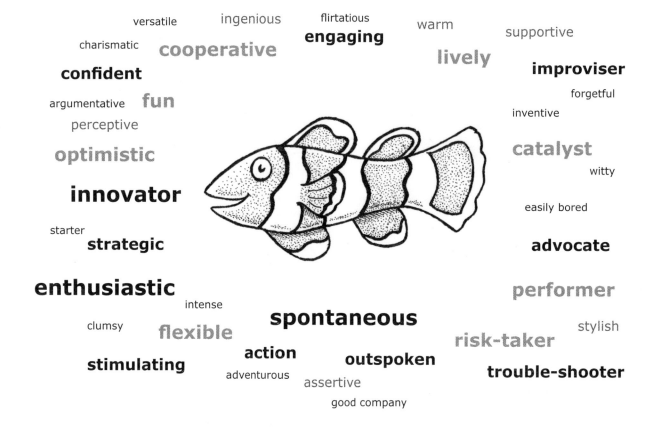

versatile
ingenious
flirtatious
warm
supportive

charismatic
cooperative
engaging
lively

confident
improviser

argumentative
fun
forgetful

perceptive
inventive

optimistic
catalyst

witty

innovator
easily bored

starter
strategic
advocate

enthusiastic
performer

intense
spontaneous
stylish

clumsy
flexible
risk-taker

stimulating
action
outspoken
trouble-shooter

adventurous
assertive

good company

Imagine drawing up a personality spec for the perfect radio DJ and you'll probably end up with a Clownfish. Each preferred letter oozes DJ attributes. The E provides quick-talking, think-out-loud repartee, the N adds imagination and off-the-wall thinking, the F delivers empathy and connection with listeners and guests and the P provides the spontaneity that breathes excitement into live shows. Graham Norton, Chris Evans, Paul O'Grady and Terry Wogan are all unique individuals but each one of them brings the best of their Clownfish personality to their radio shows. There is always potential for their spur-of-the-moment ideas to derail their positive intentions; Russell Brand and Jonathan Ross are reminders to every Clownfish that they need to learn to step back and think before launching into their next idea or project. The loss of some of their *joie de vivre* and relentlessly positive outlook ('Oh it'll be alright – yeah let's just do it, it's only a bit of fun') is a balance all Clownfish are likely to have to deal with in the classroom and beyond. Their charm carries them through most of the situations their lack of planning propels them into.

Motto: Hey, I've had another idea!

To be happy in the classroom I prefer to:

- Have fun.
- Encounter (or create) variety and action, working with different groups on a range of content.
- Develop and use my imagination and creativity to solve problems.
- Have few (or no) rules, schedules and structure.
- Improvise and innovate.
- Work in groups to discuss ideas, values and beliefs spontaneously to generate new meaning and understanding.

Teaching style:

- Aim to develop the unique potential of all students.
- Offer choice and variety in learning to motivate and inspire students.
- Value creativity and discussion in their students.
- May neglect formal assessment and evaluation.

As children:

- Enjoy variety/action, get bored easily and move on to something new.
- Imaginative and creative with ideas, words, toys and games.
- Often have a good sense of humour.
- Push boundaries and enjoy negotiating changes in the rules!
- Often precocious, versatile and risk-takers/accident-prone.
- Generally do things at the last minute.
- Strive to be unique and 'different', imposing their personal style.

- Often popular but can be a threat to some teachers/adults who don't appreciate their original thinking!

When teaching Clownfish:

- Encourage their active imaginations; let them think out loud and express their ideas without fear of ridicule.
- Don't try and win all the arguments, but do stay firm on the really important issues.
- Try not to quash their spontaneous preferences – they'll do it when they're ready (if they want to), offer choice and variety.

Team contribution:

- Imagination and ideas.
- Predict impact on people.
- Bring energy and dynamism.

Achilles heel:

- Rebellious, take on too much, forgetful.

Clownfish in numbers (%):

- UK/USA population: 6/8
- Primary teachers: 10
- Secondary teachers: 12
- University lecturers: 9
- Head teachers: 2
- Risk-taker as child (rank/16): 5/16

Dolphin   ENFJ

idealistic   peacemaker   loyal   improviser

persuasive   organised   **mentor**   **empathy**   tolerant

                                         nurturing

communicator   **friendly**

supportive

action   patient

intuitive   congenial

sociable   **outgoing**

determination   exciting

harmony   generous

cooperative   tranquil

                                              warm   considerate

sincere   gracious   spirited   catalyst

emotional   caring   **imaginative**   **leader**

exuberant   **perceptive**   inspiring

Dolphins are naturally warm, charming and engaging company. This makes them popular in classrooms as teachers and students. They are the go-to person for advice and support, sometimes finding themselves swamped as they sort out everyone's problems. They are naturally suited to pastoral roles but may prefer to apply their talents in other directions. They are consensual and driven by the highest human values, making them treasured and cherished leaders.

Motto: Let's all be friends.

To be happy in the classroom I prefer to:

- Be the catalyst, coordinating the resources available to me and the group.
- Plan strategically, creatively problem-solve and achieve on time.
- Work with others, helping each person apply their strengths to the task at hand.
- Unleash my entrepreneurial flair to generate excitement and results.
- Understand and apply rules and adhere to a clear structure.

Teaching style:

- Aim to develop the unique potential of all students.
- Offer choice and variety in learning to motivate and inspire students.
- Value creativity and discussion in their students.
- May neglect formal assessment and evaluation in favour of building positive personal relationships.

As children:

- Bundles of energy and warmth; friendly and cheerful.
- Confident, sociable and like doing new things.
- Love cuddles and wear their hearts on their sleeves.
- Natural performers.
- Tend to like school as a place to make friends and enjoy parties, playing at friends' houses and family gatherings.
- Thrive when they feel liked by teachers and other adults.
- Usually enjoy discussing opinions, values and views, especially about people.
- Can put other's feelings and needs ahead of their own.

When teaching Dolphins:

- Expect a lot of energy, enthusiasm (and noise).
- Give them lots of physical attention and praise.
- Encourage them to express their ideas and opinions; it's OK to disagree with people sometimes.

Team contribution:

- Advocate.
- Nurturer.
- Catalyst.

Achilles Heel:

- Controlling, self-doubt, oversensitive.

Dolphins in numbers (%):

- UK/USA population: 3/3
- Primary teachers: 7
- Secondary teachers: 10
- University lecturers: 8
- Head teachers: 3
- Risk-taker as child (rank/16): 14/16

Eagle   ENTJ

ideas

entrepreneurial

reliable

adroit   goal

stubborn

impact

conceptualise

forceful   managerial

stimulating

vigorous

trustworthy

knowledge

structured   critical

strong

develop

implement

plan

planner

goal-setting

risk

voracious

decisive

expert   **strategic**

process

strict   **direction**

finisher

systematic

get things done

conscientious

deliver

detached

The Eagle is a natural entrepreneur. Each letter of their preferences points in the direction of business success. The E brings natural networking qualities, the N adds stunning novel ideas and approaches, the T supplies objectivity plus a focus on task and the J adds the organisational zeal and completer-finisher edge. Wrapped up together these preferences serve teacher and student well. Eagles are under-represented in teaching, except at head teacher level. As students Eagles can be motivated best when they can see a purpose to the curriculum beyond school.

Motto: I'll be the leader.

To be happy in the classroom I prefer to:

- Be the conductor, orchestrating the resources available to me.
- Plan strategically, creatively problem-solve and achieve on time.
- Work with others, helping each person apply their strengths to the task at hand.
- Unleash my entrepreneurial flair to generate excitement and results.
- Generate a fast pace, strong work ethic and be bold and decisive.

Teaching style:

- Focus on making the curriculum engaging and challenging.
- Encourage students to be curious, think for themselves and be responsible.
- Help students understand and apply underlying theories, models and concepts so they can justify their thinking.
- May underplay the importance of the pastoral side of teaching.

As children:

- Restless, natural leaders usually 'on the go'.
- Ingenious and creative entrepreneurs.
- Usually take pride in their originality and determination.
- Enjoy facts and like to focus on a task (may need help learning about tact).
- Can become rebellious when bored – need a channel for their energy and go-for-it, problem-solving attitude.
- They prefer honest feedback to false compliments.
- Can appear to be mature from an early age.

When teaching Eagles:

- Be direct, honest, organised and logical to bring harmony (and expect it back!).
- Allow as much responsibility (within clear boundaries) for the child to flourish (it might be hard to keep up with them sometimes!).
- Help them take charge of their own lives and show people their best.
- Share your plan and stick to it if at all possible; they really don't respect teachers who appear unreliable or disorganised.

Team contribution:

- Offer hard work to complete tasks.
- Analyse and reallocate resources economically.
- Able to design and implement projects.

Achilles heel:

- Abrasive, bossy, critical.

Eagle in numbers (%):

- UK/USA Population: 3/2
- Primary teachers: 5
- Secondary teachers: 4
- University lecturers: 7
- Head teachers: 10
- Risk-taker as child (rank/16): 8/16

Falcon   ENTP

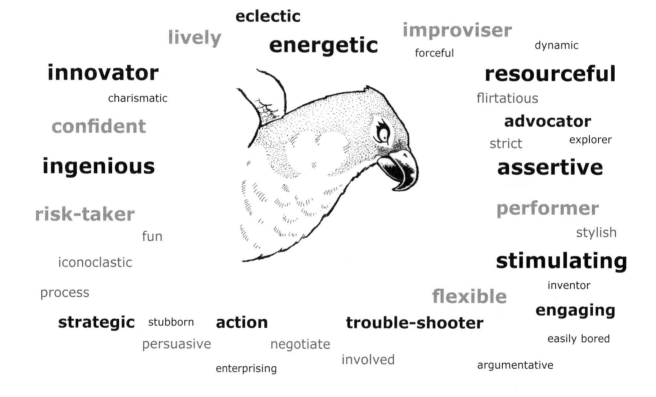

eclectic

lively

energetic

improviser

forceful

dynamic

innovator

charismatic

confident

ingenious

risk-taker

fun

iconoclastic

process

strategic   stubborn   action

persuasive   negotiate

enterprising

resourceful

flirtatious

advocator

strict   explorer

assertive

performer

stylish

stimulating

inventor

flexible

engaging

easily bored

trouble-shooter

involved   argumentative

Falcons are natural entertainers and comedians. They are usually considered sharp and engaging company. They can generally talk their way out of any situation with their naturally powerful and persuasive verbal skills. They'd probably make great cult leaders but thankfully they tend to become comedians, actors, rock stars or bingo-callers instead. Although under-represented as teachers they tend to be a very positive influence in schools, especially with students that need non-conventional role models. As natural iconoclasts there may be friction between school leaders and the Falcon teacher. In the classroom Falcon students are usually the first to be labelled as troublemakers, especially if they aren't academic high-fliers (because they'll be bored). If you're wondering what it would be like to teach a group of bored Falcons, imagine walking into a class where your first row is Tracey Beaker, Bob Geldof, Frankie Boyle and Noel Gallagher! Channelling their considerable energy in a positive direction is essential as they can influence the mood of other students with an ease most teachers only learn after ten years in the classroom.

When I was a teenager my 10-year-old sister became a vegetarian for a while. I disagreed so I surreptitiously hid meat in her food. That happened twenty years ago but I still get wound up by people making irrational choices.
Sam, who kindly supplemented his younger sister's protein intake and illustrates the intense passion and action Falcons are capable of when roused by strong ideas

Motto: But why do you say that?

To be happy in the classroom I prefer to:

- Have fun.
- Have variety and action, working with different groups on a range of content.
- Develop and use my imagination and creativity to solve problems.
- Have few (or no) rules, schedules and structure.
- Work in groups to discuss ideas, values and beliefs spontaneously and without conflict.

Teaching style:

- Focus on making the curriculum engaging and challenging.
- Encourage students to be curious, think for themselves and be responsible.
- Help students understand and apply underlying theories, models and concepts so they can justify their thinking.
- May underplay the importance of the pastoral side of teaching.

As children:

- Enjoy variety/action, get bored easily and move on to something new.
- Imaginative and creative with ideas, words, toys and games.
- Often have a good sense of humour.
- Push boundaries and enjoy negotiating changes in the rules!
- Often precocious and risk-takers, accident-prone.
- Generally do things at the last minute.
- Iconoclastic.

- Strive to be autonomous, unique and 'different', developing their own style.
- Often popular but can be a threat to some teachers/adults who don't appreciate their original thinking!

When teaching Falcons:

- Encourage their active imaginations, let them think out loud and express their ideas without fear of ridicule.
- Don't try and win all the arguments, but do stay firm on the really important issues.
- Try not to quash their spontaneity – they'll do it when they're ready (if they want to), offer choice and variety.

The phrase 'they could start an argument in an empty room' was probably first attributed to a Falcon. When harmony breaks out they can find it dull and will throw something into the mix to generate debate or action.

Team contribution:

- Understand and apply theory.
- Play devil's advocate.
- Bring energy and dynamism.

Achilles heel:

- Rebellious, combative, unfocused.

Falcon in numbers (%):

- UK/USA population: 3/3
- Primary teachers: 3
- Secondary teachers: 3
- University lecturers: 5
- Head teachers: 2
- Risk-taker as child (rank/16): 1/16

Tawny Owl   INTP

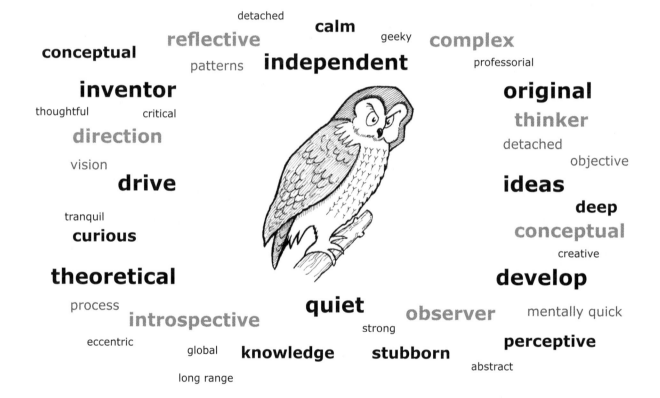

The cliché of the mad professor encapsulates the essence of the Tawny Owl. Einstein is said to have been observed lost in his thoughts as he wondered off on really long walks, unaware he was in his slippers or pyjamas. The story may be myth but Tawny Owls are the most likely candidate to lose track of reality, being so engrossed in thought and more interested in the principles underlying things than the things themselves. This is the key to understanding the Tawny Owl type. They are over-represented in teaching, especially the higher education sector. This is perhaps not surprising as they are adapted more to the intellectual and abstract world than the real world (the real world being the place for the four Cats: Cat, Lion, Panther and Tiger). As students they are liable to drift off into a world of their own. The path to success in the classroom, as teachers or students, is not to lose themselves in ever more complex and theoretical ideas. When they can capture and apply their thoughts simply, they liberate their best.

Motto: I'll analyse it to understand it.

To be happy in the classroom I prefer to:

- Develop, analyse and apply new ideas.
- Apply my energy to the process of understanding and developing my knowledge of a subject.
- Be challenged and avoid doing any stuff just to kill time.
- Avoid sentimentality.
- Work best with a minimum of people, rules and supervision.

Teaching style:

- Focus on making the curriculum engaging and challenging
- Encourage students to be curious, think for themselves and be responsible
- Help students understand and apply underlying theories, models and concepts so they can justify their thinking.
- May underplay the importance of the pastoral side of teaching.

As children:

- Enjoy learning, especially facts that help them understand how the world works.
- Very individualistic and determined to do things their way!
- Often enjoy competitive games and toys.
- May not seek or need lots of physical attention (it doesn't mean they don't respect you).
- Will question authority and don't like being fussed over.
- Imaginative problem-solvers, enjoy testing theories and ideas (including challenging their parents!).
- Enjoy privacy and may take things apart to see how they're made.

When teaching Tawny Owls:

- Delegate to your child as many decisions as you can (within clear, logical boundaries).
- Can be very self-critical so describe how they can be their best in a logical way.
- Find common interests you can share to create a strong bond.

Team contribution:

- Analyse complex theories.
- Imagination and vision.
- Flexibility.

Achilles heel:

- Sarcastic, argumentative, withdrawn.

Tawny Owl in numbers (%):

- UK/USA population: 2/3
- Primary teachers: 2
- Secondary teachers: 3
- University lecturers: 6
- Head teachers: 1
- Risk-taker as child (rank/16): 2/16

Barn Owl   INTJ

drive challenges private original
strategist deliver abrupt
decisive develop
firm structured purposeful achieve
reliable get things done
assertive vision
implement critical
natural leader finisher
theorise goals process
conceptual
patterns
independent ideas
concise perceptive goal-setting
competent determined strict
detached strategic direction
conscientious systematic
ideas long range master schedules
plan

Barn Owls are strategic leaders and usually willing and able to take charge of people and resources. Barn Owls locate prey using their acute sense of hearing and as people Barn Owls have the ability to listen, absorb and disentangle complex concepts and puzzles with similar precision and aplomb. George Lucas, Morrissey and Bill Gates are all Barn Owls. They share an awkwardness and reticence born from their ability to see more than those around them. At best this trait can catapult Barn Owl teachers into the realm of sage and guide or, at worst, to sarcastic, sneering critic and outsider. As students Barn Owls need to be encouraged to share their insights to avoid retreating into the quiet refuge of their thoughts.

Motto: I'll work it out myself.

To be happy in the classroom I prefer to:

- Enjoy exploring new ideas and information.
- Create and develop original and creative solutions to improve current systems or thinking.
- Be assessed using fair, objective and explicit standards.
- Work in a stable, friendly but hardworking environment where everyone focuses on concrete tasks, free of personal squabbles.
- Give/be given clear responsibilty, expectations and deadlines.
- Be able to work independently.

Teaching style:

- Focus on making the curriculum engaging and challenging.
- Encourage students to be curious, think for themselves and be responsible and determined.
- Help students understand and apply underlying theories, models and concepts so they can justify their thinking.
- May underplay the importance of the pastoral side of teaching.

As children:

- Often intense and serious (they're trying to make sense of their world) and appear more mature than many of the adults around them!
- Often attracted to interests that require precision and skill (may prefer solitary rather than team games/hobbies).
- Learning best by doing and being shown how to do something, prefer being corrected in private.
- Tend to value the opportunity to create new models/ideas/theories.
- Like to research topics in detail and become an 'expert' – allow them such opportunities.

When teaching Barn Owls:

- Respect their need for privacy, self-control and independence.
- Help them learn that things are not always black and white; especially to develop tact and sensitivity.
- Offer responsibility; ask their advice (around areas of interest).

Team contribution:

- Analyse theoretical concepts.
- Reflection and calm.
- Objective implementation

Achilles heel:

- Aloof, abrupt, critical.

Barn Owl in numbers (%):

- UK/USA population: 1/2
- Primary teachers: 3
- Secondary teachers: 6
- University lecturers: 11
- Head teachers: 9
- Risk-taker as child (rank/16): 6/16

Chapter 3
Recognising Personality Preferences

In this chapter:

- Learn how to recognise and develop all eight personality preferences

- Understand how crucial they are in the classroom

- Introduce activities so you and your students can increase your behavioural flexibility

One's mind, once stretched by a new idea, never regains its original dimensions.
Oliver Wendell Holmes

How are we energised?

stand out **confident** exude
limelight **E** action **outside**
outgoing not quiet
assertive interrupt movement
contribute to breadth
show

concentration
reflection gentle
calm **inside**
quiet **I** serene
part of the crowd still depth
watchful **good listener** blend in
careful
absorb take in

Our energy is either generated internally (Introvert: **I** preference) or externally (Extravert: **E** preference). The general understanding of the terms extravert and introvert do not reflect the preferences as described by Jung. In the personality type approach both preferences are equally valid. In some cultures **E** preference is considered 'better'. This can be seen on TV programmes like *The Apprentice* and *X Factor* where **E** preference characteristics are lauded at the expense of **I** preference characteristics. Cultural and religious bias exists in the promotion of one approach over the other when in reality both are equally valuable to society. The US culture generally praises **E** preference behaviour, whereas Buddhism extols **I** preference behaviour. This idea can form the basis of an interesting classroom discussion. Do schools, subjects and different teachers promote one preference above the other? If so, why?

From where do you gain your energy – inside or out?

Clues for E preference:

- I think out loud.
- I generally act quickly.
- I mostly talk more than I listen.
- I prefer to stand out.
- I tend to work best in groups.

Clues for I preference:

- I think before I speak.
- I generally act carefully
- I mostly listen more than I talk.
- I prefer to blend in.
- I tend to work best alone.

Energy in the classroom

Effective teachers control the energy in their classroom. We are all stimulated either by paying attention to things happening inside our body (thoughts, ideas, feelings) or by paying attention to things happening outside our body (the buzz of activity at a fun fair, watching a stray dog chase an Ofsted inspector across the playground). Although we all experience both, these internal and external stimuli are distinct. People do seem to have a preference for being fired up either by one or the other.

This aspect of personality has the biggest impact in the classroom (and beyond). Most problems between people are caused by poor communication – research suggests as much as up to 80%! Listening to the words, interpreting their meaning and replying (internally and/or externally) is more difficult than we think and is at the root of so many problems between individuals and communities.

There are basically two ways to communicate: we're talking *or* listening, giving *or* receiving. Both are crucial but we have a preference for one or the other. Although we all talk and listen at different times it is really useful to identify your underlying preference. It will tend to be the approach you favour in your classroom and the approach you prefer your students to use. During most of your lessons you will be expressing your preference without even knowing it. Neither is better. Neither is right or wrong. Both preferences are important and need to be expressed. An inclusive classroom is balanced and allows both preferences to contribute and flourish.

To ride or hide?

I have an **E** son and an **I** daughter. Before her last week at primary school my daughter said she didn't want to go to school for the whole week. She didn't appear to be ill so my wife and I sent her to school. By Wednesday she confessed the cause of her reticence. She had been told she would be receiving a reward from the head teacher on Friday at a whole school assembly and would be required to go up to the front to collect it with everyone looking at her. Then she'd have to shake hands with the head and walk all the way back to her seat. You could feel her fear and dread as she imagined the horror of this conspicuous public performance. Imagining the penetrating, burning gaze of 150 pairs of judging eyes! **I** preferences tend to dislike being pointed out in an assembly or in classrooms. They'd rather blend in. The event was organised by a well-meaning **E** preference head who wanted every student to be publicly displayed and praised. For many **I** preferences this represents a nightmare not a celebration.

My son, an **E** preference, would have loved such an occasion. He'd stride confidently up to greet and thank the head, acknowledging his mates in the crowd with raised thumbs and a wide grin. He is in a rock band and was deciding whether to be lead singer or lead guitarist. He eventually decided to be both so he will receive maximum attention and adulation. Not all **E** preferences are as attention-seeking as this but they do prefer to be seen and heard than melt away from the action.

E talkers:

- Do you tend to interrupt?
- Do you generally share what's on your mind?

Do you stop yourself halfway through a sentence and then move off in another direction, with an additional point to offer or story to share?

E teachers tend to have noisier classrooms with more talking from the teacher, who asks more questions, has more discussions and group activities and seeks feedback from the whole group.

I listeners:

- Do you think through your thoughts before blurting them out?
- Do you tend to lose the opportunity to share your thoughts because others speak before you?
- Do you sometimes switch off as people verbally spar around you?

I teachers tend to have quieter classrooms, they talk less, they encourage their students to talk less and think more, they offer more opportunity for quiet working alone or in pairs and seek less feedback. An **INTJ** teacher recently commented: 'I'm an **I** preference but an **E** in the classroom.'

Remember, no one is always behaving exclusively in **E** or **I** mode. Great teachers move between the two during each lesson (and the other six letter preferences too). All are needed to ensure every student is catered for. Lessons flow best when all eight preferences are present, just as a really effective workout at the gym exercises all muscle groups. Going to the gym and simply sitting in the hot tub for an hour would be the same as a lesson comprising of only one activity, such as reading from a textbook or watching a DVD.

> *My son James is* **E** *preference and my other son Matthew is* **I** *preference. I noticed when they were toddlers that almost from the moment we left the house and the front door shut behind us that James would come alive. He was being energised by the world around him; the traffic, the park, observing and meeting new people. Matthew was the opposite; he'd come alive when we got back inside the house and the door closed behind us. He would relax and look forward to playing with his familiar toys, books and computer games! They're both brilliant boys but very different.*
>
> **Sarah, a mum understanding and embracing**
> **the differences in the preferences of her sons**

I recently delivered an Inset day at a primary school. During a coffee break two job-share teachers approached me. One was **E** preference and the other **I** preference. The **E** spoke first – they usually do: 'On days we work together and I take the class straight after Jan, it takes me fifteen minutes to get the class going, to wind them up ready for my lesson.' Jan then reported the opposite experience: 'After they've been with Diane it takes me fifteen minutes to calm them down, to get them quiet and focused.' They asked if this was partly a result of their different preferences. I think so. I suggested they observe each other and record all examples of **E** and **I** they noticed, from big stuff like 'Let's have a discussion' (**E**) or 'Let's meditate' (**I**) to small stuff like the teacher interrupting a student mid-sentence (**E**) or a student interrupting the teacher (**I**). Jan emailed me a couple of months later (Diane would have talked about it but Jan would be more likely to communicate via email) to report an 80%/20% bias in their classrooms in the direction of their preference. She asked if this was dangerous! What do you think?

An **I** preference teacher recently told me he has a thirty second egg-timer he uses after every question he asks in class. Everyone then has thirty seconds to prepare an answer. I'd guess this will be really useful to the 50% **I** preferences in his class but a form of torture to the 50% **E**'s! A study by Rowe (1986) in over 300 lessons discovered that teachers ask a question and pause on average just less than one second (yes, one second!) before taking an answer from a student or rephrasing the question. When teachers were taught to wait for three seconds the impact was dramatic. The length of response tripled and less discipline was required because more of the students took part.

Research by Cotton (1998) suggests waiting longer than three seconds offers further benefits for students and teachers. Students remember more and achieve more; they ask more questions; there are more interactions between students and fewer interruptions. Teachers also benefit as they listen more, especially to students previously considered slow, and they tend to vary their question style and depth. This research is most likely to improve classroom interactions for **E** preference teachers and **I** preference students. Some **I** preference students are unlikely to contribute to classroom discussions and teacher questions. Remember to measure student participation by what they learn not what they verbally contribute in class, otherwise the **I** preferences are hugely disadvantaged.

Students with a mix of teachers will be exposed to both **E** and **I** styles. In primary schools students tend to have less contact with a range of teachers so the potential for the 50% of students who do not share their teacher's preference to suffer is greater than in secondary schools. Students will do well or not in a subject due more to their teacher's personality preferences being complementary or abrasive than the stuff observed by Ofsted inspectors. Be aware of your preference and introduce techniques for all students to excel – it's a way of truly personalising the learning experience. Without it, learning and progress, as defined by Ofsted, is unlikely. Basically, to process information, an **E** preference student needs to talk it through out loud and an **I** preference needs to think it through inside their heads. For any learning to take place each preference must be accommodated.

If you have an **E** preference you are more likely to interrupt. If you have an **I** preference you are more likely to be interrupted. During training I ask people to stand on one side of the room or the other based on the statement which best describes their behaviour:

In conversations I tend to interrupt others   or   **In conversations I tend to be interrupted**

We then explore the three communication possibilities between two people: **E**+**E**, **E**+**I** or **I**+**I**.

E+E

Both tend to get on well. They talk to/at each other. They use their mouth to think. They are both comfortable interrupting each other and being interrupted. The conversation will dart and flit from topic to topic and if they move away from the task or point neither tends to mind. They may return to the point or may not. They can always interrupt later if they remember something they consider to be useful.

E+I

The **E** will tend to dominate a conversation with an **I**. This reduces the likelihood of awkward silences in social situations but overall the potential for a poor communication experience is greatest in an **E**+**I** discussion. The **E** can misinterpret the **I** silence as disinterest or disagreement, which may not be the case. The **I** can assume the talkative **E** is not interested in what the **I** thinks because they're not giving the **I** a chance to express their thoughts. So both **E** and **I** can quickly become frustrated. The **E** needs to learn to slow down and give the **I** space and time to formulate and then express their thoughts without assuming silence is dead time. The **I** needs to remember an **E** thinks out loud and is uncomfortable with silence so will fill it with any words, not necessarily well thought-out contributions. The **I** also needs to be assertive and insist on making a contribution, if not immediately then later via email or another method of communication or risk being ignored.

This combination is likely to be the most toxic in the classroom. An **E** teacher can appear rude, aggressive and even arrogant to many **I** preference students (and some of the **E**'s). They tend to underestimate how much talking they do in an average lesson. They will naturally favour **E** preference students by praising verbal contributions. To get the best out of their **I** students they need to add **I** qualities to their repertoire. An **I** teacher can appear too slow, boring and secretive to many **E** preference students. They may also negatively label the **E** preference children in their group as boisterous, rude, unteachable or hyperactive/ADHD.

I+I

Both tend to get on well. They listen to each other. They use their ears first. They are comfortable with silence and gaps in the conversation as they assume the other person is thinking through their thoughts and will speak when they have something useful to say. The classroom environment is calm and quiet with a higher proportion of time spent on individual 'thinking inside your head' activities such as reading, watching and copying from books with minimal talking. **I** teachers need to build in opportunities for **E** preferences to talk during lessons as they absorb and retain by discussing information and ideas with others (unlike **I** preferences who absorb and retain better using internal processing). This difference highlights the importance of both preferences being accommodated by the teacher for whole classroom learning to occur.

Tip: The best way to improve **E** and **I** communication is to share this with your students so teacher and students can all develop better use of **E** and **I**. Then it becomes fun and inclusive rather than a burden for a teacher to carry alone.

The E+I karaoke test

A quick way to identify preference is to ask students if they're willing to perform karaoke. **E** preferences are generally keen to belt out their favourite songs regardless of their musical talent, whereas **I** preferences will wilt at the mere thought of it, preferring to chew off their own hand than sing in front of a group. (Alcohol can affect the above preferences – for adults, of course!)

E teacher with E student

E students can be reminiscent of hungry chicks in a tiny nest jostling for attention as they feverishly flap their wings every time food is near. The **E** teacher is able to feed their insatiable appetite. To get the best out of your naturally effusive student you need to:

- Derive pleasure from the lively repartee when it generates new energy and insights; the student learns best this way, but remember there may be others in the classroom vying for your attention.
- Stay on track, be positive and avoid badgering, as both teacher and student are easily distracted.
- Stay calm and clear, otherwise two **E** preferences can talk louder and louder with neither listening to replies.
- Do keep some thoughts to yourself as you might think of a more tactful way of expressing yourself later.
- Seek to help the student clarify and develop their thinking rather than assert your own opinions.
- Encourage each other to be quiet so the **I** preferences in the class can contribute.

E teacher with I student

I preference students present a big challenge to **E** preference teachers. Above all the student needs time to think, and time is a precious commodity usually gobbled up by **E** preference teachers or fellow **E** students. To get the best out of your naturally reserved student you need to:

- Slow down your speech and movement to present a calm and reassuring demeanour.
- Don't press the student for an immediate answer or opinion; respect their need for privacy and reflection before responding.
- Give the student time and space to work alone – don't stand over their shoulder, waiting to scold or pounce like a hungry predator.
- Avoid trying to fix problems immediately or finish their sentences.
- Don't place them in groups/teams where they are the only **I** preference in a sea of **E** preferences – they'll be ignored or overruled.
- Offer written praise, not just verbal.
- Communicate with the student one-to-one where possible – written comments, asides during group activities or as you pass them in the corridor.
- Speak softly, slowly and succinctly while both seated and standing and avoid too much eye contact, unless you're praising them.
- Suggest they can write down their questions/issues for you to reply to later.

- Above all, resist labelling the student as 'slow' or 'disinterested'; they're just different to you.

I teacher with I student

Both teacher and student share a preference for quiet reflection and usually get along well. To get the best out of your calm student you need to:

- Respect the student's desire for discretion and independence.
- Provide time for your student to think through their thoughts; they don't like being put on the spot.
- Share your ideas and thoughts regularly to check you both understand each other rather than assuming silence means all is well.
- Take time to clarify your thoughts but don't avoid confrontation; if something needs to be said be succinct and direct as you deliver it.
- Use non-verbal communication – smiles and gestures are reassuring to **I** students. You can even use sticky notes/emails to pass on feedback.

I teacher with E student

It's an effort to contain **E** preference students in the traditional classroom environment, especially for **I** preference teachers who generally seek and demand more quiet time in their lessons. To get the best out of your naturally lively student you need to:

- Listen patiently and enthusiastically to the student's ideas, stories, anecdotes and descriptions.
- Stay open to their banter and off-the-wall ramblings to see where they lead – the student is thinking out loud and this is how they learn best.
- Remember to offer your own thoughts and steer the student away from contentious subjects/topics, especially in group discussions.
- Encourage the student to think things through before talking; otherwise they'll hog the lesson.
- Build in plenty of opportunities during lessons for **E** students to talk things through with other **E** preferences (while the **I** preferences reflect and think alone).

It takes two people to speak truth, one to speak and another to hear.

Henry David Thoreau

These two activities are intended for use before you introduce **E** and **I** with the group.

Student Activity: **The Lemon Juice Test**

The amount of saliva we produce after placing a drop of lemon juice on our tongue predicts our personality preference for **E** or **I**.

The test

You will need:

- Lemon juice (either one fresh lemon per 10 students or branded juice)
- Kitchen scales
- Pipette or plastic spoons
- Cotton wool balls

Experiment

Each student places a large drop of lemon juice on their tongue and swills it around their mouth for ten seconds. They then use a cotton wool ball to mop up all the saliva produced. When they've mopped it up, place the cotton wool ball on the scales, weigh the ball and record the result. Compare the class results with the personality preferences for **E** and **I** and note the level of correlation. Standing the group in a line from most spit to least adds drama to the conclusion of the experiment. The 'most **E**' will produce least spit and the 'most **I**' the most spit.

Explaining the results

The reticular activating system (RAS) is the part of our brain which responds to stimuli like food and social contact. It controls the amount of saliva we produce in response to food. Lemon juice is a good food stimulus. Scientists think **I** preferences have more activity in their RAS and produce more saliva, even when it isn't being stimulated. An extra stimulus, such as lemon juice, will produce a large amount of saliva. But because the RAS also reacts to social contact, **I** preferences will react more strongly to meeting people too. They find group situations, such as classrooms, more stressful than **E** preferences. RAS activity and saliva production is lower in **E** preferences so they usually produce less saliva but are more comfortable with social contact. Expect up to 50% more saliva from the **I** preferences. Other factors also affect saliva production such as thirst, time of day and how competitive and inclined your students are to cheat.

If the thought of this activity disgusts you then try the next one, Undercover Mole, instead. However, if you think it's yucky, you should be relieved that I've spared you the biology experiments I did at university involving human urine, blood, dead rats and drugging fruit flies. (I should stress these were part of the course, not recreational.)

Student Activity: **Undercover Mole**

Groups of students are given a broad topic to discuss: What is the best programme currently on TV? Which celebrity would it be best to have as a close friend? Take aside one person from each group and assign them the role of scribe. They are to note everyone's name and count the number of times they start to speak, including interruptions that are ignored. A tick for each time is easiest to record.

After three of four minutes, call time and ask each scribe to reveal how many contributions were made by each student before going on to discuss **E** and **I** preferences. We would predict far more contributions from **E** preferences. Make sure you don't make any **E** or **I** preferences feel bad about the number of contributions they made. This is about understanding our differences.

Now, here are some activities to develop both **E** and **I**, because we all need both as behavioural choices to be successful.

Student Activity: **Shopping Channel (developing E preference)**

Students are placed in groups of around six. In turns they are challenged to sell something as if on a shopping channel without thinking, preparation or rehearsal time. The seller can select a random object hidden in a bag such as a pencil, board rubber, tie, hat or something from home like a banana, candle or tin of dog food. The group can time each seller. The aim is to speak for up to two minutes without a pause of more than five seconds.

E preferences tend to be good at this activity and **I** preferences usually cringe even at the thought of it. To help ease this discomfort, place students in groups with their friends and define success as (a) having a go and joining in (b) increasing the time you speak for each consecutive product.

Given almost any object, **E** preferences can think on their feet and promote it with humour and charm. **I** preferences will tend to dry up and become self-conscious. Discuss positively the merits and disadvantages of both preferences in situations where we're asked to perform on the spot.

Student Activity: **The Plot Thickens (developing I preference)**

In pairs one person will tell a story (e.g. plot of a well-known film, a favourite holiday, causes of the Second World War) and the other person has to listen without interruption or adding their own thoughts, feelings and so on. Then they swap over. Discuss who is naturally better at listening. It's usually **I**'s. When is this useful in life? When is it limiting?

Another version is to ask person A to tell a story then person B has to repeat it exactly. Will they remember all the details? Again **I**'s tend to do better.

Tip: Try to use activities in pairs. Exploring the benefits and shortcomings of **E** and **I** will allow all students to feel good about their preference as well as thinking about how and why they should develop their non-preferred style. Use the approach when introducing **S**+**N**, **F**+**T** and **J**+**P** too.

Student Activity: **Networking and Feedback (E preference at its best)**

Ask students to network and seek feedback to demonstrate their power and effectiveness.

Networking

Within your class the chances are someone will know:

- A famous person.
- A person with a very unusual job.
- A person who has a wacky hobby.
- A person who has visited an unusual country.

You (and your students) can add to this list. Find out how well connected and interesting your students are! We're told it's good to talk to people to find out what's going on. Chatting to others (in safe environments) can help us unearth job opportunities, placements, useful information on forthcoming events, gigs, trips and so on. **E** preferences are naturally good at this. They start conversations with people almost anywhere (in shop queues, on bus/train journeys). The growth of email, texting and social networking sites has made it far easier for **I** preferences to 'join the party' and be more connected. In fact, the world is now more connected than ever for both **E** and **I** preferences.

Feedback

Seeking advice or feedback from people we respect and who know us well is crucial to personal growth and learning. It's much quicker to access and use the wisdom of others rather than trying to work it all out for ourselves. Ask students to seek feedback from a friend or relative they respect on their personality type description. The feedback, when provided by someone we respect, is always revealing and valuable.

The benefit of networking and feedback are encapsulated in the Wisdom of Crowds theory. For example, if you ask a group of thirty people to guess how many sweets are in a large jar, the chances of an individual being correct are low. Individual guesses are unreliable and answers will cover a wide range. However, when researchers take the average score from the whole group they have repeatedly found the number to be unerringly accurate. The theory can be applied across other fields. **E** preferences are more likely to seek the opinions of others and are therefore more likely to benefit from the theory. **I** preferences can benefit too by overcoming their reticence.

Student Activity: **Really Listening**

> *Active listening is the process of picking flowers and presenting them back to the person as a bouquet.*
> **William Miller and Stephen Rollnick,**
> ***Motivational Interviewing: Preparing People for Change***

Researchers have discovered that **E** preferences are more accident-prone than **I** preferences (from paper cuts through to car accidents). **I** preferences are naturally more aware of and in tune with their own bodies than **E** preferences. They can 'go inside' their own mind and body and benefit from this whether in simple relaxation or more formal meditation. We all benefit from such relaxation as our heart rate slows, rates of stress related hormones reduce and we become aware of our bodies. It's the feeling most of us experience when lying on a beach in warm sunshine with the gentle and reassuring sound of waves lapping on the shore. Many schools introducing their students to basic and regular meditation sessions report a positive impact on behaviour and concentration levels. A simple way to introduce this in the classroom is listening to a piece of soothing music in silence for four minutes and asking students to close their eyes and imagine the music sinking into and filling their whole body and noticing any colours or images the music initiates.

The Benson breathing technique is an alternative to music. Simply ask students to control their breathing rate by breathing in slowly for three seconds, holding for three, and releasing for three. Repeat five times. During normal breathing we use only 16% of lung capacity. This exercise develops deeper, slower breathing and stops us talking! These are great ways to start a lesson, perhaps with the lesson objectives in view behind you.

An E fishing trip

I suggested to one group of teachers that our hobbies generally reflect our preferences. As an example I suggested fishing is a likely to be an ideal hobby for **I** preferences. One teacher immediately informed me that he was a fishing enthusiast and an **E** preference (he was **ENFP** Clownfish). I asked him to describe a typical fishing trip. He told me that he goes out with a group of around six mates in the early morning. They take a healthy supply of cans and spend the day chatting, joking and larking around until they get hungry. They stop off at the local pub before returning home to their partners. They rarely catch any fish. This sounds like an **E** spin on an **I** pastime! Type informs *how* not *what* we do. This is also true of jobs.

Delia Smith and Jamie Oliver share similar careers. They are both multimillionaire celebrity chefs. They are probably opposite personality preferences – Jamie an **ENFP** Clownfish and Delia an **ISTJ** Polar Bear. How they do their job can be predicted by type preference: Jamie is an imaginative, flexible, sociable whirlwind and Delia is a reliable, step-by-step, focused and organised institution. If they swapped approaches both careers would suffer. I can't imagine Delia trying to be cool and 'getting down wiv da kids' by wearing a baseball cap the wrong way round while rapping her recipes or Jamie in a smart suit feeding fancy food to City bankers in elitist chic restaurants.

Teachers too can use their type preferences as the basis of how best to engage and inspire their students rather than trying to be a teacher they aren't. Too many books on how to be a good teacher should really be titled 'How To Be a Copy of the Good Teacher Authoring This Book'. How they are a good teacher is not necessarily how you are a good teacher.

Student Activity: So You Think You Can't Dance

This activity is a dancing competition which explores the link between **E** and **I** preference and confidence.

Split the class into two groups – **E** preferences stand on one side of the room and **I** preferences on the other. Explain that everyone is going to take part in a psychological experiment. First, you will play some music and the **E** preferences will dance! The **I** preferences, huddled in groups of half a dozen or so (or individually if the group is small) will score the quality of dancing they see. They are marking the overall group. Collect in the scores, perhaps on pieces of paper so they remain secret. Next, repeat the activity but this time the **I** preferences dance and the **E** preferences score the overall performance.

Collect the scores and before you reveal the results you can discuss what the experiment was all about. Confidence and **E** preference are often described as the same thing. Equally, lack of confidence is often synonymous with **I** preference. This is a false correlation. Real confidence is something that comes from inside of us. It is someone comfortable with who they are. It's an 'I'm OK, you're OK,' mentality. Outer confidence is something completely different. **E** preferences often display this more than **I** preferences. An **E** recently told me: 'People think I'm confident because I talk a lot, but I'm not confident,

I'm just talking, usually rubbish. A friend of mine hardly speaks but when she does it's much better than what I've spent ten minutes trying to say.'

If this interpretation is true the **E** preferences are likely to achieve higher scores for their dancing than **I** preferences. Did this happen? Was the result influenced by context? **I** preferences often report that they don't perform well when they feel they're being watched. Many **I** preference actors are great at playing a character then become a gibbering wreck when interviewed in front of a live audience. Some **I**'s will be great dancers. Did they show this? Why?

We all need to develop inner and outer confidence, and we can apply **E** and **I** preferences to explore and develop outer confidence. To develop inner confidence we need to explore the remaining personality preferences.

Making sense of our world

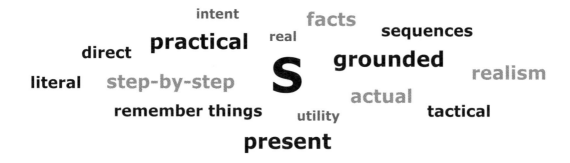

The **S** stands for Sensing and the **N** for Intuition in Jung and Myers-Briggs classifications. These words are not necessarily useful summaries of this preference but the letters are retained for simplicity and consistency (as are all of the preference letters).

Between 65–75% of people are **S** preference and only 25–35% are **N** preference. This is the only pairing where there is not roughly half of each preference in the general population. However, the ratio of classroom teachers is nearer 50% of each, which is good news for the **N** preference students but not so good for the majority who are **S** preference.

How do you take in information – detail/facts first (**S**) or big picture/ideas first (**N**)? This chunk of personality is crucial in classrooms because it's essential to how we learn.

Clues for S preference:

● I look for facts/details.
● I focus on what works now.
● I'm better at applying what I know.
● I tend to go step-by-step.
● I'm practical and grounded.

Clues for N preference:

● I look for possibilities/patterns.
● I focus on how to make it different.
● I prefer learning new things.
● I tend to join in anywhere.
● I'm a daydreamer.

Dressing up like an S or an N

My daughter is **S** preference and I'm **N** preference. She was given the part of shepherd in her school nativity play. I offered to help with her outfit. She requested a beard. We couldn't find a beard in any shop. My daughter hadn't played with her Barbie doll for a few years so I thought I could scalp it – providing a luscious blonde beard. When I informed my daughter she looked horrified. As an **S** she lives in the real world and could see how poor my scheme was. As an **N** I was carried away by the idea. **N**'s have loads of ideas, some great, some rubbish. She agreed to try on the beard but it looked evil because I'd left a tiny bit of Barbie's face on the piece of scalp I'd removed. My daughter played the shepherd without a beard. Barbie never recovered. Ken dumped her for my son's plastic Princess Leia doll.

My son and I are both **N** preferences. On a World Book Day he wanted to dress up as Dr Who. He improvised an outfit brilliantly. All he lacked was a sonic screwdriver. 'Don't worry Dad, I'll find something.' He ran off upstairs in a whir of excitement (he's also E preference). He returned a few minutes later with a joke object a friend had bought me for my birthday, a nose hair trimmer. It did look like a sonic screwdriver. It had a dull blue light at one end and was the right size and design. 'Can I take it to school, Dad?' barely disguising his enthusiasm. I admired his buzzing **N** imagination but had doubts about handing an object with a moving blade to a 10-year-old boy.

S thinking:

> *Great things are not done by impulse, but by a series of small things brought together.*
>
> **Vincent Van Gogh**

N thinking:

> *If a universe can be imagined it exists.*
>
> **Professor M. R. Franks, astronomer**

> *I shut my eyes in order to see.*
>
> **Paul Gauguin**

I can't understand why people are frightened of new ideas. I'm frightened of the old ones.

John Cage

The **S** approach prevails in secondary education; a significant advantage to **S** teachers and students within this phase. The **N** approach prevails in primary education and universities; a boost for **N** teachers and students at the beginning and end of their educational journey.

Babies, bathwater and creativity

It is an easy mistake to think **N** is more creative than **S**. The truth is they are both creative in different ways. The **N** prefers to discard the current paradigm; the **S** prefers to refine and develop it. Thus solutions proposed by an **N** are likely to appear more radical and out there. The **S** solution will look safer and less creative but the following example demonstrates the merits and place for both **S** and **N**.

In the 1960s, space travel boffins realised ballpoint pens would not write in zero gravity. NASA scientists were given six million dollars to develop a pen that would write in these extreme conditions. They did so using ingenious **N** thinking. Russian scientists had far less money and decided to take pencils instead. The Russians are using **S** thinking. One solution isn't more creative than the other but all problems can be solved with a baby in the bath (**S**) or expelled from it (**N**). More often than not, the answer is in the 'real' (**S**) world. When it isn't, 'imaginative' (**N**) thinking can come to the rescue.

Ken Robinson writes extensively on creativity. He remarks how young children tend to think they are creative and adults think they aren't. He suggests creativity (as distinct from imagination) is the greatest gift of human intelligence. Imagination uses **N** thinking and creativity uses **S** or **N** or both thinking. The more complex the world becomes the more creative we need to be to meet its challenges. Exploring **S** and **N** is a powerful way to show everyone that they can be creative either when applying their preference or when challenged to use their opposite, helping students to go beyond what they know – to truly aim higher.

Doubling toothpaste sales

The creative group at a major toothpaste manufacturer were struggling to generate new ideas to further increase sales of their product. All the marketing and advertising gimmicks had been exhausted. As they sat chewing the ends of their pencils and staring into the distance, the tea lady entered the room and as she rattled her trolley towards them she suggested they just make the hole on the tube cap bigger. There are other versions of this tale but they make the same point. Creativity is not just about big new ideas and inventions. Sometimes the answers are in the real world.

Kaizan is the Japanese business model of making progress by implementing bottom up, small, sequential improvements. It is the best of **S** preference. By applying **S** preference thinking many small improvements can be made which result in dramatic progress in the long term. **N** preference thinking will generate huge, infrequent yet sudden quantum leaps and advances. Most **N** ideas will be unworkable but some will be brilliant and paradigm shifting. **S** preferences are often great at advising **N** preferences as to which of their many ideas are the good, useful, applicable ones.

*My partner and I are **N** preferences. We go for long walks and stop somewhere nice and both sit for twenty minutes and write a story or poem about an object that catches our eye, a tree, a stone, anything. (Then we read them to each other as we're both E preferences too.)*

Brenda, ENFP Clownfish

A TV documentary recently explored creativity within the music business: Mark Ronson was challenged to create hits in a series of collaborations. Neil Tennant observed that creativity is the result of a collision of opposites, when hard and soft meet, such as Lennon and McCartney. Many creative people work in pairs rather than alone, especially in comedy. Would the Chuckle Brothers be as funny if they'd not had each other? Sting, who generally works alone, says he finds it more difficult to be creative as he ages. He notices that his children can write two songs in a day whereas it takes him two months. It probably has less to do with age and more to do with attitude. The seemingly fearless, reckless play of children breeds creativity. They will produce many ideas quickly; most are unusable but if they are not hidden away, like a crumb in an unkempt beard, a gem may be created. Risky rule-breaking is the parent of innovation and **N**+**P** preference types (Seal, Tawny Owl, Clownfish and Falcon) are the most likely to be labelled creative, as traditionally defined.

Types of creative expression in N+P preferences

- **Seal:** Writer, poet (Shakespeare, J. K. Rowling).
- **Tawny Owl:** Inventor of technological gadgets (mad professors like Albert Einstein)
- **Clownfish:** Actor, performer, radio DJ (Jonathan Ross, Graham Norton)
- **Falcon:** Musician, comedian (Noel Gallagher, Billy Connolly)

Creativity and playfulness

Creativity expert Bob McKim was not the first person to notice that children tend to be more creative than adults. The explanation he proposes is that a playful mindset is more prevalent in children. Playfulness is encouraged in pre-school and primary education but virtually shunned in secondary schools and workplaces (although there are famous exceptions such as Apple and Google). He suggests that play is associated with anarchy which is why it is progressively obliterated from the curriculum as students approach their teenage years.

He has developed two activities that measure our capacity for playfulness. The first is to ask students to quickly draw a portrait (head and face) of the person sitting next to them. Stress they only have thirty seconds and must work quickly. After thirty seconds ask each student to share their work with their partner. Amid the laughter, some people will apologise and feel embarrassed about the quality of their work. This is typical of adult groups. Others will have just immersed themselves in the activity and had fun. This is typical of younger groups. The potential disapproval of our peers is the reason most adults cite for apologising about the poor quality of their portrait. McKim argues that developing this sense of conformity as we age lowers our capacity for creativity.

His other famous test on creativity is '30 Circles'. He provides everyone with a sheet of A4 comprising thirty circles (six rows and five columns). He challenges each person to turn every circle into an object. He suggests a sun and a football as examples. He sets a time limit of sixty seconds and says the aim is to turn as many circles as possible into objects within the time limit. Afterwards he asks how many people use his examples (sun, football) and some people do. A smiley face is a common solution but few people fill in all thirty circles with one repeated design, which would have been the quickest way to fill in all of them. He suggests we don't repeat a design because we self-edit to try to be as creative as we can. He points out that this is a flaw; assuming creativity is all. There are many occasions in life when we need to focus on solutions, on experience, rather than imagination. In personality type the same message can be expressed as the need for everyone to acknowledge their preference but develop behavioural flexibility to use **S** and **N** – convergent and divergent thinking, questions and answers, explore and reflect, experiment and hypothesise.

Jung also thought playfulness was at the heart of creativity:

> The creation of something new is not accomplished by the intellect but by the play instinct. The creative mind plays with the objects it loves.

S teacher with S student

Both you and your student gather information in the same way. You both live in the present and use your past experiences to make sense of what you see. You are naturally practical, sequential and realistic in your teaching style and you encourage your students to follow suit. A solid, workman-like relationship develops; you both mutually understand what each needs to do to get the job done. To best support your naturally grounded student you need to:

- Show how learning can be applied in the real world.
- Build the student's competence by allowing them to practise until they are satisfied they can do it.
- Encourage the student to develop their imagination to add to their skill base.

S teacher with N student

Your student likes the big picture first not the details. They love to use their imagination and be original above all else. You use your experience to make sense of the world. You are naturally practical, sequential and realistic in style and encourage your students to follow suit. **N** students will at best find this approach challenging and at worst find it dreary, turgid and fusty. You must be wary of labelling the student as a daydreamer or 'away with the fairies'; it is how they take in information and make sense of the world they experience. To get the best out of your naturally imaginative student you need to:

● Celebrate the imagination and insight of your student and what it can bring to the lesson and subject.

● Help the student appreciate the value of an **S** approach – the benefits of discovering facts, details, procedure, experiments, applying experience, structure and a step-by-step model.

N teacher with N student

Both you and your student gather information by seeing the big picture first; inspiration before perspiration, using intuition and metaphor to infer meaning. You will naturally unleash your imagination in the classroom and the **N** student will respond well to this, possibly joining in with flights of fancy, anecdotes and stories. A natural affinity between you and your student is often present because you both see the world in the same way – with a burning curiosity to understand why things are as they are by exploring patterns, possibilities, ideas and theories. Be careful not to look like you're favouring **N** students to the detriment of **S** students. Every student needs to be able to contribute in their preferred way. To get the best out of your naturally imaginative student you need to:

● Offer questions and projects that can be explored creatively.

● Avoid repetitive tasks as the student will quickly tire.

● Highlight the important contribution of the **S** approach – the value of facts, details, procedure, experiments, applying experience, structure and a step-by-step model.

N teacher with S student

N teachers can inspire all students, but you do need to respect the need for **S** preference students to be given clear guidelines, structure, facts, details and procedures; otherwise they can struggle. To get the best out of your naturally grounded student you need to:

● Demonstrate how learning can be applied in the real world.

● Provide time for the student to repeat and practise until satisfied they are competent.

● Encourage the student to develop their imagination to add to their skill base.

● Be careful not to look like you're favouring **N** students to the detriment of **S** students. Every student needs to be able to contribute in their preferred way.

Use the following activities to explore **S** and **N** with your students before revealing the preference pair.

Student Activity: **Picture Quiz**

Look at the picture below:

Students then spend three minutes (no cheating – use a watch) and write down what they see. If possible use near identical big red apples for best results with groups.

(S) Is your list mostly factual and realistic?

S preferences usually answer in the following way:

a red apple
stalk in centre 1 cm long
slightly marked around top
resting on clear table
shadow cast on left base
probably a Red Delicious

(N) Does your list move off into the imaginative, figurative and metaphor?

N preferences usually answer differently:

a red apple
globe shape like a planet
food, sustenance for life
possible weapon/missile
looks like apple from *Snow White*
symbol for New York

This activity is a bit of a classic on personality type training courses. When placed in groups of all S and all N preferences, the S preferences nearly always produce the first list and the N preferences nearly always produce the second. This is fascinating because it demonstrates that we take in information about what we see differently, depending on our S or N preference. Two people looking out of the same window can see a very different view. Neither is right or wrong. An S might describe bare trees, muddy ground, grey sky; an N might see autumn, a good walk or their favourite time of year.

Ask N's to go outside and find something that symbolises what they've learned so far. In personality type courses they return happy and energised because they've been asked to use their imagination, which they love doing. They invariably come back with leaves or flowers and make the point that although all leaves or flowers follow the same basic design they all have unique differences, just like people and their personality similarities and differences. One group of N preference teachers I worked with in a hotel each returned with a different alcoholic beverage – pint of lager or beer, glass of wine, gin and tonic – and a big smile on their faces. They compared differences between alcoholic drinks with human personality differences. They also made the point that after they'd finished their drink their personalities were likely to change!

Student Activity: **The Snowman**

The type guru Jane Kise developed this activity as a professional development exercise and I've shared it with many teachers and students with fantastic and predictable results. For more details see Kise and Russell's *Differentiated School Leadership* (2008). Students need a pen/pencil and a blank sheet of paper. They are asked to write for five minutes. The instructions you supply need to be as described as below or you may prejudice the outcome.

'I'm about to reveal a title. You will have five minutes, one to think about what you'll write and four to write it, based on this title … "The Snowman".'

S preferences tend to write:

A review of *The Snowman* by Raymond Briggs.
A how-to-build-a-snowman guide.
A recollection of a childhood snowman-building experience.
A conventional chronological tale in which a snowman is made.

Personality in the Classroom

N preferences tend to write:

A metaphorical tale where there are references to themes such as life, death, love, loss and friendship or one bristling with florid descriptions and humour. For example: 'Once upon a time there was a drugs dealer called the Snowman. He was given this name due to the high quality of product he supplied in his neighbourhood …' This story was written by a primary school teacher and raised many of her colleagues' eyebrows when she read it out!

After people have written their stories it's a good idea to ask them to stand in a line with most S and most N at each end with gradations between. You then predict the likely stories at each end and ask for volunteers to read their story. The prediction is usually very accurate and helps teachers or students see how important this preference is. A selection of stories follow this activity for your pleasure!

Here is a selection of some snowman stories from Inset and student events:

N end of the scale:

Once upon a time there was a drug dealer named the Snowman. He was given this name due to the high quality of product he supplied to the local neighbourhood. He wrecked the lives of many people. For years his bony twig-like fingers swapped cash for drugs and drugs for cash. One winter there was a blizzard so severe that it kept most people off the streets. The Snowman stood on his familiar street corner and froze to death in the cold of night, his body stiff and coated in snow.

Primary teacher, Bahrain, ENFJ

The Snowman always wanted to experience a suntan but had been told by the Anti-Sun Council that it was impossible and he should erase all thoughts of sunbathing from his mind. He was determined to experience a tan and hired a pilot, using his snow dollars, and set off from Iceland on his southerly journey. While speaking to the pilot he noticed …

Mr Chapman, INTP (he also rearranged his type letters to say PINT!)

As it was such a hot day down at the beach, the Snowman melted away, just as his mum had warned him, and he, always knowing better, had ignored her, for the last time.

Primary teacher, Rochdale, INFJ

S end of the scale:

The Snowman is a famous book by Raymond Briggs and a cartoon that is often shown on TV at Christmas. It is famous for its pencil drawn animation and memorable soundtrack. Many people think the title song 'Walking in the Air' was sung by Aled Jones, but it wasn't. I don't remember who sang it but it definitely wasn't him. Definitely.

Secondary teacher, Tyneside, ISFP

To build a snowman you need the correct type of snow. Roll two balls, one bigger for the body (100 cm) and a smaller one for the head (30 cm). Decorate with small round objects for buttons. Wrap an old scarf around the neck (this acts as extra support). Carefully add eyes using pebbles and a nose using a carrot or parsnip. A hat can be added as a finishing touch.

Mr Dalston, Wales, ISTJ

And from a student using both S and N:

It was late on Christmas Eve. The children slept lightly, filled with anticipation and hope. At last it was morning. They rushed downstairs and opened their presents. They hadn't noticed the fresh fall of crisp white snow that neatly covered the whole garden. They ran out intent on building the best snowman ever. They constructed a big body and head and decorated their snowman using an old hat and scarf. Dad had been bought new ones for Christmas so he didn't mind.

Alice, Year 10 student, Suffolk, ESFJ

These two letters are so important because how tasks are given out to students will determine whether or not they'll be motivated to work enthusiastically or be bored before they even begin. N preferences need to be creative and throw their imagination into a task for it to appeal. **S** preferences need a structure and a sequence to latch on to for task satisfaction. **N** preferences like the big picture first whereas **S** preferences like to know detail and how the learning can be applied in the real world. Teachers miss an obvious, easy and powerful motivational aid if they ignore this difference between students. Satisfy both preferences and enjoy the enhanced enthusiasm you can weave into even the most challenging of topics.

Student Activity: **Story by Numbers**

Creativity can be defined as the process of bringing together two random ideas or objects and observing the result. Mostly the product will be rubbish but occasionally there will be magic. Evolutionary biologist Matt Ridley suggests sex as a metaphor for this process. Sexual reproduction produces far more variety within offspring than asexual reproduction. He argues that humans have made so much progress in the last few thousand years, compared to other species, due to an unprecedented mixing and blending of information, or as he puts it: 'when ideas have sex'. Nietzsche also described it well: 'You must have chaos within you to give birth to a dancing star.'

Here is a simple version of the parlour game Consequences which illustrates how a random process can be very creative. It's a great game for those students who use the mantra 'I'm not creative, me.'

Ask students to generate a list of answers to the following:

1   A word to describe a spider.
2   A cute animal.
3   Your favourite celebrity.
4   A room or place around school.
5   Your favourite teacher.
6   A type of fruit.

Students then put the words into the gaps below to give an insight into how creativity works:

Once upon a time there was an evil criminal called (1) …… (2) ……

He had a plan to kidnap (3) …… and imprison them in a secret cage in (4) ……

The only person who could save the day was (5) …… using a magic (6) ……. from the school kitchen.

Here are some activities to develop both **S** and **N** preferences.

Student Activity: **An Elephant in the Garden**

In pairs you have a conversation in which you cannot deny the other person's reality, only build upon it. One person takes on an **S** role and the other takes on an **N** role. You act out the roles, one person **S** and the other **N**, adding one sentence each. Swap over roles every time the teacher blows a whistle or claps. For example:

N: I have a pet elephant at home.

S: That must pose difficulties with regards to feeding.

N: No, I have Savannah grass delivered by helicopter from Africa.

S: How often?

N: Whenever the elephant is hungry. It presses our doorbell with its trunk, it can reach from its hutch you see, and this automatically triggers a delivery.

S: So it's a bit like Tesco home delivery?

N: Yes, only with helicopters, elephants and a magic goblin, trained as an animal psychologist who caters to the elephant's emotional needs.

S: The hutch must be big. Don't you live in a fifth-floor flat?

N: Yes, it's a nightmare getting the elephant in the lift; he's claustrophobic, but the goblin psychologist has made real progress lately.

This simple activity can really draw out the difference in **S** and **N** preferences. **S**'s marvel at the speed and weirdness of the **N** and the **N**'s at the clarity and grounded processing of the **S**. They understand and appreciate this difference even more when they swap roles. In many groups it may be best to work with teams of three (or four) because **S** preference people out-number **N** preferences by a ratio of two to one. The third person can perform the role of scribe and observer of the rules and can also remind the two protagonists of the **S** and **N** elements of their performance. This activity helps everyone appreciate difference and not show one approach as superior to the other per se.

Student Activity: Listen To Your Father/Comedy Improvisation

Listen to Your Father

A recent radio phone-in asked listeners to share daft things their dads told them when they were young. A long list of **N** preference ideas flooded in:

● My dad convinced me that cat's eyes on motorways were actually operated by elves with torches running up and down tunnels.
● My dad said talcum powder is made by putting moths in bags and shaking vigorously to collect dust.
● My dad said sweets and drinks bought at motorway services taste of petrol and should never be bought.

Ask your students what 'silly' **N** preference suggestions they've heard. A discussion on parental type and its influence on children can ensue.

Comedy Improvisation

Another version is asking students to riff Eddie Izzard style. I laughed for days after hearing Izzard observe that bees making honey is quite bizarre. He remarked that earwigs don't make chutney and wasps don't make mayonnaise. Invite students to mix their own combinations of insects/invertebrates and preserves/condiments/sauces and agree on the funniest combinations. This is **N** preference as applied by stand-up comedians.

Student Activity: Disney Creativity Strategy

Robert Dilts is one the pioneers and finest exponents of modelling – the neuro-linguistic programming (NLP) approach of finding experts in their fields and observing in detail how they achieve excellence. We can all then benefit from copying their process but *not* trying to be a mimic or karaoke version of the person. When we copy at the level of skill, not the level of identity, we can absorb the useful part of that we seek to learn.

Imagination and creativity are sought after qualities. Can they be taught? Robert Dilts modelled Walt Disney, renowned as a dreamer who also achieved results. Dilts discovered a process used by Disney that we can all follow to enhance our creativity. Disney basically tried on three different types of thinking in sequence (it's a bit like Thinking Hats). The model develops both **S** and **N** preferences (and **T** which is described in the next pair of preferences).

You can work individually or in teams, although it's best in teams. Identify a topic to stretch your creativity. Examples could include developing:

● A new magazine concept.
● A new brand of pet food.
● Ideas to improve school exam results (I dare you!).

● A policy think-tank to develop attractive policies for a pitch to the main political parties.

Mark out three distinct places, one for each step of the process. These could be corners of a room, separate tables or chairs or hoops placed on the floor.

The first area is *dreamer state*. Here we can imagine, daydream and ponder ideas and thoughts without fear of ridicule or judgement. All ideas should be noted briefly and quickly. It's good to explore your ideas as pictures. Look up and to your right as you daydream. Do not edit yourself at this stage as some of the best ideas start off from apparently silly and vague thoughts. Playing music and moving around can help at this point. Some people do this naturally before they drift off to sleep or while they're watching TV or staring up at the clouds or into a fire. This is **N** preference at play. Perhaps you can imagine you are all mermaids swimming in a warm lagoon or dragons flying through the skies looking for new ideas. Stop when the ideas have tailed off.

The second area is *realist state*. Here we take the list of ideas and begin to organise them into a structured plan. We ask: How would this work? What else do we need to know for it to happen in the real world? This is similar to **S** preference thinking.

The third area is *critic state*. Here we test the plan. We ask: What could go wrong? How would we put it right? Are there any unintended consequences or difficulties? What would doubters say? What are the costs and benefits? This is the equivalent of **T** (with a bit of **F**) preference.

You now begin to edit your list of ideas, not before, and then return to the dreamer state. Cycle around these three positions at least three times to refine and develop ideas before expecting great results.

Disney wanted to create full-length cartoon feature films. That was his dream. He believed there were fewer constraints to true storytelling in animated form than the traditional movie-making of the time. In realist state he researched the process. Could it be done technically? His answer was no it couldn't, so he developed new animation techniques and materials (including paints and acetates) until he knew it was now technically possible both in cost and time.

In critic state he asked, could a cartoon story sustain the interest of an audience for eighty minutes? He experimented with movie genres and settled on family friendly themes. Early drafts were not successful; audiences did not identify with animal characters. He went back into dreamer state to imagine animals drawn with faces that could show emotion. He added eyebrows and made the eyes bigger and audiences were then able to identify with the characters. Songs were incorporated as part of this process.

Most organisations neglect this process, especially dreamer state, and rush into launching something before all three positions are explored fully. *The Apprentice* illustrates this point as most tasks are completed to a frighteningly low standard (remember 'Pants Man'?).

Further techniques to develop creative thinking

John Davitt has developed a creative activity generator on his website (www.newtools.org/showtxt.php?docid=724) Type in your subject and click 'Generate' to view as many random suggestions as you like. For example, I entered the subject 'How the brain learns' and was given the following suggestions: As a U2 style rock anthem, as a letter of complaint, as a TV weather forecast with the subject in the background, as a sketch drawn with your non-dominant hand, as a one-minute play, as a twenty-second answer-phone message.

Role Play: Act out a scene such as being a passenger at an airport to develop new understanding and potential ways to improve service, or turn off the lights and go under your chair to understand what it was like to be a coal miner.

Ask Questions: Individually, then in groups, list as many questions as you can about a topic – silly questions are often the best. Philosophy for Children and Ian Gilbert's Thunks® are great examples of using questions to generate creative thinking. For example: Where does the sky start? What colour is love?

Six Thinking Hats and mind-mapping are additional approaches that produce creative thinking.

Blending the finest of **S** and **N** is best summarised as follows:

It's not wise to violate rules until you know how to observe them.

T. S. Eliot

How do you decide things – with your head or your heart?

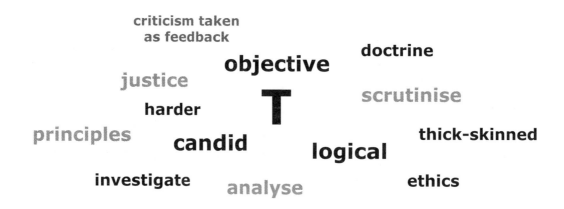

The **F** stands for Feeling and the **T** for Thinking. These labels can knock people off the scent of what this chunk of personality is all about. We all think and feel but there is a distinct variation around how we prefer to decide: objectively or subjectively. The **T/F** preference is the only one with a distinct gender difference. Around two-thirds of males report a **T** preference and one-third an **F** preference. For females the proportions are reversed: two-thirds **F** preference and one-third **T** preference.

Clues for T preference:

● I'm concerned first for the task.
● I ask 'Is it the right decision?'
● I usually think of comments as feedback.
● I'm seen as firm-minded.
● I'm more objective than subjective.

Clues for F preference:

● I'm concerned first for the people involved.
● I ask 'How will it affect people?'
● I usually think of comments as criticism.
● I'm seen as warm-hearted.
● I'm more subjective than objective.

My daughter is an **F** preference and my son a **T** preference. At the end of Year 7 I asked my daughter which subjects she liked best. As she replied I realised there was a direct link between the subjects she liked and the teachers she liked and liked her. This is typical of **F** preferences – people and relationships come first. For an **F** preference student, the relationship they have with their teacher will determine their attitude towards the subject and lesson. If they like the teacher they will like the subject. Many teachers, especially **T** preference, ignore this at their peril. If the personal relationship isn't strong, it doesn't matter how interesting you make a lesson or how brilliant your preparation.

Equally relevant is the different focus of **T** preference students. My **T** preference son has liked the same subjects through Years 7 to 11. For a **T** preference it is the content, task and process that are their focus, not relationships. To half of the students in your class content is the key. Touchy-feely stuff will put off **T** preferences. They will interpret this as weakness! They'd prefer you to be assertive and candid.

Football managers often use the cliché that good management is based on knowing which players need a kick up the backside and which players need an arm around their shoulder. This dichotomy of approach is as valid in the classroom (and staffroom) as it is in Sir Alex Ferguson's dressing room. Discovering a student's preference for **F** or **T** provides a powerful insight into how best to build a relationship and motivate individual students.

In most of the schools I visit the vibe is **F** in primary and **T** in secondary. The question of **F** or **T** as an organisational culture is interesting. What is the culture in your school? What impact does this have (on you, the students, staff and parents)? Research suggests that most businesses have a **T** preference culture and the majority of bosses have a **T** preference. Around 80% of head teachers have a **T** preference.

In the classroom, in my experience, many males will claim their preference is **T** due to peer pressure and the macho culture in which they live. Interestingly this effect is present among some groups of girls too, especially if a group leader is **T** (often Panther or Falcon) and the rest of the group will want to show they are the same as their leader. This effect also happens in organisations when staff model or copy their boss. It is important to attempt to dissipate the impact of peer pressure and other factors that can prevent someone accurately recognising and accepting their underlying preference.

Emphasising the difference between type preference and behaviour helps; we can all behave in an **F** or **T** style which doesn't undermine our preference. Describing (or showing clips) of TV advertisements can be revealing. For example, adverts for children's toys tend to be very stereotypical. An **F** style ad for a doll will tend to feature two smiling girls at the kitchen table gently combing the hair of a pony as soft twinkly music plays in the background. A **T** style ad for a doll will feature two shouting boys, outside in the rain with mud on their faces, crashing two action figures against each other, as loud thumping music blasts. Some TV programmes are very macho. You can almost smell the testosterone in an episode of *Top Gear* as the **T** preference presenters run amok in expensive cars and on pointless laddish challenges.

Personality in the Classroom

Exploring the **F/T** preference with students can be fascinating and revealing. The preference relates to how we make decisions and this means it is probably the preference most easily influenced and obscured by peer pressure and other external influences. As well as developing type theory, Jung also observed that all human cultures create similar explanations for the underlying aspects of the psyche, our deepest instincts. Jung called these archetypes – innate ways to experience and explain our urges. For example, the *shadow* archetype is our dark side, the voice of the devil we hear inside our heads. It is represented by symbols such as snakes, dragons and demons. The *anima* and *animus archetypes* are the male and female roles we play. We can all exhibit nurturing and detached behaviour depending upon the context. Even the toughest, hardest Year 11 student can be a big softy when cradling and cooing to their newly born sibling. The anima is the female aspect present in men and the animus the male aspect present in females. Jung was in no way being sexist here! He is referring to unconscious processes exhibited by both genders. We all find babies cute (and baby animals – you can check this by showing a picture of a young ape, puppy or kitten and a collective ahh! will reverberate around the classroom). Even if the tough students don't admit it they'll experience the ahh internally. Evolutionary biologists have found cuteness is directly proportionate to the size of eyes in proportion to the face; bigger is cute because babies have proportionately bigger eyes than adults. Recognising that both are present, but we have a preference, is really useful as it explains how we make decisions and interpret other people's decisions and motives in many areas of our lives.

Personality type **F** is generally associated with feminine and **T** with masculine characteristics. These are themes worthy of classroom discussion. Young people who are not their stereotype can find this revelation particularly useful. **F** preference males are naturally caring and **T** preference females naturally candid. When females are also **E** preference (Panther, Black Bear, Falcon and Eagle) they are naturally assertive, feisty and forthright. These females (e.g. Madonna, Katie Price, Victoria Beckham, Deborah Meaden) can too easily be labelled as lippy and troublemakers in school and beyond. They are the antithesis of the feminine stereotype of old-fashioned Disney films such as *Snow White* and *Sleeping Beauty*. Teaching **E** and **T** preference children to curb their 'tell it how it is, in ya face' approach will help them succeed inside and outside the classroom. Conversely, **I** and **F** preference (Koala, Seal, Cat and Seahorse) males are naturally gentle, kind and nurturing. This is against the stereotype of boys generally propagated in secondary schools. Yelling to these students 'Stand up for yourself, speak up, stop being a doormat', even if well-intentioned, is unlikely to be beneficial. Helping these students understand how their preferences impact on their approach and on how others perceive them is valuable.

Generally, we all think our preference is the correct lens from which to view and interpret the world. For example, emotional intelligence is a concept forged from an **F** perspective. The psychologist Carl Rogers also speaks from an **F** perspective when proposing that to grow and self-actualise we all need genuineness, acceptance and empathy. **F** preferences may benefit from these approaches but **T** preferences will generally not seek these conditions. Early twentieth century models of business management (treating people as units of production) were **T** preference interpretations of mass-produced goods. Interestingly, schools were developed in this period!

Knowledge of our own and other's preferences makes us better communicators. We must be careful not to treat people the way we expect to be treated ourselves, especially in relation to **F** and **T** preferences.

We do not see things as they are. We see things as we are.

Anaïs Nin

There is a saying: no good deed goes unpunished. This could be a direct warning to **F** preferences. They want to help, be nice and want everyone to get along. While discussing the essence of his comedy character David Brent, Ricky Gervais suggests Brent confused being popular with being respected. It is a characteristic of **F** preference that they will try to gain respect by being nice to people. This approach is likely to end in failure. It is especially dangerous when an **F** uses this approach to a **T** preference: they respect someone less not more if they see equivocation and 'softness'.

An **F**'s way of thinking:

If you don't like someone, the way they hold their spoon will make you furious; if you do like them, they can turn their plate over into your lap and you won't mind.

Irving Becker

A **T**'s way of thinking:

I'll always tell you what I really think. Why wouldn't I? I'll not say one thing at the dinner-table and another to the camera half an hour later. I'm not aggressive, I'm honest.

Sarah, a contestant on *Come Dine With Me*

F teacher with F student

Both you and your student are concerned first with people and relationships before the task/subject content. You like to form personal relationships with all your students, unless you don't like the student – and **F** preference teachers are more inclined than **T** preference teachers to have their favourites! You are also prone to make promises to students you may not be able to keep, overstretch yourself and even do work the students should be doing themselves. You both enjoy a warm and friendly classroom atmosphere. Compliments are likely to go in both directions boosting your confidence as well as your student's. A thank-you card will make your day! The student needs to feel you like them. If this happens they'll work hard but if not they may switch off completely. This explains why a student can be top of the class one year (with a teacher they like) and show no interest at all in the same subject the following year when they change teacher. To get the best out of your student:

- Offer learning situations that allow the application of empathy, collaboration and teamworking.
- Provide ample and regular praise while offering tactful support to overcome any blind-spots.
- Motivate by appealing to the strength of your personal belief in the student (don't let me down, I know you can do it, I like you).

F teacher with T student

The teacher is concerned with relationship first then task, whereas it's the other way round for the student. You must accept that the student is different; not cold, blunt, mean and unfriendly, just different and focused on task first. If you can accept this your relationship can be really positive. To get the best out of your naturally objective student you need to:

- Offer targeted compliments. Just saying everything is great will neither impress nor help the student; in fact, it can result in the student respecting you less and concluding you are a liar or a soft touch. When you praise you may be pressed for proof!
- Be logical and objective rather than emotional in discussions.
- Realise that if the student challenges you it is probably to clarify their thoughts rather than dispute your authority or character. Perhaps ask 'What would you do to improve/change this?' or 'What do you think?' Once they've clarified their thoughts they may be ready to ask and absorb what you think.
- Work in ways that test their skill and knowledge competitively (they raise their game).
- Encourage the student to develop tact and diplomacy because around 50% of people are **F** preference and can interpret their well-intentioned feedback as a personal attack.

T teacher with T student

Both you and your student are task-focused, direct, consistent, blunt and assertive. The classroom is likely to have a business-like atmosphere. You provide students with clear and concise guidelines on what is expected in terms of behaviour, homework and so on. At best this means everyone knows where they stand and how to behave. To get the best out of your naturally task-focused student:

- Work in ways that test their skill and knowledge competitively (they raise their game for competitions, challenges, quizzes, measuring and beating personal bests).
- Help them understand that 50% of people are **F** preference and can interpret well-intentioned feedback as personal criticism (remember this one yourself!).
- Focus on what the student has achieved and what comes next.

T teacher with F student

You focus first on task and second on people/relationships. The classroom is likely to have a purposeful atmosphere. You provide clear guidelines on what is expected in terms of behaviour, homework and so on. At best this means everyone knows where they stand and how to behave. At worst the classroom can resemble a military boot-camp full of either potentially mutinous or dispirited and brow-beaten new recruits.

Remember, the personal relationship you have with this student is key to their accord. The student needs to feel you like them. If this happens they'll work harder but if not they may switch off. This explains why a student can be top of the class one year (with a teacher they like) and show no interest at all in the same subject the following year when they change teacher. To get the best out of your naturally people-focused student you need to:

● Offer learning situations that allow for the use of empathy, collaboration and teamworking to counter-balance your natural tendency to focus on task.

● Give ample and regular praise while offering tactful support to overcome any weaknesses. Feedback can be easily interpreted as criticism so walk on egg-shells when delivering it.

● Motivate by appealing to the strength of your personal belief in the student (don't let me down, I know you can do it, I like you).

● Be prepared to compromise occasionally; the student will see you as human rather than weak.

● Avoid trying to fix something without considering potential underlying emotional causes.

Some teachers/schools are uncomfortable with the concept of saying you like a student because it could come back and haunt you later when another student complains that they haven't been presented with the accolade. Praise the behaviour not the person is the mantra. Personally, I believe that by not doing so you're missing a great opportunity to reach **F** preference students. You're not training dogs; you're attempting to inspire children. I'm an **F** preference and I still remember my art teacher telling me she liked me and my work and thought I could go on and achieve great things. I can still remember the room and where I was sitting as she said it – it was so powerful. She only said it once but once was enough. I don't think I'd be working in education if I hadn't had a handful of amazing teachers to inspire me. This approach is to be used sparingly and must be genuine to have an impact but is surely worth having in your repertoire. Researchers have found that dolphins (real dolphins not ENFJ's) will work harder for trainers who occasionally offer additional random rewards than for trainers who only provide a treat after the completion of a specific task. Dolphins, like many humans, want to be appreciated for who they are and not just how good they are at jumping through hoops.

Here are some activities which identify **F** and **T** preferences.

Student Activity: **Discussion**

The teacher reads, or displays on a screen, various scenarios for groups to discuss. Examples could include:

1   You are going out for the day with friends. One person has invited themselves who most people in the group do not like. What should you do?

   T's will lean towards the bald truth with comments such as: 'I'd tell her she couldn't come because she simply wasn't invited', 'I'd tell her she was cheeky but could come' or 'I wouldn't talk to her all day'.

   F's lean towards empathy and equivocation: 'She could still come but couldn't choose which shops we visit', 'She could spend time with the people who do like her', 'We'll let her come this time' or 'I'd think she was being cheeky but wouldn't say anything to her'.

2   Show a picture (that is busy with people and scenery) and ask students to write down what they see.

F's tend to be subjective and focus on the people and speculate on their relationships: 'It's two friends who have recently had an argument, I think they'll be OK because …'

T's tend to be more objective and focus on the scene as well as the people: 'It's autumn because the leaves are turning brown and windy because the flag is flapping and there is a party in the garden.'

3   Agony Aunt. Either (a) describe a problem from a column that is based around a relationship, misunderstanding and what-to-do-next dilemma. (Steer clear of those that could be at home on an episode of *Jeremy Kyle*; if you've never seen *Jeremy Kyle*, well done, please keep up the good work.) Ask individuals to formulate a response then discuss their opinions: do they match an **F** and **T** response? Or (b) give out a page or carefully chosen collection of letters and ask students to identify **F** and **T** replies. Upmarket broadsheet dilemma columns where readers provide answers to a question are particularly effective.

Here are some activities to develop **F** and **T** preferences.

Student Activity: **Channel Hopping**

Show a selection of TV adverts and ask students to identify **F** and **T** references. For what purpose are these references made? Are you influenced/interested in gender (and other) stereotypes? Children's toys are good examples. DIY products and lager ads are generally very **T** while cleaning products such as air fresheners and washing-up liquid are very **F**.

Student Activity: **The Three Perceptual Positions**

Position 1: *I, I feel, I think, I see*

We experience the world through our own eyes. We are mostly interpreting information based on how we feel about it and what we will or could do next.

Position 2: *They*

We empathise with another person, we see the world as they see it, we're in their shoes, we anticipate what they might think and do next. When we watch TV or films or read fiction, we regularly identify with characters. This is **F** preference at its best, like a counsellor or police psychologist trying to predict the next movement of a criminal.

Position 3: *Outsider, detached observer, detective*

We are in position of judge and jury. We do not identify with one character; we forensically examine the motives and actions of all protagonists. This is **T** preference at its best, like Inspector Morse or Jonathan Creek.

Select a clip from a scene involving two protagonists with very different viewpoints (from *EastEnders* to Shakespeare). Play the clip twice. During the first viewing students are asked to experience the scene in Position 2, as the character A or B (perhaps half the students as character A and the other half as character B) making notes and then commenting on the feelings and motivation of each character. Then repeat with the whole class experiencing the scene in Position 3 as judge/ jury deciding who is right/wrong and what might happen next. The activity illustrates **T** and **F** preferences.

In NLP the first perceptual position is I or me. What do I experience? What do I think? This equates to watching the clip and saying what *you* think not what the characters think. This is **T** preference in action. The second perceptual position is about identifying and empathising with the character, understanding their feelings/motivations and predicting what they'll do next. This is **F** preference in action. The third perceptual position is observing and analysing a situation from a distance and understanding what both characters are experiencing, like a judge/jury. This is the best of **F** and **T** in action – pulling both sources of information together and drawing accurate conclusions.

Judging and perceiving

prepared   deadlines

reach goals   **finish**   **J**   **decisive**   **on the move**

control

seek order   **organised**   complete

tidy   closure

neat   plan

relax   proposal

flexible   **start**   **seek fun**

pending   **P**   slouch

open   off the cuff

chill   **spontaneous**   adapt

change goals

guidelines

Is your attitude to life more about planning/organisation (**J**) or spontaneity and flexibility (**P**)? This preference has a massive impact in school (and life generally) because it relates to our overall approach to living. The **J** stands for Judging and the **P** for Perceiving. These words do not accurately encapsulate the meaning of these preferences. They refer to the **J** preference desire to decide and then move on, contrasted with the **P** preference desire to keep options and senses open to absorb further information.

Clues for J preference:

- I like to plan and organise.
- I like writing and using lists.
- I prefer things tidy, so I know where everything is.
- Once I start something I gain satisfaction once I've finished.
- I work at a steady pace.

Clues for P preference:

- I like to wonder how things will turn out.
- I don't like writing or using lists.
- I don't usually keep things tidy, so I often spend time looking for stuff.
- I enjoy starting things but can easily become bored and start something else.
- I work at the last minute to get things finished.

The film *Clockwise*, starring John Cleese as an ultra-organised head teacher (**J**) who used to be disorganised (**P**) on his way to speak at a conference, is a parable on the strengths and weaknesses of both **J** and **P** behaviour.

J preferences are natural organisers. They see the world as something to be organised using the systems and procedures they have developed themselves. They get things done on time and become appreciated for their reliability. Because they impose their own systems in everything they do their Achilles heel can be a lack of flexibility and an 'I know best' attitude. They are satisfied when they complete a task. **P** preferences are naturally flexible and spontaneous. They do not seek to control the world because they crave options. They like to adapt and amend as they progress, so they tend to complete work at the last minute. They are satisfied when they start a task.

Large organisations require and favour **J** preference behaviour. To succeed as a teacher or student **J** preference behaviour is required whether or not it is your preference. Disadvantaged **P** students need support if they are to thrive in schools. Most do receive this support and are successful but they'll generally find the whole experience uncomfortable and unnatural. In many schools it's cool to behave in a **P** preference way, but not very productive!

A **P** preference speaks:

> *There is no pleasure in having nothing to do; the fun is in having lots to do and not doing it.*
>
> **Mary Wilson Little**

My wife is a **J** preference and I'm **P**. Following the birth of our son, my wife spent ten days in hospital and then ten days at home. I was driving home from work on a Wednesday evening thinking she'd been indoors for nearly three weeks and perhaps we could go out to the Metro Centre at the weekend. I suggested this to my wife who – as a **J** preference likes a plan and likes to stick to it – agreed and mentally noted that we'd be visiting the Metro Centre at 10 a.m. on Saturday. To her it is a written contract, a confirmed diary entry. To me, a **P** preference, it was just an idea, a possibility, an option to throw into the pot of possible weekend activities. When Saturday morning arrived my wife was busily packing the baby bag with the seventy essential items we'd need for a two-hour trip and I asked what she was doing. She reminded me of our earlier conversation.

'What's the matter, don't you want to go?' she asked.

'It's a nice day; perhaps we could go somewhere else?'

'Do you want to go somewhere else?'

'I'm not sure – should we decide on the way?'

This type of conversation is typical between **J** and **P** preference couples. The **P** prefers options and choices whereas the **J** seeks a plan and closure. Research by Paul Tieger suggests this letter difference is the most likely source of conflict in marriages (when one partner is **J** and the other **P**) as it pervades our whole attitude to time and life. It is likely to have a big impact in the classroom too.

Marriage guidance for J's

Two **J** preferences together is an interesting combination. A marriage guidance counsellor saw a couple who had been married for forty years before seeking help. They'd been happily married for thirty-five and then the husband was made redundant. For years he'd looked after the garden and garage and she'd taken care of the house and kids. Following his redundancy he began to offer his wife helpful suggestions such as changing the day they shopped and alternative cleaning routines. His suggestions did not find favour and instead of implementing his ideas she sought marriage guidance. The counsellor identified a classic **J+J** relationship. **J**'s get on well together when they divide out the tasks. Their partnership worked when they split the tasks and left each other to get on with it. **J**'s work best together when they do this. Both will complete tasks in their own way and on time. Tension and conflict is likely if **J**'s try to organise each other. In attempting to impose their own right way onto another **J**, who already has their own right way, a skirmish or clash is almost inevitable. The counsellor recommended they divide out all the jobs again and leave each other to complete their responsibilities without interference. This is the key to a great relationship for two **J**'s whether married or in school.

The other combination is two **P** preferences together. This is a Shaggy and Scooby or Homer and Bart Simpson combination. Both are laid back and enjoy the moment. In the classroom they are relaxed and open-minded as teacher or student. A **P** preference teacher can be a great team member amongst a group of **J** teachers as they bring calm and spontaneity to the team. Their desks are likely to be cluttered and their approach apparently chaotic; so a team made up exclusively of **P** preferences could resemble a white water rafting experience.

J teacher with J student

Both you and your student are organised, decisive, like to work out a plan and are enraptured and mesmerised by it. Your classroom is a bastion of organisation, a well-oiled machine. The subject will probably be broken down into lesson-sized chunks and the year planned out with alacrity. Many **J** students are reassured by your organisational fervour. They simply accept your schedule and deliver their side of the bargain, generally completing all tasks on time. Interestingly, some **J** students will baulk at your well-intentioned thoroughness as they would prefer to create their own plan rather than have one imposed, due to their desire for control. So two **J** preferences together can clash, though at least all the work will be done. Most secondary schools require students to be so organised that two **J** preferences are the probably the most constructive combination. There may be a little bit more **P**-friendly slack in the primary, further and higher education sectors but it is being relentlessly eroded like a chalk cliff face in a gale-force storm. To get the best out of your naturally organised student:

● Rejoice in your shared desire for all things ordered, neat and respectful of deadlines.
● Allow the student independence in planning their work in their own way if they really want to.
● Be prepared to adjust your own plans if external events interfere with your careful preparations and encourage your student to also embrace flexibility when pertinent.
● Avoid making quick decisions about what needs to be done before considering all of the options.

J teacher with P student

You are organised and decisive. You develop and implement plans. Your classroom is usually an organised place, running like clockwork, your subject broken down into lesson-sized chunks and the whole year planned out. Your **P** student will either respond:

● Positively by accepting your expertise and understanding the long-term benefits they'll reap.
● Passively by just accepting your structure/plan for an easy life without really buying into the content or process you are offering.
● Negatively by rejecting you, your structure/plan and subject completely; even if they're physically in your room they will not engage and participate.

To get the best out of your naturally laid-back student you should note your student doesn't just like options and choice; they need them or they start to squirm, wriggle and rebel. The secondary school environment is difficult enough for **P** preference students so you can help to soften the pressure. To help:

- Provide as much flexibility as possible such as multiple choice homework tasks and options within the lesson.
- Avoid giving out detailed schedules unless they're essential.
- Don't be pickier with detail than is absolutely necessary and avoid scolding the student for occasional lapses if at all possible.
- Shake things up now and again to prevent predictability becoming boring for the student; random surprises and changes to routines will be energising.
- Assist the student to identify simple time-management techniques to ensure they can succeed; some organisation benefits everyone.

P teacher with P student

You and your student can be organised and efficient – it's just such an effort! While enjoying a mutual love of spontaneity, which provides each with relief from the stifling and constraining timetables and deadlines prevalent in most large organisations such as schools, you must also remember to complete essential and necessary tasks. Although you are likely to be a fun and popular teacher you must also focus on the task of preparing the student to succeed socially and academically. Both you and your student prefer to start tasks than finish them. Your initial enthusiasm can quickly wane. To get the best out of your naturally laid-back student you need to understand they don't just like options and choice; they are essential or they'll start to squirm, wriggle and rebel. The structured, timetabled and routine-rich secondary school environment is difficult for many **P** preferences. You can help by:

- Providing as much flexibility as possible (multiple choice homework tasks and options within the lesson).
- Avoiding detailed schedules unless absolutely necessary; they ossify rather than energise the student.
- Mix things up now and again to prevent boredom setting in; random surprises and changes will be energising.
- Assisting the student to adopt simple time-management techniques to ensure they can succeed academically in the **J** preference world of school and work.

P teacher with J student

There is a stark contrast between your laid-back, flexible and spontaneous style and your naturally organised student that either can be a massive chasm or a useful place to build a bridge that both of you can use. To create a positive relationship you need to play to each other's strengths. The student can benefit from your ability to adapt and change plans and you can benefit from the student's desire to have a plan they can work to and complete. You can also:

- Support the student's desire for order, neatness and respecting deadlines.
- Allow the student independence in planning their work in their own way if they really want to.
- Avoid changing plans just for the sake of it; you will frustrate rather than engage the student.
- Encourage the student to consider flexibility now and then as it can be beneficial; learning to take things in your stride rather than become flustered is a useful life lesson.

When are rules useful? When is it acceptable to break rules? Ask students how they feel about instructions and rules generally and a **J/P** difference usually emerges.

Here is an activity to introduce the **J/P** preference to your students.

Student Activity: **Perfect Portrait**

Students are given the following instruction sheet on drawing/painting a portrait. Art materials are required. The twist in this activity is to discover your students' attitude towards rules and instructions. Halfway through you stop the group and offer them the chance to complete the picture in their own way or continue to follow the instructions. Avoid paying too much attention to their work to minimise your influence! At the end of the ten minutes you can reveal the purpose and seek feedback.

What should happen is **J** preferences accept and follow the instructions. They will be more careful and deliberate. They are more likely to stay with the instructions rather than following the offer to abandon them. **P** preferences should approach the task differently. They are bored by instructions and may have abandoned these even before the offer! They prefer to improvise and are more likely to ignore the instructions early in the process.

Instruction sheet

You have ten minutes to create a self-portrait in a specific style of a famous artist.

1   Draw a circle in the middle of the page as big as you can.
2   Use blue or green paint/pencil to shade in the area outside of the circle. Leave enough space at the bottom to paint in your full name in capital letters in red.
3   Draw the outline of your eyes, nose and mouth.
4   For the skin of the face use two brushes each with a slightly different shade, matching your own skin colour, and dab as if applying dots until you cover the whole face except for the eyes and mouth.
5   Use dabs of blue for the top lip.
6   Use dabs of green for the bottom lip.
7   For the tongue use pink.
8   For hair use the brightest yellow you can find and add using S shape strokes.
9   For the eyes use only black and white paint.
10   Add eight red dots along the top and nine black dots along the bottom.
11   Well done. You have now finished.
12   Stop and await further instructions.

Here are some activities to develop **J** and **P** preferences.

Student Activity: **Cool at School**

Ask students to stand on one side of the room if they like to get things sorted and finished before they play and on the other side if they can play anytime. Encourage honesty as peer pressure tends to push teenagers towards the former statement and adults to the latter statement (particularly when they are in the same room as their boss). More teenagers will gravitate towards the second statement (**P**) than the first (**J**).

Describe the benefits of both preferences. What can they offer? Why it is cool to be **P** preference? What is it like when you have to operate in your non-preferred letter?

Student Activity: **Planning and Plans**

Ask students to line up from most **J** at one end through to most **P** at the other. Select a group of five at each end and sit them in groups on either side of the room. Everyone else joins you at the front. Explain to the two groups you are going to present a question and they are going to discuss it and note down their answers. Write up the statement: 'Describe the importance of plans and planning'.

As the groups get to work, quietly predict what their answers will be with the students at the front. This is basically a **J** question so we can predict the **J**'s will like the question and answer it sincerely. They will generally agree that plans and planning are good and provide a list of reasons to justify their viewpoint.

Predict the **P** group will be bored by the question and not really want to answer it. They are uncomfortable with plans and planning. Their answers tend to be vague and half-hearted. They may even answer a little sarcastically.

After both groups have written something ask for feedback. The results are generally as predicted and you can then discuss the differences between **J** and **P** preferences and the impact on attitude to homework and revision.

Developing awareness of all eight letters (EISNFTJP) in your classroom

I am always doing that which I cannot do, in order that I may learn how to do it.

Picasso

Learning how to use all eight preferences develops increased flexibility of behaviour. We can learn to choose the best way to behave in any situation we encounter. How cool is that!

Student Activity: Holiday of a Lifetime

Create a holiday advert to appeal to all eight preference letters. You could give each group a different location or style of holiday: skiing in Italy, beach resort in Jamaica, camping/adventure holiday in Wales, Mediterranean cruise or Ibiza clubbing experience. For example:

At our resort there are nightclubs and karaoke and Skegness has got talent [appealing to E preferences]. We also have quiet and secluded pools and beach areas where you can relax among your thoughts [appealing to I preferences] to the gentle sound of ocean waves and songbirds from our nature garden. During the day you can try your hand at crafts, dance or sporty activities [S preference] or feed your creative side with painting, poetry and drama [N preference].

Check at the end if groups have appealed to the rest of the students' preferences by voting on who likes the holiday. If all eight preferences are included everyone should be keen on the holiday.

Student Activity: **SWOT Style Analysis**

Using their personality description from this book or www.thebuzzbook.co.uk, each student carries out a self-assessment of known strengths, known weaknesses, unknown strengths and unknown weaknesses. For example an ENFP may agree they are creative and friendly (known strengths), unaware they're a catalyst (unknown strengths), aware they're disorganised (known weakness) and so on.

SWOT Analysis

Name: .... Animal type: ....

Known strengths:	Unknown strengths:
Known weaknesses:	**Unknown weaknesses:**

In pairs the students can discuss their results. Emphasise the importance of self-awareness and how positive it is to share/ discuss who we are with others. What can they do to overcome any identified weaknesses?

Student Activity: **Word Power**

Teams look at the following lists which describe **E** and **I** preferences:

E: active, loud, friendly, sociable, good talker, boisterous, aggressive

I: passive, quiet, deep, shy, good listener, slow, boring, secretive

Are some words positive? Are some negative? If so, can you think of a suitable alternative word or phrase? Are some words biased, confusing or unclear? Can you identify five good pairs of words to help people understand the preferences?

All preferences are OK. It's fine to be who we are and understand our natural strengths and styles. We need to be aware of the danger of stereotyping and using pejorative words/phrases.

Student Activity: **Typecasting**

Pairs choose a famous person they both know fairly well and work out their preferences. They can then look up the full description to see if it fits. For example: Stephen Fry is **E** not **I, N** not **S, F** not **T** and **J** not **P**; is Eminem **I, N, T** and **J**?

Student Activity: **Animal Magic**

Students work in animal groupings (Bears, Cats, Sea Animals and Birds). They could first be asked to match four descriptions to the four animal groupings. Then ask students if they exhibit their own animal preferences in school or at home.

Ask what each person in the group has in common and how they differ. Are they friends with a mixture of types or do they mostly have friends who are the same animal type? Why is that? How can this help/hinder them?

Students can also be asked to match types to suitable learning styles, school/degree course subjects or careers to generate discussions about how to plan their future based on underlying preferences. This is a good activity when dividing students into animal groupings (see Chapter 4).

The table below could be used as a worksheet. You may wish to blank out the headers (Bears, Birds, etc.) if you're going to ask the students to match up each description. Alternatively place a blanked out version on a screen and ask groups to identify each animal grouping. You can then give out this sheet for referencing the remaining tasks within this activity.

Leading animal groupings: an overview

Bears (SJ)	Cats (SP)
• Like setting rules, expect things done their way, offer plenty of dos and don'ts	• Prefer a hands-off style, flexible and bold
• Value tradition, thoroughness, defined roles and responsibilities	• Independent problem-solvers
• Enjoy finishing tasks	• Encourage others to learn by doing, developing and applying their skills
• Annoyed by unmet deadlines, neglect of procedure	• Hard to fool
• If stressed – they remove privileges from those around them	• Focused on action and process
• Favourite question: Are we following the rules?	• Under-represented in teaching
	• Annoyed by strict directions
	• If stressed – become strict or lackadaisical
	• Favourite question: Can we just get on with it now?
Bears like to be recognised for *what* they produce, the results of their endeavour, sweat and toil.	Cats like to be recognised for *how* they work and contribute.
Sea Animals (NF)	**Birds (NT)**
• Encouraging, nurturing, 'hippy' leaders	• Strategic, objective, logical leaders
• Seek harmony, shared values, common purpose	• Task-focused
• Focus on ideas and people	• Most self-critical of all types
• Annoyed by impersonal treatment, organisational violation of their values	• Self-contained (think about ideas), competitive, intellectual
• If stressed – withdraw their support/include only their 'favourites'	• Annoyed by poor logic, reason or principle and unproductive rules/tradition
• Favourite question: How can we all get along?	• If stressed – autocratic
	• Favourite question: Why?
Sea animals like to be recognised for *who* they are.	Birds like to be recognised for their *ideas*.

Personality in the Classroom © David Hodgson and Crown House Publishing, 2012.

Chapter 4
Leadership Styles

In this chapter:

- ● Learn about leadership styles

- ● Explore how type can help you lead and inspire staff, colleagues and students

- ● Apply the type temperaments model
(Cats, Birds, Sea Animals and Bears) in school and beyond

When the music changes so does the dance.
African proverb

Leadership styles

Great leaders have a strong sense of identity. They have passion and authenticity. They lead through sharing their vision. Martin Luther King had a dream, not a seventeen-point action plan including improving by 2.5% in this or that. Start leading in a school or classroom with your vision. By sharing your message you will attract followers.

The first to join you are the bravest. In marketing theory (the Law of Diffusion of Innovations) they are innovators and make up only 2.5% of a group, so don't be put off by an initially cool response to your rallying call. Next will come the 13.5% of early adopters/early majority; they like what they see and can spot the value and potential. Then it becomes easier as the 34% of late adopters/late majority join the prevailing culture. Around 16%, the laggers, may never join you and this is often the hardest part of leadership – recognising that not everyone will be able to follow your vision. Some leaders then spend a disproportionate amount of time wooing the laggers and neglecting the needs, support and advice of the majority, which can derail the whole organisation. On www.ted.com Derek Sivers illustrates this process by showing a clip from a music festival. A lone dancer struts his stuff (the metaphor being head teacher or classroom teacher). After a little while he is joined by an innovator and then a few more and then more join the mash-up. Soon most people are dancing (late adopters).

Leadership is sometimes confused with management. Most leadership courses are management courses. Resources and people can be managed but only people can be led. So leadership is about moving people (followers) from one place to another. History shows us that carrots for the bosses and sticks for the workers were the preferred twentieth-century tools available to leaders. In school leadership neither should be used. School leaders would be attempting to herd cats if they attempted such approaches. Measuring teacher performance and impact is not as simple as factory output (although the Fischer Family Trust and Ofsted have a go). Teachers are masters in their own classrooms and, like many professionals in the public sector, pretty isolated. Leading teachers is different. Leading a school is also different. Few leaders have to unite so many groups (teachers, parents, students, governors, local community, politicians, employers, etc.).

Personality type can help. Leadership is about people and the first person we need to understand is our self.

Leaders create momentum behind a clear vision based on higher values. Not a bland mission statement but a real principle. This should be something to motivate and inspire students, parents and teachers. To check yours, answer the following questions:

If your school was an animal what would it be and why?

If your students were a football team who would they be and why?

If your school was a prison/hospital/country who would be who?

Here are some answers teachers have given in recent sessions:

> *Our school would be Wigan or Wolves, not the best resourced but punching above their weight, fighting hard.*

> *Our school is like Newcastle, poor leadership but still in the Premier League.*

This reveals much about the attitude of the staff. What kind of leadership vision is required in your school?

An additional activity which reveals a teacher's thoughts on their personal strengths and their potential contribution to a team is the Retsina Game (so called because retsina is universally acknowledged as the world's most appalling drink).

The Retsina Game

Ask a group of teachers (working in same animal groupings): 'If you were a drink, other than retsina, what would you be and why?' Their answers are likely to be as entertaining as they are revealing.

Here is a sample of answers and a blank grid for your own use.

Polar Bear (ISTJ)	Koala (ISFJ)	Seahorse (INFJ)	Barn Owl (INTJ)
Whisky, neat – no nonsense. Water – essential but unexciting.	A thermos flask of weak milky tea – nice, unnoticed and just what you need to help you relax as you sit in your car (don't want to catch the sniffles) looking out to sea.	The Ocean (known as 'the drink') – deep, metaphorical, hidden, massive potential and swirling body of ideas and possibilities.	A top quality whisky – strong, quality, understated and effective.
Tiger (ISTP)	Cat (ISFP)	Seal (INFP)	Tawny Owl (INTP)
Lager – a serious session with the lads/lasses or drunk cold from the fridge at home; flexible and independent.	Cream/milk – liked by most, nourishing and nurturing.	A magic potion with the power (of imagination) to persuade people to behave in new ways.	Pure alcohol – endless possibilities and combinations, dangerous to know but exciting.
Panther (ESTP)	Lion (ESFP)	Clownfish (ENFP)	Falcon (ENTP)
A high energy drink that generates energy and fun.	A party cocktail – a bowl of punch (with bits of unnecessary fruit) that can be adapted all night to suit the mood of the party.	A spilled drink, knocked over by a Clownfish. A drink you can't remember where you put it down …	Something fizzy. Vodka – can be mixed with a variety of soft drinks to form a potent experience.
Black Bear (ESTJ)	Teddy Bear (ESFJ)	Dolphin (ENFJ)	Eagle (ENTJ)
Champagne – only the best will do for Black Bears.	A cappuccino shared with friends as gossip is exchanged.	A smoothie – full of good ingredients that help people be their best.	A top selling aspirational brand that leads the field; competitors try to emulate the natural leader.

If you were a drink what would you be and why?

Polar Bear (**ISTJ**)	Koala (**ISFJ**)	Seahorse (**INFJ**)	Barn owl (**INTJ**)
Tiger (**ISTP**)	Cat (**ISFP**)	Seal (**INFP**)	Tawny Owl (**INTP**)
Panther (**ESTP**)	Lion (**ESFP**)	Clownfish (**ENFP**)	Falcon (**ENTP**)
Black Bear (**ESTJ**)	Teddy Bear (**ESFJ**)	Dolphin (**ENFJ**)	Eagle (**ENTJ**)

Is there a 'best mix' of people for a great leadership team?

Couples provide a clue to answering this question. Over 90% of couples believe good communication is the most important indicator of a healthy relationship. At home or work, teams that communicate well perform well. People of similar types will generally communicate more effectively with each other because they are on the same wavelength. Does this mean teams comprising similar types are better leaders? No, they may get along together but they are more likely to be poorer performing if they lead a large organisation of differing personality types. Statistics on marriage reveal that couples are more likely to stay together when they share two rather than any other number of preferences.

The number appears to be more important than which pairs of letters are shared. Effective relationships benefit from variety. When different perspectives are available to couples or teams the insights and decisions are likely to be stronger. Diversity works on many levels. Bosses who recruit and promote people in their own image (type) are risking the future of their organisation. The essence of great leadership is great communication between great varieties of opinion. Different types like to lead and be led in different ways as follows:

Bears (50% of population – 75% of leaders)

The story of the *Three Little Pigs* provides both vindication and solace to the four Bear personality types. Bears build brick by brick. They believe hard work and following instructions will bring lasting rewards. They eschew the straw or stick house option both as leader and as follower. When leading Bears, make sure you give them plans and bricks and they will respond positively; busily building a strong wolf-proof school brick by brick, day by day.

- Like setting rules and expect things to be done their way.
- They ask via interpreting rules (their own or the school's) with plenty of dos and don'ts, shouldn't and must, and so on.
- Value tradition, thoroughness, defined roles and responsibilities.
- Teddy and Koala focus/purpose: people (over-represented in primary teaching).
- Black and Polar focus/purpose: task completion.
- Annoyed by unmet deadlines, neglect of procedure.
- If stressed – they remove privileges from those around them.

Bears like to be recognised for what they produce, the results of their endeavour, sweat and toil. They cope least well with change, clinging on to established ways more than any other types. They prefer evolution to revolution. Sometimes they'll be right and sometimes they'll be wrong, but good leaders introduce change carefully to Bears, stressing the sequential and logical benefits that will be harnessed with the introduction of each little change. Bears are good at consistently adhering to rules and procedures and tweaking existing systems and protocols. They're more patient with detail and routine tasks than other types. They're keen to introduce stars, house points and other symbolic rewards.

The Asian countries that successive politicians insist we should be emulating generally espouse natural **S/J** methods (and 50% of people have **S/J** preferences). It is not surprising that politicians and *Daily Mail* readers would like to embed concepts such as discipline, respect and following the rules; they're what built the British Empire. School blazer too hot, boy? Well it's preparing you to serve King and Country in the colonies!

Not only have these days long gone in British culture, they're actually worrying many Asian educators. The culture of respect for rules and tradition is strong in Asia but may well hold back their economic development for the remainder of this century. Speaking on *Newsnight* a Professor of Delinquency from the University of Beijing recently bemoaned a lack of entrepreneurial spirit and attitude of risk-taking that is essential in the young if China is to develop beyond a mass-manufacturing model. Such political and cultural repression across much of Asia perhaps gives the UK a great opportunity to flourish for a little longer. According to Professor Ken Robinson, tradition in the UK means 200 years; in the USA it is 20 years; and in China 2,000 years. As the pace of change speeds up we need ever more flexible workers to succeed but this attitude eludes many Bears. Rather than being taunted and vilified, they need to be made aware of their strengths and the benefits of developing greater flexibility of behaviour.

> *It used to take 15 years for half of workers' skills to become out-dated, this now happens in 3 years.*
>
> **Susan Nash and Courtney Bolin,**
> *Teamwork from the Inside Out Fieldbook*

Perhaps this is a useful tenet for everyone, especially teachers; what we think we know can quickly become obsolete. A greying politician making education policy based on their own school-day experiences may be just too outdated. So we must respect the strengths **SJ**'s can bring (and they make up 50% of our students) while also teaching the importance of elasticity of thought and continual development of skills to thrive throughout their working lives. Type is an excellent framework in which to develop these profitable attitudes and behaviours. **SJ**'s can be appreciated as the guardians of values and qualities such as respect and honour. But Bears, like all types, need to be encouraged to embrace the best of all letters, no matter how alien to preference, to flourish.

Communication chasm

Belligerently inquisitive Bird meets traditional conforming Bear:

Bird: What would happen if I put my finger in an electric socket?

Bear: You must never put your finger in an electric socket!

Bird: I know that, but what would happen if I did?

Bear: You'll be punished severely!

Cats (30% of population – 8% of leaders)

Alexander the Great was presented with a challenge by the God Zeus when he and his army visited the City of Gordium prior to a major battle. He studied a complicated knot and was asked to release it. After a couple of hours he raised his sword and with a spinning flourish sliced through the knot and the rope fell away. The Gordian solution was invented: solving a problem with new thinking, the magic of meeting an old problem with new eyes. Alexander's all-action approach is typical of the four Cats. They are action heroes. They lead this way and they like to be led this way. They are at their best when they can approach tasks with gusto. They were made to roam corridors with a walkie-talkie pressed against their ear as they rush urgently to trouble-shoot and melt away problems.

- Prefer a hands-off style, flexible and bold.
- Encourage others to learn by doing, developing and applying their skills.
- They quickly become impatient with ditherers.
- Hard to fool.
- Focused on action.
- Under-represented in teaching.
- Annoyed by strict directions.
- If stressed – become authoritarian.

Cats like to be recognised for how they work and contribute. Good leaders praise their all-action approach, regularly asking how they are going to implement X or Y. They're great at trialling new initiatives quickly, though they may neglect a few details in their haste. Cats are naturally restless, jittery and frequently labelled hyperactive. They are not motivated by long-term gains. 'Ten years from now you could be Head of Department' is too far away! Similarly, asking Cat students to work hard because in fifteen years they'll reap the benefits is likely to horrify rather than inspire.

Henry Fielding's Tom Jones is an eighteenth century character who still resonates today partly due to his vigorous, gutsy and kind-hearted Lion personality characteristics. His lust for life coupled with the highest integrity is reflected in the best of all four Cat personalities. His impulsive moral lapses and reckless behaviour are weaknesses many Cats are able to avoid. The Cats live life with similar intent to Tom Jones. They embrace experience in a natural way that can make other animals feel dour and contrived. When other animals learn to sit in the shade and enjoy the sunset, alive in the moment, they glimpse what it can be like to be a Cat. When we enjoy a roller-coaster ride, a view of an expansive sky, snow-topped mountains or churning sea smacking into the pier below our feet, we are alive like Cats.

Sea Animals (12% of population – 5% of leaders)

At the end of *The Wizard of Oz* the central characters discover that what they sought – courage, heart and brains – were present all along. Throughout their adventure Lion demonstrated incredible bravery, Tin Man's compassion shone through and Scarecrow was clever and ingenious. They didn't really need certificates or medals. Sea Animals lead in order to draw out the innate strengths of those around them. They are focused on nurturing potential as leaders and as teachers. They are working on a higher level than GCSE grades (which can create problems). They can be the most difficult group of animals to lead because they want to be treated as individuals and judged for their global impact (which is difficult to measure).

- Encouraging, nurturing, 'hippy' leaders.
- Seek harmony, shared values, and common purpose.
- Over-represented in teaching, especially Clownfish and Dolphin.
- Focus on ideas and people.
- Annoyed by impersonal treatment or organisational violation of their values.
- If stressed – withdraw their support/include only their 'favourites'.

Sea Animals are searching for meaning in life. They can be easily crushed if a lesson or presentation to management goes badly (as they perceive) because they consider it a slur on their identity and worth. Rather than be told to 'grow up and get over yourself', they'll need an arm around their shoulder and reassurance that they are making a valuable contribution to the school/world. This can make them appear the neediest of people to lead but thankfully they will only need a pep talk now and again.

Sea Animals like to be recognised for the unique contribution they make and acknowledged for who they are. Good leaders coach and nurture Sea Animals, motivating them by sharing a vision of the school that could be reproduced from *The Guardian*. As teachers they can sometimes side with the viewpoint of the student rather than the school rules, which can have negative, self-defeating, long-term consequences.

Stephen Fry, a Dolphin personality, often ponders the key to life during interviews, perfectly illustrating the way Sea Animals seek meaning and patterns to understand people. A common theme is his belief that craving wealth and happiness via answers or techniques is doomed to fail. A goal is the wrong target because if we reach it we will then be disappointed asking: 'Is this it?' If we don't reach it we will feel a failure. The key to life is to be interested in ideas, people and places. When we are interested in others they like our company and will share their resources and opportunities. Focus on ourselves and we are boring. Saying 'I want this', 'I need such and such', makes us self-obsessed.

The phrase 'the best way to be interesting is to be interested' captures the sense of awe underpinning Sea Animals at their best. Michael Palin, a Seal personality, is such a successful interviewer because he appears to be genuinely interested in all of the people he meets on his travels. Travel innately appeals to Sea Animals because it broadens and deepens their minds, we only learn about ourselves when we listen to others.

Another classic Sea Animal is Percy Bysshe Shelley. Sea Animals are romantic, poetic and idealistic, often with a tortured, swirling soul eternally seeking meaning thrown into the mix. Shelley could claim the full set. Expelled from university for writing a pamphlet promoting atheism, he eloped to Ireland with a lover. He later travelled around Italy before perishing at sea aged 30 leaving a grieving widow.

> *And sunlight clasps the earth,*
> *And the moonbeams kiss the sea;*
> *What are all these kissings worth If thou kiss not me?*
>
> **Shelley**

Birds (8% of population – 12% of leaders)

William of Ockham was a fourteenth century logician. He reasoned that ideas should not be complicated unnecessarily. When theories compete the simpler theory is both more elegant and nearer the truth. The concept is widely known as Occam's razor. The metaphor of shaving away all that is superfluous and irrelevant to reveal a beautiful truth encapsulates the approach of the four Birds. Unsurprisingly his idea finds favour with many Birds including Isaac Newton, Albert Einstein and Stephen Hawking. Birds lead using the razor of their intuitive logic. As leaders they present clear plans and direction for others to follow. When being led they require evidence for the road they're being asked to travel. Sharpen your razor to lead Birds effectively.

- Strategic, objective, logical leaders.
- Task-focused.
- Most self-critical of all types.

Personality in the Classroom

- Tawny/Barn Owl style – self-contained, share information on a need-to-know basis (over-represented in secondary teaching and higher education).
- Eagle/Falcon style – discuss/argue, competitive.
- Annoyed by poor logic, reason or principles and unproductive rules/tradition.
- If stressed – autocratic.

Birds like to be recognised for their ideas. They are naturally non-conformist and independent. Good leaders harness their sharp enquiring intellect, seeking advice and incorporating it into a new shared vision. If Eagles and Falcons are not on-board they can be a highly disruptive influence. Owls tend to be quieter, even socially awkward, but they are high-achievers and valuable allies for any leader.

> *I always keep a supply of stimulants handy, in case I see a snake – which I also keep handy.*
> **W. C. Fields, illustrating the natural wit and adept verbal touches of an NT preference**

A conversation with a Bird can be like a white water rafting experience as we're swept along easily and willingly, charmed by the power and clarity of their rhetoric. We marvel at the way complex ideas collide with humour and insight. Comedian Bill Hicks provides an enthralling example of a Bird in startling form during a frenzied opus at the end of his final tour when he asks: Is there a point? The clip is available on YouTube (http://wecanchangetheworld.wordpress.com/2008/03/18/youtube-john-lennon-watching-the-wheels-bill-hicks-its-just-a-ride/) and worth viewing to enjoy the intense, passionate and piercing delivery which perfectly frames the words spoken. Here is a flavour of his piece:

> *Is there a point?*
>
> *Yes, life is a ride.*
>
> *The world is like a ride in an amusement park.*
>
> *When you choose to go on, it seems real; that's how powerful it is.*
>
> *Some people have been on a long time and forget it's a ride.*
>
> *But it's just a ride.*
>
> *We can change it anytime we want.*
>
> *It's only a choice, no effort, no worries.*
>
> *It's a choice between fear and love.*
>
> *Through the eyes of fear we want to put bigger locks on our doors, buy guns and kill people.*
>
> *Through the eyes of love we see everything as one.*
>
> *We can change the world to a better ride.*
>
> *All the money spent on weapons could clothe and educate everyone, no one left out.*
>
> *Not one human excluded. Together we could explore space, both inner and outer, in peace.*

Portia, one of Shakespeare's strongest female characters, exemplifies the Bird's ability to analyse, dissect and explain with steely accuracy. She summarises the personalities of her suitors succinctly and with a sagacious wit that can so easily be mistaken as caustic and cavalier. Her transformation into a young male lawyer is a role made for all four Birds who excel when they can strategise, coordinate and reason. In the classroom the Bird teacher must learn to deploy their intellect with more compassion than Portia in the courtroom. Students too must be wary of venting their thoughts without careful analysis of their likely impact.

By preference, Birds give answers whereas Sea Animals ask questions. Leaders that recognise this can forge excellent relationships with their colleagues.

Activity: Guess the Animal

Read a speech or watch a politician on TV and see if you can predict their animal type. This is great practice for leaders. Here is an extract from a famous speech by John F. Kennedy. What animal type do you think he was? (*Answer at the bottom of the next page.)

> *The gross national product includes air pollution, advertising for cigarettes, it counts special locks for our doors, and jails for the people who break them. GNP includes the destruction of the redwoods and the death of Lake Superior.*

It grows with the production of napalm and missiles and nuclear warheads … And if GNP includes all this, there is much that it does not comprehend.

It does not allow for the health of our families, the quality of their education, or the joy of their play. It is indifferent to the decency of our factories and the safety of our streets alike. It does not include the beauty of our poetry or the strength of our marriages, or the intelligence of our public debate or the integrity of our public officials.

GNP measures neither our wit nor our courage, neither our wisdom nor our learning, neither our compassion nor our devotion to our country.

It measures everything, in short, except that which makes life worthwhile; and it can tell us everything about America – except whether we are proud to be Americans.

Putting it all together

Type offers a very practical framework for leaders, whether in a school, a group of teachers or students in the classroom.

Leading

You may have great ideas (I hope you do, but sadly poor ideas are also regularly introduced into schools and businesses across the world) but how you present these is equally important. Make sure you present your case in a style and language that appeals to all four animal groupings. Use the Leading Animal Groupings chart (on page 93) as a checklist. As well as helping you to be persuasive, it will also help you to identify (and answer) questions you are likely to be asked when you present your ideas. The best ideas give everyone something to buy into. Your new literacy strategy needs to convince:

● The Bears by appealing to their sense of tradition, offering step-by-step procedures and timescales.
● The Birds by being theoretically sound and backed up with research evidence.
● The Sea Animals by being inclusive and nurturing, recognising the impact on staff and students.
● The Cats by having a plan of action, a framework they can adapt and run with.

A presentation to a mixture of types needs to cover all bases. When presenting an idea to an individual you can focus your energy more specifically, reducing the waffle. Use the descriptions in Chapter 2 to help you prepare for meetings with individuals. This is not about manipulation; this is about more effective communication. In my experience anyone trying to lead by stealth is soon found out and will instantly lose the respect of their colleagues.

Families

Twin studies are the staple of many psychological texts. I have had the good fortune to interview genetically identical quadruplets to explore the impact of nurture and nature. The four 17-year-olds were studying A levels at the same college. Their types are ENFP (Clownfish), ESTP (Panther) and two INFJ's (Seahorses). So, although they are genetically identical and brought up together, they do not all share the same personality types. The cocktail of nature and nurture must determine personality in subtle rather than deterministic ways. This makes sense as it promotes greater variety within family groupings.

The Panther and Clownfish spoke first and for the group. The two Seahorses spoke less. The Panther and Clownfish were dressed less conservatively than their sisters and made far less eye contact. This is **E/I** preference in action. The Panther was identified by her sisters as the bossy one (she is **E** and **T** preference). They predicted that both parents were **F** preference and since an early age the family had a motto that if the Panther was happy the family was happy! The Clownfish also said she could act as a bridge between her other sisters. The two Seahorses said they were in tune with each and they were both going to the same university to study the same degree course.

What was interesting about meeting the quadruplets was how type can predict and explain much. This is reassuring to family members as personality differences can be appreciated as well as understood. Within an hour the sisters were starting to explain aspects of each other's behaviour and choices with smiles on their faces. This is a major strength of the type

*Answer: JFK is a Dolphin (**ENFJ**).

model; it is simple to understand and apply. It is also built on the principle that everyone is OK, we're just different. The sisters also reminded me that, as a tight-knit farming family that stressed how they always looked after each other, there are factors other than personality type that make us who we are. Parents and teachers influence values and beliefs which have a bigger impact on success and happiness than personality type. However, personality type is an invaluable guide to how we can express our potential and thus be happy and successful.

Chapter 5
Teacher Resources

In this chapter:

- ● Explore charts summarising type applications

- ● Find out how to use them as classroom resources

A professor is someone who talks in someone else's sleep.
W. H. Auden

Personality type is best applied in real life rather than read about in books. It can positively transform relationships between people when it is brought to life. This chapter includes resources that are meant to be laminated and photocopied, pinned up on staffroom noticeboards and classrooms walls, and taken to parties and family gatherings. People love talking about themselves and the type framework can encourage the most shrinking of violets to blossom and disperse pollen everywhere.

Type preferences

Professionals in one field often seek to blend or link their favoured theories and approaches to personality type. There are obvious links with learning theories, Multiple Intelligences, Belbin, NLP and other approaches but I generally find it is best to apply type in the form in which it has been developed since Myers-Briggs brilliantly translated Jung's work over sixty years ago. However, Gregorc's work on learning styles fits so neatly into the type model that I will include a summary here.

Phenomenological researcher Dr Anthony Gregorc discovered:

- The most successful professionals and students learn to operate in a variety of styles but understand their own preference.
- Learning involves how we perceive (let in, grasp) and how we order (organise and store) data/experiences.
- We perceive on a continuum from concrete (reality) to abstract (connections).
- We order, organise and store on a continuum from sequential (precise, structured, microscope) to random (categories, telescope).

These lead to four 'styles' – Concrete Sequential, Concrete Random, Abstract Sequential and Abstract Random – which link to personality temperaments as follows:

1   Ensure all four are available within a lesson.
2   If a student goes off-task, offer a way to continue applying their preferred style.
3   Students could work in teams, with like-minded animals, when task is differentiated by style or in complementary groups to encourage contributions from all students.

Teacher's guide to reaching every student

Children are different. Great teachers connect with all children by understanding these differences. Hints on how to reach all children are offered in the following table:

Concrete Sequential (**SJ** Bears)	Concrete Random (**SP** Cats)
Like: hands on, data and figures, checklists, clear instructions, outlines, charts, deadlines, manuals, methodical approaches, tangible outcomes, conventions, specific answers.	Like: problem-solving, investigation, up and doing, practical experiments, independence, risks, choice, exploration, options, challenges, open-ended tasks, trial and error, games, flexibility, multiple resources.
Bears relish structured practical activities with clear rules, making a model from a set of instructions, completing a list of short tasks, observing and imitating an expert, working through a booklet/manual.	Cats relish open-ended practical work such as visits, projects, experiments, making things and skill development.
Abstract Sequential (NT Birds)	**Abstract Random (NF Sea Animals)**
Like: reading, ideas, analysis, evaluation, reasoning, theories, lectures, note-taking, debate, logic, knowledge, vicarious thinking, tests, structure, objective hypothesising, comparisons.	Like: belonging, fantasy, discussion, peer teaching, group work, humour, games, stories, own ideas, drama, role-play, subjectivity, media, emotions, spontaneity, art, own timetable, self-expression.
Birds relish structured academic research such as exploring the theory behind a concept, the connections between concepts, workbooks based on puzzles and comparisons.	Sea Animals relish unstructured group working such as discussions, projects, collaborations, presentations that develop personal relationships and creative experiences.

We know children are different. Great teachers connect with all children by understanding and working with these differences, rather than using methods which suit the teacher. Hints on how to reach all children are offered in the following table:

Polar Bear (**ISTJ**)	Koala (**ISFJ**)	Seahorse (**INFJ**)	Barn Owl (**INTJ**)
BE CONCRETE	BE NICE	SEE BIG PICTURE	BE ORGANISED
Be practical and logical, provide facts and detail. Allow thinking time. **Default statement:** **This is how to do it right.**	Be specific and polite. Listen and wait for a reply, don't be pushy. **Default question:** **Are you clear about what the next steps are?**	Provide vision. Be positive and personal. Let them ruminate. **Default statement:** **Let's plan the next best step for this topic.**	Provide all necessary facts, detail and theory so they can analyse it all. **Default statement:** **If you need more info as you work on this topic just let me know.**
Tiger (**ISTP**)	Cat (**ISFP**)	Seal (**INFP**)	Tawny Owl (**INTP**)
BE ACTIVE	BE SPECIFIC	BE SENSITIVE	BE THEORETICAL
Emphasise the action and challenge involved in solving real problems. Don't push. **Default question:** **Do you have enough to get on with this yourself?**	Be clear, gentle and collaborative. **Default question:** **Do you need anything else from me before you work on this?**	Be sincere, personal and allow thinking time. Engage through their passions. **Default question:** **I'd love to hear how this topic can interest you.**	Provide enough info to ignite their curiosity; they like to ponder, sift and analyse data. **Default question:** **Would you like a challenge/puzzle?**
Panther (**ESTP**)	Lion (**ESFP**)	Clownfish (**ENFP**)	Falcon (**ENTP**)
BE PRAGMATIC	BE FRIENDLY	BE CURIOUS	BE ENTERTAINED
Motivate using fun, games, action and practical benefits. **Default question:** **Here's a challenge – can you rise to it?**	Be direct, practical and let them talk until they understand. **Default statement:** **Tell me what else you need before you start.**	Listen as they describe their ideas. Appeal to their unique imagination. Offer choice. **Default question:** **How are you going to use your imagination in this topic?**	Enjoy their wit and banter. Steer them to tasks as a way of enhancing their performing skills. **Default question:** **Before you surprise me, can I help?**
Black Bear (**ESTJ**)	Teddy Bear (**ESFJ**)	Dolphin (**ENFJ**)	Eagle (**ENTJ**)
BE ASSERTIVE	BE PERSONAL	BE NURTURING	BE PREPARED
Be direct, firm, brief, fair and consistent; they'll respect your competence. **Default statement:** **Here's the plan. Enjoy completing on time.**	Ask how they feel. They follow their values. Provide clarity and plans. Praise their contribution. **Default statement:** **I appreciate your work, thanks. Here's the next bit.**	Be consistent, friendly and consensual. Listen to their insights. **Default question:** **How are you feeling about the next topic?**	They like to challenge and debate to understand. Be bold, concise and challenging. **Default question:** **What's your strategy for the next topic going to be?**

Offering projects to motivate all types

Students are motivated by different kinds of activities. To ensure you reach all four animal groups you can use the grid below. Roll a dice to select the choice of topic or task. For example, imagine you throw a six for the subject *functions of the liver*. The four methods are draw, design, debate and interview people. These words can inspire student or teachers to create appropriate ways to learn the topic. For example, draw seven characters each illustrating a different function, design seven posters each illustrating a different function, debate which function is most important, perhaps rank the seven, arrange a vote, interview people on why they voted as they did, research interviews with people with liver failure. Allowing students choice in how they achieve the learning outcomes for the topic improves retention.

Cats		Bears	
1	Physical/hands-on challenge	1	Identify
2	Game	2	Graph
3	Song	3	Complete
4	Assemble/collect	4	Timeline (sequence/organise)
5	Visit/explore	5	Make
6	Draw	6	Design
Birds		**Sea Animals**	
1	Compare	1	Create
2	Think about	2	Imagine
3	Research	3	Pretend
4	Set up a court room/advocate	4	Drama/role-play
5	Invent	5	In groups
6	Debate	6	Interview people about …

Leadership with style!

The following approaches are those that appeal most for each style of animal grouping:

NT Birds	NF Sea Animals
Big picture themes, theoretically sound and referenced, autonomy, models and systems, challenges, analysis and logic	Humanistic vision, personal growth, creative freedom, praise and encouragement, values, inspiration, inclusivity
SJ Bears	**SP Cats**
Clear expectations and defined process, deadlines, consistency, organised, hard working, led by example	Adventure, variety, flexibility, stimulation, using initiative rather than relying on procedures, fun, task-oriented

Give a dog a bad name: negative labels often attached to each type

Negative labels can damage children for life. Teachers need to tread very carefully and avoid causing offence. The labels below, provided by teachers based on the labels they were given at school by their teachers, are commonly associated with each type. Please avoid using these.

Polar Bear (**ISTJ**)	Koala (**ISFJ**)	Seahorse (**INFJ**)	Barn Owl (**INTJ**)
Too slow, too quiet, loner/don't contribute, need spoon feeding, want everything to have a point, too hard, too competitive, rush work to finish it, too rigid/boring, bossy, stubborn	Too slow, too quiet, loner/don't contribute, never raise their hand, need spoon feeding, want to know purpose of everything, too soft and oversensitive, rush work to finish it, too rigid/boring	Too slow, too quiet, loner/don't contribute, away with the fairies, live in a dream world, don't follow instructions, too soft/oversensitive, rush work to finish it, too rigid/boring	Too slow, too quiet, loner/don't contribute, daydreamer, live in a dream world, don't follow instructions, too hard, too competitive, rush work to finish it, too stubborn, bossy
Tiger (**ISTP**)	Cat (**ISFP**)	Seal (**INFP**)	Tawny Owl (**INTP**)
Don't read enough, loner/don't contribute, want everything to have a point, too hard, too argumentative, competitive, lazy, too last minute/laid back	Too slow, too quiet, loner/don't contribute, need spoon feeding, want everything to have a point, too soft and oversensitive, lazy, too last minute/laid back	Too slow, too quiet, daydreamer, away with the fairies, don't follow instructions, too soft/oversensitive, lazy, too last minute/laid back, hippy	Too slow, too quiet, loner/don't contribute, daydreamer, live in a dream world, don't follow instructions, too hard, too competitive, lazy, too last minute/laid back, a mad professor
Panther (**ESTP**)	Lion (**ESFP**)	Clownfish (**ENFP**)	Falcon (**ENTP**)
Too fidgety, don't read enough, cheeky/answer back, attention span of a gnat, want everything to have a point, ignore instructions, too tough, too competitive, rush work to finish it, lazy, too last minute/laid back	Too fidgety, don't read enough, cheeky/answer back, want everything to have a point, too soft/oversensitive, lazy, too last minute/laid back	Too fidgety, cheeky/answer back, away with the fairies, live in a dream world, don't follow instructions, too soft/oversensitive, lazy, too last minute/laid back	Too fidgety, cheeky/answer back, ask 'why' too much, live in a dream world, don't follow instructions, too hard, too competitive, argumentative, lazy, too last minute, hyper/ADHD
Black Bear (**ESTJ**)	Teddy Bear (**ESFJ**)	Dolphin (**ENFJ**)	Eagle (**ENTJ**)
Too restless, don't read enough, answer back, want everything to have a point, too hard, too competitive, rush work to finish it, too rigid/boring, stubborn, bossy	Too chatty, don't read enough, tactless, need spoon feeding, want everything to have a point, too soft/oversensitive, rush work to finish it, too rigid/boring	Too chatty, restless, daydreamer, away with the fairies, too soft/oversensitive, weak, martyr	Too fidgety, don't read enough, cheeky/answer back, want everything to have a point, daydreamer, live in their own world, too hard, too competitive, too rigid/stubborn, bossy

Famous types

Everybody likes to compare themselves to TV/movie stars and role models. Here is a sample list of well-known and positive celebrities. Students can add their own suggestions to keep the chart up-to-date. Do you like the names next to your type? What attributes do you share? Who would you most like to be like?

Personality in the Classroom

Polar Bear (**ISTJ**)	Koala (**ISFJ**)	Seahorse (**INFJ**)	Barn Owl (**INTJ**)
Denzel Washington Mr Spock Delia Smith Queen Elizabeth II George Washington	Jerry Seinfeld Marge Simpson David Beckham Nelson Mandela Peter Andre	Oprah Winfrey Gandhi Cinderella Velma (*Scooby-Doo*)	Morrissey Willy Wonka George Lucas Bill Gates Steven Spielberg
Tiger (**ISTP**)	Cat (**ISFP**)	Seal (**INFP**)	Tawny Owl (**INTP**)
Vin Diesel Clint Eastwood Shrek James Bond Roy Keane	Paul McCartney Ray Mears Mozart Michael Jackson Bill Oddie Rembrandt	J. R. R. Tolkien Peter Jackson J. K. Rowling A. A. Milne Johnny Depp Michael Palin Shakespeare	Isaac Asimov Newton Einstein Richard Dawkins Descartes Nietzsche
Panther (**ESTP**)	Lion (**ESFP**)	Clownfish (**ENFP**)	Falcon (**ENTP**)
Jack Nicholson Liam Gallagher Tom Sawyer Bart Simpson Madonna Zorro	Ben Affleck Homer Simpson Elvis George Best Ian Botham Shaggy and Scooby	Jack Black Sinbad Jonathan Ross Graham Norton Katie Holmes Belle (*Beauty and the Beast*)	John Lennon Tracy Beaker Noel Gallagher Eddie Murphy Larry David Doc (*Back to the Future*) Dr Who Jimmy Carr
Black Bear (**ESTJ**)	Teddy Bear (**ESFJ**)	Dolphin (**ENFJ**)	Eagle (**ENTJ**)
Alan Sugar Alex Ferguson Duncan Bannatyne Victoria Beckham Katie Price	Britney Spears Kylie Minogue Gary Lineker Truly Scrumptious (*Chitty Chitty Bang Bang*) Mary Poppins Wonder Woman (1970s TV character)	Sean Connery Peter Kay Martin Luther King Stephen Fry Peter Ustinov	Harrison Ford Arnold Schwarzenegger Quentin Tarantino Steve Jobs Whoopi Goldberg

Thanks to www.typetango.com for some of the above suggestions.

Common classroom complaints (and their remedy)

Teacher complaint	Type source (and remedy)
Student talks too much	**E** preference habit (allow regular opportunities for **E** preferences to talk as part *of* the learning, not talking *between* the learning)
Student moves around class without permission	**E** preference habit (build in movement, regular short breaks and changes of pace, direction and focus – this helps everyone)

Student struggles in group activities	**I** preference habit (be careful how you group children together – create mixes that benefit quieter students)
Student does not contribute in class	**I** preference habit (don't overuse teacher-led class discussion as most children will be excluded, ask students to discuss in pairs or write down thoughts first on a personal wipe-clean board before sharing)
Student constantly asks you to check their work at each step	**S** preference habit (give clearer, detailed instructions for the student to follow)
Student doesn't use their initiative or apply their knowledge	**S** preference habit (offer prompts, random creativity generator (see page 79), ask them to see how others are approaching the task)
Student keeps asking you to repeat instructions	**N** preference habit (be patient, they tend to be more interested in the process than the rules – a clear overview plus detailed steps will help)
Student wanders off topic or answers a question you didn't ask	**N** preference habit (be clear on what needs to included but allow flexibility on how it can be presented)
Student too sensitive to teacher feedback	**F** preference habit (be clear you're questioning the piece of work not the person and how they can improve it)
Student stubborn, belligerent or unwilling to compromise	**T** preference habit (debate, state your case objectively without threats/coercion)
Student insults, annoys or agitates others	**T** preference habit (make them aware of the consequences of their approach and agree alternative strategies)
Student too interested in gossip and peer opinions	**F** preference habit (focus on task)
Student needs reassurance and wants to know they'll have enough time to complete everything required	**J** preference habit (offer clear schedules and timetables – if you can't stick to the plan say how you will fit it in later)
Student wants to make their work perfect	**J** preference habit (make them work in rough first on separate pieces of paper using mind-maps, key words, etc.)
Student takes too long to settle down and doesn't finish work regularly	**P** preference habit (settle the student down before introducing the topic, give regular updates and reminders of time limits
Student leaves everything to the last minute	**P** preference habit (break topics into smaller assignments to prevent work becoming overwhelming)

confident

stand out   exude

limelight   **E**   action   outside

assertive   outgoing   not quiet

       interrupt   movement

contribute to   breadth

show

concentration

   reflection   gentle

quiet   **calm**   inside   serene

part of the crowd   **I**   still   depth

watchful   good listener   blend in

absorb   take in   careful

intent

practical
real   facts   sequences

direct

grounded

literal   step-by-step

S

realism

remember things   actual

utility   **tactical**

present

vision   **future**   scatterbrain

random

ingenious   # N   possible   global

concoct   original

metaphor   **imaginative**   **creative**   invent

strategic

compassion   kindness

softer   **friendly**   **caring**   sympathise

passion   **F**   emotion

empathy

subjective   personal

values

**feedback taken
as criticism**

**criticism taken
as feedback**

doctrine

objective

justice

scrutinise

T

harder

principles   **thick-skinned**

candid   **logical**

investigate   analyse   **ethics**

prepared

deadlines

reach goals

finish

J

decisive

on the move

control

complete

seek order

organised

closure

tidy

plan

neat

proposal

relax

flexible

P

start

seek fun

pending

open

slouch

off the cuff

chill

spontaneous

adapt

change goals

guidelines

Part 2

Chapter 6
Explore the One-to-One Relationships You Have with Each Student

In this chapter:

- **Discover tips showing you how to overcome personality clashes and difficulties**

- **Personalise learning to ensure every student progresses**

The meeting of personalities is like the contact of two chemical substances. If there is any reaction both are transformed.
Carl Jung

Personality in the Classroom

One-to-one relationships are crucial in the classroom. Most people remember at least one teacher they really connected with – a teacher they felt was understanding, respectful and supportive. The following section is designed to help teachers connect with individual students by suggesting ways in which their personality preferences can complement each other rather than clash. If you know your own type and the type of an individual student, the grid below will enable you to access suggestions which build positive relationships.

		Student							
		Polar Bear (ISTJ)	Black Bear (ESTJ)	Teddy Bear (ESFJ)	Koala Bear (ISFJ)	Lion (ESFP)	Panther (ESTP)	Tiger (ISTP)	Cat (ISFP)
Teacher	Polar Bear (ISTJ)	4	1	12	13	7	9	5	16
	Black Bear (ESTJ)	20	17	28	29	23	25	21	32
	Teddy Bear (ESFJ)	34	35	33	46	39	38	42	43
	Koala Bear (ISFJ)	52	59	53	49	62	63	56	58
	Lion (ESFP)	77	65	66	78	70	69	73	74
	Panther (ESTP)	86	81	85	87	91	88	90	92
	Tiger (ISTP)	101	102	98	105	107	109	104	108
	Cat (ISFP)	126	113	114	128	117	116	120	121
	Seahorse (INFJ)	143	131	129	144	135	132	136	138
	Seal (INFP)	153	146	148	154	145	147	155	156
	Clownfish (ENFP)	169	162	164	170	161	163	171	172
	Dolphin (ENFJ)	189	180	179	190	182	181	185	186
	Eagle (ENTJ)	196	202	200	198	205	206	195	194
	Falcon (ENTP)	223	214	215	210	212	220	216	221
	Tawny Owl (INTP)	237	225	226	238	230	229	233	234
	Barn Owl (INTJ)	241	253	254	242	250	249	245	246

		Student							
		Seahorse (INFJ)	Seal (INFP)	Clownfish (ENFP)	Dolphin (ENFJ)	Eagle (ENTJ)	Falcon (ENTP)	Tawny Owl (INTP)	Barn Owl (INTJ)
Teacher	Polar Bear (ISTJ)	14	2	3	6	15	10	11	8
	Black Bear (ESTJ)	30	18	19	22	31	26	27	24
	Teddy Bear (ESFJ)	47	44	40	36	37	41	45	48
	Koala Bear (ISFJ)	64	60	51	55	57	50	54	61
	Lion (ESFP)	79	75	71	67	68	72	76	80
	Panther (ESTP)	95	96	82	84	83	89	94	93
	Tiger (ISTP)	100	112	110	99	106	103	97	111
	Cat (ISFP)	124	122	118	115	127	119	123	125
	Seahorse (INFJ)	141	140	137	139	134	130	133	142
	Seal (INFP)	157	159	152	151	149	150	160	158
	Clownfish (ENFP)	173	175	168	167	165	166	176	174
	Dolphin (ENFJ)	191	187	183	177	178	184	188	192
	Eagle (ENTJ)	201	208	204	199	197	203	207	193
	Falcon (ENTP)	217	213	222	224	219	209	218	211
	Tawny Owl (INTP)	239	235	231	227	228	232	236	240
	Barn Owl (INTJ)	243	247	251	255	256	252	248	244

1
Polar Bear teacher with Black Bear student
ISTJ and ESTJ

Both Bears are natural leaders in the classroom and beyond. They can hardly help themselves from taking charge and completing tasks. Their mutual understanding can form the basis of an effective relationship. Clashes can occur when the student attempts to wrestle control from their teacher. Good Polar Bear teachers work out ways to provide their student with opportunities to express their organisational talent. For the teacher to get the best out of their naturally lively student they need to:

■ Listen patiently and enthusiastically to the student's ideas and apparent ramblings.

■ Endure 'silly' ideas to see where they lead – the student is thinking out loud and this is how they learn best.

■ Steer the student away from controversial subjects/topics, especially in group discussions.

■ Build in plenty of opportunities during lessons for the **E** students to talk things through with other **E** preferences.

■ Also offer your own thoughts; if you need a timeout ask for one.

■ Encourage the student to think things through before talking otherwise they'll hog the lesson.

Both teacher and student gather information in the same way. They notice detail using their senses (aware of what they can see, hear and feel). Both are focused on the present. The teacher is instinctively practical, sensible and realistic in their teaching style and will encourage their students to follow their lead. A solid, workman-like relationship develops with both teacher and student mutually understanding what each needs to do to get the job done. For the teacher to get the best out of their essentially grounded student they need to:

■ Demonstrate how learning can be applied in the real world.

■ Allow the student opportunities to repeat and practise until satisfied they are competent.

■ Encourage the use of imagination as a useful process (it's not wasting time).

Both teacher and student are task-focused, direct, consistent and honest. The classroom is likely to have a business-like and purposeful atmosphere. Students are given clear guidelines on what is expected in terms of behaviour, homework and so on. If the student challenges the teacher it is likely to be for clarification. At best this means everyone knows where they stand and how to behave. For the teacher to get the best out of their inherently task-focused student they need to:

■ Work in ways that test their skill and knowledge competitively (they raise their game for competitions, challenges, quizzes, measuring and beating personal bests).

■ Help them appreciate that 50% of people are **F** preference and can interpret feedback as criticism.

■ Focus on what the student has achieved and what comes next.

■ Be prepared to compromise occasionally.

■ Avoid trying to fix something without considering potential underlying emotional causes.

The **J** teacher takes pleasure in scheduling their time. They are organised and decisive. They work out a plan and stick to it, often aided by an impressive to-do list. Their classroom is usually an organised place. The subject will probably be broken down into lesson-sized chunks and the year planned out whether an Ofsted inspector is due or not. Many **J** students are reassured by their teacher's organisational zeal. They simply adopt the schedule and deliver their side of the bargain, generally completing all tasks on time. Interestingly, some **J**'s will baulk at their teacher's well-intentioned thoroughness. They would like to create their own plan and work to it rather than adopt someone else's. This is due to the **J** preference desire for control. So two **J** preferences together can clash, though at least all their work will be done. Most schools require students to be so organised that two **J** preferences are, potentially, the most constructive combination. For the teacher to get the best out of their naturally organised student they need to:

■ Enjoy your shared desire for order, neatness and respecting deadlines.

■ Allow the student independence in planning their work in their own way if they really want to.

■ Be prepared to adjust your own plans if external events interfere with your careful preparations (and encourage the student to also embrace flexibility occasionally).

■ Shake things up now and again to prevent predictability becoming boredom.

■ Avoid making quick decisions about what needs to be done before considering all of the options.

2
Polar Bear teacher with Seal student
ISTJ and INFP

The naturally clear and confident Polar Bear teacher shares one type preference with their Seal student. Both like to think things through before reaching a conclusion. For these near opposites to attract they need to accept and appreciate each other's differences to create a balanced and inclusive classroom. For the teacher to get the best out of their naturally thoughtful student they need to:

■ Respect the student's need for privacy and independence.

■ Offer the student time to think through their thoughts.

■ Politely state your opinion to ensure you both know what you're doing.

■ Take time to clarify your thoughts and if something needs to be said be calm and direct as you deliver it, but avoid being confrontational.

■ Use non-verbal communication – smiles and gestures are reassuring to **I** students. You can even use sticky notes/emails to pass on feedback.

The Polar Bear teacher likes to use their experience to make sense of what is around them. The teacher is essentially practical, sequential and realistic in style and will generally encourage their students to follow suit. The Seal student may at best find this challenging and at worst find it boring and simplistic. The Bear teacher may label the student a daydreamer, lost in their own world or 'away with the fairies'. They should resist the temptation to castigate their student because this is how they take in information and learn best. In the right context daydreaming can lead to new insights. For the teacher to get the best out of their inherently imaginative student they need to:

■ Embrace the imagination and insight of the student and what it can bring to the lesson.

■ Encourage the student to become aware of the important contribution of the **S** approach (the value of facts, details, procedure, experiments, applying experience, structure, the step-by-step model).

The teacher is focused first on task and second on people/relationships. The classroom is likely to have a business-like, purposeful atmosphere. Students are given clear guidelines on what is expected in terms of behaviour, homework and so on. At best this means everyone knows where they stand and how to behave. At worst the classroom can resemble a military boot-camp full of dispirited and brow-beaten new recruits. Remember, the personal relationship the teacher develops with this student is the key to success. The Seal needs to feel they like their teacher and that the teacher likes them too. If this happens they'll work harder but if they don't they may switch off completely. This explains why a student can be top of the class one year (with a teacher they like) and show no interest at all in the subject the following year when they change teacher. For the teacher to get the best out of their instinctively people-focused student they need to:

■ Offer learning situations that allow for the use of empathy, collaboration and teamworking to counter-balance your natural tendency to focus on task.

■ Give ample and regular praise while offering tactful support to overcome any blind-spots. Feedback can be easily interpreted as criticism so walk on egg-shells when delivering it.

■ Persuade by appealing to the strength of your personal belief in the student (don't let me down, I know you can do it, I like you).

■ Be prepared to compromise occasionally.

The Polar Bear teacher takes pleasure in scheduling their time. They are organised and decisive. They work out a plan and stick to it, usually aided by an impressive to-do list. Their classroom is likely to be the most organised space in school. The subject will probably be broken down into lesson-sized chunks and the year planned out in detail with zeal. The **P** student will either respond:

■ Positively by accepting your expertise and understanding the long-term benefits they'll reap.

■ Passively by just accepting your structure/plan for an easy life without really buying into the content or process you are offering.

■ Negatively by rejecting you, your structure/plan and subject completely (even if they're physically in your room they will not engage and participate).

For the teacher to get the best out of their intrinsically laid-back student they should note the student doesn't just like options and choice; they need them or they start to itch, squirm and rebel. The secondary school environment is difficult enough for **P** preference students so teachers can help soften the pressure. To help:

■ Provide as much flexibility as possible (multiple choice homework tasks, choice within the lesson).

■ Avoid giving out detailed schedules (they'll just lose it anyway!).

■ Don't be more picky with detail than is absolutely necessary.

■ Shake things up now and again to prevent predictability becoming boredom. Introduce random surprises and changes.

■ Identify simple ways the student can organise and manage their time to complete important work without a last-minute panic.

3
Polar Bear teacher with Clownfish student
ISTJ and ENFP

Teacher and student share no type preferences. A successful relationship needs to be built on an acceptance and appreciation of each other's differences. Clashes are most frequently experienced when the teacher's task-focused, organisational zeal jars with the chatty, whimsical and fun-focused student. For the teacher to get the best out of their naturally lively student they need to:

■ Listen patiently and enthusiastically to the student's ideas and apparent ramblings.

■ Endure 'silly' ideas to see where they lead – the student is thinking out loud and this is how they learn best.

■ Steer the student away from controversial subjects/topics, especially in group discussions.

■ Build in plenty of opportunities during lessons for the **E** students to talk things through with other **E** preferences.

■ Also offer your own thoughts; if you need a timeout ask for one.

■ Encourage the student to think things through before talking otherwise they'll hog the lesson.

The Polar Bear teacher likes to use their experience to make sense of what is around them. The teacher is essentially practical, sequential and realistic in style and will generally encourage their students to follow suit. The **N** student may at best find this challenging and at worst find it boring. The Bear teacher may label the student a daydreamer, lost in their own world or 'away with the fairies'. They should resist the temptation to castigate their student because this is how they take in information and make sense of the world. In the right context daydreaming can lead to the invention of cars, planes, medicines and computers. For the teacher to get the best out of their inherently imaginative student they need to:

■ Embrace the imagination and insight of the student and what it can bring to the lesson.

■ Encourage the student to become aware of the important contribution of the **S** approach (the value of facts, details, procedure, experiments, applying experience, structure, the step-by-step model).

The teacher is focused first on task and second on people/relationships. The classroom is likely to have a business-like, purposeful atmosphere. Students are given clear guidelines on what is expected in terms of behaviour, homework and so on. At best this means everyone knows where they stand and how to behave. At worst the classroom can resemble a military boot-camp full of dispirited and brow-beaten new recruits. Remember, the personal relationship between teacher and student is the key to ensure a hard-working student; not a focus on tasks and subject content. The Clownfish needs to feel they like their teacher and that the teacher likes them too. If this happens they'll work harder but if they don't they may switch off completely. This explains why a student can be top of the class one year (with a teacher they like) and show no interest at all in the subject the following year when they change teacher. For the teacher to get the best of their instinctively people-focused student they need to:

■ Offer learning situations that allow for the use of empathy, collaboration and teamworking to counter-balance your natural tendency to focus on task.

■ Give ample and regular praise while offering tactful support to overcome any blind-spots. Feedback can be easily interpreted as criticism so walk on egg-shells when delivering it.

■ Persuade by appealing to the strength of your personal belief in the student (don't let me down, I know you can do it, I like you).

■ Be prepared to compromise occasionally.

The **J** teacher takes pleasure in scheduling their time. They are organised and decisive. They work out a plan and stick to it, usually aided by an impressive to-do list. Their classroom is likely to be the most organised space in school. The subject will probably be broken down into lesson-sized chunks and the year planned out in detail with zeal. The **P** student will either respond:

■ Positively by accepting your expertise and understanding the long-term benefits they'll reap.

■ Passively by just accepting your structure/plan for an easy life without really buying into the content or process you are offering.

■ Negatively by rejecting you, your structure/plan and subject completely (even if they're physically in your room they will not engage and participate).

For the teacher to get the best out of their intrinsically laid-back student they should note the student doesn't just like options and choice; they need them or they start to itch, squirm and rebel. The secondary school environment is difficult enough for **P** preference students so teachers can help soften the pressure. To help:

■ Provide as much flexibility as possible (multiple choice homework tasks, choice within the lesson).

■ Avoid giving out detailed schedules (they'll just lose it anyway!).

■ Don't be more picky with detail than is absolutely necessary.

■ Shake things up now and again to prevent predictability becoming boredom. Introduce random surprises and changes.

■ Identify simple ways the student can organise and manage their time to complete important work without last-minute anxiety.

4
Polar Bear teacher with Polar Bear student
ISTJ and ISTJ

Polar Bears are organised, decisive and in control. They are also task-focused and determined to succeed. These common foundations usually result in a constructive relationship. Clashes are only likely if the student's assertiveness is incorrectly interpreted as belligerence. For the teacher to get the best out of their naturally thoughtful student they need to:

■ Respect the student's need for privacy and independence.

■ Offer the student time to think through their thoughts.

■ Politely state your opinion to ensure you both know what you're doing.

■ Take time to clarify your thoughts and if something needs to be said be calm and direct as you deliver it, but avoid being confrontational.

■ Use non-verbal communication – smiles and gestures are reassuring to **I** students. You can even use sticky notes/emails to pass on feedback.

Both teacher and student gather information in the same way. They notice detail using their senses (aware of what they can see, hear and feel). Both use their experience to make sense of what they see and notice. They are both focused on the present. The teacher is instinctively practical, sensible and realistic in their teaching style and will encourage their students to follow their lead. A solid, workman-like relationship develops with both teacher and student mutually understanding what each needs to do to get the job done. For the teacher to get the best out of their essentially grounded student they need to:

■ Demonstrate how learning can be applied in the real world.

■ Allow the student opportunities to repeat and practise until satisfied they are competent.

■ Encourage the use of imagination as a useful process (it's not wasting time).

Both teacher and student are task-focused, direct, consistent and honest. The classroom is likely to have a business-like and purposeful atmosphere. Students are given clear guidelines on what is expected in terms of behaviour, homework and so on. If the student challenges the teacher it is likely to be for clarification. At best this means everyone knows where they stand and how to behave. For the teacher to get the best out of their inherently task-focused student they need to:

■ Work in ways that test their skill and knowledge competitively (they raise their game for competitions, challenges, quizzes, measuring and beating personal bests).

■ Help them appreciate that 50% of people are **F** preference and can interpret feedback as criticism.

■ Focus on what the student has achieved and what comes next.

■ Be prepared to compromise occasionally.

■ Avoid trying to fix something without considering potential underlying emotional causes.

Polar Bears must schedule their time. They are the most organised and decisive of all types. They work out a plan and stick to it and their plan is the right one. Their classroom is usually an organised place. The subject will probably be broken down into lesson-sized chunks and the year planned out whether or not an Ofsted inspector is due. Many **J** students are reassured by their teacher's organisational zeal. They simply adopt the schedule and deliver their side of the bargain, generally completing all tasks on time. Interestingly, some **J**'s will baulk at their teacher's well-intentioned thoroughness. They would like to create their own plan and work to it rather than adopt someone else's. This is due to the **J**'s desire for control. So two **J** preferences together can clash, though at least all their work will be done. Most schools require students to be so organised that two **J** preferences are likely to be the most constructive combination. For the teacher to get the best out of their naturally organised student they need to:

■ Enjoy your shared desire for order, neatness and respecting deadlines.

■ Allow the student independence in planning their work in their own way if they really want to.

■ Be prepared to adjust your own plans if external events interfere with your careful preparations (and encourage the student to also embrace flexibility occasionally).

■ Shake things up now and again to prevent predictability becoming boredom.

■ Avoid making quick decisions about what needs to be done before considering all of the options.

5
Polar Bear teacher with Tiger student
ISTJ and ISTP

Polar Bears and Tigers share a fuss-free and objective focus on the present. The differences are the desire of the student to be reflective and flexible whereas the teacher is direct and organised. For the teacher to get the best out of their naturally independent student they need to:

■ Respect the student's need for privacy and space.

■ Offer the student time to think through their thoughts.

■ Politely state your opinion to ensure you both know what you're doing.

■ Take time to clarify your thoughts and if something needs to be said be calm and direct as you deliver it, but avoid being confrontational.

■ Use non-verbal communication – smiles and gestures are reassuring to **I** students. You can even use sticky notes/emails to pass on feedback.

Both teacher and student gather information in the same way. They notice detail using their senses (aware of what they can see, hear and feel). Both are both focused on the here and now. The teacher is instinctively practical, sensible and realistic in their teaching style and will encourage their students to follow their lead. A solid, workman-like relationship develops with both teacher and student mutually understanding what each needs to do to get the job done. For the teacher to get the best out of their essentially grounded student they need to:

■ Demonstrate how learning can be applied in the real world.

■ Allow the student opportunities to repeat and practise until satisfied they are competent.

■ Encourage the use of imagination as a useful process (it's not wasting time).

Both teacher and student are task-focused, direct, consistent and honest. The classroom is likely to have a business-like and purposeful atmosphere. Students are given clear guidelines on what is expected in terms of behaviour, homework and so on. If the student challenges the teacher it is likely to be for clarification. At best this means everyone knows where they stand and how to behave. For the teacher to get the best out of their inherently task-focused student they need to:

■ Work in ways that test their skill and knowledge competitively (they raise their game for competitions, challenges, quizzes, measuring and beating personal bests).

■ Help them understand that 50% of people are **F** preference and can interpret feedback as criticism.

■ Focus on what the student has achieved and what comes next.

■ Be prepared to compromise occasionally.

■ Avoid trying to fix something without considering potential underlying emotional causes.

The **J** teacher takes pleasure in scheduling their time. They are organised and decisive. They work out a plan and stick to it, usually aided by an impressive to-do list. Their classroom is likely to be the most organised space in school. The subject will probably be broken down into lesson-sized chunks and the year planned out in detail with zeal. The **P** student will either respond:

■ Positively by accepting your expertise and understanding the long-term benefits they'll reap.

■ Passively by just accepting your structure/plan for an easy life without really buying into the content or process you are offering.

■ Negatively by rejecting you, your structure/plan and subject completely (even if they're physically in your room they will not engage and participate).

For the teacher to get the best out of their intrinsically laid-back student they should note the student doesn't just like options and choice; they need them or they start to itch, squirm and rebel. The secondary school environment is difficult enough for **P** preference students so teachers can help soften the pressure. To help:

■ Provide as much flexibility as possible (multiple choice homework tasks, choice within the lesson).

■ Avoid giving out detailed schedules (they'll just lose it anyway!).

■ Don't be more picky with detail than is absolutely necessary.

■ Shake things up now and again to prevent predictability becoming boredom. Introduce random surprises and changes.

■ Identify simple ways the student can organise and manage their time to complete important work without a last-minute rush.

6
Polar Bear teacher with Dolphin student
ISTJ and ENFJ

Teacher and student share one type preference. Both are organised and respect deadlines. They differ in the way they absorb and process information. To get the best out of the Dolphin student the teacher must embrace the imagination, subtlety and compassion they can add to classroom tasks. For the teacher to get the best out of their naturally lively student they need to:

■ Listen patiently and enthusiastically to the student's ideas and apparent ramblings.

■ Endure 'silly' ideas to see where they lead – the student is thinking out loud and this is how they learn best.

■ Steer the student away from controversial subjects/topics, especially in group discussions.

■ Build in plenty of opportunities during lessons for the **E** students to talk things through with other **E** preferences.

■ Also offer your own thoughts; if you need a timeout ask for one.

■ Encourage the student to think things through before talking otherwise they could hijack the lesson.

The Polar Bear teacher likes to use their experience to make sense of what is around them. The teacher is essentially practical, sequential and realistic in style and will generally encourage their students to follow suit. The **N** student may at best find this challenging and at worst find it boring. The teacher may label the student a daydreamer or lost in their own world. They should resist the temptation to castigate their student because this is how they take in information and make sense of the world. In the right context daydreaming can lead to new ways of absorbing and retaining course content for all students in the group. For the teacher to get the best out of their inherently imaginative student they need to:

■ Embrace the imagination and insight of the student and what it can bring to the lesson.

■ Encourage the student to become aware of the important contribution of the **S** approach (the value of facts, details, procedure, experiments, applying experience, structure, the step-by-step model).

The teacher is focused first on task and second on people/relationships. The classroom is likely to have a business-like, purposeful atmosphere. Students are given clear guidelines on what is expected in terms of behaviour, homework and so on. At best this means everyone knows where they stand and how to behave. At worst the classroom can resemble a military boot-camp full of dispirited and brow-beaten new recruits. Remember, the personal relationship the teacher develops with this student is key. The Dolphin needs to feel they like their teacher and that the teacher likes them too. If this happens they'll work harder but if they don't they may switch off completely. This explains why a student can be top of the class one year (with a teacher they like) and show no interest at all in the subject the following year when they change teacher. For the teacher to get the best out of their instinctively people-focused student they need to:

■ Offer learning situations that allow for the use of empathy, collaboration and teamworking to counter-balance your natural tendency to focus on task.

■ Give ample and regular praise while offering tactful support to overcome any blind-spots. Feedback can be easily interpreted as criticism so walk on egg-shells when delivering it.

■ Persuade/influence by appealing to the strength of your personal belief in the student (don't let me down, I know you can do it, I like you).

■ Be prepared to compromise occasionally.

The **J** teacher takes pleasure in scheduling their time. They are organised and decisive. They work out a plan and stick to it, often aided by an impressive to-do list. Their classroom is usually an organised place. The subject will probably be broken down into lesson-sized chunks and the year planned out with alacrity. Many **J** students are reassured by their teacher's organisational zeal. They simply adopt the schedule and deliver their side of the bargain, generally completing all tasks on time. Interestingly, some **J**'s will baulk at their teacher's well-intentioned thoroughness. They would like to create their own plan and work to it rather than adopt someone else's. This is due to the **J**'s desire for control. So two **J** preferences together can clash, though at least all their work will be done. Most schools require students to be so organised that two **J** preferences are, potentially, the most constructive combination. For the teacher to get the best out of their naturally organised student they need to:

■ Enjoy your shared desire for order, neatness and respecting deadlines.

■ Allow the student independence in planning their work in their own way if they really want to.

■ Be prepared to adjust your own plans if external events interfere with your careful preparations (and encourage the student to also embrace flexibility occasionally).

■ Shake things up now and again to prevent predictability becoming boredom.

■ Avoid making quick decisions about what needs to be done before considering all of the options.

7
Polar Bear teacher with Lion student
ISTJ and ESFP

Both teacher and student share an interest in understanding what makes things as they are using observation and experience. They differ in the way they develop conclusions. The Lion is drawn to consider impact on people and the Polar Bear is drawn to analyse the facts objectively. For the teacher to get the best out of their naturally playful and fun-loving student they need to:

■ Listen patiently and enthusiastically to the student's ideas and apparent ramblings.

■ Endure 'silly' ideas to see where they lead – the student is thinking out loud and this is how they learn best.

■ Steer the student away from controversial subjects/topics, especially in group discussions.

■ Build in plenty of opportunities during lessons for the **E** students to talk things through with other **E** preferences.

■ Also offer your own thoughts; if you need a timeout ask for one.

■ Encourage the student to think things through before talking otherwise they'll hog the lesson.

Both teacher and student gather information in the same way. They notice detail using their senses (aware of what they can see, hear and feel). Both use their experience to make sense of what they see and notice. They are both focused on the present. The teacher is instinctively practical, sensible and realistic in their teaching style and will encourage their students to follow their lead. A solid, workman-like relationship develops with both teacher and student mutually understanding what each needs to do to get the job done. For the teacher to get the best out of their essentially grounded student they need to:

■ Demonstrate how learning can be applied in the real world.

■ Allow the student opportunities to repeat and practise until satisfied they are competent.

■ Encourage the use of imagination as a useful process (it's not wasting time).

The student is focused first on people then task whereas the teacher operates in the opposite way. The classroom is likely to have a business-like, purposeful atmosphere. Students are given clear guidelines on what is expected in terms of behaviour, homework and so on. At best this means everyone knows where they stand and how to behave. At worst the classroom can resemble a military boot-camp full of dispirited and browbeaten new recruits. Remember, the personal relationship the teacher develops with this student is key. The Lion needs to feel they like their teacher and that the teacher likes them too. If this happens they'll work harder but if they don't they may switch off completely. This explains why a student can be top of the class one year (with a teacher they like) and show no interest at all in the subject the following year when they change teacher. For the teacher to get the best out of their instinctively people-focused student they need to:

■ Offer learning situations that allow for the use of empathy, collaboration and teamworking to counter-balance your natural tendency to focus on task.

■ Give ample and regular praise while offering tactful support to overcome any blind-spots. Feedback can be easily interpreted as criticism so walk on egg-shells when delivering it.

■ Persuade/influence by appealing to the strength of your personal belief in the student (don't let me down, I know you can do it, I like you).

■ Be prepared to compromise occasionally or the Lion may roar.

Polar Bears must schedule their time. They are the most organised and decisive of all types. They work out a plan and stick to it, usually aided by an impressive to do-list, and their plan is the right one. Their classroom is likely to be the most organised space in school. The subject will probably be broken down into lesson-sized chunks and the year planned out in detail with zeal. The **P** student will either respond:

■ Positively by accepting your expertise and understanding the long-term benefits they'll reap.

■ Passively by just accepting your structure/plan for an easy life without really buying into the content or process you are offering.

■ Negatively by rejecting you, your structure/plan and subject completely (even if they're physically in your room they will not engage and participate).

For the teacher to get the best out of their intrinsically laid-back student they should note the student doesn't just like options and choice; they need them or they start to itch, squirm and rebel. The secondary school environment is difficult enough for **P** preference students so teachers can help soften the pressure. To help:

■ Provide as much flexibility as possible (multiple choice homework tasks, choice within the lesson).

■ Avoid giving out detailed schedules (they'll just lose it anyway!).

■ Don't be more picky with detail than is absolutely necessary.

■ Shake things up now and again to prevent predictability becoming boredom. Introduce random surprises and changes.

■ Identify simple ways the student can organise and manage their time to complete important work without a last-minute panic.

8
Polar Bear teacher with Barn Owl student
ISTJ and INTJ

Barn Owls and Polar Bears share three type preferences. Both are reserved, determined, objective and conscientious. They differ in the way they collect and understand information. The Barn Owl thinks strategically and big picture whereas the Polar Bear is focused on the rational and prudent application of facts. For the teacher to get the best out of their naturally level-headed student they need to:

■ Respect the student's need for privacy and independence.

■ Offer the student time to think through their thoughts.

■ Politely state your opinion to ensure you both know what you're doing.

■ Take time to clarify your thoughts and if something needs to be said be calm and direct as you deliver it, but avoid being confrontational.

■ Use non-verbal communication – smiles and gestures are reassuring to **I** students. You can even use sticky notes/emails to pass on feedback.

- Allow the student time and space to work on their own; don't hover over their head, waiting to pounce.

The Polar Bear teacher likes to use their experience to make sense of what is around them. The teacher is essentially practical, sequential and realistic in style and will generally encourage their students to follow suit. The **N** student may at best find this challenging and at worst find it boring. The teacher may label the student a daydreamer or lost in their own world. They should resist the temptation to castigate their student because this is how they take in information and make sense of the world. In the right context daydreaming can lead to the invention of cars, planes, medicines and computers. For the teacher to get the best out of their inherently imaginative student they need to:

- Embrace the imagination and insight of the student and what it can bring to the lesson.
- Encourage the student to become aware of the important contribution of the **S** approach (the value of facts, details, procedure, experiments, applying experience, structure, the step-by-step model).

Both teacher and student are task-focused, direct, consistent and honest. The classroom is likely to have a business-like and purposeful atmosphere. Students are given clear guidelines on what is expected in terms of behaviour, homework and so on. If the student challenges the teacher it is likely to be for clarification. At best this means everyone knows where they stand and how to behave. For the teacher to get the best out of their fundamentally task-focused student they need to:

- Work in ways that test their skill and knowledge competitively (they raise their game for competitions, challenges, quizzes, measuring and beating personal bests).
- Help them understand that 50% of people are **F** preference and can interpret feedback as criticism.
- Focus on what the student has achieved and what comes next.
- Be prepared to compromise occasionally.
- Avoid trying to fix something without considering potential underlying emotional causes.

The **J** teacher takes pleasure in scheduling their time. They are organised and decisive. They work out a plan and stick to it, often aided by an impressive to-do list. Their classroom is usually an organised place. The subject will probably be broken down into lesson-sized chunks and the year planned out meticulously. Many **J** students are reassured by their teacher's organisational zeal. They simply adopt the schedule and deliver their side of the bargain, generally completing all tasks on time. Interestingly, some **J**'s will baulk at their teacher's well-intentioned thoroughness. They would like to create their own plan and work to it rather than adopt someone else's. This is due to the **J**'s desire for control. So two **J**'s together can clash, though at least all their work will be done. Most schools require students to be so organised that two **J**'s are, potentially, the most constructive combination. For the teacher to get the best out of their naturally organised student they need to:

- Enjoy your shared desire for order, neatness and respecting deadlines.
- Allow the student independence in planning their work in their own way if they really want to.

- Be prepared to adjust your own plans if external events interfere with your careful preparations (and encourage the student to also embrace flexibility occasionally).
- Shake things up now and again to prevent predictability becoming boredom.
- Avoid making quick decisions about what needs to be done before considering all of the options.

9
Polar Bear teacher with Panther student
ISTJ and ESTP

Both Polar Bear and Panther are natural leaders. The mutual understanding derives from two shared preferences and can form the basis of an effective relationship. Clashes can occur when the student attempts to wrestle control from their teacher. Good Polar Bear teachers work out ways to provide their Panther student with opportunities to express their sense of fun. For the teacher to get the best out of their naturally talkative student they need to:

- Listen patiently and enthusiastically to the student's ideas and apparent ramblings.
- Endure 'silly' ideas to see where they lead – the student is thinking out loud and this is how they learn best.
- Steer the student away from controversial subjects/topics, especially in group discussions.
- Build in plenty of opportunities during lessons for the **E** students to talk things through with other **E** preferences.
- Also offer your own thoughts; if you need a timeout ask for one.
- Encourage the student to think things through before talking otherwise they'll hog the lesson.

Both teacher and student gather information in the same way. They notice detail using their senses (aware of what they can see, hear and feel). Both use their experience to make sense of what they see and notice. They are both focused on the present. The teacher is instinctively practical, sensible and realistic in their teaching style and will encourage their students to follow their lead. A solid, workman-like relationship develops with both teacher and student mutually understanding what each needs to do to get the job done. For the teacher to get the best out of their essentially grounded student they need to:

- Demonstrate how learning can be applied in the real world.
- Allow the student opportunities to repeat and practise until satisfied they are competent.
- Encourage the use of imagination as a useful process (it's not wasting time).

Both teacher and student are task-focused, direct, consistent and honest. The classroom is likely to have a business-like and purposeful atmosphere. Students are given clear guidelines on what is expected in terms of behaviour, homework and so on. If the student challenges the teacher it is likely to be for clarification. At best this means everyone knows where they stand and how to be-

have. For the teacher to get the best out of their inherently task-focused student they need to:

- Work in ways that test their skill and knowledge competitively (they raise their game for competitions, challenges, quizzes, measuring and beating personal bests).
- Avoid trying to fix something without considering potential underlying emotional causes.
- Help them appreciate that 50% of people are **F** preference and can interpret feedback as criticism.
- Focus on what the student has achieved and what comes next.
- Be prepared to compromise occasionally or the Panther may rebel.

The **J** teacher takes pleasure in scheduling their time. They are organised and decisive. They work out a plan and stick to it, usually aided by an impressive to-do list. Their classroom is likely to be the most organised space in school. The subject will probably be broken down into lesson-sized chunks and the year planned out in detail with zeal. The **P** student will either respond:

- Positively by accepting your expertise and understanding the long-term benefits they'll reap.
- Passively by just accepting your structure/plan for an easy life without really buying into the content or process you are offering.
- Negatively by rejecting you, your structure/plan and subject completely (even if they're physically in your room they will not engage and participate).

For the teacher to get the best out of their intrinsically laid-back student they should note the student doesn't just like options and choice; they need them or they start to itch, squirm and rebel. The secondary school environment is difficult enough for **P** preference students so teachers can help soften the pressure. To help:

- Provide as much flexibility as possible (multiple choice homework tasks, choice within the lesson).
- Avoid giving out detailed schedules (they'll just lose it anyway!).
- Don't be more picky with detail than is absolutely necessary.
- Shake things up now and again to prevent predictability becoming boredom. Introduce random surprises and changes.
- Identify simple ways the student can organise and manage their time to complete important work without a last-minute panic.

10
Polar Bear teacher with Falcon student
ISTJ and ENTP

Both Polar Bears and Falcons are natural leaders. The mutual understanding derives from one shared preference (an objective and unsentimental view of the world) which can form the basis of an effective relationship. Clashes can occur when the student attempts to wrestle control from their teacher. Good teachers work out ways to provide their Falcon student with opportunities to express their need to perform and put across their often controversial and forthright views. They are often shared for shock value as the Falcon is easily bored. For the teacher to get the best out of their naturally confrontational student they need to:

■ Listen patiently and enthusiastically to the student's ideas and apparent ramblings.

■ Endure 'silly' ideas to see where they lead – the student is thinking out loud and this is how they learn best.

■ Steer the student away from controversial subjects/topics, especially in group discussions.

■ Build in plenty of opportunities during lessons for the **E** students to talk things through with other **E** preferences.

■ Also offer your own thoughts; if you need a timeout ask for one.

■ Encourage the student to think things through before talking otherwise they'll hijack the lesson.

The Polar Bear teacher likes to use their experience to make sense of what is around them. The teacher is essentially practical, sequential and realistic in style and will generally encourage their students to follow suit. The **N** student may at best find this challenging and at worst find it boring. The teacher may label the student argumentative or even arrogant. They should resist the temptation to castigate their student because this is how they take in information and make sense of the world. In the right context daydreaming can lead to the invention of cars, planes, medicines and computers. For the teacher to get the best out of their inherently imaginative student they need to:

■ Embrace the imagination and insight of the student and what it can bring to the lesson.

■ Encourage the student to become aware of the important contribution of the **S** approach (the value of facts, details, procedure, experiments, applying experience, structure, the step-by-step model).

Both teacher and student are task-focused, direct, consistent and honest. The classroom is likely to have a business-like and purposeful atmosphere. Students are given clear guidelines on what is expected in terms of behaviour, homework and so on. If the student challenges the teacher it is likely to be for clarification. At best this means everyone knows where they stand and how to behave. For the teacher to get the best out of their fundamentally task-focused student they need to:

■ Work in ways that test their skill and knowledge competitively (they raise their game for competitions, challenges, quizzes, measuring and beating personal bests).

■ Help them understand that 50% of people are **F** preference and can interpret feedback as criticism.

■ Focus on what the student has achieved and what comes next.

■ Be prepared to compromise occasionally.

■ Avoid trying to fix something without considering potential underlying emotional causes.

Polar Bears must schedule their time. They are the most organised and decisive of all types. They work out a plan and stick to it and their plan is the right one. Their classroom is likely to be the most organised space in school. The subject will probably be broken down into lesson-sized

chunks and the year planned out in detail with zeal. The **P** student will either respond:

■ Positively by accepting your expertise and understanding the long-term benefits they'll reap.

■ Passively by just accepting your structure/plan for an easy life without really buying into the content or process you are offering.

■ Negatively by rejecting you, your structure/plan and subject completely (even if they're physically in your room they will not engage and participate).

For the teacher to get the best out of their intrinsically laid-back student they should note the student doesn't just like options and choice; they need them or they start to itch, squirm and rebel. The secondary school environment is difficult enough for **P** preference students so teachers can help soften the pressure. To help:

■ Provide as much flexibility as possible (multiple choice homework tasks, choice within the lesson).

■ Avoid giving out detailed schedules (they'll just lose it anyway!).

■ Don't be more picky with detail than is absolutely necessary.

■ Shake things up now and again to prevent predictability becoming boredom. Introduce random surprises and changes.

■ Identify simple time-management strategies to ensure the student thrives.

11
Polar Bear teacher with Tawny Owl student
ISTJ and INTP

Polar Bears and Tawny Owls share two preferences. Neither is prone to sentimentality. Their differences are substantial and need to be respected for a positive relationship to flourish. The practical and direct Bear contrasts with the theoretical and professorial Owl. For the teacher to get the best out of their naturally introspective student they need to:

■ Respect the student's need for privacy and independence.

■ Offer the student time to think through their thoughts.

■ Politely state your opinion to ensure you both know what you're doing.

■ Take time to clarify your thoughts and if something needs to be said be calm and direct as you deliver it, but avoid being confrontational.

■ Use non-verbal communication – smiles and gestures are reassuring to **I** students. You can even use sticky notes/emails to pass on feedback.

The Polar Bear teacher likes to use their experience to make sense of what is around them. The teacher is essentially practical, sequential and realistic in style and will generally encourage their students to follow suit. The **N** student may at best find this challenging and at worst find it boring. The teacher may label the student argumentative or even arrogant. They should resist the temptation to castigate their student because this is how

they take in information and make sense of the world. In the right context daydreaming can lead to new insights for the whole class to enjoy. For the teacher to get the best out of their inherently imaginative student they need to:

■ Embrace the imagination and insight of the student and what it can bring to the lesson.

■ Encourage the student to become aware of the important contribution of the **S** approach (the value of facts, details, procedure, experiments, applying experience, structure, the step-by-step model).

Both teacher and student are task-focused, direct, consistent and honest. The classroom is likely to have a business-like and purposeful atmosphere. Students are given clear guidelines on what is expected in terms of behaviour, homework and so on. If the student challenges the teacher it is likely to be for clarification. At best this means everyone knows where they stand and how to behave. For the teacher to get the best out of their fundamentally task-focused student they need to:

■ Focus on what the student has achieved and what comes next.

■ Be prepared to compromise occasionally.

■ Avoid trying to fix something without considering potential underlying emotional causes.

■ Work in ways that test their skill and knowledge competitively (they raise their game for competitions, challenges, quizzes, measuring and beating personal bests).

■ Help them understand that half of people have an **F** preference and can interpret feedback as criticism.

The **J** teacher takes pleasure in scheduling their time. They are organised and decisive. They work out a plan and stick to it, usually aided by an impressive to-do list. Their classroom is likely to be the most organised space in school. The subject will probably be broken down into lesson-sized chunks and the year planned out in detail with zeal. The **P** student will either respond:

■ Positively by accepting your expertise and understanding the long-term benefits they'll reap.

■ Passively by just accepting your structure/plan for an easy life without really buying into the content or process you are offering.

■ Negatively by rejecting you, your structure/plan and subject completely (even if they're physically in your room they will not engage and participate).

For the teacher to get the best out of their intrinsically laid-back student they should note the student doesn't just like options and choice; they need them or they start to itch, squirm and rebel. The secondary school environment is difficult enough for **P** preference students so teachers can help soften the pressure. To help:

■ Provide as much flexibility as possible (multiple choice homework tasks, choice within the lesson).

■ Avoid giving out detailed schedules (they'll just lose it anyway!).

■ Don't be more picky with detail than is absolutely necessary.

■ Shake things up now and again to prevent predictability becoming boredom. Introduce random surprises and changes.

■ Identify simple ways the student can organise and manage their time to complete important work without a last-minute rush.

12
Polar Bear teacher with Teddy Bear student
ISTJ and ESFJ

Both teacher and student share an interest in understanding what makes things as they are and completing tasks efficiently and on schedule. They differ in the way they are energised and develop conclusions. The Teddy is drawn to discuss the impact on people and the Polar Bear is drawn to quietly analyse the facts objectively. For the teacher to get the best out of their naturally sociable student they need to:

- Listen patiently and enthusiastically to the student's ideas and apparent ramblings – the student is thinking out loud and this is how they process and organise information.
- Steer the student away from controversial subjects/gossip, especially in group discussions.
- Build in plenty of opportunities during lessons for the **E** students to talk things through with other **E** preferences.
- Also offer your own thoughts; if you need a timeout ask for one.
- Encourage the student to think things through before talking otherwise they'll hog the lesson.

Both teacher and student gather information in the same way. They notice detail using their senses (aware of what they can see, hear and feel). They are both focused on the present. The teacher is instinctively practical, sensible and realistic in their teaching style and will encourage their students to follow their lead. A solid, workman-like relationship develops with both teacher and student mutually understanding what each needs to do to get the job done. For the teacher to get the best out of their essentially grounded student they need to:

- Demonstrate how learning can be applied in the real world.
- Allow the student opportunities to repeat and practise until satisfied they are competent.
- Encourage the use of imagination as a useful process (it's not wasting time).

The teacher is focused first on task and second on people/relationships. The classroom is likely to have a business-like, purposeful atmosphere. Students are given clear guidelines on what is expected in terms of behaviour, homework and so on. At best this means everyone knows where they stand and how to behave. At worst the classroom can resemble a military boot-camp full of dispirited and brow-beaten new recruits. Remember, the personal relationship the teacher develops with this student is the key to success. The Teddy needs to feel they like their teacher and that the teacher likes them too. If this happens they'll work harder but if they don't they may switch off completely. This explains why a student can be top of the class one year (with a teacher they like) and show no interest at all in the subject the following year when they change teacher. For the teacher to get the best out of their instinctively people-focused student they need to:

- Offer learning situations that allow for the use of empathy, collaboration and teamworking to counter-balance your natural tendency to focus on task.
- Give ample and regular praise while offering tactful support to overcome any blind-spots. Feedback can be easily interpreted as criticism so walk on egg-shells when delivering it.
- Persuade/influence by appealing to the strength of your personal belief in the student (don't let me down, I know you can do it, I like you).
- Be prepared to compromise occasionally or the Teddy may sulk.

Polar Bears must schedule their time. They are the most organised and decisive of all types. They work out a plan and stick to it and their plan is the right one. Their classroom is usually an organised place. The subject will probably be broken down into lesson-sized chunks and the year planned out meticulously. Many **J** students are reassured by their teacher's organisational zeal. They simply adopt the schedule and deliver their side of the bargain, generally completing all tasks on time. Interestingly, some **J**'s will baulk at their teacher's well-intentioned thoroughness. They would like to create their own plan and work to it rather than adopt someone else's. This is due to the **J**'s desire for control. So two **J**'s together can clash, though at least all their work will be done. Most schools require students to be so organised that two **J**'s are, potentially, the most constructive combination. For the teacher to get the best out of their naturally organised student they need to:

- Enjoy your shared desire for order, neatness and respecting deadlines.
- Be prepared to adjust your own plans if external events interfere with your careful preparations (and encourage the student to also embrace flexibility occasionally).
- Shake things up now and again to prevent predictability becoming boredom.
- Avoid making quick decisions about what needs to be done before considering all of the options.
- Allow the student independence in planning their work in their own way if they really want to.

13
Polar Bear teacher with Koala student
ISTJ and ISFJ

Both Bears live in the real world using experience and observation to make sense of things. They differ in the way they develop conclusions. The Koala is drawn to consider impact on people and the Polar Bear to analyse the facts objectively. For the teacher to get the best out of their naturally reticent student they need to:

- Respect the student's need for privacy and independence.
- Offer the student time to think through their thoughts.
- Politely state your opinion to ensure you both know what you're doing.

- Take time to clarify your thoughts and if something needs to be said be calm and direct as you deliver it, but avoid being confrontational.
- Use non-verbal communication – smiles and gestures are reassuring to **I** students. You can even use sticky notes/emails to pass on feedback.

Both teacher and student gather information in the same way. They notice detail using their senses (aware of what they can see, hear and feel). Both are focused on the present. The teacher is instinctively practical, sensible and realistic in their teaching style and will encourage their students to follow their lead. A solid, workman-like relationship develops with both teacher and student mutually understanding what each needs to do to get the job done. For the teacher to get the best out of their essentially grounded student they need to:

- Demonstrate how learning can be applied in the real world.
- Allow the student opportunities to repeat and practise until satisfied they are competent.
- Encourage the use of imagination as a useful process (it's not wasting time).

The teacher is focused first on task and second on people/relationships. The classroom is likely to have a business-like, purposeful atmosphere. Students are given clear guidelines on what is expected in terms of behaviour, homework and so on. At best this means everyone knows where they stand and how to behave. At worst the classroom can resemble a military boot-camp. Remember, the personal relationship the teacher develops with this student is the key to success. The Koala needs to feel they like their teacher and that the teacher likes them too. If this happens they'll work harder but if they don't they may switch off completely. This explains why a student can be top of the class one year (with a teacher they like) and show no interest at all in the subject the following year when they change teacher. For the teacher to get the best out of their instinctively people-focused student they need to:

- Offer learning situations that allow for the use of empathy, collaboration and small teamworking to counter-balance your natural tendency to focus on task.
- Give ample and regular praise while offering tactful support to overcome any blind-spots. Feedback can be easily interpreted as criticism so tread carefully when delivering it.
- Engage by quietly and regularly stating your personal belief in the student (don't let me down, I know you can do it, I like you).
- Be prepared to compromise occasionally to reassure the routine-loving Koala.

Bear teachers take pleasure in scheduling their time. They are organised and decisive. They work out a plan and stick to it, often aided by an impressive to-do list. Their classroom is usually an organised place. The subject will probably be broken down into lesson-sized chunks and the year planned out whether or not an Ofsted inspector is due. Many **J** students are reassured by their teacher's organisational zeal. They simply adopt the schedule and deliver their side of the bargain, generally completing all tasks on time. Interestingly, some **J**'s will baulk at their teacher's well-intentioned thoroughness. They would like to create their own plan and work to it rather than adopt someone else's. This is due to the **J**'s desire for control. So two **J**'s together can clash, though at least all their work will be done. Most schools require students to be so organised that two **J**'s are, potentially, a very constructive combination. For the teacher to get the best out of their naturally organised student they need to:

- Enjoy your shared desire for order, neatness and respecting deadlines.
- Allow the student independence in planning their work in their own way if they really want to.
- Be prepared to adjust your own plans if external events interfere with your careful preparations (and encourage the student to also embrace flexibility occasionally).
- Shake things up now and again to prevent predictability becoming boredom.
- Avoid making quick decisions about what needs to be done before considering all of the options.

14
Polar Bear teacher with Seahorse student
ISTJ and INFJ

Polar Bears and Seahorses share two preferences. Both like to finish work on time. They differ in the way they develop conclusions. The Seahorse is drawn to fantasy and to consider impact on people whereas the Polar Bear likes to analyse the facts objectively. For the teacher to get the best out of their naturally introspective student they need to:

- Slow down and be calm and succinct.
- Leave plenty of time between question and answer; respect the student's need for time to think and reflect before responding.
- Allow the student time and space to work on their own; don't hover over their head, waiting to pounce.
- Avoid trying to fix problems immediately or finish their sentences.
- Pair them up with complementary types (Koalas, Cats and Seals).
- Avoid placing them in groups/teams where they are the only **I** preference in a sea of **E** preferences (they're likely to sit in silence).
- Provide written praise (not just verbal).

The Polar Bear teacher likes to use their experience to make sense of what is around them. The teacher is essentially practical, sequential and realistic in style and will generally encourage their students to follow suit. The **N** student may at best find this challenging and at worst find it boring. The Polar Bear teacher may label the student argumentative or even arrogant. They should resist the temptation to castigate their student because this is how they take in information and make sense of the world. In the right context daydreaming can lead to the invention of cars, planes, medicines and computers. For the teacher to get the best out of their inherently imaginative student they need to:

- Embrace the imagination and insight offered by the Seahorse student and what this can add to the lesson.

- Encourage the student to become aware of the important contribution of the **S** approach (the value of facts, details, procedure, experiments, applying experience, structure, the step-by-step model).

The teacher is focused first on task and second on people/relationships. The classroom is likely to have a business-like, purposeful atmosphere. Students are given clear guidelines on what is expected in terms of behaviour, homework and so on. At best this means everyone knows where they stand and how to behave. At worst the classroom can resemble a military boot-camp. Remember, the personal relationship the teacher develops with this student is the key to success. The Seahorse needs to feel they like their teacher and that the teacher likes them too. If this happens they'll work harder but if they don't they may switch off completely. This explains why a student can be top of the class one year (with a teacher they like) and show no interest at all in the subject the following year when they change teacher. For the teacher to get the best out of their instinctively people-focused student they need to:

- Offer learning situations that allow for the use of empathy, collaboration and teamworking to counter-balance your natural tendency to focus on task.
- Give ample and regular praise while offering tactful support to overcome any blind-spots. Feedback can be easily interpreted as criticism so walk on egg-shells when delivering it.
- Persuade/influence by appealing to the strength of your personal belief in the student (don't let me down, I know you can do it, I like you).
- Be prepared to compromise occasionally.

The **J** teacher takes pleasure in scheduling their time. They are organised and decisive. They work out a plan and stick to it, often aided by an impressive to-do list. Their classroom is usually an organised place. The subject will probably be broken down into lesson-sized chunks and the year planned out whether or not an Ofsted inspector is lurking in the corridor. Many **J** students are reassured by their teacher's organisational zeal. They simply adopt the schedule and deliver their side of the bargain, generally completing all tasks on time. Interestingly, some **J**'s will baulk at their teacher's well-intentioned thoroughness. They would like to create their own plan and work to it rather than adopt someone else's. This is due to the **J**'s desire for control. So two **J**'s together can clash, though at least all their work will be done. Most schools require students to be so organised that two **J**'s are, potentially, a very constructive combination. For the teacher to get the best out of their naturally organised student they need to:

- Enjoy your shared desire for order, neatness and respecting deadlines.
- Allow the student independence in planning their work in their own way if they really want to.
- Avoid making quick decisions about what needs to be done before considering all of the options.
- Be prepared to adjust your own plans if external events interfere with your careful preparations (and encourage the student to also embrace flexibility occasionally).
- Shake things up now and again to prevent predictability becoming boredom.

15
Polar Bear teacher with Eagle student
ISTJ and ENTJ

Both Polar Bears and Eagles like to be in charge. Mutual understanding derives from two shared type preferences and can form the basis of an effective relationship. Clashes can occur when the student attempts to wrestle control from their teacher. Effective Polar Bear teachers work out ways to provide their Eagle student with opportunities to express their need to lead and state their often forthright views. For the teacher to get the best out of their naturally confrontational student they need to:

- Listen patiently and enthusiastically to the student's ideas and apparent ramblings.
- Endure 'silly' ideas to see where they lead – the student is thinking out loud and this is how they learn best.
- Steer the student away from controversial subjects/topics, especially in group discussions.
- Build in plenty of opportunities during lessons for the **E** students to talk things through with other **E** preferences.
- Also offer your own thoughts; if you need a timeout ask for one.
- Encourage the student to think things through before talking otherwise they'll hog the lesson.

The Polar Bear teacher likes to use their experience to make sense of what is around them. The teacher is essentially practical, sequential and realistic in style and will generally encourage their students to follow suit. The **N** student may at best find this challenging and at worst find it boring. The teacher may label the student argumentative or even arrogant. They should resist the temptation to castigate their student because this is how they take in information and make sense of the world. In the right context daydreaming can lead to the invention of cars, planes, medicines and computers. For the teacher to get the best out of their inherently imaginative student they need to:

- Embrace the imagination and insight of the student and what it can bring to the lesson.
- Encourage the student to become aware of the important contribution of the **S** approach (the value of facts, details, procedure, experiments, applying experience, structure, the step-by-step model).

Both teacher and student are task-focused, direct, consistent and honest. The classroom is likely to have a business-like and purposeful atmosphere. Students are given clear guidelines on what is expected in terms of behaviour, homework and so on. If the student challenges the teacher it is likely to be for clarification. At best this means everyone knows where they stand and how to behave. For the teacher to get the best out of their characteristically task-focused Eagle they need to:

- Work in ways that test their skill and knowledge competitively (they raise their game for competitions, challenges, quizzes, measuring and beating personal bests).

- Help them understand that 50% of people are **F** preference and can interpret feedback as criticism.
- Focus on what the student has achieved and what comes next.
- Be prepared to compromise occasionally.
- Avoid trying to fix something without considering potential underlying emotional causes.

Polar Bear teachers take pleasure in scheduling their time. They are organised and decisive. They work out a plan and stick to it, often aided by an impressive to-do list. Their classroom is usually an organised place. The subject will probably be broken down into lesson-sized chunks and the year planned out whether or not an Ofsted inspector is due. Many **J** students are reassured by their teacher's organisational zeal. They simply adopt the schedule and deliver their side of the bargain, generally completing all tasks on time. Interestingly, some **J**'s will baulk at their teacher's well-intentioned thoroughness. They would like to create their own plan and work to it rather than adopt someone else's. This is due to the **J**'s desire for control. So two **J**'s together can clash, though at least all their work will be done. Most schools require students to be so organised that two **J**'s are, potentially, a very constructive combination. For the teacher to get the best out of their naturally organised student they need to:

- Enjoy your shared desire for order, neatness and respecting deadlines.
- Allow the student independence in planning their work in their own way if they really want to.
- Be prepared to adjust your own plans if external events interfere with your careful preparations (and encourage the student to also embrace flexibility occasionally).
- Shake things up now and again to prevent predictability becoming boredom.
- Avoid making quick decisions about what needs to be done before considering all of the options.

16
Polar Bear teacher with Cat student
ISTJ and ISFP

The naturally confident and assertive Polar Bear teacher shares two preferences with their Cat student. To form an effective relationship they need to accept and appreciate each other's differences. The Cat gains satisfaction when work feels like fun whereas to the Bear work is satisfying as work. For the teacher to get the best out of their naturally introspective student they need to:

- Slow down and be succinct.
- Allow the student time and space to work on their own; don't hover over their head, waiting to pounce.
- Leave plenty of time between question and answer; let the student sleep on it so they fully organise their thoughts.
- Avoid trying to fix problems immediately or finish their sentences.

- Pair them up with complementary types (Tigers, Seals and Tawny Owls).
- Avoid placing them in groups/teams where they are the only **I** preference in a sea of **E** preferences (they'll be smothered).
- Provide written praise (not just verbal).
- Let the student know they can always come and talk to you alone during breaks or they can write down their questions/issues for you to reply to later.

Both teacher and student gather information in the same way. They notice detail using their senses (aware of what they can see, hear and feel). Both use their experience to make sense of what they see and notice. They are both focused on the present. The teacher is instinctively practical, sensible and realistic in their teaching style and will encourage their students to follow their lead. A solid, workman-like relationship develops with both teacher and student mutually understanding what each needs to do to get the job done. For the teacher to get the best out of their essentially grounded student they need to:

- Show how learning can be applied in the real world.
- Allow the student opportunities to repeat and practise until satisfied they are competent.
- Encourage the use of imagination as a useful process (it's not wasting time).

The teacher is focused first on task and second on people/relationships. The classroom is likely to have a business-like, purposeful atmosphere. Students are given clear guidelines on what is expected in terms of behaviour, homework and so on. At best this means everyone knows where they stand and how to behave. At worst the classroom can resemble a military boot-camp full of dispirited and brow-beaten new recruits. Remember, the personal relationship the teacher develops with this student is the key to success. The Cat needs to feel they like their teacher and that the teacher likes them too. If this happens they'll work harder but if they don't they may switch off completely. This explains why a student can be top of the class one year (with a teacher they like) and show no interest at all in the subject the following year when they change teacher. For the teacher to get the best out of their instinctively people-focused student they need to:

- Offer learning situations that allow for the use of empathy, collaboration and teamworking to counter-balance your natural tendency to focus on task.
- Give ample and regular praise while offering tactful support to overcome any blind-spots. Feedback can be easily mistaken for criticism so walk on egg-shells when delivering it.
- Persuade/influence by appealing to the strength of your personal belief in the student (don't let me down, I know you can do it, I like you).
- Be prepared to compromise occasionally.

The Polar Bear teacher takes pleasure in scheduling their time. They are organised and decisive. They work out a plan and stick to it, usually aided by an impressive to-do list. Their classroom is likely to be the most organised space in school. The subject will probably be broken down into lesson-sized chunks and the year planned out in detail with zeal. The **P** student will either respond:

- Positively by accepting your expertise and understanding the long-term benefits they'll reap.

- Passively by just accepting your structure/plan for an easy life without really buying into the content or process you are offering.
- Negatively by rejecting you, your structure/plan and subject completely (even if they're physically in your room they will not engage and participate).

For the teacher to get the best out of their intrinsically laid-back student they should note the student doesn't just like options and choice; they need them or they start to itch, squirm and rebel. The secondary school environment is difficult enough for **P** preference students so teachers can help soften the pressure. To help:

- Provide as much flexibility as possible (multiple choice homework tasks, choice within the lesson).
- Avoid giving out detailed schedules (they'll just lose it anyway!).
- Don't be more picky with detail than is absolutely necessary.
- Shake things up now and again to prevent predictability becoming boredom. Introduce random surprises and changes.
- Help the student identify simple effective strategies to ensure they can succeed.

17
Black Bear teacher with Black Bear student
ESTJ and ESTJ

Black Bears are natural leaders. They can hardly help themselves from taking charge and completing tasks. Their mutual understanding can form the basis of an effective relationship. Clashes can occur when the student attempts to wrestle control from their teacher. Good Black Bear teachers work out ways to provide their student with opportunities to express their organisational talent. For the teacher to get the best out of their naturally effusive student they need to:

- Enjoy the lively banter when it is appropriate to spark new thoughts and ideas; the student learns best this way, but remember there may be thirty others in the classroom.
- Stick to the point and stay positive (don't nag).
- Avoid going over old ground.
- Be calm and clear, otherwise two **E** preferences can talk louder and louder like PMQs (with neither listening).
- Remember you can keep some thoughts to yourself (and you may think of a better way of expressing something, especially criticism, later).
- Be an enthusiastic and supportive listener; seek to help the student clarify and develop their thinking rather than assert your own.
- Help each other learn to be quiet and encourage the **I** preferences in the class to express themselves.

Both teacher and student gather information in the same way. They notice detail using their senses (aware of what they can see, hear and feel). Both use their experience to make sense of what they see and notice. They are both focused on the present. The teacher is instinctively practical, sensible and realistic in their teaching style and will encourage their students to follow their lead. A solid, workman-like relationship develops with both teacher and student mutually understanding what each needs to do to get the job done. For the teacher to get the best out of their essentially grounded student they need to:

■ Demonstrate how learning can be applied in the real world.

■ Allow the student opportunities to repeat and practise until satisfied they are competent.

■ Encourage the use of imagination as a useful process (it's not wasting time).

Both teacher and student are task-focused, direct, consistent and honest. The classroom is likely to have a business-like and purposeful atmosphere. Students are given clear guidelines on what is expected in terms of behaviour, homework and so on. If the student challenges the teacher it is likely to be for clarification. At best this means everyone knows where they stand and how to behave. For the teacher to get the best out of their inherently task-focused student they need to:

■ Work in ways that test their skill and knowledge competitively (they raise their game for competitions, challenges, quizzes, measuring and beating personal bests).

■ Help them understand that 50% of people are **F** preference and can interpret feedback as criticism.

■ Focus on what the student has achieved and what comes next.

■ Be prepared to compromise occasionally.

■ Avoid trying to fix something without considering potential underlying emotional causes.

The **J** teacher takes pleasure in scheduling their time. They are organised and decisive. They work out a plan and stick to it, often aided by an impressive to-do list. Their classroom is usually an organised place. The subject will probably be broken down into lesson-sized chunks and the year planned out whether an Ofsted inspector is due or not. Many **J** students are reassured by their teacher's organisational zeal. They simply adopt the schedule and deliver their side of the bargain, generally completing all tasks on time. Interestingly, some **J**'s will baulk at their teacher's well-intentioned thoroughness. They would like to create their own plan and work to it rather than adopt someone else's. This is due to the **J**'s desire for control. So two **J**'s together can clash, though at least all their work will be done. Most schools require students to be so organised that two **J**'s are, potentially, the most constructive combination. For the teacher to get the best out of their naturally organised student they need to:

■ Enjoy your shared desire for order, neatness and respecting deadlines.

■ Allow the student independence in planning their work in their own way if they really want to.

■ Be prepared to adjust your own plans if external events interfere with your careful preparations (and encourage the student to also embrace flexibility occasionally).

■ Shake things up now and again to prevent predictability becoming boredom.

■ Avoid making quick decisions about what needs to be done before considering all of the options.

18
Black Bear teacher with Seal student
ESTJ and INFP

The naturally confident and assertive Black Bear teacher shares no type preferences with their Seal student. For opposites to attract they need to accept and appreciate each other's differences. For the teacher to get the best out of their naturally introspective student they need to:

■ Slow down and be succinct.

■ Leave plenty of time between question and answer; respect the student's need for time to think and reflect before responding.

■ Allow the student time and space to work on their own; don't hover over their head, waiting to pounce.

■ Avoid trying to fix problems immediately or finish their sentences.

■ Avoid placing them in groups/teams where they are the only **I** preference in a sea of **E** preferences (they'll be smothered).

■ Provide written praise (not just verbal).

The Black Bear teacher likes to use their experience to make sense of what is around them. The teacher is essentially practical, sequential and realistic in style and will generally encourage their students to follow suit. The **N** student may at best find this challenging and at worst find it boring. The Black Bear teacher may label the student a daydreamer, lost in their own world or 'away with the fairies'. They should resist the temptation to castigate their student because this is how they take in information and make sense of the world. In the right context daydreaming can lead to the invention of cars, planes, medicines and computers. For the teacher to get the best out of their inherently imaginative student they need to:

■ Embrace the imagination and insight of the student and what it can bring to the lesson.

■ Encourage the student to become aware of the important contribution of the **S** approach (the value of facts, details, procedure, experiments, applying experience, structure, the step-by-step model).

The teacher is focused first on task and second on people/relationships. The classroom is likely to have a business-like, purposeful atmosphere. Students are given clear guidelines on what is expected in terms of behaviour, homework and so on. At best this means everyone knows where they stand and how to behave. At worst the classroom can resemble a military boot-camp full of dispirited and brow-beaten new recruits. Remember, the personal relationship the teacher develops with this student is the key to success. The Seal needs to feel they like their teacher and that the teacher likes them too. If this happens they'll work harder but if they don't they may switch off completely. This explains why a student can be top of the class one year (with a teacher they like) and show no interest at all in the subject the following year when they change teacher. For the teacher to get the best out of their instinctively people-focused student they need to:

■ Offer learning situations that allow for the use of empathy, collaboration and teamworking to counter-balance your natural tendency to focus on task.

■ Give ample and regular praise while offering tactful support to overcome any blind-spots. Feedback can be easily interpreted as criticism so walk on egg-shells when delivering it.

■ Persuade/influence by appealing to the strength of your personal belief in the student (don't let me down, I know you can do it, I like you).

■ Be prepared to compromise occasionally.

The Black Bear teacher takes pleasure in scheduling their time. They are organised and decisive. They work out a plan and stick to it, usually aided by an impressive to-do list. Their classroom is likely to be the most organised space in school. The subject will probably be broken down into lesson-sized chunks and the year planned out in detail with zeal. The **P** student will either respond:

■ Positively by accepting your expertise and understanding the long-term benefits they'll reap.

■ Passively by just accepting your structure/plan for an easy life without really buying into the content or process you are offering.

■ Negatively by rejecting you, your structure/plan and subject completely (even if they're physically in your room they will not engage and participate).

For the teacher to get the best out of their intrinsically laid-back student they should note the student doesn't just like options and choice; they need them or they start to itch, squirm and rebel. The secondary school environment is difficult enough for **P** preference students so teachers can help soften the pressure. To help:

■ Provide as much flexibility as possible (multiple choice homework tasks, choice within the lesson).

■ Avoid giving out detailed schedules (they'll just lose it anyway!).

■ Don't be more picky with detail than is absolutely necessary.

■ Shake things up now and again to prevent predictability becoming boredom. Introduce random surprises and changes.

■ Help the student identify simple effective strategies to ensure they can succeed.

19
Black Bear teacher with Clownfish student
ESTJ and ENFP

Both teacher and student are naturally energetic and assertive. They differ on three preferences which means a successful relationship needs to be built on an acceptance and appreciation of each other's differences. Clashes are most frequently experienced when the teacher's task-focused organisational zeal jars with the whimsical and fun-focused student. For the ebullient teacher and equally excitable student to gel the teacher needs to:

- Enjoy the lively banter when it is appropriate to spark new thoughts and ideas; the student learns best this way, but remember there may be thirty others in the classroom.
- Stick to the point and stay positive (don't nag), as both teacher and student are easily distracted and liable to go off track!
- Avoid going over old ground.
- Be calm and clear, otherwise two **E** preferences can talk louder and louder with neither listening.
- Remember you can keep some thoughts to yourself (and you may think of a better way of expressing something, especially criticism, later).
- Be an enthusiastic and supportive listener; seek to help the student clarify and develop their thinking rather than assert your own.
- Help each other learn to be quiet and encourage the **I** preferences in the class to express themselves.

The Black Bear teacher likes to use their experience to make sense of what is around them. The teacher is essentially practical, sequential and realistic in style and will generally encourage their students to follow suit. The **N** student may at best find this challenging and at worst find it boring. The Black Bear teacher may label the student a daydreamer or 'away with the fairies'. They should resist the temptation to castigate their student because this is how they take in information and make sense of the world. In the right context daydreaming can lead to new inventions. For the teacher to get the best out of their inherently imaginative student they need to:

- Embrace the imagination and insight of the student and what it can bring to the lesson.
- Encourage the student to become aware of the important contribution of the **S** approach (the value of facts, details, procedure, experiments, applying experience, structure, the step-by-step model).

The teacher is focused first on task and second on people/relationships. The classroom is likely to have a business-like, purposeful atmosphere. Students are given clear guidelines on what is expected in terms of behaviour, homework and so on. At best this means everyone knows where they stand and how to behave. At worst the classroom can resemble a military boot-camp full of dispirited and brow-beaten new recruits. Remember, the personal relationship the teacher develops with this student is key. The Clownfish needs to feel they like their teacher and that the teacher likes them too. If this happens they'll work harder but if they don't they may switch off completely. This explains why a student can be top of the class one year (with a teacher they like) and show no interest at all in the subject the following year when they change teacher. For the teacher to get the best out of their instinctively people-focused student they need to:

- Offer learning situations that allow for the use of empathy, collaboration and teamworking to counter-balance your natural tendency to focus on task.
- Persuade by appealing to the strength of your personal belief in the student (don't let me down, I know you can do it, I like you).
- Be prepared to compromise occasionally; Clownfish can sulk or disrupt if huffed.
- Give ample and regular praise while offering tactful support to overcome any blind-spots. Feedback can be easily interpreted as criticism so walk on egg-shells when delivering it.

The **J** teacher takes pleasure in scheduling their time. They are organised and decisive. They work out a plan and stick to it, usually aided by an impressive to-do list. Their classroom is likely to be the most organised space in school. The subject will probably be broken down into lesson-sized chunks and the year planned out in detail with zeal. The **P** student will either respond:

- Positively by accepting your expertise and understanding the long-term benefits they'll reap.
- Passively by just accepting your structure/plan for an easy life without really buying into the content or process you are offering.
- Negatively by rejecting you, your structure/plan and subject completely (even if they're physically in your room they will not engage and participate).

For the teacher to get the best out of their intrinsically laid-back student they should note the student doesn't just like options and choice; they need them or they start to itch, squirm and rebel. The secondary school environment is difficult enough for **P** preference students so teachers can help soften the pressure. To help:

- Provide as much flexibility as possible (multiple choice homework tasks, choice within the lesson).
- Avoid giving out detailed schedules (they'll just lose it anyway!).
- Don't be more picky with detail than is absolutely necessary.
- Shake things up now and again to prevent predictability becoming boredom. Introduce random surprises and changes.
- Identify simple ways the student can organise and manage their time to complete important work without a last-minute panic.

20
Black Bear teacher with Polar Bear student
ESTJ and ISTJ

Black Bears and Polar Bears are organised, decisive and in control. They are also task-focused and determined to succeed. These common foundations usually result in a constructive relationship. Clashes are only likely if the student's assertiveness is incorrectly interpreted as belligerence. For the teacher to get the best out of their student they need to:

- Slow down and be calm and succinct.
- Leave plenty of time between question and answer; respect the student's need for time to think and reflect before responding.
- Allow the student time and space to work on their own; don't hover over their head, waiting to pounce.
- Avoid trying to fix problems immediately or finish their sentences.
- Pair them up with complementary types (Bears and Owls).
- Provide written praise (not just verbal).
- Let the student know they can always come and talk to you alone during breaks or they can write down their questions/issues for you to reply to later.

Both teacher and student gather information in the same way. They notice detail using their senses (aware of what they can see, hear and feel). Both use their experience to make sense of what they see and notice. They are both focused on the present. The teacher is instinctively practical, sensible and realistic in their teaching style and will encourage their students to follow their lead. A solid, workman-like relationship develops with both teacher and student mutually understanding what each needs to do to get the job done. For the teacher to get the best out of their essentially grounded student they need to:

- Demonstrate how learning can be applied in the real world.
- Allow the student opportunities to repeat and practise until satisfied they are competent.
- Encourage the use of imagination as a useful process (it's not wasting time).

Both teacher and student are task-focused, direct, consistent and honest. The classroom is likely to have a business-like and purposeful atmosphere. Students are given clear guidelines on what is expected in terms of behaviour, homework and so on. If the student challenges the teacher it is likely to be for clarification. At best this means everyone knows where they stand and how to behave. For the teacher to get the best out of their inherently task-focused student they need to:

- Work in ways that test their skill and knowledge competitively (they raise their game for competitions, challenges, quizzes, measuring and beating personal bests).
- Help them understand that 50% of people are **F** preference and can interpret feedback as criticism.
- Focus on what the student has achieved and what comes next.
- Be prepared to compromise occasionally.
- Avoid trying to fix something without considering potential underlying emotional causes.

The Black Bear teacher takes pleasure in scheduling their time. They are organised and decisive. They work out a plan and stick to it, often aided by an impressive to-do list. Their classroom is usually an organised place. The subject will probably be broken down into lesson-sized chunks and the year planned out whether an Ofsted inspector is due or not. Many **J** students are reassured by their teacher's organisational zeal. They simply adopt the schedule and deliver their side of the bargain, generally completing all tasks on time. Interestingly, some **J**'s will baulk at their teacher's well-intentioned thoroughness. They would like to create their own plan and work to it rather than adopt someone else's. This is due to the **J**'s desire for control. So two **J**'s together can clash, though at least all their work will be done. Most schools require students to be so organised that two **J**'s are, potentially, the most constructive combination. For the teacher to get the best out of their naturally organised student they need to:

- Enjoy your shared desire for order, neatness and respecting deadlines.
- Allow the student independence in planning their work in their own way if they really want to.
- Be prepared to adjust your own plans if external events interfere with your careful preparations (and encourage the student to also embrace flexibility occasionally).
- Shake things up now and again to prevent predictability becoming boredom.

■ Avoid making quick decisions about what needs to be done before considering all of the options.

21
Black Bear teacher with Tiger student
ESTJ and ISTP

Black Bears and Tigers share an objective focus on the present. The differences are in the desire of the student to be reflective and flexible whereas the teacher is direct and organised. For the teacher to get the best out of their naturally reserved student they need to:

■ Slow down and be calm and succinct.

■ Leave plenty of time between question and answer; respect the student's need for time to think and reflect before responding.

■ Allow the student time and space to work on their own; don't hover over their head, waiting to pounce.

■ Avoid trying to fix problems immediately or finish their sentences.

■ Pair them up with complementary types (Cats, Panthers and Tawny Owls).

■ Avoid placing them in groups/teams where they are the only **I** preference in a sea of **E** preferences (they'll be ignored).

■ Provide written praise (not just verbal).

■ Let the student know they can always come and talk to you alone during breaks or they can write down their questions/issues for you to reply to later.

Both teacher and student gather information in the same way. They notice detail using their senses (aware of what they can see, hear and feel). Both use their experience to make sense of what they see and notice. They are both focused on the present. The teacher is instinctively practical, sensible and realistic in their teaching style and will encourage their students to follow their lead. A solid, workman-like relationship develops with both teacher and student mutually understanding what each needs to do to get the job done. For the teacher to get the best out of their essentially grounded student they need to:

■ Demonstrate how learning can be applied in the real world.

■ Allow the student opportunities to repeat and practise until satisfied they are competent.

■ Encourage the use of imagination as a useful process (it's not wasting time).

Both teacher and student are task-focused, direct, consistent and honest. The classroom is likely to have a business-like and purposeful atmosphere. Students are given clear guidelines on what is expected in terms of behaviour, homework and so on. If the student challenges the teacher it is likely to be for clarification. At best this means everyone knows where they stand and how to behave. For the teacher to get the best out of their inherently task-focused student they need to:

■ Work in ways that test their skill and knowledge competitively (they raise their game for competitions, challenges, quizzes, measuring and beating personal bests).

■ Help them understand that 50% of people are **F** preference and can interpret feedback as criticism.

■ Focus on what the student has achieved and what comes next.

■ Be prepared to compromise occasionally.

■ Avoid trying to fix something without considering potential underlying emotional causes.

The **J** teacher takes pleasure in scheduling their time. They are organised and decisive. They work out a plan and stick to it, usually aided by an impressive to-do list. Their classroom is likely to be the most organised space in school. The subject will probably be broken down into lesson-sized chunks and the year planned out in detail with zeal. The **P** student will accept your expertise and understand the long-term benefits they'll reap. For the teacher to get the best out of their intrinsically laid-back student they should note the student doesn't just like options and choice; they need them or they start to itch, squirm and rebel. The secondary school environment is difficult enough for **P** preference students so teachers can help soften the pressure. To help:

■ Provide as much flexibility as possible (multiple choice homework tasks, choice within the lesson).

■ Avoid giving out detailed schedules (they'll just lose it anyway!).

■ Don't be more picky with detail than is absolutely necessary.

■ Shake things up now and again to prevent predictability becoming boredom. Introduce random surprises and changes.

■ Identify simple ways the student can organise and manage their time to complete important work without a last-minute rush.

22
Black Bear teacher with Dolphin student
ESTJ and ENFJ

Black Bears and Dolphins share energy and a desire to finish on time. They differ in the way they absorb and process information. To get the best out of the Dolphin student the teacher must embrace the imagination, subtlety and compassion they can add to classroom tasks. For the teacher to get the best out of their naturally effusive student they need to:

■ Enjoy the lively banter when it is appropriate to spark new thoughts and ideas; the student learns best this way, but remember there may be thirty others in the classroom.

■ Stick to the point and stay positive (don't nag), as both teacher and student are easily distracted and liable to go off track!

■ Avoid going over old ground.

■ Be calm and clear, otherwise two **E** preferences can talk louder and louder like PMQs (with neither listening).

■ Remember you can keep some thoughts to yourself (and you may think of a better way of expressing something, especially criticism, later).

■ Be an enthusiastic and supportive listener; seek to help the student clarify and develop their thinking rather than assert your own.

■ Help each other learn to be quiet and encourage the **I** preferences in the class to express themselves.

The Black Bear likes to use their experience to make sense of what is around them. The teacher is essentially practical, sequential and realistic in style and will generally encourage their students to follow suit. The **N** student may at best find this challenging and at worst find it boring. The teacher may label the Dolphin a daydreamer, lost in their own world or 'away with the fairies'. They should resist the temptation to castigate their student because this is how they take in information and make sense of the world. In the right context daydreaming can lead to the invention of cars, planes, medicines and computers. For the teacher to get the best out of their inherently imaginative student they need to:

■ Embrace the imagination and insight of the student and what it can bring to the lesson.

■ Encourage the student to become aware of the important contribution of the **S** approach (the value of facts, details, procedure, experiments, applying experience, structure, the step-by-step model).

The teacher is focused first on task and second on people/relationships. The classroom is likely to have a business-like, purposeful atmosphere. Students are given clear guidelines on what is expected in terms of behaviour, homework and so on. At best this means everyone knows where they stand and how to behave. At worst the classroom can resemble a military bootcamp full of dispirited and brow-beaten new recruits. Remember, the personal relationship the teacher develops with this student is key. The Dolphin needs to feel they like their teacher and that the teacher likes them too. If this happens they'll work harder but if not they may switch off completely. This explains why a student can be top of the class one year (with a teacher they like) and show no interest at all in the subject the following year when they change teacher. For the teacher to get the best out of their instinctively people-focused student they need to:

■ Offer learning situations that allow for the use of empathy, collaboration and teamworking to counter-balance your natural tendency to focus on task.

■ Give ample and regular praise while offering tactful support to overcome any blind-spots. Feedback can be easily interpreted as criticism so walk on egg-shells when delivering it.

■ Persuade/influence by appealing to the strength of your personal belief in the student (don't let me down, I know you can do it, I like you).

■ Be prepared to compromise occasionally.

The Black Bear takes pleasure in scheduling their time. They are organised and decisive. They work out a plan and stick to it, often aided by an impressive to-do list. Their classroom is usually an organised place. The subject will probably be broken down into lesson-sized chunks and the year planned out whether or not an Ofsted inspector is due. Many **J** students are reassured by their teacher's organisational zeal. They simply adopt the schedule and deliver their side of the bargain, generally completing all tasks on time. Interestingly, some **J**'s will baulk at their teacher's well-intentioned thoroughness. They would like to create their own plan and work to it rather than adopt someone else's plan. This is due to the J's desire for control. So two J's together can clash, though at least all their work will be done. Most schools require students to be so organised that two J's are, potentially, the most constructive combination. To help the student progress:

■ Enjoy your shared desire for order, neatness and respecting deadlines.

■ Allow the student independence in planning their work in their own way if they really want to.

■ Be prepared to adjust your own plans if external events interfere with your careful preparations (and encourage the student to also embrace flexibility occasionally).

■ Shake things up now and again to prevent predictability becoming boredom.

■ Avoid making quick decisions about what needs to be done before considering all of the options.

23
Black Bear teacher with Lion student
ESTJ and ESFP

Black Bears and Lions share an interest in understanding what makes things as they are using energy and observation. They differ in the way they develop conclusions. The Lion is drawn to consider impact on people and the Black Bear to analyse the facts objectively. For the teacher to get the best out of their naturally playful and fun-loving student they need to:

■ Enjoy the lively banter when it is appropriate to spark new thoughts and ideas; the student learns best this way, but remember there may be thirty others in the classroom.

■ Stick to the point and stay positive (don't nag), as both teacher and student are easily distracted and liable to go off track!

■ Avoid going over old ground.

■ Be calm and clear, otherwise two E preferences can talk louder and louder like PMQs (with neither listening).

■ Remember you can keep some thoughts to yourself (and you may think of a better way of expressing something, especially criticism, later).

■ Be an enthusiastic and supportive listener; seek to help the student clarify and develop their thinking rather than assert your own.

■ Help each other learn to be quiet and encourage the I preferences in the class to express themselves.

Both teacher and student gather information in the same way. They take in detail using their senses (aware of what they can see, hear and feel). Both use their experience to make sense of what they see and notice. They are both focused on the present. The teacher is instinctively practical, sensible and realistic in their teaching style and will encourage their students to follow their lead. A solid, workman-like relationship develops with both teacher and student mutually understanding what each needs to do to get the job done. For the teacher to get the best out of their essentially grounded student they need to:

■ Demonstrate how learning can be applied in the real world.

■ Allow the student opportunities to repeat and practise until satisfied they are competent.

■ Encourage the use of imagination as a useful process (it's not wasting time).

The teacher is focused first on task and second on people/relationships. The classroom is likely to have a business-like, purposeful atmosphere. Students are given clear guidelines on what is expected in terms of behaviour, homework and so on. At best this means everyone knows where they stand and how to behave. At worst the classroom can resemble a military boot-camp full of dispirited and brow-beaten new recruits. Remember, the personal relationship the teacher develops with this student is crucial. The Lion needs to feel they like their teacher and that the teacher likes them too. If this happens they'll work harder but if not they may switch off completely. This explains why a student can be top of the class one year (with a teacher they like) and show no interest at all in the subject the following year when they change teacher. For the teacher to get the best out of their instinctively people-focused student they need to:

■ Offer learning situations that allow for the use of empathy, collaboration and teamworking to counter-balance your natural tendency to focus on task.

■ Give ample and regular praise while offering tactful support to overcome any blind-spots. Feedback can be easily interpreted as criticism so walk on egg-shells when delivering it.

■ Persuade/influence by appealing to the strength of your personal belief in the student (don't let me down, I know you can do it, I like you).

■ Be prepared to compromise occasionally.

The J teacher takes pleasure in scheduling their time. They are organised and decisive. They work out a plan and stick to it, usually aided by an impressive to-do list. Their classroom is likely to be the most organised space in school. The subject will probably be broken down into lesson-sized chunks and the year planned out in detail with zeal. The P student will either respond:

■ Positively by accepting your expertise and understanding the long-term benefits they'll reap.

■ Passively by just accepting your structure/plan for an easy life without really buying into the content or process you are offering.

■ Negatively by rejecting you, your structure/plan and subject completely (even if they're physically in your room they will not engage and participate).

For the teacher to get the best out of their intrinsically laid-back student they should note the student doesn't just like options and choice; they need them or they start to itch, squirm and rebel. The secondary school environment is difficult enough for P preference students so teachers can help soften the pressure. To help:

■ Provide as much flexibility as possible (multiple choice homework tasks, choice within the lesson).

■ Avoid giving out detailed schedules (they'll just lose it anyway!).

■ Don't be more picky with detail than is absolutely necessary.

■ Shake things up now and again to prevent predictability becoming boredom. Introduce random surprises and changes.

■ Identify simple ways the student can organise and manage their time to complete important work without a last-minute rush.

24
Black Bear teacher with Barn Owl student
ESTJ and INTJ

Black Bears and Barn Owls share the same objective approach to developing conclusions. They differ in their methods of collecting and understanding information. The practical and direct Bear contrasts with the theoretical and strategic Owl. For the teacher to get the best out of their naturally reserved student they need to:

■ Slow down and be calm and succinct.

■ Leave plenty of time between question and answer; respect the student's need for time to think and reflect before responding.

■ Allow the student time and space to work on their own; don't hover over their head, waiting to pounce.

■ Avoid trying to fix problems immediately or finish their sentences.

■ Pair them up with complementary types (Bears and Tawny Owls).

■ Avoid placing them in groups/teams where they are the only I preference in a sea of E preferences (they'll be smothered).

■ Provide written praise (not just verbal).

■ Let the student know they can always come and talk to you alone during breaks or they can write down their questions/issues for you to reply to later.

The Black Bear likes to use their experience to make sense of what is around them. The teacher is essentially practical, sequential and realistic in style and will generally encourage their students to follow suit. The N student may at best find this challenging and at worst find it boring. The teacher may label the Barn Owl a daydreamer or lost in their own world. They should resist the temptation to castigate their student because this is how they take in information and make sense of the world. In the right context daydreaming can lead to the invention of cars, planes, medicines and computers. For the teacher to get the best out of their inherently imaginative student they need to:

■ Embrace the imagination and insight of the student and what it can bring to the lesson.

■ Encourage the student to become aware of the important contribution of the S approach (the value of facts, details, procedure, experiments, applying experience, structure, the step-by-step model).

Both teacher and student are task-focused, direct, consistent and honest. The classroom is likely to have a business-like and purposeful atmosphere. Students are given clear guidelines on what is expected in terms of behaviour, homework and so on. If the student challenges the teacher it is likely to be for clarification. At best this means everyone knows where they stand and how to behave. For the teacher to get the best out of their fundamentally task-focused student they need to:

- Work in ways that test their skill and knowledge competitively (they raise their game for competitions, challenges, quizzes, measuring and beating personal bests).
- Help them understand that 50% of people are **F** preference and can interpret feedback as criticism.
- Focus on what the student has achieved and what comes next.
- Be prepared to compromise occasionally.
- Avoid trying to fix something without considering potential underlying emotional causes.

The **J** teacher takes pleasure in scheduling their time. They are organised and decisive. They work out a plan and stick to it, often aided by an impressive to-do list. Their classroom is usually an organised place. The subject will probably be broken down into lesson-sized chunks and the year planned out whether an Ofsted inspector is due or not. Many **J** students are reassured by their teacher's organisational zeal. They simply adopt the schedule and deliver their side of the bargain, generally completing all tasks on time. Interestingly, some **J**'s will baulk at their teacher's well-intentioned thoroughness. They would like to create their own plan and work to it rather than adopt someone else's. This is due to the **J**'s desire for control. So two **J**'s together can clash, though at least all their work will be done. Most schools require students to be so organised that two **J**'s are, potentially, the most constructive combination. For the teacher to maximise student progress:

- Enjoy your shared desire for order, neatness and respecting deadlines.
- Allow the student independence in planning their work in their own way if they really want to.
- Be prepared to adjust your own plans if external events interfere with your careful preparations (and encourage the student to also embrace flexibility occasionally).
- Shake things up now and again to prevent predictability becoming boredom.
- Avoid making quick decisions about what needs to be done before considering all of the options.

25
Black Bear teacher with Panther student
ESTJ and ESTP

Black Bears and Panthers are natural leaders. The mutual understanding derives from three shared preferences and can form the basis of an effective relationship. Clashes can occur when the student attempts to wrestle control from their teacher. Good Black Bear teachers work out ways to provide their Panther student with opportunities to express their sense of fun. For the teacher to get the best out of their naturally talkative student they need to:

- Enjoy the lively banter when it is appropriate to spark new thoughts and ideas; the student learns best this way, but remember there may be thirty others in the classroom.

- Stick to the point and stay positive (don't nag).
- Avoid going over old ground.
- Be calm and clear, otherwise two **E** preferences can talk louder and louder with neither listening.
- Remember you can keep some thoughts to yourself (and you may think of a better way of expressing something, especially criticism, later).
- Be an enthusiastic and supportive listener; seek to help the student clarify and develop their thinking rather than assert your own.
- Help each other learn to be quiet and encourage the **I** preferences in the class to express themselves.

Both teacher and student gather information in the same way. Both use their experience to make sense of what they see and notice. They are both focused on the present. The teacher is instinctively practical, sensible and realistic in their teaching style and will encourage their students to follow their lead. A solid, workman-like relationship develops with both teacher and student mutually understanding what each needs to do to get the job done. For the teacher to get the best out of their essentially grounded student they need to:

- Demonstrate how learning can be applied in the real world.
- Allow the student opportunities to repeat and practise until satisfied they are competent.
- Encourage the use of imagination as a useful process (it's not wasting time).

Both teacher and student are task-focused, direct, consistent and honest. The classroom is likely to have a business-like and purposeful atmosphere. Students are given clear guidelines on what is expected in terms of behaviour, homework and so on. If the student challenges the teacher it is likely to be for clarification. At best this means everyone knows where they stand and how to behave. For the teacher to get the best out of their inherently task-focused student they need to:

- Work in ways that test their skill and knowledge competitively (they raise their game for competitions, challenges, quizzes, measuring and beating personal bests).
- Help them appreciate that 50% of people are **F** preference and can interpret feedback as criticism.
- Focus on what the student has achieved and what comes next.
- Be prepared to compromise occasionally.
- Avoid trying to fix something without considering potential underlying emotional causes.

The **J** teacher takes pleasure in scheduling their time. They are organised and decisive. They work out a plan and stick to it, usually aided by an impressive to-do list. Their classroom is likely to be the most organised space in school. The subject will probably be broken down into lesson-sized chunks and the year planned out in detail. The **P** student will either respond:

- Positively by accepting your expertise and understanding the long-term benefits they'll reap.
- Passively by just accepting your structure/plan for an easy life without really buying into the content or process you are offering.

- Negatively by rejecting you, your structure/ plan and subject completely (even if they're physically in your room they will not engage and participate).

For the teacher to get the best out of their intrinsically laid-back student they should note the student doesn't just like options and choice; they need them or they start to itch, squirm and rebel. The secondary school environment is difficult enough for **P** preference students so teachers can help soften the pressure. To help:

- Provide as much flexibility as possible (multiple choice homework tasks, choice within the lesson).
- Avoid giving out detailed schedules (they'll just lose it anyway!).
- Don't be more picky with detail than is absolutely necessary.
- Shake things up now and again to prevent predictability becoming boredom. Introduce random surprises and changes.
- Identify simple ways the student can organise and manage their time to complete important work without a last-minute rush.

26
Black Bear teacher with Falcon student
ESTJ and ENTP

Black Bears and Falcons are natural leaders. The mutual understanding derives from two shared preferences and can form the basis of an effective relationship. Clashes can occur when the student attempts to wrestle control from their teacher. Good Black Bear teachers work out ways to provide their Falcon student with opportunities to express their need to perform and put across their often controversial and forthright views. They are often shared for shock value as the Falcon is easily bored. For the teacher to get the best out of their naturally confrontational student they need to:

- Enjoy the lively banter when it is appropriate to spark new thoughts and ideas; the student learns best this way, but remember there may be thirty others in the classroom.
- Stick to the point and stay positive (don't nag).
- Avoid going over old ground.
- Be calm and clear, otherwise two **E** preferences can talk louder and louder with neither listening.
- Remember you can keep some thoughts to yourself (and you may think of a better way of expressing something, especially criticism, later).
- Be an enthusiastic and supportive listener; seek to help the student clarify and develop their thinking rather than assert your own.
- Help each other learn to be quiet and encourage the **I** preferences in the class to express themselves.

The Black Bear likes to use their experience to make sense of what is around them. The teacher is essentially practical, sequential and realistic in style and will generally encourage their students to follow suit. The **N** student may at best find this challenging and at worst find it boring. The teacher may label the Falcon argumentative or even arrogant. They should resist the temptation to castigate their student because this is how they take in information and make sense of the world. In the right context daydreaming can lead to the invention of cars, planes, medicines and computers. For the teacher to get the best out of their inherently imaginative student they need to:

■ Embrace the imagination and insight of the student and what it can bring to the lesson.

■ Encourage the student to become aware of the important contribution of the **S** approach (the value of facts, details, procedure, experiments, applying experience, structure, the step-by-step model).

Both teacher and student are task-focused, direct, consistent and honest. The classroom is likely to have a business-like and purposeful atmosphere. Students are given clear guidelines on what is expected in terms of behaviour, homework and so on. If the student challenges the teacher it is likely to be for clarification. At best this means everyone knows where they stand and how to behave. For the teacher to get the best out of their fundamentally task-focused student they need to:

■ Work in ways that test their skill and knowledge competitively (they raise their game for competitions, challenges, quizzes, measuring and beating personal bests).

■ Help them understand that 50% of people are **F** preference and can interpret feedback as criticism.

■ Focus on what the student has achieved and what comes next.

■ Be prepared to compromise occasionally.

■ Avoid trying to fix something without considering potential underlying emotional causes.

The **J** teacher takes pleasure in scheduling their time. They are organised and decisive. They work out a plan and stick to it, usually aided by an impressive to-do list. Their classroom is likely to be the most organised space in school. The subject will probably be broken down into lesson-sized chunks and the year planned out in detail with zeal. The **P** student will either respond:

■ Positively by accepting your expertise and understanding the long-term benefits they'll reap.

■ Passively by just accepting your structure/plan for an easy life without really buying into the content or process you are offering.

■ Negatively by rejecting you, your structure/plan and subject completely (even if they're physically in your room they will not engage and participate).

For the teacher to get the best out of their intrinsically laid-back student they should note the student doesn't just like options and choice; they need them or they start to itch, squirm and rebel. The secondary school environment is difficult enough for **P** preference students so teachers can help soften the pressure. To help:

■ Provide as much flexibility as possible (multiple choice homework tasks, choice within the lesson).

■ Avoid giving out detailed schedules (they'll just lose it anyway!).

■ Don't be more picky with detail than is absolutely necessary.

■ Shake things up now and again to prevent predictability becoming boredom. Introduce random surprises and changes.

■ Identify simple ways the student can organise and manage their time to complete important work without last-minute angst.

27
Black Bear teacher with Tawny Owl student
ESTJ and INTP

Black Bears and Tawny Owls share only one preference. Neither is prone to sentimentality. Their differences are substantial and need to be respected for a positive relationship to flourish. The practical and direct Bear contrasts with the theoretical and professorial Owl. For the teacher to get the best out of their naturally introspective student they need to:

■ Slow down and be calm and succinct.

■ Leave plenty of time between question and answer; respect the student's need for time to think and reflect before responding.

■ Allow the student time and space to work on their own; don't hover over their head, waiting to pounce.

■ Avoid trying to fix problems immediately or finish their sentences.

■ Pair them up with complementary types (Owls and Polar Bears).

■ Avoid placing them in groups/teams where they are the only **I** preference in a sea of **E** preferences (they'll be smothered).

■ Provide written praise (not just verbal).

The Black Bear likes to use their experience to make sense of what is around them. The teacher is essentially practical, sequential and realistic in style and will generally encourage their students to follow suit. The **N** student may at best find this challenging and at worst find it boring. The teacher may label the Tawny Owl argumentative or even arrogant. They should resist the temptation to castigate their student because this is how they take in information and make sense of the world. In the right context daydreaming can lead to the invention of cars, planes, medicines and computers. For the teacher to get the best out of their inherently imaginative student they need to:

■ Embrace the imagination and insight of the student and what it can bring to the lesson.

■ Encourage the student to become aware of the important contribution of the **S** approach (the value of facts, details, procedure, experiments, applying experience, structure, the step-by-step model).

Both teacher and student are task-focused, direct, consistent and honest. The classroom is likely to have a business-like and purposeful atmosphere. Students are given clear guidelines on what is expected in terms of behaviour, homework and so on. If the student challenges the teacher it is likely to be for clarification. At best this means everyone knows where they stand and how to behave. For the teacher to get the best out of their characteristically task-focused student they need to:

■ Work in ways that test their skill and knowledge competitively (they raise their game for competitions, challenges, quizzes, measuring and beating personal bests).

■ Help them understand that 50% of people are **F** preference and can interpret feedback as criticism.

■ Focus on what the student has achieved and what comes next.

■ Be prepared to compromise occasionally.

■ Avoid trying to fix something without considering potential underlying emotional causes.

The **J** teacher takes pleasure in scheduling their time. They are organised and decisive. They work out a plan and stick to it, usually aided by an impressive to-do list. Their classroom is likely to be the most organised space in school. The subject will probably be broken down into lesson-sized chunks and the year planned out in colour-coded detail. The **P** student will either respond:

■ Positively by accepting your expertise and understanding the long-term benefits they'll reap.

■ Passively by just accepting your structure/plan for an easy life without really buying into the content or process you are offering.

■ Negatively by rejecting you, your structure/plan and subject completely (even if they're physically in your room they will not engage and participate).

For the teacher to get the best out of their intrinsically laid-back student they should note the student doesn't just like options and choice; they need them or they start to itch, squirm and rebel. The secondary school environment is difficult enough for **P** preference students so teachers can help soften the pressure. To help:

■ Provide as much flexibility as possible (multiple choice homework tasks, choice within the lesson).

■ Avoid giving out detailed schedules (they'll just lose it anyway!).

■ Don't be more picky with detail than is absolutely necessary.

■ Shake things up now and again to prevent predictability becoming boredom. Introduce random surprises and changes.

■ Identify simple ways the student can organise and manage their time to complete important work without a last-minute rush.

28
Black Bear teacher with Teddy Bear student
ESTJ and ESFJ

Both Bears share an interest in understanding what makes things as they are using energy and observation. They differ in the way they develop conclusions. The Teddy is drawn to consider impact on people and the Black Bear to analyse the facts objectively. For the teacher to get the best out of their naturally sociable student they need to:

■ Enjoy the lively banter when it is appropriate to spark new thoughts and ideas; the student learns best this way, but remember there may be thirty others in the classroom.

■ Stick to the point and stay positive (don't nag), as both teacher and student are easily distracted and liable to go off track!

■ Avoid going over old ground.

■ Remember you can keep some thoughts to yourself (and you may think of a better way of expressing something, especially criticism, later).

■ Help each other learn to be quiet and encourage the **I** preferences in the class to express themselves.

■ Be an enthusiastic and supportive listener; seek to help the student clarify and develop their thinking rather than assert your own.

Both teacher and student gather information in the same way. Both use their experience to make sense of what they see and notice. They are both focused on the present. The teacher is instinctively practical, sensible and realistic in their teaching style and will encourage their students to follow their lead. A solid, workman-like relationship develops with both teacher and student mutually understanding what each needs to do to get the job done. For the teacher to get the best out of their essentially grounded student they need to:

■ Demonstrate how learning can be applied in the real world.

■ Allow the student opportunities to repeat and practise until satisfied they are competent.

■ Encourage the use of imagination as a useful process (it's not wasting time).

The teacher is focused first on task and second on people/relationships. The classroom is likely to have a business-like, purposeful atmosphere. Students are given clear guidelines on what is expected in terms of behaviour, homework and so on. At best this means everyone knows where they stand and how to behave. At worst the classroom can resemble a military boot-camp full of dispirited and brow-beaten new recruits. Remember, the personal relationship the teacher develops with this student is the key to success. The Teddy needs to feel they like their teacher and that the teacher likes them too. If this happens they'll work harder but if not they may switch off completely. This explains why a student can be top of the class one year (with a teacher they like) and show no interest at all in the subject the following year when they change teacher. For the teacher to get the best out of their instinctively people-focused student they need to:

■ Offer learning situations that allow for the use of empathy, collaboration and teamworking to counter-balance your natural tendency to focus on task.

■ Give ample and regular praise while offering tactful support to overcome any blind-spots. Feedback can be easily interpreted as criticism so walk on egg-shells when delivering it.

■ Motivate by appealing to the strength of your personal belief in the student (don't let me down, I know you can do it, I like you).

■ Be prepared to compromise occasionally.

The **J** teacher takes pleasure in scheduling their time. They are organised and decisive. They work out a plan and stick to it, often aided by an impressive to-do list. Their classroom is usually an organised place. The subject will probably be broken down into lesson-sized chunks and the year planned out whether or not an Ofsted inspector is sitting at the back of the classroom. Many **J** students are reassured by their teacher's organisational zeal. They simply adopt the schedule and deliver their side of the bargain, generally completing all tasks on time. Interestingly, some **J**'s will baulk at their teacher's well-intentioned thoroughness. They would like to create their own plan and work to it rather than adopt someone else's. This is due to the **J**'s desire for control. Two **J** preferences together can clash, though at least all their work will be done. Most schools require students to be so organised that two **J** preferences are, potentially, the most constructive combination. The teacher can help their characteristically organised student by:

■ Enjoying your shared desire for order, neatness and respecting deadlines.

■ Allowing the student independence in planning their work in their own way if they really want to.

■ Being prepared to adjust your own plans if external events interfere with your careful preparations and encourage the student to also embrace flexibility occasionally.

■ Mixing things up now and again to prevent predictability becoming boredom.

■ Avoiding making quick decisions about what needs to be done before considering all of the options.

29
Black Bear teacher with Koala student
ESTJ and ISFJ

Both Bears live in the real world using experience and observation to make sense of things. They differ in the way they develop conclusions. The Koala is drawn to consider impact on people and the Black Bear to analyse the facts objectively. For the teacher to get the best out of their naturally reticent student they need to:

■ Slow down and be calm and succinct.

■ Leave plenty of time between question and answer; respect the student's need for time to think and reflect before responding.

■ Allow the student time and space to work on their own; don't hover over their head, waiting to pounce.

■ Avoid trying to fix problems immediately or finish their sentences.

■ Pair them up with complementary types (Seahorses, Cats and Seals).

■ Avoid placing them in groups/teams where they are the only **I** preference in a sea of **E** preferences (they're likely to sit in silence).

■ Provide written praise (not just verbal).

Both teacher and student gather information in the same way. They notice detail using their senses (aware of what they can see, hear and feel) and use their experience to make sense of their environment. They are both focused on the present. The teacher is instinctively practical, sensible and realistic in their teaching style and will encourage their students to follow their lead. A solid, workman-like relationship develops with both teacher and student mutually understanding what each needs to do to get the job done. For the teacher

to get the best out of their essentially grounded student they need to:

■ Demonstrate how learning can be applied in the real world.

■ Allow the student opportunities to repeat and practise until satisfied they are competent.

■ Encourage the use of imagination as a useful process (it's not wasting time).

The teacher is focused first on task and second on people/relationships. The classroom is likely to have a business-like, purposeful atmosphere. Students are given clear guidelines on what is expected in terms of behaviour, homework and so on. At best this means everyone knows where they stand and how to behave. At worst the classroom can resemble a military boot-camp. Remember, the personal relationship the teacher develops with this student is the key to success. The Koala needs to feel they like their teacher and that the teacher likes them too. If this happens they'll work harder but if not they may switch off completely. This explains why a student can be top of the class one year (with a teacher they like) and show no interest at all in the subject the following year when they change teacher. For the teacher to get the best out of their instinctively people-focused student they need to:

■ Offer learning situations that allow for the use of empathy, collaboration and small teamworking to counter-balance your natural tendency to focus on task.

■ Give ample and regular praise while offering tactful support to overcome any blind-spots. Feedback can be easily interpreted as criticism so tread carefully when delivering it.

■ Engage by quietly and regularly stating your personal belief in the student (don't let me down, I know you can do it, I like you).

■ Be prepared to compromise occasionally to reassure the routine-loving Koala.

The **J** teacher takes pleasure in scheduling their time. They are organised and decisive. They work out a plan and stick to it, often aided by an impressive to-do list. Their classroom is usually an organised place. The subject will probably be broken down into lesson-sized chunks and the year planned out whether or not an Ofsted inspector is lurking in the corridor clasping their clipboard. Many **J** students are reassured by their teacher's organisational zeal. They simply adopt the schedule and deliver their side of the bargain, generally completing all tasks on time. Interestingly, some **J**'s will baulk at their teacher's well-intentioned thoroughness. They would like to create their own plan and work to it rather than adopt someone else's. This is due to the **J**'s desire for control. So two **J**'s together can clash, though at least all their work will be done. Most schools require students to be so organised that two **J**'s are, potentially, a very constructive combination. For the teacher to get the best out of their naturally organised student they need to:

■ Enjoy your shared desire for order, neatness and respecting deadlines.

■ Allow the student independence in planning their work in their own way if they really want to.

■ Be prepared to adjust your own plans if external events interfere with your careful preparations and also encourage the student to embrace flexibility.

■ Shake things up now and again to prevent predictability becoming boredom.

■Avoid making quick decisions about what needs to be done before considering all of the options.

30
Black Bear teacher with Seahorse student
ESTJ and INFJ

Black Bears and Seahorses share one preference. Both like to finish work on time. They differ in the way they develop conclusions. The Seahorse is drawn to fantasy and to consider impact on people whereas the Black Bear is drawn to analyse the facts objectively. For the teacher to get the best out of their naturally introspective student they need to:

■Slow down and be calm and succinct.

■Leave plenty of time between question and answer; respect the student's need for time to think and reflect before responding.

■Allow the student time and space to work on their own; don't hover over their head, waiting to pounce.

■Avoid trying to fix problems immediately or finish their sentences.

■Pair them up with complementary types (Koalas, Cats and Seals).

■Avoid placing them in groups/teams where they are the only **I** preference in a sea of **E** preferences (they're likely to sit in silence).

■Provide written praise (not just verbal).

The Black Bear likes to use their experience to make sense of what is around them. The teacher is essentially practical, sequential and realistic in style and will generally encourage their students to follow suit. The **N** student may at best find this challenging and at worst find it boring. The teacher may label the Seahorse argumentative or even arrogant. They should resist the temptation to castigate their student because this is how they take in information and make sense of the world. In the right context daydreaming can lead to the invention of cars, planes, medicines and computers. For the teacher to get the best out of their inherently imaginative student they need to:

■Embrace the imagination and insight offered by the Seahorse student and what this can add to the lesson.

■Encourage the student to become aware of the important contribution of the **S** approach (the value of facts, details, procedure, experiments, applying experience, structure, the step-by-step model).

The teacher is focused first on task and second on people/relationships. The classroom is likely to have a business-like, purposeful atmosphere. Students are given clear guidelines on what is expected in terms of behaviour, homework and so on. At best this means everyone knows where they stand and how to behave. At worst the classroom can resemble a military boot-camp. Remember, the personal relationship the teacher develops with this student is the key to success. The Seahorse needs to feel they like their teacher and that the teacher likes them too. If this happens they'll work harder but if they don't they may switch off completely. This explains why a

student can be top of the class one year (with a teacher they like) and show no interest at all in the subject the following year when they change teacher. For the teacher to get the best out of their instinctively people-focused student they need to:

■Offer learning situations that allow for the use of empathy, collaboration and teamworking to counter-balance your natural tendency to focus on task.

■Give ample and regular praise while offering tactful support to overcome any blind-spots. Feedback can be easily interpreted as criticism so walk on egg-shells when delivering it.

■Inspire by appealing to the strength of your personal belief in the student (don't let me down, I know you can do it, I like you).

■Be prepared to compromise occasionally to avoid the Seahorse withdrawing inside their shell.

The **J** teacher takes pleasure in scheduling their time. They are organised and decisive. They work out a plan and stick to it, often aided by an impressive to-do list. Their classroom is usually an organised place. The subject will probably be broken down into lesson-sized chunks and the year planned out whether or not an Ofsted inspection is due. Many **J** students are reassured by their teacher's organisational competence. They simply adopt the schedule and deliver their side of the bargain, generally completing all tasks on time. Interestingly, some **J**'s will baulk at their teacher's well-intentioned thoroughness. They would like to create their own plan and work to it rather than adopt someone else's. This is due to the **J**'s desire for control. Two **J** preferences together can clash, though at least all their work will be done. Most schools require students to be so organised that two **J** preferences are, potentially, a very constructive combination. For the teacher to get the best out of their naturally organised student they need to:

■Enjoy your shared desire for order, neatness and respecting deadlines.

■Allow the student independence in planning their work in their own way if they really want to.

■Be prepared to adjust your own plans if external events interfere with your careful preparations and encourage the student to embrace flexibility.

■Avoid making quick decisions about what needs to be done before considering all of the options.

■Shake things up now and again to prevent predictability becoming boredom.

31
Black Bear teacher with Eagle student
ESTJ and ENTJ

Black Bears and Eagles are natural leaders. Mutual understanding derives from three shared preferences and can form the basis of an effective relationship. Clashes can occur when the student attempts to wrestle control from their teacher. Effective Black Bear teachers work out

ways to provide their Eagle student with opportunities to express their need to show leadership and put across their often forthright views. For the teacher to get the best out of their naturally confrontational student they need to:

■Enjoy the lively banter when it is appropriate to spark new thoughts and ideas; the student learns best this way, but remember there may be thirty others in the classroom.

■Stick to the point and stay positive (don't nag).

■Avoid going over old ground.

■Be calm and clear, otherwise two **E** preferences can talk louder and louder like PMQs (with neither listening).

■Remember you can keep some thoughts to yourself (and you may think of a better way of expressing something, especially criticism, later).

■Be an enthusiastic and supportive listener; seek to help the student clarify and develop their thinking rather than assert your own.

■Help each other learn to be quiet and encourage the **I** preferences in the class to express themselves.

The Black Bear likes to use their experience to make sense of what is around them. The teacher is essentially practical, sequential and realistic in style and will generally encourage their students to follow suit. The **N** student may at best find this challenging and at worst find it boring. The teacher may label the Eagle argumentative or even arrogant. They should resist the temptation to castigate their student because this is how they take in information and make sense of the world. In the right context daydreaming can lead to the invention of cars, planes, medicines and computers. For the teacher to get the best out of their inherently imaginative student they need to:

■Embrace the imagination and insight of the student and what it can bring to the lesson.

■Encourage the student to become aware of the important contribution of the **S** approach (the value of facts, details, procedure, experiments, applying experience, structure, the step-by-step model).

Both teacher and student are task-focused, direct, consistent and honest. The classroom is likely to have a business-like and purposeful atmosphere. Students are given clear guidelines on what is expected in terms of behaviour, homework and so on. If the student challenges the teacher it is likely to be for clarification. At best this means everyone knows where they stand and how to behave. For the teacher to get the best out of their fundamentally task-focused Eagle they need to:

■Work in ways that test their skill and knowledge competitively (they raise their game for competitions, challenges, quizzes, measuring and beating personal bests).

■Focus on what the student has achieved and what comes next.

■Be prepared to compromise occasionally.

■Avoid trying to fix something without considering potential underlying emotional causes.

■Help them appreciate that half the population are **F** preference and can interpret feedback as criticism.

The **J** teacher takes pleasure in scheduling their time. They are organised and decisive. They work out a plan and stick to it, often aided by an impressive to-do list. Their classroom is usually an organised place. The subject will probably be broken down into lesson-sized chunks and the year planned out whether or not an Ofsted inspector is due. Many **J** students are reassured by their teacher's organisational fervour. They simply adopt the schedule and deliver their side of the bargain, generally completing all tasks on time. Interestingly, some **J**'s will baulk at their teacher's well-intentioned thoroughness. They would like to create their own plan and work to it rather than adopt someone else's. This is due to the **J**'s desire for control. Two **J** preferences together can clash, though at least all their work will be done. Most schools require students to be so organised that two **J** preferences are, potentially, a very constructive combination. For the teacher to get the best out of their naturally organised student they need to:

■ Allow the student independence in planning their work in their own way if they really want to.

■ Be prepared to adjust your own plans if external events interfere with your careful preparations.

■ Shake things up now and again to prevent predictability becoming boredom.

■ Avoid making quick decisions about what needs to be done before considering all of the options.

■ Enjoy your shared desire for order, neatness and respecting deadlines.

32
Black Bear teacher with Cat student
ESTJ and ISFP

The naturally confident and assertive Black Bear teacher shares only one preference with their Cat student. For such opposites to attract they need to accept and appreciate each other's differences. The Cat gains satisfaction when work feels like fun whereas to the Bear work is satisfying as work. For the teacher to get the best out of their naturally introspective student they need to:

■ Slow down and be succinct.

■ Leave plenty of time between question and answer; respect the student's need for time to think and reflect before responding.

■ Allow the student time and space to work on their own; don't hover over their head, waiting to pounce.

■ Avoid trying to fix problems immediately or finish their sentences.

■ Pair them up with complementary types (Tigers, Seals and Tawny Owls).

■ Avoid placing them in groups/teams where they are the only **I** preference in a sea of **E** preferences (they'll be smothered).

■ Provide written praise (not just verbal).

■ Let the student know they can always come and talk to you alone during breaks or they can write down their questions/issues for you to reply to later.

Both teacher and student gather information in the same way. They notice detail using their senses (aware of what they can see, hear and feel). Both use their experience to make sense of what they see and notice. They are both focused on

the present. The teacher is instinctively practical, sensible and realistic in their teaching style and will encourage their students to follow their lead. A solid, workman-like relationship develops with both teacher and student mutually understanding what each needs to do to get the job done. For the teacher to get the best out of their essentially grounded student they need to:

■ Show how learning can be applied in the real world.

■ Allow the student opportunities to repeat and practise until satisfied they are competent.

■ Encourage the use of imagination as a useful process (it's not wasting time).

The teacher is focused first on task and second on people/relationships. The classroom is likely to have a business-like, purposeful atmosphere. Students are given clear guidelines on what is expected in terms of behaviour, homework and so on. At best this means everyone knows where they stand and how to behave. At worst the classroom can resemble a military boot-camp full of dispirited and brow-beaten new recruits. Remember, the personal relationship the teacher develops with this student is the key to success. The Cat needs to feel they like their teacher and that the teacher likes them too. If this happens they'll work harder but if not they may switch off completely. This explains why a student can be top of the class one year (with a teacher they like) and show no interest at all in the subject the following year when they change teacher. For the teacher to get the best out of their instinctively people-focused student they need to:

■ Offer learning situations that allow for the use of empathy, collaboration and teamworking to counter-balance your natural tendency to focus on task.

■ Give ample and regular praise while offering tactful support to overcome any blind-spots. Feedback can be easily mistaken for criticism so walk on egg-shells when delivering it.

■ Persuade by appealing to the strength of your personal belief in the student (don't let me down, I know you can do it, I like you).

■ Be prepared to compromise occasionally or the Cat can sulk.

The Black Bear teacher takes pleasure in scheduling their time. They are organised and decisive. They work out a plan and stick to it, usually aided by an impressive to-do list. Their classroom is likely to be the most organised space in school. The subject will probably be broken down into lesson-sized chunks and the year planned out in detail with zeal. The **P** student will either respond:

■ Positively by accepting your expertise and understanding the long-term benefits they'll reap.

■ Passively by just accepting your structure/plan for an easy life without really buying into the content or process you are offering.

■ Negatively by rejecting you, your structure/plan and subject completely (even if they're physically in your room they will not engage and participate).

For the teacher to get the best out of their intrinsically laid-back student they should note the student doesn't just like options and choice; they need them or they start to itch, squirm and rebel. The secondary school environment is difficult enough for **P** preference students so teachers can help soften the pressure. To help:

■ Provide as much flexibility as possible (multiple choice homework tasks, choice within the lesson).

■ Avoid giving out detailed schedules (they'll just lose it anyway!).

■ Don't be more picky with detail than is absolutely necessary.

■ Shake things up now and again to prevent predictability becoming boredom. Introduce random surprises and changes.

■ Help the student identify effective time-management strategies to ensure they can cope with the organisational challenges of school.

33
Teddy Bear teacher with Teddy Bear student
ESFJ and ESFJ

The naturally sociable and caring teacher with the similarly orientated student is a potentially perfect pairing. The teacher can be a great role model showing their student how well Teddies can combine hard work and warmth. For the teacher to get the best out of their effusive student they need to:

■ Enjoy the lively chit-chat when it is appropriate to spark new thoughts and ideas; the student learns best this way, but remember there may be thirty others in the classroom.

■ Stick to the point and stay positive (don't nag), as both teacher and student are easily distracted and liable to go off track!

■ Remember you can keep some thoughts to yourself (and you may think of a better way of expressing something, especially criticism, later).

■ Be an enthusiastic and supportive listener; seek to help the student clarify and develop their thinking rather than assert your own.

■ Help each other learn to be quiet and encourage the **I** preferences in the class to express themselves.

■ Avoid raking over old ground.

■ Be calm and clear, otherwise two **E** preferences can talk louder and louder with neither side listening.

Both teacher and student gather information in the same way. They notice detail using their senses (aware of what they can see, hear and feel). Both primarily use their experience to make sense of their environment. They both live in the present. The teacher is naturally practical, sequential, sensible and realistic in their teaching style and will encourage their students to follow suit. When a solid and warm relationship develops both teacher and student mutually understand what each needs to do to get the job done. For the teacher to get the best out of their naturally grounded student they need to:

■ Demonstrate how learning can be applied in the real world.

■ Allow the student opportunities to repeat and practise until satisfied they are competent.

■ Encourage the use of imagination as a useful process (it's not wasting time).

The teacher and student are both concerned first with people and relationships before the task/subject content. They like to form personal relationships with all their students, unless they don't like the student. Teddy teachers are likely to have their favourites, but are usually able to mask it. Teddy students can be among their pets as they share all preferences. Because they operate at an emotional level these teachers are more likely to make promises to students, overstretch themselves and even do work the students should be doing themselves. Teacher and student both enjoy a classroom atmosphere that is warm and friendly. A lesson could be reminiscent of a trip to the hairdressers when Teddies start to swap gossip and biographical details! Compliments are likely to go in both directions boosting the sometimes fragile confidence of teacher as well as student. The Teddy student needs to feel they like their teacher and that the teacher likes them too. If this happens they'll work harder but if not they may lose interest. This explains why a student can be top of the class one year (with a teacher they like) and show no interest at all in the subject the following year when they change teacher. For the teacher to get the best out of their relationship-focused student they need to:

■ Offer learning situations that allow for the use of empathy, collaboration and teamworking.

■ Give ample and regular praise while offering tactful support to overcome any blind-spots.

■ Motivate by appealing to the strength of your personal belief in the student (don't let me down, I know you can do it).

The Teddy teacher takes pleasure in scheduling their time. They are organised and decisive. They work out a plan and stick to it, often aided by an impressive to-do list. Their classroom is usually an organised place. The subject will probably be broken down into lesson-sized chunks and the year planned out whether an Ofsted inspector is due or not. Many Teddy students are reassured by their teacher's organisational prowess (they're only usually knocked off schedule by a good gossip). They simply adopt the schedule and deliver their side of the bargain, generally completing all tasks on time. Interestingly, some **J**'s will baulk at their teacher's well-intentioned thoroughness. They would like to create their own plan and work to it rather than adopt someone else's. This is due to the Teddy student's desire for control. So two **J**'s together can clash, though at least all their work will be done. Most secondary schools require students to be so organised that two **J**'s are the best combination. For the teacher to get the best out of their characteristically organised student they need to:

■ Enjoy your shared desire for order, neatness and respecting deadlines.

■ Allow the student independence in planning their work in their own way if they really want to.

■ Be prepared to adjust your own plans if external events interfere with your careful preparations (and encourage the student to also embrace flexibility occasionally).

■ Shake things up now and again to prevent predictability becoming boredom.

■ Avoid making quick decisions about what needs to be done before considering all of the options.

34
Teddy Bear teacher with Polar Bear student
ESFJ and ISTJ

These two Bears share much in common. Both respect authority and are mindful of the purpose of school. The student is keen to stick to the point and may become frustrated with the teacher's socialising. The student may consider this wasted time. For the teacher to get the best out of their more internally focused student they need to:

■ Slow down and be calm and succinct.

■ Avoid pressing the student for an answer or opinion; respect their need for time to think and reflect before responding.

■ Allow the student time and space to work on their own; don't hover over their head, as if waiting to pounce.

■ Avoid trying to fix problems immediately or finish their sentences.

■ Provide written praise (not just verbal).

■ Let the student know they can always come and talk to you alone during breaks or they can write down their questions/issues for you to reply to later.

■ Respect their preference for privacy (even asking 'How's your mum?' after she's had a baby can be very embarrassing in front of other students).

Both teacher and student gather information in the same way. They notice detail using their senses (aware of what they can see, hear and feel). Both use their experience to make sense of what they notice. They both live in the present. The teacher is naturally practical, sequential, sensible and realistic in their teaching style. Polar Bears need little encouragement to adopt the same approach. A solid, workman-like relationship develops with both teacher and student mutually understanding what each needs to do to get the job done. For the teacher to get the best out of their naturally grounded student they need to:

■ Demonstrate how learning can be applied in the real world.

■ Allow the student opportunities to repeat and practise until satisfied they are competent.

■ Encourage the use of imagination as a useful process and explain it is not time-wasting.

The teacher is concerned with relationship then task whereas the student is the other way round. The teacher must learn to accept that the student is different; not cold, blunt and unfriendly, but simply focused on task first. If the teacher can accept this the relationship can be really positive for both teacher and student. For the teacher to get the best out of their inherently objective student they need to:

■ Offer targeted compliments. Just saying everything is great will not impress or help the student; in fact, it can result in the student not respecting the teacher, concluding they lie and/or are a soft touch. When you praise you may be pressed for proof!

■ Be logical and objective rather than emotional in discussions.

■ Accept that if the student challenges you it is probably to clarify their thoughts rather than a test of your authority or character. Perhaps ask 'What would you do to improve/change this?' or 'What do you think?' Once they've clarified their thoughts they may be ready to ask and absorb what you think.

■ Work in ways that test their skill and knowledge competitively (they raise their game).

■ Help them understand that 50% of people are **F** preference and can interpret feedback as criticism; this seems an especially valuable lesson for male Polar Bears.

Both teacher and student derive pleasure from scheduling their time. They are organised and decisive. They work out a plan and stick to it, often aided by an impressive to-do list. Their classroom is usually an organised place. The subject will probably be broken down into lesson-sized chunks and the year planned out whether an Ofsted inspector is due or not. Some **J** students will be reassured by their teacher's organisational zeal. They simply adopt the schedule and deliver their side of the bargain, generally completing all tasks on time. Interestingly, some **J**'s will baulk at their teacher's well-intentioned thoroughness. They would like to create their own plan and work to it rather than adopt someone else's. This is due to the **J**'s desire for control. So two **J**'s together can clash, though at least all their work will be done. Most secondary schools require students to be so organised that two **J**'s are the best combination. For the teacher to get the best out of their naturally organised student they need to:

■ Enjoy your shared desire for order, neatness and respecting deadlines.

■ Allow the student independence in planning their work in their own way if they really want to.

■ Avoid making quick decisions about what needs to be done before considering all of the options.

■ Be prepared to adjust your own plans if external events interfere with your careful preparations (and encourage the student to also embrace flexibility occasionally).

■ Shake things up now and again to prevent predictability becoming boredom.

35
Teddy Bear teacher with Black Bear student
ESFJ and ESTJ

Bears share much in common. They are interested in establishing the facts and then working clearly on the task in hand until the work is completed efficiently. The difference lies in their focus of attention; task for the student and relationships for the teacher. This can create tension as the teacher tends to focus more on the personal than the student feels they need. For the teacher to get the best out of their naturally assertive student they need to:

- Enjoy the lively banter when it is appropriate to spark new thoughts and ideas; the student learns best this way, but remember there may be thirty others in the classroom.
- Stick to the point; Teddy teachers are easily distracted and liable to go off track!
- Avoid going over old ground unless requested by the student.
- Be calm and clear, otherwise two **E** preferences can talk louder and louder like PMQs (with neither listening).
- Remember you can keep some thoughts to yourself.
- Be an enthusiastic and supportive listener; seek to help the student clarify and develop their thinking rather than assert your own.
- Help each other learn to be quiet and encourage the **I** preferences in the class to express themselves.

Both teacher and student gather information in the same way. They notice detail using their senses (aware of what they can see, hear and feel). They both use their experience to make sense of what they notice. They both live in the present. The teacher is naturally practical, sequential, sensible and realistic in their teaching style and encourages their students to follow suit. A solid, workman-like relationship develops with both teacher and student mutually understanding what each needs to do to get the job done. For the teacher to get the best out of their grounded student they need to:

- Demonstrate how learning can be applied in the real world.
- Allow the student opportunities to repeat and practise until satisfied they are competent.
- Encourage the use of imagination as a useful process (it's not wasting time).

The teacher is concerned with relationship then task whereas the student is the other way round. The teacher must learn to accept that the student is different; not cold, blunt and unfriendly, but simply focused on task first. If the teacher can accept this the relationship can be really positive for both teacher and student. For the teacher to get the best out of their fundamentally assertive student they need to:

- Offer targeted compliments. Just saying everything is great will not impress or help the student; in fact, it can result in the student not respecting the teacher, concluding they lie and/or are a soft touch. When you praise you may be pressed for proof!
- Be logical and objective rather than emotional in discussions.
- Accept that if the student challenges you it is probably to clarify their thoughts rather than meant as a slight to your authority or character. Perhaps ask 'What would you do to improve/change this?' or 'What do you think?' Once they've clarified their thoughts they may be ready to ask and absorb what you think.
- Help them understand that around 50% of people are **F** preference and can interpret feedback as criticism.
- Work in ways that test their skill and knowledge competitively (they raise their game).

Bears take pleasure in scheduling their time. They are organised and decisive. They work out a plan and stick to it, often aided by an impressive to-do list. Their classroom is usually an organised place. The subject will probably be broken down into lesson-sized chunks and the year

planned out whether or not an Ofsted inspector is due. Many **J** students are reassured by their teacher's organisational zeal. They simply adopt the schedule and deliver their side of the bargain, generally completing all tasks on time. Interestingly, some **J**'s will baulk at their teacher's well-intentioned thoroughness. They would like to create their own plan and work to it rather than adopt someone else's. This is due to the **J**'s desire for control. So two **J**'s together can clash, though at least all their work will be done. Most secondary schools require students to be so organised that two **J**'s are the best combination. For the teacher to get the best out of their intrinsically organised student they need to:

- Enjoy your shared desire for order, neatness and respecting deadlines.
- Allow the student independence in planning their work in their own way if they really want to.
- Be prepared to adjust your own plans if external events interfere with your careful preparations (and encourage the student to also embrace flexibility occasionally).
- Shake things up now and again to prevent predictability becoming boredom.
- Avoid making quick decisions about what needs to be done before considering all of the options.

36
Teddy Bear teacher with Dolphin student
ESFJ and ENFJ

Teddies and Dolphins share three type preferences. Both are sociable and organised. They can be like a pair of hairdressers catching up on each other's weekend when they're relaxed! Providing they avoid too much chat, especially about people, they should work well together. For the teacher to get the best out of their naturally effusive student they need to:

- Enjoy the lively banter when it is appropriate to spark new thoughts and ideas; the student learns best this way, but remember there may be thirty others in the classroom.
- Stick to the point and stay positive (don't nag), as both teacher and student are easily distracted and liable to go off track!
- Avoid going over old ground unless it is curriculum focused.
- Be calm and clear, otherwise two **E** preferences can talk louder and louder like PMQs (with neither listening).
- Remember you can keep some thoughts to yourself (and you may think of a better way of expressing something, especially criticism, later).
- Be an enthusiastic and supportive listener; seek to help the student clarify and develop their thinking rather than assert your own.
- Help each other learn to be quiet and encourage the **I** preferences in the class to express themselves.

The Teddy teacher likes to use their experience to make sense of the world. They are naturally sequential and realistic in style and encourage

their students to follow suit. The **N** student may at best find this perplexing and at worst find it uninteresting. The teacher is likely to see the student as a daydreamer. They should resist the temptation to chastise their student because this is how they take in information and make sense of their world. In the right context daydreaming can lead to new insights. For the teacher to get the best out of their inherently imaginative student they need to:

- Embrace the imagination and insight of the student and what it can bring to the lesson.
- Encourage the student to become aware of the important contribution of the **S** approach (the value of facts, details, procedure, experiments, applying experience, structure, the step-by-step model).

The teacher and student are both concerned with people and relationships before the task/subject content. Teddies like to form personal relationships with all their students, unless they don't like the student (**F** teachers are more inclined than **T** preference teachers to have their favourites!). Because they operate at an emotional level these teachers are more likely to make promises to students, overstretch themselves and even do work the students should be doing themselves. Teacher and student both enjoy a classroom atmosphere that is warm and friendly. Compliments are likely to go in both directions boosting the confidence of teacher as well as student. The Dolphin needs to feel they like their teacher and that the teacher likes them too. If this happens they'll work harder. This explains why a student can be top of the class one year (with a teacher they like) and show no interest at all in the same subject the following year when they change teacher. For the teacher to get the best out of their relationship-focused student they need to:

- Offer learning situations that allow for the use of empathy, collaboration and teamworking.
- Give ample and regular praise while offering tactful support to overcome any blind-spots.
- Persuade/influence by appealing to the strength of your personal belief in the student (don't let me down, I know you can do it, I like you).

The Teddy teacher takes pleasure in scheduling their time. They are organised and decisive. They work out a plan and stick to it, often aided by an impressive to-do list. Their classroom is usually an organised place. The subject will probably be broken down into lesson-sized chunks and the year meticulously planned. Many Dolphins are reassured by their teacher's organisational zeal. They simply adopt the schedule and deliver their side of the bargain, generally completing all tasks on time. Interestingly, some Dolphins will baulk at their teacher's well-intentioned thoroughness. They would like to create their own plan and work to it rather than adopt someone else's. This is due to the **J**'s desire for control. So two **J** preferences together can clash, though at least all their work will be done. Most secondary schools require students to be so organised that two **J** preferences are the best combination. For the teacher to get the best out of their naturally organised student they need to:

- Enjoy your shared desire for order, neatness and respecting deadlines.
- Allow the student independence in planning their work in their own way if they really want to.
- Shake things up now and again to prevent predictability becoming boredom.

■ Avoid making quick decisions about what needs to be done before considering all of the options.

■ Be prepared to adjust your own plans if external events interfere with your careful preparations (also encourage the Dolphin to also embrace flexibility now and again).

37
Teddy Bear teacher with Eagle student
ESFJ and ENTJ

Teddy Bears and Eagles share two type preferences. Both are outwardly confident and organised. They differ in the way they absorb information and make decisions. The practical and social teacher and the theoretical and assertive student may clash over these differences. For the teacher to get the best out of their naturally forthright student they need to:

■ Enjoy the lively banter when it is appropriate to spark new thoughts and ideas; the student learns best this way, but remember there may be thirty others in the classroom.

■ Stick to the point and stay positive (don't nag), as both teacher and student are easily distracted and liable to go off track!

■ Be calm and clear, otherwise two **E** preferences can talk louder and louder with neither listening.

■ Remember you can keep some thoughts to yourself (and you may think of a better way of expressing something, especially criticism, later).

■ Be an enthusiastic and supportive listener; seek to help the student clarify and develop their thinking rather than assert your own.

■ Help each other learn to be quiet and encourage the **I** preferences in the class to express themselves.

Teddy teachers like to use their experience to make sense of what they see. They live in the present. The teacher is naturally practical, sequential and realistic in style and will encourage their students to follow suit. The **N** student will at best find this challenging and at worst find it turgid. The teacher may see the student as lost in their own world. They should resist the temptation to rebuke their student because this is how they take in information and make sense of the world. In the right context daydreaming can lead to amazing new discoveries. For the teacher to get the best out of their inherently imaginative student they need to:

■ Embrace the imagination and insight of the student and what it can bring to the lesson.

■ Encourage the student to become aware of the important contribution of the **S** approach (the value of facts, details, procedure, experiments, applying experience, structure, the step-by-step model).

The Teddy teacher is concerned with relationship then task whereas the student is the other way round. The teacher must learn to accept that the student is different; not cold, blunt and unfriendly, but simply focused on task first. If the teacher can accept this the relationship can be

really positive for both teacher and student. For the teacher to get the best out of their essentially emphatic student they need to:

■ Offer targeted compliments. Just saying everything is great will not impress or help the student; in fact, it can result in the student not respecting the teacher, concluding they lie and/or are a soft touch. When you praise you may be pressed for proof!

■ Be logical and objective rather than emotional in discussions.

■ Accept that if the student challenges you it is probably to clarify their thoughts rather than meant as a slight to your authority or character. Perhaps ask 'What would you do to improve/change this?' or 'What do you think?' Once they've clarified their thoughts they may be ready to ask and absorb what you think.

■ Work in ways that test their skill and knowledge competitively (they raise their game).

■ Help them understand that around 50% of people are **F** preference and can interpret feedback as criticism.

The Teddy teacher takes pleasure in scheduling their time. They are organised and decisive. They work out a plan and stick to it, often aided by an impressive to-do list. Their classroom is usually an organised place. The subject will probably be broken down into lesson-sized chunks. Some Eagles will be reassured by their teacher's organisational fervour. They simply adopt the schedule and deliver their side of the bargain, generally completing all tasks on time. Interestingly, some Eagles will baulk at their teacher's well-intentioned thoroughness. They would like to create their own plan and work to it rather than adopt someone else's proposal. This is due to the **J**'s desire for control. So two **J**'s together can clash, though at least all their work will be done. Most secondary schools require students to be so organised that two **J**'s are the best combination. For the teacher to get the best out of their instinctively organised student they need to:

■ Enjoy your shared desire for order, neatness and respecting deadlines.

■ Allow the student independence in planning their work in their own way if they really want to.

■ Be prepared to adjust your own plans if external events interfere with your careful preparations (and encourage the student to also embrace flexibility occasionally).

■ Shake things up now and again to prevent predictability becoming boredom.

■ Avoid making quick decisions about what needs to be done before considering all of the options; the Eagle is likely to spot any mistakes you make.

38
Teddy Bear teacher with Panther student
ESFJ and ESTP

Teddies and Panthers share two type preferences. Both are gregarious and demonstrative. They prefer to do rather than theorise. Clashes

are most likely when student liveliness gets out of hand and they interpret the teacher's warmth and attention to detail as tethering and smothering. For the teacher to get the best out of their naturally effusive student they need to:

■ Enjoy the lively banter when it is appropriate to spark new thoughts and ideas; the student learns best this way, but remember there may be thirty others in the classroom.

■ Stick to the point and stay positive (don't nag), as both teacher and student are easily distracted and liable to go off track!

■ Avoid going over old ground.

■ Be calm and clear, otherwise two **E** preferences can talk louder and louder like PMQs (with neither listening).

■ Remember you can keep some thoughts to yourself (and you may think of a better way of expressing something, especially criticism, later).

■ Be an enthusiastic and supportive listener; seek to help the student clarify and develop their thinking rather than assert your own.

■ Help each other learn to be quiet and encourage the **I** preferences in the class to express themselves.

Both teacher and student gather information in the same way. They notice detail using their senses (aware of what they can see, hear and feel). The teacher is naturally sequential and realistic in their teaching style and encourages their students to follow suit. A solid, workman-like relationship develops with both teacher and student mutually understanding what each needs to do to get the job done. For the teacher to get the best out of their grounded student they need to:

■ Show how learning can be applied in the real world.

■ Provide opportunities for the student to repeat and practise something until it is mastered.

■ Encourage the use of imagination as a useful addition to their learning repertoire.

The teacher is concerned with relationship then task whereas the student is the other way round. The teacher must learn to accept that the student is different; not cold, blunt and unfriendly, but simply focused on task first. If the teacher can accept this the relationship can be really positive for both teacher and student. For the teacher to get the best out of their fundamentally assertive Panther they need to:

■ Offer targeted compliments. Just saying everything is great will not impress or help the student; in fact, it can result in the student not respecting the teacher, concluding they lie and/or are a soft touch. When you praise you may be pressed for proof!

■ Be logical and objective rather than emotional in discussions.

■ Accept that if the student challenges you it is probably to clarify their thoughts rather than meant as a slight to your authority or character. Perhaps ask 'What would you do to improve/change this?' or 'What do you think?' Once they've clarified their thoughts they may be ready to ask and absorb what you think.

■ Work in ways that test their skill and knowledge competitively (they raise their game).

■ Help them appreciate that around 50% of people are **F** preference and can interpret feedback as criticism.

The **J** teacher takes pleasure in scheduling their time. They are organised and decisive. They work out a plan and stick to it, often aided by an impressive to-do list. Their classroom is usually an organised place. The subject will probably be broken down into lesson-sized chunks and the year planned out whether an Ofsted inspector is due or not. The **P** student will either respond:

- Positively by accepting your expertise and understanding the long-term benefits they'll reap.
- Passively by just accepting your structure/plan for an easy life without really buying into the content or process you are offering.
- Negatively by rejecting you, your structure/plan and subject completely (even if they're physically in your room they will not engage and participate).

For the teacher to get the best out of their naturally laid-back student they should note the student doesn't just like options and choice; they need them or they start to itch, squirm and rebel. The secondary school environment is tough for many **P** preference students. Teachers can help soften the pressure by:

- Providing as much flexibility as possible (multiple choice homework tasks, choice within the lesson).
- Resisting the temptation to burden the student with detailed schedules.
- Not being more picky with detail than is absolutely necessary.
- Shaking things up now and again to prevent predictability becoming boredom. Introduce random surprises and changes.
- Helping the student identify ways they can organise and manage their time to complete important work without a last-minute rush.

39
Teddy Bear teacher with Lion student
ESFJ and ESFP

Teddies and Lions share three type preferences. Both are earnest and warm. Clashes are most likely when the Lion is reluctant to get on with required tasks and complete work on time. For the teacher to get the best out of their naturally vociferous student they need to:

- Enjoy the lively banter when it is appropriate to spark new thoughts and ideas; the student learns best this way, but remember there may be thirty others in the classroom.
- Stick to the point and stay positive (don't nag), as both teacher and student are easily distracted and liable to go off track!
- Avoid going over old ground unless requested by the student.
- Be calm and clear, otherwise two **E** preferences can talk louder and louder with neither listening.
- Remember you can keep some thoughts to yourself (and you may think of a better way of expressing something, especially criticism, later).

- Be an enthusiastic and supportive listener; seek to help the student clarify and develop their thinking rather than assert your own.
- Help each other learn to be quiet and encourage the **I** preferences in the class to express themselves.

Both teacher and student gather information in the same way. They notice detail using their senses (aware of what they can see, hear and feel). The teacher is naturally sequential and realistic in their teaching style and encourages their students to follow suit. A solid, workman-like relationship develops with both teacher and student mutually understanding what each needs to do to get the job done. For the teacher to get the best out of their grounded student they need to:

- Show how learning can be applied in the real world.
- Provide opportunities for the student to repeat and practise something until it is mastered.
- Encourage the use of imagination as a useful addition to their learning repertoire.

Both teacher and student are interested in people and relationships before the task/subject content. The teacher likes to form personal relationships with all their students, unless they don't like the student (**F** teachers are more inclined than **T** preference teachers to have their favourites!). Because they operate at an emotional level these teachers are more likely to make promises to students, overstretch themselves and even do work the students should be doing themselves. Teacher and student both enjoy a classroom atmosphere that is warm and friendly. Compliments are likely to go in both directions boosting the confidence of teacher as well as student. For the teacher to get the best out of their relationship-focused student they need to:

- Offer learning situations that allow for the use of empathy, collaboration and teamworking.
- Give ample and regular praise while offering tactful support to overcome any blind-spots.
- Motivate by appealing to the strength of your personal belief in the student (don't let me down, I know you can do it, I like you).

The **J** teacher takes pleasure in scheduling their time. They are organised and decisive. They work out a plan and stick to it, often aided by an impressive to-do list. Their classroom is usually an organised place. The subject will probably be broken down into lesson-sized chunks and the year planned out with alacrity. The **P** student will either respond:

- Positively by accepting your expertise and understanding the long-term benefits they'll reap.
- Passively by just accepting your structure/plan for an easy life without really buying into the content or process you are offering.
- Negatively by rejecting you, your structure/plan and subject completely (even if they're physically in your room they will not engage and participate).

For the teacher to get the best out of their naturally laid-back student they should note the student doesn't just like options and choice; they need them or they start to squirm and rebel. The secondary school environment is tough for many **P** preference students. Teachers can help soften the pressure by:

- Providing as much flexibility as possible (multiple choice homework tasks, choice within the lesson).

- Resisting the temptation to burden the student with detailed schedules.
- Not being more picky with detail than is absolutely necessary.
- Shaking things up now and again to prevent predictability becoming boredom.
- Helping the student identify ways they can organise and manage their time to complete important work without a last-minute rush.
- Introducing random surprises and changes to keep the student enthused.

40
Teddy Bear teacher with Clownfish student
ESFJ and ENFP

The Teddy and Clownfish share two type preferences. Both enjoy talking and like a friendly and positive classroom environment. Clashes are more likely due to their similarities rather than their differences, such as being oversensitive and talking too much. For the teacher to get the best out of their naturally bubbly student they need to:

- Enjoy the lively banter when it is appropriate to spark new thoughts and ideas; the student learns best this way, but remember there may be thirty others in the classroom.
- Stick to the point and stay positive (don't nag), as both teacher and student are easily distracted and liable to go off track!
- Avoid going over old ground.
- Be calm and clear, otherwise two **E** preferences can talk louder and louder like PMQs (with neither listening).
- Remember you can keep some thoughts to yourself (and you may think of a better way of expressing something, especially criticism, later).
- Be an enthusiastic and supportive listener; seek to help the student clarify and develop their thinking rather than assert your own.
- Help each other learn to be quiet and encourage the **I** preferences in the class to express themselves.

The Teddy teacher likes to use their experience to make sense of their learning. The teacher is naturally sequential, sensible and realistic in style and encourages their students to follow suit. The **N** student can find this approach dull. The teacher is likely to see the student as a daydreamer. They should resist the temptation to castigate their student because this is how they take in information and make sense of the world. In the right context daydreaming can lead to better absorption and retention of the topic. To get the best out of their inherently ingenious student the teacher can:

- Embrace the imagination and insight of the student and what it can bring to the lesson.
- Encourage the student to become aware of the important contribution of the **S** approach (the value of facts, details, procedure, experiments, applying experience, structure, the step-by-step model).

Both teacher and student are interested in people and relationships before the task/subject content.

The teacher likes to form personal relationships with all their students, unless they don't like the student (**F** teachers are more inclined than **T** preference teachers to have their favourites!). Because they operate at an emotional level these teachers are more likely to make promises to students, overstretch themselves and even do work the students should be doing themselves. Teacher and student both enjoy a classroom atmosphere that is warm and friendly. Compliments are likely to go in both directions boosting the confidence of teacher as well as student. For the teacher to get the best out of their relationship-focused student they need to:

- Offer learning situations that allow for the use of empathy, collaboration and teamworking.
- Give ample and regular praise while offering tactful support to overcome any blind-spots.
- Motivate by appealing to the strength of your personal belief in the student (don't let me down, I know you can do it, I like you).

The **J** teacher takes pleasure in scheduling their time. They are organised and decisive. They work out a plan and stick to it, often aided by an impressive to-do list. Their classroom is usually an organised place. The subject will probably be broken down into lesson-sized chunks and the year planned out whether or not an Ofsted inspector is due. The **P** student will either respond:

- Positively by accepting your expertise and understanding the long-term benefits they'll reap.
- Passively by just accepting your structure/plan for an easy life without really buying into the content or process you are offering.
- Negatively by rejecting you, your structure/plan and subject completely (even if they're physically in your room they will not engage and participate).

For the teacher to get the best out of their naturally laid-back student they should note the student doesn't just like options and choice; they need them or they start to itch, squirm and rebel. The secondary school environment is tough for many **P** preference students. Teachers can help soften the pressure by:

- Providing as much flexibility as possible (multiple choice homework tasks, choice within the lesson).
- Resisting the temptation to burden the student with detailed schedules.
- Not being more picky with detail than is absolutely necessary.
- Shaking things up now and again to prevent predictability becoming boredom. Introduce random surprises and changes.
- Helping the Clownfish identify ways they can organise and manage their time to complete important work without a last-minute panic.

41
Teddy Bear teacher with Falcon student
ESFJ and ENTP

The Teddy and Falcon share one type preference. Both are sociable. Their differences can easily lead to confusion or conflict. The grounded and

harmony-seeking Teddy contrasts with the Falcon's quirky imagination and insatiable need to play devil's advocate to understand things. For the teacher to get the best out of their naturally effusive student they need to:

- Enjoy the lively banter when it is appropriate to spark new thoughts and ideas; the student learns best this way, but remember there may be thirty others in the classroom.
- Stick to the point and stay positive (don't nag), as both teacher and student are easily distracted and liable to go off track!
- Avoid going over old ground.
- Be calm and clear, otherwise two **E** preferences can talk louder and louder with neither listening.
- Remember you can keep some thoughts to yourself (and you may think of a better way of expressing something, especially criticism, later).
- Be an enthusiastic and supportive listener; seek to help the student clarify and develop their thinking rather than assert your own.
- Help each other learn to be quiet and encourage the **I** preferences in the class to express themselves.

The teacher likes to use their experience to make sense of their learning. The teacher is naturally sequential, sensible and realistic in style and encourages their students to follow suit. The **N** student can find this approach mind-numbingly dull. The teacher is likely to see the student as a daydreamer. They should resist the temptation to castigate their student because this is how they take in information and make sense of the world. In the right context daydreaming can lead to better absorption and retention of the topic. To get the best out of their intrinsically ingenious student the teacher can:

- Embrace the imagination and insight of the student and what it can bring to the lesson.
- Encourage the student to become aware of the important contribution of the **S** approach (the value of facts, details, procedure, experiments, applying experience, structure, the step-by-step model).

The teacher is concerned with relationship then task whereas the student is the other way round. The teacher must learn to accept that the student is different; not cold, blunt and unfriendly, but simply focused on task first. If the teacher can accept this the relationship can be really positive for both teacher and student. For the teacher to get the best out of their fundamentally assertive student they need to:

- Offer targeted compliments. Just saying everything is great will not impress or help the student; in fact, it can result in the student not respecting the teacher, concluding they lie and/or are a soft touch. When you praise you may be pressed for proof!
- Be logical and objective rather than emotional in discussions.
- Accept that if the student challenges you it is probably to clarify their thoughts rather than meant as a slight to your authority or character. Perhaps ask 'What would you do to improve/change this?' or 'What do you think?' Once they've clarified their thoughts they may be ready to ask and absorb what you think.
- Work in ways that test their skill and knowledge competitively (they raise their game).

- Help them understand that around 50% of people are **F** preference and can interpret feedback as criticism.

The **J** teacher takes pleasure in scheduling their time. They are organised and decisive. They work out a plan and stick to it, often aided by an impressive to-do list. Their classroom is usually an organised place. The subject will probably be broken down into lesson-sized chunks and the year planned out whether or not an Ofsted inspector is lurking in the corridor. The **P** student will either respond:

- Positively by accepting your expertise and understanding the long-term benefits they'll reap.
- Passively by just accepting your structure/plan for an easy life without really buying into the content or process you are offering.
- Negatively by rejecting you, your structure/plan and subject completely (even if they're physically in your room they will not engage and participate).

For the teacher to get the best out of their naturally laid-back student they should note the student doesn't just like options and choice; they need them or they start to itch, squirm and rebel. The secondary school environment is tough for many **P** preference students. Teachers can help soften the pressure by:

- Providing as much flexibility as possible (multiple choice homework tasks, choice within the lesson).
- Resisting the temptation to burden the student with detailed schedules.
- Not being more picky with detail than is absolutely necessary.
- Shaking things up now and again to prevent predictability becoming boredom. Introduce random surprises and changes.
- Helping the student identify simple effective strategies to organise and complete their work.

42
Teddy Bear teacher with Tiger student
ESFJ and ISTP

Teddies and Tigers share one type preference. Both are practical. Their differences can be significant. The warm and nurturing teacher needs to quickly learn that the Tiger student values and needs independence and space to complete their work. For the teacher to get the best out of their naturally reserved student they need to:

- Slow down and be calm and succinct.
- Leave plenty of time between question and answer; respect the student's need for time to think and reflect before responding.
- Allow the student time and space to work on their own; don't hover over their head, waiting to pounce.
- Avoid trying to fix problems immediately or finish their sentences.
- Avoid placing them in groups/teams where they are the only **I** preference in a sea of **E** preferences (they'll be smothered).

■ Provide written praise (not just verbal).

Both teacher and student gather information in the same way. They notice detail using their senses (aware of what they can see, hear and feel). The teacher is naturally sequential and realistic in their teaching style and encourages their students to follow suit. A solid, workman-like relationship develops with both teacher and student mutually understanding what each needs to do to get the job done. For the teacher to get the best out of their grounded student they need to:

■ Show how learning can be applied in the real world.

■ Provide opportunities for the student to repeat and practise something until it is mastered.

■ Encourage the use of imagination as a useful addition to their learning repertoire.

The teacher likes to use their experience to make sense of their learning. The teacher is naturally sequential, sensible and realistic in style and encourages their students to follow suit. The **N** student can find this approach dull. The teacher is likely to see the student as a daydreamer. They should resist the temptation to castigate their student because this is how they take in information and make sense of the world. In the right context daydreaming can lead to better absorption and retention of the topic. To get the best out of their inherently ingenious student the teacher can:

■ Embrace the imagination and insight of the student and what it can bring to the lesson.

■ Encourage the student to become aware of the important contribution of the **S** approach (the value of facts, details, procedure, experiments, applying experience, structure, the step-by-step model).

The teacher is concerned with relationship then task whereas the student is the other way round. The teacher must learn to accept that the student is different; not cold, blunt and unfriendly, but simply focused on task first. If the teacher can accept this the relationship can be really positive for both teacher and student. For the teacher to get the best out of their naturally objective Tiger they need to:

■ Offer targeted compliments. Just saying everything is great will not impress or help the student; in fact, it can result in the student not respecting the teacher, concluding they lie and/or are a soft touch. When you praise you may be pressed for proof!

■ Be logical and objective rather than emotional in discussions.

■ Accept that if the student challenges you it is probably to clarify their thoughts rather than test your authority or character. Perhaps ask 'What would you do to improve/change this?' or 'What do you think?' Once they've clarified their thoughts they may be ready to ask and absorb what you think.

■ Work in ways that test their skill and knowledge competitively (they raise their game).

■ Help them understand that around 50% of people are **F** preference and can interpret feedback as criticism.

The **J** teacher takes pleasure in scheduling their time. They are organised and decisive. They work out a plan and stick to it, often aided by an impressive to-do list. Their classroom is usually an organised place. The subject will probably be broken down into lesson-sized chunks and the year planned out whether an Ofsted inspector is due or not. The **P** student will either respond:

■ Positively by accepting your expertise and understanding the long-term benefits they'll reap.

■ Passively by just accepting your structure/plan for an easy life without really buying into the content or process you are offering.

■ Negatively by rejecting you, your structure/plan and subject completely (even if they're physically in your room they will not engage and participate).

For the teacher to get the best out of their naturally laid-back student they should note the student doesn't just like options and choice; they need them or they start to itch, squirm and rebel. The secondary school environment is tough for many **P** preference students. Teachers can help soften the pressure by:

■ Providing as much flexibility as possible (multiple choice homework tasks, choice within the lesson).

■ Resisting the temptation to burden the student with detailed schedules.

■ Not being more picky with detail than is absolutely necessary.

■ Shaking things up now and again to prevent predictability becoming boredom. Introduce random surprises and changes.

■ Helping the student identify ways they can organise and manage their time to complete important work without a last-minute rush.

43
Teddy Bear teacher with Cat student
ESFJ and ISFP

Teddies and Cats share two type preferences. Both are grounded and sociable. Clashes are likely when the teacher smothers and attempts to over-organise the independence loving Cat. For the teacher to get the best out of their naturally reserved student they need to:

■ Slow down and be calm and succinct.

■ Leave plenty of time between question and answer; respect the student's need for time to think and reflect before responding.

■ Allow the student time and space to work on their own; don't hover over their head, waiting to pounce.

■ Avoid trying to fix problems immediately or finish their sentences.

■ Avoid placing them in groups/teams where they are the only **I** preference in a sea of **E** preferences (they'll be smothered).

■ Provide written praise (not just verbal).

Both teacher and student gather information in the same way. They notice detail using their senses (aware of what they can see, hear and feel). The teacher is naturally sequential and realistic in their teaching style and encourages their students to follow suit. A solid, workman-like relationship develops with both teacher and student mutually understanding what each needs to do to get the job done. For the teacher to get the best out of their grounded student they need to:

■ Show how learning can be applied in the real world.

■ Provide opportunities for the student to repeat and practise something until it is mastered.

■ Encourage the use of imagination as a useful addition to their learning repertoire.

Both teacher and student are interested in people and relationships before the task/subject content. The teacher likes to form personal relationships with all their students, unless they don't like the student (**F** teachers are more inclined than **T** preference teachers to have their favourites!). Because they operate at an emotional level these teachers are more likely to make promises to students, overstretch themselves and even do work the students should be doing themselves. Teacher and student both enjoy a classroom atmosphere that is warm and friendly. Compliments are likely to go in both directions boosting the confidence of teacher as well as student. For the teacher to get the best out of their relationship-focused student they need to:

■ Offer learning situations that allow for the use of empathy, collaboration and teamworking.

■ Give ample and regular praise while offering tactful support to overcome any blind-spots.

■ Motivate by appealing to the strength of your personal belief in the student (don't let me down, I know you can do it, I like you).

The **J** teacher takes pleasure in scheduling their time. They are organised and decisive. They work out a plan and stick to it, often aided by an impressive to-do list. Their classroom is usually an organised place. The subject will probably be broken down into lesson-sized chunks and the year planned out whether an Ofsted inspector is due or not. The **P** student will either respond:

■ Positively by accepting your expertise and understanding the long-term benefits they'll reap.

■ Passively by just accepting your structure/plan for an easy life without really buying into the content or process you are offering.

■ Negatively by rejecting you, your structure/plan and subject completely (even if they're physically in your room they will not engage and participate).

For the teacher to get the best out of their naturally laid-back student they should note the student doesn't just like options and choice; they need them or they start to itch, squirm and rebel. The secondary school environment is tough for many **P** preference students. Teachers can help alleviate the pressure by:

■ Shaking things up now and again to prevent predictability becoming boredom.

■ Introducing random surprises and changes as variety is the spice of life.

■ Helping the student identify simple effective strategies to ensure they can succeed.

■ Providing as much flexibility as possible (multiple choice homework tasks, choice within the lesson).

■ Resisting the temptation to burden the student with detailed schedules.

■ Not being more picky with detail than is absolutely necessary.

44
Teddy Bear teacher with Seal student
ESFJ and INFP

Teddies and Seals share one type preference. Both seek a harmonious classroom environment. Their differences can be complementary with the grounded and organised teacher cajoling the more dreamy Seal into making the most of their potential. For the teacher to get the best out of their naturally reserved student they need to:

■ Slow down and be calm and succinct.

■ Leave plenty of time between question and answer; respect the student's need for time to think and reflect before responding.

■ Allow the student time and space to work on their own; don't hover over their head, waiting to pounce.

■ Avoid trying to fix problems immediately or finish their sentences.

■ Pair them up with complementary types (Seahorses, Teddy Bears and Dolphins).

■ Avoid placing them in groups/teams where they are the only **I** preference in a sea of **E** preferences (they'll be smothered).

■ Provide written praise (not just verbal).

The teacher likes to use their experience to make sense of their learning. The teacher is naturally sequential, sensible and realistic in style and encourages their students to follow suit. The **N** student can find this approach dull. The teacher is likely to see the student as a daydreamer. They should resist the temptation to castigate their student because this is how they take in information and make sense of the world. In the right context daydreaming can lead to better absorption and retention of a topic. To get the best out of their inherently ingenious student the teacher can:

■ Embrace the imagination and insight of the student and what it can bring to the lesson.

■ Encourage the student to become aware of the important contribution of the **S** approach (the value of facts, details, procedure, experiments, applying experience, structure, the step-by-step model).

Both teacher and student are interested in people and relationships before the task/subject content. The teacher likes to form personal relationships with all their students, unless they don't like the student (**F** teachers are more inclined than **T** preference teachers to have their favourites!). Because they operate at an emotional level these teachers are more likely to make promises to students, overstretch themselves and even do work the students should be doing themselves. Teacher and student both enjoy a classroom atmosphere that is warm and friendly. Compliments are likely to go in both directions boosting the confidence of teacher as well as student. For the teacher to get the best out of their relationship-focused student they need to:

■ Offer learning situations that allow for the use of empathy, collaboration and teamworking.

■ Give ample and regular praise while offering tactful support to overcome any blind-spots.

■ Motivate by appealing to the strength of your personal belief in the student (don't let me down, I know you can do it).

The **J** teacher takes pleasure in scheduling their time. They are organised and decisive. They work out a plan and stick to it, often aided by an impressive to-do list. Their classroom is usually an organised place. The subject will probably be broken down into lesson-sized chunks and the year planned out whether an Ofsted inspector is due or not. The **P** student will either respond:

■ Positively by accepting your expertise and understanding the long-term benefits they'll reap.

■ Passively by just accepting your structure/plan for an easy life without really buying into the content or process you are offering.

■ Negatively by rejecting you, your structure/plan and subject completely (even if they're physically in your room they will not engage and participate).

For the teacher to get the best out of their naturally laid-back student they should note the student doesn't just like options and choice; they need them or they start to itch, squirm and rebel. The secondary school environment is tough for many **P** preference students. Teachers can help soften the pressure by:

■ Providing as much flexibility as possible (multiple choice homework tasks, choice within the lesson).

■ Resisting the temptation to burden the student with detailed schedules.

■ Helping the student identify ways they can organise and manage their time to complete important work without a last-minute rush.

■ Not being more picky with detail than is absolutely necessary.

■ Shaking things up now and again to prevent predictability becoming boredom.

45
Teddy Bear teacher with Tawny Owl student
ESFJ and INTP

Truly Scrumptious meets Caractacus Potts! Opposites can help each other grow and develop. For the teacher to get the best out of their naturally reserved student they need to:

■ Slow down and be calm and succinct.

■ Leave plenty of time between question and answer; respect the student's need for time to think and reflect before responding.

■ Allow the student time and space to work on their own; don't hover over their head, waiting to pounce.

■ Avoid trying to fix problems immediately or finish their sentences.

■ Avoid placing them in groups/teams where they are the only **I** preference in a sea of **E** preferences (they'll be smothered).

■ Provide written praise (not just verbal).

The teacher likes to use their experience to make sense of their learning. The teacher is naturally sequential, sensible and realistic in style and encourages their students to follow suit. The **N** student can find this approach dull. The teacher is likely to see the student as a daydreamer. They should resist the temptation to castigate their student because this is how they take in information and make sense of the world. In the right context daydreaming can lead to better absorption and retention of the topic. To get the best out of their naturally ingenious student the teacher can:

■ Embrace the imagination and insight of the student and what it can bring to the lesson.

■ Encourage the student to become aware of the important contribution of the **S** approach (the value of facts, details, procedure, experiments, applying experience, structure, the step-by-step model).

The teacher is concerned with relationship then task whereas the student is the other way round. The teacher must learn to accept that the student is different; not cold, blunt and unfriendly, but simply focused on task first. If the teacher can accept this the relationship can be really positive for both teacher and student. For the teacher to get the best out of their fundamentally objective student they need to:

■ Offer targeted compliments. Just saying everything is great will not impress or help the student; in fact, it can result in the student not respecting the teacher, concluding they lie and/or are a soft touch. When you praise you may be pressed for proof!

■ Be logical and objective rather than emotional in discussions.

■ Accept that if the student challenges you it is probably to clarify their thoughts rather than meant as a slight to your authority or character. Perhaps ask 'What would you do to improve/change this?' or 'What do you think?' Once they've clarified their thoughts they may be ready to ask and absorb what you think.

■ Work in ways that test their skill and knowledge competitively (they raise their game).

■ Help them understand that around half the population are **F** preference and can interpret feedback as criticism.

The **J** teacher takes pleasure in scheduling their time. They are organised and decisive. They work out a plan and stick to it, often aided by an impressive to-do list. Their classroom is usually an organised place. The subject will probably be broken down into lesson-sized chunks and the year planned out whether or not an Ofsted inspector is due. The **P** student will either respond:

■ Positively by accepting your expertise and understanding the long-term benefits they'll reap.

■ Passively by just accepting your structure/plan for an easy life without really buying into the content or process you are offering.

■ Negatively by rejecting you, your structure/plan and subject completely (even if they're physically in your room they will not engage and participate).

For the teacher to get the best out of their naturally laid-back student they should note the student doesn't just like options and choice; they need them or they start to itch, squirm and rebel. The secondary school environment is tough for many **P** preference students. Teachers can help soften the pressure by:

■ Providing as much flexibility as possible (multiple choice homework tasks, choice within the lesson).

■ Resisting the temptation to burden the student with detailed schedules.

- Not being more picky with detail than is absolutely necessary.
- Shaking things up now and again to prevent predictability becoming boredom. Introduce random surprises and changes.
- Helping the student identify ways they can organise and manage their time to complete important work without a last-minute panic.

46
Teddy Bear teacher with Koala student
ESFJ and ISFJ

Teddies and Koalas share three type preferences. Both are warm, practical and organised and usually work well together, especially when the teacher learns to listen and avoids speaking over their student. To get the best out of their naturally reserved student they need to:

- Slow down and be calm and succinct.
- Leave plenty of time between question and answer; respect the student's need for time to think and reflect before responding.
- Allow the student time and space to work on their own; don't hover over their head, waiting to pounce.
- Avoid trying to fix problems immediately or finish their sentences.
- Pair them up with complementary types (Seahorses, Seals, Teddy Bears and Dolphins).
- Avoid placing them in groups/teams where they are the only **I** preference in a sea of **E** preferences (they'll be smothered).
- Provide written praise (not just verbal).

Both teacher and student gather information in the same way. They notice detail using their senses (aware of what they can see, hear and feel). The teacher is naturally sequential and realistic in their teaching style and encourages their students to follow suit. A solid, workman-like relationship develops with both teacher and student mutually understanding what each needs to do to get the job done. For the teacher to get the best out of their grounded student they need to:

- Show how learning can be applied in the real world.
- Provide opportunities for the student to repeat and practise something until it is mastered.
- Encourage the use of imagination as a useful addition to their learning repertoire.

Both teacher and student are interested in people and relationships before the task/subject content. The Teddy likes to form personal relationships with all their students, unless they don't like the student (**F** teachers are more inclined than **T** preference teachers to have their favourites!). Because they operate at an emotional level these teachers are more likely to make promises to students, overstretch themselves and even do work the students should be doing themselves. Teacher and student both enjoy a classroom atmosphere that is warm and friendly. Compliments are likely to go in both directions boosting the confidence of teacher as well as student. For the teacher to get the best out of their relationship-focused student they need to:

- Offer learning situations that allow for the use of empathy, collaboration and teamworking.
- Give ample and regular praise while offering tactful support to overcome any blind-spots.
- Motivate by appealing to the strength of your personal belief in the student (don't let me down, I know you can do it, I like you).

The **J** teacher takes pleasure in scheduling their time. They are organised and driven to complete. They work out a plan and stick to it, often aided by an impressive to-do list. Their classroom is usually an organised place. The subject will probably be broken down into lesson-sized chunks and the whole year planned out on a colour-coded spreadsheet. Many **J** students are reassured by their teacher's insatiable appetite to stick to the plan. They simply embrace the schedule and deliver their side of the bargain, generally completing all tasks on time. Interestingly, some **J** preferences will baulk at their teacher's well-intentioned thoroughness. They would like to create their own plan and work to it rather than adopt someone else's. This is due to the **J**'s desire for control. So two **J**'s together can clash, though at least all the work will be done. Most secondary schools require students to be so organised that two **J**'s are a welcome combination. For the teacher to get the best out of their characteristically organised student they need to:

- Be prepared to adjust your own plans if external events interfere with your careful preparations (and encourage the student to also embrace flexibility occasionally).
- Shake things up now and again to prevent predictability becoming boredom.
- Avoid making quick decisions about what needs to be done before considering all of the options.
- Enjoy your shared desire for order, neatness and respecting deadlines.
- Allow the student independence in planning their work in their own way if they really want to.

47
Teddy Bear teacher with Seahorse student
ESFJ and INFJ

The Teddy Bear and Seahorse share two type preferences. Both are organised and friendly. The teacher can help the daydreaming student focus their energies for academic success. To get the best out of their naturally introspective student they need to:

- Slow down and be calm and succinct.
- Leave plenty of time between question and answer; respect the student's need for time to think and reflect before responding.
- Allow the student time and space to work on their own; don't hover over their head, waiting to pounce.
- Avoid trying to fix problems immediately or finish their sentences.
- Avoid placing them in groups/teams where they are the only **I** preference in a sea of **E** preferences (they'll be smothered).
- Provide written praise (not just verbal).

The teacher likes to use their experience to make sense of their learning. The teacher is naturally sequential, sensible and realistic in style and encourages their students to follow suit. The **N** student can find this approach dull. The teacher is likely to see the student as a daydreamer. They should resist the temptation to castigate their student because this is how they take in information and make sense of the world. In the right context daydreaming can lead to better absorption and retention of the topic. To get the best out of their inherently ingenious student the teacher can:

- Embrace the imagination and insight of the student and what it can bring to the lesson.
- Encourage the student to become aware of the important contribution of the **S** approach (the value of facts, details, procedure, experiments, applying experience, structure, the step-by-step model).

Both teacher and student are interested in people and relationships before the task/subject content. The teacher likes to form personal relationships with all their students, unless they don't like the student (**F** teachers are more inclined than **T** preference teachers to have their favourites!). Because they operate at an emotional level these teachers are more likely to make promises to students, overstretch themselves and even do work the students should be doing themselves. Teacher and student both enjoy a classroom atmosphere that is warm and friendly. Compliments are likely to go in both directions boosting the confidence of teacher as well as student. For the teacher to get the best out of their relationship-focused student they need to:

- Offer learning situations that allow for the use of empathy, collaboration and teamworking.
- Give ample and regular praise while offering tactful support to overcome any blind-spots.
- Motivate by appealing to the strength of your personal belief in the student (don't let me down, I know you can do it, I like you).

The **J** teacher takes pleasure in scheduling their time. They are organised and driven to complete. They work out a plan and stick to it, often aided by an impressive to-do list. Their classroom is usually an organised place. The subject will probably be broken down into lesson-sized chunks and the whole year planned out on a colour-coded spreadsheet. Many **J** students are reassured by their teacher's insatiable appetite to stick to the plan. They simply embrace the schedule and deliver their side of the bargain, generally completing all tasks on time. Interestingly, some **J** preferences will baulk at their teacher's well-intentioned thoroughness. They would like to create their own plan and work to it rather than adopt someone else's. This is due to the **J**'s desire for control. So two **J**'s together can clash, though at least all the work will be done. Most secondary schools require students to be so organised that two **J**'s are a welcome combination. For the teacher to get the best out of their instinctively organised student they need to:

- Enjoy your shared desire for order, neatness and respecting deadlines.
- Allow the student independence in planning their work in their own way if they really want to.
- Be prepared to adjust your own plans if external events interfere with your careful preparations (and encourage the student to also embrace flexibility occasionally).

- Shake things up now and again to prevent predictability becoming boredom.
- Avoid making quick decisions about what needs to be done before considering all of the options.

48
Teddy Bear teacher with Barn Owl student
ESFJ and INTJ

Teddy Bears and Barn Owls share one type preference. Both are organised. The naturally introspective and astute theoretical approach of the Owl can be challenging to some Teddy teachers who are uncomfortable with this alien method of absorbing and processing information. To help their student excel they need to:

- Slow down and be calm and succinct.
- Leave plenty of time between question and answer; respect the student's need for time to think and reflect before responding.
- Allow the student time and space to work on their own; don't hover over their head, waiting to pounce.
- Avoid trying to fix problems immediately or finish their sentences.
- Pair them up with complementary types (Seahorses, Seals, Teddy Bears and Dolphins).
- Avoid placing them in groups/teams where they are the only **I** preference in a sea of **E** preferences (they'll be smothered).
- Provide written praise (not just verbal).
- Let the student know they can always come and talk to you alone during breaks or they can write down their questions/issues for you to reply to later.

The teacher likes to use their experience to make sense of their learning. The teacher is naturally sequential, sensible and realistic in style, and encourages their students to follow suit. The **N** student can find this approach dull. The teacher is likely to see the student as a daydreamer. They should resist the temptation to castigate their student because this is how they take in information and make sense of the world. In the right context daydreaming can lead to better absorption and retention of the topic. To get the best out of their naturally ingenious student the teacher can:

- Embrace the imagination and insight of the student and what it can bring to the lesson.
- Encourage the student to become aware of the important contribution of the **S** approach (the value of facts, details, procedure, experiments, applying experience, structure, the step-by-step model).

The teacher is concerned with relationship then task whereas the student is the other way round. The teacher must learn to accept that the student is different; not cold, blunt and unfriendly, but simply focused on task first. If the teacher can accept this the relationship can be really positive for both teacher and student. For the teacher to get the best out of their naturally objective Barn Owl they need to:

- Offer targeted compliments. Just saying everything is great will not impress or help the student; in fact, it can result in the student not respecting the teacher, concluding they lie and/or are a soft touch. When you praise you may be pressed for proof!
- Be logical and objective rather than emotional in discussions.
- Work in ways that test their skill and knowledge competitively (they raise their game).
- Help them understand that around 50% of people are **F** preference and can interpret feedback as criticism.
- Accept that if the student challenges you it is probably to clarify their thoughts rather than demean your authority or character. Perhaps ask 'What would you do to improve/change this?' or 'What do you think?' Once they've clarified their thoughts they may be ready to ask and absorb what you think.

The **J** teacher takes pleasure in scheduling their time. They are organised and driven to complete. They work out a plan and stick to it, often aided by an impressive to-do list. Their classroom is usually an organised place. The subject will probably be broken down into lesson-sized chunks and the whole year planned in glorious detail. Many **J** students are reassured by their teacher's insatiable appetite to stick to the plan. They simply embrace the schedule and deliver their side of the bargain, generally completing all tasks on time. Interestingly, some **J** preferences will baulk at their teacher's well-intentioned thoroughness. They would like to create their own plan and work to it rather than adopt someone else's. This is due to the **J**'s preference for control. So two **J** preferences together can clash, though at least all the work will be done. Most secondary schools require students to be so organised that two **J** preferences are a welcome combination. For the teacher to get the best out of their fundamentally organised student need to:

- Enjoy your shared desire for order, neatness and respecting deadlines.
- Allow the student independence in planning their work in their own way if they really want to.
- Be prepared to adjust your own plans if external events interfere with your careful preparations (and encourage the student to also embrace flexibility occasionally).
- Shake things up now and again to prevent predictability becoming boredom.
- Avoid making quick decisions about what needs to be done before considering all of the options; the Barn Owl will spot any inconsistency and probably inform you of the error.

49
Koala teacher with Koala student
ISFJ and ISFJ

The naturally reserved and warm Koala teacher–student combination is a recipe for mutual understanding and quiet, determined application.

They may not wish to be labelled 'nice', but the word captures their ideal Koala classroom environment and temperament. For the teacher to get the best out of their inherently caring and careful student they need to:

- Respect the student's need for privacy and independence.
- Allow the student plenty of time to think through their thoughts.
- Take time to clarify your thoughts but don't avoid confrontation; if something needs to be said, be calm and direct as you deliver it.
- Use non-verbal communication – smiles and gestures are especially reassuring. You can even use sticky notes/emails to pass on feedback.
- Offer the student opportunities to see you one-to-one away from the sometimes hurly-burly environment of the classroom.

Both teacher and student gather information in the same way. They notice detail using their senses – fully absorbed in what they can see, hear and feel. Both use their experience to understand their environment. They both live in the present. The teacher is naturally practical, sensible and realistic in their teaching style and encourages their students to follow suit. A solid, workmanlike relationship develops with both teacher and student mutually understanding what each needs to do to get the job done. For the teacher to get the best out of their naturally grounded student they need to:

- Show how learning can be applied in the real world.
- Allow the student opportunities to repeat and practise until satisfied they are competent.
- Encourage the use of imagination as a useful process (it's not wasting time).

Both teacher and student are concerned first with people and relationships before the task and subject content. Koala teachers like to form personal relationships with all their students, unless they don't like the student (**F** teachers are more inclined than **T** preference teachers to have their favourites!). Because they operate at an emotional level these teachers are more likely to make promises to students, overstretch themselves and even do work the students should be doing themselves. Teacher and student both enjoy a classroom atmosphere that is warm and friendly. Compliments are likely to go in both directions boosting the confidence of teacher as well as student. The Koala student needs to feel they like their teacher and that the teacher likes them too. If this happens they'll work harder but if they don't they may switch off completely. This explains why a student can be top of the class one year (with a teacher they like) and take little interest the following year when they change teacher. For the teacher to get the best out of their relationship-focused Koala student they need to:

- Offer learning situations that allow for the use of empathy, collaboration and teamworking.
- Provide ample and regular praise while offering tactful support to overcome any blind-spots.
- Influence by appealing to the strength of your personal belief in the student (don't let me down, I know you can do it, I like you).

The **J** teacher takes pleasure in organising time. They are structured, work out a plan and stick to it, often aided by an impressive to-do list. Their classroom is usually a calm place. The subject will be broken down into lesson-sized chunks and the year planned out whether or not an Ofsted inspector is due. Many **J** students are reassured by their teacher's organisational zeal. They simply adopt the schedule and deliver their side of the bargain, generally completing all tasks on time. Interestingly, some **J**'s will baulk at their teacher's well-intentioned thoroughness. They would like to create their own plan and work to it rather than adopt someone else's. This is due to the **J**'s desire for control. So two **J**'s together can clash, though at least all their work will be done. Most secondary schools require students to be so organised that two **J**'s are the best combination. For the teacher to get the best out of their naturally organised student they need to:

- Enjoy your shared desire for order, neatness and respecting deadlines.
- Allow the student independence in planning their work in their own way if they really want to.
- Be prepared to adjust your own plans if external events interfere with your careful preparations (and encourage the student to also embrace flexibility occasionally).
- Shake things up now and again to prevent predictability becoming boredom.
- Avoid making quick decisions about what needs to be done before considering all of the options.

50
Koala teacher with Falcon student
ISFJ and ENTP

Difference in all four personality preferences can so easily be a recipe for conflict in the classroom. A naturally confident and assertive Falcon student with a fundamentally placid and consensual Koala teacher could easily clash. The teacher needs to remember that the eternally restless and fidgety student is not trying to destroy everything the teacher is attempting to create; they are expressing their true preferences. If the teacher can't find a way to incorporate the student's preferences they will merely become bored and potentially even more disruptive. Opposites can also learn much from each other. The nurturing Koala teacher can bring a calm and steady focus while the iconoclastic Falcon can inject jest, energy and fun. The right mix benefits the whole class. For the teacher to get the best out of the liveliest of students they need to:

- Listen patiently and enthusiastically to the student's brainstorming and ramblings.
- Stay open to 'silly' ideas to see where they lead – the student is thinking out loud and this is how they learn best.
- Also offer your own thoughts; if you need a timeout ask for one.
- Encourage the student to think things through before talking otherwise they'll hog the lesson.
- Steer the student away from controversial subjects/topics, especially in group discussions.
- Build in plenty of opportunities during lessons for the **E** students to talk things through with other **E** preferences.

The teacher likes to use their experience to make sense of what they notice. Koalas live in the present. The teacher is naturally practical, sequential, sensible and realistic in style and encourages their students to follow suit. The **N** student will at best find this challenging and at worst find it boring. The teacher is likely to see the student as a daydreamer, lost in their own world or 'away with the fairies'. They should resist the temptation to castigate their student because this is how they take in information and make sense of the world. In the right context daydreaming can lead to the invention of cars, planes, medicines and computers. For the teacher to get the best out of their naturally imaginative student they need to:

- Embrace the imagination and insight of the student and what it can bring to the lesson.
- Encourage the student to become aware of the important contribution of the **S** approach (the value of facts, details, procedure, experiments, applying experience, structure, the step-by-step model).

The teacher is concerned with relationship then task whereas the student is the other way round. The teacher must learn to accept that the student is different; not cold, blunt and argumentative, but different and focused on task first. If the teacher can accept this the relationship can be really positive for both teacher and student. For the teacher to get the best out of their essentially ebullient student they need to:

- Offer targeted compliments. Just saying everything is great will not impress or help the student; in fact, it can result in the student not respecting the teacher, concluding they lie and/or are a soft touch. When you praise you may be pressed for proof!
- Be logical and objective rather than emotional in discussions.
- Accept that if the student challenges you it is probably to clarify their thoughts rather than as a slight to your authority or character. Perhaps ask 'What would you do to improve/change this?' or 'What do you think?' Once they've clarified their thoughts they may be ready to ask and absorb what you think.
- Work in ways that test their skill and knowledge competitively (they raise their game).
- Help them understand that 50% of people are **F** preference and can interpret feedback as criticism.

The Koala teacher takes pleasure in scheduling time. They are organised and decisive. They work out a plan and stick to it, usually aided by their meticulous preparation. Their classroom may resemble a well-oiled machine. The subject will be clearly broken down into lesson-sized chunks. The **P** student will either respond:

- Positively by accepting your expertise and understanding the long-term benefits they'll reap.
- Passively by just accepting your structure/plan for an easy life without really buying into the content or process you are offering.
- Negatively by rejecting you, your structure/plan and subject completely (even if they're physically in your room they will not engage and participate).

For the teacher to get the best out of their naturally laid-back student they should note the student doesn't just like options and choice; they need them or they start to itch, squirm and rebel. The secondary school environment is difficult enough for **P** preference students so teachers can help soften the pressure. To help:

- Provide as much flexibility as possible (multiple choice homework tasks, choice within the lesson).
- Avoid giving out detailed schedules (they'll just lose it anyway!).
- Don't be more picky with detail than is absolutely necessary.
- Shake things up now and again to prevent predictability becoming boredom. Introduce random surprises and changes.
- Provide tips to help the student organise and manage their time to complete important work without a last-minute rush.

51
Koala teacher with Clownfish student
ISFJ and ENFP

Sharing one preference **F** means student and teacher are united in their desire to create a nurturing and personal relationship. The potent clash of the remaining preferences – teacher craving quiet structure and stability and student craving excitement and chaos – is potentially corrosive. When the teacher embraces the Clownfish's spontaneity and imagination the whole class can benefit. For the Koala teacher to get the best out of their innately excitable student they need to:

- Listen patiently and enthusiastically to the student's ideas, brainstorming and ramblings.
- Stay open to 'silly' ideas to see where they lead – the student is thinking out loud and this is how they process information and learn best.
- Also offer your own thoughts; if you need a timeout ask for one.
- Encourage the student to think things through before talking otherwise they'll hog the lesson.
- Steer the student away from controversial subjects/topics, especially in group discussions.
- Build in plenty of opportunities during lessons for the **E** students to talk things through with other **E** preferences.

The teacher likes to use their experience to make sense of what they notice. They both live in the present. The teacher is naturally sequential and realistic in style and encourages their students to follow suit. The **N** student will at best find this challenging and at worst find it boring. The teacher is likely to see the student as a daydreamer, lost in their own world or 'away with the fairies'. They should resist the temptation to castigate their student because this is how they take in information and make sense of the world. In the right context daydreaming can lead to the invention of cars, planes, medicines and computers. For the teacher to get the best out of their naturally imaginative student they need to:

- Incorporate the imagination and insight of the student and what it can bring to the lesson.

■ Encourage the student to become aware of the important contribution of the **S** approach (the value of facts, details, procedure, experiments, applying experience, structure, the step-by-step model).

The teacher and student are both concerned first with people and relationships before the task/subject content. They like to form personal relationships with all their students, unless they don't like the student (**F** teachers are more inclined than **T** preference teachers to have their favourites!). Because they operate at an emotional level these teachers are more likely to make promises to students, overstretch themselves and even do work the students should be doing themselves. Teacher and student both enjoy a classroom atmosphere that is warm and friendly. Compliments are likely to go in both directions boosting the confidence of teacher as well as student. The Clownfish needs to feel they like their teacher and that the teacher likes them too. If this happens they'll work harder but if they don't they may switch off completely. This explains why a student can be top of the class one year (with a teacher they like) and show no interest at all in the subject the following year when they change teacher. For the teacher to get the best out of their relationship-focused student they need to:

■ Prepare learning situations that allow for the use of empathy, collaboration and teamworking.

■ Provide ample and regular praise while offering tactful support to overcome any blind-spots.

■ Influence by appealing to the strength of your personal belief in the student (don't let me down, I know you can do it, I like you).

The **J** teacher takes pleasure in scheduling their time. They are organised and decisive. They work out a plan and stick to it, usually aided by their meticulous preparation. Their classroom may resemble a well-oiled machine. The subject will be clearly broken down into lesson-sized chunks. The **P** student will either respond:

■ Positively by accepting your expertise and understanding the long-term benefits they'll reap.

■ Passively by just accepting your structure/plan for an easy life without really buying into the content or process you are offering.

■ Negatively by rejecting you, your structure/plan and subject completely (even if they're physically in your room they will not engage and participate).

For the teacher to get the best out of their innately laid-back student they should note the student doesn't just like options and choice; they need them or they start to itch, squirm and rebel. The secondary school environment is difficult enough for **P** preference students so teachers can help soften the pressure. To help:

■ Provide as much flexibility as possible (multiple choice homework tasks, choice within the lesson).

■ Avoid giving out detailed schedules (they'll just lose it anyway!).

■ Don't be more picky with detail than is absolutely necessary.

■ Shake things up now and again to prevent predictability becoming boredom. Introduce random surprises and changes.

■ Help the student identify simple effective time-management methods to ensure they succeed.

52
Koala teacher with Polar Bear student
ISFJ and ISTJ

The Koala and Polar Bear share three of the four preferences. They both value routine, tradition and hard work. As long as the teacher respects the student's need for privacy and corrects any errors quietly their relationship should be smooth and business-like. For the teacher to get the best out of their naturally cautious student they need to:

■ Help the student develop independence while being aware of the needs of others.

■ Allow the student plenty of time to think through their thoughts.

■ Share your ideas and thoughts regularly to ensure you both know what you're doing.

■ Take time to clarify your thoughts but don't dodge confrontation; if something needs to be said be calm and direct as you deliver it.

■ Use non-verbal communication – smiles and gestures are reassuring to **I** students. You can even use sticky notes/emails to pass on feedback.

■ Provide opportunities for the student to see you one-to-one away from the sometimes hectic environment of the classroom.

Both teacher and student gather information in the same way. They notice detail using their senses (aware of what they can see, hear and feel) and they both use their experience to make sense of what they notice. They both live in the present. The teacher is naturally practical, sequential, sensible and realistic in their teaching style and encourages their students to follow suit. A solid, workman-like relationship develops with both teacher and student mutually understanding what each needs to do to get the job done. For the teacher to get the best out of their grounded student they need to:

■ Demonstrate how learning can be applied in the real world.

■ Allow the student opportunities to repeat and practise until satisfied they are competent.

■ Encourage the use of imagination as a useful process (it's not wasting time).

The teacher is concerned with relationship then task whereas the student is the other way round. The teacher must learn to accept that the student is different; not cold, blunt and unfriendly, but different and focused on task first. If the teacher can accept this the relationship can be really positive for both teacher and student. For the teacher to get the best out of their inherently objective student they need to:

■ Offer targeted compliments. Just saying everything is great will not impress or help the student; in fact, it can result in the student not respecting the teacher, concluding they lie and/or are a soft touch. When you praise you may be pressed for proof!

■ Be logical and objective rather than emotional in discussions.

■ Accept that if the student challenges you it is probably to clarify their thoughts rather than a slight to your authority or character. Perhaps ask 'What would you do to improve/change this?' or 'What do you think?' Once they've clarified their thoughts they may be ready to ask and absorb what you think.

■ Work in ways that test their skill and knowledge competitively (they raise their game).

■ Help them understand that 50% of people are **F** preference and can interpret feedback as criticism.

The **J** teacher takes pleasure in organising time. They are structured and decisive. They work out a plan and stick to it, often aided by an impressive to-do list. Their classroom is usually an organised place. The subject will probably be broken down into lesson-sized chunks and the year planned out whether an Ofsted inspector is due or not. Many **J** students are reassured by their teacher's organisational zeal. They simply adopt the schedule and deliver their side of the bargain, generally completing all tasks on time. Interestingly, some **J**'s will baulk at their teacher's well-intentioned thoroughness. They would like to create their own plan and work to it rather than adopt someone else's. This is due to the **J**'s desire for control. So two **J**'s together can clash, though at least all their work will be done. Most secondary schools require students to be so organised that two **J**'s are the best combination. For the teacher to get the best out of their intrinsically organised Polar Bear student they need to:

■ Enjoy your shared desire for order, neatness and respecting deadlines.

■ Allow the student independence in planning their work in their own way if they really want to.

■ Be prepared to adjust your own plans if external events interfere with your careful preparations (and encourage the student to also embrace flexibility occasionally).

■ Shake things up now and again to prevent predictability becoming boredom.

■ Avoid making quick decisions about what needs to be done before considering all of the options.

53
Koala teacher with Teddy Bear student
ISFJ and ESFJ

Bears share much in common. They are down-to-earth, orderly and hard-working which helps to keep things moving in the classroom. Koalas and Teddies also share a desire to develop a nurturing and caring group. Clashes are likely to be based on their different energy levels. The socially adept Teddy is inclined to chat instead of working or chat while they work. This can tire and annoy the more focused teacher. To get the best out of their naturally talkative student the teacher can:

■ Listen patiently and enthusiastically to the Teddy's stories, observations and ramblings.

- Stay open to the student as they think out loud as this is how they learn best.
- Also offer your own thoughts; if you need a timeout ask for one.
- Encourage the student to think things through before talking otherwise they'll hog the lesson.
- Steer the student away from controversial subjects/topics, especially in group discussions.
- Build in plenty of opportunities during lessons for the **E** students to talk things through with other **E** preferences.

Both teacher and student gather information in the same way. They notice detail using their senses (aware of what they can see, hear and feel) and they both use their experience to make sense of what they notice. They both live in the present. The teacher is naturally sequential, sensible and realistic in their teaching style and encourages their students to follow suit. A solid, workman-like relationship develops with both teacher and student mutually understanding what each needs to do to get the job done. For the teacher to get the best out of their innately grounded student they need to:

- Demonstrate how learning can be applied in the real world.
- Allow the student opportunities to repeat and practise until satisfied they are competent.
- Encourage the use of imagination as a useful process (it's not wasting time).

The teacher and student are both concerned first with people and relationships before the task/subject content. Teachers like to form personal relationships with all their students, unless they don't like the student (**F** teachers are more inclined than **T** preference teachers to have their favourites!). Because they operate at an emotional level these teachers are more likely to make promises to students, overstretch themselves and even do work the students should be doing themselves. Teacher and student both enjoy a classroom atmosphere that is warm and friendly. Compliments are likely to go in both directions boosting the confidence of teacher as well as student. The Teddy needs to feel they like their teacher and that the teacher likes them too. If this happens they'll work harder but if not they may switch off completely. This explains why a student can be top of the class one year (with a teacher they like) and show no interest at all in the subject the following year when they change teacher. For the teacher to get the best out of their relationship-focused student they need to:

- Offer learning situations that allow for the use of empathy, collaboration and teamworking.
- Provide ample and regular praise while offering tactful support to overcome any blind-spots.
- Persuade by appealing to the strength of your personal belief in the student (don't let me down, I know you can do it, I like you).

The **J** teacher takes pleasure in organising time. They are structured and decisive. They work out a plan and stick to it, often aided by an impressive to-do list. Their classroom is usually an organised place. The subject will probably be broken down into lesson-sized chunks and the year planned out whether an Ofsted inspector is due or not. Many **J** students are reassured by their teacher's organisational zeal. They simply adopt the schedule and deliver their side of the bargain, generally completing all tasks on time. Interestingly, some **J**'s will baulk at their teacher's well-intentioned thoroughness. They would like to create their own plan and work to it rather than adopt someone else's. This is due to the **J**'s desire for control. So two **J**'s together can clash, though at least all their work will be done. Most secondary schools require students to be so organised that two **J**'s are the best combination. For the teacher to get the best out of their characteristically organised student they need to:

- Enjoy your shared desire for order, neatness and respecting deadlines.
- Allow the student independence in planning their work in their own way if they really want to.
- Be prepared to adjust your own plans if external events interfere with your careful preparations (and encourage the student to also embrace flexibility occasionally).
- Shake things up now and again to prevent predictability becoming boredom.
- Avoid making quick decisions about what needs to be done before considering all of the options.

54
Koala teacher with Tawny Owl student
ISFJ and INTP

The Koala and Tawny Owl only share one preference. They both think things through carefully before contributing. The remaining differences can lead to clashes. The conservative Koala can be surprised by the Tawny Owl's investigative and tenacious imagination or embrace their different way of exploring and understanding the world around them. For the teacher to get the best out of their naturally lively student they need to:

- Respect the student's need for privacy and independence.
- Allow the student plenty of time to think through their thoughts.
- Share your ideas and thoughts regularly to ensure you both know what you're doing.
- Take time to clarify your thoughts but don't dodge confrontation; if something needs to be said be calm and direct as you deliver it.
- Use non-verbal communication – smiles and gestures are reassuring to **I** students. You can even use sticky notes/emails to pass on feedback.
- Provide opportunities for the student to see you one-to-one away from the sometimes hectic environment of the classroom.

The teacher likes to use their experience to make sense of what they notice. They both live in the present. The teacher is naturally practical, sequential and realistic in style and encourages their students to follow suit. The **N** student will at best find this challenging and at worst find it boring. The teacher is likely to see the student as a daydreamer, lost in their own world or 'away with the fairies'. They should resist the temptation to castigate their student because this is how they take in information and make sense of the world. In the right context daydreaming can lead to the invention of cars, planes, medicines and computers. For the teacher to get the best out of their imaginative student they need to:

- Embrace the imagination and insight of the student and what it can bring to the lesson.
- Help the student to become aware of the important contribution of the **S** approach (the value of facts, details, procedure, experiments, applying experience, structure, the step-by-step model).

The teacher is concerned with relationship then task whereas the student is the other way round. The teacher must learn to accept that the student is different; not cold, blunt and unfriendly, but different and focused on task first. If the teacher can accept this the relationship can be really positive for both teacher and student.

For the teacher to get the best out of their intrinsically analytical student they need to:

- Offer targeted compliments. Just saying everything is great will not impress or help the student; in fact, it can result in the student not respecting the teacher, concluding they lie and/or are a soft touch. If you praise you may be pressed for proof!
- Be logical and objective rather than emotional in discussions.
- Accept that if the student challenges you it is probably to clarify their thoughts rather than a slur on your character. Perhaps ask 'What would you do to improve/change this?' or 'What do you think?' Once they've clarified their thoughts they may be ready to ask and absorb what you think.
- Engage in ways that test their skill and knowledge competitively (they raise their game).
- Help them appreciate that half the population are **F** preference and can interpret feedback as criticism.

The **J** teacher takes pleasure in scheduling their time. They are organised and decisive. They work out a plan and stick to it, usually aided by their meticulous preparation. Their classroom may resemble a well-oiled machine. The subject will be deliberately broken down into lesson-sized chunks. The **P** student will either respond:

- Positively by accepting your expertise and understanding the long-term benefits they'll reap.
- Passively by just accepting your structure/plan for an easy life without really buying into the content or process you are offering.
- Negatively by rejecting you, your structure/plan and subject completely (even if they're physically in your room they will not engage and participate).

For the teacher to get the best out of their naturally laid-back student they should note the student doesn't just like options and choice; they need them or they start to itch, squirm and rebel. The secondary school environment is difficult enough for **P** preference students so teachers can help soften the pressure. To help:

- Provide as much flexibility as possible (multiple choice homework tasks, choice within the lesson).
- Introduce random surprises and changes.
- Avoid giving out detailed schedules (they'll just lose it anyway!).
- Don't be more picky with detail than is absolutely necessary.
- Shake things up now and again to prevent predictability becoming boredom.

55
Koala teacher with Dolphin student
ISFJ and ENFJ

The Koala teacher shares two preferences with their Dolphin student. Both are friendly, warm and efficient. The contrast is in their way of taking in information – the quiet and realistic Koala versus the effervescent and imaginative Dolphin. For the Koala teacher to get the best out of their sociable student they need to:

■ Listen patiently and enthusiastically to the Dolphin's ideas and ramblings.

■ Stay open to 'silly' ideas to see where they lead – the student is thinking out loud and this is how they learn best.

■ Also offer your own thoughts; if you need a timeout ask for one.

■ Push the student to think things through before talking otherwise they'll hog the lesson.

■ Plan plenty of opportunities during lessons for the **E** students to talk things through with other **E** preferences.

The Koala teacher likes to use their experience to make sense of what they notice. They both live in the present. The teacher is naturally practical, sequential, sensible and realistic in style and encourages their students to follow suit. The **N** student will at best find this challenging and at worst find it boring. The teacher is likely to see the student as a daydreamer, lost in their own world or 'away with the fairies'. They should resist the temptation to castigate their student because this is how they take in information and make sense of the world. In the right context daydreaming can lead to amazing inventions. For the teacher to get the best out of their inherently imaginative student they need to:

■ Embrace the imagination and insight of the student and what it can bring to the lesson.

■ Encourage the student to become aware of the important contribution of the **S** approach (the value of facts, details, procedure, experiments, applying experience, structure, the step-by-step model).

The teacher and student are both concerned first with people and relationships before the task/subject content. Teachers like to form personal relationships with all their students, unless they don't like the student (**F** teachers are more inclined than **T** preference teachers to have their favourites!). Because they operate at an emotional level these teachers are more likely to make promises to students, overstretch themselves and even do work the students should be doing themselves. Teacher and student both enjoy a classroom atmosphere that is warm and friendly. Compliments are likely to go in both directions boosting the confidence of teacher as well as student. The Dolphin needs to feel they like their teacher and that the teacher likes them too. If this happens they'll work harder but if they don't they may switch off completely. This explains why a student can be top of the class one year (with a teacher they like) and show no interest at all in the subject the following year when they change teacher. For the teacher to get the best out of their relationship-focused student they need to:

■ Offer learning situations that allow for the use of empathy, collaboration and teamworking.

■ Provide ample and regular praise while offering tactful support to overcome any blind-spots.

■ Persuade by appealing to the strength of your personal belief in the student (don't let me down, I know you can do it, I like you).

■ Don't brush issues under the carpet – discuss them early before they become major problems.

The **J** teacher takes pleasure in organising time. They are structured and decisive. They work out a plan and stick to it, often aided by an impressive to-do list. Their classroom is usually an organised place. The subject will probably be broken down into lesson-sized chunks and the year planned out whether an Ofsted inspector is due or not. Many **J** students are reassured by their teacher's organisational zeal. They simply adopt the schedule and deliver their side of the bargain, generally completing all tasks on time. Interestingly, some Dolphins will baulk at their teacher's well-intentioned thoroughness. They would like to create their own plan and work to it rather than adopt someone else's. This is due to the **J**'s desire for control. So two **J** preferences together can clash, though at least all their work will be done. Most secondary schools require students to be so organised that two **J** preferences are the best combination. For the teacher to get the best out of their characteristically organised student they need to:

■ Enjoy your shared desire for order, neatness and respecting deadlines.

■ Offer the student independence in planning their work in their own way if they really want to.

■ Be prepared to adjust your own plans if external events interfere with your careful preparations (and encourage the student to also embrace flexibility occasionally).

■ Shake things up now and again to prevent predictability becoming boredom.

■ Avoid making quick decisions about what needs to be done before considering all of the options.

56
Koala teacher with Tiger student
ISFJ and ISTP

The Koala teacher shares two preferences with their Tiger student. Both are down to earth and communicate literally. The differences in the conservative approach of the teacher and the more rebellious and adventurous student can lead to problems. All Cats seek action and often like to learn by moving and doing, so the Koala needs to provide ample opportunities for action to prevent boredom from setting in. For the teacher to get the best out of their inherently reflective student they need to:

■ Respect the student's need for privacy and independence.

■ Allow the student plenty of time to think through their thoughts.

■ Share your ideas and thoughts regularly to ensure you both know what you're doing.

■ Take time to clarify your thoughts but don't avoid confrontation; if something needs to be said be calm and direct as you deliver it.

■ Use non-verbal communication – smiles and gestures are reassuring to **I** students. You can even use sticky notes/emails to pass on feedback.

■ Suggest the student can see you one-to-one away from the sometimes hectic environment of the classroom.

Both teacher and student gather information in the same way. They notice detail using their senses (aware of what they can see, hear and feel) and they both use their experience to make sense of what they notice. They both live in the present. The teacher is naturally practical, sequential, sensible and realistic in their teaching style and encourages their students to follow suit. A solid, workman-like relationship develops with both teacher and student mutually understanding what each needs to do to get the job done. For the teacher to get the best out of their down-to-earth student they need to:

■ Demonstrate how learning can be applied in the real world.

■ Allow the student opportunities to repeat and practise until satisfied they are competent.

■ Encourage the use of imagination as a useful process (it's not wasting time).

The Koala teacher is concerned with relationship then task whereas the student is the other way round. The teacher must learn to accept that the student is different; not cold, blunt and unfriendly, but different and focused on task first. If the teacher can accept this the relationship can be really positive for both teacher and student. For the teacher to get the best out of their naturally grounded student they need to:

■ Offer targeted compliments. Just saying everything is great will not impress or help the student; in fact, it can result in the student not respecting the teacher, concluding they lie and/or are a soft touch. When you praise you may be pressed for proof!

■ Be logical and objective rather than emotional in discussions.

■ Accept that if the student challenges you it is probably to clarify their thoughts rather than besmirch your validity as a human being. Perhaps ask 'What would you do to improve/change this?' or 'What do you think?' Once they've clarified their thoughts they may be ready to ask and absorb what you think.

■ Work in ways that test their skill and knowledge competitively (they raise their game).

■ Help them understand that 50% of people are **F** preference and can interpret feedback as criticism.

The **J** teacher takes pleasure in scheduling their time. They are organised and decisive. They work out a plan and stick to it, usually aided by their meticulous preparation. Their classroom may resemble a well-oiled machine. The subject will be clearly broken down into lesson-sized chunks. The **P** student will either respond:

■ Positively by accepting your expertise and understanding the long-term benefits they'll reap.

■ Passively by just accepting your structure/plan for an easy life without really buying into the content or process you are offering.

■ Negatively by rejecting you, your structure/plan and subject completely (even if they're physically in your room they will not engage and participate).

For the teacher to get the best out of their instinctively laid-back student they should note the student doesn't just like options and choice; they need them or they start to itch, squirm and rebel. The secondary school environment is difficult enough for **P** preference students so teachers can help soften the pressure. To help:

■ Provide as much flexibility as possible (multiple choice homework tasks, choice within the lesson).

■ Introduce random surprises and changes.

■ Avoid giving out detailed schedules (they'll just lose it anyway!).

■ Don't be more picky with detail than is absolutely necessary.

■ Shake things up now and again to prevent predictability becoming boredom.

57
Koala teacher with Eagle student
ISFJ and ENTJ

The Koala is likely to find Birds the most challenging of students. The naturally confident, strategic and assertive Eagle student can question the systems and rules carefully introduced by the Koala teacher. The Eagle can't really help being a leader so a teacher who finds a way to incorporate this trait will create a positive learning environment for all students. For the teacher to get the best out of their inherently lively student they need to:

■ Listen patiently and enthusiastically to the student's riff and rambles.

■ Stay open to 'silly' ideas to see where they lead – the student is thinking out loud and this is how they learn best.

■ Also offer your own thoughts; if you need a timeout ask for one.

■ Encourage the student to think things through before talking otherwise they'll hog the lesson.

■ Steer the student away from controversial subjects/topics, especially in group discussions.

■ Build in plenty of opportunities during lessons for the **E** students to talk things through with other **E** preferences.

The teacher is concerned with relationship then task whereas the student is the other way round. The teacher must learn to accept that the student is different; not cold, blunt and unfriendly, but different and focused on task first. If the teacher can accept this the relationship can be really positive for both teacher and student. For the teacher to get the best out of their naturally assertive student they need to:

■ Offer targeted compliments. Just saying everything is great will not impress or help the student; in fact, it can result in the student not respecting the teacher, concluding they lie and/or are a soft touch. When you praise you may be pressed for proof!

■ Be logical and objective rather than emotional in discussions.

■ Accept that if the student challenges you it is probably to clarify their thoughts rather than a slight to your authority or character. Perhaps ask 'What would you do to improve/change this?' or 'What do you think?' Once they've clarified their thoughts they may be ready to ask and absorb what you think.

■ Work in ways that test their skill and knowledge competitively (they raise their game).

■ Help them understand that 50% of people are **F** preference and can interpret feedback as criticism.

The Koala teacher takes pleasure in organising time. They are structured and decisive. They work out a plan and stick to it, often aided by an impressive to-do list. Their classroom is usually an organised place. The subject will probably be meticulously broken down into lesson-sized chunks and the year planned out. Many **J** students are reassured by their teacher's organisational zeal. They simply adopt the schedule and deliver their side of the bargain, generally completing all tasks on time. Interestingly, some **J**'s will baulk at their teacher's well-intentioned thoroughness. They would like to create their own plan and work to it rather than adopt another's plan. This is due to the **J**'s desire for control. So two **J**'s together can clash, though at least all their work will be done. Most secondary schools require students to be so organised that two **J**'s are the best combination. For the teacher to get the best out of their fundamentally organised student they need to:

■ Allow the student independence in planning their work in their own way if they really want to.

■ Be prepared to adjust your own plans if external events interfere with your careful preparations (and encourage the student to also embrace flexibility occasionally).

■ Shake things up now and again to prevent predictability becoming boredom.

■ Avoid making quick decisions about what needs to be done before considering all of the options.

■ Enjoy your shared desire for order, neatness and respecting deadlines.

58
Koala teacher with Cat student
ISFJ and ISFP

The Koala and Cat share three of the four preferences. Both like to work on tasks in a friendly and structured environment. The differences in the conservative approach of the teacher and the more adventurous student can lead to problems. All Cats seek action and often like to learn by moving and doing, so the Koala needs to provide ample opportunities for action to prevent boredom from setting in. For the teacher to get the best out of their naturally self-contained student they need to:

■ Respect the student's need for privacy and independence.

■ Allow the student plenty of time to think through their thoughts.

■ Share your ideas and thoughts regularly to ensure you both know what you're doing.

■ Take time to clarify your thoughts but don't avoid confrontation; if something needs to be said be calm and direct as you deliver it.

■ Use non-verbal communication – smiles and gestures are reassuring to **I** students. You can even use sticky notes/emails to pass on feedback.

■ Provide opportunities for the student to see you one-to-one away from the sometimes hectic environment of the classroom.

Both teacher and student gather information in the same way. They notice detail using their senses (aware of what they can see, hear and feel) and they both use their experience to make sense of what they see. They both live in the present. The teacher is naturally practical, sequential, sensible and realistic in their teaching style and encourages their students to follow suit. A solid, workman-like relationship develops with both teacher and student mutually understanding what each needs to do to get the job done. For the teacher to get the best out of their intrinsically grounded student they need to:

■ Encourage the use of imagination as a useful process (it's not time-wasting).

■ Demonstrate how learning can be applied in the real world.

■ Allow the student opportunities to repeat and practise until satisfied they are competent.

The teacher and student are both concerned first with people and relationships before the task/subject content. They like to form personal relationships with all their students, unless they don't like the student (**F** teachers are more inclined than **T** preference teachers to have their favourites!). Because they operate at an emotional level these teachers are more likely to make promises to students, overstretch themselves and even do work the students should be doing themselves. Teacher and student both enjoy a classroom atmosphere that is warm and friendly. Compliments are likely to go in both directions boosting the confidence of teacher as well as student. The Cat needs to feel they like their teacher and that the teacher likes them too. For the teacher to get the best out of their essentially relationship-focused student they need to:

■ Offer learning situations that allow for the use of empathy, collaboration and teamworking.

■ Provide ample and regular praise while offering tactful support to overcome any blind-spots.

■ Motivate by stressing the strength of your personal belief in the student (don't let me down, I know you can do it, I like you).

The Koala teacher takes pleasure in scheduling their time. They are organised and decisive. They work out a plan and stick to it, usually aided by their meticulous preparation. Their classroom may resemble a well-oiled machine. The subject will be clearly broken down into lesson-sized chunks. The **P** student will either respond:

■ Positively by accepting your expertise and understanding the long-term benefits they'll reap.

■ Passively by just accepting your structure/plan for an easy life without really buying into the content or process you are offering.

■ Negatively by rejecting you, your structure/plan and subject completely (even if they're physically in your room they will not engage and participate).

For the teacher to get the best out of their inherently laid-back student they should note the student doesn't just like options and choice; they need them or they start to itch, squirm and rebel. The secondary school environment is difficult enough for **P** preference students so teachers can help soften the pressure. To help:

■ Provide as much flexibility as possible (multiple choice homework tasks, choice within the lesson).

■ Avoid giving out detailed schedules (they'll just lose it anyway!).

■ Don't be more picky with detail than is absolutely necessary.

■ Shake things up now and again to prevent predictability becoming boredom. Introduce random surprises and changes.

■ Identify simple ways the student can organise and manage their time to complete important work without a last-minute rush.

59
Koala teacher with Black Bear student
ISFJ and ESTJ

Bears share much in common. They are down-to-earth, orderly and hard-working which helps to keep things moving in the classroom. Koalas and Black Bears differ in their preferred approach to tasks. The Koala is reserved and people centred whereas the Black Bear is forthright and task centred. This can lead to conflict but the following tips should minimise misunderstanding. For the teacher to get the best out of their driven student they need to:

■ Listen patiently and enthusiastically to the student's plans, ideas and advice.

■ Stay open to ambitious contributions to see where they lead – the student is thinking out loud and this is how they learn best.

■ Also offer your own thoughts; if you need a timeout ask for one.

■ Encourage the student to think things through before talking otherwise they'll hog the lesson.

■ Steer the student away from controversial subjects/topics, especially in group discussions.

■ Build in plenty of opportunities during lessons for the **E** students to talk things through with other **E** preferences.

Both teacher and student gather information in the same way. They notice detail using their senses (aware of what they can see, hear and feel) and they both use their experience to make sense of what they see. They both live in the present. The teacher is naturally practical, sequential, sensible and realistic in their teaching style and encourages their students to follow suit. A solid, workman-like relationship develops with both teacher and student mutually understanding what each needs to do to get the job done. For the teacher

to get the best out of their naturally grounded student they need to:

■ Demonstrate how learning can be applied in the real world.

■ Allow the student opportunities to repeat and practise until satisfied they are competent.

■ Encourage the use of imagination as a useful process (it's not wasting time).

The Koala is concerned with relationship then task whereas the Black Bear is the other way round. The teacher must learn to accept that the student is different; not cold, blunt and unfriendly, but different and focused on task first. If the teacher can accept this the relationship can be really positive for both teacher and student. For the teacher to get the best out of their characteristically assertive student they need to:

■ Offer targeted compliments. Just saying everything is great will not impress or help the student; in fact, it can result in the student not respecting the teacher, concluding they lie and/or are a soft touch. When you praise you may be pressed for proof!

■ Be logical and objective rather than emotional in discussions.

■ Help them understand that 50% of people are **F** preference and can interpret feedback as criticism.

■ Accept that if the student challenges you it is probably to clarify their thoughts, not to embarrass you. Perhaps ask 'What would you do to improve/change this?' or 'What do you think?' Once they've clarified their thoughts they may be ready to ask and absorb what you think.

■ Work in ways that test their skill and knowledge competitively (they raise their game).

The **J** teacher takes pleasure in organising time. They are structured and decisive. They work out a plan and stick to it, often aided by an impressive to-do list. Their classroom is usually an organised place. The subject will probably be broken down into lesson-sized chunks and the year planned out whether an Ofsted inspector is due or not. Many **J** students are reassured by their teacher's organisational zeal. They simply adopt the schedule and deliver their side of the bargain, generally completing all tasks on time. Interestingly, some **J**'s will baulk at their teacher's well-intentioned thoroughness. They would like to create their own plan and work to it rather than adopt someone else's. This is due to the **J**'s desire for control. So two **J**'s together can clash, though at least all their work will be done. Most secondary schools require students to be so organised that two **J** preferences are the best combination. For the teacher to get the best out of their naturally organised student they need to:

■ Enjoy your shared desire for order, neatness and respecting deadlines.

■ Allow the student independence in planning their work in their own way if they really want to.

■ Avoid making quick decisions about what needs to be done before considering all of the options.

■ Be prepared to adjust your own plans if external events interfere with your careful preparations (and encourage the student to also embrace flexibility occasionally).

■ Stir things up now and again to prevent predictability becoming boredom.

60
Koala teacher with Seal student
ISFJ and INFP

The Koala and Seal share a desire to work in a quietly nurturing environment. Seals are the biggest daydreamers and will often lose themselves in their thoughts. This could annoy the more focused and practical Koala. However, Seals can't really stay in the 'real world' for too long. Koalas who incorporate the Seal's active imagination will benefit. To get the best out of their naturally creative student they need to:

■ Respect the student's need for privacy and independence.

■ Allow the student plenty of time to think through their thoughts.

■ Share your ideas and thoughts regularly to ensure you both know what you're doing.

■ Take time to clarify your thoughts but don't avoid confrontation; if something needs to be said be calm and direct as you deliver it.

■ Use non-verbal communication – smiles and gestures are reassuring to **I** students. You can even use sticky notes/emails to pass on feedback.

■ Provide opportunities for the student to see you one-to-one away from the sometimes hectic environment of the classroom.

The teacher likes to use their experience to make sense of what they notice. They both live in the present. The teacher is naturally practical, sequential, sensible and realistic in style and encourages their students to follow suit. The **N** student will at best find this challenging and at worst find it boring. The teacher is likely to see the student as a daydreamer, lost in their own world or 'away with the fairies'. They should resist the temptation to castigate their student because this is how they take in information and make sense of the world. In the right context daydreaming can lead to amazing new ideas and inventions. For the teacher to get the best out of their inherently imaginative student they need to:

■ Embrace the imagination and insight of the student and what it can bring to the lesson.

■ Encourage the student to become aware of the important contribution of the **S** approach (the value of facts, details, procedure, experiments, applying experience, structure, the step-by-step model).

The teacher and student are both concerned first with people and relationships before the task/subject content. They like to form personal relationships with all their students, unless they don't like the student (**F** teachers are more inclined than **T** preference teachers to have their favourites!). Because they operate at an emotional level these teachers are more likely to make promises to students, overstretch themselves and even do work the students should be doing themselves. Teacher and student both enjoy a classroom atmosphere that is warm and friendly. Compliments are likely to go in both directions boosting the confidence of teacher as well as student. The Seal needs to feel they like their teacher and that the teacher likes them too. For the teacher to get the best out of their relationship-focused student they need to:

- Offer learning situations that allow for the use of empathy, collaboration and teamworking.
- Provide ample and regular praise while offering tactful support to overcome any blind-spots.
- Persuade/influence by appealing to the strength of your personal belief in the student (don't let me down, I know you can do it, I like you).

The Koala teacher takes pleasure in scheduling their time. They are organised and decisive. They work out a plan and stick to it, usually aided by their painstaking preparation. Their classroom may resemble a well-oiled machine. The subject will be clearly broken down into lesson-sized chunks. The **P** student will either respond:

- Positively by accepting your expertise and understanding the long-term benefits they'll reap.
- Passively by just accepting your structure/plan for an easy life without really buying into the content or process you are offering.
- Negatively by rejecting you, your structure/plan and subject completely (even if they're physically in your room they will not engage and participate).

For the teacher to get the best out of their naturally laid-back student they should note the student doesn't just like options and choice; they need them or they start to itch, squirm and rebel. The secondary school environment is difficult enough for **P** preference students so teachers can help soften the pressure. To help:

- Provide as much flexibility as possible (multiple choice homework tasks, choice within the lesson).
- Avoid giving out detailed schedules (they'll just lose it anyway!).
- Don't be more picky with detail than is absolutely necessary.
- Shake things up now and again to prevent predictability becoming boredom. Introduce random surprises and changes.
- Identify simple ways the student can organise and manage their time to complete important work without a last-minute rush.

61
Koala teacher with Barn Owl student
ISFJ and INTJ

The Koala is likely to face a dilemma with a Barn Owl student. The naturally confident, strategic and quietly assertive Barn Owl is liable to question the systems and rules carefully introduced by the Koala teacher for the benefit of all. The Barn Owl can't really help being a leader so a Koala teacher who finds a way to incorporate this trait without feeling threatened will create a positive learning environment. For the teacher to get the best out of their naturally lively student they need to:

- Respect the student's need for privacy and independence.
- Allow the student plenty of time to think through their thoughts.

- Share your ideas and thoughts regularly to ensure you both know what you're doing.
- Take time to clarify your thoughts but don't avoid confrontation; if something needs to be said be calm and direct as you deliver it.
- Use non-verbal communication – smiles and gestures are reassuring to **I** students. You can even use sticky notes/emails to pass on feedback.
- Provide opportunities for the student to see you one-to-one away from the sometimes hectic environment of the classroom.

The teacher likes to use their experience to make sense of what they notice. They both live in the present. The teacher is naturally practical, sequential, sensible and realistic in style and encourages their students to follow suit. The **N** student will at best find this challenging and at worst find it boring. The teacher is likely to see the student as a daydreamer, lost in their own world or 'away with the fairies'. They should resist the temptation to castigate their student because this is how they take in information and make sense of the world. In the right context daydreaming can lead to the invention of cars, planes, medicines and computers. For the teacher to get the best out of their inherently imaginative student they need to:

- Embrace the imagination and insight of the student and what it can bring to the lesson.
- Encourage the student to become aware of the important contribution of the **S** approach (the value of facts, details, procedure, experiments, applying experience, structure, the step-by-step model).

The teacher is concerned with relationship then task whereas the student is the other way round. The teacher must learn to accept that the student is different; not cold, blunt and unfriendly, but different and focused on task first. If the teacher can accept this the relationship can be really positive for both teacher and student. For the teacher to get the best out of their fundamentally objective student they need to:

- Work in ways that test their skill and knowledge competitively (they raise their game).
- Help them understand that 50% of people are **F** preference and can interpret feedback as criticism.
- Offer targeted compliments. Just saying everything is great will not impress or help the student; in fact, it can result in the student not respecting the teacher, concluding they lie and/or are a soft touch. When you praise you may be pressed for proof!
- Be logical and objective rather than emotional in discussions.
- Accept that if the student challenges you it is probably to clarify their thoughts rather than meant as a slur on your character. Perhaps ask 'What would you do to improve/change this?' or 'What do you think?' Once they've clarified their thoughts they may be ready to ask and absorb what you think.

The **J** teacher takes pleasure in organising time. They are structured and thorough. They work out a plan and stick to it, often aided by an impressive to-do list. Their classroom is usually an organised place. The subject will probably be broken down into lesson-sized chunks and the year planned out whether an Ofsted inspector is due or not. Many **J** students are reassured by their teacher's organisational zeal. They simply adopt the schedule and deliver their side of the

bargain, generally completing all tasks on time. Interestingly, some **J**'s will baulk at their teacher's well-intentioned fastidiousness. They would like to create their own plan and work to it rather than adopt someone else's. This is due to the **J** desire for control. So two **J** preferences together can clash, though at least all their work will be done. Most secondary schools require students to be so organised that two **J** preferences are the best combination. For the teacher to get the best out of their naturally organised student they need to:

- Enjoy your shared desire for order, neatness and respecting deadlines.
- Allow the student independence in planning their work in their own way if they really want to.
- Be prepared to adjust your own plans if external events interfere with your careful preparations (and encourage the student to also embrace flexibility occasionally).
- Shake things up now and again to prevent predictability becoming boredom.
- Avoid making quick decisions about what needs to be done before considering all of the options.

62
Koala teacher with Lion student
ISFJ and ESFP

The Koala and Lion share two of the four preferences. Both enjoy a structured and friendly environment in which to work. The differences in the conservative approach of teacher and the more rebellious and adventurous student can lead to problems. All Cats seek action and often like to learn by moving, doing and talking, so the Koala needs to provide ample opportunities for such action to prevent boredom from setting in. For the teacher to get the best out of their inherently lively student they need to:

- Endure patiently and enthusiastically the student's ideas and rambling stories.
- Remain open to 'silly' ideas to see where they lead – the student is thinking out loud and this is how they learn best.
- Also offer your own thoughts; if you need a timeout ask for one.
- Encourage the student to think things through before talking otherwise they'll hog the lesson.
- Steer the student away from controversial subjects/topics, especially in group discussions.
- Plan plenty of opportunities during lessons for the **E** students to talk things through with other **E** preferences.

Both teacher and student gather information in the same way. They notice detail using their senses (aware of what they can see, hear and feel) and they both use their experience to make sense of what they see. They both live in the present. The teacher is naturally practical, sequential, sensible and realistic in their teaching style and encourages their students to follow suit. A solid, workman-like relationship develops with both teacher and student mutually understanding what each needs to do to get the job done. For the teacher to get the best out of their naturally grounded student they need to:

■ Demonstrate how learning can be applied in the real world.

■ Allow the student opportunities to repeat and practise until satisfied they are competent.

■ Encourage the use of imagination as a useful process (it's not wasting time).

The teacher and student are both concerned first with people and relationships before the task/subject content. They like to form personal relationships with all their students, unless they don't like the student (**F** teachers are more inclined than **T** preference teachers to have their favourites!). Because they operate at an emotional level these teachers are more likely to make promises to students, overstretch themselves and even do work the students should be doing themselves. Teacher and student both enjoy a classroom atmosphere that is warm and friendly. Compliments are likely to go in both directions boosting the confidence of teacher as well as student. The Lion needs to feel they like their teacher and that the teacher likes them too. If this happens they'll work harder but if not they may switch off completely. This explains why a student can be top of the class one year (with a teacher they like) and show no interest at all in the subject the following year when they change teacher. For the teacher to get the best out of their relationship-focused student they need to:

■ Offer learning situations that allow for the use of empathy, collaboration and teamworking.

■ Influence by appealing to the strength of your personal belief in the student (don't let me down, I know you can do it, I like you).

■ Supply ample and regular praise while offering tactful support to overcome any blind-spots.

The Koala teacher takes pleasure in scheduling their time. They are organised and decisive. They work out a plan and stick to it, usually aided by their meticulous preparation. Their classroom may resemble a well-oiled machine. The subject will be clearly broken down into lesson-sized chunks. The **P** student will either respond:

■ Positively by accepting your expertise and understanding the long-term benefits they'll reap.

■ Passively by just accepting your structure/plan for an easy life without really buying into the content or process you are offering.

■ Negatively by rejecting you, your structure/plan and subject completely (even if they're physically in your room they will not engage and participate).

For the teacher to get the best out of their naturally laid-back student they should note the student doesn't just like options and choice; they need them or they start to itch, squirm and rebel. The secondary school environment is difficult enough for **P** preference students so teachers can help soften the pressure. To help:

■ Provide as much flexibility as possible (multiple choice homework tasks, choice within the lesson).

■ Avoid giving out detailed schedules (they'll just lose it anyway!).

■ Don't be more picky with detail than is absolutely necessary.

■ Shake things up now and again to prevent predictability becoming boredom. Introduce random surprises and changes.

■ Identify simple ways the student can organise and manage their time to complete important work without a last-minute rush.

63
Koala teacher with Panther student
ISFJ and ESTP

Difference in three of the four personality preferences can so easily lead to conflict in the classroom. The naturally playful and assertive Panther student with the inherently placid Koala teacher could easily clash. The teacher needs to constantly remember that the eternally restless and fidgety student is not trying to devour everything the teacher is attempting to create; they are expressing their true anarchic preferences. If the teacher can't find a way to incorporate the student's preferences they will merely become bored and potentially more disruptive. Opposites can also learn much from each other. The nurturing Koala teacher can bring a calm and steady focus while the intrepid and impulsive Panther can inject jest, energy and humour. The right mix benefits the whole class. For the teacher to draw out the potential of such a lively student they need to:

■ Listen patiently and enthusiastically to the student's ideas and contributions.

■ Remain open to off-the-wall ideas to see where they lead – the student is thinking out loud and this is how they learn best.

■ Also offer your own thoughts; if you need a timeout ask for one.

■ Encourage the student to think things through before talking otherwise they'll hog the lesson.

■ Teach the Panther how to dodge controversial subjects/topics, especially in group discussions.

■ Build in plenty of opportunities during lessons for the **E** students to talk things through with other **E** preferences.

Both teacher and student gather information in the same way. They notice detail using their senses (aware of what they can see, hear and feel) and they both use their experience to make sense of what they see. They both live in the present. The teacher is naturally practical, sequential, sensible and realistic in their teaching style and encourages their students to follow suit. A solid relationship develops, both teacher and student mutually understanding what each needs to do to get the job done. For the teacher to get the best out of their naturally boisterous student they need to:

■ Demonstrate how learning can be applied in the real world.

■ Allow the student opportunities to repeat and practise until satisfied they are competent.

■ Encourage the use of imagination as a useful process to solve problems.

The Koala teacher is concerned with relationship then task whereas the Panther student is the other way round. The teacher must learn to accept that the student is different; not cold, blunt and unfriendly, but different and focused on task first. If the teacher can accept this the relationship can be really positive for both teacher and student. For the teacher to get the best out of their essentially assertive student they need to:

■ Offer targeted compliments. Just saying everything is great will not impress or help the student; in fact, it can result in the student not respecting the teacher, concluding they lie and/or are a soft touch. When you praise you may be pressed for proof!

■ Be logical and objective rather than emotional in discussions.

■ Accept that if the student challenges you it is probably to clarify their thoughts rather than as a slight to your authority or character. Perhaps ask 'What would you do to improve/change this?' or 'What do you think?' Once they've clarified their thoughts they may be ready to ask and absorb what you think.

■ Work in ways that test their skill and knowledge competitively (they raise their game).

■ Help them understand that 50% of people are **F** preference and can interpret feedback as criticism.

The **J** teacher takes pleasure in scheduling their time. They are organised and decisive. They work out a plan and stick to it, usually aided by their meticulous preparation. Their classroom may resemble a well-oiled machine. The subject will be clearly broken down into lesson-sized chunks. The **P** student will either respond:

■ Positively by accepting your expertise and understanding the long-term benefits they'll reap.

■ Passively by just accepting your structure/plan for an easy life without really buying into the content or process you are offering.

■ Negatively by rejecting you, your structure/plan and subject completely (even if they're physically in your room they will not engage and participate).

For the teacher to get the best out of their naturally laid-back student they should note the student doesn't just like options and choice; they need them or they start to itch, squirm and rebel. The secondary school environment is difficult enough for **P** preference students so teachers can help soften the pressure. To help:

■ Provide as much flexibility as possible (multiple choice homework tasks, choice within the lesson).

■ Avoid giving out detailed schedules (they'll just lose it anyway!).

■ Don't be more picky with detail than is absolutely necessary.

■ Shake things up now and again to prevent predictability becoming boredom. Introduce random surprises and changes.

■ Help the student identify simple time-management strategies to ensure they complete important work on time.

64
Koala teacher with Seahorse student
ISFJ and INFJ

The Koala and Seahorse share three preferences. They generally understand each other well. Both value politeness, warmth, good manners and work efficiently on tasks. Both are likely to excel in the primary school arena but may find the hurly-burly of secondary schools more challenging. They can be so comfortable together that the teacher may not stretch the student fully. The Koala may achieve this by encouraging the active imagination of the Seahorse. For the teacher to get the best out of their naturally introverted student they need to:

■ Respect the student's need for privacy and independence.

■ Allow the student plenty of time to think through their thoughts.

■ Share your ideas and thoughts regularly to ensure you both know what you're doing.

■ Take time to clarify your thoughts but don't avoid confrontation; if something needs to be said be calm and direct as you deliver it.

■ Use non-verbal communication – smiles and gestures are reassuring to **I** students. You can even use sticky notes/emails to pass on feedback.

■ Provide opportunities for the student to see you one-to-one away from the sometimes hectic environment of the classroom.

The Koala teacher likes to use their experience to make sense of what they notice. They both live in the present. The teacher is naturally practical, sequential, sensible and realistic in style and encourages their students to follow suit. The **N** student will at best find this challenging and at worst find it boring. The teacher is likely to see the student as a daydreamer, lost in their own world or 'away with the fairies'. They should resist the temptation to castigate their student because this is how they take in information and make sense of the world. In the right context daydreaming can lead to the invention of cars, planes, medicines and computers. For the teacher to get the best out of their inherently imaginative student they need to:

■ Embrace the imagination and insight of the student and what it can bring to the lesson.

■ Encourage the student to become aware of the important contribution of the **S** approach (the value of facts, details, procedure, experiments, applying experience, structure, the step-by-step model).

The teacher and student are both concerned first with people and relationships before the task/subject content. They like to form personal relationships with all their students, unless they don't like the student (**F** teachers are more inclined than **T** preference teachers to have their favourites!). Because they operate at an emotional level these teachers are more likely to make promises to students, overstretch themselves and even do work the students should be doing themselves. Teacher and student both enjoy a classroom atmosphere that is warm and friendly. Compliments are likely to go in both directions boosting the confidence of teacher as well as student. The Seahorse needs to feel they like their teacher and that the teacher likes them too. If this happens they'll work harder but if not they may switch off. For the teacher to get the best out of their relationship-focused student they need to:

■ Offer learning situations that allow for the use of empathy, collaboration and teamworking.

■ Provide ample and regular praise while offering tactful support to overcome any blind-spots.

■ Influence by sharing your personal belief in the student (don't let me down, I know you can do it, I like you).

The **J** teacher takes pleasure in organisation. They are structured and decisive. They work out a plan and stick to it, often aided by an impressive to-do list. Their classroom is usually an organised place. Lessons will probably be broken down into lesson-sized chunks and the year planned out whether an Ofsted inspector is due or not. Many **J** students are reassured by their teacher's organisational zeal. They simply adopt the schedule and deliver their side of the bargain, generally completing all tasks on time. Interestingly, some **J**'s will baulk at their teacher's well-intentioned thoroughness. They would like to create their own plan and work to it rather than adopt someone else's plan. This is due to the **J**'s desire for control. So two **J**'s together can clash, though at least all their work will be done. Most secondary schools require students to be so organised that two **J**'s are the best combination. For the teacher to get the best out of their naturally organised student they need to:

■ Enjoy your shared desire for order, neatness and respecting deadlines.

■ Allow the student independence in planning their work in their own way if they really want to.

■ Be prepared to adjust your own plans if external events interfere with your careful preparations (and encourage the student to also embrace flexibility occasionally).

■ Avoid making quick decisions about what needs to be done before considering all of the options.

■ Shake things up now and again to prevent predictability becoming boredom.

65
Lion teacher with Black Bear student
ESFP and ESTJ

Lions and Black Bears share two type preferences. Both are assertive and grounded in reality. The playful and sociable teacher balances the driven and objective student. Conflict is most likely when the natural leadership attributes of the Bear challenge the fun and perky style of their teacher. For the teacher to get the best out of their naturally effusive student they need to:

■ Enjoy the lively banter when it is appropriate to spark new thoughts and ideas; the student learns best this way, but remember there may be thirty others in the classroom.

■ Stick to the point, stay positive and don't nag.

■ Avoid going over old ground unless requested to do so by the student.

■ Be calm and clear, otherwise two **E** preferences can talk louder and louder with neither listening.

■ Remember you can keep some thoughts to yourself (and you may think of a better way of expressing something, especially criticism, later).

■ Be an enthusiastic and supportive listener; seek to help the student clarify and develop their thinking rather than assert your own.

■ Help each other learn to be quiet and encourage the **I** preferences in the class to express themselves.

Both teacher and student gather information in the same way. They notice detail using their senses (aware of what they can see, hear and feel). The teacher is naturally sequential and realistic in their teaching style and encourages their students to follow suit. A solid relationship develops with both teacher and student mutually understanding what each needs to do to get the job done. For the teacher to get the best out of their grounded student they need to:

■ Show how learning can be applied in the real world.

■ Provide opportunities for the student to repeat and practise something until it is mastered.

■ Encourage the use of imagination as a useful addition to their learning repertoire.

The teacher is concerned with relationship then task whereas the student is the other way round. The teacher must learn to accept that the student is different; not cold, blunt and unfriendly, but simply focused on task first. If the teacher can accept this the relationship can be really positive for both teacher and student. For the teacher to get the best out of the fundamentally self-assured Black Bear they need to:

■ Offer targeted compliments. Just saying everything is great will not impress or help the student; in fact, it can result in the student not respecting the teacher, concluding they lie and/or are a soft touch. When you praise you may be pressed for proof!

■ Be logical and objective rather than emotional in discussions.

■ Help them understand that around 50% of people are **F** preference and can interpret feedback as criticism.

■ Accept that if the student challenges you it is probably to clarify their thoughts rather than meant as a slight to your authority or character. Perhaps ask 'What would you do to improve/change this?' or 'What do you think?' Once they've clarified their thoughts they may be ready to ask and absorb what you think.

■ Work in ways that test their skill and knowledge competitively (they raise their game).

The laid-back, flexible and spontaneous teacher with the naturally organised student can be a dream team or a disaster. To create a positive relationship they need to play to each other's strengths. The student can benefit from the teacher's ability to adapt and change plans and the teacher can benefit from the student's desire to have a plan they can work to and complete. The teacher can also:

■ Encourage and support the student's desire for order, neatness and respecting deadlines.

- Allow the student independence in planning their work in their own way if they really want to.
- Avoid changing plans just for the sake of it; this will only frustrate the student.
- Encourage the Black Bear to embrace fun and flexibility now and again.

66
Lion teacher with Teddy Bear student
ESFP and ESFJ

The Lion and Teddy Bear share three type preferences. Both are lively, sociable and grounded in reality. The playful and sociable teacher balances the organised and focused student. Conflict is most likely when the more serious attributes of the Teddy challenge the fun and spontaneous style of their teacher. For the teacher to get the best out of their naturally effusive student they need to:

- Enjoy the lively banter when it is appropriate to spark new thoughts and ideas; the student learns best this way, but remember there may be thirty others in the classroom.
- Stick to the point and stay positive (don't nag), as both teacher and student are easily distracted and liable to go off track!
- Avoid going over old ground.
- Be calm and clear, otherwise two **E** preferences can talk louder and louder with neither listening to each other.
- Remember you can keep some thoughts to yourself (and you may think of a better way of expressing something, especially criticism, later).
- Be an enthusiastic and supportive listener; seek to help the student clarify and develop their thinking rather than assert your own.
- Help each other learn to be quiet and encourage the **I** preferences in the class to express themselves.

Both teacher and student gather information in the same way. They notice detail using their senses (aware of what they can see, hear and feel). The teacher is naturally sequential and realistic in their teaching style and encourages their students to follow suit. A solid, workman-like relationship develops with both teacher and student mutually understanding what each needs to do to get the job done. For the teacher to get the best out of their grounded student they need to:

- Show how learning can be applied in the real world.
- Provide opportunities for the student to repeat and practise something until it is mastered.
- Encourage the use of imagination as a useful addition to their learning repertoire.

Both teacher and student are interested in people and relationships before the task/subject content. The teacher likes to form personal relationships with all their students, unless they don't like the student (**F** teachers are more inclined than **T** preference teachers to have their favourites!). Because they operate at an emotional level these teachers are more likely to make promises to stu-

dents, overstretch themselves and even do work the students should be doing themselves. Teacher and student both enjoy a classroom atmosphere that is warm and friendly. Compliments are likely to go in both directions boosting the confidence of teacher as well as student. For the teacher to get the best out of their relationship-focused student they need to:

- Offer learning situations that allow for the use of empathy, collaboration and teamworking.
- Give ample and regular praise while offering tactful support to overcome any blind-spots.
- Motivate by appealing to the strength of your personal belief in the student (don't let me down, I know you can do it, I like you).

The laid-back, flexible and spontaneous teacher with the naturally organised student can be a dream team or a disaster. To create a positive relationship they need to play to each other's strengths. The student can benefit from the teacher's ability to adapt and change plans and the teacher can benefit from the student's desire to have a plan they can work to and complete. The teacher can also:

- Encourage and support the student's desire for order, neatness and respecting deadlines.
- Allow the student independence in planning their work in their own way if they really want to.
- Encourage the student to embrace flexibility occasionally.
- Avoid changing plans just for the sake of it; this will only frustrate the student.

67
Lion teacher with Dolphin student
ESFP and ENFJ

Dolphins and Lions share two type preferences – both exuding energy and warmth. Clashes are likely if the teacher fails to appreciate the Dolphin's core desire to build secure relationships and use their imagination to shine. Lessons delivered by the sensation-seeking Lion can be too spontaneous and spur-of-the-moment for some Dolphins. To fully develop their natural team-player student they need to:

- Enjoy the lively banter when it is appropriate to spark new thoughts and ideas; the student learns best this way, but remember there may be thirty others in the classroom.
- Stick to the point and stay positive (don't nag), as both teacher and student are easily distracted and liable to go off track!
- Avoid going over old ground.
- Be calm and clear, otherwise two **E** preferences can talk louder and louder with neither listening.
- Remember you can keep some thoughts to yourself (and you may think of a better way of expressing something, especially criticism, later).
- Be an enthusiastic and supportive listener; seek to help the student clarify and develop their thinking rather than assert your own.

- Help each other learn to be quiet and encourage the **I** preferences in the class to express themselves.

The teacher likes to use their experience to make sense of their learning. The teacher is naturally sequential, sensible and realistic in style and encourages their students to follow suit. The **N** student can find this approach dull. The teacher is likely to see the student as a daydreamer. They should resist the temptation to castigate their student because this is how they take in information and make sense of the world. In the right context daydreaming can lead to better absorption and retention of the topic. To get the best out of their ingenious Dolphin student the teacher can:

- Embrace the imagination and insight of the student and what it can bring to the lesson.
- Encourage the student to become aware of the important contribution of the **S** approach (the value of facts, details, procedure, experiments, applying experience, structure, the step-by-step model).

Both teacher and student are interested in people and relationships before the task/subject content. The teacher likes to form personal relationships with all their students, unless they don't like the student (**F** teachers are more inclined than **T** preference teachers to have their favourites!). Because they operate at an emotional level these teachers are more likely to make promises to students, overstretch themselves and even do work the students should be doing themselves. Teacher and student both enjoy a classroom atmosphere that is warm and friendly. Compliments are likely to go in both directions boosting the confidence of teacher as well as student. To get the best out of their relationship-focused student the teacher should:

- Offer learning situations that allow for the use of empathy, collaboration and teamworking.
- Give ample and regular praise while offering tactful support to overcome any blind-spots.
- Motivate by appealing to the strength of your personal belief in the student (don't let me down, I know you can do it, I value your contribution).

The laid-back, flexible and spontaneous teacher with the naturally organised student can be a dream team or a disaster. To create a positive relationship they need to play to each other's strengths. The student can benefit from the teacher's ability to adapt and change plans and the teacher can benefit from the student's desire to have a plan they can work to and complete. The teacher can also:

- Encourage and support the student's desire for order, neatness and respecting deadlines.
- Allow the student independence in planning their work in their own way if they really want to.
- Avoid changing plans just for the sake of it; this will only frustrate the student.
- Encourage the student to change their routine now and again.

68
Lion teacher with Eagle student
ESFP and ENTJ

Lions and Eagles share two type preferences. Both are assertive and enjoy action. The playful and sociable teacher balances the driven and imaginative student. Conflict is most likely when the natural leadership attributes of the Eagle challenge the fun and bouncy style of their teacher. For the teacher to get the best out of their naturally systematic student they need to:

■ Enjoy the lively banter when it is appropriate to spark new thoughts and ideas; the student learns best this way, but remember there may be thirty others in the classroom.

■ Stick to the point and stay positive (don't nag), as both teacher and student are easily distracted and liable to go off track!

■ Avoid going over old ground.

■ Be calm and clear, otherwise two **E** preferences can talk louder and louder without either listening.

■ Remember you can keep some thoughts to yourself (and you may think of a better way of expressing something, especially criticism, later).

■ Be an enthusiastic and supportive listener; seek to help the student clarify and develop their thinking rather than assert your own.

■ Help each other learn to be quiet and encourage the **I** preferences in the class to express themselves.

The teacher likes to use their experience to make sense of their learning. The teacher is naturally sequential, sensible and realistic in style and encourages their students to follow suit. The **N** student can find this approach dull. The teacher is likely to see the student as a daydreamer. They should resist the temptation to castigate their student because this is how they take in information and make sense of the world. In the right context daydreaming can lead to better absorption and retention of the topic. To get the best out of their ingenious student the teacher can:

■ Encourage the student to become aware of the important contribution of the **S** approach (the value of facts, details, procedure, experiments, applying experience, structure, the step-by-step model).

■ Embrace the imagination and insight of the student and what it can bring to the lesson.

The teacher is concerned with relationship then task whereas the student is the other way round. The teacher must learn to accept that the student is different; not cold, blunt and unfriendly, but simply focused on task first. If the teacher can accept this the relationship can be really positive for both teacher and student. For the teacher to get the best out of their fundamentally assertive student they need to:

■ Offer targeted compliments. Just saying everything is great will not impress or help the student; in fact, it can result in the student not respecting the teacher, concluding they lie and/or are a soft touch. When you praise you may be pressed for proof!

■ Be logical and objective rather than emotional in discussions.

■ Accept that if the student challenges you it is probably to clarify their thoughts rather than meant as a slight to your authority or character. Perhaps ask 'What would you do to improve/change this?' or 'What do you think?' Once they've clarified their thoughts they may be ready to ask and absorb what you think.

■ Help them understand that around 50% of people are **F** preference and can interpret feedback as criticism.

■ Work in ways that test their skill and knowledge competitively (they raise their game).

The laid-back, flexible and spontaneous teacher with the naturally organised student can be a dream team or a disaster. To create a positive relationship they need to play to each other's strengths. The student can benefit from the teacher's ability to adapt and change plans and the teacher can benefit from the student's desire to have a plan they can work to and complete. The teacher can also:

■ Avoid changing plans just for the sake of it; this will only frustrate the student.

■ Encourage the student to embrace flexibility occasionally.

■ Encourage and support the student's desire for order, neatness and respecting deadlines.

■ Allow the student independence in planning their work in their own way if they really want to.

69
Lion teacher with Panther student
ESFP and ESTP

All four Cats are realistic, adaptable and action-oriented. Traditional classroom teaching does not play to their natural strengths. The Lion teacher can help draw out the best in their Panther students, especially in secondary schools, by utilising their interest in learning from experience, fun and action. The combination of the naturally confident and assertive teacher with the equally excitable student is likely to create a carnival classroom environment. For the teacher to get the best out of their playful student they need to:

■ Enjoy the lively banter when it is appropriate to spark new thoughts and ideas; the student learns best this way, but remember there may be thirty others in the classroom.

■ Stick to the point and stay positive (don't nag), as both teacher and student are easily distracted and liable to go off track!

■ Avoid going over old ground.

■ Be calm and clear, otherwise two **E** preferences can talk louder and louder with neither listening; embrace the saying 'seek first to understand then to be understood'.

■ Remember you can keep some thoughts to yourself (and you may think of a better way of expressing something, especially criticism, later).

■ Be an enthusiastic and supportive listener; seek to help the student clarify and develop their thinking rather than assert your own.

■ Help each other learn to be quiet and encourage the **I** preferences in the class to express themselves.

Both teacher and student gather information in the same way. They notice detail using their senses (aware of what they can see, hear and feel). The teacher is naturally sequential and realistic in their teaching style and encourages their students to follow suit. A solid, workman-like relationship develops with both teacher and student mutually understanding what each needs to do to get the job done. For the teacher to get the best out of their grounded student they need to:

■ Show how learning can be applied in the real world.

■ Provide opportunities for the student to repeat and practise something until it is mastered.

■ Encourage the use of imagination as a useful addition to their learning repertoire.

The teacher is concerned with relationship then task whereas the student is the other way round. The teacher must learn to accept that the student is different; not cold, blunt and unfriendly, but simply focused on task first. If the teacher can accept this the relationship can be really positive for both teacher and student. For the teacher to get the best out of their naturally assertive student they need to:

■ Offer targeted compliments. Just saying everything is great will not impress or help the student; in fact, it can result in the student not respecting the teacher, concluding they lie and/or are a soft touch. When you praise you may be pressed for proof!

■ Be logical and objective rather than emotional in discussions.

■ Accept that if the student challenges you it is probably to clarify their thoughts rather than meant as a slight to your authority or character. Perhaps ask 'What would you do to improve/change this?' or 'What do you think?' Once they've clarified their thoughts they may be ready to ask and absorb what you think.

■ Help them understand that around 50% of people are **F** preference and can easily interpret feedback as criticism.

■ Work in ways that test their skill and knowledge competitively (they raise their game).

Lions and Panthers can learn to be organised and efficient but it is tolerated rather than embraced enthusiastically. While enjoying a mutual love of spontaneity, which provides each with relief from the stifling and constraining timetables and deadlines essential in large organisations such as schools, they must also remember to complete any necessary tasks. Although likely to be fun and popular teachers, they also need to focus on the task of preparing the student to succeed socially and academically. Both prefer to start tasks than finish them. Their initial enthusiasm can quickly drain. Both need to ensure they identify and complete the important tasks or the student (or their parents) may eventually ask awkward questions. For the teacher to get the best out of their naturally laid-back student they need to understand the student doesn't just like options and choice; they are essential or they start to itch, squirm and rebel. The structured, timetabled and routine-rich secondary school environment is difficult for many **P** preferences. Teachers can help by:

- Providing as much flexibility as possible (multiple choice homework tasks, choice within the lesson).
- Avoiding detailed schedules (they'll just lose it anyway!).
- Shaking things up now and again to prevent predictability becoming boredom. Introduce random surprises and changes.
- Helping the student identify ways they can organise and manage their time to complete important work without a last-minute panic.

70
Lion teacher with Lion student
ESFP and ESFP

All four Cats are realistic, adaptable and action-oriented. Traditional classroom teaching does not play to their natural strengths. The Lion teacher can help draw out the best in their Lion student and help them succeed using their interest in learning from experience, fun and action. The combination of the naturally confident and assertive teacher with the equally excitable student is likely to create a roller-coaster classroom environment. For the teacher to get the best out of their effusive student they need to:

- Enjoy the lively banter when it is appropriate to spark new thoughts and ideas; the student learns best this way, but remember there may be thirty others in the classroom.
- Stick to the point and stay positive (don't nag), as both teacher and student are easily distracted and liable to go off track!
- Avoid going over old ground.
- Be calm and clear, otherwise two **E** preferences can talk louder and louder with neither listening.
- Remember you can keep some thoughts to yourself (and you may think of a better way of expressing something, especially criticism, later).
- Be an enthusiastic and supportive listener; seek to help the student clarify and develop their thinking rather than assert your own.
- Help each other learn to be quiet and encourage the **I** preferences in the class to express themselves.

Both teacher and student gather information in the same way. They notice detail using their senses (aware of what they can see, hear and feel). The teacher is naturally sequential and realistic in their teaching style and encourages their students to follow suit. A solid, workman-like relationship develops with both teacher and student mutually understanding what each needs to do to get the job done. For the teacher to get the best out of their grounded student they need to:

- Show how learning can be applied in the real world.
- Provide opportunities for the student to repeat and practise something until it is mastered.
- Encourage the use of imagination as a useful addition to their learning repertoire.

Both teacher and student are interested in people and relationships before the task/subject content.

The Lion teacher likes to form personal relationships with all their students, unless they don't like the student (**F** teachers are more inclined than **T** preference teachers to have their favourites!). Because they operate at an emotional level these teachers are more likely to make promises to students, overstretch themselves and even do work the students should be doing themselves. Teacher and student both enjoy a classroom atmosphere that is warm and friendly. Compliments are likely to go in both directions boosting the confidence of teacher as well as student. For the teacher to get the best out of their relationship-focused student they need to:

- Offer learning situations that allow for the use of empathy, collaboration and teamworking.
- Give ample and regular praise while offering tactful support to overcome any blind-spots.
- Motivate by appealing to the strength of your personal belief in the student (don't let me down, I know you can do it, I like you).

Lions abhor to-do-lists, schedules and predictability; they rarely reach the status of an acquired taste or a honed skill. While enjoying their mutual love of spontaneity, which provides each with relief from the stifling and constraining timetables and deadlines essential in large organisations such as schools, they must also remember to complete any necessary tasks. Although likely to be fun and popular teachers, they also need to focus on the task of preparing the student to succeed socially and academically. Both prefer to start tasks than finish them. Their initial enthusiasm can quickly evaporate. Both need to ensure they identify and complete the important tasks or the student (or their parents) may eventually ask awkward questions. For the teacher to get the best out of their naturally laid-back student they need to understand the student doesn't just like options and choice; they are essential or they start to itch, squirm and rebel. The structured, timetabled and routine-rich secondary school environment is difficult for many **P** preferences. Teachers can help by:

- Helping the student identify ways they can organise and manage their time to complete important work without a last-minute rush.
- Providing as much flexibility as possible (multiple choice homework tasks, choice within the lesson).
- Not giving out detailed schedules (they'll just lose it anyway!).
- Shaking things up now and again to prevent predictability becoming boredom.

71
Lion teacher with Clownfish student
ESFP and ENFP

Lions and Clownfish share three type preferences. Both are gregarious and flexible, although the grounded teacher differs from the imaginative student. Clashes are likely when the student's sense of fun impinges on the need to complete serious tasks in detail and on time. For the teacher to get the best out of their naturally impulsive student they need to:

- Enjoy the lively banter when it is appropriate to spark new thoughts and ideas; the student learns best this way, but remember there may be thirty others in the classroom.
- Stick to the point and stay positive (don't nag), as both teacher and student are easily distracted and liable to go off track!
- Avoid going over old ground.
- Be calm and clear, otherwise two **E** preferences can compete for attention and talk louder and louder without listening.
- Remember you can keep some thoughts to yourself (and you may think of a better way of expressing criticism later).
- Be an enthusiastic and supportive listener; seek to help the student clarify and develop their thinking rather than assert your own.
- Help each other learn to be quiet and encourage the **I** preferences in the class to express themselves.

The teacher likes to use their experience to make sense of their learning. The teacher is sequential, sensible and realistic in style and encourages their students to follow suit. The **N** student can find this approach dull. The teacher is likely to see the student as a daydreamer. They should resist the temptation to castigate their student because this is how they take in information and make sense of the world. In the right context daydreaming can lead to better absorption and retention of the topic. To get the best out of their ingenious student the teacher can:

- Embrace the imagination and insight of the student and what it can bring to the lesson.
- Encourage the student to become aware of the important contribution of the **S** approach (the value of facts, details, procedure, experiments, applying experience, structure, the step-by-step model).

Both teacher and student are interested in people and relationships before the task/subject content. The teacher likes to form personal relationships with all their students, unless they don't like the student (**F** teachers are more inclined than **T** preference teachers to have their favourites!). Because they operate at an emotional level these teachers are more likely to make promises to students, overstretch themselves and even do work the students should be doing themselves. Teacher and student both enjoy a classroom atmosphere that is warm and friendly. Compliments may fly in both directions boosting the confidence of teacher as well as student. For the teacher to get the best out of their relationship-focused student they need to:

- Offer learning situations that allow for the use of empathy, collaboration and teamworking.
- Give ample and regular praise while offering tactful support to overcome any blind-spots.
- Motivate by appealing to the strength of your personal belief in the student (don't let me down, I know you can do it, I like you).

P preferences can be organised and efficient; it's just rarely worth the aggravation. While enjoying a mutual love of spontaneity, which provides each with relief from the stifling and constraining timetables and deadlines essential in large organisations such as schools, they must also remember to complete any necessary tasks. Although likely to be fun and popular teachers, they also need to focus on the task of preparing the student to succeed socially and academically. Both prefer to start tasks than finish them. Their initial enthusiasm can quickly wane. Both need to ensure they identify and complete the important tasks or the student (or their parents) may eventually ask awkward questions. For the teacher to get the best out of their naturally laid-back student they need to understand the student doesn't just like options and choice; they are essential or they start to itch, squirm and rebel. The structured, timetabled and routine-rich secondary school environment is difficult for many **P** preferences. Teachers can help by:

■ Providing as much flexibility as possible (multiple choice homework tasks, choice within the lesson).

■ Helping the student identify ways they can organise and manage their time to complete important work without a last-minute rush.

■ Avoiding detailed schedules (they'll just lose it anyway!).

■ Introducing random surprises and changes to keep the student interested.

72
Lion teacher with Falcon student
ESFP and ENTP

The Lion and Falcon share two type preferences. Both are gregarious and flexible. The warm, grounded teacher differs from the imaginative and controversial student. Clashes are likely when the Falcon's sense of fun impinges on the need to complete serious tasks in detail and on time. For the Lion to get the best out of their naturally impulsive student they need to:

■ Enjoy the lively banter when it is appropriate to spark new thoughts and ideas; the student learns best this way, but remember there may be thirty others in the classroom.

■ Stick to the point and stay positive (don't nag), as both teacher and student are easily distracted and liable to go off track!

■ Avoid going over old ground.

■ Be calm and clear, otherwise two **E** preferences can talk louder and louder like PMQs (with neither listening).

■ Be an enthusiastic and supportive listener; seek to help the student clarify and develop their thinking rather than assert your own.

■ Help each other learn to be quiet and encourage the **I** preferences in the class to express themselves. Their verbal sparring and camaraderie, as seen in *Top Gear*, can be nauseous to other students in the class.

The Lion teacher likes to use their experience to make sense of their learning. The teacher is sequential, sensible and realistic in style and encourages their students to follow suit. The **N** student can find this approach leaden. The teacher is likely to see the student as a daydreamer. They should resist the temptation to castigate their student because this is how they take in information and make sense of the world. In the right context daydreaming can lead to better absorption and retention of the topic. To get the best out of their ingenious student the teacher can:

■ Embrace the imagination and insight of the student and what it can bring to the lesson.

■ Encourage the student to become aware of the important contribution of the **S** approach (the value of facts, details, procedure, experiments, applying experience, structure, the step-by-step model).

The teacher is concerned with relationship then task whereas the student is the other way round. The teacher must learn to accept that the student is different; not cold, blunt and unfriendly, but simply focused on task first. If the teacher can accept this the relationship can be really positive for both teacher and student. For the teacher to get the best out of their characteristically inventive student they need to:

■ Offer targeted compliments. Just saying everything is great will not impress or help the student; in fact, it can result in the student not respecting the teacher, concluding they lie and/or are a soft touch. When you praise you may be pressed for proof!

■ Be logical and objective rather than emotional in discussions.

■ Accept that if the student challenges you it is probably to clarify their thoughts rather than a test of your authority or character. Perhaps ask 'What would you do to improve/change this?' or 'What do you think?' Once they've clarified their thoughts they may be ready to ask and absorb what you think.

■ Work in ways that test their skill and knowledge competitively (they raise their game).

■ Help them understand that around 50% of people are **F** preference and can interpret feedback as criticism.

P preferences can learn to be organised and efficient but it is tolerated rather than embraced enthusiastically. While enjoying a mutual love of spontaneity, which provides each with relief from the stifling and constraining timetables and deadlines essential in large organisations such as schools, they must also remember to complete any necessary tasks. Although likely to be fun and popular teachers, they also need to focus on the task of preparing the student to succeed socially and academically. Both prefer to start tasks than finish them. Their initial enthusiasm can quickly dissipate. Both need to ensure they identify and complete the important tasks or the student (or their parents) may eventually ask awkward questions. For the teacher to get the best out of their naturally laid-back student they need to understand the student doesn't just like options and choice; they are essential or they start to itch, squirm and rebel. The structured, timetabled and routine-rich secondary school environment is difficult for many **P** preferences. Teachers can help by:

■ Providing as much flexibility as possible (multiple choice homework tasks, choice within the lesson).

■ Avoiding detailed schedules (they'll just lose it anyway!).

■ Shaking things up now and again to prevent predictability becoming boredom. Introduce random surprises and changes.

■ Helping the student identify simple time-management techniques to ensure they can succeed; these are especially useful for the scattergun Falcon.

73
Lion teacher with Tiger student
ESFP and ISTP

All four Cats are realistic, adaptable and action-oriented. Traditional classroom teaching does not play to their natural strengths. The Lion teacher can help draw out the best in the Tiger and encourage them to succeed by using their interest in learning independently from experience and action. They can also:

■ Slow down and be calm and succinct.

■ Leave plenty of time between question and answer; respect the student's need for time to think and reflect before responding.

■ Allow the student time and space to work on their own; don't hover over their head, waiting to pounce.

■ Avoid trying to fix problems immediately or finish their sentences.

■ Avoid placing them in groups/teams where they are the only **I** preference in a sea of **E** preferences (they'll be smothered).

■ Provide written praise (not just verbal).

Both teacher and student gather information in the same way. They notice detail using their senses (aware of what they can see, hear and feel). The teacher is naturally sequential and realistic in their teaching style and encourages their students to follow suit. A solid, workman-like relationship develops with both teacher and student mutually understanding what each needs to do to get the job done. For the teacher to get the best out of their grounded student they need to:

■ Show how learning can be applied in the real world.

■ Provide opportunities for the student to repeat and practise something until it is mastered.

■ Encourage the use of imagination as a useful addition to their learning repertoire.

The teacher is concerned with relationship then task whereas the student is the other way round. The teacher must learn to accept that the student is different; not cold, blunt and unfriendly, but simply focused on task first. If the teacher can accept this the relationship can be really positive for both teacher and student. For the teacher to get the best out of their naturally objective student they need to:

■ Offer targeted compliments. Just saying everything is great will not impress or help the student; in fact, it can result in the student not respecting the teacher, concluding they lie and/or are a soft touch. When you praise you may be pressed for proof!

■ Be logical and objective rather than emotional in discussions.

■ Accept that if the student challenges you it is probably to clarify their thoughts rather than meant as a slight to your authority or character. Perhaps ask 'What would you do to improve/change this?' or 'What do you think?' Once they've clarified their thoughts they may be ready to ask and absorb what you think.

■ Work in ways that test their skill and knowledge competitively (they raise their game).

◼ Help them understand that around 50% of people are **F** preference and can interpret feedback as criticism.

Lions and Tigers abhor to-do-lists, schedules and predictability; they rarely reach the status of an acquired taste or a honed skill. While enjoying their mutual love of spontaneity, which provides each with relief from the stifling and constraining timetables and deadlines essential in large organisations such as schools, they must also remember to complete any necessary tasks. Although likely to be fun and popular teachers, they also need to focus on the task of preparing the student to succeed socially and academically. Both prefer to start tasks than finish them. Their initial enthusiasm can quickly dissolve. Both need to ensure they identify and complete the important tasks or the student (or their parents) may eventually ask awkward questions. For the teacher to get the best out of their naturally laid-back student they need to understand the student doesn't just like options and choice; they are essential or they start to itch, squirm and rebel. The structured, timetabled and routine-rich secondary school environment is difficult for many **P** preferences. Teachers can help by:

◼ Providing as much flexibility as possible (multiple choice homework tasks, choice within the lesson).

◼ Avoiding detailed schedules (they'll just lose it anyway!).

◼ Helping the student identify ways they can organise and manage their time to complete important work without a last-minute rush.

◼ Shaking things up now and again to prevent predictability becoming boredom. Random surprises and changes will delight the Tiger.

74
Lion teacher with Cat student
ESFP and ISFP

All four Cats are realistic, adaptable and action-oriented. Traditional classroom teaching does not play to their natural strengths. The Lion teacher can help draw out the best in their Cat students and encourage them to succeed using their interest in learning from experience and action. The teacher can also:

◼ Slow down and be calm and succinct.

◼ Leave plenty of time between question and answer; respect the student's need for time to think and reflect before responding.

◼ Allow the student time and space to work on their own; don't hover over their head, waiting to pounce.

◼ Avoid trying to fix problems immediately or finish their sentences.

◼ Avoid placing them in groups/teams where they are the only **I** preference in a sea of **E** preferences (they'll be smothered).

◼ Provide written praise (not just verbal).

◼ Let the student know they can always come and talk to you alone during breaks or they can write down their questions/issues for you to reply to later.

Both teacher and student gather information using their senses (aware of what they can see, hear and feel). The teacher is naturally sequential and realistic in their teaching style and encourages their students to follow suit. A solid, workmanlike relationship develops with both teacher and student mutually understanding what each needs to do to get the job done. For the teacher to get the best out of their grounded student they need to:

◼ Show how learning can be applied in the real world.

◼ Provide opportunities for the student to repeat and practise something until it is mastered.

◼ Encourage the use of imagination as a useful addition to their learning repertoire.

Both teacher and student are interested in people and relationships before the task/subject content. Because they operate at an emotional level Lion teachers are more likely to make promises to students, overstretch themselves and even do work the students should be doing themselves. Teacher and student both enjoy a classroom atmosphere that is warm and friendly. Compliments are likely to go in both directions boosting the confidence of teacher as well as student. To help their student make progress Lions can:

◼ Offer learning situations that allow for the use of empathy, collaboration and teamworking.

◼ Give ample and regular praise while offering tactful support to overcome any blind-spots.

◼ Motivate by appealing to the strength of your personal belief in the student (don't let me down, I know you can do it, I like you).

Lions and Cats can be organised and efficient; it's just such an effort! While enjoying a mutual love of spontaneity, which provides each with relief from the stifling and constraining timetables and deadlines characteristic of large organisations such as schools, they must also remember to complete any necessary tasks. Although likely to be fun and popular teachers, they also need to focus on the task of preparing the student to succeed socially and academically. Both prefer to start tasks than finish them. Their initial enthusiasm can quickly wane. Both need to ensure they identify and complete the important tasks or the student (or their parents) may eventually ask awkward questions. For the teacher to get the best out of their naturally laid-back student they need to understand the student doesn't just like options and choice; they are essential or they start to itch, squirm and rebel. The structured, timetabled and routine-rich secondary school environment is difficult for many **P** preferences. Teachers can help by:

◼ Avoiding detailed schedules (they'll just lose it anyway!).

◼ Shaking things up now and again to prevent predictability becoming boredom.

◼ Helping the student identify ways they can organise and manage their time to complete important work without a last-minute rush.

◼ Providing as much flexibility as possible (multiple choice homework tasks, choice within the lesson).

75
Lion teacher with Seal student
ESFP and INFP

Lions and Seals share two type preferences. Both are warm and adaptable. Clashes are likely if the Lion imposes their full-on energetic style onto the more reflective and introspective Seal. For the Lion teacher to get the best out of their naturally inquisitive student they need to:

◼ Slow down and be calm and succinct.

◼ Leave plenty of time between question and answer; respect the student's need for time to think and reflect before responding.

◼ Allow the student time and space to work on their own; don't hover over their head, waiting to pounce.

◼ Avoid trying to fix problems immediately or finish their sentences.

◼ Avoid placing them in groups/teams where they are the only **I** preference in a sea of **E** preferences (they'll be smothered).

◼ Provide written praise (not just verbal).

The teacher likes to use their experience to make sense of their world. Lions are sequential, sensible and realistic in style and encourage their students to follow suit. The Seal can find this approach dull and predictable. The teacher is likely to see the student as a daydreamer. They should resist the temptation to castigate their student because this is how they take in information and make sense of the world. In the right context daydreaming can lead to better absorption and retention of the topic. To get the best out of their ingenious student the teacher can:

◼ Embrace the imagination and insight of the student and what it can bring to the lesson.

◼ Encourage the student to become aware of the important contribution of the **S** approach (the value of facts, details, procedure, experiments, applying experience, structure, the step-by-step model).

Both teacher and student are interested in people and relationships before the task/subject content. The teacher likes to form personal relationships with all their students, unless they don't like the student (**F** teachers are more inclined than **T** preference teachers to have their favourites!). Because they operate at an emotional level these teachers are more likely to make promises to students, overstretch themselves and even do work the students should be doing themselves. Teacher and student both enjoy a classroom atmosphere that is warm and friendly. Compliments are likely to flow in both directions boosting the confidence of teacher as well as student. For the teacher to get the best out of their relationship-focused student they need to:

◼ Offer learning situations that allow for the use of empathy, collaboration and teamworking.

◼ Give ample and regular praise while offering tactful support to overcome any blind-spots.

◼ Motivate by appealing to the strength of your personal belief in the student (don't let me down, I know you can do it, I like you).

P preferences can learn to be organised and efficient but it is tolerated reluctantly rather than embraced enthusiastically. While enjoying a mutual love of spontaneity, which provides each with relief from the stifling and constraining timetables and deadlines prevalent in large organisations such as schools, they must also remember to complete any necessary tasks. Although likely to be fun and popular teachers, they also need to focus on the task of preparing the student to succeed academically. Both prefer to start tasks than finish them. Their initial enthusiasm can quickly wane. Both need to ensure they identify and complete the important tasks or the student (or their parents) may eventually ask awkward questions. For the teacher to get the best out of their naturally laid-back student they need to understand the student doesn't just like options and choice; they are essential or they start to itch, squirm and rebel. The structured, timetabled and routine-rich secondary school environment is difficult for many **P** preferences. Teachers can help by:

▧ Providing as much flexibility as possible (multiple choice homework tasks, choice within the lesson).

▧ Avoiding detailed schedules (they'll just lose it anyway!).

▧ Shaking things up now and again to prevent predictability becoming boredom.

▧ Helping the Seal identify ways they can organise and manage their time to complete important work without last-minute terror.

76
Lion teacher with Tawny Owl student
ESFP and INTP

Lions and Tawny Owls share only one type preference. The playful and sociable teacher can be balanced by the investigative and introspective student. Conflict is most likely when the reflective and curious attributes of the Owl challenge the fun, grounded and bubbly style of their teacher. For the teacher to get the best out of their naturally analytical student they need to:

▧ Slow down and be calm and succinct.

▧ Leave plenty of time between question and answer; respect the student's need for time to think and reflect before responding.

▧ Allow the student time and space to work on their own; don't hover over their head, waiting to pounce like a hungry Lion!

▧ Avoid trying to fix problems immediately or finish their sentences.

▧ Avoid placing them in groups/teams where they are the only **I** preference in a sea of **E** preferences (they'll be smothered).

▧ Provide written praise (not just verbal).

The teacher likes to use their experience to make sense of their learning. The teacher is naturally sequential, sensible and realistic in style and encourages their students to follow suit. The **N** student can find this approach dull. The teacher is likely to see the student as a daydreamer. They should resist the temptation to castigate their student because this is how they take in information and make sense of the world. In the right context daydreaming can lead to better absorption and retention of the topic. To get the best out of their ingenious student the teacher can:

▧ Embrace the imagination and insight of the student and what it can bring to the lesson.

▧ Encourage the student to become aware of the important contribution of the **S** approach (the value of facts, details, procedure, experiments, applying experience, structure, the step-by-step model).

The Lion teacher is concerned with relationship then task whereas the Tawny Owl student is the other way round. The teacher must learn to accept that the student is different; not cold, blunt and unfriendly, but simply focused on task first. If the teacher can accept this the relationship can be really positive for both teacher and student. For the teacher to get the best out of their characteristically objective student they need to:

▧ Offer targeted compliments. Just saying everything is great will not impress or help the student; in fact, it can result in the student not respecting the teacher, concluding they lie and/or are a soft touch. When you praise you may be pressed for proof!

▧ Be logical and objective rather than emotional in discussions.

▧ Accept that if the student challenges you it is probably to clarify their thoughts rather than meant as a slight to your authority or character. Perhaps ask 'What would you do to improve/change this?' or 'What do you think?' Once they've clarified their thoughts they may be ready to ask and absorb what you think.

▧ Work in ways that test their skill and knowledge competitively (they raise their game).

▧ Help them understand that around 50% of people are **F** preference and can interpret feedback as criticism.

If pushed, **P** preferences can be organised and efficient; it's just such an effort! While enjoying a mutual love of spontaneity, which provides each with relief from the stifling and constraining timetables and deadlines essential in large organisations such as schools, they must also remember to complete any necessary tasks. Although likely to be fun teachers, they also need to focus on the task of preparing the student to succeed socially and academically. Both prefer to start tasks than finish them. Their initial enthusiasm can quickly evaporate. Both need to ensure they identify and complete the important tasks or the student (or their parents) may eventually ask awkward questions. For the teacher to get the best out of their naturally laid-back student they need to understand the student doesn't just like options and choice; they are essential or they start to itch, wriggle and rebel. The structured, timetabled and routine-rich secondary school environment is difficult for many **P** preferences. Teachers can help by:

▧ Providing as much flexibility as possible (multiple choice homework tasks, choice within the lesson).

▧ Avoiding detailed schedules (they'll just lose it anyway!).

▧ Shaking things up now and again to prevent predictability becoming boredom. Introduce random surprises and changes.

▧ Helping the student identify simple time-management strategies to ensure they can succeed.

77
Lion teacher with Polar Bear student
ESFP and ISTJ

The Lion and Polar Bear share one type preference. Both are self-assured and grounded in reality. The playful and sociable teacher balances the driven and objective student. Conflict is most likely when the natural leadership attributes of the Bear challenge the fun and sprightly style of their teacher. For the teacher to get the best out of their characteristically serious student they need to:

▧ Slow down and be calm and succinct.

▧ Leave plenty of time between question and answer; respect the student's need for time to think and reflect before responding.

▧ Allow the student time and space to work on their own; don't hover over their head, waiting to pounce.

▧ Avoid trying to fix problems immediately or finish their sentences.

▧ Avoid placing them in groups/teams where they are the only **I** preference in a sea of **E** preferences (they'll be smothered).

▧ Provide written praise (not just verbal).

Both teacher and student gather information using their senses (aware of what they can see, hear and feel). The teacher is naturally sequential and realistic in their teaching style and encourages their students to follow suit. A solid, workmanlike relationship develops with both teacher and student mutually understanding what each needs to do to get the job done. For the teacher to help their grounded student they need to:

▧ Show how learning can be applied in the real world.

▧ Provide opportunities for the student to repeat and practise something until it is mastered.

▧ Encourage the use of imagination as a useful addition to their learning repertoire.

The teacher is concerned with relationship then task whereas the student is the other way round. The teacher must learn to accept that the student is different; not cold, blunt and unfriendly, but simply focused on task first. If the teacher can accept this the relationship can be really positive for both teacher and student. For the teacher to get the best out of their naturally assertive student they need to:

▧ Offer targeted compliments. Just saying everything is great will not impress or help the student; in fact, it can result in the student not respecting the teacher, concluding they lie and/or are a soft touch. When you praise you may be pressed for proof!

▧ Be logical and objective rather than emotional in discussions.

▧ Accept that if the student challenges you it is probably to clarify their thoughts rather than test your authority or character. Perhaps ask 'What would you do to improve/change this?' or 'What do you think?' Once they've clarified their thoughts they may be ready to ask and absorb what you think.

▧ Help them understand that around 50% of people are **F** preference and can interpret feedback as criticism.

■ Work in ways that test their skill and knowledge competitively (they raise their game).

The laid-back, flexible and spontaneous teacher with the organised student can be a dream team or a disaster. To create a positive relationship they need to play to each other's strengths. The student can benefit from the teacher's ability to adapt and change plans and the teacher can benefit from the student's desire to have a plan they can work to and complete. The teacher can also:

■ Encourage and support the student's desire for order, neatness and respecting deadlines.

■ Allow the student independence in planning their work in their own way if they really want to.

■ Encourage the student to embrace flexibility occasionally.

■ Avoid changing plans just for the sake of it; this will only frustrate the student.

78
Lion teacher with Koala student
ESFP and ISFJ

The naturally confident and assertive Lion teacher shares two type preferences with the reticent and dependable Koala. Koalas rarely pop their heads above the parapet and are therefore unlikely to cause trouble. It is more probable they'll be swamped by the strength of the Lion personality and become invisible. For the teacher to get the best out of their reserved student they need to:

■ Slow down and be calm and succinct.

■ Leave plenty of time between question and answer; respect the student's need for time to think and reflect before responding.

■ Allow the student time and space to work on their own; don't hover over their head, waiting to pounce.

■ Pair them up with complementary types (Seahorses, Seals and Cats).

■ Avoid placing them in groups where they are the only **I** preference in a sea of **E** preferences (they'll be smothered).

■ Provide written praise (not just verbal).

■ Avoid trying to fix problems immediately or finish their sentences.

Both teacher and student gather information in the same way. They notice detail using their senses (aware of what they can see, hear and feel). The teacher is naturally sequential and realistic in their teaching style and encourages their students to follow suit. A solid, workman-like relationship develops with both teacher and student mutually understanding what each needs to do to get the job done. For the teacher to get the best out of their grounded student they need to:

■ Provide opportunities for the student to repeat and practise something until it is mastered.

■ Show how learning can be applied in the real world.

■ Encourage the use of imagination as a useful addition to their learning repertoire.

Both teacher and student are interested in people and relationships before the task/subject content. The teacher likes to form personal relationships with all their students, unless they don't like the student (**F** teachers are more inclined than **T** preference teachers to have their favourites!). Because they operate at an emotional level these teachers are more likely to make promises to students, overstretch themselves and even do work the students should be doing themselves. Teacher and student both enjoy a classroom atmosphere that is warm and friendly. Compliments are likely to go in both directions boosting the confidence of teacher as well as student. For the teacher to get the best out of their relationship-focused student they need to:

■ Offer learning situations that allow for the use of empathy, collaboration and teamworking.

■ Give ample and regular praise while offering tactful support to overcome any blind-spots.

■ Motivate by appealing to the strength of your personal belief in the student (don't let me down, I know you can do it).

The laid-back, flexible and spontaneous teacher with the naturally organised student can be a dream team or a disaster. To create a positive relationship they need to play to each other's strengths. The student can benefit from the teacher's ability to adapt and change plans and the teacher can benefit from the student's desire to have a plan they can work to and complete. The teacher can also:

■ Allow the student independence in planning their work in their own way if they really want to.

■ Avoid changing plans just for the sake of it; this will only frustrate the student.

■ Encourage the student to embrace flexibility now and again.

■ Support the student's desire for order, neatness and respecting deadlines.

79
Lion teacher with Seahorse student
ESFP and INFJ

The naturally gregarious Lion teacher shares one type preference with the reticent and dependable Seahorse. Seahorses are quiet and introspective and are therefore unlikely troublemakers. It is more probable they'll be swamped by the strength of the Lion personality and become invisible. For the teacher to get the best out of their reserved student they need to:

■ Slow down and be calm and succinct.

■ Leave plenty of time between question and answer; respect the student's need for time to think and reflect before responding.

■ Allow the student time and space to work on their own; don't hover over their head, waiting to pounce.

■ Avoid trying to fix problems immediately or finish their sentences.

■ Pair them up with complementary types (Seals, Teddy Bears, Koalas and Dolphins).

■ Avoid placing them in groups/teams where they are the only **I** preference in a sea of **E** preferences (they'll be smothered).

■ Provide written praise (not just verbal).

The teacher likes to use their experience to make sense of their learning. The teacher is naturally sequential, sensible and realistic in style and encourages their students to follow suit. The **N** student can find this approach dull. The teacher is likely to see the student as a daydreamer. They should resist the temptation to castigate their student because this is how they take in information and make sense of the world. In the right context daydreaming can lead to better absorption and retention of the topic. To get the best out of their ingenious student the teacher can:

■ Embrace the imagination and insight of the student and what it can bring to the lesson.

■ Encourage the student to become aware of the important contribution of the **S** approach (the value of facts, details, procedure, experiments, applying experience, structure, the step-by-step model).

Both teacher and student are interested in people and relationships before the task/subject content. The Lion teacher likes to form personal relationships with all their students, unless they don't like the student (**F** teachers are more inclined than **T** preference teachers to have their favourites!). Because they operate at an emotional level these teachers are more likely to make promises to students, overstretch themselves and even do work the students should be doing themselves. Teacher and student both enjoy a classroom atmosphere that is warm and friendly. Compliments are likely to go in both directions boosting the confidence of teacher as well as student. For the teacher to get the best out of their relationship-focused student they need to:

■ Offer learning situations that allow for the use of empathy, collaboration and teamworking.

■ Give ample and regular praise while offering tactful support to overcome any blind-spots.

■ Motivate by appealing to the strength of your personal belief in the student (don't let me down, I know you can do it, I like you).

The laid-back, flexible and spontaneous teacher with the naturally organised student can be a dream team or a disaster. To create a positive relationship they need to play to each other's strengths. The student can benefit from the teacher's ability to adapt and change plans and the teacher can benefit from the student's desire to have a plan they can work to and complete. The teacher can also:

■ Encourage and support the student's desire for order, neatness and respecting deadlines.

■ Allow the student independence in planning their work in their own way if they really want to.

■ Avoid changing plans just for the sake of it; this will only frustrate the student.

■ Encourage the student to try new approaches and activities; variety is the spice of life.

80
Lion teacher with Barn Owl student
ESFP and INTJ

The Lion and Barn Owl share no type preferences. The playful and sociable teacher can be balanced by the investigative and organised student. Conflict is most likely when the quiet leadership attributes of the Owl challenge the fun, grounded and bouncy style of their teacher. When opposites don't attract they should try to appreciate their differences. The teacher can also help the naturally analytical Barn Owl progress when they:

- Slow down and are calm and succinct.
- Leave plenty of time between question and answer; respect the student's need for time to think and reflect before responding.
- Allow the student time and space to work on their own; don't hover over their head, waiting to pounce.
- Avoid trying to fix problems immediately or finish their sentences.
- Avoid placing them in groups/teams where they are the only **I** preference in a sea of **E** preferences (they'll be smothered).
- Provide written praise (not just verbal).

The teacher likes to use their experience to make sense of their learning. The teacher is naturally sequential, sensible and realistic in style and encourages their students to follow suit. The **N** student can find this approach dull. The teacher is likely to see the student as a daydreamer. They should resist the temptation to castigate their student because this is how they take in information and make sense of the world. In the right context daydreaming can lead to better absorption and retention of the topic. To get the best out of their ingenious student the teacher can:

- Embrace the imagination and insight of the student and what it can bring to the lesson.
- Encourage the student to become aware of the important contribution of the **S** approach (the value of facts, details, procedure, experiments, applying experience, structure, the step-by-step model).

The teacher is concerned with relationship then task whereas the student is the other way round. The teacher must learn to accept that the student is different; not cold, blunt and unfriendly, but simply focused on task first. If the teacher can accept this the relationship can be really positive for both teacher and student. For the teacher to get the best out of their characteristically assertive student they need to:

- Offer targeted compliments. Just saying everything is great will not impress or help the student; in fact, it can result in the student not respecting the teacher, concluding they lie and/or are a soft touch. When you praise you may be pressed for proof!
- Be logical and objective rather than emotional in discussions.
- Accept that if the student challenges you it is probably to clarify their thoughts. Perhaps ask 'What would you do to improve/change this?' or 'What do you think?' Once they've clarified their thoughts they may be ready to ask and absorb what you think.

- Work in ways that test their skill and knowledge competitively (they raise their game).
- Help them understand that around 50% of people are **F** preference and can interpret feedback as criticism.

When the laid-back, flexible and spontaneous teacher meets the naturally organised student they can complement each other or clash spectacularly. To build a positive relationship they need to play to each other's strengths. The student can benefit from the teacher's ability to adapt and change plans and the teacher can benefit from the student's desire to have a plan they can work to and complete. The teacher can also:

- Encourage and support the student's desire for order, neatness and respecting deadlines.
- Encourage the student to occasionally embrace flexibility.
- Allow the student independence in planning their work in their own way if they really want to.
- Avoid changing plans just for the sake of it; this will only frustrate the student.

81
Panther teacher with Black Bear student
ESTP and ESTJ

Panthers and Black Bears share three preferences. Both are direct, assertive and buoyed when wrestling with a task. The more playful and flexible approach of the teacher can jar with the natural business-like focus of the student. When they learn to appreciate and embrace this difference they can be an effective classroom combination. For the teacher to get the best out of their naturally effusive student they need to:

- Enjoy the lively banter when it is appropriate to spark new thoughts and ideas; the student learns best this way, but remember there may be thirty others in the classroom.
- Stick to the point and stay positive (don't nag), as both teacher and student are easily distracted and liable to go off track!
- Avoid going over old ground.
- Be calm and clear, otherwise two **E** preferences can talk louder and louder like PMQs (with neither listening).
- Remember you can keep some thoughts to yourself (and you may think of a better way of expressing something, especially criticism, later).
- Be an enthusiastic and supportive listener; seek to help the student clarify and develop their thinking rather than assert your own.
- Help each other learn to be quiet and encourage the **I** preferences in the class to express themselves.

Both teacher and student gather information in the same way. They notice detail using their senses (aware of what they can see, hear and feel). Both rely on experience to make sense of their world. Both live in the present. The teacher is generally practical, sequential and realistic in their teaching style and encourages their Black Bear student to follow suit. A solid, workman-

like relationship can develop with both teacher and student mutually understanding what each needs to do to get the job done. For the teacher to get the best out of the most grounded student they need to:

- Demonstrate how learning can be applied in the real world.
- Allow the student opportunities to repeat and practise until satisfied they are competent.
- Encourage the use of imagination as a useful process (it's not wasting time).

Both teacher and student are task-focused, direct, consistent and honest. The classroom is likely to have a business-like, purposeful atmosphere. Students are given clear guidelines on what is expected in terms of behaviour, homework and so on. If the student challenges the teacher it is likely to be for clarification. At best this means everyone knows where they stand and how to behave. For the teacher to get the best out of their fundamentally task-focused student they need to:

- Work in ways that test their skill and knowledge competitively (they raise their game for competitions, challenges, quizzes, measuring and beating personal bests).
- Help them understand that 50% of people are **F** preference and can interpret feedback as criticism.
- Focus on what the student has achieved and what comes next.
- Be prepared to compromise occasionally.
- Avoid trying to fix something without considering potential underlying emotional causes.

The more laid-back, flexible and spontaneous teacher with the naturally organised student can be a dream team or a disaster. To create a positive relationship they need to play to each other's strengths. The student can benefit from the teacher's ability to adapt and change plans and the teacher can benefit from the student's desire to have a plan they can work to and complete. The teacher can also:

- Encourage and support the student's desire for order, neatness and respecting deadlines.
- Allow the student independence in planning their work in their own way if they really want to.
- Avoid changing plans just for the sake of it; this will only frustrate the student.
- Encourage the student to embrace change; Bears will benefit from increased flexibility.

82
Panther teacher with Clownfish student
ESTP and ENFP

Panthers and Clownfish share two preferences. Both are flexible and enjoy the opportunity to be spontaneous in the classroom. They absorb and process information differently which is more likely to lead to confusion than conflict in the classroom. To bring out the best of their essentially outgoing student the teacher needs to:

- Enjoy the lively banter when it is appropriate to spark new thoughts and ideas; the student learns best this way but remember there may be thirty others in the classroom.
- Stick to the point and stay positive (don't nag), as both teacher and student are easily distracted and liable to go off track!
- Avoid going over old ground.
- Provide written praise (not just verbal).
- Let the student know they can always come and talk to you alone during breaks or they can write down their questions/issues for you to reply to later.
- Be calm and clear, otherwise two **E** preferences can talk louder and louder like PMQs (with neither listening).
- Remember you can keep some thoughts to yourself (and you may think of a better way of expressing something, especially criticism, later).
- Be an enthusiastic and supportive listener; seek to help the student clarify and develop their thinking rather than assert your own.
- Help each other learn to be quiet and encourage the **I** preferences in the class to express themselves.

The Panther likes to use their experience to make sense of what they notice. They both live in the present. The teacher is naturally practical and realistic in style and encourages their students to follow suit. The Clownfish may find this style too simplistic and lacking in depth. The teacher is likely to see the student as a daydreamer or 'away with the fairies'. They should resist the temptation to castigate their student because this is how they take in information and make sense of the world. In the right context the daydreaming Clownfish can be incredibly creative and insightful. For the teacher to get the best out of their naturally imaginative student they need to:

- Embrace the imagination and insight of the student and what it can bring to the lesson.
- Encourage the student to become aware of the important contribution of the **S** approach (the value of facts, details, procedure, experiments, applying experience, structure, the step-by-step model).

The teacher is focused first on task and second on people/relationships. The classroom is likely to have a purposeful atmosphere. Students are given clear guidelines on what is expected in terms of behaviour, homework and so on. At best this means everyone knows where they stand and how to behave. At worst the classroom can feel combative and tough. Remember the personal relationship you have with this student is key. The Clownfish needs to feel they like their teacher and that the teacher likes them too. If this happens they'll work harder but if not they may completely switch off. This explains why a student can be top of the class one year (with a teacher they like) and show no interest at all in the subject the following year when they change teacher. For the teacher to get the best out of their empathetic student they need to:

- Offer learning situations that allow for the use of empathy, collaboration and teamworking to counter-balance your natural tendency to focus on task.
- Give ample and regular praise while offering tactful support to overcome any blind-spots. Feedback can be easily interpreted as criticism so walk on egg-shells when delivering it.

- Influence by appealing to the strength of your personal belief in the student (don't let me down, I know you can do it, I like you).
- Be prepared to occasionally compromise your brusque approach to protect the frail self-belief of many outwardly confident Clownfish.

Panthers and Clownfish can be organised and efficient; it's just such an effort! While enjoying a mutual love of spontaneity, which provides each with relief from the stifling and constraining timetables dominating large organisations such as schools, they must also remember to complete any necessary tasks. Although likely to be fun and popular teachers, they also need to focus on the task of preparing the student to succeed socially and academically. Both prefer to start tasks than finish them. Their initial enthusiasm can quickly wane. Both need to ensure they identify and complete the important tasks or the student (or their parents) may eventually ask awkward questions. For the teacher to get the best out of their naturally laid-back student they need to understand the student doesn't just like options and choice; they are essential. The secondary school environment is difficult enough for **P** preference students so teachers can help their student achieve by:

- Providing as much flexibility as possible (multiple choice homework tasks, choice within the lesson).
- Avoiding giving out detailed schedules (they'll just lose it anyway!).
- Mixing things up now and again to prevent predictability becoming boredom. Introduce random surprises and changes.
- Providing time-management tips to ensure the Clownfish can overcome their naturally chaotic approach.

83 Panther teacher with Eagle student
ESTP and ENTJ

Panthers and Eagles share two preferences. Both are assertive and direct. Clashes are likely when assertiveness is interpreted as belligerence or mutiny. It's more likely to be the Eagle student stretching their analytical powers. For teachers with a deft touch the Eagle will become a useful ally rather than a cantankerous insurgent. To bring out the best of their essentially outgoing and 'natural leader' student the teacher needs to:

- Enjoy the lively banter when it is appropriate to spark new thoughts and ideas; the student learns best this way, but remember there may be thirty others in the classroom.
- Stick to the point and stay positive (don't nag), as both teacher and student are easily distracted and liable to go off track!
- Avoid going over old ground.
- Provide written praise (not just verbal).
- Let the student know they can always come and talk to you alone during breaks or they can write down their questions/issues for you to reply to later.

- Be calm and clear, otherwise two **E** preferences can talk louder and louder like PMQs (with neither listening).
- Remember you can keep some thoughts to yourself (and you may think of a better way of expressing something, especially criticism, later).
- Be an enthusiastic and supportive listener; seek to help the student clarify and develop their thinking rather than assert your own.
- Help each other learn to be quiet and encourage the **I** preferences in the class to express themselves.

The teacher likes to use their experience to make sense of what they notice. The teacher is naturally practical and realistic in style and encourages their students to follow suit. The Eagle student may find this superficial and in need of further scrutiny. The teacher is apt to embrace the analytical appetite of the Eagle or experience bewilderment at a perceived slight to their authority. The Panther should resist the temptation to castigate their student because this is how they take in information and make sense of the world. In the right context the confrontational, querying style will lead to a deeper absorption and retention of the subject content. For the teacher to get the best out of their naturally competitive student they need to:

- Embrace the imagination and insight of the student and what it can bring to the lesson.
- Encourage the student to become aware of the important contribution of the **S** approach (the value of facts, details, procedure, experiments, applying experience, structure, the step-by-step model).

Both teacher and student are task-focused, direct, consistent and open. The classroom is likely to have a carnival atmosphere. Students are given clear guidelines on what is expected in terms of behaviour, homework and so on. If the student challenges the teacher it is likely to be for clarification. At best this means everyone knows where they stand and how to behave. For the teacher to get the best out of their fundamentally task-focused student they need to:

- Work in ways that test their skill and knowledge competitively (they raise their game for competitions, challenges, quizzes, measuring and beating personal bests).
- Help them understand that half the population are **F** preference and can interpret feedback as criticism.
- Avoid trying to fix something without considering potential underlying emotional causes.

The more laid-back, flexible and spontaneous teacher with the naturally organised student can be a dream team or a disaster. To create a positive relationship they need to play to each other's strengths. The student can benefit from the teacher's ability to adapt and change plans and the teacher can benefit from the student's desire to have a plan they can work to and complete. The teacher can also:

- Encourage and support the student's desire for order, neatness and respecting deadlines.
- Allow the student independence in planning their work in their own way if they really want to.
- Avoid changing plans just for the sake of it; this will only frustrate the student.
- Encourage the student to embrace plasticity; Eagles will benefit from increased flexibility.

84
Panther teacher with Dolphin student
ESTP and ENFJ

Panthers and Dolphins share one preference. Both are sociable and outgoing. They differ in the way they take in information, make decisions and in their attitude to school and life; the objective and flexible manner of the Panther contrasts with the organised and empathetic style of the Dolphin. To bring out the best of their innately warm and friendly student the teacher needs to:

■ Enjoy the lively banter when it is appropriate to spark new thoughts and ideas; the student learns best this way, but remember there may be thirty others in the classroom.

■ Stick to the point and stay positive (don't nag), as both teacher and student are easily distracted and liable to go off track!

■ Avoid going over old ground.

■ Provide written praise (not just verbal).

■ Let the student know they can always come and talk to you alone during breaks or they can write down their questions/issues for you to reply to later.

■ Be calm and clear, otherwise two **E** preferences can talk louder and louder like PMQs (with neither listening).

■ Remember you can keep some thoughts to yourself (and you may think of a better way of expressing something, especially criticism, later).

■ Be an enthusiastic and supportive listener; seek to help the student clarify and develop their thinking rather than assert your own.

■ Help each other learn to be quiet and encourage the **I** preferences in the class to express themselves.

The teacher likes to use their experience to make sense of what they notice. The teacher is naturally practical and realistic in style and encourages their students to follow suit. The Dolphin student may find this challenging or superficial. The teacher is likely to see the student as a daydreamer or 'away with the fairies'. They should resist the temptation to castigate their student because this is how they take in information and make sense of the world. In the right context daydreaming can lead to the absorption and retention of subject content. For the teacher to get the best out of their naturally imaginative student they need to:

■ Embrace the imagination and insight of the student and what it can bring to the lesson.

■ Encourage the student to become aware of the important contribution of the **S** approach (the value of facts, details, procedure, experiments, applying experience, structure, the step-by-step model).

The teacher is focused first on task and second on people/relationships. The classroom is likely to have a purposeful atmosphere. Students are given clear guidelines on what is expected in terms of behaviour, homework and so on. At best this means everyone knows where they stand and how to behave. At worst the classroom can feel combative and tough to the nurturing Dolphin. Remember the personal relationship you have with this student is key. The Dolphin needs to feel they like their teacher and that the teacher

likes them too. If this happens they'll work harder but if not they may completely switch off. This explains why a student can be top of the class one year (with a teacher they like) and show no interest at all in the subject the following year when they change teacher. For the teacher to get the best out of their fundamentally people-focused student they need to:

■ Offer learning situations that allow for the use of empathy and personal reflection to counter-balance your natural tendency to focus on task and discussion.

■ Give ample and regular praise while offering tactful support to overcome any blind-spots. Feedback can be easily interpreted as criticism so walk on egg-shells when delivering it.

■ Influence by appealing to the strength of your personal belief in the student (don't let me down, I know you can do it, I like you).

■ Be prepared to compromise your ebullient approach to protect the feelings of the Dolphin.

The more laid-back, flexible and spontaneous teacher with the naturally organised student can be a dream team or a disaster. To create a positive relationship they need to play to each other's strengths. The student can benefit from the teacher's ability to adapt and change plans and the teacher can benefit from the student's desire to have a plan they can work to and complete. The teacher can also:

■ Encourage and support the student's desire for order, neatness and respecting deadlines.

■ Allow the student independence in planning their work in their own way if they really want to.

■ Avoid changing plans just for the sake of it; this will only frustrate the student.

■ Encourage the student to embrace flexibility occasionally as it will help the Dolphin to chill out.

85
Panther teacher with Teddy Bear student
ESTP and ESFJ

Panthers and Teddy Bears share two preferences. Both are focused in the real world of facts, learn from experience and are sociable. They differ in the way they make decisions and their attitude to school and life; the objective and flexible manner of the Panther contrasts with the organised and empathetic style of the Teddy. To bring out the best of their innately warm and friendly student the teacher needs to:

■ Enjoy the lively banter when it is appropriate to spark new thoughts and ideas; the student learns best this way, but remember there may be thirty others in the classroom.

■ Stick to the point and stay positive (don't nag), as both teacher and student are easily distracted and liable to go off track!

■ Avoid going over old ground.

■ Provide written praise (not just verbal).

■ Let the student know they can always come and talk to you alone during breaks or they can write down their questions/issues for you to reply to later.

■ Be calm and clear, otherwise two **E** preferences can talk louder and louder like PMQs (with neither listening).

■ Remember you can keep some thoughts to yourself (and you may think of a better way of expressing something, especially criticism, later).

■ Be an enthusiastic and supportive listener; seek to help the student clarify and develop their thinking rather than assert your own.

■ Help each other learn to be quiet and encourage the **I** preferences in the class to express themselves.

The Panther and Teddy prefer to use their experience to make sense of what they notice. They both live in the present. The teacher is naturally practical and realistic in style and encourages their students to follow suit. A strong relationship can flourish with both teacher and student understanding what each needs to do to get the job done. For the teacher to get the best out of their naturally grounded student they need to:

■ Demonstrate how learning can be applied in the real world.

■ Allow the student opportunities to repeat and practise until satisfied they are competent.

■ Encourage the use of imagination as a useful process (it's not wasting time).

The teacher is focused first on task and second on people/relationships. The classroom is likely to have a purposeful atmosphere. Students are given clear guidelines on what is expected in terms of behaviour, homework and so on. At best this means everyone knows where they stand and how to behave. At worst the classroom can feel combative and tough to the nurturing Teddy. Remember the personal relationship you have with this student is key. The Teddy needs to feel they like their teacher and that the teacher likes them too. If this happens they'll work harder but if not they may completely switch off. This explains why a student can be top of the class one year (with a teacher they like) and show no interest at all in the subject the following year when they change teacher. For the teacher to get the best out of their fundamentally people-focused student they need to:

■ Offer learning situations that allow for the use of empathy and personal reflection to counter-balance your natural tendency to focus on task and discussion.

■ Give ample and regular praise while offering tactful support to overcome any blind-spots. Feedback can be easily interpreted as criticism so walk on egg-shells when delivering it.

■ Influence by appealing to the strength of your personal belief in the student (don't let me down, I know you can do it, I like you).

■ Be prepared to compromise your domineering approach to protect the frail self-belief of many Teddies.

When the laid-back, flexible and spontaneous teacher meets the naturally organised student they can complement each other or clash spectacularly. To build a positive relationship they need to play to each other's strengths. The student can benefit from the teacher's ability to adapt and change plans and the teacher can benefit from the student's desire to have a plan they can work to and complete. The teacher can also:

- Encourage and support the student's desire for order, neatness and respecting deadlines.
- Allow the student independence in planning their work in their own way if they really want to.
- Avoid changing plans just for the sake of it; this will only frustrate the student.
- Encourage the student to embrace flexibility as it will help the Teddy relax.

86
Panther teacher with Polar Bear student
ESTP and ISTJ

Panthers and Polar Bears share two preferences. Both are direct, objective and prefer learning from experience. The fun-loving Panther is likely to clash with the more serious and sombre Polar Bear if the teacher does not respect the Bear's need for a business-like approach to work. To avoid this Panther needs to:

- Slow down and be calm and succinct.
- Leave plenty of time between question and answer; respect the student's need for time to think and reflect before responding.
- Allow the student time and space to work on their own; don't hover over their head, waiting to pounce.
- Avoid trying to fix problems immediately or finish their sentences.
- Pair them up with complementary types (Bears and Tigers).
- Avoid placing them in groups/teams where they are the only **I** preference in a sea of **E** preferences (they'll be smothered).
- Provide written praise (not just verbal).

Both Panther and Polar Bear tend to use their past experiences to make sense of the present. The teacher is naturally practical and realistic in style and encourages their students to follow suit. A strong relationship can flourish with both teacher and student understanding what each needs to do to get the job done. For the teacher to get the best out of their naturally grounded student they need to:

- Demonstrate how learning can be applied in the real world.
- Allow the student opportunities to repeat and practise until satisfied they are competent.
- Encourage the use of imagination as a useful process (it's not wasting time).

Both teacher and student are task-focused, direct, consistent and open. The classroom is likely to have a carnival atmosphere. Students are given clear guidelines on what is expected in terms of behaviour, homework and so on. If the student challenges the teacher it is likely to be for clarification. At best this means everyone knows where they stand and how to behave. For the teacher to get the best out of their fundamentally task-focused student they need to:

- Work in ways that test their skill and knowledge competitively (they raise their game for competitions, challenges, quizzes, measuring and beating personal bests).

- Help them understand that 50% of people are **F** preference and can interpret feedback as criticism.
- Avoid trying to fix something without considering potential underlying emotional causes.
- Focus on what the student has achieved and what comes next.
- Be prepared to compromise occasionally.

The more laid-back, flexible and spontaneous Panther teacher with the naturally organised Polar Bear student can be a dream team or a disaster. To create a positive relationship they need to play to each other's strengths. The student can benefit from the teacher's ability to adapt and change plans and the teacher can benefit from the student's desire to have a plan they can work to and complete. The teacher can also:

- Encourage and support the student's desire for order, neatness and respecting deadlines.
- Allow the student independence in planning their work in their own way if they really want to.
- Encourage the student to embrace flexibility now and again, but avoid changing plans just for the sake of it; this will only frustrate the Polar Bear.

87
Panther teacher with Koala student
ESTP and ISFJ

Panthers and Koalas share one preference. Both are focused on the real world of facts and both learn from experience. Rather than clash the teacher is more likely to ignore the potentially invisible Koala. To prevent this possibility:

- Slow down and be calm and succinct.
- Leave plenty of time between question and answer; respect the student's need for time to think and reflect before responding.
- Allow the student time and space to work on their own; don't hover over their head, waiting to pounce.
- Avoid trying to fix problems immediately or finish their sentences.
- Avoid placing them in groups/teams where they are the only **I** preference in a sea of **E** preferences (they'll be smothered).
- Provide written praise (not just verbal).

The Panther and Koala prefer to use their experience to make sense of what they notice. They both live in the present. The teacher is naturally practical and realistic in style and encourages their students to follow suit. A strong relationship can flourish with both teacher and student understanding what each needs to do to get the job done. For the teacher to get the best out of their naturally grounded student they need to:

- Demonstrate how learning can be applied in the real world.
- Allow the student opportunities to repeat and practise until satisfied they are competent.
- Encourage the use of imagination as a useful process (it's not wasting time).

The teacher is focused first on task and second on people/relationships. The classroom is likely to have a purposeful atmosphere. Students are given clear guidelines on what is expected in terms of behaviour, homework and so on. At best this means everyone knows where they stand and how to behave. At worst the classroom can feel combative, tough and overwhelm the coy Koala. Remember the personal relationship you have with this student is key. The Koala needs to feel they like their teacher and that the teacher likes them too. If this happens they'll work harder but if not they may completely switch off. This explains why a student can be top of the class one year (with a teacher they like) and show no interest at all in the subject the following year when they change teacher. For the teacher to get the best out of their fundamentally people-focused student they need to:

- Offer learning situations that allow for the use of empathy, collaboration and small teamworking to counter-balance your natural tendency to focus on task.
- Give ample and regular praise while offering tactful support to overcome any blind-spots. Feedback can be easily interpreted as criticism so tread carefully when delivering it.
- Engage by quietly and regularly stating your personal belief in the student (don't let me down, I know you can do it, I like you).
- Be prepared to compromise your domineering approach to avoid shattering the frail self-belief of many Koalas.

When the laid-back, flexible and spontaneous teacher meets the naturally organised student they can complement each other or clash spectacularly. To build a positive relationship they need to play to each other's strengths. The student can benefit from the teacher's ability to adapt and change plans and the teacher can benefit from the student's desire to have a plan they can work to and complete. The teacher can also:

- Encourage and support the student's desire for order, neatness and respecting deadlines.
- Allow the student independence in planning their work in their own way if they really want to.
- Avoid changing plans just for the sake of it; this will only frustrate the student.
- Nurture flexibility as this will help agitated Koalas to chill out.

88
Panther teacher with Panther student
ESTP and ESTP

The naturally assertive teacher and student share all four preferences. Panthers are rare as teachers so Panther students can benefit greatly from being with a role model they can identify with and emulate. Clashes are likely to centre on the student's desire for drama and fun to be a constant feature in the classroom. This can test the patience even of the like-minded teacher. To get the best out of their innately ebullient student the teacher needs to:

- Enjoy the lively banter when it is appropriate to spark new thoughts and ideas; the student learns best this way, but remember there may be thirty others in the classroom.
- Stick to the point and stay positive (don't nag), as both teacher and student are easily distracted and liable to go off track!
- Avoid going over old ground.
- Provide written praise (not just verbal).
- Let the student know they can always come and talk to you alone during breaks or they can write down their questions/issues for you to reply to later.
- Be calm and clear, otherwise two **E** preferences can talk louder and louder with neither listening.
- Remember you can keep some thoughts to yourself (and you may think of a better way of expressing something, especially criticism, later).
- Be an enthusiastic and supportive listener; seek to help the student clarify and develop their thinking rather than assert your own.
- Help each other learn to be quiet and encourage the **I** preferences in the class to express themselves.

Both teacher and student gather information in the same urgent way. They notice detail using their senses (aware of what they can see, hear and feel). They both use their experience to make sense of their world. They both live in the moment. A strong relationship can flourish with both teacher and student understanding what each needs to do to get the job done. For the teacher to get the best out of their naturally grounded student they need to:

- Demonstrate how learning can be applied in the real world.
- Allow the student opportunities to repeat and practise until satisfied they are competent.
- Encourage the use of imagination as a useful process (it's not wasting time).

Both teacher and student are task-focused, direct, consistent and open. The classroom is likely to have a carnival atmosphere. Students are given clear guidelines on what is expected in terms of behaviour, homework and so on. If the student challenges the teacher it is likely to be for clarification. At best this means everyone knows where they stand and how to behave. For the teacher to get the best out of their fundamentally task-focused student they need to:

- Work in ways that test their skill and knowledge competitively (they raise their game for competitions, challenges, quizzes, measuring and beating personal bests).
- Help them understand that 50% of people are **F** preference and can interpret feedback as criticism.
- Avoid trying to fix something without considering potential underlying emotional causes.
- Focus on what the student has achieved and what comes next.
- Be prepared to compromise occasionally.

Panthers can learn to be organised and efficient but it is tolerated rather than embraced enthusiastically. While enjoying a mutual love of spontaneity, which provides each with relief from the stifling and constraining timetables and deadlines essential in large organisations such as schools, they must also remember to complete any necessary tasks. Although likely to be fun and popular teachers, they also need to focus on the

task of preparing the student to succeed socially and academically. Both prefer to start tasks than finish them. Their initial enthusiasm can quickly wane. Both need to ensure they identify and complete the important tasks or the student (or their parents) may eventually ask awkward questions. For the teacher to get the best out of their naturally laid-back student they need to understand the student doesn't just like options and choice; they are essential. The secondary school environment is difficult enough for **P** preference students so teachers can help their student achieve by:

- Helping the student identify ways they can organise and manage their time to complete important work without a last-minute rush.
- Providing as much flexibility as possible (multiple choice homework tasks, choice within the lesson).
- Being wary of providing detailed schedules (they'll just be lost!).
- Stirring things up now and again to prevent predictability becoming boredom. Introduce random surprises and changes.

89
Panther teacher with Falcon student
ESTP and ENTP

Bart Simpson meets Bob Geldof! The irrepressibly confident and assertive Panther teacher with the equally excitable Falcon student is a rare combination. Both are naturally rebellious and restless. Both crave action. They will gel when the subject is deemed interesting enough to stop their minds wandering into other areas. Falcon students can be the most challenging in the traditional classroom environment. Teachers that create an unconventional classroom tend to have most success with Falcon students. For the teacher to get the best out of their naturally effusive student they need to:

- Enjoy the lively banter when it is appropriate to spark new thoughts and ideas; the student learns best this way, but remember there may be thirty others in the classroom.
- Stick to the point and stay positive (don't nag), as both teacher and student are easily distracted and liable to go off track!
- Avoid going over old ground.
- Remember you can keep some thoughts to yourself (and you may think of a better way of expressing something, especially criticism, later).
- Be an enthusiastic and supportive listener; seek to help the student clarify and develop their thinking rather than assert your own.
- Be calm and clear, otherwise two **E** preferences can talk louder and louder like PMQs (with neither listening).
- Help each other learn to be quiet and encourage the **I** preferences in the class to express themselves.

The teacher likes to use their experience to make sense of what they notice. The teacher is naturally practical and realistic in style and encourages their students to follow suit. The **N** prefer-

ence Falcon student may find this challenging or boring. The teacher is likely to see the student as a daydreamer or 'away with the fairies'. They should resist the temptation to castigate their student because this is how they take in information and make sense of the world. In the right context daydreaming can lead to the invention of cars, planes, medicines and computers. For the teacher to get the best out of their imaginative student they need to:

- Embrace the imagination and insight of the student and what it can bring to the lesson.
- Encourage the student to become aware of the important contribution of the **S** approach (the value of facts, details, procedure, experiments, applying experience, structure, the step-by-step model).

Both teacher and student are task-focused, direct, consistent and honest. The classroom is likely to have a business-like, purposeful atmosphere. Students are given clear guidelines on what is expected in terms of behaviour, homework and so on. If the student challenges the teacher it is likely to be for clarification. At best this means everyone knows where they stand and how to behave. For the teacher to get the best out of their fundamentally task-focused student they need to:

- Work in ways that test their skill and knowledge competitively (they raise their game for competitions, challenges, quizzes, measuring and beating personal bests).
- Help them understand that 50% of people are **F** preference and can interpret feedback as criticism.
- Focus on what the student has achieved and what comes next.
- Be prepared to compromise occasionally.
- Avoid trying to fix something without considering potential underlying emotional causes.

Panthers and Falcons abhor to-do-lists, schedules and predictability; they rarely reach the status of an acquired taste or a honed skill. While enjoying their mutual love of spontaneity, which provides each with relief from the stifling and constraining timetables and deadlines essential in large organisations such as schools, they must also remember to complete any necessary tasks. Although likely to be fun and popular teachers, they also need to focus on the task of preparing the student to succeed socially and academically. Both prefer to start tasks than finish them. Their initial enthusiasm can quickly wane. Both need to ensure they identify and complete the important tasks or the student (or their parents) may eventually ask awkward questions. For the teacher to get the best out of their naturally laid-back student they need to understand the student doesn't just like options and choice; they are essential. The secondary school environment is difficult enough for **P** preference students so teachers can help their student achieve by:

- Providing as much flexibility as possible (multiple choice homework tasks, choice within the lesson).
- Avoiding giving out detailed schedules (they'll just lose it anyway!).
- Mixing things up now and again to prevent predictability becoming boredom. Introduce random surprises and changes.
- Helping the student identify ways they can organise and manage their time to complete important work without a last-minute rush.

90
Panther teacher with Tiger student
ESTP and ISTP

All four Cats are realistic, adaptable and action-oriented. Traditional 'sit still and listen' teaching does not play to their natural strengths. The teacher can help draw out the best of the Tiger and help them succeed by using their interest in learning independently from experience and action. Both like action and variety and excel when learning is fun as well as purposeful. For the Panther teacher to get the best out of their more reserved Tiger student they need to:

■ Slow down and be calm and succinct.

■ Shun hectoring the student for an answer or opinion; respect their need for time to think and reflect before answering.

■ Provide written praise (not just verbal).

■ Allow the student time and space to work on their own; don't hover over their head, waiting to pounce.

■ Let the student know they can always come and talk to you alone during breaks or they can write down their questions/issues for you to reply to later.

■ Avoid trying to fix problems immediately or finish their sentences.

■ Avoid placing them in groups/teams where they are the only **I** preference in a sea of **E** preferences (they'll be smothered).

Both teacher and student gather information in the same way. They notice detail using their senses (aware of what they can see, hear and feel). Both use their experience to make sense of their world. They both live in the present. The teacher is naturally sequential and realistic in their teaching style and likes their students to follow suit. A solid, workman-like relationship develops with both teacher and student mutually understanding what each needs to do to get the job done. For the teacher to get the best out of their down-to-earth student they need to:

■ Describe how learning can be applied in the real world.

■ Provide opportunities for the student to repeat and practise until satisfied they are competent.

■ Encourage the use of imagination as a useful process (it's not wasting time).

Both teacher and student are task-focused, consistent and honest. The classroom is likely to have a purposeful atmosphere. Students are given clear guidelines on what is expected in terms of behaviour, homework and so on. If the student challenges the teacher it is likely to be for clarification. At best this means everyone knows where they stand and how to behave. For the teacher to get the best out of their naturally grounded student they need to:

■ Work in ways that test their skill and knowledge competitively (they raise their game for competitions, challenges, quizzes, measuring and beating personal bests).

■ Help them understand that 50% of people are **F** preference and can interpret feedback as criticism.

■ Be prepared to compromise occasionally.

■ Focus on what the student has achieved and what comes next.

■ Avoid trying to fix something without considering potential underlying emotional causes.

P preferences can be organised and efficient; it's just such an effort! While enjoying a mutual love of spontaneity which provides each with relief from the stifling and constraining timetables and deadlines essential in large organisations such as schools, they must also remember to complete any necessary tasks. Although likely to be fun and popular teachers, they also need to focus on the task of preparing the student to succeed socially and academically. Both prefer to start tasks than finish them. Their initial enthusiasm can quickly evaporate. Both need to ensure they identify and complete the important tasks or the student (or their parents) may eventually ask awkward questions. For the teacher to get the best out of their naturally laid-back student they need to understand the student doesn't just like options and choice; they are essential. The secondary school environment is difficult enough for **P** preference students so teachers can help their student achieve by:

■ Providing as much flexibility as possible (multiple choice homework tasks, choice within the lesson).

■ Avoiding giving out detailed schedules (they'll just lose it anyway!).

■ Mixing things up now and again to prevent predictability becoming boredom. Introduce random surprises and changes.

■ Introducing simple time-management techniques to ensure the Tiger completes important work on time.

91
Panther teacher with Lion student
ESTP and ESFP

The Panther teacher and Lion student share three preferences. Both seek out action and variety and thrive when learning is fun as well as purposeful. But, like an episode of *Top Gear*, the reckless camaraderie can be nauseous, so the teacher needs to:

■ Enjoy the lively banter when it is appropriate to spark new thoughts and ideas; the student learns best this way, but remember there may be thirty others in the classroom.

■ Stick to the point and stay positive (don't nag), as both teacher and student are easily distracted and liable to go off track!

■ Help each other learn to be quiet and encourage the **I** preferences in the class to express themselves.

■ Avoid going over old ground.

■ Be calm and clear, otherwise two **E** preferences can talk louder and louder like PMQs (with neither listening).

■ Remember you can keep some thoughts to yourself (and you may think of a better way of expressing something, especially criticism, later).

■ Be an enthusiastic and supportive listener; seek to help the student clarify and develop their thinking rather than assert your own.

Both teacher and student gather information in the same way. They notice detail using their senses (aware of what they can see, hear and feel) They both use their experience to make sense of their world. They both live in the present. The teacher is naturally sequential and realistic in their teaching style and likes their students to follow suit. A solid, workman-like relationship develops with both teacher and student mutually understanding what each needs to do to get the job done. For the teacher to get the best out of their naturally grounded student they need to:

■ Demonstrate how learning can be applied in the real world.

■ Encourage the use of imagination as a useful process (it's not wasting time).

■ Allow the student opportunities to repeat and practise until satisfied they are competent.

The teacher is focused first on task and second on people/relationships. The classroom is likely to have a business-like, purposeful atmosphere. Students are given clear guidelines on what is expected in terms of behaviour, homework and so on. At best this means everyone knows where they stand and how to behave. At worst the classroom can feel combative and tough. Remember the personal relationship you have with this student is key. The Lion needs to feel they like their teacher and that the teacher likes them too. If this happens they'll work harder but if not they may completely switch off. This explains why a student can be top of the class one year (with a teacher they like) and show no interest at all in the subject the following year when they change teacher. For the teacher to get the best out of their fundamentally people-focused student they need to:

■ Influence by appealing to the strength of your personal belief in the student (don't let me down, I know you can do it, I like you).

■ Offer learning situations that allow for the use of empathy, collaboration and teamworking to counter-balance your natural tendency to focus on task.

■ Give ample and regular praise while offering tactful support to overcome any blind-spots. Feedback can be easily interpreted as criticism so walk on egg-shells if you need to reprimand.

■ Be prepared to compromise occasionally.

Panthers and Lions abhor to-do-lists, schedules and predictability; they rarely reach the status of an acquired taste or a honed skill. While enjoying their mutual love of spontaneity, which provides each with relief from the stifling and constraining timetables and deadlines essential in large organisations such as schools, they must also remember to complete any necessary tasks. Although likely to be fun and popular teachers, they also need to focus on the task of preparing the student to succeed socially and academically. Both prefer to start tasks than finish them. Their initial enthusiasm can quickly wane. Both need to ensure they identify and complete the important tasks or the student (or their parents) may eventually ask awkward questions. For the teacher to get the best out of their naturally laid-back student they need to understand the student doesn't just like options and choice; they are essential. The secondary school environment is difficult enough for **P** preference students so teachers can help their student achieve by:

- Providing as much flexibility as possible (multiple choice homework tasks, choice within the lesson).
- Helping the student identify simple but effective strategies to ensure they can succeed.
- Avoiding giving out detailed schedules (they'll just lose it anyway!).
- Mixing things up now and again to prevent predictability becoming boredom. Introduce random surprises and changes.

92
Panther teacher with Cat student
ESTP and ISFP

All four Cats are realistic, adaptable and action-oriented. Traditional classroom teaching does not play to their natural strengths. The Panther teacher can help draw out the best of the Cat and help them succeed by using their interest in learning independently from experience and action. The Panther and Cat share two preferences. Both like variety and prefer learning when it is fun as well as purposeful. For the teacher to get the best out of their naturally reserved student they need to:

- Avoid trying to fix problems immediately or finish their sentences.
- Pair them up with complementary types (Seahorses, Seals, Teddy Bears and Dolphins).
- Avoid placing them in groups/teams where they are the only **I** preference in a sea of **E** preferences (they'll be smothered).
- Provide written praise (not just verbal).
- Let the student know they can always come and talk to you alone during breaks or they can write down their questions/issues for you to reply to later.
- Slow down and be calm and succinct.
- Leave plenty of time between question and answer; respect the student's need for time to think and reflect before responding.
- Allow the student time and space to work on their own; don't hover over their head, waiting to pounce.

Both teacher and student gather information in the same way. They notice detail using their senses (aware of what they can see, hear and feel). They both use their experience to make sense of their world. They both live in the present. The teacher is naturally sequential and realistic in their teaching style and likes their students to follow suit. A solid, workman-like relationship develops with both teacher and student mutually understanding what each needs to do to get the job done. For the teacher to get the best out of their grounded student they need to:

- Demonstrate how learning can be applied in the real world.
- Allow the student opportunities to repeat and practise until satisfied they are competent.
- Encourage the use of imagination as a useful process (it's not wasting time).

The teacher is focused first on task and second on people/relationships. The classroom is likely to have a business-like, purposeful atmosphere.

Students are given clear guidelines on what is expected in terms of behaviour, homework and so on. At best this means everyone knows where they stand and how to behave. At worst the classroom can feel as unnecessarily combative as an episode of *Top Gear*. Remember the personal relationship you have with this student is key. The Cat needs to feel they like their teacher and that the teacher likes them too. If this happens they'll work harder but if not they may completely switch off. This explains why a student can be top of the class one year (with a teacher they like) and show no interest at all in the subject the following year when they change teacher. For the teacher to get the best out of their fundamentally people-focused student they need to:

- Offer learning situations that allow for the use of empathy, collaboration and teamworking to counter-balance your natural tendency to focus on task.
- Give ample and regular praise while offering tactful support to overcome any blind-spots. Feedback can be easily interpreted as criticism so walk on egg-shells when delivering it.
- Influence by appealing to the strength of your personal belief in the student (don't let me down, I know you can do it, I like you).
- Be prepared to compromise occasionally.

Panthers and Cats can be organised and efficient; it's just such an effort! While enjoying a mutual love of spontaneity, which provides each with relief from the stifling and constraining time-tables and deadlines essential in large organisations such as schools, they must also remember to complete any necessary tasks. Although likely to be fun and popular teachers, they also need to focus on the task of preparing the student to succeed socially and academically. Both prefer to start tasks than finish them. Their initial enthusiasm can quickly dissipate. Both need to ensure they identify and complete the important tasks or the student (or their parents) may eventually ask awkward questions. For the teacher to get the best out of their naturally laid-back student they need to understand the student doesn't just like options and choice; they are essential. The secondary school environment is difficult enough for **P** preference students so teachers can assist their student to achieve by:

- Providing as much flexibility as possible (multiple choice homework tasks, choice within the lesson).
- Avoiding giving out detailed schedules (they'll just lose it anyway!).
- Mixing things up now and again to prevent predictability becoming boredom. Introduce random surprises and changes.
- Helping the student identify ways they can organise and manage their time to complete important work without a last-minute rush.

93
Panther teacher with Barn Owl student
ESTP and INTJ

The Panther teacher shares just one preference with their Barn Owl student. Both are assertive and direct. Clashes are likely when assertiveness

is interpreted as belligerence or mutiny. It's more likely to be the Owl student stretching their analytical powers. For teachers with a deft touch the Barn Owl will become a useful ally rather than a cantankerous insurgent. To get the best out of the naturally introspective Owl student:

- Slow down and be calm and succinct.
- Leave plenty of time between question and answer; respect the student's need for time to think and reflect before responding.
- Allow the student time and space to work on their own; don't hover over their head, waiting to pounce.
- Avoid trying to fix problems immediately or finish the Barn Owl's sentences.
- Pair them up with complementary types (Owls, Tigers and Polar Bears).
- Avoid placing them in groups/teams where they are the only **I** preference in a sea of **E** preferences (they'll be annoyed or ignored).
- Provide written praise (not just verbal).
- Let the student know they can always come and talk to you alone during breaks or they can write down their questions/issues for you to reply to later.

The Panther teacher likes to use their experience to make sense of what they notice. They live in the present. The teacher is naturally practical and impulsive in style and encourages their students to follow suit. The Barn Owl student may find this challenging or boring. The teacher is likely to see the student as a tactician or daydreamer. They should resist the temptation to castigate their student because this is how they take in information and make sense of the world. In the right context daydreaming can lead to new insights and inventions. For the teacher to get the best out of their rational student they need to:

- Embrace the imagination and insight of the student and what it can bring to the lesson.
- Encourage the student to become aware of the important contribution of the **S** approach (the value of facts, details, procedure, experiments, applying experience, structure, the step-by-step model).

Both teacher and student are objective and direct. The classroom is likely to have a purposeful atmosphere. Students are given clear guidelines on what is expected in terms of behaviour, homework and so on. If the student challenges the teacher it is likely to be for clarification. At best this means both know where they stand and how to behave. For the teacher to get the best out of their naturally analytical student they need to:

- Work in ways that test their skill and knowledge competitively (they raise their game for competitions, challenges, quizzes, measuring and beating personal bests).
- Help them understand that 50% of people are **F** preference and can take well-intentioned feedback as criticism.
- Focus on what the student has achieved and what comes next.
- Be prepared to compromise occasionally.
- Avoid trying to fix something without considering potential underlying emotional causes.

The laid-back, flexible and spontaneous teacher with the naturally organised student can be a dream team or a disaster. To create a positive relationship they need to play to each other's strengths. The student can benefit from the teacher's ability to adapt and change plans and the teacher can benefit from the student's desire to have a plan they can work to and complete. The teacher can also:

- Encourage and support the student's desire for order, neatness and respecting deadlines.
- Allow the student independence in planning their work in their own way if they really want to.
- Avoid changing plans just for the sake of it; this will only frustrate the student.
- Encourage the student to embrace flexibility as this helps Barn Owls to chill out.

94
Panther teacher with Tawny Owl student
ESTP and INTP

The Panther teacher shares two preferences with their Tawny Owl student. Both are assertive and direct. Clashes are likely when assertiveness is interpreted as belligerence or disinterest. It's more likely to be the Owl student stretching their analytical powers. For teachers with a deft touch the Tawny Owl will become a useful ally rather than an interfering 'mad professor'. For the teacher to get the best out of their inherently introspective student they need to:

- Slow down and be calm and succinct.
- Leave plenty of time between question and answer; respect the student's need for time to think and reflect before responding.
- Allow the student time and space to work on their own; don't hover over their head, waiting to pounce.
- Avoid trying to fix problems immediately or finish the Owl's sentences.
- Pair them up with complementary types (Owls, Tigers and Polar Bears).
- Avoid placing them in groups/teams where they are the only **I** preference in a sea of **E** preferences (they'll be annoyed or ignored).
- Provide written praise (not just verbal).

The Panther teacher likes to use their experience to make sense of what they notice. They live in the present. The teacher is naturally practical and impulsive in style and encourages their students to follow suit. The Tawny Owl student may find this challenging or boring. The teacher is likely to see the student as a daydreamer. They should resist the temptation to scold their student because this is how they take in information and make sense of the world. In the right context daydreaming can lead to new insights and inventions. For the teacher to get the best out of their rational student they need to:

- Embrace the imagination and insight of the student and what it can bring to the lesson.
- Encourage the student to become aware of the important contribution of the **S** approach (the value of facts, details, procedure, experiments, applying experience, structure, the step-by-step model).

Both teacher and student are objective and direct. The classroom is likely to have a purposeful atmosphere. Students are given clear guidelines on what is expected in terms of behaviour, homework and so on. If the student challenges the teacher it is likely to be for clarification. At best this means both know where they stand and how to behave. For the teacher to get the best out of their naturally analytical student they need to:

- Work in ways that test their skill and knowledge competitively (they raise their game for competitions, challenges, quizzes, measuring and beating personal bests).
- Help them understand that 50% of people are **F** preference and can take well-intentioned feedback as criticism.
- Focus on what the student has achieved and what comes next.
- Be prepared to compromise occasionally.
- Avoid trying to fix something without considering potential underlying emotional causes.

Panthers and Tawny Owls can be organised and efficient; it's just such an effort! While enjoying a mutual love of spontaneity, which provides each with relief from the stifling and constraining timetables and deadlines essential in large organisations such as schools, they must also remember to complete any necessary tasks. Although likely to be fun and popular teachers, they also need to focus on the task of preparing the student to succeed socially and academically. Both prefer to start tasks than finish them. Their initial enthusiasm can quickly wane. Both need to ensure they identify and complete the important tasks or the student (or their parents) may eventually ask awkward questions. For the teacher to get the best out of their naturally laid-back student they need to understand the student doesn't just like options and choice; they are essential. The secondary school environment is tough enough for **P** preference students so teachers can help their student achieve by:

- Avoiding giving out detailed schedules (they'll just lose it anyway!).
- Mixing things up now and again to prevent predictability becoming boredom. Introduce random surprises and changes.
- Helping the student identify time-management strategies to ensure they can succeed.
- Providing as much flexibility as possible (multiple choice homework tasks, choice within the lesson).

95
Panther teacher with Seahorse student
ESTP and INFJ

Panthers and Seahorses share no type preferences. Opposites can attract when they genuinely embrace and appreciate each other's contributions. When the teacher respects and utilises the student's desire for space to ponder, daydream, personalise learning and organise their work a strong relationship is likely. The Seahorse is naturally very empathetic which requires the more abrasive Panther to:

- Slow down and be calm and succinct.
- Leave plenty of time between question and answer; respect the student's need for time to think and reflect before responding.

- Allow the student time and space to work on their own; don't hover over their head, waiting to pounce.
- Avoid trying to fix problems immediately or finish their sentences.
- Avoid placing them in groups/teams where they are the only **I** preference in a sea of **E** preferences (they'll be swamped).
- Provide written praise (not just verbal).

The Panther likes to use their experience to make sense of what they notice. They both live in the present. The teacher is naturally practical and realistic in style and encourages their students to follow suit. The Seahorse may find this style too simplistic and lacking in depth. The teacher is likely to see the student as a daydreamer or 'away with the fairies'. They should resist the temptation to dismiss the student's imagination because this is how they take in information and make sense of the world. In the right context the daydreaming Seahorse can absorb and retain more learning using their preference. For the teacher to get the best out of their imaginative student they need to:

- Embrace the imagination and insight of the student and what it can bring to the lesson.
- Encourage the student to become aware of the important contribution of the **S** approach (the value of facts, details, procedure, experiments, applying experience, structure, the step-by-step model).

The teacher is focused first on task and second on people/relationships. The classroom is likely to have a purposeful atmosphere. Students are given clear guidelines regarding what is expected in terms of behaviour, homework and so on. At best this means everyone knows where they stand and how to behave. At worst the classroom can feel combative and tough. Remember the personal relationship you have with this student is key. The Seahorse needs to feel they like their teacher and that the teacher likes them too. If this happens they'll work harder but if not they may completely switch off. This explains why a student can be top of the class one year (with a teacher they like) and show no interest at all in the subject the following year when they change teacher. To get the best out of the fundamentally people-focused student:

- Offer learning situations that allow for the use of empathy, collaboration and teamworking to counter-balance your natural tendency to focus on task.
- Give ample and regular praise while offering tactful support to overcome any blind-spots. Feedback can be easily interpreted as criticism so walk on egg-shells when delivering it.
- Influence by appealing to the strength of your personal belief in the student (don't let me down, I know you can do it, I like you).
- Be prepared to compromise your brusque approach to protect the frail self-belief of many Seahorses.

The more laid-back, flexible and spontaneous teacher with the naturally organised student can be a dream team or a disaster. To create a positive relationship they need to play to each other's strengths. The student can benefit from the teacher's ability to adapt and change plans and the teacher can benefit from the student's desire to have a plan they can work to and complete. The teacher can also:

- Encourage and support the student's desire for order, neatness and respecting deadlines.

- Allow the student independence in planning their work in their own way if they really want to.
- Avoid changing plans just for the sake of it; this will only frustrate the student.
- Encourage the student to embrace flexibility – even Seahorses need to relax occasionally.

96
Panther teacher with Seal student
ESTP and INFP

Panthers and Seals share just one preference. Both are flexible and enjoy the opportunity to be spontaneous in the classroom. When the teacher respects and utilises the Seal's desire for space to ponder, daydream and personalise learning a strong relationship is likely. The Seal is the most inclusive and empathetic of all types, which requires the naturally cavalier Panther to:

- Slow down and be calm and succinct.
- Leave plenty of time between question and answer; respect the student's need for time to think and reflect before responding.
- Allow the student time and space to work on their own; don't hover over their head, waiting to pounce.
- Avoid trying to fix problems immediately or finish their sentences.
- Avoid placing them in groups/teams where they are the only **I** preference in a sea of **E** preferences (they'll be smothered).
- Provide written praise (not just verbal).

The Panther likes to use their experience to make sense of what they notice. They both live in the present. The teacher is naturally practical and realistic in style and encourages their students to follow suit. The Seal may find this style too simplistic and lacking in depth. The teacher is likely to see the student as a daydreamer or 'away with the fairies'. They should resist the temptation to castigate their student because this is how they take in information and make sense of the world. In the right context the daydreaming Seal can write novels, poems and philosophy. For the teacher to get the best out of their inherently imaginative student they need to:

- Embrace the imagination and insight of the student and what it can bring to the lesson.
- Encourage the student to become aware of the important contribution of the **S** approach (the value of facts, details, procedure, experiments, applying experience, structure, the step-by-step model).

The teacher is focused first on task and second on people/relationships. The classroom is likely to have a purposeful atmosphere. Students are given clear guidelines on what is expected in terms of behaviour, homework and so on. At best this means everyone knows where they stand and how to behave. At worst the classroom can feel combative and tough. Remember the personal relationship you have with this student is key. The Seal needs to feel they like their teacher and that the teacher likes them too. If this happens they'll work harder but if not they may completely switch off. This explains why a student

can be top of the class one year (with a teacher they like) and show no interest at all in the subject the following year when they change teacher. For the teacher to get the best out of their fundamentally people-focused student they need to:

- Offer learning situations that allow for the use of empathy, collaboration and teamworking to counter-balance your natural tendency to focus on task.
- Give ample and regular praise while offering tactful support to overcome any blind-spots. Feedback can be easily interpreted as criticism so walk on egg-shells when delivering it.
- Influence by appealing to the strength of your personal belief in the student (don't let me down, I know you can do it, I like you).
- Be prepared to occasionally compromise your curt approach to protect the fragile self-belief of many Seals.

Panthers and Seals can be organised and efficient; it's just such an effort! While enjoying a mutual love of spontaneity, which provides each with relief from the stifling and constraining time-tables and deadlines essential in large organisations such as schools, they must also remember to complete any necessary tasks. Although likely to be fun and popular teachers, they also need to focus on the task of preparing the student to succeed socially and academically. Both prefer to start tasks than finish them. Their initial enthusiasm can quickly wane. Both need to ensure they identify and complete the important tasks or the student (or their parents) may eventually ask awkward questions. For the teacher to get the best out of their naturally laid-back student they need to understand the student doesn't just like options and choice; they are essential. The secondary school environment is difficult enough for **P** preference students so teachers can help their student achieve by:

- Providing as much flexibility as possible (multiple choice homework tasks, choice within the lesson).
- Avoiding giving out detailed schedules (they'll just lose it anyway!).
- Mixing things up now and again to prevent predictability becoming boredom. Introduce random surprises and changes.
- Introducing time-management tips to help the Seal complete important tasks on time.

97
Tiger teacher with Tawny Owl student
ISTP and INTP

Tigers and Tawny Owls share three type preferences. Both are reserved, detached observers and fiercely autonomous. Their similarities can form the basis of a strong relationship. Clashes are likely when their independent streak prevents the student from seeking help when it is needed. For the teacher to get the best out of their naturally reserved student they need to:

- Respect the student's need for privacy and independence.

- Take time to clarify your thoughts but don't avoid confrontation; if something needs to be said be calm and direct as you deliver it.
- Use non-verbal communication – smiles and gestures are reassuring to **I** students; you can even use sticky notes/emails to pass on feedback.
- Allow the student plenty of time to think through their thoughts.
- Share your ideas and thoughts regularly to ensure you both know what you're doing.

The teacher likes to use their experience to make sense of things. The one-step-at-a-time teacher encourages their students to follow suit. The **N** student will at best find this over-simplistic and at worst find it boring. The teacher is likely to label the student as 'away with the fairies'. They should resist the temptation to castigate their student because this is how they take in information and make sense of the subject. In the right context daydreaming can lead to new ways of absorbing and retaining information. For the teacher to get the best out of their inherently imaginative student they need to:

- Embrace the imagination and insight of the student and what it can bring to the lesson.
- Encourage the student to become aware of the important contribution of the **S** approach (the value of facts, details, procedure, experiments, applying experience, structure, the step-by-step model).

Both teacher and student are task-focused, direct, consistent and honest. The classroom is likely to have a business-like, purposeful atmosphere. Students are given clear guidelines on what is expected in terms of behaviour, homework and so on. If the student challenges the teacher it is likely to be for clarification. At best this means everyone knows where they stand and how to behave. At worst the classroom can be an assembly line of serious learning modules devoid of fun and real engagement. For the teacher to get the best out of their fundamentally task-focused student they need to:

- Work in ways that test their skill and knowledge competitively (they raise their game for competitions, challenges, quizzes, measuring and beating personal bests).
- Help them understand that 50% of people are **F** preference and can interpret feedback as criticism.
- Focus on what the student has achieved and what comes next.
- Be prepared to compromise occasionally.
- Avoid trying to fix something without considering potential underlying emotional causes.

Tigers and Tawny Owls can be organised and efficient; it's just such an effort! While enjoying a mutual love of spontaneity, which provides each with relief from the stifling and constraining timetables and deadlines essential in large organisations such as schools, they must also remember to complete any necessary tasks. Although likely to be fun and popular teachers, they also need to focus on the task of preparing the student to succeed socially and academically. Both prefer to start tasks than finish them. Their initial enthusiasm can quickly wane. Both need to ensure they identify and complete the important tasks or the student (or their parents) may eventually ask awkward questions. For the teacher to get the best out of their naturally laid-back student they need to understand the student doesn't just like options and choice; they are essential or they start to itch, squirm and rebel. The secondary school environment is difficult enough for **P** preference students so teachers can help their student achieve by:

- Providing as much flexibility as possible (multiple choice homework tasks, choice within the lesson).
- Avoiding detailed schedules (they'll just lose it anyway!).
- Shaking things up now and again to prevent predictability becoming boredom. Introduce random surprises and changes.
- Identifying clear strategies to ensure they can manage their workload successfully.

98
Tiger teacher with Teddy Bear student
ISTP and ESFJ

Tigers and Teddy Bears share one type preference. When they gel they can help stretch each other which will benefit the whole class. For the teacher to get the best out of their Teddy student they need to accept and embrace the Bear's need to socialise and organise their work. To support their naturally lively student they can also:

- Listen patiently and enthusiastically to the student impulsively expressing their thoughts.
- Stay open to 'silly' ideas to see where they lead – the student is thinking out loud and this is how they learn best.
- Also offer your own thoughts; if you need a timeout ask for one.
- Encourage the student to think things through before talking otherwise they may sabotage the lesson.
- Steer the student away from controversial subjects, especially in group discussions.
- Build in plenty of opportunities during lessons for the **E** students to talk things through with other **E** preferences.

Both teacher and student gather information in the same way. They notice detail using their senses (aware of what they can see, hear and feel). Both live in the present. The teacher is naturally sequential and realistic in their teaching style and encourages their students to follow suit. A solid, workman-like relationship develops with both teacher and student mutually understanding what each needs to do to get the job done. For the teacher to get the best out of their grounded student they need to:

- Allow the student opportunities to repeat and practise until satisfied they are competent.
- Describe how learning can be applied in the real world.
- Encourage the use of imagination as a useful process (it's not wasting time).

The teacher is focused first on task and second on people/relationships. The classroom is likely to have a business-like, purposeful atmosphere. Students are given clear guidelines on what is expected in terms of behaviour, homework and so on. At best this means everyone knows where they stand and how to behave. At worst the classroom can resemble a military boot-camp devoid of fun. Remember the personal relationship you

have with this student is key. The Teddy needs to feel they like their teacher and that the teacher likes them too. If this happens they'll work harder but if not they may switch off. This explains why a student can be top of the class one year (with a teacher they like) and show no interest at all in the subject the following year when they change teacher. For the teacher to get the best out of their fundamentally people-focused student they need to:

- Offer learning situations that allow for the use of empathy, collaboration and teamworking to counter-balance your natural tendency to focus on task.
- Give ample and regular praise while offering tactful support to overcome any blind-spots. Feedback can be easily interpreted as criticism so walk on egg-shells when delivering it.
- Influence by appealing to the strength of your personal belief in the student (don't let me down, I know you can do it, I like you).
- Be prepared to compromise occasionally as Teddies can sulk.

The laid-back, flexible and spontaneous Tiger with the naturally organised Teddy can be a dream team or a disaster. To create a positive relationship they need to play to each other's strengths. The student can benefit from the teacher's ability to adapt and change plans and the teacher can benefit from the student's desire to have a plan they can work to and complete. The teacher can also:

- Encourage and support the student's desire for order, neatness and respecting deadlines.
- Allow the student independence in planning their work in their own way if they really want to.
- Avoid changing plans just for the sake of it; this will only frustrate the student.
- Encourage the student to embrace flexibility occasionally.

99
Tiger teacher with Dolphin student
ISTP and ENFJ

Tigers and Dolphins are opposite types. When they gel they can help stretch each other which will assist the whole class. For the teacher to get the best out of their Dolphin student they need to accept and embrace the Dolphin's need to discuss ideas and their impact on people. For the teacher to get the best out of their naturally erudite student they need to:

- Listen patiently and enthusiastically to the student impulsively expressing their thoughts.
- Stay open to 'silly' ideas to see where they lead – the student is thinking out loud and this is how they learn best.
- Also offer your own thoughts; if you need a timeout ask for one.
- Encourage the student to think things through before talking otherwise they may sabotage the lesson.
- Steer the student away from controversial subjects, especially in group discussions.

- Build in plenty of opportunities during lessons for the **E** students to talk things through with other **E** preferences.

The teacher likes to use their experience to make sense of things. The one-step-at-a-time teacher encourages their students to follow suit. The **N** student will at best find this over-simplistic and at worst find it boring. The teacher is likely to label the student as 'away with the fairies'. They should resist the temptation to castigate their student because this is how they take in information and make sense of the subject. In the right context daydreaming can lead to new ways of absorbing and retaining information. For the teacher to get the best out of their imaginative student they need to:

- Embrace the imagination and insight of the student and what it can bring to the lesson.
- Encourage the student to become aware of the important contribution of the **S** approach (the value of facts, details, procedure, experiments, applying experience, structure, the step-by-step model).

The teacher is focused first on task and second on people/relationships. The classroom is likely to have a business-like, purposeful atmosphere. Students are given clear guidelines on what is expected in terms of behaviour, homework and so on. At best this means everyone knows where they stand and how to behave. At worst the classroom can resemble a military boot-camp devoid of fun. Remember the personal relationship you have with this student is key. The Dolphin needs to feel they like their teacher and that the teacher likes them too. If this happens they'll work harder but if they don't they may switch off. This explains why a student can be top of the class one year (with a teacher they like) and show no interest at all in the subject the following year when they change teacher. For the teacher to get the best out of their fundamentally people-focused student they need to:

- Offer learning situations that allow for the use of empathy, collaboration and teamworking to counter-balance your natural tendency to focus on task.
- Give ample and regular praise while offering tactful support to overcome any blind-spots. Feedback can be easily interpreted as criticism so walk on egg-shells when delivering it.
- Persuade by appealing to the strength of your personal belief in the student (don't let me down, I know you can do it, I like you).
- Be prepared to compromise occasionally to show the Dolphin that you really appreciate their contributions.

The laid-back, flexible and spontaneous teacher with the naturally organised student can be a dream team or a disaster. To create a positive relationship they need to play to each other's strengths. The student can benefit from the teacher's ability to adapt and change plans and the teacher can benefit from the student's desire to have a plan they can work to and complete. The teacher can also:

- Encourage and support the student's desire for order, neatness and respecting deadlines.
- Allow the student independence in planning their work in their own way if they really want to.
- Avoid changing plans just for the sake of it; this will only frustrate the student.
- Encourage the student to embrace flexibility occasionally as it may lead to new insights.

100
Tiger teacher with Seahorse student
ISTP and INFJ

Its Cowboys and Indians when Tiger and Seahorse meet, with Clint Eastwood (Tiger) and spiritual Native American (Seahorse) sharing the classroom! Both are naturally self-contained. The remaining differences can present challenges for the teacher. To reach the imaginative, compassionate and organised student the teacher needs to hold back on their more 'macho' style. For the teacher to get the best out of their naturally self-contained student they also need to:

■ Respect the student's need for privacy and independence.

■ Take time to clarify your thoughts but don't avoid confrontation; if something needs to be said be calm and direct as you deliver it.

■ Use non-verbal communication – smiles and gestures are reassuring to **I** students; you can even use sticky notes/emails to pass on feedback.

■ Allow the student plenty of time to think through their thoughts.

■ Share your ideas and thoughts regularly to ensure you both know what you're doing.

The teacher likes to use their experience to make sense of things. The one-step-at-a-time teacher encourages their students to follow suit. The **N** student will at best find this over-simplistic and at worst find it boring. The teacher is likely to label the student as 'away with the fairies'. They should resist the temptation to castigate their student because this is how they take in information and make sense of the subject. In the right context daydreaming can lead to new ways of absorbing and retaining information. For the teacher to get the best of their imaginative student they need to:

■ Embrace the imagination and insight of the student and what it can bring to the lesson.

■ Encourage the student to become aware of the important contribution of the **S** approach (the value of facts, details, procedure, experiments, applying experience, structure, the step-by-step model).

The teacher is focused first on task and second on people/relationships. The classroom is likely to have a business-like, purposeful atmosphere. Students are given clear guidelines on what is expected in terms of behaviour, homework and so on. At best this means everyone knows where they stand and how to behave. At worst the classroom can resemble a brutish boot-camp devoid of fun. Remember the personal relationship you have with this student is key. The Seahorse needs to feel they like their teacher and that the teacher likes them too. If this happens they'll work harder but if not they may switch off. This explains why a student can be top of the class one year (with a teacher they like) and show no interest at all in the subject the following year when they change teacher. For the teacher to get the best out of their fundamentally people-focused student they need to:

■ Offer learning situations that allow for the use of empathy, collaboration and teamworking to counter-balance your natural tendency to focus on task.

■ Give ample and regular praise while offering tactful support to overcome any blind-spots. Feedback can be easily interpreted as criticism so tread carefully when delivering it.

■ Persuade by appealing to the strength of your personal belief in the student (don't let me down, I know you can do it, I like you).

■ Be prepared to compromise occasionally or the student may sulk.

The laid-back, flexible and spontaneous teacher with the naturally organised student can be a dream team or a disaster. To create a positive relationship they need to play to each other's strengths. The student can benefit from the teacher's ability to adapt and change plans and the teacher can benefit from the student's desire to have a plan they can work to and complete. The teacher can also:

■ Encourage and support the student's desire for order, neatness and respecting deadlines.

■ Allow the student independence in planning their work in their own way if they really want to.

■ Avoid changing plans just for the sake of it; this will only frustrate the student.

■ Encourage the student to embrace flexibility now and again.

101
Tiger teacher with Polar Bear student
ISTP and ISTJ

Tigers and Polar Bears share three type preferences. Both are realistic, objective and seek independence. Clashes are most likely when the energetic leadership tendencies of the Polar Bear threaten the more understated plans presented by the Tiger. For the teacher to get the best out of their naturally grounded student they need to:

■ Respect the student's need for privacy and independence.

■ Take time to clarify your thoughts but don't avoid confrontation; if something needs to be said be calm and direct as you deliver it.

■ Use non-verbal communication – smiles and gestures are reassuring to **I** students; you can even use sticky notes/emails to pass on feedback.

■ Allow the student plenty of time to think through their thoughts.

■ Share your ideas and thoughts regularly to ensure you both know what you're doing.

Both teacher and student gather information in the same way. They notice detail using their senses (aware of what they can see, hear and feel). Both live in the present. The teacher is naturally sequential and realistic in their teaching style and encourages their students to follow suit. A solid, workman-like relationship develops with both teacher and student mutually understanding what each needs to do to get the job done. For the teacher to get the best out of their rule loving student they need to:

■ Allow the student opportunities to repeat and practise until satisfied they are competent.

■ Describe how learning can be applied in the real world.

■ Encourage the use of imagination as a useful process (it's not wasting time).

Both teacher and student are task-focused, direct, consistent and honest. The classroom is likely to have a business-like, purposeful atmosphere. Students are given clear guidelines on what is expected in terms of behaviour, homework and so on. If the student challenges the teacher it is likely to be for clarification. At best this means everyone knows where they stand and how to behave. At worst the classroom can be an assembly line of serious learning modules devoid of fun and real engagement. For the teacher to get the best out of their naturally task-focused student they need to:

■ Work in ways that test their skill and knowledge competitively (they raise their game for competitions, challenges, quizzes, measuring and beating personal bests).

■ Help them understand that 50% of people are **F** preference and can interpret feedback as criticism.

■ Focus on what the student has achieved and what comes next.

■ Be prepared to compromise occasionally.

■ Avoid trying to fix something without considering potential underlying emotional causes.

The laid-back, flexible and spontaneous teacher with the naturally organised student can be a dream team or a disaster. To create a positive relationship they need to play to each other's strengths. The student can benefit from the teacher's ability to adapt and change plans and the teacher can benefit from the student's desire to have a plan they can work to and complete. The teacher can also:

■ Encourage and support the student's desire for order, neatness and respecting deadlines.

■ Allow the student independence in planning their work in their own way if they really want to.

■ Encourage the student to deviate from their routines now and again.

■ Avoid changing plans just for the sake of it; this will only frustrate the student.

102
Tiger teacher with Black Bear student
ISTP and ESTJ

Tigers and Black Bears share two type preferences. Both are practical, realistic and crave independence. Clashes are most likely when the energetic leadership qualities of the Bear threaten to engulf the more understated plans presented by the Tiger. For the teacher to get the best out of their naturally lively student they need to:

■ Listen patiently and enthusiastically to the student as they express their thoughts.

■ Stay open to off-the-cuff ideas to see where they lead – the student is thinking out loud and this is how they learn best.

■ Offer your own thoughts; if you need a timeout ask for one.

■ Encourage the student to think things through before talking otherwise they may sabotage the lesson.

■ Steer the student away from controversial subjects, especially in group discussions.

■ Build in plenty of opportunities during lessons for the **E** students to talk things through with other **E** preferences.

Both teacher and student gather information in the same way. They notice detail using their senses (aware of what they can see, hear and feel). Both live in the present. The teacher is naturally sequential in their teaching style and encourages their students to follow suit. A solid, workman-like relationship develops with both teacher and student mutually understanding what each needs to do to get the job done. For the teacher to get the best out of their grounded student they need to:

■ Allow the student opportunities to repeat and practise until satisfied they are competent.

■ Describe how learning can be applied in the real world.

■ Encourage the use of imagination as a useful process (it's not wasting time).

Both teacher and student are task-focused, direct, consistent and honest. The classroom is likely to have a business-like, purposeful atmosphere. Students are given clear guidelines on what is expected in terms of behaviour, homework and so on. If the student challenges the teacher it is likely to be for clarification. At best this means everyone knows where they stand and how to behave. At worst the classroom can be an assembly line of serious learning modules devoid of fun and real engagement. For the teacher to get the best out of their fundamentally task-focused student they need to:

■ Work in ways that test their skill and knowledge competitively (they raise their game for competitions, challenges, quizzes, measuring and beating personal bests).

■ Help them understand that 50% of people are **F** preference and can interpret feedback as criticism.

■ Focus on what the student has achieved and what comes next.

■ Be prepared to compromise occasionally.

■ Avoid trying to fix something without considering potential underlying emotional causes.

The laid-back, flexible and spontaneous teacher with the naturally organised student can be a dream team or a disaster. To create a positive relationship they need to play to each other's strengths. The student can benefit from the teacher's ability to adapt and change plans and the teacher can benefit from the student's desire to have a plan they can work to and complete. The teacher can also:

■ Encourage and support the student's desire for order, neatness and respecting deadlines.

■ Allow the student independence in planning their work in their own way if they really want to.

■ Avoid changing plans just for the sake of it; this will only frustrate the student.

■ Encourage the Black Bear to embrace flexibility occasionally to add some spice to life.

103
Tiger teacher with Falcon student
ISTP and ENTP

Tigers and Falcons share two preferences. Both are fiercely independent analysers. Their independence is the most likely source of conflict. If the teacher can let go some of the outrageous behaviour they can be a great classroom combination. For the teacher to get the best out of their naturally 'hyperactive' student they need to:

■ Listen patiently and enthusiastically to the student impulsively expressing their thoughts.

■ Stay open to 'silly' ideas to see where they lead – the student is thinking out loud and this is how they learn best.

■ Also offer your own thoughts; if you need a timeout ask for one.

■ Encourage the student to think things through before talking otherwise they may sabotage the lesson.

■ Steer the student away from controversial subjects, especially in group discussions.

■ Build in plenty of opportunities during lessons for the **E** students to talk things through with other **E** preferences.

The Tiger teacher likes to use their experience to make sense of things. The one-step-at-a-time teacher encourages their students to follow suit. The **N** student will at best find this over-simplistic and at worst find it boring. The teacher is likely to label the student as 'away with the fairies'. They should resist the temptation to castigate their student because this is how they take in information and make sense of the subject. In the right context daydreaming can lead to new ways of absorbing and retaining information. For the teacher to get the best out of their inherently imaginative student they need to:

■ Embrace the imagination and insight of the student and what it can bring to the lesson.

■ Encourage the student to become aware of the important contribution of the **S** approach (the value of facts, details, procedure, experiments, applying experience, structure, the step-by-step model).

Both teacher and student are task-focused, direct, consistent and honest. The classroom is likely to have a business-like, purposeful atmosphere. Students are given clear guidelines on what is expected in terms of behaviour, homework and so on. If the student challenges the teacher it is likely to be for clarification. At best this means everyone knows where they stand and how to behave. At worst the classroom can be an assembly line of serious learning modules devoid of fun and real engagement. For the teacher to get the best out of their fundamentally task-focused student they need to:

■ Work in ways that test their skill and knowledge competitively (they raise their game for competitions, challenges, quizzes, measuring and beating personal bests).

■ Help them appreciate that 50% of people are **F** preference and can interpret feedback as criticism.

■ Focus on what the student has achieved and what comes next.

■ Be prepared to compromise occasionally.

■ Avoid trying to fix something without considering potential underlying emotional causes.

Tigers and Falcons can be organised and efficient; it's just such an effort! While enjoying a mutual love of spontaneity, which provides each with relief from the stifling and constraining timetables and deadlines essential in large organisations such as schools, they must also remember to complete any necessary tasks. Although likely to be fun and popular teachers, they also need to focus on the task of preparing the student to succeed socially and academically. Both prefer to start tasks than finish them. Their initial enthusiasm can quickly wane. Both need to ensure they identify and complete the important tasks or the student (or their parents) may eventually ask awkward questions. For the teacher to get the best out of their naturally laid-back student they need to understand the student doesn't just like options and choice; they are essential or they start to itch, squirm and rebel. The secondary school environment is difficult enough for **P** preference students so teachers can help their student achieve by:

■ Providing as much flexibility as possible (multiple choice homework tasks, choice within the lesson).

■ Avoiding giving out detailed schedules (they'll just lose it anyway!).

■ Shaking things up now and again to prevent predictability becoming boredom. Introduce random surprises and changes.

■ Helping the Falcon identify simple time-management techniques to ensure they can succeed.

104
Tiger teacher with Tiger student
ISTP and ISTP

Tigers are the most 'macho' of types. This can be the basis of a strong classroom relationship, the student benefiting from a role model with whom they can easily identify and emulate. Clashes are likely if the student is denied their preference for independence. To get the best out of their reflective student the teacher can:

■ Respect the student's need for privacy and independence.

■ Take time to clarify your thoughts but don't avoid confrontation; if something needs to be said be calm and direct as you deliver it.

■ Use non-verbal communication – smiles and gestures are reassuring to **I** students; you can even use sticky notes/emails to pass on feedback.

■ Allow the student plenty of time to think through their thoughts.

■ Share your ideas and thoughts regularly to ensure you both know what you're doing.

Tigers gather their information in the same way. They notice detail using their senses (aware of what they can see, hear and feel). Both live in the present. The teacher is naturally sequential and realistic in their teaching style and encourages their students to follow suit. A solid, no-nonsense relationship develops with both teacher and student mutually understanding what each needs to do to get the job done. For the teacher to get the best out of their grounded student they need to:

■ Allow the student opportunities to repeat and practise until satisfied they are competent.

■ Describe how learning can be applied in the real world.

■ Encourage the use of imagination as a useful process (it's not wasting time).

Both teacher and student are task-focused, direct, consistent and honest. The classroom is likely to have a business-like, purposeful atmosphere. Students are given clear guidelines on what is expected in terms of behaviour, homework and so on. If the student challenges the teacher it is likely to be for clarification. At best this means everyone knows where they stand and how to behave. At worst the classroom can be an assembly line of serious learning modules devoid of fun and real engagement. For the teacher to get the best out of their naturally task-focused student they need to:

■ Help them understand that 50% of people are **F** preference and can interpret feedback as criticism.

■ Focus on what the student has achieved and what comes next.

■ Be prepared to compromise occasionally.

■ Avoid trying to fix something without considering potential underlying emotional causes.

■ Work in ways that test their skill and knowledge competitively (they raise their game for competitions, challenges, quizzes, measuring and beating personal bests).

Tigers abhor to-do-lists, schedules and predictability; they rarely reach the status of an acquired taste or a honed skill. While enjoying their mutual love of spontaneity, which provides each with relief from the stifling and constraining timetables and deadlines essential in large organisations such as schools, they must also remember to complete any necessary tasks. Although likely to be fun and popular teachers, they also need to focus on the task of preparing the student to succeed socially and academically. Both prefer to start tasks than finish them. Their initial enthusiasm can quickly wane. Both need to ensure they identify and complete the important tasks or the student (or their parents) may eventually ask awkward questions. For the teacher to get the best out of their naturally laid-back student they need to understand the student doesn't just like options and choice; they are essential or they start to itch, squirm and rebel. The secondary school environment is difficult enough for **P** preference students so teachers can help their student achieve by:

■ Providing as much flexibility as possible (multiple choice homework tasks, choice within the lesson).

■ Avoiding giving out detailed schedules (they'll just lose it anyway!).

■ Shaking things up now and again to prevent predictability becoming boredom. Introduce random surprises and changes.

■ Helping the student identify simple time-management strategies to ensure they can succeed.

105
Tiger teacher with Koala student
ISTP and ISFJ

Tigers and Koalas share two type preferences. Both are reserved and systematic in their approach to tasks. Koalas are unlikely to make a fuss in class but they can be easily ignored and cast adrift if the teacher does not temper their matter-of-fact and tough-love style. For the teacher to get the best out of their intrinsically conservative student they need to:

■ Respect the student's need for privacy and independence.

■ Take time to clarify your thoughts but don't avoid confrontation; if something needs to be said be calm and direct as you deliver it.

■ Use non-verbal communication – smiles and gestures are reassuring to **I** students; you can even use sticky notes/emails to pass on feedback.

■ Allow the student plenty of time to think through their thoughts.

■ Share your ideas and thoughts regularly to ensure you both know what you're doing.

Both teacher and student gather information in the same way. They notice detail using their senses (aware of what they can see, hear and feel). Both live in the present. The teacher is naturally sequential and realistic in their teaching style and encourages their students to follow suit. A solid, workman-like relationship develops with both teacher and student mutually understanding what each needs to do to get the job done. For the teacher to get the best out of their grounded student they need to:

■ Allow the student opportunities to repeat and practise until satisfied they are competent.

■ Describe how learning can be applied in the real world.

■ Encourage the use of imagination as a useful process (it's not wasting time).

The teacher is focused first on task and second on people/relationships. The classroom is likely to have a business-like, purposeful atmosphere. Students are given clear guidelines on what is expected in terms of behaviour, homework and so on. At best this means everyone knows where they stand and how to behave. At worst the classroom can resemble a military boot-camp devoid of fun. Remember the personal relationship you have with this student is key. The Koala needs to feel they like their teacher and that the teacher likes them too. If this happens they'll work harder but if they don't they may switch off. This explains why a student can be top of the class one year (with a teacher they like) and show no interest at all in the subject the following year when they change teacher. For the teacher to get the best out of their naturally people-focused student they need to:

■ Offer learning situations that allow for the use of empathy, collaboration and teamworking to counter-balance your natural tendency to focus on task.

■ Give ample and regular praise while offering tactful support to overcome any blind-spots. Feedback can be easily interpreted as criticism so walk on egg-shells when delivering it.

■ Influence by appealing to the strength of your personal belief in the student (don't let me down, I know you can do it, I like you).

■ Be prepared to compromise occasionally.

The laid-back, flexible and spontaneous teacher with the naturally organised student can be a dream team or a disaster. To create a positive relationship they need to play to each other's strengths. The student can benefit from the teacher's ability to adapt and change plans and the teacher can benefit from the student's desire to have a plan they can work to and complete. The teacher can also:

■ Encourage and support the student's desire for order, neatness and respecting deadlines.

■ Allow the student independence in planning their work in their own way if they really want to.

■ Encourage the student to embrace flexibility occasionally.

■ Avoid changing plans just for the sake of it; this will only frustrate the student.

106
Tiger teacher with Eagle student
ISTP and ENTJ

Tigers and Eagles share one type preference. Both crave independence. Clashes are most likely when the energetic leadership qualities of the Eagle threaten the more understated plans presented by the Tiger. For the teacher to get the best out of their naturally lively student they need to:

■ Listen patiently and enthusiastically to the student impulsively expressing their thoughts.

■ Stay open to 'silly' ideas to see where they lead – the student is thinking out loud and this is how they learn best.

■ Also offer your own thoughts; if you need a timeout ask for one.

■ Encourage the student to think things through before talking otherwise they may sabotage the lesson.

■ Steer the student away from controversial subjects, especially in group discussions.

■ Build in plenty of opportunities during lessons for the **E** students to talk things through with other **E** preferences.

The teacher likes to use their experience to make sense of things. The one-step-at-a-time teacher encourages their students to follow suit. The **N** student will at best find this over-simplistic and at worst find it boring. The teacher is likely to label the student as 'away with the fairies'. They should resist the temptation to castigate their student because this is how they take in information and make sense of the subject. In the right context daydreaming can lead to new ways of absorbing and retaining information. For the teacher to get the best out of their inherently imaginative student they need to:

■ Embrace the imagination and insight of the student and what it can bring to the lesson.

- Encourage the student to become aware of the important contribution of the **S** approach (the value of facts, details, procedure, experiments, applying experience, structure, the step-by-step model).

Both teacher and student are task-focused, direct, consistent and honest. The classroom is likely to have a business-like, purposeful atmosphere. Students are given clear guidelines on what is expected in terms of behaviour, homework and so on. If the student challenges the teacher it is likely to be for clarification. At best this means everyone knows where they stand and how to behave. At worst the classroom can be an assembly line of serious learning modules devoid of fun and real engagement. For the teacher to get the best out of their fundamentally task-focused student they need to:

- Work in ways that test their skill and knowledge competitively (they raise their game for competitions, challenges, quizzes, measuring and beating personal bests).
- Help them understand that 50% of people are **F** preference and can interpret feedback as criticism.
- Focus on what the student has achieved and what comes next.
- Be prepared to compromise occasionally.
- Avoid trying to fix something without considering potential underlying emotional causes.

The laid-back, flexible and spontaneous teacher with the naturally organised student can be a dream team or a disaster. To create a positive relationship they need to play to each other's strengths. The student can benefit from the teacher's ability to adapt and change plans and the teacher can benefit from the student's desire to have a plan they can work to and complete. The teacher can also:

- Encourage and support the student's desire for order, neatness and respecting deadlines.
- Encourage the student to embrace flexibility occasionally.
- Allow the student independence in planning their work in their own way if they really want to.
- Avoid changing plans just for the sake of it; this will only frustrate the student.

107
Tiger teacher with Lion student
ISTP and ESFP

Tigers and Lions share two type preferences. Both are action-orientated realists. The Lion may be too chatty and personal for the independent and cool teacher. For the teacher to get the best out of their naturally effervescent student they need to:

- Listen patiently and enthusiastically to the student impulsively expressing their thoughts.
- Stay open to 'silly' ideas to see where they lead – the student is thinking out loud and this is how they learn best.
- Also offer your own thoughts; if you need a timeout ask for one.

- Encourage the student to think things through before talking otherwise they may sabotage the lesson.
- Steer the student away from controversial subjects, especially in group discussions.
- Build in plenty of opportunities during lessons for the **E** students to talk things through with other **E** preferences.

All four Cats gather their information in the same way. They notice detail using their senses (aware of what they can see, hear and feel). Both live in the present. The teacher is naturally sequential and realistic in their teaching style and encourages their students to follow suit. A solid, workman-like relationship develops with both teacher and student mutually understanding what each needs to do to get the job done. For the teacher to get the best out of their grounded student they need to:

- Allow the student opportunities to repeat and practise until satisfied they are competent.
- Describe how learning can be applied in the real world.
- Encourage the use of imagination as a useful process (it's not wasting time).

The teacher is focused first on task and second on people/relationships. The classroom is likely to have a business-like, purposeful atmosphere. Students are given clear guidelines on what is expected in terms of behaviour, homework and so on. At best this means everyone knows where they stand and how to behave. At worst the classroom can resemble a military boot-camp devoid of fun. Remember the personal relationship you have with this student is key. The Lion needs to feel they like their teacher and that the teacher likes them too. If this happens they'll work harder but if they don't they may switch off. This explains why a student can be top of the class one year (with a teacher they like) and show no interest at all in the subject the following year when they change teacher. For the teacher to get the best out of their fundamentally people-focused student they need to:

- Offer learning situations that allow for the use of empathy, collaboration and teamworking to counter-balance your natural tendency to focus on task.
- Give ample and regular praise while offering tactful support to overcome any blind-spots. Feedback can be easily seen as criticism so walk on egg-shells when delivering it.
- Persuade/influence by appealing to the strength of your personal belief in the student (don't let me down, I know you can do it, I like you).
- Be prepared to compromise occasionally; if the Lion wins a few battles you can win the war.

The four Cats can be organised and efficient; it's just such an effort! While enjoying a mutual love of spontaneity, which provides each with relief from the stifling and constraining timetables and deadlines essential in large organisations such as schools, they must also remember to complete any necessary tasks. Although likely to be fun and popular teachers, they also need to focus on the task of preparing the student to succeed socially and academically. Both prefer to start tasks than finish them. Their initial enthusiasm can quickly wane. Both need to ensure they identify and complete the important tasks or the student (or their parents) may eventually ask awkward questions. For the teacher to get the best out of their naturally laid-back student they need to understand

the student doesn't just like options and choice; they are essential or they start to itch, squirm and rebel. The secondary school environment is difficult enough for **P** preference students so teachers can help their student achieve by:

- Providing as much flexibility as possible (multiple choice homework tasks, choice within the lesson).
- Avoiding detailed schedules (they'll just lose it anyway!).
- Shaking things up now and again to prevent predictability becoming boredom.
- Introducing random surprises and changes.
- Identifying effective strategies to ensure they can manage their workload successfully.

108
Tiger teacher with Cat student
ISTP and ISFP

All four Cats are realistic, adaptable and action-orientated. Traditional classroom teaching does not play to their natural strengths. The Tiger teacher can help draw out the best of the Cat and help them succeed by using their interest in learning independently from experience and action. For the teacher to get the best out of their fundamentally private student they need to:

- Respect the student's need for privacy and independence.
- Take time to clarify your thoughts but don't avoid confrontation; if something needs to be said be calm and direct as you deliver it.
- Use non-verbal communication – smiles and gestures are reassuring to **I** students; you can even use sticky notes/emails to pass on feedback.
- Allow the student plenty of time to think through their thoughts.
- Remember to share your ideas and thoughts regularly to ensure you both know what you're doing.

Both teacher and student gather information in the same way. They notice detail using their senses (aware of what they can see, hear and feel). Both live in the present. The Tiger teacher is naturally realistic and 'lead by example' in their teaching style and encourages their students to follow suit. A solid, workman-like relationship develops with both teacher and student mutually understanding what each needs to do to get the job done. For the teacher to get the best out of their grounded student they need to:

- Allow the student opportunities to repeat and practise until satisfied they are competent.
- Describe how learning can be applied in the real world.
- Encourage the use of imagination as a useful process (it's not wasting time).

The teacher is focused first on task and second on people/relationships. The classroom is likely to have a purposeful atmosphere. Students are given clear guidelines on what is expected in terms of behaviour, homework and so on. At best this means everyone knows where they stand and how to behave. At worst the classroom can resemble a military boot-camp devoid of fun. Remember, the personal relationship you have with this student is key. The Cat needs to feel they like their teacher and that the teacher likes them too. If this happens they'll work harder but if not they may switch off. This explains why a student can be top of the class one year (with a teacher they like) and show no interest at all in the same subject the following year when they change teacher. For the teacher to get the best out of their naturally people-focused student they need to:

■ Offer learning situations that allow for the use of empathy, collaboration and teamworking to counter-balance your natural tendency to focus on task.

■ Give ample and regular praise while offering tactful support to overcome any blind-spots. Feedback can be easily interpreted as criticism so be careful when delivering it.

■ Persuade by appealing to the strength of your personal belief in the student (don't let me down, I know you can do it, I like you).

■ Be prepared to compromise occasionally or the Cat may sulk.

Tigers and Cats can be organised and efficient; it's just such an effort! While enjoying a mutual love of spontaneity, which provides each with relief from the stifling and constraining timetables and deadlines essential in large organisations such as schools, they must also remember to complete any necessary tasks. Although likely to be fun and popular teachers, they also need to focus on the task of preparing the student to succeed socially and academically. Both prefer to start tasks than finish them. Their initial enthusiasm can quickly wane. Both need to ensure they identify and complete the important tasks or the student (or their parents) may eventually ask awkward questions. For the teacher to get the best out of their naturally laid-back student they need to understand that they need options and choice or they start to itch, squirm and rebel. The secondary school environment is difficult enough for **P** preference students so teachers can help their student achieve by:

■ Providing as much flexibility as possible (multiple choice homework tasks, choice within the lesson).

■ Not giving out detailed schedules (they'll just lose it anyway!).

■ Shaking things up now and again to prevent predictability becoming boredom. Introduce random surprises and changes.

■ Helping the student identify simple time-management techniques to ensure they can succeed.

109
Tiger teacher with Panther student
ISTP and ESTP

All four Cats are realistic, adaptable and action-oriented. Traditional classroom teaching does not play to their natural strengths. The Tiger teacher can help draw out the best of the Panther and encourage them to succeed by using their interest in learning independently from experience and action. For the teacher to get the best out of their ebullient student they need to:

■ Listen patiently and enthusiastically to the student impulsively expressing their thoughts.

■ Steer the student away from controversial subjects, especially in group discussions.

■ Build in plenty of opportunities during lessons for the **E** students to talk things through with other **E** preferences.

■ Stay open to 'silly' ideas and banter to see where they lead – the student is thinking out loud and this is how they learn best.

■ Also offer your own thoughts; if you need a timeout ask for one.

■ Encourage the student to think things through before talking otherwise they may sabotage the lesson.

Both teacher and student gather information in the same way. They notice detail using their senses (aware of what they can see, hear and feel). Both live in the present. The teacher is naturally sequential and realistic in their teaching style and likes their students to follow suit. A solid, workman-like relationship develops with both teacher and student mutually understanding what each needs to do to get the job done. For the teacher to get the best out of their grounded student they need to:

■ Allow the student opportunities to repeat and practise until satisfied they are competent.

■ Describe how learning can be applied in the real world.

■ Encourage the use of imagination as a useful process (it's not wasting time).

Both teacher and student are task-focused, direct, consistent and honest. The classroom is likely to have a business-like, purposeful atmosphere. Students are given clear guidelines on what is expected in terms of behaviour, homework and so on. If the student challenges the teacher it is likely to be for clarification. At best this means everyone knows where they stand and how to behave. At worst the classroom can be an assembly line of serious learning modules devoid of fun and real engagement. For the teacher to get the best out of their naturally task-focused student they need to:

■ Work in ways that test their skill and knowledge competitively (they raise their game for competitions, challenges, quizzes, measuring and beating personal bests).

■ Help them understand that 50% of people are **F** preference and can interpret feedback as criticism.

■ Focus on what the student has achieved and what comes next.

■ Be prepared to compromise occasionally.

■ Avoid trying to fix something without considering potential underlying emotional causes.

Tigers and Panthers can be organised and efficient; it's just such an effort! While enjoying a mutual love of spontaneity, which provides each with relief from the stifling and constraining timetables and deadlines essential in large organisations such as schools, they must also remember to complete any necessary tasks. Although likely to be fun and popular teachers, they also need to focus on the task of preparing the student to succeed socially and academically. Both prefer to start tasks than finish them. Their initial enthusiasm can quickly vanish. Both need to ensure they identify and complete the important tasks or the student (or their parents) may eventually ask awkward questions. For the teacher to get the best out of their naturally laid-back stu-

dent they need to understand the student doesn't just like options and choice; they are essential or they start to itch, squirm and rebel. The secondary school environment is difficult enough for **P** preference students so teachers can help their student achieve by:

■ Providing as much flexibility as possible (multiple choice homework tasks, choice within the lesson).

■ Avoiding giving out detailed schedules (they'll just lose it anyway!).

■ Shaking things up now and again to prevent predictability becoming boredom. Introduce random surprises and changes.

■ Identifying simple but effective time-management strategies to help the naturally disorganised Panther succeed.

110
Tiger teacher with Clownfish student
ISTP and ENFP

Tigers and Clownfish share one type preference. Both are flexible. For the teacher to get the best out of their naturally effusive student they need to accept their differences, especially their need to discuss, share ideas and be reassured. The teacher can also:

■ Enjoy the lively banter when it is appropriate to spark new thoughts and ideas; the student learns best this way, but remember there are other students in the classroom.

■ Stick to the point and stay positive (don't nag **T** or mother **F** students), as both teacher and student are easily distracted and liable to go off track!

■ Avoid going over old ground.

■ Be aware that you can keep some thoughts to yourself (and you may think of a better way of expressing something, especially criticism, later).

■ Be an enthusiastic and supportive listener; seek to help the student clarify and develop their thinking rather than assert your own.

■ Practise listening skills and encourage the **I** preferences in the class to contribute.

■ Be calm and clear, otherwise two **E** preferences can talk louder and louder at each other with neither listening.

The teacher likes to use their experience to make sense of things. The one-step-at-a-time teacher encourages their students to follow suit. The **N** student will at best find this over-simplistic and at worst find it boring. The teacher is likely to label the student as 'away with the fairies'. They should resist the temptation to castigate their student because this is how they take in information and make sense of the subject. In the right context daydreaming can lead to new ways of absorbing and retaining information. For the teacher to get the best out of their naturally imaginative student they need to:

■ Embrace the imagination and insight of the student and what it can bring to the lesson.

■ Encourage the student to become aware of the important contribution of the **S** approach (the value of facts, details, procedure, experiments, applying experience, structure, the step-by-step model).

The student is focused first on people then task whereas the teacher operates in the opposite way. The classroom is likely to have a business-like, purposeful atmosphere. Students are given clear guidelines on what is expected in terms of behaviour, homework and so on. At best this means everyone knows where they stand and how to behave. At worst the classroom can resemble a military boot-camp devoid of compassion. Remember the personal relationship you have with this student is key. The Clownfish needs to feel they like their teacher and that the teacher likes them too. If this happens they'll work harder but if not they may switch off. This explains why a student can be top of the class one year (with a teacher they like) and show no interest at all in the subject the following year when they change teacher. For the teacher to get the best out of their fundamentally people-focused student they need to:

■ Offer learning situations that allow for the use of empathy, collaboration and teamworking to counter-balance your natural tendency to focus on task.

■ Give ample and regular praise while offering tactful support to overcome any blind-spots. Feedback can be easily interpreted as criticism so walk on egg-shells when delivering it.

■ Persuade by appealing to the strength of your personal belief in the student (don't let me down, I know you can do it, I like you).

■ Be prepared to compromise occasionally, otherwise the Clownfish can be disruptive.

Tigers and Clownfish can be organised and efficient; it's just such an effort! While enjoying a mutual love of spontaneity, which provides each with relief from the stifling and constraining timetables and deadlines essential in large organisations such as schools, they must also remember to complete any necessary tasks. Although likely to be fun and popular teachers, they also need to focus on the task of preparing the student to succeed socially and academically. Both prefer to start tasks than finish them. Their initial enthusiasm can quickly wane. Both need to ensure they identify and complete the important tasks or the student (or their parents) may eventually ask awkward questions. For the teacher to get the best out of their naturally laid-back student they need to understand the student doesn't just like options and choice; they are essential. The secondary school environment is difficult enough for **P** preference students so teachers can help their student progress by:

■ Providing as much flexibility as possible (multiple choice homework tasks, choice within the lesson).

■ Avoiding giving out detailed schedules (they'll just lose it anyway!).

■ Shaking things up now and again to prevent predictability becoming boredom. Introduce random surprises and changes.

■ Helping the student identify ways they can organise and manage their time to complete important work without a last-minute rush.

111
Tiger teacher with Barn Owl student
ISTP and INTJ

Tigers and Barn Owls share two type preferences. Both are reserved, detached observers and fiercely autonomous. Their similarities can form the basis of a strong relationship. Clashes are likely when their independent streak prevents the student from seeking help when it is needed. For the teacher to get the best out of their naturally reserved student they need to:

■ Respect the student's need for privacy and independence.

■ Take time to clarify your thoughts but don't avoid confrontation; if something needs to be said be calm and direct as you deliver it.

■ Use non-verbal communication – smiles and gestures are reassuring to **I** students; you can even use sticky notes/emails to pass on feedback.

■ Allow the student plenty of time to think through their thoughts.

■ Share your ideas and thoughts regularly to ensure you both know what you're doing.

The teacher likes to use their experience to make sense of things. The one-step-at-a-time teacher encourages their students to follow suit. The **N** student will at best find this over-simplistic and at worst find it boring. The teacher is likely to label the student as 'away with the fairies'. They should resist the temptation to castigate their student because this is how they take in information and make sense of the subject. In the right context daydreaming can lead to new ways of absorbing and retaining information. For the teacher to get the best out of their imaginative student they need to:

■ Embrace the imagination and insight of the student and what it can bring to the lesson.

■ Encourage the student to become aware of the important contribution of the **S** approach (the value of facts, details, procedure, experiments, applying experience, structure, the step-by-step model).

Both teacher and student are task-focused, direct, consistent and honest. The classroom is likely to have a business-like, purposeful atmosphere. Students are given clear guidelines on what is expected in terms of behaviour, homework and so on. If the student challenges the teacher it is likely to be for clarification. At best this means everyone knows where they stand and how to behave. At worst the classroom can be an assembly line of serious learning modules devoid of fun and real engagement. For the teacher to get the best out of their fundamentally task-focused student they need to:

■ Work in ways that test their skill and knowledge competitively (they raise their game for competitions, challenges, quizzes, measuring and beating personal bests).

■ Help them understand that 50% of people are **F** preference and can interpret feedback as criticism.

■ Focus on what the student has achieved and what comes next.

■ Be prepared to compromise occasionally.

■ Avoid trying to fix something without considering potential underlying emotional causes.

The laid-back, flexible and spontaneous teacher with the naturally organised student can be a dream team or a disaster. To create a positive relationship they need to play to each other's strengths. The student can benefit from the teacher's ability to adapt and change plans and the teacher can benefit from the student's desire to have a plan they can work to and complete. The teacher can also:

■ Allow the student independence in planning their work in their own way if they really want to.

■ Avoid changing plans just for the sake of it; this will only frustrate the student.

■ Encourage the student to embrace flexibility occasionally.

■ Encourage and support the Barn Owl's desire for order, neatness and respecting deadlines.

112
Tiger teacher with Seal student
ISTP and INFP

Tigers and Seals share two type preferences. Both are private and adaptable. Conflict is unlikely but can result from the personal and imaginative style of the student clashing with the cool and practical teacher. For the Tiger to get the best out of their idealistic student they need to:

■ Respect the student's need for privacy and independence.

■ Take time to clarify your thoughts but don't avoid confrontation; if something needs to be said be calm and direct as you deliver it.

■ Use non-verbal communication – smiles and gestures are reassuring to **I** students; you can even use sticky notes/emails to pass on feedback.

■ Allow the student plenty of time to think through their thoughts.

■ Share your ideas and thoughts regularly to ensure you both know what you're doing.

The teacher likes to use their experience to make sense of things. The one-step-at-a-time teacher encourages their students to follow suit. The **N** student will at best find this over-simplistic and at worst find it boring. The teacher is likely to label the student as 'away with the fairies'. They should resist the temptation to castigate their student because this is how they take in information and make sense of the subject. In the right context daydreaming can lead to new ways of absorbing and retaining information. For the teacher to get the best out of their naturally imaginative student they need to:

■ Embrace the imagination and insight of the student and what it can bring to the lesson.

■ Encourage the student to become aware of the important contribution of the **S** approach (the value of facts, details, procedure, experiments, applying experience, structure, the step-by-step model).

The teacher is focused first on task and second on people/relationships. The classroom is likely to have a business-like, purposeful atmosphere. Students are given clear guidelines on what is expected in terms of behaviour, homework and so on. At best this means everyone knows where they stand and how to behave. At worst the classroom can resemble a military boot-camp devoid of warmth. Remember the personal relationship you have with this student is key. The Seal needs to feel they like their teacher and that the teacher likes them too. If present they'll work harder but if not they can quickly switch off. This explains why a student can be top of the class one year (with a teacher they like) and show no interest at all in the same subject the following year when they change teacher. For the teacher to get the best out of their fundamentally people-focused student they need to:

■ Offer learning situations that allow for the use of empathy, collaboration and teamworking to counter-balance your natural tendency to focus on task.

■ Give ample and regular praise while offering tactful support to overcome any blind-spots. Feedback can be easily interpreted as criticism so walk on egg-shells when delivering it.

■ Persuade by appealing to the strength of your personal belief in the student (don't let me down, I know you can do it, I like you).

■ Be prepared to compromise or the Seal may withdraw.

P preferences can be organised and efficient; it's just such an effort! While enjoying a mutual love of spontaneity, which provides each with relief from the stifling and constraining timetables and deadlines prevalent in large organisations such as schools, they must also remember to complete any necessary tasks. Although likely to be resolute teachers, they also need to focus on the task of preparing the student to succeed socially and academically. Both prefer to start tasks than finish them. Their initial enthusiasm can quickly evaporate. Both need to ensure they identify and complete the important tasks or the student (or their parents) may eventually ask awkward questions. For the teacher to get the best out of their naturally laid-back student they need to understand the student doesn't just like options and choice; they are essential or they start to itch, squirm and rebel. The secondary school environment is difficult enough for **P** preference students so teachers can help their student achieve by:

■ Providing as much flexibility as possible (multiple choice homework tasks, choice within the lesson).

■ Avoiding giving out detailed schedules (they'll just lose it anyway!).

■ Shaking things up now and again to prevent predictability becoming boredom. Introduce random surprises and changes.

■ Identifying simple time-management strategies to ensure the Seal can flourish.

113
Cat teacher with Black Bear student
ISFP and ESTJ

Cats and Black Bears share one type preference. Both are grounded and learn in a step-by-step way. Conflict is most likely if the student attempts to take charge of the more laid-back classroom preferred by Cat teachers. For the teacher to get the best out of their naturally lively student they need to:

■ Listen patiently and enthusiastically to the student impulsively expressing their thoughts.

■ Stay open to 'silly' ideas to see where they lead – the student is thinking out loud and this is how they learn best.

■ Also offer your own thoughts; if you need a timeout ask for one.

■ Encourage the student to think things through before talking otherwise they may sabotage the lesson.

■ Steer the student away from controversial subjects, especially in group discussions.

■ Build in plenty of opportunities during lessons for the **E** students to talk things through with other **E** preferences.

Both teacher and student gather information in the same way. They notice detail using their senses (aware of what they can see, hear and feel). Both live in the present. The teacher is naturally sequential and realistic in their teaching style. They encourage their students to follow suit. A solid, workman-like relationship develops with both teacher and student mutually understanding what each needs to do to get the job done. For the teacher to get the best from their grounded student:

■ Allow the student opportunities to repeat and practise until satisfied they are competent.

■ Describe how learning can be applied in the real world.

■ Encourage the use of imagination as a useful process (it's not wasting time).

The teacher is concerned with relationship then task whereas the student is the other way round. The teacher must learn to accept that the student is different; not cold, blunt and unfriendly, but different and focused on task first. If the teacher can accept this the relationship can be really positive for both teacher and student. For the teacher to get the best out of their intrinsically self-assured Black Bear student they need to:

■ Offer targeted compliments. Just saying everything is great will not impress or help the student; in fact, it can result in the student not respecting the teacher, concluding they lie and/or are a soft touch. When you praise you may be pressed for proof!

■ Be logical and objective rather than emotional in discussions.

■ Accept that if the student challenges you it is probably to clarify their thoughts rather than meant as a slight to your authority or character. Perhaps ask 'What would you do to improve/change this?' or 'What do you think?' Once they've clarified their thoughts they may be ready to ask and absorb what you think.

■ Work in ways that test their skill and knowledge competitively (they raise their game).

■ Help them understand that 50% of people are **F** preference and can interpret feedback as criticism.

The laid-back, flexible and spontaneous teacher with the naturally organised student can be a dream team or a disaster. To create a positive relationship they need to play to each other's strengths. The student can benefit from the teacher's ability to adapt and change plans and the teacher can benefit from the student's desire to have a plan they can work to and complete. The teacher can also:

■ Encourage and support the student's desire for order, neatness and respecting deadlines.

■ Allow the student independence in planning their work in their own way if they really want to.

■ Avoid changing plans just for the sake of it; this will only frustrate the student.

■ Encourage the student to embrace flexibility as a way to broaden their experiences.

114
Cat teacher with Teddy Bear student
ISFP and ESFJ

Cats and Teddies share two type preferences. Both are warm-natured and grounded; more thermos of milky tea than intoxicating cocktail. For the teacher to get the best out of their naturally lively student they need to:

■ Listen patiently and enthusiastically to the student impulsively expressing their thoughts.

■ Stay open to 'silly' ideas to see where they lead – the student is thinking out loud and this is how they learn best.

■ Also offer your own thoughts; if you need a timeout ask for one.

■ Encourage the student to think things through before talking otherwise they may sabotage the lesson.

■ Steer the student away from controversial subjects, especially in group discussions.

■ Build in plenty of opportunities during lessons for the **E** students to talk things through with other **E** preferences.

Both Cat and Teddy gather their information in the same way. They notice detail using their senses (aware of what they can see, hear and feel). Both live in the present. The teacher is naturally sequential and realistic in their teaching style and will encourage their students to follow suit. A solid, workman-like relationship develops with both teacher and student mutually understanding what each needs to do to get the job done. For the teacher to get the best out of their grounded student they need to:

■ Allow the student opportunities to repeat and practise until satisfied they are competent.

■ Describe how learning can be applied in the real world.

■ Encourage the use of imagination as a useful process (it's not wasting time).

Both teacher and student are both concerned first with people and relationships before the task/subject content. They like to form warm personal relationships. Compliments are likely to go in both directions boosting the confidence of teacher as well as student. The Teddy needs to feel they like their teacher and that the teacher likes them too. If this happens they'll work harder but if not they may switch off completely. This explains why a student can be top of the class one year (with a teacher they like) and show no interest at all in the subject the following year when they change teacher. For the teacher to get the best out of their relationship-focused student they need to:

■ Offer learning situations that allow for the use of empathy, collaboration and teamworking.

■ Give ample and regular praise while offering tactful support to overcome any blind-spots.

■ Motivate by appealing to the strength of your personal belief in the student (don't let me down, I know you can do it, I like you).

When the laid-back, flexible and spontaneous teacher meets the naturally organised student they can complement each other or clash spectacularly. To build a positive relationship they need to play to each other's strengths. The student can benefit from the teacher's ability to adapt and change plans and the teacher can benefit from the student's desire to have a plan they can work to and complete. The teacher can also:

■ Encourage and support the student's desire for order, neatness and respecting deadlines.

■ Allow the student independence in planning their work in their own way if they really want to.

■ Encourage the student to embrace flexibility occasionally.

■ Avoid changing plans just for the sake of it; this will only frustrate the student.

115
Cat teacher with Dolphin student
ISFP and ENFJ

Cats and Dolphins share one type preference. Both are interested in contributing to a friendly classroom environment. For the teacher to get the best out of their naturally sociable student they need to:

■ Listen patiently and enthusiastically to the student impulsively expressing their thoughts.

■ Stay open to 'silly' ideas to see where they lead – the student is thinking out loud and this is how they learn best.

■ Also offer your own thoughts; if you need a timeout ask for one.

■ Encourage the student to think things through before talking otherwise they may sabotage the lesson.

■ Steer the student away from controversial subjects, especially in group discussions.

■ Build in plenty of opportunities during lessons for the **E** students to talk things through with other **E** preferences.

The teacher likes to use their experience to make sense of things. The one-step-at-a-time teacher encourages their students to follow suit. The **N** student will at best find this over-simplistic and at worst find it boring. The teacher is likely to label the student as 'away with the fairies'. They should resist the temptation to castigate their student because this is how they take in information and make sense of the subject. In the right context daydreaming can lead to new ways of absorbing and retaining information. For the teacher to get the best out of their inherently imaginative student they need to:

■ Embrace the imagination and insight of the student and what it can bring to the lesson.

■ Encourage the student to become aware of the important contribution of the **S** approach (the value of facts, details, procedure, experiments, applying experience, structure, the step-by-step model).

Both teacher and student are concerned first with people and relationships before the task/subject content. They like to form warm personal relationships. Compliments are likely to go in both directions boosting the confidence of teacher as well as student. The Dolphin needs to feel they like their teacher and that the teacher likes them too. If this happens they'll work harder but if they don't they may switch off completely. This explains why a student can be top of the class one year (with a teacher they like) and show no interest at all in the subject the following year when they change teacher. For the teacher to get the best out of their relationship-focused student they need to:

■ Offer learning situations that allow for the use of empathy, collaboration and teamworking.

■ Give ample and regular praise while offering tactful support to overcome any blind-spots.

■ Persuade/influence by appealing to the strength of your personal belief in the student (don't let me down, I know you can do it, I like you).

The laid-back, flexible and spontaneous teacher with the naturally organised student can be a dream team or a disaster. To create a positive relationship they need to play to each other's strengths. The student can benefit from the teacher's ability to adapt and change plans and the teacher can benefit from the student's desire to have a plan they can work to and complete. The teacher can also:

■ Encourage and support the student's desire for order, neatness and respecting deadlines.

■ Encourage the student to embrace flexibility occasionally.

■ Allow the student independence in planning their work in their own way if they really want to.

■ Avoid changing plans just for the sake of it; this will only frustrate the organised Dolphin.

116
Cat teacher with Panther student
ISFP and ESTP

Cats and Panthers share two type preferences. Like all cats they both seek and need action and variety. If the teacher can direct the boundless energy of the Panther the pair can flourish. For the teacher to get the best out of their naturally lively student they need to:

■ Listen patiently and enthusiastically to the student impulsively expressing their thoughts.

■ Stay open to 'silly' ideas to see where they lead – the student is thinking out loud and this is how they learn best.

■ Also offer your own thoughts; if you need a timeout ask for one.

■ Encourage the student to think things through before talking otherwise they may sabotage the lesson.

■ Steer the student away from controversial subjects, especially in group discussions.

■ Build in plenty of opportunities during lessons for the **E** students to talk things through with other **E** preferences.

Both teacher and student gather information in the same way. They notice detail using their senses (aware of what they can see, hear and feel). Both live in the present. The teacher is naturally sequential and realistic in their teaching style and encourages their students to follow suit. A solid, workman-like relationship develops with both teacher and student mutually understanding what each needs to do to get the job done. For the teacher to get the best out of their grounded student they need to:

■ Allow the student opportunities to repeat and practise until satisfied they are competent.

■ Describe how learning can be applied in the real world.

■ Encourage the use of imagination as a useful process (it's not wasting time).

The teacher is concerned with relationship then task whereas the student is the other way round. The teacher must learn to accept that the student is different; not cold, blunt and unfriendly, but different and focused on task first. If the teacher can accept this the relationship can be really positive for both teacher and student. For the teacher to get the best out of their intrinsically objective student they need to:

■ Offer targeted compliments. Just saying everything is great will not impress or help the student; in fact, it can result in the student not respecting the teacher, concluding they lie and/or are a soft touch. When you praise you may be pressed for proof!

■ Be logical and objective rather than emotional in discussions.

■ Accept that if the student challenges you it is probably to clarify their thoughts rather than meant as a slight to your authority or character. Perhaps ask 'What would you do to improve/change this?' or 'What do you think?' Once they've clarified their thoughts they may be ready to ask and absorb what you think.

■ Work in ways that test their skill and knowledge competitively (they raise their game).

■ Help them understand that 50% of people are **F** preference and can interpret feedback as criticism.

Cats and Panthers abhor to-do-lists, schedules and predictability; they rarely reach the status of an acquired taste or a honed skill. While enjoying their mutual love of spontaneity, which provides each with relief from the stifling and constraining timetables and deadlines ubiquitous in large organisations such as schools, they must also remember to complete any necessary tasks. Although likely to be fun and quietly popular teachers, they also need to focus on the task of preparing the student to succeed socially and academically. Both prefer to start tasks than finish them. Their initial enthusiasm can quickly wane. Both need to make sure they identify and complete the important tasks or the student (or their parents) may eventually ask awkward questions. For the teacher to get the best out of their naturally laid-back student they need to understand the student doesn't just like options and choice; they are essential or they start to itch, squirm and rebel. The secondary school environment is difficult enough for **P** preference students so teachers can help their student achieve by:

■ Providing as much flexibility as possible (multiple choice homework tasks, choice within the lesson).

■ Avoiding giving out detailed schedules (they'll just lose it anyway!).

■ Introducing random surprises and changes to prevent predictability morphing into boredom.

■ Helping the student identify ways they can organise and manage their time to complete important work without a last-minute rush.

117
Cat teacher with Lion student
ISFP and ESFP

Cats and Lions share three type preferences. Both seek action, variety and fun. But, like an episode of *Top Gear*, the reckless camaraderie can be nauseous; so reigning in and taming the Lion is often necessary for classroom harmony. For the teacher to get the best out of their naturally lively student they need to:

■ Listen patiently and enthusiastically to the student impulsively expressing their thoughts.

■ Stay open to 'silly' ideas to see where they lead – the student is thinking out loud and this is how they learn best.

■ Also offer your own thoughts; if you need a timeout ask for one.

■ Encourage the student to think things through before talking otherwise they may sabotage the lesson.

■ Steer the student away from controversial subjects, especially in group discussions.

■ Build in plenty of opportunities during lessons for the **E** students to talk things through with other **E** preferences.

Both teacher and student gather information in the same way. They notice detail using their senses (aware of what they can see, hear and feel). Both live in the present. The teacher is naturally sequential in their teaching style and encourages their students to follow suit. A solid, workman-like relationship can develop with both teacher and student mutually understanding what each needs to do to get the job done. For the teacher to get the best out of their grounded student they need to:

■ Allow the student opportunities to repeat and practise until satisfied they are competent.

■ Describe how learning can be applied in the real world.

■ Encourage the use of imagination as a useful process (it's not wasting time).

Both teacher and student are concerned first with people and relationships before the task/subject content. They like to form warm personal relationships. Compliments may move in both directions boosting the confidence of teacher as well as student. The Lion needs to feel they like their teacher and that the teacher likes them too. For the teacher to get the best out of their relationship-focused student they need to:

■ Offer learning situations that allow for the use of empathy, collaboration and teamworking.

■ Give ample and regular praise while offering tactful support to overcome any blind-spots.

■ Persuade/influence by appealing to the strength of your personal belief in the student (don't let me down, I know you can do it, I like you).

Cats and Lions can be organised and efficient; it's just such an effort! While enjoying a mutual love of spontaneity, which provides each with relief from the stifling and constraining timetables and deadlines essential in large organisations such as schools, they must also remember to complete any necessary tasks. Although likely to be fun and popular teachers, they also need to focus on the task of preparing the student to succeed socially and academically. Both prefer to start tasks than finish them. Their initial enthusiasm can quickly wane. Both need to ensure they identify and complete the important tasks or the student (or their parents) may eventually ask awkward questions. For the teacher to get the best out of their naturally laid-back student they need to understand the student doesn't just like options and choice; they are essential or they start to itch, wriggle and rebel. The secondary school environment is difficult enough for **P** preference students so teachers can help their student achieve by:

■ Providing as much flexibility as possible (multiple choice homework tasks, choice within the lesson).

■ Avoiding giving out detailed schedules (they'll just lose it anyway!).

■ Reorganising things now and again to prevent predictability becoming boredom.

■ Helping the student identify ways they can organise and manage their time to complete important work without a last-minute rush.

■ Introducing random surprises and changes to satisfy the fidgety Lion.

118
Cat teacher with Clownfish student
ISFP and ENFP

Cats and Clownfish share two type preferences. Both like a sociable and flexible classroom environment. Clashes are most likely when the student can't settle into the quiet and reflective style of many Cats. For the teacher to get the best out of their naturally lively student they need to:

■ Listen patiently and enthusiastically to the student impulsively expressing their thoughts.

■ Stay open to 'silly' ideas to see where they lead – the student is thinking out loud and this is how they learn best.

■ Also offer your own thoughts; if you need a timeout ask for one.

■ Encourage the student to think things through before talking otherwise they may sabotage the lesson.

■ Steer the student away from controversial subjects, especially in group discussions.

■ Build in plenty of opportunities during lessons for the **E** students to talk things through with other **E** preferences.

The teacher likes to use their experience to make sense of things. The one-step-at-a-time teacher encourages their students to follow suit. The **N** student will at best find this over-simplistic and at worst find it boring. The teacher is likely to label the student as 'away with the fairies'. They should resist the temptation to castigate their student because this is how they take in information and make sense of the subject. In the right context daydreaming can lead to new ways of absorbing and retaining information. For the teacher to get the best out of their inherently imaginative student they need to:

■ Embrace the imagination and insight of the student and what it can bring to the lesson.

■ Encourage the student to become aware of the important contribution of the **S** approach (the value of facts, details, procedure, experiments, applying experience, structure, the step-by-step model).

Both teacher and student are concerned first with people and relationships before the task/subject content. They like to form warm personal relationships. Compliments are usually traded in both directions boosting the confidence of teacher as well as student. The Clownfish needs to feel they like their teacher and that the teacher likes them too. If this happens they'll work harder but if not they may switch off. This explains why a student can be top of the class one year (with a teacher they like) and show no interest at all in the subject the following year when they change teacher. For the teacher to get the best out of their relationship-focused student they need to:

■ Offer learning situations that allow for the use of empathy, collaboration and teamworking.

■ Give ample and regular praise while offering tactful support to overcome any blind-spots.

■ Persuade/influence by appealing to the strength of your personal belief in the student (don't let me down, I know you can do it, I like you).

P preferences abhor to-do-lists, schedules and predictability; they rarely reach the status of an acquired taste or a honed skill. While enjoying their mutual love of spontaneity, which provides each with relief from the stifling and constraining timetables and deadlines essential in large organisations such as schools, they must also remember to complete any necessary tasks. Although likely to be fun and popular teachers, they also need to focus on the task of preparing the student to succeed socially and academically. Both prefer to start tasks than finish them. Their initial enthusiasm can quickly wane. Both need to ensure they identify and complete the important tasks or the student (or their parents) may eventually ask awkward questions. For the teacher to get the best out of their naturally laid-back student they need to understand the student doesn't just like options and choice; they are essential or they start to itch, squirm and rebel.

The secondary school environment is difficult enough for **P** preference students so teachers can help their student achieve by:

■ Providing as much flexibility as possible (multiple choice homework tasks, choice within the lesson).

■ Avoiding giving out detailed schedules (they'll just lose it anyway!).

■ Helping the student identify ways they can organise and manage their time to complete important work without a last-minute rush.

■ Introducing random surprises and changes to engage the restless Clownfish.

119
Cat teacher with Falcon student
ISFP and ENTP

Cats and Falcons share one type preference. Both like a flexible and spontaneous working environment. Falcons often need to be calmed and directed and a purring Cat teacher is well placed to deliver. For the teacher to get the best out of their naturally lively student they need to:

■ Listen patiently and enthusiastically to the student impulsively expressing their thoughts.

■ Stay open to 'silly' ideas to see where they lead – the student is thinking out loud and this is how they learn best.

■ Also offer your own thoughts; if you need a timeout ask for one.

■ Encourage the student to think things through before talking otherwise they may sabotage the lesson.

■ Steer the student away from controversial subjects, especially in group discussions.

■ Build in plenty of opportunities during lessons for the **E** students to talk things through with other **E** preferences.

The teacher likes to use their experience to make sense of things. The one-step-at-a-time teacher encourages their students to follow suit. The **N** student will at best find this over-simplistic and at worst find it boring. The teacher is likely to label the student as 'away with the fairies'. They should resist the temptation to castigate their student because this is how they take in information and make sense of the subject. In the right context daydreaming can lead to new ways of absorbing and retaining information. For the teacher to get the best out of their inherently imaginative student they need to:

■ Embrace the imagination and insight of the student and what it can bring to the lesson.

■ Encourage the student to become aware of the important contribution of the **S** approach (the value of facts, details, procedure, experiments, applying experience, structure, the step-by-step model).

The teacher is concerned with relationship then task whereas the student is the other way round. The teacher must learn to accept that the student is different; not cold, blunt and unfriendly, but different and focused on task first. If the teacher can accept this the relationship can be really positive for both teacher and student. For the teacher

to get the best out of their naturally assertive Falcon student they need to:

■ Offer targeted compliments. Just saying everything is great will not impress or help the student; in fact, it can result in the student not respecting the teacher, concluding they lie and/or are a soft touch. When you praise you may be pressed for proof!

■ Be logical and objective rather than emotional in discussions.

■ Accept that if the student challenges you it is probably to clarify their thoughts rather than meant as a slight to your authority or character. Perhaps ask 'What would you do to improve/change this?' or 'What do you think?' Once they've clarified their thoughts they may be ready to ask and absorb what you think.

■ Work in ways that test their skill and knowledge competitively (they raise their game).

■ Help them understand that 50% of people are **F** preference and can interpret feedback as criticism.

Cats and Falcons can be organised and efficient; it's just such an effort! While enjoying a mutual love of spontaneity, which provides each with relief from the stifling and constraining timetables and deadlines essential in large organisations such as schools, they must also remember to complete any necessary tasks. Although likely to be fun and popular teachers, they also need to focus on the task of preparing the student to succeed socially and academically. Both prefer to start tasks than finish them. Their initial enthusiasm can quickly wane. Both need to ensure they identify and complete the important tasks or the student (or their parents) may eventually ask awkward questions. For the teacher to get the best out of their naturally laid-back student they need to understand the student doesn't just like options and choice; they are essential or they start to itch, squirm and rebel. The secondary school environment is difficult enough for **P** preference students so teachers can help their student achieve by:

■ Providing as much flexibility as possible (multiple choice homework tasks, choice within the lesson).

■ Avoiding giving out detailed schedules (they'll just lose it anyway!).

■ Helping the student identify ways they can organise and manage their time to complete important work without a last-minute rush.

■ Introducing random changes to the routine to energise the feisty Falcon.

120
Cat teacher with Tiger student
ISFP and ISTP

Cats and Tigers share three type preferences. Both like an experience-rich and relaxed working environment. Both prefer minimal supervision. For the teacher to get the best out of their naturally lively student they need to:

■ Respect the student's need for privacy and independence

■ Take time to clarify your thoughts but don't avoid confrontation; if something needs to be said be calm and direct as you deliver it.

■ Use non-verbal communication – smiles and gestures are reassuring to **I** students; you can even use sticky notes/emails to pass on feedback.

■ Allow the student plenty of time to think through their thoughts.

■ Share your ideas and thoughts regularly to ensure you both know what you're doing.

Both teacher and student gather information in the same way. They notice detail using their senses (aware of what they can see, hear and feel). Both live in the present. The teacher is naturally realistic in their teaching style and encourages their students to follow suit. A solid, workman-like relationship develops with both teacher and student mutually understanding what each needs to do to get the job done. For the teacher to get the best out of their grounded student they need to:

■ Allow the student opportunities to repeat and practise until satisfied they are competent.

■ Describe how learning can be applied in the real world.

■ Encourage the use of imagination as a useful process (it's not wasting time).

The teacher is concerned with relationship then task whereas the student is the other way round. The teacher must learn to accept that the student is different; not cold, blunt and unfriendly, but different and focused on task first. If the teacher can accept this the relationship can be really positive for both teacher and student. For the teacher to get the best out of their intrinsically objective student they need to:

■ Offer targeted compliments. Just saying everything is great will not impress or help the student; in fact, it can result in the student not respecting the teacher, concluding they lie and/or are a soft touch. When you praise you may be pressed for proof!

■ Be logical and objective rather than emotional in discussions.

■ Accept that if the student challenges you it is probably to clarify their thoughts rather than meant as a slight to your authority or character. Perhaps ask 'What would you do to improve/change this?' or 'What do you think?' Once they've clarified their thoughts they may be ready to ask and absorb what you think.

■ Work in ways that test their skill and knowledge competitively (they raise their game).

■ Help them understand that 50% of people are **F** preference and can interpret feedback as criticism.

P preferences can be organised and efficient; it's just such an effort! While enjoying a mutual love of spontaneity, which provides each with relief from the stifling and constraining timetables and deadlines essential in large organisations such as schools, they must also remember to complete any necessary tasks. Although likely to be fun and popular teachers, they also need to focus on the task of preparing the student to succeed socially and academically. Both prefer to start tasks than finish them. Their initial enthusiasm can quickly wane. Both need to ensure they identify and complete the important tasks or the student (or their parents) may eventually ask awkward questions. For the teacher to get the best out of their naturally laid-back student they need to understand the student doesn't just like options and choice;

they are essential or they start to itch, squirm and rebel. The secondary school environment is difficult enough for **P** preference students so teachers can help their student achieve by:

- Providing as much flexibility as possible (multiple choice homework tasks, choice within the lesson).
- Avoiding giving out detailed schedules (they'll just lose it anyway!).
- Shaking things up now and again to prevent predictability becoming boredom. Introduce random surprises and changes.
- Helping identify simple time-management strategies to ensure the Tiger can prosper.

121
Cat teacher with Cat student
ISFP and ISFP

Sharing all four preferences can help teacher and student understand each other for good or ill. Cats like their independence and this is the most likely source of conflict. For the teacher to get the best out of their naturally reserved student they need to:

- Respect the student's need for privacy.
- Take time to clarify your thoughts but don't avoid confrontation; if something needs to be said be calm and direct as you deliver it.
- Use non-verbal communication – smiles and gestures are reassuring to **I** students; you can even use sticky notes/emails to pass on feedback.
- Allow the student plenty of time to think through their thoughts.
- Share your ideas and thoughts regularly to ensure you both know what you're doing.

Cats gather information in the same way. They notice detail using their senses (aware of what they can see, hear and feel). Both live in the present. The teacher is naturally utilitarian in their teaching style and encourages their students to follow suit. A solid, workman-like relationship develops with both teacher and student mutually understanding what each needs to do to get the job done. For the teacher to get the best out of their grounded student they need to:

- Allow the student opportunities to repeat and practise until satisfied they are competent.
- Describe how learning can be applied in the real world.
- Encourage the use of imagination as a useful process (it's not wasting time).

Cats are concerned first with people and relationships before the task/subject content. They like to form warm personal relationships. The Cat student needs to feel they like their teacher and that the teacher likes them too. If this happens they'll work harder but if not they may switch off completely. This explains why a student can be top of the class one year (with a teacher they like) and show no interest at all in the same subject the following year when they change teacher. For the teacher to get the best out of their relationship-focused student they need to:

- Offer learning situations that allow for the use of empathy, collaboration and teamworking.

- Give ample and regular praise while offering tactful support to overcome any blind-spots.
- Motivate by appealing to the strength of your personal belief in the student (don't let me down, I know you can do it, I like you).

Cats can be organised and efficient; it's just such an effort! While enjoying a mutual love of spontaneity, which provides each with relief from the stifling and constraining timetables and deadlines essential in large organisations such as schools, they must also remember to complete any necessary tasks. Although likely to be fun and popular teachers. they also need to focus on the task of preparing the student to succeed socially and academically. Both prefer to start tasks than finish them. Their initial enthusiasm can quickly wane. Both need to ensure they identify and complete the important tasks or the student (or their parents) may eventually ask awkward questions. For the teacher to get the best out of their naturally laid-back student they need to understand the student doesn't just like options and choice; they are essential or they start to itch, squirm and rebel. The secondary school environment is difficult enough for **P** preference students so teachers can help their student achieve by:

- Providing as much flexibility as possible (multiple choice homework tasks, choice within the lesson).
- Avoiding giving out detailed schedules (they'll just lose it anyway!).
- Shaking things up now and again to prevent predictability becoming boredom.
- Helping the Cat student identify simple time-management techniques to ensure they can be successful.

122
Cat teacher with Seal student
ISFP and INFP

Cats and Seals share three type preferences. Both enjoy time to work alone in a laid-back, low key and supportive atmosphere. For the teacher to get the best out of their naturally sensitive student they need to:

- Respect the student's need for privacy and independence.
- Take time to clarify your thoughts but don't avoid confrontation; if something needs to be said be calm and direct as you deliver it.
- Use non-verbal communication – smiles and gestures are reassuring to **I** students; you can even use sticky notes/emails to pass on feedback.
- Allow the student plenty of time to think through their thoughts.
- Share your ideas and thoughts regularly to ensure you both know what you're doing.

The teacher likes to use their experience to make sense of things. The one-step-at-a-time teacher encourages their students to follow suit. The **N** student will at best find this over-simplistic and at worst find it dreary. The teacher is likely to label the student as 'away with the fairies'. They should resist the temptation to castigate their student because this is how they take in infor-

mation and make sense of the subject. In the right context daydreaming can lead to new ways of absorbing and retaining information. For the teacher to get the best out of their inherently imaginative student they need to:

- Embrace the imagination and insight of the student and what it can bring to the lesson.
- Encourage the student to become aware of the important contribution of the **S** approach (the value of facts, details, procedure, experiments, applying experience, structure, the step-by-step model).

Both teacher and student are concerned first with people and relationships before the task/subject content. They like to form warm personal relationships. Compliments may flow in both directions boosting the confidence of teacher as well as student. The Seal needs to feel they like their teacher and that the teacher likes them too. If this happens they'll work harder but if not they may switch off completely. For the teacher to get the best out of their relationship-focused student they need to:

- Offer learning situations that allow for the use of empathy, collaboration and teamworking.
- Give ample and regular praise while offering tactful support to overcome any blind-spots.
- Persuade/influence by appealing to the strength of your personal belief in the student (don't let me down, I know you can do it, I like you).

Cats and Seals abhor to-do-lists, schedules and predictability; they rarely reach the status of an acquired taste or a honed skill. While enjoying their mutual love of spontaneity, which provides each with relief from the stifling and constraining timetables and deadlines essential in large organisations such as schools, they must also remember to complete any necessary tasks. Although likely to be fun and popular teachers, they also need to focus on the task of preparing the student to succeed socially and academically. Both prefer to start tasks than finish them. Their initial enthusiasm can quickly wane. Both need to ensure they identify and complete the important tasks or the student (or their parents) may eventually ask awkward questions. For the teacher to get the best out of their naturally laid-back student they need to understand the student doesn't just like options and choice; they are essential or they start to itch, squirm and rebel. The secondary school environment is difficult enough for **P** preference students so teachers can help their student achieve by:

- Providing as much flexibility as possible (multiple choice homework tasks, choice within the lesson).
- Avoiding giving out detailed schedules (they'll just lose it anyway!).
- Shaking things up now and again to prevent predictability becoming boredom.
- Helping the student identify ways they can organise and manage their time to complete important work without a last-minute rush.

123
Cat teacher with Tawny Owl student
ISFP and INTP

Cats and Tawny Owls share two type preferences. Both are quietly determined and respond well to being offered choices in how they complete tasks. For the teacher to get the best out of their naturally thoughtful student they need to:

■ Respect the student's need for privacy and independence

■ Take time to clarify your thoughts but don't avoid confrontation; if something needs to be said be calm and direct as you deliver it.

■ Use non-verbal communication – smiles and gestures are reassuring to **I** students; you can even use sticky notes/emails to pass on feedback.

■ Allow the student plenty of time to think through their thoughts.

■ Share your ideas and thoughts regularly to ensure you both know what you're doing.

The teacher likes to use their experience to make sense of things. The one-step-at-a-time teacher encourages their students to follow suit. The **N** student will at best find this over-simplistic and at worst find it tedious. The teacher is likely to label the student as 'away with the fairies'. They should resist the temptation to castigate their student because this is how they take in information and make sense of the subject. In the right context daydreaming can lead to new ways of absorbing and retaining information. For the teacher to get the best out of their inherently imaginative student they need to:

■ Embrace the imagination and insight of the student and what it can bring to the lesson.

■ Encourage the student to become aware of the important contribution of the **S** approach (the value of facts, details, procedure, experiments, applying experience, structure, the step-by-step model).

The teacher is concerned with relationship then task whereas the student is the other way round. The teacher must learn to accept that the student is different; not cold, blunt and unfriendly, but different and focused on task first. If the teacher can accept this the relationship can be really positive for both teacher and student. For the teacher to get the best out of their naturally objective Tawny Owl student they need to:

■ Offer targeted compliments. Just saying everything is great will not impress or help the student; in fact, it can result in the student not respecting the teacher, concluding they lie and/or are a soft touch. When you praise you may be pressed for proof!

■ Be logical and objective rather than emotional in discussions.

■ Accept that if the student challenges you it is probably to clarify their thoughts rather than meant as a slight to your authority or character. Perhaps ask 'What would you do to improve/change this?' or 'What do you think?' Once they've clarified their thoughts they may be ready to ask and absorb what you think.

■ Work in ways that test their skill and knowledge competitively (they raise their game).

■ Help them understand that 50% of people are **F** preference and can interpret feedback as criticism.

Cats and Tawny Owls can be organised and efficient; it's just such an effort! While enjoying a mutual love of spontaneity, which provides each with relief from the stifling and constraining timetables and deadlines essential in large organisations such as schools, they must also remember to complete any necessary tasks. Although likely to be fun and popular teachers, they also need to focus on the task of preparing the student to succeed socially and academically. Both prefer to start tasks than finish them. Their initial enthusiasm can quickly wane. Both need to ensure they identify and complete the important tasks or the student (or their parents) may eventually ask awkward questions. For the teacher to get the best out of their naturally laid-back student they need to understand the student doesn't just like options and choice; they are essential or they start to itch, squirm and rebel. The secondary school environment is difficult enough for **P** preference students so teachers can help their student achieve by:

■ Providing as much flexibility as possible (multiple choice homework tasks, choice within the lesson).

■ Avoiding giving out detailed schedules (they'll just lose it anyway!).

■ Introducing random surprises and changes.

■ Identifying simple time-management strategies to ensure the Tawny Owl can blossom.

124
Cat teacher with Seahorse student
ISFP and INFJ

Cats and Seahorses share two type preferences. Both are polite and warm. For the teacher to get the best out of their naturally introspective student they need to:

■ Respect the student's need for privacy and independence.

■ Take time to clarify your thoughts but don't avoid confrontation; if something needs to be said be calm and direct as you deliver it.

■ Use non-verbal communication – smiles and gestures are reassuring to **I** students; you can even use sticky notes/emails to pass on feedback.

■ Allow the student plenty of time to think through their thoughts.

■ Share your ideas and thoughts regularly to ensure you both know what you're doing.

The teacher likes to use their experience to make sense of things. The one-step-at-a-time teacher encourages their students to follow suit. The **N** student will at best find this over-simplistic and at worst find it boring. The teacher is likely to label the student as 'away with the fairies'. They should resist the temptation to castigate their student because this is how they take in information and make sense of the subject. In the right context daydreaming can lead to new ways of absorbing and retaining information. For the

teacher to get the best out of their inherently imaginative student they need to:

■ Embrace the imagination and insight of the student and what it can bring to the lesson.

■ Encourage the student to become aware of the important contribution of the **S** approach (the value of facts, details, procedure, experiments, applying experience, structure, the step-by-step model).

Both teacher and student are concerned first with people and relationships before the task/subject content. They like to form warm personal relationships. The Seahorse needs to feel they like their teacher and that the teacher likes them too. If this happens they'll work harder but if not they may switch off. This explains why a student can be top of the class one year (with a teacher they like) and show no interest at all in the subject the following year when they change teacher. For the teacher to get the best out of their relationship-focused student they need to:

■ Offer learning situations that allow for the use of empathy, collaboration and teamworking.

■ Give ample and regular praise while offering tactful support to overcome any blind-spots.

■ Influence by appealing to the strength of your personal belief in the student (don't let me down, I know you can do it).

The laid-back, flexible and spontaneous teacher with the naturally organised student can be a dream team or a disaster. To create a positive relationship they need to play to each other's strengths. The student can benefit from the teacher's ability to adapt and change plans and the teacher can benefit from the student's desire to have a plan they can work to and complete. The teacher can also:

■ Encourage the student to embrace flexibility occasionally.

■ Encourage and support the student's desire for order, neatness and respecting deadlines.

■ Allow the student independence in planning their work in their own way if they really want to.

■ Avoid changing plans just for the sake of it; this will only frustrate the Seahorse.

125
Cat teacher with Barn Owl student
ISFP and INTJ

Cats and Barn Owls share one type preference. Both are naturally reserved and thoughtful. For the teacher to get the best out of their naturally lively but introspective student they need to:

■ Respect the student's need for privacy and independence.

■ Take time to clarify your thoughts but don't avoid confrontation; if something needs to be said be calm and direct as you deliver it.

■ Use non-verbal communication – smiles and gestures are reassuring to **I** students; you can even use sticky notes/emails to pass on feedback.

■ Allow the student plenty of time to think through their thoughts.

■ Share your ideas and thoughts regularly to ensure you both know what you're doing.

The teacher likes to use their experience to make sense of things. The one-step-at-a-time teacher encourages their students to follow suit. The **N** student will at best find this over-simplistic and at worst find it lacklustre. The teacher is likely to label the student as 'away with the fairies'. They should resist the temptation to castigate their student because this is how they take in information and make sense of the subject. In the right context daydreaming can lead to new ways of absorbing and retaining information. For the teacher to get the best out of their inherently imaginative student they need to:

■ Embrace the imagination and insight of the student and what it can bring to the lesson.

■ Encourage the student to become aware of the important contribution of the **S** approach (the value of facts, details, procedure, experiments, applying experience, structure, the step-by-step model).

The teacher is concerned with relationship then task whereas the student is the other way round. The teacher must learn to accept that the student is different; not cold, blunt and unfriendly, but different and focused on task first. If the teacher can accept this the relationship can be really positive for both teacher and student. For the teacher to get the best out of their naturally analytical student they need to:

■ Offer targeted compliments. Just saying everything is great will not impress or help the student; in fact, it can result in the student not respecting the teacher, concluding they lie and/or are a soft touch. When you praise you may be pressed for proof!

■ Be logical and objective rather than emotional in discussions.

■ Accept that if the student challenges you it is probably to clarify their thoughts rather than defy your authority or character. Perhaps ask 'What would you do to improve/change this?' or 'What do you think?' Once they've clarified their thoughts they may be ready to ask and absorb what you think.

■ Work in ways that test their skill and knowledge competitively (they raise their game).

■ Help them understand that 50% of people are **F** preference and can interpret feedback as criticism.

The laid-back, flexible and spontaneous teacher with the naturally organised student can be a dream team or a disaster. To create a positive relationship they need to play to each other's strengths. The student can benefit from the teacher's ability to adapt and change plans and the teacher can benefit from the student's desire to have a plan they can work to and complete. The teacher can also:

■ Encourage and support the student's desire for order, neatness and respecting deadlines.

■ Allow the student independence in planning their work in their own way if they really want to.

■ Avoid changing plans just for the sake of it; this will only frustrate the student.

126
Cat teacher with Polar Bear student
ISFP and ISTJ

Cats and Polar Bears share two type preferences. Both are reserved, considered and like to get on with the task in hand. They differ in their approach to the task; the laid-back and personal Cat contrasting with the objective and precise Bear. For the teacher to get the best out of their naturally private student they need to:

■ Respect the student's need for privacy and independence.

■ Take time to clarify your thoughts but don't avoid confrontation; if something needs to be said be calm and direct as you deliver it.

■ Use non-verbal communication – smiles and gestures are reassuring to **I** students; you can even use sticky notes/emails to pass on feedback.

■ Allow the student plenty of time to think through their thoughts.

■ Share your ideas and thoughts regularly to ensure you both know what you're doing.

Both teacher and student gather information in the same way. They notice detail using their senses (aware of what they can see, hear and feel). Both live in the present. The teacher is naturally realistic in their teaching style and encourages their students to follow suit. A solid, workmanlike relationship develops with both teacher and student mutually understanding what each needs to do to get the job done. For the teacher to get the best out of their grounded student they need to:

■ Allow the student opportunities to repeat and practise until satisfied they are competent.

■ Describe how learning can be applied in the real world.

■ Encourage the use of imagination as a useful process (it's not wasting time).

The teacher is concerned with relationship then task whereas the student is the other way round. The teacher must learn to accept that the student is different; not cold, blunt and unfriendly, but different and focused on task first. If the teacher can accept this the relationship can be really positive for both teacher and student. For the teacher to get the best out of their inherently objective student they need to:

■ Offer targeted compliments. Just saying everything is great will not impress or help the student; in fact, it can result in the student not respecting the teacher, concluding they lie and/or are a soft touch. When you praise you may be pressed for proof!

■ Be logical and objective rather than emotional in discussions.

■ Accept that if the student challenges you it is probably to clarify their thoughts rather than meant as a slight to your authority or character. Perhaps ask 'What would you do to improve/change this?' or 'What do you think?' Once they've clarified their thoughts they may be ready to ask and absorb what you think.

■ Work in ways that test their skill and knowledge competitively (they raise their game).

■ Help them understand that 50% of people are **F** preference and can interpret feedback as criticism.

The laid-back, flexible and spontaneous teacher with the naturally organised student can be a dream team or a disaster. To create a positive relationship they need to play to each other's strengths. The student can benefit from the teacher's ability to adapt and change plans and the teacher can benefit from the student's desire to have a plan they can work to and complete. The teacher can also:

■ Encourage and support the student's desire for order, neatness and respecting deadlines.

■ Encourage the student to embrace flexibility occasionally.

■ Avoid changing plans just for the sake of it; this will only frustrate the student.

■ Allow the student independence in planning their work in their own way if they really want to.

127
Cat teacher with Eagle student
ISFP and ENTJ

Cats and Eagles share no type preferences. For opposites to attract they need to embrace each other's differences. The laid-back teacher and potentially bossy student can learn from their different classroom styles. For the teacher to get the best out of their naturally lively student they need to:

■ Encourage the student to think things through before talking otherwise they may sabotage the lesson.

■ Steer the student away from controversial subjects, especially in group discussions.

■ Build in plenty of opportunities during lessons for the **E** students to talk things through with other **E** preferences.

■ Listen patiently and enthusiastically to the student impulsively expressing their thoughts.

■ Stay open to 'silly' ideas to see where they lead – the student is thinking out loud and this is how they learn best.

■ Also offer your own thoughts; if you need a timeout ask for one.

The teacher likes to use their experience to make sense of things. The one-step-at-a-time teacher encourages their students to follow suit. The **N** student will at best find this over-simplistic and at worst find it boring. The teacher is likely to label the student as 'away with the fairies'. They should resist the temptation to castigate their student because this is how they take in information and make sense of the subject. In the right context daydreaming can lead to new ways of absorbing and retaining information. For the teacher to get the best out of their inherently imaginative student they need to:

■ Embrace the imagination and insight of the student and what it can bring to the lesson.

■ Encourage the student to become aware of the important contribution of the **S** approach (the value of facts, details, procedure, experiments, applying experience, structure, the step-by-step model).

The teacher is concerned with relationship then task whereas the student is the other way round. The teacher must learn to accept that the student is different; not cold, blunt and unfriendly, but different and focused on task first. If the teacher can accept this the relationship can be really positive for both teacher and student. For the teacher to get the best out of their fundamentally assertive Eagle student they need to:

■ Accept that if the student challenges you it is probably to clarify their thoughts rather than meant as a slight to your authority or character. Perhaps ask 'What would you do to improve/change this?' or 'What do you think?' Once they've clarified their thoughts they may be ready to ask and absorb what you think.

■ Work in ways that test their skill and knowledge competitively (they raise their game).

■ Help them understand that 50% of people are **F** preference and can interpret feedback as criticism.

■ Offer targeted compliments. Just saying everything is great will not impress or help the student; in fact, it can result in the student not respecting the teacher, concluding they lie and/or are a soft touch. When you praise you may be pressed for proof!

■ Be logical and objective rather than emotional in discussions.

The laid-back, flexible and spontaneous teacher with the naturally organised student can be a dream team or a disaster. To create a positive relationship they need to play to each other's strengths. The student can benefit from the teacher's ability to adapt and change plans and the teacher can benefit from the student's desire to have a plan they can work to and complete. The teacher can also:

■ Avoid changing plans just for the sake of it; this will only frustrate the student.

■ Encourage the student to embrace flexibility occasionally.

■ Encourage and support the student's desire for order, neatness and respecting deadlines.

■ Allow the student independence in planning their work in their own way if they really want to; Eagles respond positively to responsibility.

128
Cat teacher with Koala student
ISFP and ISFJ

Cats and Koalas share three type preferences. Both are quiet, grounded, warm and likely to see eye-to-eye in the classroom. For the teacher to get the best out of their naturally sensitive student they need to:

■ Respect the student's need for privacy and independence.

■ Take time to clarify your thoughts but don't avoid confrontation; if something needs to be said be calm and direct as you deliver it.

■ Use non-verbal communication – smiles and gestures are reassuring to **I** students; you can even use sticky notes/emails to pass on feedback.

■ Allow the student plenty of time to think through their thoughts.

■ Share your ideas and thoughts regularly to ensure you both know what you're doing.

Both teacher and student gather information in the same way. They notice detail using their senses (aware of what they can see, hear and feel). Both live in the present. The teacher is naturally realistic in their teaching style and encourages their students to follow suit. A solid, workmanlike relationship develops with both teacher and student mutually understanding what each needs to do to get the job done. For the teacher to get the best out of their grounded student they need:

■ Allow the student opportunities to repeat and practise until satisfied they are competent.

■ Describe how learning can be applied in the real world.

■ Encourage the use of imagination as a useful process (it's not wasting time).

Both teacher and student are concerned first with people and relationships before the task/subject content. They like to form warm personal relationships. Compliments are likely to go in both directions boosting the confidence of teacher as well as student. The Koala needs to feel they like their teacher and that the teacher likes them too. If this happens they'll work harder but if they don't they may completely switch off. This explains why a student can be top of the class one year (with a teacher they like) and show no interest at all in the subject the following year when they change teacher. For the teacher to get the best out of their relationship-focused student they need to:

■ Offer learning situations that allow for the use of empathy, collaboration and teamworking.

■ Give ample and regular praise while offering tactful support to overcome any blind-spots.

■ Persuade/influence by appealing to the strength of your personal belief in the student (don't let me down, I know you can do it, I like you).

The laid-back, flexible and spontaneous teacher with the naturally organised student can be a dream team or a disaster. To create a positive relationship they need to play to each other's strengths. The student can benefit from the teacher's ability to adapt and change plans and the teacher can benefit from the student's desire to have a plan they can work to and complete. The teacher can also:

■ Encourage and support the student's desire for order, neatness and respecting deadlines.

■ Allow the student independence in planning their work in their own way if they really want to.

■ Avoid changing plans just for the sake of it; this only frustrates the student.

■ Encourage the student to embrace change; sometimes it is necessary and useful.

129
Seahorse teacher with Teddy Bear student
INFJ and ESFJ

Seahorses and Bears share a desire to be organised. The reality-first approach of the Teddy contrasts with the imagination-first approach of the teacher. Clashes are most likely when the more gregarious student contrasts with the more reserved teacher. For the teacher to get the best out of their naturally lively student they need to:

■ Listen patiently and enthusiastically to the student impulsively expressing their thoughts.

■ Stay open to 'silly' ideas to see where they lead – the student is thinking out loud and this is how they learn best.

■ Also offer your own thoughts; if you need a timeout ask for one.

■ Encourage the student to think things through before talking otherwise they may sabotage the lesson.

■ Steer the student away from controversial subjects, especially in group discussions.

■ Build in plenty of opportunities during lessons for the **E** students to talk things through with other **E** preferences.

The imaginative teacher can inspire all students, but they do need to respect the need for around 65% of students to be given clear guidelines, structure, facts, details and procedures; otherwise they can flounder. For the teacher to get the best out of their intrinsically grounded student they need to:

■ Demonstrate how learning can be applied in the real world.

■ Allow the student opportunities to repeat and practise until satisfied they are competent.

■ Encourage the use of imagination as a useful process (it's not wasting time).

■ Be careful not to look like you're favouring **N** students to the detriment of **S** students. Every student needs to be able to contribute in their preferred way.

Both teacher and student are both concerned first with people and relationships before the task/subject content. They like to form warm personal relationships. Compliments are likely to go in both directions boosting the confidence of teacher as well as student. The Teddy needs to feel they like their teacher and that the teacher likes them too. If this happens they'll work harder but if they don't they may switch off completely. This explains why a student can be top of the class one year (with a teacher they like) and show no interest at all in the subject the following year when they change teacher. For the teacher to get the best out of their relationship-focused student they need to:

■ Offer learning situations that allow for the use of empathy, collaboration and teamworking.

■ Give ample and regular praise while offering tactful support to overcome any blind-spots.

■ Influence by appealing to the strength of your personal belief in the student (don't let me down, I know you can do it, I like you).

The **J** teacher takes pleasure in scheduling their time. They are organised and decisive. They work out a plan and stick to it, often aided by an impressive to-do list. Their classroom is usually organised. The subject will probably be broken down into lesson-sized chunks and the year planned out whether or not an Ofsted inspector is due. Many **J** preference students are reassured by their teacher's organisational zeal. They simply adopt the schedule and deliver their side of the bargain, generally completing all tasks on time. Interestingly, some **J** preferences will baulk at their teacher's well-intentioned thoroughness. They would like to create their own plan and work to it rather than adopt someone else's. This is due to the **J**'s desire for control. So two **J**'s together can clash, though at least all their work will be done. Most secondary schools require students to be so organised that two **J**'s are the best combination. For the teacher to get the best out of their naturally organised student they need to:

■ Enjoy your shared desire for order, neatness and respecting deadlines.

■ Allow the student independence in planning their work in their own way if they really want to.

■ Be prepared to adjust your own plans if external events interfere with your careful preparations (and encourage the student to also embrace flexibility occasionally).

■ Shake things up now and again to prevent predictability becoming boredom.

■ Avoid making quick decisions about what needs to be done before considering all of the options.

130
Seahorse teacher with Falcon student
INFJ and ENTP

Seahorses and Birds use their imagination to make sense of their world. The Falcon applies their imagination to solve technical problems which can clash with the personal approach of the Seahorse. The student's desire for flexibility can also conflict with the teacher's quietly organised approach. For the teacher to get the best out of their naturally lively student they need to:

■ Listen patiently and enthusiastically to the student impulsively expressing their thoughts.

■ Stay open to 'silly' ideas to see where they lead – the student is thinking out loud and this is how they learn best.

■ Also offer your own thoughts; if you need a timeout ask for one.

■ Encourage the student to think things through before talking otherwise they may sabotage the lesson.

■ Steer the student away from controversial subjects, especially in group discussions.

■ Build in plenty of opportunities during lessons for the **E** students to talk things through with other **E** preferences.

Both teacher and student gather information by seeing the big picture first, using hunches, inferences and imagination to infer meaning. The teacher will naturally use their imagination in the classroom and the **N** student will respond well to this, possibly joining in with flights of fancy, anecdotes and stories. A natural affinity between teacher and student is often present because they both look at the world in the same way – with a burning curiosity to understand why things are as they are by exploring patterns, possibilities, ideas and theories. Be careful not to look like you're favouring **N** preference students to the detriment of the **S** preference students. Every student needs to be able to contribute in their preferred way. For the teacher to get the best out of their inherently imaginative student they need to:

■ Offer questions/projects that can be explored creatively.

■ Avoid repetitive tasks as they'll quickly lose interest.

■ Encourage the student to become aware of the important contribution of the **S** approach (the value of facts, details, procedure, experiments, applying experience, structure, the step-by-step model).

The teacher is concerned with relationship then task whereas the student is the other way round. The teacher must learn to accept that the student is different; not cold, blunt and unfriendly, but different and focused on task first. If the teacher can accept this the relationship can be really positive for both teacher and student. For the teacher to get the best out of their assertive Falcon they need to:

■ Offer targeted compliments. Just saying everything is great will not impress or help the student; in fact, it can result in the student not respecting the teacher, concluding they lie and/or are a soft touch. When you praise you may be pressed for proof!

■ Be logical and objective rather than emotional in discussions.

■ Accept that if the student challenges you it is probably to clarify their thoughts rather than meant as a slight to your authority or character. Perhaps ask 'What would you do to improve/change this?' or 'What do you think?' Once they've clarified their thoughts they may be ready to ask and absorb what you think.

■ Work in ways that test their skill and knowledge competitively (they raise their game).

■ Help them understand that half the population are **F** preference and can interpret feedback as criticism.

The **J** teacher takes pleasure in scheduling their time. They are organised and decisive. They work out a plan and stick to it, often aided by an impressive to-do list. Their classroom is usually an organised place. The subject will probably be broken down into lesson-sized chunks and the year planned out with military precision. The **P** student will either respond:

■ Positively by accepting your expertise and understanding the long-term benefits they'll reap.

■ Passively by just accepting your structure/plan for an easy life without really buying into the content or process you are offering.

■ Negatively by rejecting you, your structure/plan and subject completely (even if they're physically in your room they will not engage and participate).

For the teacher to get the best out of their naturally laid-back student they should note the student doesn't just like options and choice; they need them or they start to itch, squirm and rebel. The secondary school environment is difficult enough for **P** preference students so teachers can help soften the pressure. To help:

■ Provide as much flexibility as possible (multiple choice homework tasks, choice within the lesson).

■ Shake things up now and again to prevent predictability becoming boredom. Introduce random surprises and changes.

■ Identify effective strategies to ensure they can manage their workload successfully.

■ Avoid giving out detailed schedules (they'll just lose it anyway!).

■ Don't be more picky with detail than is absolutely necessary.

131
Seahorse teacher with Black Bear student
INFJ and ESTJ

Seahorses and Bears share a desire to be organised. The reality-first approach of the Black Bear contrasts with the imagination-first style of the teacher. Clashes are most likely when the more gregarious and objective student contrasts with the more reserved and nurturing teacher. For the teacher to get the best out of their naturally lively student they need to:

■ Listen patiently and enthusiastically to the student impulsively expressing their thoughts.

■ Stay open to 'silly' ideas to see where they lead – the student is thinking out loud and this is how they learn best.

■ Also offer your own thoughts; if you need a timeout ask for one.

■ Encourage the student to think things through before talking otherwise they may sabotage the lesson.

■ Steer the student away from controversial subjects, especially in group discussions.

■ Build in plenty of opportunities during lessons for the **E** students to talk things through with other **E** preferences.

The imaginative teacher can inspire all students, but they do need to respect the need for Black Bears to be given clear guidelines, structure, facts, details and procedures; otherwise they can flounder. For the teacher to get the best out of their grounded student they need to:

■ Demonstrate how learning can be applied in the real world.

■ Allow the student opportunities to repeat and practise until satisfied they are competent.

■ Encourage the use of imagination as a useful process (it's not wasting time).

■ Be careful not to look like you're favouring **N** students to the detriment of **S** students. Every student needs to be able to contribute in their preferred way.

The teacher is concerned with relationship then task whereas the student is the other way round. The teacher must learn to accept that the student is different; not cold, blunt and unfriendly, but different and focused on task first. If the teacher can accept this the relationship can be really positive for both teacher and student. For the teacher to get the best out of their intrinsically assertive student they need to:

- Offer targeted compliments. Just saying everything is great will not impress or help the student; in fact, it can result in the student not respecting the teacher, concluding they lie and/or are a soft touch. When you praise you may be pressed for proof!
- Be logical and objective rather than emotional in discussions.
- Accept that if the student challenges you it is probably to clarify their thoughts rather than meant as a slight to your authority or character. Perhaps ask 'What would you do to improve/change this?' or 'What do you think?' Once they've clarified their thoughts they may be ready to ask and absorb what you think.
- Work in ways that test their skill and knowledge competitively (they raise their game).
- Help them understand that 50% of people are **F** preference and can interpret feedback as criticism.

The **J** teacher takes pleasure in scheduling their time. They are organised and decisive. They work out a plan and stick to it, often aided by an impressive to-do list. Their classroom is usually organised. The subject will probably be broken down into lesson-sized chunks and the year planned out whether or not an Ofsted inspector is due. Many **J** preference students are reassured by their teacher's organisational zeal. They simply adopt the schedule and deliver their side of the bargain, generally completing all tasks on time. Interestingly, some **J** preferences will baulk at their teacher's well-intentioned thoroughness. They would like to create their own plan and work to it rather than adopt someone else's plan. This is due to the **J**'s desire for control. So two **J**'s together can clash, though at least all their work will be done. Most secondary schools require students to be so organised that two **J**'s are the best combination. For the teacher to get the best out of their naturally organised student they need to:

- Enjoy your shared desire for order, neatness and respecting deadlines.
- Allow the student independence in planning their work in their own way if they really want to.
- Be prepared to adjust your own plans if external events interfere with your careful preparations (and encourage the student to also embrace flexibility occasionally).
- Shake things up now and again to prevent predictability becoming boredom.
- Avoid making quick decisions about what needs to be done before considering all of the options.

132
Seahorse teacher with Panther student
INFJ and ESTP

Seahorses and Panthers are opposite personality types. Opposites can share a blessed or cursed relationship. The naturally imaginative, reserved and organised Seahorse can draw out these qualities in their student. The teacher must also accept and steer the spontaneous, lively and hedonistic Panther to calm and safe shores. For the teacher to get the best out of their naturally effusive student they need to:

- Listen patiently and enthusiastically to the student impulsively expressing their thoughts.
- Stay open to 'silly' ideas to see where they lead – the student is thinking out loud and this is how they learn best.
- Also offer your own thoughts; if you need a timeout ask for one.
- Encourage the student to think things through before talking otherwise they may sabotage the lesson.
- Steer the student away from controversial subjects, especially in group discussions.
- Build in plenty of opportunities during lessons for the **E** students to talk things through with other **E** preferences.

The imaginative teacher can inspire all students, but they do need to respect the need for Panthers to be given clear guidelines, structure, facts, details and procedures; otherwise they can be easily distracted. For the teacher to get the best out of their grounded student they need to:

- Demonstrate how learning can be applied in the real world.
- Allow the student opportunities to repeat and practise until satisfied they are competent.
- Encourage the use of imagination as a useful process (it's not wasting time).
- Be careful not to look like you're favouring **N** students to the detriment of **S** students. Every student needs to be able to contribute in their preferred way.

The teacher is concerned with relationship then task whereas the student is the other way round. The teacher must learn to accept that the student is different; not cold, blunt and unfriendly, but different and focused on task first. If the teacher can accept this the relationship can be really positive for both teacher and student. For the teacher to get the best out of their fundamentally assertive student they need to:

- Offer targeted compliments. Just saying everything is great will not impress or help the student; in fact, it can result in the student not respecting the teacher, concluding they lie and/or are a soft touch. When you praise you may be pressed for proof!
- Be logical and objective rather than emotional in discussions.
- Accept that if the student challenges you it is probably to clarify their thoughts rather than meant as a slight your authority or character. Perhaps ask 'What would you do to improve/ change this?' or 'What do you think?' Once they've clarified their thoughts they may be ready to ask and absorb what you think.
- Work in ways that test their skill and knowledge competitively (they raise their game).
- Help them understand that 50% of people are **F** preference and can interpret feedback as criticism.

Seahorses have to schedule their time. They are naturally organised. They work out a plan and stick to it, often aided by an impressive to-do list. Their classroom is usually an organised place. The **P** student will either respond:

- Positively by accepting your expertise and understanding the long-term benefits they'll reap.
- Passively by just accepting your structure/plan for an easy life without really buying into the content or process you are offering.
- Negatively by rejecting you, your structure/ plan and subject completely (even if they're physically in your room they will not engage and participate).

For the teacher to get the best out of their naturally laid-back student they should note the student doesn't just like options and choice; they need them or they start to itch, squirm and rebel. The secondary school environment is difficult enough for **P** preference students so teachers can help soften the pressure. To help:

- Provide as much flexibility as possible (multiple choice homework tasks, choice within the lesson).
- Avoid giving out detailed schedules (they'll just lose it anyway!).
- Don't be more picky with detail than is absolutely necessary.
- Shake things up now and again to prevent predictability becoming boredom. Introduce random surprises and changes.
- Show the student how to implement simple time-management techniques to ensure they succeed.

133
Seahorse teacher with Tawny Owl student
INFJ and INTP

Seahorses and Tawny Owls use their imagination to make sense of their world. The Owl applies their imagination to solve technical problems which can clash with the personal approach of the Seahorse. The Tawny Owl's desire for flexibility can also conflict with the teacher's quietly organised approach. For the teacher to get the best out of their naturally reserved student they need to:

- Respect the student's need for privacy and independence.
- Take time to clarify your thoughts but don't avoid confrontation; if something needs to be said be calm and direct as you deliver it.
- Use non-verbal communication – smiles and gestures are reassuring to **I** students; you can even use sticky notes/emails to pass on feedback.
- Allow the student plenty of time to think through their thoughts.
- Share your ideas and thoughts regularly to ensure you both know what you're doing.

Both teacher and student gather information by seeing the big picture first, using hunches, inferences and imagination to infer meaning. The teacher will naturally use their imagination in the classroom and the **N** student will respond well to this, possibly joining in with flights of fancy, anecdotes and stories. A natural affinity between teacher and student is often present because they both look at the world in the same way – with a burning curiosity to understand why things are as they are by exploring patterns, possibilities, ideas and theories. Be careful not to look like you're favouring **N** preference students to the detriment of **S** preference students. Every student needs to be able to contribute in their preferred way. For the teacher to get the best out of their inherently imaginative student they need to:

◼ Offer questions/projects that can be explored creatively.

◼ Avoid repetitive tasks as they'll quickly lose interest.

◼ Encourage the student to become aware of the important contribution of the **S** approach (the value of facts, details, procedure, experiments, applying experience, structure, the step-by-step model).

The teacher is concerned with relationship then task whereas the student is the other way round. The teacher must learn to accept that the student is different; not cold, blunt and unfriendly, but different and focused on task first. If the teacher can accept this the relationship can be really positive for both teacher and student. For the teacher to get the best out of their naturally analytical student they need to:

◼ Offer targeted compliments. Just saying everything is great will not impress or help the student; in fact, it can result in the student not respecting the teacher, concluding they lie and/or are a soft touch. When you praise you may be pressed for proof!

◼ Be logical and objective rather than emotional in discussions.

◼ Accept that if the student challenges you it is probably to clarify their thoughts rather than meant as a slight your authority or character. Perhaps ask 'What would you do to improve/change this?' or 'What do you think?' Once they've clarified their thoughts they may be ready to ask and absorb what you think.

◼ Work in ways that test their skill and knowledge competitively (they raise their game).

◼ Help them understand that half of people are **F** preference and can interpret feedback as criticism.

The **J** teacher takes pleasure in scheduling their time. They are organised and decisive. They work out a plan and stick to it, often aided by an impressive to-do list. Their classroom is usually an organised place. The subject will probably be broken down into lesson-sized chunks and the year planned out in detail. The **P** student will either respond:

◼ Positively by accepting your expertise and understanding the long-term benefit they'll reap.

◼ Passively by just accepting your structure/plan for an easy life without really buying into the content or process you are offering.

◼ Negatively by rejecting you, your structure/plan and subject completely (even if they're physically in your room they will not engage and participate).

For the teacher to get the best out of their naturally laid-back student they should note the student doesn't just like options and choice; they need them or they start to itch, squirm and rebel. The secondary school environment is difficult enough for **P** preference students so teachers can help soften the pressure. To help:

◼ Provide as much flexibility as possible (multiple choice homework tasks, choice within the lesson).

◼ Avoid giving out detailed schedules (they'll just lose it anyway!).

◼ Don't be more picky with detail than is absolutely necessary.

◼ Shake things up now and again to prevent predictability becoming boredom. Introduce random surprises and changes.

◼ Identify effective time-management strategies to ensure the Tawny Owl can succeed.

134
Seahorse teacher with Eagle student
INFJ and ENTJ

Seahorses and Eagles use their imagination to make sense of their world. The Eagle applies their imagination to solve technical problems which can clash with the more personal approach of the Seahorse. The student's desire for control and independence can also conflict with the teacher's quietly organised approach. For the teacher to get the best out of their naturally lively student they need to:

◼ Listen patiently and enthusiastically to the student impulsively expressing their thoughts.

◼ Stay open to 'silly' ideas to see where they lead – the student is thinking out loud and this is how they learn best.

◼ Also offer your own thoughts; if you need a timeout ask for one.

◼ Encourage the student to think things through before talking otherwise they may sabotage the lesson.

◼ Steer the student away from controversial subjects, especially in group discussions.

◼ Build in plenty of opportunities during lessons for the **E** students to talk things through with other **E** preferences.

Both teacher and student gather information by seeing the big picture first, using hunches, inferences and imagination to infer meaning. The teacher will naturally use their imagination in the classroom and the **N** student will respond well to this, possibly joining in with flights of fancy, anecdotes and stories. A natural affinity between teacher and student is often present because they both look at the world in the same way – with a burning curiosity to understand why things are as they are by exploring patterns, possibilities, ideas and theories. Be careful not to look like you're favouring **N** preference students to the detriment of the 65% of **S** preference students. Every student needs to be able to contribute in their preferred way. For the teacher to get the best out of their imaginative student they need to:

◼ Offer questions/projects that can be explored creatively.

◼ Avoid repetitive tasks as they'll quickly lose interest.

◼ Encourage the student to become aware of the important contribution of the **S** approach (the value of facts, details, procedure, experiments, applying experience, structure, the step-by-step model).

The teacher is concerned with relationship then task whereas the student is the other way round. The teacher must learn to accept that the student

is different; not cold, blunt and unfriendly, but different and focused on task first. If the teacher can accept this the relationship can be really positive for both teacher and student. For the teacher to get the best out of their fundamentally assertive student they need to:

◼ Offer targeted compliments. Just saying everything is great will not impress or help the student; in fact, it can result in the student not respecting the teacher, concluding they lie and/or are a soft touch. When you praise you may be pressed for proof!

◼ Be logical and objective rather than emotional in discussions.

◼ Accept that if the student challenges you it is probably to clarify their thoughts rather than smite your authority or character. Perhaps ask 'What would you do to improve/change this?' or 'What do you think?' Once they've clarified their thoughts they may be ready to ask and absorb what you think.

◼ Work in ways that test their skill and knowledge competitively (they raise their game).

◼ Help them understand that 50% of people are **F** preference and can interpret feedback as criticism.

The **J** teacher takes pleasure in scheduling their time. They are organised and decisive. They work out a plan and stick to it, often aided by an impressive to-do list. Their classroom is usually very organised. The subject will probably be broken down into lesson-sized chunks and the year planned out in detail. Many **J** preference students are reassured by their teacher's organisational zeal. They simply adopt the schedule and deliver their side of the bargain, generally completing all tasks on time. Interestingly, some **J** preferences will baulk at their teacher's well-intentioned thoroughness. They would like to create their own plan and work to it rather than adopt someone else's. This is due to the **J**'s desire for control. So two **J**'s together can clash, though at least all their work will be done. Most secondary schools require students to be so organised that two **J**'s are the best combination. For the teacher to get the best out of their naturally organised student they need to:

◼ Enjoy your shared desire for order, neatness and respecting deadlines.

◼ Allow the student independence in planning their work in their own way if they really want to.

◼ Be prepared to adjust your own plans if external events interfere with your careful preparations (and encourage the student to also embrace flexibility occasionally).

◼ Shake things up now and again to prevent predictability becoming boredom.

◼ Avoid making quick decisions about what needs to be done before considering all of the options.

135
Seahorse teacher with Lion student
INFJ and ESFP

Seahorses and Lions share one type preference. Their differences can be the most likely source of conflict. The really organised Seahorse can find the spontaneous, spur-of-the-moment Lion challenging. For the teacher to get the best out of their naturally lively student they need to:

■ Listen patiently and enthusiastically to the student impulsively expressing their thoughts.

■ Stay open to 'silly' ideas to see where they lead – the student is thinking out loud and this is how they learn best.

■ Also offer your own thoughts; if you need a timeout ask for one.

■ Encourage the student to think things through before talking otherwise they may sabotage the lesson.

■ Steer the student away from controversial subjects, especially in group discussions.

■ Build in plenty of opportunities during lessons for the **E** students to talk things through with other **E** preferences.

The imaginative teacher can inspire all students, but they do need to respect the need for Lions to be given clear guidelines, structure, facts, details and procedures; otherwise they can flounder. For the teacher to get the best out of their grounded student they need to:

■ Demonstrate how learning can be applied in the real world.

■ Allow the student opportunities to repeat and practise until satisfied they are competent.

■ Encourage the use of imagination as a useful process (it's not wasting time).

■ Be careful not to look like you're favouring **N** students to the detriment of **S** students. Every student needs to be able to contribute in their preferred way.

Both teacher and student are concerned first with people and relationships before the task/subject content. They like to form warm personal relationships. Compliments are likely to go in both directions boosting the confidence of teacher as well as student. The Lion needs to feel they like their teacher and that the teacher likes them too. If this happens they'll work harder but if not they may switch off completely. This explains why a student can be top of the class one year (with a teacher they like) and show no interest at all in the subject the following year when they change teacher. For the teacher to get the best out of their relationship-focused student they need to:

■ Offer learning situations that allow for the use of empathy, collaboration and teamworking.

■ Give ample and regular praise while offering tactful support to overcome any blind-spots.

■ Persuade/influence by appealing to the strength of your personal belief in the student (don't let me down, I know you can do it, I like you).

The **J** teacher takes pleasure in scheduling their time. They are organised and decisive. They work out a plan and stick to it, often aided by an impressive to-do list. Their classroom is usually an organised place. The subject will probably be broken down into lesson-sized chunks and the year planned out whether or not an Ofsted inspector is due. The **P** student will either respond:

■ Positively by accepting your expertise and understanding the long-term benefits they'll reap.

■ Passively by just accepting your structure/plan for an easy life without really buying into the content or process you are offering.

■ Negatively by rejecting you, your structure/plan and subject completely (even if they're physically in your room they will not engage and participate).

For the teacher to get the best out of their naturally laid-back student they should note the student doesn't just like options and choice; they need them or they start to itch, squirm and rebel. The secondary school environment is difficult enough for **P** preference students so teachers can help soften the pressure. To help:

■ Provide as much flexibility as possible (multiple choice homework tasks, choice within the lesson).

■ Avoid giving out detailed schedules (they'll just lose it anyway!).

■ Don't be more picky with detail than is absolutely necessary.

■ Shake things up now and again to prevent predictability becoming boredom. Introduce random surprises and changes.

■ Identify simple time-management techniques to ensure the Lion can thrive.

136
Seahorse teacher with Tiger student
INFJ and ISTP

Seahorses and Tigers share one type preference. Their differences are the most likely source of conflict. The really organised Seahorse can find the spontaneous, action-orientated Tiger challenging. For the teacher to get the best out of their fiercely independent student they need to:

■ Respect the student's need for privacy.

■ Take time to clarify your thoughts but don't avoid confrontation; if something needs to be said be calm and direct as you deliver it.

■ Use non-verbal communication – smiles and gestures are reassuring to **I** students; you can even use sticky notes/emails to pass on feedback.

■ Allow the student plenty of time to think through their thoughts.

■ Share your ideas and thoughts regularly to ensure you both know what you're doing.

Both teacher and student gather information in the same way. They notice detail using their senses (aware of what they can see, hear and feel). Both live in the present. The teacher is naturally sequential and realistic in their teaching style and encourages their students to follow suit. A solid, workman-like relationship develops with both teacher and student mutually understanding what each needs to do to get the job done. For the teacher to get the best out of their naturally grounded student they need to:

■ Allow the student opportunities to repeat and practise until satisfied they are competent.

■ Describe how learning can be applied in the real world.

■ Encourage the use of imagination as a useful process (it's not wasting time).

The teacher is concerned with relationship then task whereas the student is the other way round. The teacher must learn to accept that the student is different; not cold, blunt and unfriendly, but different and focused on task first. If the teacher can accept this the relationship can be really positive for both teacher and student. For the teacher to get the best out of their fundamentally independent student they need to:

■ Offer targeted compliments. Just saying everything is great will not impress or help the student; in fact, it can result in the student not respecting the teacher, concluding they lie and/or are a soft touch. When you praise you may be pressed for proof!

■ Be logical and objective rather than emotional in discussions.

■ Accept that if the student challenges you it is probably to clarify their thoughts rather than trash your authority or character. Perhaps ask 'What would you do to improve/change this?' or 'What do you think?' Once they've clarified their thoughts they may be ready to ask and absorb what you think.

■ Help them understand that 50% of people are **F** preference and can interpret feedback as criticism.

■ Work in ways that test their skill and knowledge competitively (they raise their game).

The Seahorse teacher takes pleasure in scheduling their time. They are organised and decisive. They work out a plan and stick to it, often aided by an impressive to-do list. Their classroom is usually an organised place. The subject will probably be broken down into lesson-sized chunks and the year planned out in meticulous detail. The **P** student will either respond:

■ Positively by accepting your expertise and understanding the long-term benefits they'll reap.

■ Passively by just accepting your structure/plan for an easy life without really buying into the content or process you are offering.

■ Negatively by rejecting you, your structure/plan and subject completely (even if they're physically in your room they will not engage and participate).

For the teacher to get the best out of their naturally laid-back student they should note the student doesn't just like options and choice; they need them or they start to itch, squirm and rebel. The secondary school environment is difficult enough for **P** preference students so teachers can help soften the pressure. To help:

■ Provide as much flexibility as possible (multiple choice homework tasks, choice within the lesson).

■ Avoid giving out detailed schedules (they'll just lose it anyway!).

■ Don't be more picky with detail than is absolutely necessary.

■ Shake things up now and again to prevent predictability becoming boredom. Introduce random surprises and changes.

■ Provide time-management tips to ensure they can be successful.

137
Seahorse teacher with Clownfish student
INFJ and ENFP

Seahorses and Clownfish share two preferences. Both are 'hippies', interested in education as a way to grow and develop personally. When the student feels nurtured by their teacher they will respond well. The disorganised and chatty student can be a challenge for the organised and reserved teacher. To help their naturally lively student they need to:

■ Listen patiently and enthusiastically to the student impulsively expressing their thoughts.

■ Stay open to 'silly' ideas to see where they lead – the student is thinking out loud and this is how they learn best.

■ Also offer your own thoughts; if you need a timeout ask for one.

■ Encourage the student to think things through before talking otherwise they may sabotage the lesson.

■ Steer the student away from controversial subjects, especially in group discussions.

■ Build in plenty of opportunities during lessons for the **E** students to talk things through with other **E** preferences.

Both teacher and student gather information by seeing the big picture first, using hunches, inferences and imagination to infer meaning. The teacher will naturally use their imagination in the classroom and the **N** student will respond well to this, possibly joining in with flights of fancy, anecdotes and stories. A natural affinity between teacher and student is often present because they both look at the world in the same way – with a burning curiosity to understand why things are as they are by exploring patterns, possibilities, ideas and theories. Be careful not to look like you're favouring **N** preference students to the detriment of the 65% of **S** preference students. Every student needs to be able to contribute in their preferred way. For the teacher to get the best out of their inherently imaginative student they need to:

■ Offer questions/projects that can be explored creatively.

■ Avoid repetitive tasks as they'll quickly lose interest.

■ Encourage the student to become aware of the important contribution of the **S** approach (the value of facts, details, procedure, experiments, applying experience, structure, the step-by-step model).

Both teacher and student are both concerned first with people and relationships before the task/subject content. They like to form warm personal relationships. Compliments are likely to go in both directions boosting the confidence of teacher as well as student. The Clownfish needs to feel they like their teacher and that the teacher likes them too. If this happens they'll work harder but if not they may switch off. This explains why a student can be top of the class one year (with a teacher they like) and show no interest at all in the subject the following year when they change teacher. For the teacher to get the best out of their relationship-focused student they need to:

■ Offer learning situations that allow for the use of empathy, collaboration and teamworking.

■ Persuade by appealing to the strength of your personal belief in the student (don't let me down, I know you can do it, I like you).

■ Give ample and regular praise while offering tactful support to overcome any blind-spots.

The **J** teacher takes pleasure in scheduling their time. They are organised and decisive. They work out a plan and stick to it, often aided by an impressive to-do list. Their classroom is usually an organised place. The subject will probably be broken down into lesson-sized chunks and the year planned out in meticulous detail. The **P** student will either respond:

■ Positively by accepting your expertise and understanding the long-term benefits they'll reap.

■ Passively by just accepting your structure/plan for an easy life without really buying into the content or process you are offering.

■ Negatively by rejecting you, your structure/plan and subject completely (even if they're physically in your room they will not engage and participate).

For the teacher to get the best out of their naturally laid-back student they should note the student doesn't just like options and choice; they need them or they start to itch, squirm and rebel. The secondary school environment is difficult enough for **P** preference students so teachers can help soften the pressure. To help:

■ Provide as much flexibility as possible (multiple choice homework tasks, choice within the lesson).

■ Don't be more picky with detail than is absolutely necessary.

■ Shake things up now and again to prevent predictability becoming boredom. Introduce random surprises and changes.

■ Identify effective strategies to ensure they can manage their workload successfully.

■ Avoid giving out detailed schedules (they'll just lose it anyway!).

138
Seahorse teacher with Cat student
INFJ and ISFP

Seahorses and Cats share two type preferences. The really imaginative and organised Seahorse can find the realistic and spontaneous Cat challenging. For the teacher to get the best out of their naturally reserved student they need to:

■ Respect the student's need for privacy and independence.

■ Take time to clarify your thoughts but don't avoid confrontation; if something needs to be said be calm and direct as you deliver it.

■ Use non-verbal communication – smiles and gestures are reassuring to **I** students; you can even use sticky notes/emails to pass on feedback.

■ Allow the student plenty of time to think through their thoughts.

■ Share your ideas and thoughts regularly to ensure you both know what you're doing.

The imaginative teacher can inspire all students, but they do need to respect the need for Cats to be given clear guidelines, structure, facts, details and procedures; otherwise they can flounder. For the teacher to get the best out of their fundamentally grounded student they need to:

■ Demonstrate how learning can be applied in the real world.

■ Allow the student opportunities to repeat and practise until satisfied they are competent.

■ Encourage the use of imagination as a useful process (it's not wasting time).

■ Be careful not to look like you're favouring **N** students to the detriment of **S** students. Every student needs to be able to contribute in their preferred way.

Both teacher and student are concerned first with people and relationships before the task/subject content. They like to form warm personal relationships. Compliments are likely to go in both directions boosting the confidence of teacher as well as student. The Cat needs to feel they like their teacher and that the teacher likes them too. If this happens they'll work harder but if not they may switch off. This explains why a student can be top of the class one year (with a teacher they like) and show no interest at all in the subject the following year when they change teacher. For the teacher to get the best out of their relationship-focused student they need to:

■ Offer learning situations that allow for the use of empathy, collaboration and teamworking.

■ Give ample and regular praise while offering tactful support to overcome any blind-spots.

■ Persuade/influence by appealing to the strength of your personal belief in the student (don't let me down, I know you can do it).

The **J** teacher takes pleasure in scheduling their time. They are organised and decisive. They work out a plan and stick to it, often aided by an impressive to-do list. Their classroom is usually an organised place. The subject will probably be broken down into lesson-sized chunks and the year planned out meticulously. The **P** student will either respond:

■ Positively by accepting your expertise and understanding the long-term benefits they'll reap.

■ Passively by just accepting your structure/plan for an easy life without really buying into the content or process you are offering.

■ Negatively by rejecting you, your structure/plan and subject completely (even if they're physically in your room they will not engage and participate).

For the teacher to get the best out of their naturally laid-back student they should note the student doesn't just like options and choice; they need them or they start to itch, squirm and rebel. The secondary school environment is difficult enough for **P** preference students so teachers can help soften the pressure. To help:

■ Provide as much flexibility as possible (multiple choice homework tasks, choice within the lesson).

■ Avoid giving out detailed schedules (they'll just lose it anyway!).

■ Shake things up now and again to prevent predictability becoming boredom. Introduce random surprises and changes.

■ Identify effective strategies to ensure they can manage their workload successfully.

- Don't be more picky with detail than is absolutely necessary.

139
Seahorse teacher with Dolphin student
INFJ and ENFJ

Seahorses and Dolphins share three preferences. Both are 'hippies', interested in education as a way to grow and develop personally. When the student feels nurtured by their teacher they'll respond well. The chatty, sociable student can be a challenge for the organised and reserved teacher. To get the best out of their naturally lively student they need to:

- Listen patiently and enthusiastically to the student impulsively expressing their thoughts.
- Stay open to 'silly' ideas to see where they lead – the student is thinking out loud and this is how they learn best.
- Also offer your own thoughts; if you need a timeout ask for one.
- Build in plenty of opportunities during lessons for the **E** students to talk things through with other **E** preferences.
- Encourage the student to think things through before talking otherwise they may sabotage the lesson.
- Steer the student away from controversial subjects, especially in group discussions.

Both teacher and student gather information by seeing the big picture first, using hunches and imagination to infer meaning. The teacher will naturally use their imagination in the classroom and the **N** student will respond well to this, possibly joining in with flights of fancy, anecdotes and stories. A natural affinity between teacher and student is often present because they both look at the world in the same way – with a burning curiosity to understand why things are as they are by exploring patterns, possibilities, ideas and theories. Be careful not to look like you're favouring **N** preference students to the detriment of the 65% of **S** preference students. Every student needs to be able to contribute in their preferred way. For the teacher to get the best out of their imaginative student they need to:

- Offer questions/projects that can be explored creatively.
- Avoid repetitive tasks as they'll quickly lose interest.
- Encourage the student to become aware of the important contribution of the **S** approach (the value of facts, details, procedure, experiments, applying experience, structure, the step-by-step model).

Both teacher and student are concerned first with people and relationships before the task/subject content. They like to form warm personal relationships. Compliments are likely to go in both directions boosting the confidence of teacher as well as student. The Dolphin needs to feel they like their teacher and that the teacher likes them too. If this happens they'll work harder but if they don't they may switch off completely. This explains why a student can be top of the class one year (with a teacher they like) and show no inter-

est at all in the subject the following year when they change teacher. For the teacher to get the best out of their relationship-focused student they need to:

- Offer learning situations that allow for the use of empathy, collaboration and teamworking.
- Give ample and regular praise while offering tactful support to overcome any blind-spots.
- Persuade by appealing to the strength of your personal belief in the student (don't let me down, I know you can do it, I like you).

The **J** teacher takes pleasure in scheduling their time. They are organised and decisive. They work out a plan and stick to it, often aided by an impressive to-do list. Their classroom is usually incredibly organised. The subject will probably be broken down into lesson-sized chunks and the year planned out carefully. Many Dolphins are reassured by their teacher's organisational zeal. They simply adopt the schedule and deliver their side of the bargain, generally completing all tasks on time. Interestingly, some Dolphins will baulk at their teacher's well-intentioned thoroughness. They would like to create their own plan and work to it rather than adopt someone else's. This is due to the **J**'s desire for control. So two **J**'s together can clash, though at least all their work will be done. Most secondary schools require students to be so organised that two **J**'s are the best combination. For the teacher to get the best out of their naturally organised student they need to:

- Enjoy your shared desire for order, neatness and respecting deadlines.
- Allow the student independence in planning their work in their own way if they really want to.
- Be prepared to adjust your own plans if external events interfere with your careful preparations (and encourage the student to also embrace flexibility occasionally).
- Avoid making quick decisions about what needs to be done before considering all of the options.
- Shake things up now and again to prevent predictability becoming boredom.

140
Seahorse teacher with Seal student
INFJ and INFP

Seahorse and Seal share three preferences. Both are 'hippies', interested in education as a way to grow and develop personally. When the student feels nurtured by their teacher they'll respond well. The disorganised student can be a challenge for the organised teacher. For the teacher to get the best out of their naturally lively student they need to:

- Respect the student's need for privacy and independence.
- Take time to clarify your thoughts but don't avoid confrontation; if something needs to be said be calm and direct as you deliver it.

- Use non-verbal communication – smiles and gestures are reassuring to **I** students; you can even use sticky notes/emails to pass on feedback.
- Allow the student plenty of time to think through their thoughts.
- Share your ideas and thoughts regularly to ensure you both know what you're doing.

Both teacher and student gather information by seeing the big picture first, using hunches, inferences and imagination to infer meaning. The teacher will naturally use their imagination in the classroom and the **N** student will respond well to this, possibly joining in with flights of fancy, anecdotes and stories. A natural affinity between teacher and student is often present because they both look at the world in the same way – with a burning curiosity to understand why things are as they are by exploring patterns, possibilities, ideas and theories. Be careful not to look like you're favouring **N** preference students to the detriment of the 65% of **S** preference students. Every student needs to be able to contribute in their preferred way. For the teacher to get the best out of their inherently imaginative student they need to:

- Offer questions/projects that can be explored creatively.
- Avoid repetitive tasks as they'll quickly lose interest.
- Encourage the student to become aware of the important contribution of the **S** approach (the value of facts, details, procedure, experiments, applying experience, structure, the step-by-step model).

Both teacher and student are concerned first with people and relationships before the task/subject content. They like to form warm personal relationships. Compliments are likely to go in both directions boosting the confidence of teacher as well as student. The Seal needs to feel they like their teacher and that the teacher likes them too. If this happens they'll work harder but if they don't they may switch off completely. This explains why a student can be top of the class one year (with a teacher they like) and show no interest at all in the subject the following year when they change teacher. For the teacher to get the best out of their relationship-focused student they need to:

- Offer learning situations that allow for the use of empathy, collaboration and teamworking.
- Give ample and regular praise while offering tactful support to overcome any blind-spots.
- Inspire by appealing to the strength of your personal belief in the student (don't let me down, I know you can do it, I like you).

The **J** teacher takes pleasure in scheduling their time. They are organised and decisive. They work out a plan and stick to it, often aided by an impressive to-do list. Their classroom is usually an organised place. The subject will probably be broken down into lesson-sized chunks. The **P** student will either respond:

- Positively by accepting your expertise and understanding the long-term benefits they'll reap.
- Passively by just accepting your structure/plan for an easy life without really buying into the content or process you are offering.
- Negatively by rejecting you, your structure/plan and subject completely (even if they're physically in your room they will not engage and participate).

For the teacher to get the best out of their naturally laid-back student they should note the student doesn't just like options and choice; they need them or they start to itch, squirm and rebel. The secondary school environment is difficult enough for **P** preference students so teachers can help soften the pressure. To help:

■ Provide as much flexibility as possible (multiple choice homework tasks, choice within the lesson).

■ Avoid giving out detailed schedules (they'll just lose it anyway!).

■ Don't be more picky with detail than is absolutely necessary.

■ Shake things up now and again to prevent predictability becoming boredom. Introduce random surprises and changes.

■ Identify time-management tips to ensure the Seal can excel.

141
Seahorse teacher with Seahorse student
INFJ and INFJ

Seahorses are 'hippies', interested in education as a way to grow and develop personally. When the student feels nurtured by their teacher they'll respond well. However identical types can clash. Both are quietly determined and this can fester into resentment if not resolved by the teacher. For the teacher to get the best out of their naturally quiet student they need to:

■ Respect the student's need for privacy and independence.

■ Take time to clarify your thoughts but don't avoid confrontation; if something needs to be said be calm and direct as you deliver it.

■ Use non-verbal communication – smiles and gestures are reassuring to **I** students; you can even use sticky notes/emails to pass on feedback.

■ Allow the student plenty of time to think through their thoughts.

■ Share your ideas and thoughts regularly to ensure you both know what you're doing.

Seahorses gather information by seeing the big picture first, using hunches, inferences and imagination to infer meaning. The teacher will naturally use their imagination in the classroom and the **N** student will respond well to this, possibly joining in with flights of fancy, anecdotes and stories. A natural affinity between teacher and student is often present because they both see the world with a burning curiosity to understand why things are as they are by exploring patterns, possibilities, ideas and stories. Be careful not to look like you're favouring **N** preference students to the detriment of the **S** preference students. Every student needs to be able to contribute in their preferred way. For the teacher to get the best out of their inherently imaginative student they need to:

■ Offer questions/projects that can be explored creatively.

■ Avoid repetitive tasks as they'll quickly lose interest.

■ Encourage the student to become aware of the important contribution of the **S** approach (the value of facts, details, procedure, experiments, applying experience, structure, the step-by-step model).

Both teacher and student are concerned first with people and relationships before the task/subject content. They like to form warm personal relationships. Compliments are likely to go in both directions boosting the confidence of teacher as well as student. The Seahorse student needs to feel they like their teacher and that the teacher likes them too. If this happens they'll work harder but if not they may switch off or quibble over minutiae. This explains why a student can be top of the class one year (with a teacher they like) and show no interest at all in the subject the following year when they change teacher. For the teacher to get the best out of their relationship-focused student they need to:

■ Offer learning situations that allow for the use of empathy, collaboration and teamworking.

■ Give ample and regular praise while offering tactful support to overcome any blind-spots.

■ Influence by appealing to the strength of your personal belief in the student (don't let me down, I know you can do it, I like you).

The **J** teacher takes pleasure in scheduling their time. They are organised and decisive. They work out a plan and stick to it, often aided by an impressive to-do list. Their classroom is usually very organised. The subject will probably be broken down into lesson-sized chunks and the year planned meticulously. Many **J** preference students are reassured by their teacher's organisational zeal. They simply adopt the schedule and deliver their side of the bargain, generally completing all tasks on time. Interestingly, some **J** preferences will baulk at their teacher's well-intentioned thoroughness. They would like to create their own plan and work to it rather than adopt someone else's. This is due to the **J**'s desire for control. So two **J**'s together can clash, though at least all their work will be done. Most secondary schools require students to be so organised that two **J**'s are the best combination. For the teacher to get the best out of their naturally organised student they need to:

■ Shake things up now and again to prevent predictability becoming boredom.

■ Avoid making quick decisions about what needs to be done before considering all of the options.

■ Enjoy your shared desire for order, neatness and respecting deadlines.

■ Allow the student independence in planning their work in their own way if they really want to.

■ Be prepared to adjust your own plans if external events interfere with your careful preparations (and encourage the student to also embrace flexibility occasionally).

142
Seahorse teacher with Barn Owl student
INFJ and INTJ

Seahorses and Barn Owls both use imagination to make sense of their world. The Owl applies their imagination to solve technical problems which can clash with the personal approach of the Seahorse. The student's desire for control and independence can also conflict with the teacher's quietly organised approach. For the teacher to get the best out of their naturally lively student they can:

■ Respect the student's need for privacy and independence.

■ Take time to clarify your thoughts but don't avoid confrontation; if something needs to be said be calm and direct as you deliver it.

■ Use non-verbal communication – smiles and gestures are reassuring to **I** students; you can even use sticky notes/emails to pass on feedback.

■ Allow the student plenty of time to think through their thoughts.

■ Share your ideas and thoughts regularly to ensure you both know what you're doing.

The teacher likes to use their experience to make sense of things. The one-step-at-a-time teacher encourages their students to follow suit. The **N** student will at best find this over-simplistic and at worst find it boring. The teacher is likely to label the student as 'away with the fairies'. They should resist the temptation to castigate their student because this is how they take in information and make sense of the subject. In the right context daydreaming can lead to new ways of absorbing and retaining information. For the teacher to get the best out of their inherently imaginative student they need to:

■ Embrace the imagination and insight of the student and what it can bring to the lesson.

■ Encourage the student to become aware of the important contribution of the **S** approach (the value of facts, details, procedure, experiments, applying experience, structure, the step-by-step model).

The teacher is concerned with relationship then task whereas the student is the other way round. The teacher must learn to accept that the student is different; not cold, blunt and unfriendly, but different and focused on task first. If the teacher can accept this the relationship can be really positive for both teacher and student. For the teacher to get the best out of their naturally objective student they need to:

■ Offer targeted compliments. Just saying everything is great will not impress or help the student; in fact, it can result in the student not respecting the teacher, concluding they lie and/or are a soft touch. When you praise you may be pressed for proof!

■ Be logical and objective rather than emotional in discussions.

- Accept that if the student challenges you it is probably to clarify their thoughts rather than trash your authority or character. Perhaps ask 'What would you do to improve/change this?' or 'What do you think?' Once they've clarified their thoughts they may be ready to ask and absorb what you think.
- Work in ways that test their skill and knowledge competitively (they raise their game).
- Help them remember that half of the population are **F** preference and can interpret feedback as criticism.

The **J** teacher takes pleasure in scheduling their time. They are organised and decisive. They work out a plan and stick to it, often aided by an impressive to-do list. Their classroom is usually very organised. The subject will probably be broken down into lesson-sized chunks and the year planned out carefully. Many Barn Owls are reassured by their teacher's organisational zeal. They simply adopt the schedule and deliver their side of the bargain, generally completing all tasks on time. Interestingly, some Barn Owls will baulk at their teacher's well-intentioned thoroughness. They would like to create their own plan and work to it rather than adopt someone else's. This is due to the **J**'s desire for control. So two **J**'s together can clash, though at least all their work will be done. Most secondary schools require students to be so organised that two **J**'s are the best combination. For the teacher to get the best out of their intrinsically organised student they need to:

- Enjoy your shared desire for order, neatness and respecting deadlines.
- Allow the student independence in planning their work in their own way if they really want to.
- Be prepared to adjust your own plans if external events interfere with your careful preparations (and encourage the student to also embrace flexibility occasionally).
- Shake things up now and again to prevent predictability becoming boredom.
- Avoid making quick decisions about what needs to be done before considering all of the options.

143
Seahorse teacher with Polar Bear student
INFJ and ISTJ

Seahorses and Polar Bears share a desire to be organised. The reality-first approach of the Bear contrasts with the imagination-first style of the teacher. Clashes are most likely when the coolly objective student contrasts with the more nurturing teacher. For the teacher to get the best out of their naturally self-contained student they need to:

- Respect the student's need for privacy and independence.
- Take time to clarify your thoughts but don't avoid confrontation; if something needs to be said be calm and direct as you deliver it.

- Use non-verbal communication – smiles and gestures are reassuring to **I** students; you can even use sticky notes/emails to pass on feedback.
- Allow the student plenty of time to think through their thoughts.
- Share your ideas and thoughts regularly to ensure you both know what you're doing.

The imaginative teacher can inspire all students, but they do need to respect the need for Polar Bears to be given clear guidelines, structure, facts, details and procedures; otherwise they can flounder. For the teacher to get the best out of their grounded student they need to:

- Demonstrate how learning can be applied in the real world.
- Allow the student opportunities to repeat and practise until satisfied they are competent.
- Encourage the use of imagination as a useful process (it's not wasting time).
- Be careful not to look like you're favouring **N** students to the detriment of **S** students. Every student needs to be able to contribute in their preferred way.

The teacher is concerned with relationship then task whereas the student is the other way round. The teacher must learn to accept that the student is different; not cold, blunt and unfriendly, but different and focused on task first. If the teacher can accept this the relationship can be really positive for both teacher and student. For the teacher to get the best out of their fundamentally objective student they need to:

- Offer targeted compliments. Just saying everything is great will not impress or help the student; in fact, it can result in the student not respecting the teacher, concluding they lie and/or are a soft touch. When you praise you may be pressed for proof!
- Be logical and objective rather than emotional in discussions.
- Accept that if the student challenges you it is probably to clarify their thoughts rather than meant as a slight to your authority or character. Perhaps ask 'What would you do to improve/change this?' or 'What do you think?' Once they've clarified their thoughts they may be ready to ask and absorb what you think.
- Work in ways that test their skill and knowledge competitively (they raise their game).
- Help them understand that 50% of people are **F** preference and can interpret feedback as criticism.

The **J** teacher takes pleasure in scheduling their time. They are organised and decisive. They work out a plan and stick to it, often aided by an impressive to-do list. Their classroom is usually very organised. The subject will probably be broken down into lesson-sized chunks and the year planned out whether or not an Ofsted inspector is due. Many **J** preference students are reassured by their teacher's organisational zeal. They simply adopt the schedule and deliver their side of the bargain, generally completing all tasks on time. Interestingly, some **J** preferences will baulk at their teacher's well-intentioned thoroughness. They would like to create their own plan and work to it rather than adopt someone else's. This is due to the **J**'s desire for control. So two **J** preferences together can clash, though at least all their work will be done. Most secondary schools require students to be so organised that two **J** preferences are the best combination. For

the teacher to get the best out of their naturally organised student they need to:

- Enjoy your shared desire for order, neatness and respecting deadlines.
- Be prepared to adjust your own plans if external events interfere with your careful preparations (and encourage the student to also embrace flexibility occasionally).
- Shake things up now and again to prevent predictability becoming boredom.
- Avoid making quick decisions about what needs to be done before considering all of the options.
- Allow the student independence in planning their work in their own way if they really want to.

144
Seahorse teacher with Koala student
INFJ and ISFJ

Seahorses and Koalas share three type preferences. Both are reserved, warm and organised. This can form the basis of an effective relationship. Clashes are unlikely, although the coy Koala needs to be carefully and gently coaxed to contribute and develop. For the teacher to get the best out of their naturally timid student they need to:

- Respect the student's need for privacy and independence.
- Take time to clarify your thoughts but don't avoid confrontation; if something needs to be said be calm and direct as you deliver it.
- Use non-verbal communication – smiles and gestures are reassuring to **I** students; you can even use sticky notes/emails to pass on feedback.
- Allow the student plenty of time to think through their thoughts.
- Share your ideas and thoughts regularly to ensure you both know what you're doing.

The imaginative teacher can inspire all students, but they do need to respect the need for Koalas to be given clear guidelines, structure, facts, details and procedures; otherwise they can struggle. For the teacher to get the best out of their grounded student they need to:

- Demonstrate how learning can be applied in the real world.
- Allow the student opportunities to repeat and practise until satisfied they are competent.
- Encourage the use of imagination as a useful process (it's not wasting time).
- Be careful not to look like you're favouring **N** students to the detriment of **S** students. Every student needs to be able to contribute in their preferred way.

Both teacher and student are concerned first with people and relationships before the task/subject content. They like to form warm personal relationships. Compliments are likely to go in both directions boosting the confidence of teacher as well as student. The Koala needs to feel they like their teacher and that the teacher likes them too. If this happens they'll work harder but if not they may switch off completely. This explains why a student can be top of the class one year (with a teacher they like) and show no interest at all in the same subject the following year when they change teacher. For the teacher to get the best out of their relationship-focused student they need to:

■ Offer learning situations that allow for the use of empathy, collaboration and teamworking.

■ Give ample and regular praise while offering tactful support to overcome any blind-spots.

■ Persuade/influence by appealing to the strength of your personal belief in the student (don't let me down, I know you can do it).

The Seahorse teacher takes pleasure in scheduling their time. They are organised and decisive. They work out a plan and stick to it, often aided by an impressive to-do list. Their classroom is usually organised. The subject will probably be broken down into lesson-sized chunks and the year planned out whether or not an Ofsted inspector is due on the premises. Many **J** preference students are reassured by their teacher's organisational zeal. They simply adopt the schedule and deliver their side of the bargain, generally completing all tasks on time. Interestingly, some **J** preferences will baulk at their teacher's well-intentioned thoroughness. They would like to create their own plan and work to it rather than adopt someone else's. This is due to the **J**'s desire for control. So two **J**'s together can clash, though at least all their work will be done. Most secondary schools require students to be so organised that two **J**'s are the best combination. For the teacher to get the best out of their equally organised student they need to:

■ Enjoy your shared desire for order, neatness and respecting deadlines.

■ Allow the student independence in planning their work in their own way if they really want to.

■ Be prepared to adjust your own plans if external events interfere with your careful preparations (and encourage the student to also embrace flexibility occasionally).

■ Shake things up now and again to prevent predictability becoming boredom.

■ Avoid making quick decisions about what needs to be done before considering all of the options.

145
Seal teacher with Lion student
INFP and ESFP

Seals and Lions share two of the four preferences. Both thrive in a friendly and relaxed classroom atmosphere. Conflict is only likely when the 'party' ends and hard work is required. It can be done but it just isn't enough fun. For the teacher to get the best out of their naturally effusive student they need to:

■ Listen patiently and enthusiastically to the student's ideas, brainstorming and ramblings.

■ Stay open to 'silly' ideas to see where they lead – the student is thinking out loud and this is how they learn best.

■ Also offer your own thoughts; if you need a timeout ask for one.

■ Encourage the student to think things through before talking otherwise they'll hog the lesson.

■ Steer the student away from controversial subjects/topics, especially in group discussions.

■ Build in plenty of opportunities during lessons for the **E** students to talk things through with other **E** preferences.

The imaginative Seal teacher can quietly inspire all students, but they do need to respect the need for around two-thirds of students to be given clear guidelines, structure, facts, details and procedures; otherwise they can flounder. For the teacher to get the best out of their more grounded student they need to:

■ Demonstrate how learning can be applied in the real world.

■ Allow the student opportunities to repeat and practise until satisfied they are competent.

■ Encourage the use of imagination as a useful process and explain how it's not time-wasting.

■ Be careful not to look like you're favouring **N** students to the detriment of **S** students. Every student needs to be able to contribute in their preferred way.

Both teacher and student are concerned with people and relationships before the task/subject content. Seals like to form personal relationships with all their students, unless they don't like the student (**F** teachers are more inclined than **T** preference teachers to have their favourites!). Because they operate at an emotional level these teachers are more likely to make promises to students, overstretch themselves and even do work the students should be doing themselves. Teacher and student both enjoy a classroom atmosphere that is warm and friendly. Compliments are likely to go in both directions boosting the confidence of teacher as well as student. The Lion needs to feel they like their teacher and that the teacher likes them too. If this happens they'll work harder but if not they may switch off completely. This explains why a student can be top of the class one year (with a teacher they like) and show no interest at all in the subject the following year when they change teacher. For the teacher to get the best out of their relationship-focused student they need to:

■ Offer learning situations that allow for the use of empathy, collaboration and teamworking.

■ Give ample and regular praise and offer tactful support to overcome any blind-spots.

■ Motivate by appealing to the strength of your personal belief in the student (don't let me down, I know you can do it).

P preferences can be organised and efficient; it's just such an effort! While enjoying a mutual love of spontaneity, which provides each with relief from the stifling and constraining timetables and deadlines essential in large organisations such as schools, they must also remember to complete any necessary tasks. Although likely to be fun and popular teachers, they also need to focus on the task of preparing the student to succeed socially and academically. Both prefer to start tasks than finish them. Their initial enthusiasm can quickly evaporate. Both need to ensure they identify and complete the important tasks or the student (or their parents) may eventually ask awkward questions. For the teacher to get the best out of their naturally laid-back student they need to understand the student doesn't just like options and

choice; they are essential or they start to itch, squirm and rebel. The secondary school environment is difficult enough for **P** preference students so teachers can help their student achieve by:

■ Providing as much flexibility as possible (multiple choice homework tasks, choice within the lesson).

■ Avoiding giving out detailed schedules (they'll just lose it anyway!).

■ Shaking things up now and again to prevent predictability becoming boredom. Introduce random surprises and changes.

■ Helping the student identify ways they can organise and manage their time to complete important work without a last-minute rush.

146
Seal teacher with Black Bear student
INFP and ESTJ

A Seal teacher and their Black Bear student are personality type opposites. Clashes are most likely when the perceived seriousness of the student and laid-back imagination of the teacher grate. For the teacher to get the best out of their naturally assertive student they need to respect difference and:

■ Listen patiently and enthusiastically to the student's ideas, brainstorming and ramblings.

■ Stay open to 'silly' ideas to see where they lead – the student is thinking out loud and this is how they learn best.

■ Also offer your own thoughts; if you need a timeout ask for one.

■ Encourage the student to think things through before talking otherwise they'll hog the lesson.

■ Steer the student away from controversial subjects/topics, especially in group discussions.

■ Build in plenty of opportunities during lessons for the **E** students to talk things through with other **E** preferences.

The imaginative Seal teacher can inspire all students, but they do need to acknowledge that Black Bears benefit from clear guidelines, structure, facts, details and procedures. For the teacher to get the best out of their more grounded student they need to:

■ Demonstrate how learning can be applied in the real world.

■ Allow the student opportunities to repeat and practise until satisfied they are competent.

■ Encourage the use of imagination as a useful process and explain how it's not time-wasting.

■ Be careful not to look like you're favouring **N** students to the detriment of **S** students. Every student needs to be able to contribute in their preferred way.

The teacher is concerned with relationship then task whereas the student is the other way round. The teacher must learn to accept that the student is different; not cold, blunt and unfriendly, but simply focused on task first. If the teacher can accept this the relationship can be really positive for both teacher and student. For the teacher to get the best out of their characteristically assertive student they need to:

■ Offer targeted compliments. Just saying everything is great will not impress or help the student; in fact, it can result in the student losing respect for the teacher, concluding they lie and/or are a soft touch. When you praise you may be pressed for proof!

■ Be logical and objective rather than emotional in discussions.

■ Accept that if the student challenges you it is probably to clarify their thoughts rather than test your authority or besmirch your character. Perhaps ask 'What would you do to improve/change this?' or 'What do you think?' Once they've clarified their thoughts they may be ready to ask and absorb what you think.

■ Work in ways that test their skill and knowledge competitively (they raise their game).

■ Help them appreciate that 50% of people are **F** preference and can interpret feedback as criticism.

The laid-back, flexible and spontaneous teacher with the naturally organised student can be a dream team or a disaster. To create a positive relationship they need to play to each other's strengths. The student can benefit from the teacher's ability to adapt and change plans and the teacher can benefit from the student's desire to have a plan they can work to and complete. The teacher can also:

■ Encourage and support the student's desire for order, neatness and respecting deadlines.

■ Allow the student independence in planning their work in their own way if they really want to.

■ Encourage the student to embrace flexibility occasionally.

■ Avoid changing plans just for the sake of it; this will only frustrate the student.

147
Seal teacher with Panther student
INFP and ESTP

Seals and Panthers share one preference. Both enjoy a relaxed and flexible classroom environment. Clashes are likely when the hard work has to start. For the teacher to get the best out of their naturally effusive and playful student they need to:

■ Listen patiently and enthusiastically to the student's ideas, brainstorming and pranks.

■ Stay open to 'silly' ideas to see where they lead – the student is thinking out loud and this is how they learn best.

■ Also offer your own thoughts; if you need a timeout ask for one.

■ Encourage the student to think things through before talking otherwise they'll hog the lesson.

■ Steer the student away from controversial subjects/topics, especially in group discussions.

■ Build in plenty of opportunities during lessons for the **E** students to talk things through with other **E** preferences, or else the Panther can pounce!

The imaginative Seal teacher can inspire all students, but they do need to respect the need for Panthers to be given clear guidelines, structure, facts, details and procedures; otherwise they can stumble. For the teacher to get the best out of their more grounded student they need to:

■ Demonstrate how learning can be applied in the real world.

■ Allow the student opportunities to repeat and practise until satisfied they are competent.

■ Encourage the use of imagination as a useful process and explain how it's not time-wasting.

■ Be careful not to look like you're favouring **N** students to the detriment of **S** students. Every student needs to be able to contribute in their preferred way.

The teacher is concerned with relationship then task whereas the student is the other way round. The teacher must learn to accept that the student is different; not cold, blunt and unfriendly, but simply focused on task first. If the teacher can accept this the relationship can be really positive for both teacher and student. For the teacher to get the best out of their fundamentally assertive student they need to:

■ Offer targeted compliments. Just saying everything is great will not impress or help the student; in fact, it can result in the student losing respect for the teacher, concluding they lie and/or are a soft touch. When you praise you may be pressed for proof!

■ Be logical and objective rather than emotional in discussions.

■ Accept that if the student challenges you it is probably to clarify their thoughts rather than test your authority or besmirch your character. Perhaps ask 'What would you do to improve/change this?' or 'What do you think?' Once they've clarified their thoughts they may be ready to ask and absorb what you think.

■ Help them understand that 50% of people are **F** preference and can interpret honest feedback as personal criticism.

■ Work in ways that test their skill and knowledge competitively (they raise their game).

Seals and Panthers can learn to be organised and efficient but it is tolerated rather than embraced enthusiastically. While enjoying a mutual love of spontaneity, which provides each with relief from the stifling and constraining timetables and deadlines essential in large organisations such as schools, they must also remember to complete any necessary tasks. Although likely to be fun and popular teachers, they also need to focus on the task of preparing the student to succeed socially and academically. Both prefer to start tasks than finish them. Their initial enthusiasm can quickly evaporate. Both need to ensure they identify and complete the important tasks or the student (or their parents) may eventually ask awkward questions. For the teacher to get the best out of their naturally laid-back student they need to understand the student doesn't just like options and choice; they are essential or they start to itch, squirm and rebel. The secondary school environment is difficult enough for **P** preference students so teachers can help their student achieve by:

■ Providing as much flexibility as possible (multiple choice homework tasks, choice within the lesson).

■ Avoiding detailed schedules (they'll just be lost anyway!).

■ Shaking things up now and again to prevent predictability becoming boredom. Introduce random surprises and changes.

■ Identifying simple ways the Panther can organise and manage their time to complete important work without a last-minute rush.

148
Seal teacher with Teddy Bear student
INFP and ESFJ

Seals and Teddy Bears share one preference. Both are warm, caring and inclusive. Both thrive in a harmonious classroom atmosphere. Their differences – in perceiving the world and how to live in it – can be a source of conflict. The quietly creative teacher can confuse or lose the more traditional and chatty student. For the teacher to get the best out of their naturally gregarious student they need to:

■ Listen patiently and enthusiastically to the student's observations and thoughts.

■ Stay open to 'silly' ideas to see where they lead – the student is thinking out loud and this is how they learn best.

■ Also offer your own thoughts; if you need a timeout ask for one.

■ Encourage the student to think things through before talking otherwise they'll hog the lesson.

■ Steer the student away from controversial subjects/topics, especially in group discussions.

■ Build in plenty of opportunities during lessons for the **E** students to talk things through with other **E** preferences – Teddies need to socialise!

The imaginative Seal teacher can be an inspiration to all students, but they do need to respect the Teddy's preference for clear guidelines, structure, facts, details and procedures; otherwise they can flounder. To get the best out of their more grounded student they need to:

■ Demonstrate how learning can be applied in the real world.

■ Allow the student opportunities to repeat and practise until satisfied they are competent.

■ Encourage the use of imagination as a useful process and explain how it's not time-wasting.

■ Be careful not to look like you're favouring **N** students to the detriment of **S** students. Every student needs to be able to contribute in their preferred way.

The teacher and student are both concerned with people and relationships before the task/subject content. Seals like to form personal relationships with all their students, unless they don't like the student (**F** teachers are more inclined than **T** preference teachers to have their favourites!). Because they operate at an emotional level these teachers are more likely to make promises to students, overstretch themselves and even do work the students should be doing themselves. Teacher and student both enjoy a classroom atmosphere that is warm and friendly. Compliments are likely to go in both directions boosting the confidence of teacher as well as student. The Teddy needs to feel they like their teacher and that the teacher likes them too. If this happens they'll work harder but if not they may switch off completely. This explains why a student can be top of the class one year (with a teacher they like) and show no interest at all in the subject the following year when they change teacher. For the teacher to get the best out of their relationship-focused student they need to:

■ Offer learning situations that allow for the use of empathy, collaboration and teamworking.

■ Give ample and regular praise and offer tactful support to overcome any blind-spots.

■ Motivate by appealing to the strength of your personal belief in the student (don't let me down, I know you can do it, I like you).

The laid-back, flexible and spontaneous Seal teacher with the naturally organised Teddy student can be a dream team or a disaster. To create a positive relationship they need to play to each other's strengths. The student can benefit from the teacher's ability to adapt and change plans and the teacher can benefit from the student's desire to have a plan they can work to and complete. The teacher can also:

■ Encourage and support the student's desire for order, neatness and respecting deadlines.

■ Allow the student independence in planning their work in their own way if they really want to.

■ Avoid changing plans just for the sake of it; this will only frustrate the student.

■ Encourage the student to embrace the thrill of flexibility, if only occasionally.

149
Seal teacher with Eagle student
INFP and ENTJ

Seals and Eagles share one preference. Both are naturally imaginative and ingenious. Clashes are most likely when the student's desire to take the lead interferes with the teacher's performance! For the teacher to get the best out of their inherently confident student they need to:

■ Listen patiently and enthusiastically to the student's ideas, theories and insights.

■ Stay open to 'silly' ideas to see where they lead – the student is thinking out loud and this is how they learn best.

■ Also offer your own thoughts; if you need a timeout ask for one.

■ Encourage the student to think things through before talking otherwise they'll hog the lesson.

■ Steer the student away from controversial subjects/topics, especially in group discussions.

■ Build in plenty of opportunities during lessons for the **E** students to talk things through with other **E** preferences.

Both teacher and student gather information by seeing the big picture first, using hunches, inferences and imagination to infer meaning. The Seal teacher will naturally use their imagination in the classroom and the **N** student will respond well to this, possibly joining in with flights of fancy, anecdotes and stories. A natural affinity between teacher and student is often present because they both look at the world in the same way – with a burning curiosity to understand why things are as they are by exploring patterns, possibilities, ideas and theories. Be careful not to look like you're favouring **N** students to the detriment of **S** students. Every student needs to be able to contribute in their preferred way. For the teacher to get the best out of their naturally imaginative student they need to:

■ Offer questions/projects that can be explored creatively.

■ Avoid repetitive tasks as they'll quickly lose interest.

■ Encourage the student to become aware of the important contribution of the **S** approach (the value of facts, details, procedure, experiments, applying experience, structure, the step-by-step model).

The Seal teacher is concerned with relationship then task whereas the student is the other way round. The teacher must learn to accept that the student is different; not cold, blunt and unfriendly, but simply focused on task first. If the teacher can accept this the relationship can be really positive for both teacher and student. For the teacher to get the best out of their fundamentally assertive student they need to:

■ Offer targeted compliments. Just saying everything is great will not impress or help the student; in fact, it can result in the student losing respect for the teacher, concluding they lie and/or are a soft touch. When you praise you may be pressed for proof!

■ Be logical and objective rather than emotional in discussions.

■ Accept that if the student challenges you it is probably to clarify their thoughts rather than test your authority or besmirch your character. Perhaps ask 'What would you do to improve/change this?' or 'What do you think?' Once they've clarified their thoughts they may be ready to ask and absorb what you think.

■ Work in ways that test their skill and knowledge competitively (they raise their game).

■ Help them understand that 50% of people are **F** preference and can interpret feedback as criticism.

The laid-back, flexible and spontaneous teacher with the naturally organised student can be a dream team or a disaster. To create a positive relationship they need to play to each other's strengths. The student can benefit from the teacher's ability to adapt and change plans and the teacher can benefit from the student's desire to have a plan they can work to and complete. The teacher can also:

■ Encourage and support the student's desire for order, neatness and respecting deadlines.

■ Allow the student independence in planning their work in their own way if they really want to.

■ Avoid changing plans just for the sake of it; this will only frustrate the student.

■ Encourage the student to embrace flexibility occasionally.

150
Seal teacher with Falcon student
INFP and ENTP

Seals and Falcons share two preferences. Both possess a fecund imagination and Falcons are not afraid to use it! Falcons are often misunderstood as education doesn't suit their natural, domineering, in-your-face style (though drama school does). Seal teachers can bring out the best in Falcons by steering their student to calmer waters. For the teacher to get the best out of their confrontational Falcon they need to:

■ Listen patiently and enthusiastically to the student's brainstorming and monologues.

■ Stay open to 'silly' ideas to see where they lead – the student is thinking out loud and this is how they learn best.

■ Also offer your own thoughts; if you need a timeout ask for one.

■ Encourage the student to think things through before talking otherwise they'll hijack the lesson.

■ Steer the student away from controversial subjects/topics, especially in group discussions.

■ Build in plenty of opportunities during lessons for the **E** students to talk things through with other **E** preferences.

Both teacher and student gather information by seeing the big picture first, using hunches, inferences and imagination to infer meaning. The Seal teacher will naturally use their imagination in the classroom and the **N** student will respond well to this, possibly joining in with flights of fancy, anecdotes and stories. A natural affinity between teacher and student is often present because they both look at the world in the same way – with a burning curiosity to understand why things are as they are by exploring patterns, possibilities, ideas and theories. Be careful not to look like you're favouring **N** students to the detriment of **S** students. Every student needs to be able to contribute in their preferred way. For the teacher to get the best out of their naturally imaginative student they need to:

■ Offer questions/projects that can be explored creatively.

■ Avoid repetitive tasks as they'll quickly lose interest.

■ Encourage the student to become aware of the important contribution of the **S** approach (the value of facts, details, procedure, experiments, applying experience, structure, the step-by-step model).

The teacher is concerned with relationship then task whereas the student is the other way round. The teacher must learn to accept that the student is different; not cold, blunt and unfriendly, but simply focused on task first. If the teacher can accept this the relationship can be really positive for both teacher and student.

For the teacher to get the best out of their fundamentally assertive student they need to:

■ Offer targeted compliments. Just saying everything is great will not impress or help the student; in fact, it can result in the student losing respect for the teacher, concluding they lie and/or are a soft touch. When you praise you may be pressed for proof!

■ Be logical and objective rather than emotional in discussions.

■ Accept that if the student challenges you it is probably to clarify their thoughts rather than test your authority or besmirch your character. Perhaps ask 'What would you do to improve/change this?' or 'What do you think?' Once they've clarified their thoughts they may be ready to ask and absorb what you think.

■ Work in ways that test their skill and knowledge competitively (they raise their game).

■ Help them understand that 50% of people are **F** preference and can interpret feedback as criticism.

P preferences can learn to be organised and efficient but it is tolerated rather than embraced enthusiastically. While enjoying a mutual love of spontaneity, which provides each with relief from the stifling and constraining timetables and deadlines essential in large organisations such as schools, they must also remember to complete any necessary tasks. Although likely to be fun and popular teachers, they also need to focus on the task of preparing the student to succeed socially and academically. Both prefer to start tasks than finish them. Their initial enthusiasm can quickly wane. Both need to ensure they identify and complete the important tasks or the student (or their parents) may eventually ask awkward questions. For the teacher to get the best out of their naturally laid-back student they need to understand the student doesn't just like options and choice; they are essential or they start to itch, squirm and rebel. The secondary school environment is difficult enough for **P** preference students so teachers can help their student achieve by:

■ Providing as much flexibility as possible (multiple choice homework tasks, choice within the lesson).

■ Avoiding giving out detailed schedules (they'll just lose it anyway!).

■ Shaking things up now and again to prevent predictability becoming boredom.

■ Introducing random surprises and changes.

■ Helping the student identify ways they can organise and manage their time to complete important work without a last-minute rush.

151
Seal teacher with Dolphin student
INFP and ENFJ

Seals and Dolphins share two preferences. Both are warm, sociable and imaginative. Both seek a harmonious classroom environment. Clashes are only likely when the personal relationship between teacher and student breaks down. For the teacher to get the best out of their naturally gregarious student they need to:

■ Listen patiently and enthusiastically to the student's ideas and contributions.

■ Stay open to 'silly' ideas to see where they lead – the student is thinking out loud and this is how they learn best.

■ Also offer your own thoughts; if you need a timeout ask for one.

■ Encourage the student to think things through before talking otherwise they'll hog the lesson.

■ Steer the student away from controversial subjects/topics, especially in group discussions.

■ Build in plenty of opportunities during lessons for the **E** students to talk things through with other **E** preferences.

Both teacher and student gather information by seeing the big picture first, using hunches, inferences and imagination to infer meaning. The Seal teacher will naturally use their imagination in the classroom and the **N** student will respond well to this, possibly joining in with flights of fancy, anecdotes and stories. A natural affinity between teacher and student is often present because they both look at the world in the same way – with a burning curiosity to understand why things are as they are by exploring patterns, possibilities, ideas and theories. Be careful not to look like you're favouring **N** students to the detriment of **S** students. Every student needs to be able to contribute in their preferred way. For the teacher to get the best out of their inherently imaginative student they need to:

■ Offer questions/projects that can be explored creatively.

■ Avoid repetitive tasks as they'll quickly lose interest.

■ Encourage the student to become aware of the important contribution of the **S** approach (the value of facts, details, procedure, experiments, applying experience, structure, the step-by-step model).

The teacher and student are both concerned with people and relationships before the task/subject content. Seals like to form personal relationships with all their students, unless they don't like the student (**F** teachers are more inclined than **T** preference teachers to have their favourites!). Because they operate at an emotional level these teachers are more likely to make promises to students, overstretch themselves and even do work the students should be doing themselves. Teacher and student both enjoy a classroom atmosphere that is warm and friendly. Compliments are likely to go in both directions boosting the confidence of teacher as well as student. The Dolphin needs to feel they like their teacher and that the teacher likes them too. If this happens they'll work harder but if not they may switch off completely. This explains why a student can be top of the class one year (with a teacher they like) and show no interest at all in the subject the following year when they change teacher. For the teacher to get the best out of their relationship-focused student they need to:

■ Offer learning situations that allow for the use of empathy, collaboration and teamworking.

■ Give ample and regular praise and offer tactful support to overcome any blind-spots.

■ Motivate by appealing to the strength of your personal belief in the student (don't let me down, I know you can do it, I like you).

The laid-back, flexible and spontaneous Seal teacher with the naturally organised Dolphin student can be a dream team or a disaster. To create a positive relationship they need to play to each other's strengths. The student can benefit from the teacher's ability to adapt and change plans and the teacher can benefit from the student's desire to have a plan they can work to and complete. The teacher can also:

■ Avoid changing plans just for the sake of it; this will only frustrate the student.

■ Encourage the student to embrace flexibility occasionally.

■ Encourage and support the student's desire for order, neatness and respecting deadlines.

■ Allow the student independence in planning their work in their own way if they really want to.

152
Seal teacher with Clownfish student
INFP and ENFP

Seals and Clownfish share three preferences. Both are at heart imaginative, 'hippy' daydreamers. Clashes are most likely when the gregarious Clownfish rails against the more modest style of the Seal. For the teacher to get the best out of their naturally lively student they need to:

■ Listen patiently and enthusiastically indulge the student's spontaneous performances (up to a point).

■ Stay open to off-the-wall ideas to see where they lead – the student is thinking out loud and this is how they learn best.

■ Also offer your own thoughts; if you need a timeout ask for one.

■ Encourage the student to think things through before talking otherwise they'll hog the lesson.

■ Build in plenty of opportunities during lessons for the **E** students to talk things through with other **E** preferences.

Both teacher and student gather information by seeing the big picture first, using hunches, inferences and imagination to infer meaning. The Seal teacher will naturally use their imagination in the classroom and the student will respond well to this, possibly joining in with flights of fancy, anecdotes and stories. A natural affinity between teacher and student is often present because they both look at the world in the same way – with a deep curiosity to understand why things are as they are by exploring patterns, possibilities, ideas and people. Be careful not to look like you're favouring **N** students to the detriment of **S** students. Every student needs to be able to contribute in their preferred way. For the teacher to get the best out of their inherently imaginative student they need to:

■ Offer questions/projects that can be explored creatively.

■ Avoid repetitive tasks as they'll quickly lose interest.

■ Encourage the student to become aware of the important contribution of the **S** approach (the value of facts, details, procedure, experiments, applying experience, structure, the step-by-step model).

The teacher and student are both concerned with people and relationships before the task/subject content. Seals like to form personal relationships with all their students, unless they don't like the student (**F** teachers are more inclined than **T** preference teachers to have their favourites!). Because they operate at an emotional level these teachers are more likely to make promises to students, overstretch themselves and even do work the students should be doing themselves. Teacher and student both enjoy a classroom atmosphere that is warm and friendly. Compliments are likely to go in both directions boosting the confidence of teacher as well as student. The Clownfish needs to feel they like their teacher and that the teacher likes them too. If this happens they'll work harder but if not they may switch off completely. This explains why a student can be top of the class one year (with a teacher they like) and show no interest at all in the subject the following year when they change teacher. For the teacher to get the best out of their relationship-focused student they need to:

■ Offer learning situations that allow for the use of empathy, collaboration and teamworking.

■ Give ample and regular praise and offer tactful support to overcome any blind-spots.

■ Motivate by appealing to the strength of your personal belief in the student (don't let me down, I know you can do it, I like you).

P preferences can be organised and efficient; it's just such an effort! While enjoying a mutual love of spontaneity, which provides each with relief from the stifling and constraining timetables and deadlines essential in large organisations such as schools, they must also remember to complete any necessary tasks. Although likely to be fun and popular teachers, they also need to focus on the task of preparing the student to succeed socially and academically. Both prefer to start tasks than finish them. Their initial enthusiasm can quickly wane. Both need to ensure they identify and complete the important tasks or the student (or their parents) may eventually ask awkward questions. For the teacher to get the best out of their naturally laid-back student they need to understand the student doesn't just like options and choice; they are essential or they start to itch, squirm and rebel. The secondary school environment is difficult enough for **P** preference students so teachers can help their student achieve by:

■ Providing as much flexibility as possible (multiple choice homework tasks, choice within the lesson).

■ Avoiding giving out detailed schedules (they'll just be lost).

■ Shaking things up now and again to prevent predictability becoming boredom.

■ Introducing random surprises and changes.

■ Helping the student identify ways they can organise and manage their time to complete important work without a last-minute panic.

153
Seal teacher with Polar Bear student
INFP and ISTJ

Near opposites can be useful to each other because together they cover all bases. The naturally organised and grounded student can keep the daydreamer teacher on track. Clashes are likely when differences in approach are misinterpreted as personal (by the teacher) or unprofessional (by the student). For the teacher to get the best out of their characteristically serious student they need to:

■ Respect the student's need for privacy and independence.

■ Allow the student plenty of time to think through their thoughts.

■ Share your ideas and thoughts regularly to ensure you both know what you're doing.

■ Take time to clarify your thoughts but don't avoid confrontation; if something needs to be said be calm and direct as you deliver it.

■ Use non-verbal communication – smiles and gestures are reassuring to **I** students. You can even use sticky notes/emails to pass on feedback.

■ Provide opportunities for the student to see you one-to-one away from the sometimes hectic environment of the classroom.

The imaginative Seal teacher can be an inspiration to all students, but they do need to respect the need for Polar Bears to be given clear guidelines, structure, facts, details and procedures; otherwise they can flounder. For the teacher to get the best out of their more grounded student they need to:

■ Demonstrate how learning can be applied in the real world.

■ Allow the student opportunities to repeat and practise until satisfied they are competent.

■ Encourage the use of imagination as a useful process and explain how it's not time-wasting.

■ Be careful not to look like you're favouring **N** students to the detriment of **S** students. Every student needs to be able to contribute in their preferred way.

The teacher is concerned with relationship then task whereas the student is the other way round. The teacher must learn to accept that the student is different; not cold, blunt and unfriendly, but simply focused on task first. If the teacher can accept this the relationship can be really positive for both teacher and student. For the teacher to get the best out of their naturally objective student they need to:

■ Offer targeted compliments. Just saying everything is great will not impress or help the student; in fact, it can result in the student losing respect for the teacher, concluding they lie and/or are a soft touch. When you offer praise you may be pressed for proof!

■ Be logical and objective rather than emotional in discussions.

■ Accept that if the student challenges you it is probably to clarify their thoughts rather than test your authority or besmirch your character. Perhaps ask 'What would you do to improve/change this?' or 'What do you think?' Once they've clarified their thoughts they may be ready to ask and absorb what you think.

■ Work in ways that test their skill and knowledge competitively (they raise their game).

■ Help them understand that 50% of people are **F** preference and can interpret feedback as criticism.

The laid-back, flexible and spontaneous teacher with the naturally organised student can be a dream team or a disaster. To create a positive relationship they need to play to each other's strengths. The student can benefit from the teacher's ability to adapt and change plans and the teacher can benefit from the student's desire to have a plan they can work to and complete. The teacher can also:

■ Encourage and support the student's desire for order, neatness and respecting deadlines.

■ Allow the student independence in planning their work in their own way if they really want to.

■ Avoid changing plans just for the sake of it; this will only frustrate the student.

154
Seal teacher with Koala student
INFP and ISFJ

Seals and Koalas share two preferences. Both value harmony and good manners. This can form the basis of a mutually beneficial relationship. The Seal can draw out the hidden strengths of the timid Koala. The Koala can show their teacher the value of careful planning and attention to detail. For the teacher to support their naturally reserved student they need to:

■ Respect the student's need for privacy and independence.

■ Allow the student plenty of time to think through their thoughts.

■ Share your ideas and thoughts regularly to ensure you both know what you're doing.

■ Take time to clarify your thoughts but don't avoid confrontation; if something needs to be said be calm and direct as you deliver it.

■ Use non-verbal communication – smiles and gestures are reassuring to **I** students. You can even use sticky notes/emails to pass on feedback.

■ Provide opportunities for the student to see you one-to-one away from the sometimes hectic environment of the classroom during breaks or suggest they write down their questions/issues for you to reply to later.

The imaginative Seal teacher can inspire all students, but they do need to respect the need for around two-thirds of students to be given clear guidelines, structure, facts, details and procedures; otherwise they can flounder. This is especially true of the quiet Koala student. For the teacher to get the best out of their practical student they need to:

- Demonstrate how learning can be applied in the real world.
- Allow the student opportunities to repeat and practise until satisfied they are competent.
- Encourage the use of imagination as a useful process and explain how it's not time-wasting.
- Be careful not to look like you're favouring **N** students to the detriment of **S** students. Every student needs to be able to contribute in their preferred way.

The teacher and student are both concerned with people and relationships before the task/subject content. Seals like to form personal relationships with all their students, unless they don't like the student. Because they operate at an emotional level these teachers are more likely to make promises to students, overstretch themselves and even do work the students should be doing themselves. Teacher and student both enjoy a classroom atmosphere that is warm and friendly. Compliments are likely to go in both directions boosting the confidence of teacher as well as student. The Koala needs to feel they like their teacher and that the teacher likes them too. If this happens they'll work harder but if not they may switch off completely. This explains why a student can be top of the class one year (with a teacher they like) and show no interest at all in the subject the following year when they change teacher. For the teacher to get the best out of their relationship-focused student they need to:

- Offer learning situations that allow for the use of empathy, collaboration and teamworking.
- Give ample and regular praise and offer tactful support to overcome any blind-spots.
- Motivate by appealing to the strength of your personal belief in the student (don't let me down, I know you can do it, I like you).

The flexible and fidgety teacher with the naturally organised and calm student can be a dream team or a disaster. To create a positive relationship they need to play to each other's strengths. The student can benefit from the teacher's ability to adapt and change plans and the teacher can benefit from the student's desire to have a plan they can work to and complete. The teacher can also:

- Encourage the student to embrace flexibility occasionally.
- Avoid changing plans just for the sake of it; this will only frustrate the student.
- Encourage and support the student's desire for order, neatness and respecting deadlines.
- Allow the student independence in planning their work in their own way if they really want to.

155
Seal teacher with Tiger student
INFP and ISTP

Seals and Tigers share two preferences. Both prefer a calm and laid-back classroom environment. The Tiger dislikes being told what to do and how to do it! Recognising this can prevent classroom clashes. If the Tiger is given choice and flexibility they will normally complete work without fuss or fanfare. For the teacher to get the best out of their naturally reserved student they need to:

- Respect the student's need for privacy and independence.
- Allow the student plenty of time to think through their thoughts.
- Share your ideas and thoughts regularly to ensure you both know what you're doing.
- Take time to clarify your thoughts but don't avoid confrontation; if something needs to be said be calm and direct as you deliver it.
- Use non-verbal communication – smiles and gestures are reassuring to **I** students. You can even use sticky notes/emails to pass on feedback.

The creative Seal teacher can inspire all students, but they do need to respect the need for Tigers to be given clear guidelines, structure, facts, details and procedures; otherwise they can flounder. For the teacher to get the best out of their more grounded student they need to:

- Demonstrate how learning can be applied in the real world.
- Allow the student opportunities to repeat and practise until satisfied they are competent.
- Encourage the use of imagination as a useful process and explain how it's not time-wasting.
- Be careful not to look like you're favouring **N** students to the detriment of **S** students. Every student needs to be able to contribute in their preferred way.

The teacher is concerned with relationship then task whereas the student is the other way round. The teacher must learn to accept that the student is different; not cold, blunt and unfriendly, but simply focused on task first. If the teacher can accept this relationship can be really positive for both teacher and student. To boost the student:

- Offer targeted compliments. Just saying everything is great will not impress or help the student; in fact, it can result in the student losing respect for the teacher, concluding they lie and/or are a soft touch. When you praise you may be pressed for proof!
- Be logical and objective rather than emotional in discussions.
- Accept that if the student challenges you it is probably to clarify their thoughts rather than test your authority or besmirch your character. Perhaps ask 'What would you do to improve/change this?' or 'What do you think?' Once they've clarified their thoughts they may be ready to ask and absorb what you think.
- Work in ways that test their skill and knowledge competitively (they raise their game).
- Help them understand that 50% of people are **F** preference and can interpret feedback as criticism.

P preferences abhor to-do-lists, schedules and predictability; they rarely reach the status of an acquired taste or a honed skill. While enjoying their mutual love of spontaneity, which provides each with relief from the stifling and constraining timetables and deadlines essential in large organisations such as schools, they must also remember to complete any necessary tasks. Although likely to be fun and popular teachers, they also need to focus on the task of preparing the student to succeed socially and academically. Both prefer to start tasks than finish them. Their

initial enthusiasm can quickly wane. Both need to ensure they identify and complete the important tasks or the student (or their parents) may eventually ask awkward questions. For the teacher to get the best out of their naturally laid-back student they need to understand the student doesn't just like options and choice; they are essential or they start to itch, squirm and rebel. The secondary school environment is difficult enough for Tigers so the Seal teacher can help by:

- Avoiding giving out detailed schedules (they'll just lose it anyway!).
- Shaking things up now and again to prevent predictability becoming boredom. Introduce random surprises and changes.
- Helping the student identify a few simple but effective strategies to ensure they can succeed.
- Offering as much flexibility as possible (multiple choice homework tasks, choice within the lesson).

156
Seal teacher with Cat student
INFP and ISFP

Seals and Cats share three preferences. Both enjoy a quietly sociable and laid-back classroom. Cats like to work things out for themselves. Recognising this can prevent classroom clashes. If the Cat is given choice and flexibility they will normally complete work without fuss or fanfare. For the teacher to get the best out of their naturally reserved student they need to:

- Respect the student's need for privacy and independence.
- Allow the student plenty of time to think through their thoughts.
- Share your ideas and thoughts regularly to ensure you both know what you're doing.
- Take time to clarify your thoughts but don't avoid confrontation; if something needs to be said be calm and direct as you deliver it.
- Use non-verbal communication – smiles and gestures are reassuring to **I** students. You can even use sticky notes/emails to pass on feedback.
- Provide opportunities for the student to see you one-to-one away from the sometimes hectic environment of the classroom.

The imaginative Seal teacher can inspire all students, but they do need to respect the need for around two-thirds of students to be given clear guidelines, structure, facts, details and procedures; otherwise they can flounder. For the teacher to get the best out of their more grounded student they need to:

- Demonstrate how learning can be applied in the real world.
- Allow the student opportunities to repeat and practise until satisfied they are competent.
- Encourage the use of imagination as a useful process and explain how it's not time-wasting.
- Be careful not to look like you're favouring **N** students to the detriment of **S** students. Every student needs to be able to contribute in their preferred way.

The Seal teacher and Cat student are both concerned with people and relationships before the task/subject content. Seals like to form personal relationships with all their students, unless they don't like the student (**F** teachers are more inclined than **T** preference teachers to have their favourites!). Because they operate at an emotional level these teachers are more likely to make promises to students, overstretch themselves and even do work the students should be doing themselves. Teacher and student both enjoy a classroom atmosphere that is warm and friendly. Compliments are likely to go in both directions boosting the confidence of teacher as well as student. The Cat needs to feel they like their teacher and that the teacher likes them too. If this happens they'll work harder but if not they may switch off completely. This explains why a student can be top of the class one year (with a teacher they like) and show no interest at all in the subject the following year when they change teacher. For the teacher to get the best out of their relationship-focused student they need to:

■ Offer learning situations that allow for the use of empathy, collaboration and teamworking.

■ Give ample and regular praise and offer tactful support to overcome any blind-spots.

■ Motivate by appealing to the strength of your personal belief in the student (don't let me down, I know you can do it, I like you).

Seals and Cats can be organised and efficient; it's just such an effort! While enjoying a mutual love of spontaneity, which provides each with relief from the stifling and constraining timetables and deadlines essential in large organisations such as schools, they must also remember to complete any necessary tasks. Although likely to be fun and popular teachers, they also need to focus on the task of preparing the student to succeed socially and academically. Both prefer to start tasks than finish them. Their initial enthusiasm can quickly evaporate. Both need to ensure they identify and complete the important tasks or the student (or their parents) may eventually ask awkward questions. For the teacher to get the best out of their naturally laid-back student they need to understand the student doesn't just like options and choice; they are essential or they start to itch, squirm and rebel. To help the student progress:

■ Offer as much flexibility as possible (multiple choice homework tasks, choice within the lesson).

■ Avoid giving out detailed schedules (they'll just lose it anyway!).

■ Shake things up now and again to prevent predictability becoming boredom. Introduce random surprises and changes.

■ Identify simple ways the student can organise and manage their time to complete important work without a last-minute rush.

157
Seal teacher with Seahorse student
INFP and INFJ

Seals and Seahorses share three preferences. Both are 'hippies' – interested in education as a way to grow and develop personally. When the student feels nurtured by their teacher they'll respond well. Clashes are most likely when the intense and private student fails to connect with their equally reserved teacher. For the teacher to get the best out of their naturally deep student they need to:

■ Respect the student's need for privacy and independence.

■ Allow the student plenty of time to think through their thoughts.

■ Share your ideas and thoughts regularly to ensure you both know what you're doing.

■ Take time to clarify your thoughts but don't avoid confrontation; if something needs to be said be calm and direct as you deliver it.

■ Use non-verbal communication – smiles and gestures are reassuring to **I** students. You can even use sticky notes/emails to pass on feedback.

Both teacher and student gather information by seeing the big picture first, using hunches, inferences and imagination to decipher meaning. The Seal teacher will naturally use their imagination in the classroom and the **N** student will respond well to this, possibly joining in with flights of fancy, anecdotes and stories. A natural affinity between teacher and student is often present because they both look at the world in the same way – with a burning curiosity to understand why things are as they are by exploring patterns, possibilities, ideas and theories. Be careful not to look like you're favouring **N** students to the detriment of **S** students. Every student needs to be able to contribute in their preferred way. For the teacher to get the best out of their inherently imaginative student they need to:

■ Offer questions/projects that can be explored creatively.

■ Avoid repetitive tasks as they'll quickly lose interest.

■ Encourage the student to become aware of the important contribution of the **S** approach (the value of facts, details, procedure, experiments, applying experience, structure, the step-by-step model).

The teacher and student are both concerned with people and relationships before the task/subject content. Seals like to form personal relationships with all their students, unless they don't like the student. Because they operate at an emotional level these teachers are more likely to make promises to students, overstretch themselves and even do work the students should be doing themselves. Teacher and student both enjoy a classroom atmosphere that is warm and friendly. Compliments are likely to go in both directions boosting the confidence of teacher as well as student. The Seahorse needs to feel they like their teacher and that the teacher likes them too. If this happens they'll work harder but if not they may switch off completely. This explains why a student can be top of the class one year (with a teacher they like) and show no interest at all in the subject the following year when they change teacher. For the teacher to get the best out of their relationship-focused student they need to:

■ Offer learning situations that allow for the use of empathy, collaboration and teamworking.

■ Give ample and regular praise and offer tactful support to overcome any blind-spots.

■ Motivate by appealing to the strength of your personal belief in the student (don't let me down, I know you can do it, I like you).

The laid-back, flexible and spontaneous teacher with the naturally organised student can be a dream team or a disaster. To create a positive relationship they need to play to each other's strengths. The student can benefit from the teacher's ability to adapt and change plans and the teacher can benefit from the student's desire to have a plan they can work to and complete. The teacher can also:

■ Encourage and support the student's desire for order, neatness and respecting deadlines.

■ Allow the student independence in planning their work in their own way if they really want to.

■ Avoid changing plans just for the sake of it; this will only frustrate the student.

158
Seal teacher with Barn Owl student
INFP and INTJ

Seals and Barn Owls share two preferences. Both enjoy using their imagination to make sense of the world around them. The warm, personal Seal contrasts with the strategic, objective Barn Owl and this is the usual source of conflict. For the teacher to get the best out of their naturally introspective student they need to:

■ Respect the student's need for privacy and independence.

■ Allow the student plenty of time to think through their thoughts.

■ Share your ideas and thoughts regularly to ensure you both know what you're doing.

■ Take time to clarify your thoughts but don't avoid confrontation; if something needs to be said be calm and direct as you deliver it.

■ Use non-verbal communication – smiles and gestures are reassuring to **I** students. You can even use sticky notes/emails to pass on feedback.

■ Provide opportunities for the student to see you one-to-one away from the sometimes hectic environment of the classroom.

Both teacher and student gather information by seeing the big picture first, using hunches, inferences and imagination to absorb meaning. The Seal teacher will naturally use their imagination in the classroom and the **N** student will respond well to this, possibly joining in with flights of fancy, anecdotes and stories. A natural affinity between teacher and student is often present because they both look at the world in the same way – with a burning curiosity to understand why things are as they are by exploring patterns, possibilities, ideas and theories. Be careful not to look like you're favouring **N** students to the detriment of **S** students. Every student needs to be able to contribute in their preferred way. For the teacher to get the best out of their inherently imaginative student they can:

■ Offer questions/projects that can be explored creatively.

■ Avoid repetitive tasks as they'll quickly lose interest.

- Encourage the student to become aware of the important contribution of the **S** approach (the value of facts, details, procedure, experiments, applying experience, structure, the step-by-step model).

The Seal teacher is concerned with relationship then task whereas the Owl student is the other way round. The teacher must learn to accept that the student is different; not cold, blunt and unfriendly, but simply focused on task first. If the teacher can accept this the relationship can be really positive for both teacher and student. For the teacher to get the best out of their fundamentally objective student they need to:

- Offer targeted compliments. Just saying everything is great will not impress or help the student; in fact, it can result in the student losing respect for the teacher, concluding they lie and/or are a soft touch. When you offer praise you may be pressed to provide proof!
- Be logical and objective rather than emotional in discussions.
- Accept that if the student challenges you it is probably to clarify their thoughts rather than test your authority or besmirch your character. Perhaps ask 'What would you do to improve/change this?' or 'What do you think?' Once they've clarified their thoughts they may be ready to ask and absorb what you think.
- Work in ways that test their skill and knowledge competitively (they raise their game).
- Help them understand that 50% of people are **F** preference and can interpret feedback as criticism.

The laid-back, flexible and spontaneous Seal teacher with the naturally organised Barn Owl student can be a dream team or a disaster. To create a positive relationship they need to play to each other's strengths. The student can benefit from the teacher's ability to adapt and change plans and the teacher can benefit from the student's desire to have a plan they can work to and complete. The teacher can also:

- Avoid changing plans just for the sake of it; this will only frustrate the student.
- Encourage the student to embrace flexibility occasionally.
- Encourage and support the student's desire for order, neatness and respecting deadlines.
- Allow the student independence in planning their work in their own way if they really want to.

159
Seal teacher with Seal student
INFP and INFP

Sharing all four preferences can be a strong platform. Both Seals seek a harmonious classroom environment. This shared desire can cement a positive relationship. Clashes are most likely when the student's need for privacy to think things through is misinterpreted as disinterest in subject or teacher. For the teacher to get the best out of their naturally reserved student they need to:

- Respect the student's need for privacy and independence.
- Allow the student plenty of time to think through their thoughts.
- Share your ideas and thoughts regularly to ensure you both know what you're doing.
- Take time to clarify your thoughts but don't avoid confrontation; if something needs to be said be calm and direct as you deliver it.
- Use non-verbal communication – smiles and gestures are reassuring to **I** students. You can even use sticky notes/emails to pass on feedback.
- Provide opportunities for the student to see you one-to-one away from the sometimes hectic environment of the classroom.

Both teacher and student gather information by seeing the big picture first, using hunches, inferences and imagination to garner meaning. The Seal teacher will naturally use their imagination in the classroom and the **N** student will respond well to this, possibly joining in with flights of fancy, anecdotes and stories. A natural affinity between teacher and student is often present because they both look at the world in the same way – with a burning curiosity to understand why things are as they are by exploring patterns, possibilities, ideas and theories. Be careful not to look like you're favouring **N** students to the detriment of **S** students. Every student needs to be able to contribute in their preferred way. For the teacher to help their inherently imaginative student progress they need to:

- Offer questions/projects that can be explored creatively.
- Avoid repetitive tasks as they'll quickly lose interest.
- Encourage the student to become aware of the important contribution of the **S** approach (the value of facts, details, procedure, experiments, applying experience, structure, the step-by-step model).

Seals are concerned with people and relationships before the task/subject content. Teachers like to form personal relationships with all their students, unless they don't like the student (**F** teachers are more inclined than **T** preference teachers to have their favourites!). Because they operate at an emotional level these teachers are more likely to make promises to students, overstretch themselves and even do work the students should be doing themselves. Teacher and student both enjoy a classroom atmosphere that is warm and friendly. Compliments are likely to go in both directions boosting the confidence of teacher as well as student. The Seal student needs to feel they like their teacher and that the teacher likes them too. If this happens they'll work harder but if not they may switch off completely. This explains why a student can be top of the class one year (with a teacher they like) and show no interest at all in the subject the following year when they change teacher. For the teacher to get the best out of their relationship-focused student they need to:

- Offer learning situations that allow for the use of empathy, collaboration and teamworking.
- Give ample and regular praise and offer tactful support to overcome any blind-spots.
- Motivate by appealing to the strength of your personal belief in the student (don't let me down, I know you can do it, I like you).

Seals abhor to-do-lists, schedules and predictability; they rarely reach the status of an acquired taste or a honed skill. While enjoying their mutual love of spontaneity, which provides each with relief from the stifling and constraining time-tables and deadlines essential in large organisations such as schools, they must also remember to complete any necessary tasks. Although likely to be fun and popular teachers, they also need to focus on the task of preparing the student to succeed socially and academically. Both prefer to start tasks than finish them. Their initial enthusiasm can quickly wane. Both need to ensure they identify and complete the important tasks or the student (or their parents) may eventually ask awkward questions. For the teacher to get the best out of their naturally laid-back student they need to understand the student doesn't just like options and choice; they are essential or they start to itch, squirm and rebel. The secondary school environment is difficult enough for **P** preference students so teachers can help when they:

- Provide as much flexibility as possible (multiple choice homework tasks, choice within the lesson).
- Avoid giving out detailed schedules.
- Shake things up now and again to prevent predictability becoming boredom.
- Introduce random surprises and changes.
- Identify simple ways the student can organise and manage their time to complete important work without a last-minute rush.

160
Seal teacher with Tawny Owl student
INFP and INTP

Seals and Tawny Owls share three preferences. Both enjoy using their imagination unfettered by practicality and deadlines. This common interest can cement their relationship. Differences in decision making – the subjective Seal versus the objective Tawny Owl – are usually the source of conflict in the classroom. For the teacher to get the best out of their naturally reserved student they need to:

- Respect the student's need for privacy and independence.
- Allow the student plenty of time to think through their thoughts.
- Share your ideas and thoughts regularly to ensure you both know what you're doing.
- Take time to clarify your thoughts but don't avoid confrontation; if something needs to be said be calm and direct as you deliver it.
- Use non-verbal communication – smiles and gestures are reassuring to **I** students. You can even use sticky notes/emails to pass on feedback.
- Provide opportunities for the student to see you one-to-one away from the sometimes hectic environment of the classroom.

Both teacher and student gather information by seeing the big picture first, using hunches, inferences and imagination to infer meaning. The Seal teacher will naturally use their imagination in the classroom and the Tawny Owl student will respond well to this, possibly joining in with flights of fancy, anecdotes and stories. A natural affinity between teacher and student is often present because they both look at the world in the same way – with a burning curiosity to understand why things are as they are by exploring patterns, possibilities, ideas and theories. Be careful not to look like you're favouring **N** students to the detriment of **S** students. Every student needs to be able to contribute in their preferred way. For the teacher to get the best out of their inherently imaginative student they need to:

■ Offer questions/projects that can be explored creatively.

■ Avoid repetitive tasks as they'll quickly lose interest.

■ Encourage the student to become aware of the important contribution of the **S** approach (the value of facts, details, procedure, experiments, applying experience, structure, the step-by-step model).

The Seal teacher is concerned with relationship then task whereas the Owl student is the other way round. The teacher must learn to accept that the student is different; not cold, blunt and unfriendly, but simply focused on task first. If the teacher can accept this the relationship can be really positive for both teacher and student. To help the student progress:

■ Offer targeted compliments. Just saying everything is great will not impress or help the student; in fact, it can result in the student losing respect for the teacher, concluding they lie and/or are a soft touch. When you praise you may be pressed for proof!

■ Be logical and objective rather than emotional in discussions.

■ Accept that if the student challenges you it is probably to clarify their thoughts rather than test your authority or besmirch your character. Perhaps ask 'What would you do to improve/change this?' or 'What do you think?' Once they've clarified their thoughts they may be ready to ask and absorb what you think.

■ Work in ways that test their skill and knowledge competitively (they raise their game).

■ Help the Owl develop tact around the 50% of people who have an **F** preference as they can interpret well-intentioned feedback as blunt criticism.

Seals and Tawny Owls can be organised and efficient; it's just such an effort! While enjoying a mutual love of spontaneity, which provides each with relief from the stifling and constraining timetables and deadlines essential in large organisations such as schools, they must also remember to complete any necessary tasks. Although likely to be fun and popular teachers, they also need to focus on the task of preparing the student to succeed socially and academically. Both prefer to start tasks than finish them. Their initial enthusiasm can soon evaporate. Both need to ensure they identify and complete the important tasks or the student (or their parents) may eventually ask awkward questions. For the teacher to get the best out of their naturally laid-back student they need to understand the student doesn't just like options and choice; they are essential or they start to squirm, wriggle and rebel. The secondary school environment is difficult enough for **P** preference students so teachers can help their student achieve by:

■ Providing as much flexibility as possible (multiple choice homework tasks, choice within the lesson).

■ Shaking things up now and again to prevent predictability becoming boredom.

■ Helping the student adopt time-management strategies to ensure they can complete important work on time.

161
Clownfish teacher with Lion student
ENFP and ESFP

Clownfish and Lions share three of the four preferences. Both thrive in a sociable and entertaining classroom atmosphere. Conflict is only likely when the 'party' ends and hard work is required. It can be done but it just isn't fun. For the teacher to get the best out of their naturally effusive student they need to:

■ Enjoy the lively banter when it is appropriate to spark new thoughts and ideas; the student learns best this way, but remember there may be thirty others in the classroom.

■ Stick to the point and stay positive (don't nag), as both teacher and student are easily distracted and liable to go off track!

■ Avoid going over old ground.

■ Be calm and clear, otherwise two **E** preferences can talk louder and louder with neither listening.

■ Remember you can keep some thoughts to yourself (and you may think of a better way of expressing something, especially criticism, later).

■ Be an enthusiastic and supportive listener; seek to help the student clarify and develop their thinking rather than assert your own.

■ Help each other learn to be quiet and encourage the **I** preferences in the class to express themselves.

The imaginative Clownfish teacher can inspire all students, but they do need to respect the need for around two-thirds of students to be given clear guidelines, structure, facts, details and procedures; otherwise they can flounder. For the teacher to get the best out of their more grounded Lion student they need to:

■ Demonstrate how learning can be applied in the real world.

■ Allow the student opportunities to repeat and practise until satisfied they are competent.

■ Encourage the use of imagination as a useful process and explain how it's not time-wasting.

■ Be careful not to look like you're favouring **N** students to the detriment of **S** students. Every student needs to be able to contribute in their preferred way.

Both teacher and student are concerned with people and relationships before the task/subject content. They like to form personal relationships with all their students, unless they don't like the student (**F** teachers are more inclined than **T** preference teachers to have their favourites!). Because they operate at an emotional level these teachers are more likely to make promises to students, overstretch themselves and even do work the students should be doing themselves. Teacher and student both enjoy a classroom atmosphere that is warm and friendly. Compliments are likely to go in both directions boosting the confidence of teacher as well as student.

The Lion needs to feel they like their teacher and that the teacher likes them too. If this happens they'll work harder but if not they may switch off completely. This explains why a student can be top of the class one year (with a teacher they like) and show no interest at all in the subject the following year when they change teacher. For the teacher to get the best out of their relationship-focused student they need to:

■ Offer learning situations that allow for the use of empathy, collaboration and teamworking.

■ Give ample and regular praise and offer tactful support to overcome any blind-spots.

■ Motivate by appealing to the strength of your personal belief in the student (don't let me down, I know you can do it, I like you).

P preferences can be organised and efficient; it's just such an effort! While enjoying a mutual love of spontaneity, which provides each with relief from the stifling and constraining timetables and deadlines essential in large organisations such as schools, they must also remember to complete any necessary tasks. Although likely to be fun and popular teachers, they also need to focus on the task of preparing the student to succeed socially and academically. Both prefer to start tasks than finish them. Their initial enthusiasm can quickly evaporate. Both need to ensure they identify and complete the important tasks or the student (or their parents) may eventually ask awkward questions. For the teacher to get the best out of their naturally laid-back student they need to understand the student doesn't just like options and choice; they are essential or they start to itch, squirm and rebel. The secondary school environment is difficult enough for **P** preference students so teachers can help their student achieve by:

■ Providing as much flexibility as possible (multiple choice homework tasks, choice within the lesson).

■ Avoiding giving out detailed schedules (they'll just lose it anyway!).

■ Shaking things up now and again to prevent predictability becoming boredom. Introduce random surprises and changes.

■ Identifying simple ways the student can organise and manage their time to complete important work without a last-minute panic.

162
Clownfish teacher with Black Bear student
ENFP and ESTJ

A Clownfish teacher shares only one preference with their Black Bear student. They are both sociable, will speak their mind and stand their ground. Clashes are most likely when the perceived seriousness of the student and playfulness of the teacher grate. For the teacher to get the best out of their naturally assertive student they need to:

■ Enjoy the lively banter when it is appropriate to spark new thoughts and ideas; the student learns best this way, but remember there may be thirty others in the classroom.

- Stick to the point and stay positive (don't nag), as both teacher and student are easily distracted and liable to go off track!
- Avoid going over old ground.
- Be calm and clear, otherwise two **E** preferences can talk louder and louder with neither listening.
- Remember you can keep some thoughts to yourself (and you may think of a better way of expressing something, especially criticism, later).
- Be an enthusiastic and supportive listener; seek to help the student clarify and develop their thinking rather than assert your own.
- Help each other learn to be quiet and encourage the **I** preferences in the class to express themselves.

The imaginative Clownfish teacher can inspire all students, but they do need to respect the need for around two-thirds of students to be given clear guidelines, structure, facts, details and procedures; otherwise they can flounder. For the teacher to get the best out of their more grounded student they need to:

- Demonstrate how learning can be applied in the real world.
- Allow the student opportunities to repeat and practise until satisfied they are competent.
- Encourage the use of imagination as a useful process and explain how it's not time-wasting.
- Be careful not to look like you're favouring **N** students to the detriment of **S** students. Every student needs to be able to contribute in their preferred way.

The teacher is concerned with relationship then task whereas the student is the other way round. The teacher must learn to accept that the student is different; not cold, blunt and unfriendly, but different and focused on task first. If the teacher can accept this the relationship can be really positive for both teacher and student. For the teacher to get the best out of their instinctively assertive student they need to:

- Offer targeted compliments. Just saying everything is great will not impress or help the student; in fact, it can result in the student losing respect for the teacher, concluding they lie and/or are a soft touch. When you praise you may be pressed for proof!
- Be logical and objective rather than emotional in discussions.
- Accept that if the student challenges you it is probably to clarify their thoughts rather than to test your authority or besmirch your character. Perhaps ask 'What would you do to improve/change this?' or 'What do you think?' Once they've clarified their thoughts they may be ready to ask and absorb what you think.
- Work in ways that test their skill and knowledge competitively (they raise their game).
- Help them understand that 50% of people are **F** preference and can interpret feedback as criticism.

When the laid-back, flexible and spontaneous teacher meets the naturally organised student they can complement each other or clash spectacularly. To build a positive relationship they need to play to each other's strengths. The student can benefit from the teacher's ability to adapt and change plans and the teacher can benefit from the student's desire to have a plan they can work to and complete. The teacher can also:

- Encourage and support the student's desire for order, neatness and respecting deadlines.
- Allow the student independence in planning their work in their own way if they really want to.
- Avoid changing plans just for the sake of it; this will only frustrate the student.

163 Clownfish teacher with Panther student
ENFP and ESTP

Clownfish and Panthers share two preferences. Both enjoy a relaxed and sociable classroom environment. Clashes are likely when the hard work has to start. For the teacher to get the best out of their naturally effusive student they need to:

- Enjoy the lively banter when it is appropriate to spark new thoughts and ideas; the student learns best this way, but remember there may be thirty others in the classroom.
- Stick to the point and stay positive (don't nag), as both teacher and student are easily distracted and liable to go off track!
- Avoid going over old ground.
- Be calm and clear, otherwise two **E** preferences can talk louder and louder like PMQs (with neither listening).
- Remember you can keep some thoughts to yourself (and you may think of a better way of expressing something, especially criticism, later).
- Be an enthusiastic and supportive listener; seek to help the student clarify and develop their thinking rather than assert your own.
- Help each other learn to be quiet and encourage the **I** preferences in the class to express themselves.

The imaginative Clownfish teacher can inspire all students, but they do need to respect the need for around two-thirds of students to be given clear guidelines, structure, facts, details and procedures; otherwise they can flounder. For the teacher to get the best out of their more grounded student they need to:

- Demonstrate how learning can be applied in the real world.
- Allow the student opportunities to repeat and practise until satisfied they are competent.
- Encourage the use of imagination as a useful process and explain how it's not time-wasting.
- Be careful not to look like you're favouring **N** students to the detriment of **S** students. Every student needs to be able to contribute in their preferred way.

The teacher is concerned with relationship then task whereas the student is the other way round. The teacher must learn to accept that the student is different; not cold, blunt and unfriendly, but simply focused on task first. If the teacher can accept this the relationship can be really positive for both teacher and student. For the teacher to get the best out of their essentially assertive student they need to:

- Offer targeted compliments. Just saying everything is great will not impress or help the student; in fact, it can result in the student losing respect for the teacher, concluding they lie and/or are a soft touch. When you praise you may be pressed for proof!
- Be logical and objective rather than emotional in discussions.
- Accept that if the student challenges you it is probably to clarify their thoughts rather than test your authority or besmirch your character. Perhaps ask 'What would you do to improve/change this?' or 'What do you think?' Once they've clarified their thoughts they may be ready to ask and absorb what you think.
- Work in ways that test their skill and knowledge competitively (they raise their game).
- Help them understand that 50% of people are **F** preference and can interpret feedback as criticism.

P preferences can be organised and efficient; it's just such an effort! While enjoying a mutual love of spontaneity, which provides each with relief from the stifling and constraining timetables and deadlines essential in large organisations such as schools, they must also remember to complete any necessary tasks. Although likely to be fun and popular teachers, they also need to focus on the task of preparing the student to succeed socially and academically. Both prefer to start tasks than finish them. Their initial enthusiasm can quickly wane. Both need to ensure they identify and complete the important tasks or the student (or their parents) may eventually ask awkward questions. For the teacher to get the best out of their naturally laid-back student they need to understand the student doesn't just like options and choice; they are essential or they start to itch, squirm and rebel. The secondary school environment is difficult enough for **P** preference students so teachers can help their student achieve by:

- Providing as much flexibility as possible (multiple choice homework tasks, choice within the lesson).
- Avoiding giving out detailed schedules (they'll just lose it anyway!).
- Shaking things up now and again to prevent predictability becoming boredom. Introduce random surprises and changes.
- Helping the student identify simple time-management strategies to ensure they flourish.

164 Clownfish teacher with Teddy Bear student
ENFP and ESFJ

Clownfish and Teddies share two preferences. Both are sociable and caring, but their differences – in perceiving the world and how to live in it – can be a source of annoyance. The spontaneous and creative teacher can confuse or lose the more traditional and down-to-earth student. For the teacher to get the best out of their naturally effusive student they need to:

■ Enjoy the lively banter when it is appropriate to spark new thoughts and ideas; the student learns best this way, but remember there may be thirty others in the classroom.

■ Stick to the point and stay positive (don't nag), as both teacher and student are easily distracted and liable to go off track!

■ Avoid going over old ground.

■ Be calm and clear, otherwise two **E** preferences can talk louder and louder like PMQs (with neither listening).

■ Remember you can keep some thoughts to yourself (and you may think of a better way of expressing something, especially criticism, later).

■ Be an enthusiastic and supportive listener; seek to help the student clarify and develop their thinking rather than assert your own.

■ Help each other learn to be quiet and encourage the **I** preferences in the class to express themselves.

The imaginative Clownfish teacher can inspire all students, but they do need to respect the need for around two-thirds of students to be given clear guidelines, structure, facts, details and procedures; otherwise they can flounder. For the teacher to get the best out of their more grounded student they need to:

■ Demonstrate how learning can be applied in the real world.

■ Allow the student opportunities to repeat and practise until satisfied they are competent.

■ Encourage the use of imagination as a useful process and explain how it's not time-wasting.

■ Be careful not to look like you're favouring **N** students to the detriment of **S** students. Every student needs to be able to contribute in their preferred way.

The teacher and student are both concerned with people and relationships before the task/subject content. Clownfish like to form personal relationships with all their students, unless they don't like the student (**F** teachers are more inclined than **T** preference teachers to have their favourites!). Because they operate at an emotional level these teachers are more likely to make promises to students, overstretch themselves and even do work the students should be doing themselves. Teacher and student both enjoy a classroom atmosphere that is warm and friendly. Compliments are likely to go in both directions boosting the confidence of teacher as well as student. The Teddy needs to feel they like their teacher and that the teacher likes them too. If this happens they'll work harder but if not they may switch off completely. This explains why a student can excel one year (with a teacher they like) and show no interest at all in the subject the following year when they change teacher. For the teacher to get the best out of their relationship-focused student they need to:

■ Offer learning situations that allow for the use of empathy, collaboration and teamworking.

■ Give ample and regular praise and offer tactful support to overcome any blind-spots.

■ Motivate by appealing to the strength of your personal belief in the student (don't let me down, I know you can do it, I like you).

When the laid-back, flexible and spontaneous teacher meets the naturally organised student they can complement each other or clash spectacularly. To build a positive relationship they need to play to each other's strengths. The student can benefit from the teacher's ability to

adapt and change plans and the teacher can benefit from the student's desire to have a plan they can work to and complete. The teacher can also:

■ Encourage and support the student's desire for order, neatness and respecting deadlines.

■ Allow the student independence in planning their work in their own way if they really want to.

■ Avoid changing plans just for the sake of it; this will only frustrate the student.

■ Encourage the student to embrace flexibility occasionally – variety is the spice of life.

165
Clownfish teacher with Eagle student
ENFP and ENTJ

Clownfish and Eagles share two preferences. Both are naturally assertive and ingenious. Clashes are most likely when the student's desire to take the lead interferes with the teacher's performance! For the teacher to get the best out of their inherently effusive student they need to:

■ Enjoy the lively banter when it is appropriate to spark new thoughts and ideas; the student learns best this way, but remember there may be thirty others in the classroom.

■ Stick to the point and stay positive (don't nag), as both teacher and student are easily distracted and liable to go off track!

■ Avoid going over old ground.

■ Be calm and clear, otherwise two **E** preferences can talk louder and louder with neither listening.

■ Remember you can keep some thoughts to yourself (and you may think of a better way of expressing something, especially criticism, later).

■ Be an enthusiastic and supportive listener; seek to help the student clarify and develop their thinking rather than assert your own.

■ Help each other learn to be quiet and encourage the **I** preferences in the class to express themselves.

Both teacher and student gather information by seeing the big picture first, using hunches, inferences and imagination to infer meaning. The Clownfish teacher will naturally use their imagination in the classroom and the **N** student will respond well to this, possibly joining in with flights of fancy, anecdotes and stories. A natural affinity between teacher and student is often present because they both look at the world in the same way – with a burning curiosity to understand why things are as they are by exploring patterns, possibilities, ideas and theories. Be careful not to look like you're favouring **N** students to the detriment of **S** students. Every student needs to be able to contribute in their preferred way. For the teacher to get the best out of their naturally imaginative student they need to:

■ Offer questions/projects that can be explored creatively.

■ Avoid repetitive tasks as they'll quickly lose interest.

■ Encourage the student to become aware of the important contribution of the **S** approach (the value of facts, details, procedure, experiments, applying experience, structure, the step-by-step model).

The teacher is concerned with relationship then task whereas the student is the other way round. The teacher must learn to accept that the student is different; not cold, blunt and unfriendly, but simply focused on task first. If the teacher can accept this the relationship can be really positive for both teacher and student. For the teacher to get the best out of their fundamentally assertive student they need to:

■ Offer targeted compliments. Just saying everything is great will not impress or help the student; in fact, it can result in the student losing respect for the teacher, concluding they lie and/or are a soft touch. When you praise you may be pressed for proof!

■ Be logical and objective rather than emotional in discussions.

■ Accept that if the student challenges you it is probably to clarify their thoughts rather than test your authority or besmirch your character. Perhaps ask 'What would you do to improve/change this?' or 'What do you think?' Once they've clarified their thoughts they may be ready to ask and absorb what you think.

■ Help them understand that 50% of people are **F** preference and can interpret feedback as criticism.

■ Work in ways that test their skill and knowledge competitively (they raise their game).

The laid-back, flexible and spontaneous teacher with the naturally organised student can be a dream team or a disaster. To create a positive relationship they need to play to each other's strengths. The student can benefit from the teacher's ability to adapt and change plans and the teacher can benefit from the student's desire to have a plan they can work to and complete. The teacher can also:

■ Encourage and support the student's desire for order, neatness and respecting deadlines.

■ Allow the student independence in planning their work in their own way if they really want to.

■ Encourage the student to embrace flexibility occasionally.

■ Avoid changing plans just for the sake of it; this will only frustrate the student.

166
Clownfish teacher with Falcon student
ENFP and ENTP

Clownfish and Falcons share three preferences and are very similar. They share a fecund imagination and are not afraid to use it! Falcons are often misunderstood as education doesn't suit their natural, domineering, in-your-face style (though drama school does). Clownfish can be the teachers to bring out the best in Falcons. To get the best out of their 'could start an argument in an empty room' Falcon they need to:

- Embrace the lively banter when it is appropriate to spark new thoughts and ideas; the student learns best this way, but remember there may be thirty others in the classroom.

- Stick to the point and stay positive (don't nag), as both teacher and student are easily distracted and liable to go off track!

- Avoid going over old ground (unless it's crucial detail).

- Be calm and clear, otherwise two **E** preferences can talk louder and louder, with neither listening.

- Remember you can keep some thoughts to yourself (and you may think of a better way of expressing something, especially criticism, later).

- Be an enthusiastic and supportive listener; seek to help the student clarify and develop their thinking rather than assert your own.

- Help each other learn to be quiet and encourage the **I** preferences in the class to express themselves.

Both teacher and student gather information by seeing the big picture first, using hunches, inferences and imagination to decipher meaning. The Clownfish teacher will naturally use their imagination in the classroom and the **N** student will respond well to this, possibly joining in with flights of fancy, anecdotes and stories. A natural affinity between teacher and student is often present because they both look at the world in the same way – with a burning curiosity to understand why things are as they are by exploring patterns, possibilities, ideas and theories. Be careful not to look like you're favouring **N** students to the detriment of **S** students. Every student needs to be able to contribute in their preferred way. To get the best out of the naturally imaginative student:

- Offer questions/projects that can be explored creatively.

- Avoid repetitive tasks as they'll quickly lose interest.

- Encourage the student to become aware of the important contribution of the **S** approach (the value of facts, details, procedure, experiments, applying experience, structure, the step-by-step model).

The teacher is concerned with relationship then task whereas the student is the other way round. The teacher must learn to accept that the student is different; not cold, blunt and unfriendly, but simply focused on task first. If the teacher can accept this the relationship can be really positive for both teacher and student. To help the essentially assertive Falcon:

- Offer targeted compliments. Just saying everything is great neither impresses nor helps the student; in fact, it can result in the student losing respect for the teacher, concluding they lie and/or are a soft touch. When you praise you may be pressed for proof!

- Be logical and objective rather than emotional in discussions.

- Accept that if the student challenges you it is probably to clarify their thoughts rather than test your authority or besmirch your character. Perhaps ask 'What would you do to improve/change this?' or 'What do you think?' Once they've clarified their thoughts they may be ready to ask and absorb what you think.

- Work in ways that test their skill and knowledge competitively (they raise their game).

- Help them understand that 50% of people are **F** preference and can interpret feedback as criticism.

P preferences can be organised and efficient; it's just such an effort! While enjoying a mutual love of spontaneity, which provides each with relief from the stifling and constraining timetables and deadlines essential in large organisations such as schools, they must also remember to complete any necessary tasks. Although likely to be fun and popular teachers, they also need to focus on the task of preparing the student to succeed socially and academically. Both prefer to start tasks than finish them. Their initial enthusiasm can quickly wane. Both need to ensure they identify and complete the important tasks or the student (or their parents) may eventually ask awkward questions. For the teacher to get the best out of their naturally laid-back student they need to understand the student doesn't just like options and choice; they are essential or they start to itch, squirm and rebel. The secondary school environment is difficult enough for **P** preference students so teachers can help their student achieve by:

- Providing as much flexibility as possible (multiple choice homework tasks, choice within the lesson).

- Avoiding giving out detailed schedules (they'll just lose it anyway!).

- Shaking things up now and again to prevent predictability becoming boredom. Introduce random surprises and changes.

- Helping the student identify simple time-management strategies to ensure they succeed.

167
Clownfish teacher with Dolphin student
ENFP and ENFJ

Clownfish and Dolphins share three preferences. Both are 'hippies' – interested in education as a way to grow and develop personally. When the student feels nurtured by their teacher they'll respond well. Clashes are likely when chat consumes the time for work or personal grudges are allowed to fester. For the teacher to get the best out of their naturally gregarious student they need to:

- Enjoy the lively banter when it is appropriate to spark new thoughts and ideas; the student learns best this way, but remember there may be thirty others in the classroom.

- Stick to the point and stay positive (don't nag), as both teacher and student are easily distracted and liable to go off track!

- Avoid going over old ground.

- Be calm and clear, otherwise two **E** preferences can talk louder and louder like PMQs (with neither listening).

- Remember you can keep some thoughts to yourself (and you may think of a better way of expressing something, especially criticism, later).

- Be an enthusiastic and supportive listener; seek to help the student clarify and develop their thinking rather than assert your own.

- Help each other learn to be quiet and encourage the **I** preferences in the class to express themselves.

Both teacher and student gather information by seeing the big picture first, using hunches, inferences and imagination to infer meaning. The Clownfish teacher will naturally use their imagination in the classroom and the **N** student will respond well to this, possibly joining in with flights of fancy, anecdotes and stories. A natural affinity between teacher and student is often present because they both look at the world in the same way – with a burning curiosity to understand why things are as they are by exploring patterns, possibilities, ideas and theories. Be careful not to look like you're favouring **N** students to the detriment of **S** students. Every student needs to be able to contribute in their preferred way. For the teacher to get the best out of their inherently imaginative student they need to:

- Offer questions/projects that can be explored creatively.

- Avoid repetitive tasks as they'll quickly lose interest.

- Encourage the student to become aware of the important contribution of the **S** approach (the value of facts, details, procedure, experiments, applying experience, structure, the step-by-step model).

The teacher and student are both concerned first with people and relationships before the task/subject content. They like to form personal relationships with all their students, unless they don't like the student (**F** teachers are more inclined than **T** preference teachers to have their favourites!). Because they operate at an emotional level these teachers are more likely to make promises to students, overstretch themselves and even do work the students should be doing themselves. Teacher and student both enjoy a classroom atmosphere that is warm and friendly. Compliments are likely to go in both directions boosting the confidence of teacher as well as student. The Dolphin needs to feel they like their teacher and that the teacher likes them too. If this happens they'll work harder but if they don't they may switch off completely. This explains why a student can be top of the class one year (with a teacher they like) and show no interest at all in the subject the following year when they change teacher. For the teacher to get the best out of their relationship-focused student they need to:

- Offer learning situations that allow for the use of empathy, collaboration and teamworking.

- Give ample and regular praise and offer tactful support to overcome any blind-spots.

- Motivate by appealing to the strength of your personal belief in the student (don't let me down, I know you can do it, I like you).

The laid-back, flexible and spontaneous teacher with the naturally organised student can be a dream team or a disaster. To create a positive relationship they need to play to each other's strengths. The student can benefit from the teacher's ability to adapt and change plans and the teacher can benefit from the student's desire to have a plan they can work to and complete. The teacher can also:

- Allow the student independence in planning their work in their own way if they really want to.

- Avoid changing plans just for the sake of it; this will only frustrate the student.

- Encourage the student to embrace flexibility occasionally.

■ Encourage and support the student's desire for order, neatness and respecting deadlines.

168
Clownfish teacher with Clownfish student
ENFP and ENFP

Identical types can get along like a house on fire based on their mutual values and habits. Clashes are likely when their zest for life obscures the academic side of education. Their relationship can be like an episode of *Top Gear*, with the reckless, jousting camaraderie becoming nauseous at times. For the teacher to get the best out of their naturally gregarious student they need to:

■ Enjoy the lively banter when it is appropriate to spark new thoughts and ideas; the student learns best this way, but remember there may be thirty others in the classroom.

■ Stick to the point and stay positive (don't nag), as both teacher and student are easily distracted and liable to go off track!

■ Avoid going over old ground.

■ Be calm and clear, otherwise two **E** preferences can talk louder and louder with neither listening.

■ Remember you can keep some thoughts to yourself (and you may think of a better way of expressing something, especially criticism, later).

■ Be an enthusiastic and supportive listener; seek to help the student clarify and develop their thinking rather than assert your own.

■ Help each other learn to be quiet and encourage the **I** preferences in the class to express themselves.

Both teacher and student gather information by seeing the big picture first, using hunches, inferences and imagination to infer meaning. The Clownfish teacher will naturally use their imagination in the classroom and the student will respond well to this, possibly joining in with flights of fancy, anecdotes and stories. A natural affinity between teacher and student is often present because they both look at the world in the same way – with a burning curiosity to understand why things are as they are by exploring patterns, possibilities, ideas and theories. Be careful not to look like you're favouring **N** students to the detriment of **S** students. Every student needs to be able to contribute in their preferred way. For the teacher to get the best out of their inherently imaginative student they need to:

■ Offer questions/projects that can be explored creatively.

■ Avoid repetitive tasks as they'll quickly lose interest.

■ Encourage the student to become aware of the important contribution of the **S** approach (the value of facts, details, procedure, experiments, applying experience, structure, the step-by-step model).

The teacher and student are both concerned with people and relationships before the task/subject content. The teacher likes to form personal relationships with all their students, unless they don't like the student (**F** teachers are

more inclined than **T** preference teachers to have their favourites!). Because they operate at an emotional level these teachers are more likely to make promises to students, overstretch themselves and even do work the students should be doing themselves. Teacher and student both enjoy a warm and friendly classroom atmosphere. Compliments are likely to go in both directions boosting the confidence of teacher as well as student. The Clownfish needs to feel they like their teacher and that the teacher likes them too. If this happens they'll work harder but if not they may switch off completely. This explains why a student can be top of the class one year (with a teacher they like) and show no interest at all in the subject the following year when they change teacher. For the teacher to get the best out of their relationship-focused student they need to:

■ Offer learning situations that allow for the use of empathy, collaboration and teamworking.

■ Give ample and regular praise and offer tactful support to overcome any blind-spots.

■ Motivate by appealing to the strength of your personal belief in the student (don't let me down, I know you can do it, I like you).

Clownfish abhor to-do-lists, schedules and predictability; they rarely reach the status of an acquired taste or a honed skill. While enjoying their mutual love of spontaneity, which provides each with relief from the stifling and constraining timetables and deadlines prevalent in large organisations such as schools, they must also remember to complete any necessary tasks. Although likely to be fun and popular teachers, they also need to focus on the task of preparing the student to succeed socially and academically. Both prefer to start tasks than finish them. Their initial enthusiasm can quickly wane. Both need to ensure they identify and complete the important tasks or the student (or their parents) may eventually ask awkward questions. For the teacher to get the best out of their naturally laid-back student they need to understand the student doesn't just like options and choice; they are essential or they start to itch, squirm and rebel. The secondary school environment is difficult enough for **P** preference students so teachers can help their student achieve by:

■ Providing as much flexibility as possible (multiple choice homework tasks, choice within the lesson).

■ Avoiding giving out detailed schedules (they'll just lose it anyway!).

■ Shaking things up now and again to prevent predictability becoming boredom. Introduce random surprises and changes.

■ Identifying simple ways the student can organise and manage their time to complete important work without a last-minute rush.

169
Clownfish teacher with Polar Bear student
ENFP and ISTJ

Clownfish and Polar Bears share no preferences. However, opposites can be useful to each other because together they cover all bases. The naturally organised and grounded student can keep

the mischievous teacher on track. Clashes are likely when differences in approach are misinterpreted as cold and personal (by the teacher) or unprofessional and roguish (by the student). For the teacher to get the best out of their characteristically serious student they need to:

■ Slow down and be calm and succinct.

■ Leave plenty of time between question and answer; respect the student's need for time to think and reflect before responding.

■ Allow the student time and space to work on their own; don't hover over their head, waiting to pounce.

■ Avoid trying to fix problems immediately or finish their sentences.

■ Avoid placing them in groups/teams where they are the only **I** preference in a sea of **E** preferences (they'll be smothered).

■ Don't be surprised if group work and class discussions are greeted with sighs of disappointment.

■ Provide written praise (not just verbal).

■ Let the student know they can always come and talk to you during breaks or they can write down their questions/issues for you to reply to later.

The imaginative Clownfish teacher can inspire all students, but they do need to respect the need for Polar Bears to be given clear guidelines, structure, facts, details and procedures; otherwise they can flounder. For the teacher to get the best out of their more grounded student they need to:

■ Demonstrate how learning can be applied in the real world.

■ Allow the student opportunities to repeat and practise until satisfied they are competent.

■ Encourage the use of imagination as a useful process and explain how it's not time-wasting.

■ Be careful not to look like you're favouring **N** students to the detriment of **S** students. Every student needs to be able to contribute in their preferred way.

The teacher is concerned with relationship then task whereas the student is the other way round. The teacher must learn to accept that the student is different; not cold, blunt and unfriendly, but simply focused on task first. If the teacher can accept this the relationship can be really positive for both teacher and student. For the teacher to get the best out of their naturally objective Polar Bear they need to:

■ Offer targeted compliments. Just saying everything is great will not impress or help the student; in fact, it can result in the student losing respect for the teacher, concluding they lie and/or are a soft touch. When you praise you may be pressed for proof!

■ Be logical and objective rather than emotional in discussions.

■ Accept that if the student challenges you it is probably to clarify their thoughts rather than test your authority or besmirch your character. Perhaps ask 'What would you do to improve/change this?' or 'What do you think?' Once they've clarified their thoughts they may be ready to ask and absorb what you think.

■ Work in ways that test their skill and knowledge competitively (they raise their game).

■ Help them understand that 50% of people are **F** preference and can interpret feedback as criticism.

The laid-back, flexible and spontaneous teacher with the naturally organised student can be a dream team or a disaster. To create a positive relationship they need to play to each other's strengths. The student can benefit from the teacher's ability to adapt and change plans and the teacher can benefit from the student's desire to have a plan they can work to and complete. The teacher can also:

■ Encourage and support the student's desire for order, neatness and respecting deadlines.

■ Allow the student independence in planning their work in their own way if they really want to.

■ Encourage the student to embrace flexibility occasionally.

■ Avoid changing plans just for the sake of it; this will only frustrate the student.

170
Clownfish teacher with Koala student
ENFP and ISFJ

Clownfish and Koalas share one preference. Both value harmony. This can form the basis of a mutually beneficial relationship. The Clownfish can draw out the hidden strengths of the reticent Koala. The Koala can show their teacher the value of listening, planning and attention to detail. The teacher needs to be careful not to make off-the-cuff personal comments that could hurt the feelings of the Koala. For the teacher to support their naturally reserved student they need to:

■ Slow down and be calm and succinct.

■ Leave plenty of time between question and answer; respect the student's need for time to think and reflect before responding.

■ Allow the student time and space to work on their own; don't hover over their head, waiting to pounce.

■ Avoid trying to fix problems immediately or finish their sentences.

■ Avoid placing them in groups/teams where they are the only **I** preference in a sea of **E** preferences (they'll be smothered).

■ Don't be surprised if group work and class discussions are greeted with sighs of disappointment.

■ Provide written praise (not just verbal).

■ Let the student know they can always come and talk to you later.

The imaginative Clownfish teacher can inspire all students, but they do need to respect the need for around two-thirds of students to be given clear guidelines, structure, facts, details and procedures; otherwise they can flounder. This is especially true of the Koala student. To get the best out of their grounded student they need to:

■ Demonstrate how learning can be applied in the real world.

■ Allow the student opportunities to repeat and practise until satisfied they are competent.

■ Encourage the use of imagination as a useful process and explain how it's not time-wasting.

■ Be careful not to look like you're favouring **N** students to the detriment of **S** students. Every student needs to be able to contribute in their preferred way.

The teacher and student are both concerned with people and relationships before the task/subject content. Clownfish like to form personal relationships with all their students, unless they don't like the student (**F** teachers are more inclined than **T** preference teachers to have their favourites!). Because they operate at an emotional level these teachers are more likely to make promises to students, overstretch themselves and even do work the students should be doing themselves. Teacher and student both enjoy a classroom atmosphere that is warm and friendly. The Koala needs to feel they like their teacher and that the teacher likes them too. If this happens they'll work harder but if not they may switch off completely. This explains why a student can be top of the class one year (with a teacher they like) and show no interest at all in the subject the following year when they change teacher. For the teacher to get the best out of their relationship-focused student they need to:

■ Offer learning situations that allow for the use of empathy, collaboration and teamworking.

■ Give ample and regular praise and offer tactful support to overcome any blind-spots.

■ Motivate by appealing to the strength of your personal belief in the student (don't let me down, I know you can do it, I like you).

The flexible and fidgety teacher with the naturally organised and calm student can be a dream team or a disaster. To create a positive relationship they need to play to each other's strengths. The student can benefit from the teacher's ability to adapt and change plans and the teacher can benefit from the student's desire to have a plan they can work to and complete. The teacher can also:

■ Encourage and support the student's desire for order, neatness and respecting deadlines.

■ Allow the student independence in planning their work in their own way if they really want to.

■ Encourage the student to embrace flexibility occasionally.

■ Avoid changing plans just for the sake of it; this will only frustrate the student.

171
Clownfish teacher with Tiger student
ENFP and ISTP

Clownfish and Tigers share one preference. Neither likes being told what to do and how to do it! Recognising this can prevent classroom clashes. If the Tiger is given choice and flexibility they will normally complete work without fuss or fanfare. For the teacher to get the best out of their naturally independent student they need to:

■ Slow down and be calm and succinct.

■ Leave plenty of time between question and answer; respect the student's need for time to think and reflect before responding.

■ Allow the student time and space to work on their own; don't hover over their head, waiting to pounce.

■ Avoid trying to fix problems immediately or finish their sentences.

■ Avoid placing them in groups/teams where they are the only **I** preference in a sea of **E** preferences (they'll be smothered).

■ Don't be surprised if group work and class discussions are greeted with sighs of disappointment.

■ Provide written praise (not just verbal).

The imaginative Clownfish teacher can inspire all students, but they do need to respect the need for Tigers to be given clear guidelines, structure, facts, details and procedures; otherwise they can struggle. For the teacher to get the best out of their more grounded student they need to:

■ Demonstrate how learning can be applied in the real world.

■ Allow the student opportunities to repeat and practise until satisfied they are competent.

■ Encourage the use of imagination as a useful process and explain how it's not time-wasting.

■ Be careful not to look like you're favouring **N** students to the detriment of **S** students. Every student needs to be able to contribute in their preferred way.

The teacher is concerned with relationship then task whereas the student is the other way round. The teacher must learn to accept that the student is different; not cold, blunt and unfriendly, but simply focused on task first. If the teacher can accept this the relationship can be really positive for both teacher and student. For the teacher to get the best out of their instinctively objective student they need to:

■ Offer targeted compliments. Just saying everything is great will not impress or help the student; in fact, it can result in the student losing respect for the teacher, concluding they lie and/or are a soft touch. When you praise you may be pressed for proof!

■ Be logical and objective rather than emotional in discussions.

■ Accept that if the student challenges you it is probably to clarify their thoughts rather than test your authority or besmirch your character. Perhaps ask 'What would you do to improve/change this?' or 'What do you think?' Once they've clarified their thoughts they may be ready to ask and absorb what you think.

■ Work in ways that test their skill and knowledge competitively (they raise their game).

■ Help them understand that 50% of people are **F** preference and can interpret feedback as criticism.

P preferences can be organised and efficient; it's just such an effort! While enjoying a mutual love of spontaneity, which provides each with relief from the stifling and constraining timetables and deadlines essential in large organisations such as schools, they must also remember to complete any necessary tasks. Although likely to be fun and popular teachers, they also need to focus on the task of preparing the student to succeed socially and academically. Both prefer to start tasks than finish them. Their initial enthusiasm can quickly evaporate. Both need to ensure they identify and complete the important tasks or the student (or their parents) may eventually ask awkward questions. For the teacher to get the best out of their naturally laid-back student they need to understand the student doesn't just like options and choice; they are essential or they start to itch, squirm and rebel. The secondary school environment is difficult enough for **P** preference students so teachers can help their student achieve by:

- Avoiding giving out detailed schedules (they'll just lose it anyway!).
- Shaking things up now and again to prevent predictability becoming boredom. Introduce random surprises and changes.
- Helping the student identify ways they can organise and manage their time to complete important work without a last-minute rush.
- Providing as much flexibility as possible (multiple choice homework tasks, choice within the lesson).

172
Clownfish teacher with Cat student
ENFP and ISFP

Clownfish and Cats share two preferences. Both enjoy a sociable and laid-back classroom. Neither likes being told what to do and how to do it! Recognising this can prevent classroom clashes. If the Cat is given choice and flexibility they will normally complete work with minimal fuss and fanfare. For the teacher to get the best out of their naturally private student they need to:

- Slow down and be calm and succinct.
- Leave plenty of time between question and answer; respect the student's need for time to think and reflect before responding.
- Allow the student time and space to work on their own; don't hover over their head, waiting to pounce.
- Avoid trying to fix problems immediately or finish their sentences.
- Avoid placing them in groups/teams where they are the only **I** preference in a sea of **E** preferences (they'll be smothered).
- Don't be surprised if group work and class discussions are greeted with sighs of disappointment.
- Provide written praise (not just verbal).
- Let the student know they can always come and talk to you alone during breaks or they can write down their questions/issues for you to reply to later.

The imaginative Clownfish teacher can inspire all students, but they do need to respect the need for Cats to be given clear guidelines, structure, facts, details and procedures; otherwise they can flounder. For the teacher to get the best out of their more grounded student they need to:

- Demonstrate how learning can be applied in the real world.
- Allow the student opportunities to repeat and practise until satisfied they are competent.
- Encourage the use of imagination as a useful process and explain how it's not time-wasting.
- Be careful not to look like you're favouring **N** students to the detriment of **S** students. Every student needs to be able to contribute in their preferred way.
- Be clear about what is involved in the tasks you set but offer choice in how the task can be approached.

The teacher and student are both concerned with people and relationships before the task/subject content. Clownfish like to form personal relationships with all their students, unless they don't like the student (**F** teachers are more inclined than **T** preference teachers to have their favourites!). Because they operate at an emotional level these teachers are more likely to make promises to students, overstretch themselves and even do work the students should be doing themselves. Teacher and student both enjoy a classroom atmosphere that is warm and friendly. Compliments are likely to go in both directions boosting the confidence of teacher as well as student. The Cat needs to feel they like their teacher and that the teacher likes them too. If this happens they'll work harder but if not they may switch off. For the teacher to get the best out of their relationship-focused student they need to:

- Offer learning situations that allow for the use of empathy, collaboration and teamworking.
- Give ample and regular praise and offer tactful support to overcome any blind-spots.
- Motivate by appealing to the strength of your personal belief in the student (don't let me down, I know you can do it, I like you).

Clownfish and Cats can be organised and efficient; it's just such an effort! While enjoying a mutual love of spontaneity, which provides each with relief from the stifling and constraining timetables and deadlines essential in large organisations such as schools, they must also remember to complete any necessary tasks. Although likely to be fun and popular teachers, they also need to focus on the task of preparing the student to succeed socially and academically. Both prefer to start tasks than finish them. Their initial enthusiasm can quickly wane. Both need to ensure they identify and complete the important tasks or the student (or their parents) may eventually ask awkward questions. For the teacher to get the best out of their naturally laid-back student they need to understand the student doesn't just like options and choice; they are essential or they start to itch, squirm and rebel. The secondary school environment is difficult enough for **P** preference students so teachers can help their student achieve by:

- Providing as much flexibility as possible (multiple choice homework tasks, choice within the lesson).
- Avoiding supplying detailed schedules (they'll just lose it anyway!).
- Shaking things up now and again to prevent predictability becoming boredom. Introduce random surprises and changes.
- Helping the student identify ways they can organise and manage their time to complete important work without a last-minute rush.

173
Clownfish teacher with Seahorse student
ENFP and INFJ

Clownfish and Seahorses share two preferences. Both use their imagination to empathise with people and both strive for a harmonious classroom environment. Clashes are most likely when the intense and private student fails to connect with the ebullient and open-ended teacher. For

the teacher to get the best out of their naturally reserved student they need to:

- Avoid trying to fix problems immediately or finish their sentences.
- Slow down and be calm and succinct.
- Leave plenty of time between question and answer; respect the student's need for time to think and reflect before responding.
- Allow the student time and space to work on their own; don't hover over their head, waiting to pounce.
- Avoid placing them in groups/teams where they are the only **I** preference in a sea of **E** preferences (they'll be smothered).
- Don't be surprised if group work and class discussions are greeted with sighs of disappointment.
- Provide written praise (not just verbal).
- Let the student know they can always come and talk to you alone during breaks or they can write down their questions/issues for you to reply to later.

Both teacher and student gather information by seeing the big picture first, using hunches, inferences and imagination to infer meaning. The Clownfish teacher will naturally use their imagination in the classroom and the **N** student will respond well to this, possibly joining in with flights of fancy, anecdotes and stories. A natural affinity between teacher and student is often present because they both look at the world in the same way – with a burning curiosity to understand why things are as they are by exploring patterns, possibilities, ideas and theories. Be careful not to look like you're favouring **N** students to the detriment of **S** students. Every student needs to be able to contribute in their preferred way. For the teacher to get the best out of their inherently imaginative student they need to:

- Offer questions/projects that can be explored creatively.
- Avoid repetitive tasks as they'll quickly lose interest.
- Encourage the student to become aware of the important contribution of the **S** approach (the value of facts, details, procedure, experiments, applying experience, structure, the step-by-step model).

The teacher and student are both concerned first with people and relationships before the task/subject content. Clownfish like to form personal relationships with all their students, unless they don't like the student (**F** teachers are more inclined than **T** preference teachers to have their favourites!). Because they operate at an emotional level these teachers are more likely to make promises to students, overstretch themselves and even do work the students should be doing themselves. Teacher and student both enjoy a classroom atmosphere that is warm and friendly. Compliments are likely to go in both directions boosting the confidence of teacher as well as student. The Seahorse needs to feel they like their teacher and that the teacher likes them too. If this happens they'll work harder but if not they may switch off completely. This explains why a student can be top of the class one year (with a teacher they like) and show no interest at all in the subject the following year when they change teacher. For the teacher to get the best out of their relationship-focused student they need to:

- Offer learning situations that allow for the use of empathy, collaboration and teamworking.
- Give ample and regular praise and offer tactful support to overcome any blind-spots.

■ Motivate by appealing to the strength of your personal belief in the student (don't let me down, I know you can do it, I like you).

The laid-back, flexible and spontaneous teacher with the naturally organised student can be a dream team or a disaster. To create a positive relationship they need to play to each other's strengths. The student can benefit from the teacher's ability to adapt and change plans and the teacher can benefit from the student's desire to have a plan they can work to and complete. The teacher can also:

■ Encourage and support the student's desire for order, neatness and respecting deadlines.

■ Encourage the student to embrace flexibility occasionally.

■ Allow the student independence in planning their work in their own way if they really want to.

■ Avoid changing plans just for the sake of it; this will only frustrate the student.

174
Clownfish teacher with Barn Owl student
ENFP and INTJ

Clownfish and Barn Owls share one preference. Both enjoy using their imagination to make sense of the world around them. The warm, exuberant Clownfish contrasts with the strategic, objective Barn Owl and this is the usual source of conflict. For the teacher to get the best out of their naturally introspective student they need to:

■ Leave plenty of time between question and answer; let the student sleep on it so they fully organise their thoughts.

■ Avoid trying to fix problems immediately or finish their sentences.

■ Avoid placing them in groups/teams where they are the only **I** preference in a sea of **E** preferences (they'll be smothered).

■ Don't be surprised if group work and class discussions are greeted with sighs of disappointment.

■ Provide written praise (not just verbal).

■ Slow down and be calm and succinct.

■ Allow the student time and space to work on their own; don't hover over their head, waiting to pounce.

Both teacher and student gather information by seeing the big picture first, using hunches, inferences and imagination to create meaning. The Clownfish teacher will naturally use their imagination in the classroom and the **N** student will respond well to this, possibly joining in with flights of fancy, anecdotes and stories. A natural affinity between teacher and student is often present because they both look at the world in the same way – with a burning curiosity to understand why things are as they are by exploring patterns, possibilities, ideas and theories. Be careful not to look like you're favouring **N** students to the detriment of **S** students. Every student needs to be able to contribute in their preferred way. For the teacher to get the best out of their inherently imaginative student they need to:

■ Offer questions/projects that can be explored creatively.

■ Avoid repetitive tasks as they'll quickly lose interest.

■ Encourage the student to become aware of the important contribution of the **S** approach (the value of facts, details, procedure, experiments, applying experience, structure, the step-by-step model).

The teacher is concerned with relationship then task whereas the student is the other way round. The teacher must learn to accept that the student is different; not cold, blunt and unfriendly, but simply focused on task first. If the teacher can accept this the relationship can be really positive for both teacher and student. To get the best out of their naturally objective student they need to:

■ Offer targeted compliments. Just saying everything is great will not impress or help the student; in fact, it can result in the student losing respect for the teacher, concluding they lie and/or are a soft touch. When you offer praise you may be pressed to provide proof!

■ Work in ways that test their skill and knowledge competitively (they raise their game).

■ Help them understand that 50% of people are **F** preference and can interpret feedback as criticism.

■ Be logical and objective rather than emotional in discussions.

■ Accept that if the student challenges you it is probably to clarify their thoughts rather than test your authority or besmirch your character. Perhaps ask 'What would you do to improve/change this?' or 'What do you think?' Once they've clarified their thoughts they may be ready to ask and absorb what you think.

When the laid-back, flexible and spontaneous teacher meets the naturally organised student they can complement each other or clash spectacularly. To build a positive relationship they need to play to each other's strengths. The student can benefit from the teacher's ability to adapt and change plans and the teacher can benefit from the student's desire to have a plan they can work to and complete. The teacher can also:

■ Encourage and support the student's desire for order, neatness and respecting deadlines.

■ Allow the student independence in planning their work in their own way if they really want to.

■ Avoid changing plans just for the sake of it; this will only frustrate the student.

■ Encourage the student to embrace flexibility now and again.

175
Clownfish teacher with Seal student
ENFP and INFP

Clownfish and Seals share three preferences. Both prefer a harmonious classroom environment. This shared desire can cement a positive relationship. Clashes are most likely when the Seal's need for privacy to think things through is misinterpreted as disinterest in subject or teacher. To get the best out of their naturally reserved student they need to:

■ Leave plenty of time between question and answer; let the student sleep on it so they fully organise their thoughts.

■ Avoid trying to fix problems immediately or finish their sentences.

■ Avoid placing them in groups/teams where they are the only **I** preference in a sea of **E** preferences (they'll be smothered).

■ Don't be surprised if group work and class discussions are greeted with sighs of disappointment.

■ Provide written praise (not just verbal).

■ Slow down and be calm and succinct.

■ Allow the student time and space to work on their own; don't hover over their head, waiting to pounce.

■ Let the student know they can always come and talk to you later.

Both teacher and student gather information by seeing the big picture first, using hunches, inferences and imagination to reap meaning. The Clownfish teacher will naturally use their imagination in the classroom and the **N** student will respond well to this, possibly joining in with flights of fancy, anecdotes and stories. A natural affinity between teacher and student is often present because they both look at the world in the same way – with a burning curiosity to understand why things are as they are by exploring patterns, possibilities, ideas and theories. Be careful not to look like you're favouring **N** students to the detriment of **S** students. Every student needs to be able to contribute in their preferred way. To fully harness the Seal's potential:

■ Offer questions/projects that can be explored creatively.

■ Avoid repetitive tasks as they'll quickly lose interest.

■ Encourage the student to become aware of the important contribution of the **S** approach (the value of facts, details, procedure, experiments, applying experience, structure, the step-by-step model).

Both teacher and student are concerned with people and relationships before the task/subject content. Clownfish like to form personal relationships with all their students, unless they don't like the student (**F** teachers are more inclined than **T** preference teachers to have their favourites!). Because they operate at an emotional level these teachers are more likely to make promises to students, overstretch themselves and even do work the students should be doing themselves. Teacher and student both enjoy a classroom atmosphere that is warm and friendly. Compliments are likely to go in both directions boosting the confidence of teacher as well as student. The Seal needs to feel they like their teacher and that the teacher likes them too. If this happens they'll work harder. To get the best out of their relationship-focused student they should:

■ Offer learning situations that allow for the use of empathy, collaboration and teamworking.

■ Give ample and regular praise and offer tactful support to overcome any blind-spots.

■ Motivate by appealing to the strength of your personal belief in the student (don't let me down, I know you can do it, I like you).

Clownfish and Seals can be organised and efficient; it's just so difficult! While enjoying a mutual love of spontaneity, which provides each with relief from the stifling and constraining timetables and deadlines widespread in large organisations such as schools, they must also remember to complete any necessary tasks. Although likely to be fun and popular teachers, they also need to focus on the task of preparing the student to succeed socially and academically. Both prefer to start tasks than finish them. Their initial enthusiasm can quickly wane. Both need to ensure they identify and complete the important tasks or the student (or their parents) may eventually ask awkward questions. For the teacher to get the best out of their naturally laid-back student they need to understand the student doesn't just like options and choice; they are essential or they start to itch, squirm and rebel. The secondary school environment is difficult enough for **P** preference students so teachers can help their student achieve by:

- Providing as much flexibility as possible (multiple choice homework tasks, choice within the lesson).
- Avoiding giving out detailed schedules (they'll just lose it anyway!).
- Shaking things up now and again to prevent predictability becoming boredom. Introduce random surprises and changes.
- Identifying ways they can organise and manage their work to complete important tasks on time without a last-minute rush.

176
Clownfish teacher with Tawny Owl student
ENFP and INTP

Clownfish and Tawny Owls share two preferences. Both enjoy using their imagination, unfettered by practicality and deadlines. This common interest can cement their relationship. Differences in style – the in-your-face Clownfish and the diffident, introspective Tawny Owl – are usually the source of any conflict in the classroom. For the teacher to get the best out of their naturally reserved student they need to:

- Avoid trying to fix problems immediately or finish their sentences.
- Slow down and be calm and succinct.
- Leave plenty of time between question and answer; respect the student's need for time to think and reflect before responding.
- Allow the student time and space to work on their own; don't hover over their head, waiting to pounce.
- Avoid placing them in groups/teams where they are the only **I** preference in a sea of **E** preferences (they'll be smothered).
- Don't be surprised if group work and class discussions are greeted with sighs of disappointment.
- Provide written praise (not just verbal).
- Let the student know they can always come and talk to you alone during breaks or they can write down their questions/issues for you to reply to later.

Both teacher and student gather information by seeing the big picture first, using hunches, inferences and imagination to infer meaning. The Clownfish teacher will naturally use their imagination in the classroom and the **N** student will respond well to this, possibly joining in with flights of fancy, anecdotes and stories. A natural affinity between teacher and student is often present because they both look at the world in the same way – with a burning curiosity to understand why things are as they are by exploring patterns, possibilities, ideas and theories. Be careful not to look like you're favouring **N** students to the detriment of **S** students. Every student needs to be able to contribute in their preferred way. For the teacher to get the best out of their inherently imaginative student they need to:

- Offer questions/projects that can be explored creatively.
- Avoid repetitive tasks as they'll quickly lose interest.
- Encourage the student to become aware of the important contribution of the **S** approach (the value of facts, details, procedure, experiments, applying experience, structure, the step-by-step model).

The teacher is concerned with relationship then task whereas the student is the other way round. The teacher must learn to accept that the student is different; not cold, blunt and unfriendly, but simply focused on task first. If the teacher can accept this the relationship can be really positive for both teacher and student. To harness the professorial potential of their student they should:

- Offer targeted compliments. Just saying everything is great will not impress or help the student; in fact, it can result in the student losing respect for the teacher, concluding they lie and/or are a soft touch. When you praise you may be pressed for proof!
- Be logical and objective rather than emotional in discussions.
- Work in ways that test their skill and knowledge competitively (they raise their game).
- Help them understand that 50% of people are **F** preference and can interpret feedback as criticism.
- Accept that if the student challenges you it is probably to clarify their thoughts rather than test your authority or besmirch your character. Perhaps ask 'What would you do to improve/change this?' or 'What do you think?' Once they've clarified their thoughts they may be ready to ask and absorb what you think.

P preferences can be organised and efficient; it's just so alien! While enjoying a mutual love of spontaneity, which provides each with relief from the stifling and constraining timetables and deadlines essential in large organisations such as schools, they must also remember to complete any necessary tasks. Although likely to be fun and popular teachers, they also need to focus on the task of preparing the student to succeed socially and academically. Both prefer to start tasks than finish them. Their initial enthusiasm can quickly wane. Both need to ensure they identify and complete the important tasks or the student (or their parents) may eventually ask awkward questions. For the teacher to get the best out of their naturally laid-back student they need to understand the student doesn't just like options and choice; they are essential or they start to itch, squirm and rebel. The secondary school environment is difficult enough for **P** preference students so teachers can help their student achieve by:

- Providing as much flexibility as possible (multiple choice homework tasks, choice within the lesson).

- Avoiding giving out detailed schedules (they'll just lose it anyway!).
- Shaking things up now and again to prevent predictability becoming boredom. Introduce random surprises and changes.
- Helping the student identify time-management strategies to ensure they can complete important work.

177
Dolphin teacher with Dolphin student
ENFJ and ENFJ

Dolphins are naturally confident, warm and friendly. Teacher and student can enjoy each other's desire to create a harmonious classroom environment. Clashes are unlikely but liable to be caused by oversensitivity. For the teacher to get the best out of their naturally effusive student they need to:

- Enjoy the lively banter when it is appropriate to spark new thoughts and ideas; the student learns best this way, but remember there may be thirty others in the classroom.
- Stick to the point and stay positive (don't nag), as both teacher and student are easily distracted and liable to go off track!
- Avoid going over old ground.
- Be calm and clear, otherwise two **E** preferences can talk louder and louder with neither listening.
- Remember you can keep some thoughts to yourself (and you may think of a better way of expressing something, especially criticism, later).
- Be an enthusiastic and supportive listener; seek to help the student clarify and develop their thinking rather than assert your own.
- Help each other learn to be quiet and encourage the **I** preferences in the class to express themselves.

Dolphins gather information by seeing the big picture first, using hunches, inferences and imagination to infer meaning. The teacher will naturally use their imagination in the classroom and the **N** student will respond well to this, possibly joining in with flights of fancy, anecdotes and stories. A natural affinity between teacher and student is often present because they both look at the world in the same way – with a burning curiosity to understand why things are as they are by exploring patterns, possibilities, ideas and theories. Be careful not to look like you're favouring **N** students to the detriment of **S** students. Every student needs to be able to contribute in their preferred way. For the teacher to get the best out of their inherently imaginative student they need to:

- Offer questions/projects that can be explored creatively.
- Avoid repetitive tasks as they'll quickly lose interest.
- Encourage the student to become aware of the important contribution of the **S** approach (the value of facts, details, procedure, experiments, applying experience, structure, the step-by-step model).

Personality in the Classroom

Dolphins are interested in people and relationships before the task/subject content. The teacher likes to form personal relationships with all their students, unless they don't like the student (**F** teachers are more inclined than **T** preference teachers to have their favourites!). Because they operate at an emotional level these teachers are more likely to make promises to students, over-stretch themselves and even do work the students should be doing themselves. Teacher and student both enjoy a classroom atmosphere that is warm and friendly. Compliments are likely to go in both directions boosting the confidence of teacher as well as student. For the teacher to get the best out of their relationship-focused student they need to:

- Offer learning situations that allow for the use of empathy, collaboration and teamworking.
- Give ample and regular praise while offering tactful support to overcome any blind-spots.
- Motivate by appealing to the strength of your personal belief in the student (don't let me down, I know you can do it, I like you).

Dolphins take pleasure in scheduling their time. They are organised and driven to complete. They work out a plan and stick to it, often aided by an impressive to-do list. The classroom is usually an organised place. The subject will probably be broken down into lesson-sized chunks and the whole year planned in detail. Many Dolphin students are reassured by their teacher's insatiable appetite to develop a plan. They simply embrace the schedule and deliver their side of the bargain, generally completing all tasks on time. Interestingly, some **J** preferences will baulk at their teacher's well-intentioned thoroughness. They would like to create their own plan and work to it. This is due to the **J**'s desire for control. So two **J**'s together can clash, though at least all the work will be done. Most secondary schools require students to be so organised that two **J**'s are a welcome combination. For the teacher to get the best out of their characteristically organised student they need to:

- Enjoy your shared desire for order, neatness and respecting deadlines.
- Allow the student independence in planning their work in their own way if they really want to.
- Be prepared to adjust your own plans if external events interfere with your careful preparations (and encourage the student to also embrace flexibility occasionally).
- Shake things up now and again to prevent predictability becoming boredom.
- Avoid making quick decisions about what needs to be done before considering all of the options.

Dolphins and Eagles share three type preferences. Both are naturally organised, confident and assertive which can be the basis of a strong relationship. The most likely source of conflict is the objective approach of the student jarring with the subjective approach of the teacher. For the teacher to get the best out of their naturally voracious student they need to:

- Enjoy the lively banter when it is appropriate to spark new thoughts and ideas; the student learns best this way, but remember there may be thirty others in the classroom.
- Stick to the point and stay positive (don't nag), as both teacher and student are easily distracted and liable to go off track!
- Avoid going over old ground.
- Be calm and clear, otherwise two **E** preferences can talk louder and louder with neither listening.
- Remember you can keep some thoughts to yourself (and you may think of a better way of expressing something, especially criticism, later).
- Be an enthusiastic and supportive listener; seek to help the student clarify and develop their thinking rather than assert your own.
- Help each other learn to be quiet and encourage the **I** preferences in the class to express themselves.

Both teacher and student gather information by seeing the big picture first, using hunches, inferences and imagination to infer meaning. The teacher will naturally use their imagination in the classroom and the **N** student will respond well to this, possibly joining in with flights of fancy, anecdotes and stories. A natural affinity between teacher and student is often present because they both look at the world in the same way – with a burning curiosity to understand why things are as they are by exploring patterns, possibilities, ideas and theories. Be careful not to look like you're favouring **N** students to the detriment of **S** students. Every student needs to be able to contribute in their preferred way. For the teacher to get the best out of their inherently imaginative student they need to:

- Offer questions/projects that can be explored creatively.
- Avoid repetitive tasks as they'll quickly lose interest.
- Encourage the student to become aware of the important contribution of the **S** approach (the value of facts, details, procedure, experiments, applying experience, structure, the step-by-step model).

The teacher is concerned with relationship then task whereas the student is the other way round. The teacher must learn to accept that the student is different; not cold, blunt and unfriendly, but simply focused on task first. If the teacher can accept this the relationship can be really positive for both teacher and student. For the teacher to get the best out of their fundamentally assertive student they need to:

- Offer targeted compliments. Just saying everything is great will not impress or help the student; in fact, it can result in the student not respecting the teacher, concluding they lie and/or are a soft touch. When you praise you may be pressed for proof!
- Help them understand that around 50% of people are **F** preference and can interpret feedback as criticism.
- Be logical and objective rather than emotional in discussions.

- Accept that if the student challenges you it is probably to clarify their thoughts rather than test your authority or character. Perhaps ask 'What would you do to improve/change this?' or 'What do you think?' Once they've clarified their thoughts they may be ready to ask and absorb what you think.
- Work in ways that test their skill and knowledge competitively (they raise their game).

The **J** teacher takes pleasure in scheduling their time. They are organised and driven to complete. They work out a plan and stick to it, often aided by an impressive to-do list. Their classroom is usually an organised place. The subject will probably be broken down into lesson-sized chunks. Many **J** students are reassured by their teacher's insatiable appetite to stick to the plan. They simply embrace the schedule and deliver their side of the bargain, generally completing all tasks on time. Interestingly, some **J** preferences will baulk at their teacher's well-intentioned thoroughness. They would like to create their own plan and work to it rather than adopt their teacher's. This is due to the **J**'s desire for control. So two **J**'s together can clash, though at least all the work will be done. Most secondary schools require students to be so organised that two **J**'s are a welcome combination. For the teacher to get the best out of their naturally organised student they need to:

- Enjoy your shared desire for order, neatness and respecting deadlines.
- Shake things up now and again to prevent predictability becoming boredom.
- Avoid making quick decisions about what needs to be done before considering all of the options.
- Allow the student independence in planning their work in their own way if they really want to.
- Be prepared to adjust your own plans if external events interfere with your careful preparations and encourage the student to also embrace flexibility.

Dolphins and Teddies share three type preferences. Both are sociable and organised. They can be like a pair of hairdressers catching up on each other's weekend when they're relaxed! Providing they avoid too much chat, especially about people, they should work well together. For the teacher to get the best out of their naturally effusive student they need to:

- Enjoy the lively banter when it is appropriate to spark new thoughts and ideas; the student learns best this way, but remember there may be thirty others in the classroom.
- Stick to the point and stay positive (don't nag), as both teacher and student are easily distracted and liable to go off track!
- Avoid going over old ground.

■ Remember you can keep some thoughts to yourself (and you may think of a better way of expressing something, especially criticism, later).

■ Be an enthusiastic and supportive listener; seek to help the student clarify and develop their thinking rather than assert your own.

■ Be calm and clear, otherwise two **E** preferences can talk louder and louder with neither listening.

■ Help each other learn to be quiet and encourage the **I** preferences in the class to express themselves.

The imaginative Dolphin teacher can inspire all students, but they do need to respect the need for Teddies to be given clear guidelines, structure, facts, details and procedures; otherwise they can flounder. For the teacher to get the best out of their grounded student they need to:

■ Demonstrate how learning can be applied in the real world.

■ Allow the student opportunities to repeat and practise until satisfied they are competent.

■ Encourage the use of imagination as a useful process (it's not wasting time).

■ Be careful not to look like you're favouring **N** students to the detriment of **S** students. Every student needs to be able to contribute in their preferred way.

Both teacher and student are interested in people and relationships before the task/subject content. The Dolphin likes to form personal relationships with all their students, unless they don't like the student (**F** teachers are more inclined than **T** preference teachers to have their favourites!). Because they operate at an emotional level these teachers are more likely to make promises to students, overstretch themselves and even do work the students should be doing themselves. Teacher and student both enjoy a classroom atmosphere that is warm and friendly. Compliments are likely to go in both directions boosting the confidence of teacher as well as student. For the teacher to get the best out of their relationship-focused student they need to:

■ Offer learning situations that allow for the use of empathy, collaboration and teamworking.

■ Give ample and regular praise while offering tactful support to overcome any blind-spots.

■ Motivate by appealing to the strength of your personal belief in the student (don't let me down, I know you can do it, I like you).

The **J** teacher takes pleasure in scheduling their time. They are organised and driven to complete. They work out a plan and stick to it, often aided by an impressive to-do list. Their classroom is usually an organised place. The subject will probably be broken down into lesson-sized chunks. Many **J** students are reassured by their teacher's insatiable appetite to stick to the plan. They simply embrace the schedule and deliver their side of the bargain, generally completing all tasks on time. Interestingly, some **J** preferences will baulk at their teacher's well-intentioned thoroughness. They would like to create their own plan and work to it rather than adopt someone else's. This is due to the **J**'s desire for control. So two **J**'s together can clash, though at least all the work will be done. Most secondary schools require students to be so organised that two **J**'s are a welcome combination. For the teacher to get the best out of their characteristically organised student they need to:

■ Enjoy your shared desire for order, neatness and respecting deadlines.

■ Allow the student independence in planning their work in their own way if they really want to.

■ Be prepared to adjust your own plans if external events interfere with your careful preparations (and encourage the student to also embrace flexibility occasionally).

■ Avoid making quick decisions about what needs to be done before considering all of the options.

■ Shake things up now and again to prevent predictability becoming boredom.

180
Dolphin teacher with Black Bear student
ENFJ and ESTJ

Dolphins and Black Bears share two preferences. Both are naturally organised and assertive. Clashes are most likely when the student, a natural leader, attempts to take over the classroom like an Apprentice hopeful in front of a bewildered and crumple-faced Lord Sugar. For the teacher to get the best out of their naturally determined student they need to:

■ Enjoy the lively banter when it is appropriate to spark new thoughts and ideas; the student learns best this way, but remember there may be thirty others in the classroom.

■ Stick to the point and stay positive (don't nag), as both teacher and student are easily distracted and liable to go off track!

■ Be calm and clear, otherwise two **E** preferences can talk louder and louder.

■ Be an enthusiastic and supportive listener; seek to help the student clarify and develop their thinking rather than assert your own.

■ Help each other learn to be quiet and encourage the **I** preferences in the class to express themselves.

The imaginative Dolphin teacher can inspire all students, but they do need to respect the need for Black Bears to be given clear guidelines, structure, facts, details and procedures; otherwise they can flounder. For the teacher to get the best out of their grounded student they need to:

■ Demonstrate how learning can be applied in the real world.

■ Allow the student opportunities to repeat and practise until satisfied they are competent.

■ Encourage the use of imagination as a useful process (it's not wasting time).

■ Be careful not to look like you're favouring **N** students to the detriment of **S** students. Every student needs to be able to contribute in their preferred way.

The teacher is concerned with relationship then task whereas the student is the other way round. The teacher must learn to accept that the student is different; not cold, blunt and unfriendly, but simply focused on task first. If the teacher can accept this the relationship can be really positive for both teacher and student. For the teacher to get the best out of their fundamentally assertive Bear student they need to:

■ Offer targeted compliments. Just saying everything is great will not impress or help the student; in fact, it can result in the student not respecting the teacher, concluding they lie and/or are a soft touch. When you praise you may be pressed for proof!

■ Be logical and objective rather than emotional in discussions.

■ Accept that if the student challenges you it is probably to clarify their thoughts rather than meant as a slight to your authority or character. Perhaps ask 'What would you do to improve/change this?' or 'What do you think?' Once they've clarified their thoughts they may be ready to ask and absorb what you think.

■ Help them understand that around 50% of people are **F** preference and can interpret feedback as criticism.

■ Work in ways that test their skill and knowledge competitively (they raise their game).

The **J** teacher takes pleasure in scheduling their time. They are organised and driven to complete. They work out a plan and stick to it, often aided by an impressive to-do list. Their classroom is usually an organised place. The subject will probably be broken down into lesson-sized chunks. Many **J** students are reassured by their teacher's insatiable appetite to stick to the plan. They simply embrace the schedule and deliver their side of the bargain, generally completing all tasks on time. Interestingly, some **J** preferences will baulk at their teacher's well-intentioned thoroughness. They would like to create their own plan and work to it rather than adopt someone else's. This is due to the **J**'s desire for control. So two **J**'s together can clash, though at least all the work will be done. Most secondary schools require students to be so organised that two **J**'s are a welcome combination. For the teacher to get the best out of their naturally organised student they need to:

■ Enjoy your shared desire for order, neatness and respecting deadlines.

■ Allow the student independence in planning their work in their own way if they really want to.

■ Be prepared to adjust your own plans if external events interfere with your careful preparations (and encourage the student to also embrace flexibility occasionally).

■ Shake things up now and again to prevent predictability becoming boredom.

■ Avoid making quick decisions about what needs to be done before considering all of the possibilities.

181
Dolphin teacher with Panther student
ENFJ and ESTP

Dolphins and Panthers share one type preference. Both are sociable. Clashes are most likely when the teacher is unable to channel the student's natural hyperactivity. To get the best out of their naturally energetic student they need to:

- Enjoy the lively banter when it is appropriate to spark new thoughts and ideas; the student learns best this way, but remember there may be thirty others in the classroom.
- Stick to the point and stay positive (don't nag), as both teacher and student are easily distracted and liable to go off track!
- Avoid going over old ground.
- Be calm and clear, otherwise two **E** preferences can talk louder and louder like PMQs (with neither listening).
- Remember you can keep some thoughts to yourself (and you may think of a better way of expressing something, especially criticism, later).
- Be an enthusiastic and supportive listener; seek to help the student clarify and develop their thinking rather than assert your own.
- Help each other learn to be quiet and encourage the **I** preferences in the class to express themselves.

The imaginative teacher can inspire all students, but they do need to respect the need for Panthers to be given clear guidelines, structure, facts, details and procedures; otherwise they can flounder. For the teacher to get the best out of their grounded student they need to:

- Demonstrate how learning can be applied in the real world.
- Allow the fidgety student opportunities to repeat and practise until satisfied they are competent.
- Encourage the use of imagination as a useful process.
- Be careful not to look like you're favouring **N** students to the detriment of **S** students. Every student needs to be able to contribute in their preferred way.

The teacher is concerned with relationship then task whereas the student is the other way round. The teacher must learn to accept that the student is different; not cold, blunt and unfriendly, but simply focused on task first. If the teacher can accept this the relationship can be really positive for both teacher and student. For the teacher to get the best out of their insatiable student they need to:

- Offer targeted compliments. Just saying everything is great will not impress or help the student; in fact, it can result in the student not respecting the teacher, concluding they lie and/or are a soft touch. When you praise you may be pressed for proof!
- Be logical and objective rather than emotional in discussions.
- Work in ways that test their skill and knowledge competitively (they raise their game).
- Help them understand that around 50% of people are **F** preference and can interpret feedback as criticism.
- Accept that if the student challenges you it is probably to clarify their thoughts rather than meant as a slight to your authority or character. Perhaps ask 'What would you do to improve/change this?' or 'What do you think?' Once they've clarified their thoughts they may be ready to ask and absorb what you think.

The Dolphin teacher takes pleasure in scheduling their time. They are organised and decisive. They work out a plan and stick to it, often aided by an impressive to-do list. Their classroom is usually an organised place. The subject will probably be broken down into lesson-sized chunks and the

year planned out whether or not an Ofsted inspector is due. The **P** student will either respond:

- Positively by accepting your expertise and understanding the long-term benefits they'll reap.
- Passively by just accepting your structure/plan for an easy life without really buying into the content or process you are offering.
- Negatively by rejecting you, your structure/plan and subject completely (even if they're physically in your room they will not engage and participate).

For the teacher to get the best out of their naturally laid-back student they should note the student doesn't just like options and choice; they need them or they start to itch, squirm and rebel. The secondary school environment is tough for many **P** preference students. Teachers can soften the pressure by:

- Providing as much flexibility as possible (multiple choice homework tasks, choice within the lesson).
- Resisting the temptation to burden the student with detailed schedules.
- Not being more picky with detail than is absolutely necessary.
- Introducing random surprises and changes; Panthers thrive on unpredictability.

182
Dolphin teacher with Lion student
ENFJ and ESFP

Dolphins and Lions share two type preferences – both exuding energy and warmth. Clashes are likely if the teacher fails to direct the 'party animal' Lion towards the task at hand. For the teacher to get the best out of their naturally effusive student they need to:

- Enjoy the lively banter when it is appropriate to spark new thoughts and ideas; the student learns best this way, but remember there may be thirty others in the classroom.
- Remember you can keep some thoughts to yourself (and you may think of a better way of expressing something, especially criticism, later).
- Be an enthusiastic and supportive listener; seek to help the student clarify and develop their thinking rather than assert your own.
- Stick to the point and stay positive (don't nag), as both teacher and student are easily distracted and liable to go off track!
- Stay calm and clear, otherwise two **E** preferences can talk louder and louder with neither listening.
- Help each other learn to be quiet and encourage the **I** preferences in the class to express themselves.

The imaginative Dolphin teacher can inspire all students, but they do need to respect the need for around 65% of students to be given clear guidelines, structure, facts, details and procedures; otherwise they can flounder. For the teacher to get the best out of their grounded student they need to:

- Demonstrate how learning can be applied in the real world.
- Allow the student opportunities to repeat and practise until satisfied they are competent.
- Encourage the use of imagination as a useful process (it's not wasting time).
- Be careful not to look like you're favouring **N** students to the detriment of **S** students. Every student needs to be able to contribute in their preferred way.

Both teacher and student are interested in people and relationships before the task/subject content. The teacher likes to form personal relationships with all their students, unless they don't like the student (**F** teachers are more inclined than **T** preference teachers to have their favourites!). Because they operate at an emotional level these teachers are more likely to make promises to students, overstretch themselves and even do work the students should be doing themselves. Teacher and student both enjoy a classroom atmosphere that is warm and friendly. Compliments are likely to go in both directions boosting the confidence of teacher as well as student. For the teacher to get the best out of their relationship-focused student they need to:

- Offer learning situations that allow for the use of empathy, collaboration and teamworking.
- Give ample and regular praise while offering tactful support to overcome any blind-spots.
- Motivate by appealing to the strength of your personal belief in the student (don't let me down, I know you can do it, I like you).

The **J** teacher takes pleasure in scheduling their time. They are organised and decisive. They work out a plan and stick to it, often aided by an impressive to-do list. Their classroom is usually an organised place. The subject will probably be broken down into lesson-sized chunks and the year planned out whether or not an Ofsted inspector is due. The **P** student will either respond:

- Positively by accepting your expertise and understanding the long-term benefits they'll reap.
- Passively by just accepting your structure/plan for an easy life without really buying into the content or process you are offering.
- Negatively by rejecting you, your structure/plan and subject completely (even if they're physically in your room they will not engage and participate).

For the teacher to get the best out of their naturally laid-back student they should note the student doesn't just like options and choice; they need them or they start to itch, squirm and rebel. The secondary school environment is tough for many **P** preference students. Teachers can help soften the pressure by:

- Providing as much flexibility as possible (multiple choice homework tasks, choice within the lesson).
- Resisting the temptation to burden the student with detailed schedules.
- Not being more picky with detail than is absolutely necessary.
- Shaking things up now and again to prevent predictability becoming boredom. Introduce random surprises and changes.
- Helping the student identify ways they can organise and manage their time to complete important work without a last-minute panic.

183
Dolphin teacher with Clownfish student
ENFJ and ENFP

Dolphins and Clownfish share three type preferences. Both are naturally sociable and imaginative. If the Dolphin indulges the student's need for positive attention they can channel their energy towards task completion. To get the best out of their inherently effusive student they need to:

- Enjoy the lively banter when it is appropriate to spark new thoughts and ideas; the student learns best this way, but remember there may be thirty others in the classroom.
- Remember you can keep some thoughts to yourself (and you may think of a better way of expressing something, especially criticism, later).
- Be an enthusiastic and supportive listener; seek to help the student clarify and develop their thinking rather than assert your own.
- Stick to the point and stay positive, as both teacher and student are easily distracted and liable to go off track!
- Avoid going over old ground.
- Be calm and clear, otherwise two **E** preferences can talk louder and louder with neither listening.
- Help each other learn to be quiet and encourage the **I** preferences in the class to express themselves.

Both teacher and student gather information by seeing the big picture first, using hunches, inferences and imagination to infer meaning. The teacher will naturally use their imagination in the classroom and the **N** student will respond well to this, possibly joining in with flights of fancy, anecdotes and stories. A natural affinity between teacher and student is often present because they both look at the world in the same way – with a burning curiosity to understand why things are as they are by exploring patterns, possibilities, ideas and theories. Be careful not to look like you're favouring **N** students to the detriment of **S** students. Every student needs to be able to contribute in their preferred way. For the teacher to get the best out of their naturally imaginative student they need to:

- Offer questions/projects that can be explored creatively.
- Avoid repetitive tasks as they'll quickly lose interest.
- Encourage the student to become aware of the important contribution of the **S** approach (the value of facts, details, procedure, experiments, applying experience, structure, the step-by-step model).

Both teacher and student are interested in people and relationships before the task/subject content. The Dolphin teacher likes to form personal relationships with all their students, unless they don't like the student (**F** teachers are more inclined than **T** preference teachers to have their favourites!). Because they operate at an emotional level these teachers are more likely to make promises to students, overstretch themselves and even do work the students should be doing themselves. Teacher and student both enjoy a classroom atmosphere that is warm and friendly.

Compliments are likely to go in both directions boosting the confidence of teacher as well as student. For the teacher to get the best out of their relationship-focused student they need to:

- Offer learning situations that allow for the use of empathy, collaboration and teamworking.
- Give ample and regular praise while offering tactful support to overcome any blind-spots.
- Motivate by appealing to the strength of your personal belief in the student (don't let me down, I know you can do it, I like you).

The **J** teacher takes pleasure in scheduling their time. They are organised and decisive. They work out a plan and stick to it, often aided by an impressive to-do list. Their classroom is usually an organised place. The subject will probably be broken down into lesson-sized chunks and the year planned out whether an Ofsted inspector is due or not. The **P** student will either respond:

- Positively by accepting your expertise and understanding the long-term benefits they'll reap.
- Passively by just accepting your structure/plan for an easy life without really buying into the content or process you are offering.
- Negatively by rejecting you, your structure/plan and subject completely (even if they're physically in your room they will not engage and participate).

For the teacher to get the best out of their naturally laid-back student they should note the student doesn't just like options and choice; they need them or they start to itch, squirm and rebel. The secondary school environment is tough for many **P** preference students. Teachers can help soften the pressure by:

- Providing as much flexibility as possible (multiple choice homework tasks, choice within the lesson).
- Resisting the temptation to burden the student with detailed schedules.
- Not being more picky with detail than is absolutely necessary!
- Shaking things up now and again to prevent predictability becoming boredom. Introduce random surprises and changes.
- Helping the student identify ways they can organise and manage their time to complete important work without a last-minute rush.

184
Dolphin teacher with Falcon student
ENFJ and ENTP

Dolphins and Falcons share two type preferences. Both are like fireworks spraying ideas and words everywhere. Their active and urgent style can bind them together. The potentially tactless contributions and scattergun approach of the student are the most likely causes of conflict. For the teacher to get the best out of their naturally effusive student they need to:

- Remember you can keep some thoughts to yourself (and you may think of a better way of expressing something, especially criticism, later).

- Be an enthusiastic and supportive listener; seek to help the student clarify and develop their thinking rather than assert your own.
- Help each other learn to be quiet and encourage the **I** preferences in the class to express themselves.
- Enjoy the lively banter when it is appropriate to spark new thoughts and ideas; the student learns best this way, but remember there may be thirty others in the classroom.
- Stick to the point and stay positive (don't nag), as both teacher and student are easily distracted and liable to go off track!
- Avoid going over old ground.
- Be calm and clear, otherwise two **E** preferences can talk louder and louder with neither listening.

Both teacher and student gather information by seeing the big picture first, using hunches, inferences and imagination to infer meaning. The teacher will naturally use their imagination in the classroom and the **N** student will respond well to this, possibly joining in with flights of fancy, anecdotes and stories. A natural affinity between teacher and student is often present because they both look at the world in the same way – with a burning curiosity to understand why things are as they are by exploring patterns, possibilities, ideas and theories. Be careful not to look like you're favouring **N** students to the detriment of **S** students. Every student needs to be able to contribute in their preferred way. For the teacher to get the best out of their inherently imaginative student they need to:

- Offer questions/projects that can be explored creatively.
- Avoid repetitive tasks as they'll quickly lose interest.
- Encourage the student to become aware of the important contribution of the **S** approach (the value of facts, details, procedure, experiments, applying experience, structure, the step-by-step model).

The teacher is concerned with relationship then task whereas the student is the other way round. The teacher must learn to accept that the student is different; not cold, blunt and unfriendly, but simply focused on task first. If the teacher can accept this the relationship can be really positive for both teacher and student. For the teacher to get the best out of their characteristically assertive student they need to:

- Offer targeted compliments. Just saying everything is great will not impress or help the student; in fact, it can result in the student not respecting the teacher, concluding they lie and/or are a soft touch. When you praise you may be pressed for proof!
- Work in ways that test their skill and knowledge competitively (they raise their game).
- Help them understand that around 50% of people are **F** preference and can interpret feedback as criticism.
- Accept that if the student challenges you it is probably to clarify their thoughts rather than meant as a slight to your authority or character. Perhaps ask 'What would you do to improve/change this?' or 'What do you think?' Once they've clarified their thoughts they may be ready to ask and absorb what you think.
- Be logical and objective rather than emotional in discussions.

The **J** teacher takes pleasure in scheduling their time. They are organised and decisive. They work out a plan and stick to it, often aided by an impressive to-do list. Their classroom is usually an organised place. The subject will probably be broken down into lesson-sized chunks and the year planned out whether or not an Ofsted inspector is due. The **P** student will either respond:

- Positively by accepting your expertise and understanding the long-term benefits they'll reap.
- Passively by just accepting your structure/plan for an easy life without really buying into the content or process you are offering.
- Negatively by rejecting you, your structure/plan and subject completely (even if they're physically in your room they will not engage and participate).

For the teacher to get the best out of their naturally laid-back student they should note the student doesn't just like options and choice; they need them or they start to squirm, wriggle and rebel. The secondary school environment is tough for many **P** preference students. Teachers can help soften the pressure by:

- Providing as much flexibility as possible (multiple choice homework tasks, choice within the lesson).
- Resisting the temptation to burden the student with detailed schedules.
- Not being more picky with detail than is absolutely necessary.
- Shaking things up now and again to prevent predictability becoming boredom. Introduce random surprises and changes.
- Helping the student identify simple time-management strategies to ensure they can shine.

185
Dolphin teacher with Tiger student
ENFJ and ISTP

Dolphins and Tigers share no type preferences. Opposites can help each other grow or become entrenched in their conflicting approaches. The independent Tiger can feel smothered by the warm and attentive Dolphin teacher. When the teacher liberates the student through action-orientated and autonomous activities they will usually shine. To reach their naturally reserved student teachers should:

- Slow down and be calm and succinct.
- Leave plenty of time between question and answer; respect the student's need for time to think and reflect before responding.
- Allow the student time and space to work on their own; don't hover over their head, waiting to pounce.
- Avoid trying to fix problems immediately or finish their sentences.
- Avoid placing them in groups/teams where they are the only **I** preference in a sea of **E** preferences (they'll be smothered).
- Provide written praise (not just verbal).

The imaginative Dolphin teacher can inspire all students, but they do need to respect the need for Tigers to be given clear guidelines, structure, facts, details and procedures; otherwise they can struggle. For the teacher to get the best out of their grounded student they need to:

- Demonstrate how learning can be applied in the real world.
- Allow the student opportunities to repeat and practise until satisfied they are competent.
- Encourage the use of imagination as a useful process (it's not wasting time).
- Be careful not to look like you're favouring **N** students to the detriment of **S** students. Every student needs to be able to contribute in their preferred way.

The teacher is concerned with relationship then task whereas the student is the other way round. The teacher must learn to accept that the student is different; not cold, blunt and unfriendly, but simply focused on task first. If the teacher can accept this the relationship can be really positive for both teacher and student. For the teacher to get the best out of their fundamentally objective Tiger they need to:

- Offer targeted compliments. Just saying everything is great will not impress or help the student; in fact, it can result in the student not respecting the teacher, concluding they lie and/or are a soft touch. When you praise you may be pressed for proof!
- Be logical and objective rather than emotional in discussions.
- Accept that if the student challenges you it is probably to clarify their thoughts rather than meant as a slight to your authority or character. Perhaps ask 'What would you do to improve/change this?' or 'What do you think?' Once they've clarified their thoughts they may be ready to ask and absorb what you think.
- Work in ways that test their skill and knowledge competitively (they raise their game).
- Help them understand that around 50% of people are **F** preference and can interpret feedback as criticism.

The **J** teacher takes pleasure in scheduling their time. They are organised and decisive. They work out a plan and stick to it, often aided by an impressive to-do list. Their classroom is usually an organised place. The subject will probably be broken down into lesson-sized chunks and the year planned out whether an Ofsted inspector is due or not. The **P** student will either respond:

- Positively by accepting your expertise and understanding the long-term benefits they'll reap.
- Passively by just accepting your structure/plan for an easy life without really buying into the content or process you are offering.
- Negatively by rejecting you, your structure/plan and subject completely (even if they're physically in your room they will not engage and participate).

For the teacher to get the best out of their naturally laid-back student they should note the student doesn't just like options and choice; they need them or they start to itch, squirm and rebel. The secondary school environment is tough for many **P** preference students. Teachers can help soften the pressure by:

- Providing as much flexibility as possible (multiple choice homework tasks, choice within the lesson).

- Resisting the temptation to burden the student with detailed schedules.
- Not being more picky with detail than is absolutely necessary.
- Shaking things up now and again to prevent predictability becoming boredom.
- Introducing random surprises and changes to appeal to the Tiger's fondness for action.

186
Dolphin teacher with Cat student
ENFJ and ISFP

Dolphins and Cats share one type preference. Both like to work in a friendly atmosphere. The independent Cat may feel smothered by the attentive Dolphin teacher. When the teacher liberates the student through action-orientated and autonomous activities they will generally thrive. For the teacher to get the best out of their naturally reserved student they need to:

- Slow down and be calm and succinct.
- Leave plenty of time between question and answer; respect the student's need for time to think and reflect before responding.
- Allow the student time and space to work on their own; don't hover over their head, waiting to pounce.
- Avoid trying to fix problems immediately or finish their sentences.
- Pair them up with complementary types (Seahorses, Seals and Koalas).
- Avoid placing them in groups/teams where they are the only **I** preference in a sea of **E** preferences (they'll be smothered).
- Provide written praise (not just verbal).

The imaginative teacher can inspire all students, but they do need to respect the need for Cats to be given clear guidelines, structure, facts, details and procedures; otherwise they can stumble. For the teacher to get the best out of their grounded student they need to:

- Demonstrate how learning can be applied in the real world.
- Allow the student opportunities to repeat and practise until satisfied they are competent.
- Encourage the use of imagination as a useful process (it's not wasting time).
- Be careful not to look like you're favouring **N** students to the detriment of **S** students. Every student needs to be able to contribute in their preferred way.

Both teacher and student are interested in people and relationships before the task/subject content. The Dolphin teacher likes to form personal relationships with all their students, unless they don't like the student (**F** teachers are more inclined than **T** preference teachers to have their favourites!). Because they operate at an emotional level these teachers are more likely to make promises to students, overstretch themselves and even do work the students should be doing themselves. Teacher and student both enjoy a classroom atmosphere that is warm and friendly. Compliments are likely to go in both directions boosting the confidence of teacher as well as student. For the teacher to get the best out of their relationship-focused student they need to:

◼ Offer learning situations that allow for the use of empathy, collaboration and teamworking.

◼ Give ample and regular praise while offering tactful support to overcome any blind-spots.

◼ Motivate by appealing to the strength of your personal belief in the student (don't let me down, I know you can do it, I like you).

The **J** teacher takes pleasure in scheduling their time. They are organised and decisive. They work out a plan and stick to it, often aided by an impressive to-do list. Their classroom is usually an organised place. The subject will probably be broken down into lesson-sized chunks and the year planned out whether an Ofsted inspector is due or not. The **P** student will either respond:

◼ Positively by accepting your expertise and understanding the long-term benefits they'll reap.

◼ Passively by just accepting your structure/plan for an easy life without really buying into the content or process you are offering.

◼ Negatively by rejecting you, your structure/ plan and subject completely (even if they're physically in your room they will not engage and participate).

For the teacher to get the best out of their naturally laid-back student they should note the student doesn't just like options and choice; they need them or they start to itch, squirm and rebel. The secondary school environment is tough for many **P** preference students. Teachers can help soften the pressure by:

◼ Providing as much flexibility as possible (multiple choice homework tasks, choice within the lesson).

◼ Resisting the temptation to burden the student with detailed schedules.

◼ Not being more picky with detail than is absolutely necessary.

◼ Introducing random surprises and changes to prevent predictability becoming boredom.

◼ Helping the student identify simple time-management strategies to ensure they can succeed academically.

187
Dolphin teacher with Seal student
ENFJ and INFP

Dolphins and Seals share two type preferences. Both bring warmth and imagination into the classroom. Seals are daydreamers and the teacher needs to channel this creativity towards task completion for success. To reach their naturally introspective student they should:

◼ Slow down and be calm and succinct.

◼ Leave plenty of time between question and answer; respect the student's need for time to think and reflect before responding.

◼ Allow the student time and space to work on their own; don't hover over their head, waiting to pounce.

◼ Avoid trying to fix problems immediately or finish their sentences.

◼ Avoid placing them in groups/teams where they are the only **I** preference in a sea of **E** preferences (they'll be smothered).

◼ Provide written praise (not just verbal).

Sea Animals gather information by seeing the big picture first, using hunches, inferences and imagination to deduce meaning. The teacher will naturally use their mind's eye in the classroom and the **N** student will respond well to this, possibly joining in with flights of fancy, anecdotes and stories. A natural affinity between teacher and student is often present because they both look at the world in the same way – with a burning curiosity to understand why things are as they are by exploring patterns, possibilities, ideas and theories. Be careful not to look like you're favouring **N** students to the detriment of **S** students. Every student needs to be able to contribute in their preferred way. For the teacher to get the best out of their inherently imaginative student they need to:

◼ Offer questions/projects that can be explored creatively.

◼ Avoid repetitive tasks as they'll quickly lose interest.

◼ Encourage the student to become aware of the important contribution of the **S** approach (the value of facts, details, procedure, experiments, applying experience, structure, the step-by-step model).

Both teacher and student are interested in people and relationships before the task/subject content. The teacher likes to form personal relationships with all their students, unless they don't like the student (**F** teachers are more inclined than **T** preference teachers to have their favourites!). Because they operate at an emotional level these teachers are more likely to make promises to students, overstretch themselves and even do work the students should be doing themselves. Teacher and student both enjoy a classroom atmosphere that is warm and friendly. Compliments are likely to go in both directions boosting the confidence of teacher as well as student. For the teacher to get the best out of their relationship-focused student they need to:

◼ Offer learning situations that allow for the use of empathy, collaboration and teamworking.

◼ Give ample and regular praise while offering tactful support to overcome any blind-spots.

◼ Motivate by appealing to the strength of your personal belief in the student (don't let me down, I know you can do it, I like you).

The Dolphin teacher takes pleasure in scheduling their time. They are organised and decisive. They work out a plan and stick to it, often aided by an impressive to-do list. Their classroom is usually an organised place. The subject will probably be broken down into lesson-sized chunks and the year planned out whether or not an Ofsted inspector is due. The **P** student will either respond:

◼ Positively by accepting your expertise and understanding the long-term benefits they'll reap.

◼ Passively by just accepting your structure/plan for an easy life without really buying into the content or process you are offering.

◼ Negatively by rejecting you, your structure/ plan and subject completely (even if they're physically in your room they will not engage and participate).

For the teacher to get the best out of their naturally laid-back student they should note the student doesn't just like options and choice; they need them or they start to itch, squirm and rebel.

The secondary school environment is tough for many **P** preference students. Teachers can help soften the pressure by:

◼ Providing as much flexibility as possible (multiple choice homework tasks, choice within the lesson).

◼ Resisting the temptation to burden the student with detailed schedules.

◼ Not being more picky with detail than is absolutely necessary.

◼ Introducing random surprises and changes to prevent predictability becoming boredom.

188
Dolphin teacher with Tawny Owl student
ENFJ and INTP

Dolphins and Tawny Owls share one type preference. Both use their imagination to make sense of the world. The warm and attentive teacher needs to allow the Owl space and time to think things through in their own way to bring out the best in their student. They can also:

◼ Slow down and be calm and succinct.

◼ Leave plenty of time between question and answer; respect the student's need for time to think and reflect before responding.

◼ Allow the student time and space to work on their own; don't hover over their head, waiting to pounce.

◼ Avoid trying to fix problems immediately or finish their sentences.

◼ Pair them up with complementary Owl types.

◼ Avoid placing them in groups/teams where they are the only **I** preference in a sea of **E** preferences (they'll be smothered).

◼ Provide written praise (not just verbal).

Both teacher and student gather information by seeing the big picture first, using hunches, inferences and imagination to infer meaning. The teacher will naturally use their imagination in the classroom and the **N** student will respond well to this, possibly joining in with flights of fancy, anecdotes and stories. A natural affinity between teacher and student is often present because they both look at the world in the same way – with a burning curiosity to understand why things are as they are by exploring patterns, possibilities, ideas and theories. Be careful not to look like you're favouring **N** students to the detriment of **S** students. Every student needs to be able to contribute in their preferred way. For the teacher to get the best out of their naturally imaginative student they need to:

◼ Offer questions/projects that can be explored creatively.

◼ Avoid repetitive tasks as they'll quickly lose interest.

◼ Encourage the student to become aware of the important contribution of the **S** approach (the value of facts, details, procedure, experiments, applying experience, structure, the step-by-step model).

The Dolphin teacher is concerned with relationship then task whereas the student is the other way round. The teacher must learn to accept that the student is different; not cold, blunt and un-friendly, but simply focused on task first. If the teacher can accept this the relationship can be really positive for both teacher and student. For the teacher to get the best out of their instinctively analytical student they need to:

■ Offer targeted compliments. Just saying everything is great will not impress or help the student; in fact, it can result in the student not respecting the teacher, concluding they lie and/or are a soft touch. When you praise you may be pressed for proof!

■ Be logical and objective rather than emotional in discussions.

■ Accept that if the student challenges you it is probably to clarify their thoughts rather than meant as a slight to your authority or character. Perhaps ask 'What would you do to improve/change this?' or 'What do you think?' Once they've clarified their thoughts they may be ready to ask and absorb what you think.

■ Work in ways that test their skill and knowledge competitively (they raise their game).

■ Help them appreciate that around 50% of people are **F** preference and can interpret feedback as criticism.

The Dolphin teacher takes pleasure in scheduling their time. They are organised and decisive. They work out a plan and stick to it, often aided by an impressive to-do list. Their classroom is usually an organised place. The subject will probably be broken down into lesson-sized chunks and the year planned out in great detail. The **P** student will either respond:

■ Positively by accepting your expertise and understanding the long-term benefits they'll reap.

■ Passively by just accepting your structure/plan for an easy life without really buying into the content or process you are offering.

■ Negatively by rejecting you, your structure/plan and subject completely (even if they're physically in your room they will not engage and participate).

For the teacher to get the best out of their naturally laid-back student they should note the student doesn't just like options and choice; they need them or they start to itch, squirm and rebel. The secondary school environment is tough for many **P** preference students. Teachers can help soften the pressure by:

■ Providing as much flexibility as possible (multiple choice homework tasks, choice within the lesson).

■ Resisting the temptation to burden the student with detailed schedules.

■ Not being more picky with detail than is absolutely necessary.

■ Shaking things up now and again to prevent predictability becoming boredom.

■ Introducing random surprises and changes to engage the insatiable curiosity of the Tawny Owl.

189
Dolphin teacher with Polar Bear student
ENFJ and ISTJ

Dolphins and Polar Bears share one type preference. Both are naturally organised. For the teacher to get the best out of their student they need to respect their need to apply logic, objectivity and reflection to learn. The teacher can also:

■ Slow down and be calm and succinct.

■ Leave plenty of time between question and answer; respect the student's need for time to think and reflect before responding.

■ Allow the student time and space to work on their own; don't hover over their head, waiting to pounce.

■ Avoid trying to fix problems immediately or finish their sentences.

■ Avoid placing them in groups/teams where they are the only **I** preference in a sea of **E** preferences (they'll be smothered).

■ Provide written praise (not just verbal).

The imaginative Dolphin teacher can inspire all students, but they do need to respect the need for Polar Bears to be given clear guidelines, structure, facts, details and procedures; otherwise they can flounder. For the teacher to get the best out of their naturally grounded student they need to:

■ Demonstrate how learning can be applied in the real world.

■ Allow the student opportunities to repeat and practise until satisfied they are competent.

■ Encourage the use of imagination as a useful process (it's not wasting time).

■ Be careful not to look like you're favouring **N** students to the detriment of **S** students. Every student needs to be able to contribute in their preferred way.

The teacher is concerned with relationship then task whereas the student is the other way round. The teacher must learn to accept that the student is different; not cold, blunt and unfriendly, but simply focused on task first. If the teacher can accept this the relationship can be really positive for both teacher and student. For the teacher to get the best out of their logical student they need to:

■ Offer targeted compliments. Just saying everything is great will not impress or help the student; in fact, it can result in the student not respecting the teacher, concluding they lie and/or are a soft touch. When you praise you may be pressed for proof!

■ Be logical and objective rather than emotional in discussions.

■ Accept that if the student challenges you it is probably to clarify their thoughts rather than meant as a slight to your authority or character. Perhaps ask 'What would you do to improve/change this?' or 'What do you think?' Once they've clarified their thoughts they may be ready to ask and absorb what you think.

■ Work in ways that test their skill and knowledge competitively (they raise their game).

■ Help them understand that around 50% of people are **F** preference and can interpret feedback as criticism.

The **J** teacher takes pleasure in scheduling their time. They are organised and driven to complete. They work out a plan and stick to it, often aided by an impressive to-do list. Their classroom is usually an organised place. The subject will probably be broken down into lesson-sized chunks and the whole year planned out on a colour-coded spreadsheet. Many **J** students are reassured by their teacher's insatiable appetite to stick to the plan. They simply embrace the schedule and deliver their side of the bargain, generally completing all tasks on time. Interestingly, some **J** preferences will baulk at their teacher's well-intentioned thoroughness. They would like to create their own plan and work to it rather than adopt someone else's. This is due to the **J**'s desire for control. So two **J**'s together can clash, though at least all the work will be done. Most secondary schools require students to be so organised that two **J**'s are a welcome combination. For the teacher to get the best out of their fundamentally organised student they need to:

■ Enjoy your shared desire for order, neatness and respecting deadlines.

■ Shake things up now and again to prevent predictability becoming boredom.

■ Avoid making quick decisions about what needs to be done before considering all of the options.

■ Allow the student independence in planning their work in their own way if they really want to.

■ Be prepared to adjust your own plans if external events interfere with your careful preparations.

190
Dolphin teacher with Koala student
ENFJ and ISFJ

Dolphins and Koalas share two type preferences. Both are friendly and organised. For the teacher to get the best out of their potentially invisible student they need:

■ Slow down and be calm and succinct.

■ Leave plenty of time between question and answer; respect the student's need for time to think and reflect before responding.

■ Allow the student time and space to work on their own; don't hover over their head, waiting to pounce.

■ Avoid trying to fix problems immediately or finish their sentences.

■ Pair them up with complementary types (Seahorses, Seals, Teddy Bears and Dolphins).

■ Avoid placing them in groups/teams where they are the only **I** preference in a sea of **E** preferences (they'll be smothered).

■ Provide written praise (not just verbal).

The imaginative Dolphin teacher can inspire all students, but they do need to respect the need for Koalas to be given clear guidelines, structure, facts, details and procedures; otherwise they can flounder. For the teacher to get the best out of their naturally grounded student they need to:

■ Demonstrate how learning can be applied in the real world.

■ Allow the student opportunities to repeat and practise until satisfied they are competent.

■ Encourage the use of imagination as a useful process (it's not wasting time).

■ Be careful not to look like you're favouring **N** students to the detriment of **S** students. Every student needs to be able to contribute in their preferred way.

Both teacher and student are interested in people and relationships before the task/subject content. The teacher likes to form personal relationships with all their students, unless they don't like the student (**F** teachers are more inclined than **T** preference teachers to have their favourites!). Because they operate at an emotional level these teachers are more likely to make promises to students, overstretch themselves and even do work the students should be doing themselves. Teacher and student both enjoy a classroom atmosphere that is warm and friendly. Compliments are likely to go in both directions boosting the confidence of teacher as well as student. For the teacher to get the best out of their relationship-focused student they need to:

■ Offer learning situations that allow for the use of empathy, collaboration and teamworking.

■ Give ample and regular praise while offering tactful support to overcome any blind-spots.

■ Motivate by appealing to the strength of your personal belief in the student (don't let me down, I know you can do it, I like you).

The Dolphin teacher takes pleasure in scheduling their time. They are organised and driven to complete. They work out a plan and stick to it, often aided by an impressive to-do list. Their classroom is usually an organised place. The subject will probably be broken down into lesson-sized chunks and the whole year planned with military precision. Many **J** students are reassured by their teacher's insatiable appetite to stick to the plan. They simply embrace the schedule and deliver their side of the bargain, generally completing all tasks on time. Interestingly, some **J** preferences will baulk at their teacher's well-intentioned thoroughness. They would like to develop their own strategy and work to it rather than adopt someone else's. This is due to the **J**'s desire for control. So two **J** preferences together can clash, though at least all the work will be done. Most secondary schools require students to be so organised that two **J** preferences are a welcome combination. For the teacher to get the best out of their inherently organised student they need to:

■ Enjoy your shared desire for order, neatness and respecting deadlines.

■ Allow the student independence in planning their work in their own way if they really want to.

■ Be prepared to adjust your own plans if external events interfere with your careful preparations (and encourage the student to also embrace flexibility occasionally).

■ Avoid making quick decisions about what needs to be done before considering all of the options.

■ Shake things up now and again to prevent predictability becoming boredom.

191
Dolphin teacher with Seahorse student
ENFJ and INFJ

The Dolphin and Seahorse share three type preferences. Both crave a harmonious, nurturing and workman-like classroom. To avoid their different preferred methods of communication resulting in confusion the teacher can:

■ Slow down and be calm and succinct.

■ Leave plenty of time between question and answer; respect the student's need for time to think and reflect before responding.

■ Allow the student time and space to work on their own; don't hover over their head, waiting to pounce.

■ Avoid trying to fix problems immediately or finish their sentences.

■ Pair them up with complementary types (Seals, Koalas and Cats).

■ Avoid placing them in groups/teams where they are the only **I** preference in a sea of **E** preferences (they'll be smothered).

■ Provide written praise (not just verbal).

Sea Animals gather information by seeing the big picture first, using hunches, inferences and imagination to create meaning. The teacher will naturally use their imagination in the classroom and the **N** student will respond well to this, possibly joining in with flights of fancy, anecdotes and stories. A natural affinity between teacher and student is often present because they both look at the world in the same way – with a burning curiosity to understand why things are as they are by exploring patterns, possibilities, ideas and theories. Be careful not to look like you're favouring **N** students to the detriment of **S** students. Every student needs to be able to contribute in their preferred way. For the teacher to get the best out of their naturally imaginative student they need to:

■ Offer questions/projects that can be explored creatively.

■ Avoid repetitive tasks as they'll quickly lose interest.

■ Encourage the student to become aware of the important contribution of the **S** approach (the value of facts, details, procedure, experiments, applying experience, structure, the step-by-step model).

Sea Animals are interested in people and relationships before the task/subject content. The teacher likes to form personal relationships with all their students, unless they don't like the student (**F** teachers are more inclined than **T** preference teachers to have their favourites!). Because they operate at an emotional level these teachers are more likely to make promises to students, overstretch themselves and even do work the students should be doing themselves. Teacher and student both enjoy a classroom atmosphere that is warm and friendly. Compliments are likely to go in both directions boosting the confidence of teacher as well as student. For the teacher to get the best out of their relationship-focused student they need to:

■ Offer learning situations that allow for the use of empathy, collaboration and teamworking.

■ Give ample and regular praise while offering tactful support to overcome any blind-spots.

■ Motivate by appealing to the strength of your personal belief in the student (don't let me down, I know you can do it).

The **J** teacher takes pleasure in scheduling their time. They are organised and driven to complete. They work out a plan and stick to it, often aided by an impressive to-do list. Their classroom is usually an organised place. The subject will probably be broken down into lesson-sized chunks and the whole year planned meticulously. Many **J** students are reassured by their teacher's insatiable appetite to stick to the plan. They simply embrace the schedule and deliver their side of the bargain, generally completing all tasks on time. Interestingly, some **J** preferences will baulk at their teacher's well-intentioned thoroughness. They would like to create their own plan and work to it rather than adopt someone else's. This is due to the **J**'s desire for control. So two **J** preferences together can clash, though at least all the work will be done. Most secondary schools require students to be so organised that two **J** preferences are a welcome combination. For the teacher to get the best out of their fundamentally organised student they need to:

■ Enjoy your shared desire for order, neatness and respecting deadlines.

■ Allow the student independence in planning their work in their own way if they really want to.

■ Be prepared to adjust your own plans if external events interfere with your careful preparations (and encourage the student to also embrace flexibility occasionally).

■ Shake things up now and again to prevent predictability becoming boredom.

■ Avoid making quick decisions about what needs to be done before considering all of the options.

192
Dolphin teacher with Barn Owl student
ENFJ and INTJ

Dolphins and Barn Owls share two type preferences. Both are imaginative and organised. The warm and attentive teacher needs to allow the Owl space and time to think things through in their own way to bring out the best in their student. For the teacher to encourage their naturally reserved student they need to:

■ Slow down and be calm and succinct.

■ Leave plenty of time between question and answer; respect the student's need for time to think and reflect before responding.

■ Allow the student time and space to work on their own; don't hover over their head, waiting to pounce.

■ Avoid trying to fix problems immediately or finish their sentences.

■ Avoid placing them in groups/teams where they are the only **I** preference in a sea of **E** preferences (they'll be smothered).

■ Provide written praise (not just verbal).

Both teacher and student gather information by seeing the big picture first, using hunches, inferences and imagination to infer meaning. The teacher will naturally use their imagination in the classroom and the **N** student will respond well to this, possibly joining in with flights of fancy, anecdotes and stories. A natural affinity between teacher and student is often present because they both look at the world in the same way – with a burning curiosity to understand why things are as they are by exploring patterns, possibilities, ideas and theories. Be careful not to look like you're favouring **N** students to the detriment of **S** students. Every student needs to be able to contribute in their preferred way. For the teacher to get the best out of their inherently imaginative student they need to:

■ Offer questions/projects that can be explored creatively.

■ Avoid repetitive tasks as they'll quickly lose interest.

■ Encourage the student to become aware of the important contribution of the **S** approach (the value of facts, details, procedure, experiments, applying experience, structure, the step-by-step model).

The teacher is concerned with relationship then task whereas the student is the other way round. The teacher must learn to accept that the student is different; not cold, blunt and unfriendly, but simply focused on task first. If the teacher can accept this the relationship can be really positive for both teacher and student. For the teacher to get the best out of their essentially objective student they need to:

■ Offer targeted compliments. Just saying everything is great will not impress or help the student; in fact, it can result in the student not respecting the teacher, concluding they lie and/or are a soft touch. When you praise you may be pressed for proof!

■ Be logical and objective rather than emotional in discussions.

■ Accept that if the student challenges you it is probably to clarify their thoughts rather than meant as a slight to your authority or character. Perhaps ask 'What would you do to improve/change this?' or 'What do you think?' Once they've clarified their thoughts they may be ready to ask and absorb what you think.

■ Work in ways that test their skill and knowledge competitively (they raise their game).

■ Help them understand that around 50% of people are **F** preference and can interpret feedback as criticism.

The **J** teacher takes pleasure in scheduling their time. They are organised and driven to complete. They work out a plan and stick to it, often aided by an impressive to-do list. Their classroom is usually an organised place. The subject will probably be broken down into lesson-sized chunks and the whole year planned in detail. Many **J** students are reassured by their teacher's insatiable appetite to stick to the plan. They simply embrace the schedule and deliver their side of the bargain, generally completing all tasks on time. Interestingly, some **J** preferences will baulk at their teacher's well-intentioned thoroughness. They would like to create their own plan and work to it rather than adopt someone else's. This is due to the **J**'s desire for control. So two **J** preferences together can clash, though at least all the work will be done. Most secondary schools require students to be so organised that two **J**

preferences are a welcome combination. For the teacher to get the best out of their naturally organised student they need to:

■ Enjoy your shared desire for order, neatness and respecting deadlines.

■ Allow the student independence in planning their work in their own way if they really want to.

■ Be prepared to adjust your own plans if external events interfere with your careful preparations (and encourage the student to also embrace flexibility occasionally).

■ Shake things up now and again to prevent predictability becoming boredom.

■ Avoid making quick decisions about what needs to be done before considering all of the options.

193
Eagle teacher with Barn Owl student
ENTJ and INTJ

Eagles and Barn Owls share three type preferences. Both are independent leaders. This similarity is their most likely source of conflict. For the teacher to get the best out of their naturally watchful student they need to:

■ Slow down and be calm and succinct.

■ Leave plenty of time between question and answer; respect the student's need for time to think and reflect before responding.

■ Allow the student time and space to work on their own; don't stand over their shoulder, waiting to pounce.

■ Avoid trying to fix problems immediately or finish their sentences.

■ Provide written praise (not just verbal).

Both teacher and student gather information by seeing the big picture first, using hunches, inferences and imagination to infer meaning. The teacher will naturally use their imagination in the classroom and the **N** student will respond well to this, possibly joining in with flights of fancy, anecdotes and stories. A natural affinity between teacher and student is often present because they both look at the world in the same way – with a burning curiosity to understand why things are as they are by exploring patterns, possibilities, ideas and theories. Be careful not to look like you're favouring **N** preference students to the detriment of **S** preference students. Every student needs to be able to contribute in their preferred way. For the teacher to get the best out of their inherently imaginative student they need to:

■ Offer questions/projects that can be explored creatively.

■ Avoid repetitive tasks as they'll quickly lose interest.

■ Encourage the student to become aware of the important contribution of the **S** approach (the value of facts, details, procedure, experiments, applying experience, structure, the step-by-step model).

Both teacher and student are task-focused, direct, consistent and honest. The classroom is likely to

have a business-like, purposeful atmosphere. Students are given clear guidelines on what is expected in terms of behaviour, homework and so on. If the student challenges the teacher it is likely to be for clarification. At best this means everyone knows where they stand and how to behave. At worst the classroom can be an assembly line of serious learning modules devoid of fun and real engagement. For the teacher to get the best out of their fundamentally task-focused student they need to:

■ Work in ways that test their skill and knowledge competitively (they raise their game for competitions, challenges, quizzes, measuring and beating personal bests).

■ Help them understand that 50% of people are **F** preference and can interpret feedback as criticism.

■ Focus on what the student has achieved and what comes next.

■ Be prepared to compromise occasionally as Owls can be stubborn.

■ Avoid trying to fix something without considering potential underlying emotional causes.

The Eagle teacher takes pleasure in scheduling their time. They are organised and decisive. They work out a plan and stick to it, often aided by an impressive to-do list. Their classroom is usually organised. The subject will probably be broken down into lesson-sized chunks and the year planned out whether or not an Ofsted inspector is expected. Many Barn Owls may be reassured by their teacher's organisational zeal. They simply embrace the schedule and deliver their side of the bargain, generally completing all tasks on time. However, some Owls will reject their teacher's well-intentioned thoroughness. They would like to create their own plan and work to it rather than adopt someone else's. This is due to the **J**'s desire for control. So two **J**'s together can clash, though at least all their work will be done. Most secondary schools require students to be so organised that two **J**'s are the best combination. For the teacher to get the best out of their naturally organised student they need to:

■ Enjoy your shared desire for order, neatness and respecting deadlines.

■ Allow the student independence in planning their work in their own way if they really want to.

■ Be prepared to adjust your own plans if external events interfere with your careful preparations (and encourage the student to also embrace flexibility occasionally).

■ Shake things up now and again to prevent predictability becoming boredom.

■ Avoid making quick decisions about what needs to be done before considering all of the options.

For the teacher to get the best out of their naturally laid-back student they need to understand the student doesn't just like options and choice; they are essential or they start to itch, squirm and rebel. The secondary school environment is difficult enough for **P** preference students so teachers can help their student achieve by:

■ Providing as much flexibility as possible (multiple choice homework tasks, choice within the lesson).

■ Avoiding giving out detailed schedules (they'll just lose it anyway!).

■ Shaking things up now and again to prevent predictability becoming boredom. Introduce random surprises and changes.

■ Helping the student identify simple time-management strategies to ensure they can do well.

194
Eagle teacher with Cat student
ENTJ and ISFP

Eagles and Cats share no type preferences. For opposites to attract they need to embrace each other's differences. The laid-back student and potentially domineering teacher can learn from their different classroom styles. For the teacher to get the best out of their naturally reserved student they need to:

■ Slow down and be calm and succinct.
■ Leave plenty of time between question and answer; respect the student's need for time to think and reflect before responding.
■ Allow the student time and space to work on their own; don't stand over their shoulder, waiting to pounce.
■ Avoid trying to fix problems immediately or finish their sentences.
■ Provide written praise (not just verbal).

The imaginative teacher can inspire all students, but they do need to respect the need for Cats to be given clear guidelines, structure, facts, details and procedures; otherwise they can flounder. For the teacher to get the best out of their grounded student they need to:

■ Demonstrate how learning can be applied in the real world.
■ Allow the student opportunities to repeat and practise until satisfied they are competent.
■ Encourage the use of imagination as a useful process (it's not wasting time).
■ Be careful not to look like you're favouring **N** students to the detriment of **S** students. Every student needs to be able to contribute in their preferred way.

The student is focused first on people then task whereas the teacher operates in the opposite way. The classroom is likely to have a business-like, purposeful atmosphere. Students are given clear guidelines on what is expected in terms of behaviour, homework and so on. At best this means everyone knows where they stand and how to behave. At worst the classroom can resemble a military boot-camp devoid of fun. Remember the personal relationship you have with this student is key. The Cat needs to feel they like their teacher and that the teacher likes them too. If this happens they'll work harder but if they don't they may switch off. This explains why a student can be top of the class one year (with a teacher they like) and show no interest at all in the subject the following year when they change teacher. For the teacher to get the best out of their fundamentally people-focused student they need to:

■ Offer learning situations that allow for the use of empathy, collaboration and teamworking to counter-balance your natural tendency to focus on task.

■ Give ample and regular praise while offering tactful support to overcome any blind-spots. Feedback can be easily interpreted as criticism so walk on egg-shells when delivering it.
■ Persuade by appealing to the strength of your personal belief in the student (don't let me down, I know you can do it, I like you).
■ Be prepared to compromise occasionally or you may lose your Cat.

The **J** teacher takes pleasure in scheduling their time. They are organised and decisive. They work out a plan and stick to it, often aided by an impressive to-do list. Their classroom is usually an organised place. The subject will probably be broken down into lesson-sized chunks and the year planned out whether or not an Ofsted inspection is looming. The **P** student will either respond:

■ Positively by accepting your expertise and understanding the long-term benefits they'll reap.
■ Passively by just accepting your structure/plan for an easy life without really buying into the content or process you are offering.
■ Negatively by rejecting you, your structure/plan and subject completely (even if they're physically in your room they will not engage and participate).

For the teacher to get the best out of their naturally laid-back student they should note the student doesn't just like options and choice; they need them or they start to itch, squirm and rebel. The secondary school environment is difficult enough for **P** preference students so teachers can help soften the pressure. To help:

■ Provide as much flexibility as possible (multiple choice homework tasks, choice within the lesson).
■ Avoid giving out detailed schedules (they'll just lose it anyway!).
■ Don't be more picky with detail than is absolutely necessary.
■ Shake things up now and again to prevent predictability becoming boredom. Introduce random surprises and changes.
■ Help the student identify simple time-management strategies to ensure they can thrive.

195
Eagle teacher with Tiger student
ENTJ and ISTP

Eagles and Tigers share one type preference. Both are objective and eschew sentimentality. If the teacher allows the student independence their relationship is likely to flourish. To get the best out of their naturally reserved student they need to:

■ Slow down and be calm and succinct.
■ Leave plenty of time between question and answer; respect the student's need for time to think and reflect before responding.
■ Allow the student time and space to work on their own; don't stand over their shoulder, waiting to pounce.

■ Avoid trying to fix problems immediately or finish their sentences.
■ Provide written praise (not just verbal).

The imaginative teacher can inspire all students, but they do need to respect the need for Tigers to be given clear guidelines, structure, facts, details and procedures; otherwise they can flounder. For the teacher to get the best out of their grounded student they need to:

■ Demonstrate how learning can be applied in the real world.
■ Allow the student opportunities to repeat and practise until satisfied they are competent.
■ Encourage the use of imagination as a useful process (it's not wasting time).
■ Be careful not to look like you're favouring **N** students to the detriment of the Tiger. Every student needs to be able to contribute in their preferred way.

Both teacher and student are task-focused, direct, consistent and honest. The classroom is likely to have a business-like, purposeful atmosphere. Students are given clear guidelines on what is expected in terms of behaviour, homework and so on. If the student challenges the teacher it is likely to be for clarification. At best this means everyone knows where they stand and how to behave. At worst the classroom can be an assembly line of serious learning modules devoid of fun and real engagement. For the teacher to get the best out of their fundamentally task-focused student they need to:

■ Work in ways that test their skill and knowledge competitively (they raise their game for competitions, challenges, quizzes, measuring and beating personal bests).
■ Help them understand that 50% of people are **F** preference and can interpret feedback as criticism.
■ Focus on what the student has achieved and what comes next.
■ Be prepared to compromise occasionally.
■ Avoid trying to fix something without considering potential underlying emotional causes.

The **J** teacher takes pleasure in scheduling their time. They are organised and decisive. They work out a plan and stick to it, often aided by an impressive to-do list. Their classroom is usually an organised place. The subject will probably be broken down into lesson-sized chunks and the year planned out in colour-coordinated detail. The **P** student will either respond:

■ Positively by accepting your expertise and understanding the long-term benefits they'll reap.
■ Passively by just accepting your structure/plan for an easy life without really buying into the content or process you are offering.
■ Negatively by rejecting you, your structure/plan and subject completely (even if they're physically in your room they will not engage and participate).

To support their naturally laid-back student they should note the Tiger doesn't just like options and choice; they need them or they start to itch, squirm and rebel. The secondary school environment is difficult enough for **P** preference students so teachers can help soften the pressure. To help:

■ Provide as much flexibility as possible (multiple choice homework tasks, choice within the lesson).

■ Help the student identify simple effective strategies to ensure they can succeed.

■ Avoid giving out detailed schedules (they'll just lose it anyway!).

■ Don't be more picky with detail than is absolutely necessary.

■ Shake things up now and again to prevent predictability becoming tiresome.

196
Eagle teacher with Polar Bear student
ENTJ and ISTJ

Eagles and Polar Bears share two type preferences. Both are objective and organised. They differ in how they make sense of the world. The grounded student can sometimes tire of the imagination and power of their teacher. For the teacher to get the best out of their naturally reserved student they need to:

■ Slow down and be calm and succinct.

■ Leave plenty of time between question and answer; respect the student's need for time to think and reflect before responding.

■ Allow the student time and space to work on their own; don't stand over their shoulder, waiting to pounce.

■ Avoid trying to fix problems immediately or finish their sentences.

■ Provide written praise (not just verbal).

The imaginative teacher can inspire all students, but they do need to respect the need for Polar Bears to be given clear guidelines, structure, facts, details and procedures; otherwise they can struggle. For the teacher to get the best out of their grounded student they need to:

■ Demonstrate how learning can be applied in the real world.

■ Allow the student opportunities to repeat and practise until satisfied they are competent.

■ Encourage the use of imagination as a useful process (it's not wasting time).

■ Be careful not to look like you're favouring **N** students to the detriment of **S** students. Every student needs to be able to contribute in their preferred way.

Both teacher and student are task-focused, direct, consistent and authentic. The classroom is likely to have a business-like, purposeful atmosphere. Students are given clear guidelines on what is expected in terms of behaviour, homework and so on. If the student challenges the teacher it is likely to be for clarification. At best this means everyone knows where they stand and how to behave. At worst the classroom can be an assembly line of serious learning modules devoid of fun and real engagement. For the teacher to get the best out of their fundamentally task-focused student they need to:

■ Work in ways that test their skill and knowledge competitively (they raise their game for competitions, challenges, quizzes, measuring and beating personal bests).

■ Help them understand that 50% of people are **F** preference and can interpret feedback as criticism.

■ Focus on what the student has achieved and what comes next.

■ Be prepared to compromise occasionally.

■ Avoid trying to fix something without considering potential underlying emotional causes.

The J teacher takes pleasure in scheduling their time. They are organised and decisive. They work out a plan and stick to it, often aided by an impressive to-do list. Their classroom is usually well organised. The subject will probably be broken down into lesson-sized chunks and the year planned out whether or not an Ofsted inspector is due. Many Polar Bears are reassured by their teacher's organisational zeal. They simply accept the schedule and deliver their side of the bargain, generally completing all tasks on time. Interestingly, some Polar Bears will reject their teacher's well-intentioned thoroughness. They would like to create their own plan and work to it rather than adopt someone else's. This is due to the J's desire for control. So two J's together can clash, though at least all their work will be done. Most secondary schools require students to be so organised that two J's are the best combination. For the teacher to get the best out of their naturally organised student they need to:

■ Enjoy your shared desire for order, neatness and respecting deadlines.

■ Allow the student independence in planning their work in their own way if they really want to.

■ Be prepared to adjust your own plans if external events interfere with your careful preparations (and encourage the student to also embrace flexibility occasionally).

■ Shake things up now and again to prevent predictability becoming boredom.

■ Avoid making quick decisions about what needs to be done before considering all of the options.

197
Eagle teacher with Eagle student
ENTJ and ENTJ

Eagles like to be in charge whether or not they're the teacher. This can cause conflict as two leaders in one classroom can be one too many! When they bond their shared desire to innovate, analyse and organise benefits the whole class. For the teacher to get the best out of their irrepressibly assertive student they need to:

■ Enjoy the lively banter when it is appropriate to spark new thoughts and ideas; the student learns best this way, but remember there are other students in the classroom.

■ Stick to the point and stay positive (don't nag **T** or mother **F** students), as both teacher and student are easily distracted and liable to go off track!

■ Avoid going over old ground.

■ Be calm and clear, otherwise two **E** preferences can talk louder and louder at each other with neither listening.

■ Be aware that you can keep some thoughts to yourself (and you may think of a better way of expressing something, especially criticism, later).

■ Be an enthusiastic and supportive listener; seek to help the student clarify and develop their thinking rather than assert your own.

■ Practise listening skills and encourage the **I** preferences in the class to contribute.

Both teacher and student gather information by seeing the big picture first, using hunches, inferences and imagination to infer meaning. The teacher will naturally use their imagination in the classroom and the **N** student will respond well to this, possibly joining in with flights of fancy, anecdotes and stories. A natural affinity between teacher and student is often present because they both look at the world in the same way – with a burning curiosity to understand why things are as they are by exploring patterns, possibilities, ideas and theories. Be careful not to look like you're favouring **N** preference students to the detriment of **S** preference students. Every student needs to be able to contribute in their preferred way. For the teacher to get the best out of their naturally imaginative student they need to:

■ Offer questions/projects that can be explored creatively.

■ Avoid repetitive tasks as they'll quickly lose interest.

■ Encourage the student to become aware of the important contribution of the **S** approach (the value of facts, details, procedure, experiments, applying experience, structure, the step-by-step model).

Both teacher and student are task-focused, direct, consistent and honest. The classroom is likely to have a business-like, purposeful atmosphere. Students are given clear guidelines on what is expected in terms of behaviour, homework and so on. If the student challenges the teacher it is likely to be for clarification. At best this means everyone knows where they stand and how to behave. At worst the classroom can be an assembly line of serious learning modules devoid of fun and real engagement. For the teacher to get the best out of their fundamentally task-focused student they need to:

■ Work in ways that test their skill and knowledge competitively (they raise their game for competitions, challenges, quizzes, measuring and beating personal bests).

■ Help them understand that 50% of people are **F** preference and can interpret feedback as criticism.

■ Focus on what the student has achieved and what comes next.

■ Be prepared to compromise occasionally.

■ Avoid trying to fix something without considering potential underlying emotional causes.

The Eagle teacher takes pleasure in scheduling their time. They are organised and decisive. They work out a plan and stick to it, often aided by an impressive to-do list. Their classroom is organised. The subject will probably be broken down into lesson-sized chunks and the year planned out in detail. Many **J** preference students are reassured by their teacher's organisational zeal. They simply adopt the schedule and deliver their side of the bargain, generally completing all tasks on time. Interestingly, some Eagles will baulk at their teacher's well-intentioned thoroughness. They would like to create their own plan and work to it rather than accept someone else's. This is due to the Eagle's desire for control. So two Eagles can clash and ruffle each other's feathers, but at least all their work will be done. Most secondary schools require students to be so organised that two **J**'s are the most constructive combination. For the teacher to get the best out of their naturally organised student they need to:

■ Enjoy your shared desire for order, neatness and respecting deadlines.

■ Shake things up now and again to prevent predictability becoming boredom.

■ Avoid making quick decisions about what needs to be done before considering all of the options,

■ Allow the student independence in planning their work in their own way if they really want to.

■ Be prepared to adjust your own plans if external events interfere with your careful preparations (and encourage the student to also embrace flexibility occasionally).

198
Eagle teacher with Koala student
ENTJ and ISFJ

Eagles and Koalas share one type preference. Both are naturally organised. The quiet Koala is more likely to be invisible in the Eagle's classroom than a source of trouble. For the teacher to get the best out of their reserved student they need to:

■ Slow down and be calm and succinct.

■ Leave plenty of time between question and answer; respect the student's need for time to think and reflect before responding.

■ Allow the student time and space to work on their own; don't stand over their shoulder, waiting to pounce.

■ Avoid trying to fix problems immediately or finish their sentences.

■ Provide written praise (not just verbal).

The imaginative Eagle teacher can inspire all students, but they do need to respect the Koala's need to be given clear guidelines, structure, facts, details and procedures; otherwise they can flounder. For the teacher to get the best out of their naturally grounded student they need to:

■ Allow the student opportunities to repeat and practise until satisfied they are competent.

■ Encourage the use of imagination as a useful process (it's not wasting time).

■ Be careful not to look like you're favouring **N** students to the detriment of **S** students. Every student needs to be able to contribute in their preferred way.

■ Demonstrate how learning can be applied in the real world.

The Koala student is focused first on people then task whereas the teacher operates in the opposite way. The classroom is likely to have a business-like, purposeful atmosphere. Students are given clear guidelines on what is expected in terms of behaviour, homework and so on. At best the Koala appreciates knowing where they stand and

the expected behaviour. At worst the classroom can resemble a harsh Victorian workhouse devoid of warmth. Remember the personal relationship you have with the Koala is key. The student needs to feel they like their teacher and that the teacher likes them too. If this happens they'll work harder; if not they may switch off. This explains why a student can be top of the class one year (with a teacher they like) and show no interest at all in the subject the following year when they change teacher. For the teacher to get the best out of their fundamentally people-focused student they need to:

■ Offer learning situations that allow for the use of empathy, collaboration and small teamworking to counter-balance your natural tendency to focus on task.

■ Give ample and regular praise while offering tactful support to overcome any blind-spots. Feedback can be easily interpreted as criticism so tread carefully when delivering it.

■ Engage by quietly and regularly stating your personal belief in the student (don't let me down, I know you can do it, I like you).

■ Be prepared to compromise occasionally to reassure the routine-loving Koala.

The **J** teacher takes pleasure in scheduling their time. They are organised and decisive. They work out a plan and stick to it, usually aided by an impressive to-do list. Their classroom is well organised. The subject will probably be broken down into lesson-sized chunks and the year planned out meticulously. Most Koalas will be reassured by their teacher's organisational excellence. They simply accept the schedule and deliver their side of the bargain, generally completing all tasks on time. Interestingly, some Koalas may baulk at their teacher's well-intentioned thoroughness. They would like to create their own plan and work to it rather than follow someone else's. This is due to the Koala's desire for autonomy. Rather than actually clash an underground resistance is the likely result. Most secondary schools require students to be so organised that two **J**'s are the best combination. For the teacher to get the best out of their naturally organised student they need to:

■ Enjoy your shared desire for order, neatness and respecting deadlines.

■ Allow the student independence in planning their work in their own way if they really want to.

■ Be prepared to adjust your own plans if external events interfere with your careful preparations (and encourage the student to also embrace flexibility occasionally).

■ Avoid making quick decisions about what needs to be done before considering all of the options.

■ Shake things up now and again to prevent routine turning into stagnation.

199
Eagle teacher with Dolphin student
ENTJ and ENFJ

Eagle and Dolphin share three type preferences. Both are energetic, inimitable and natural organisers. Eagles focus their intellect to solve technical problems whereas Dolphins use their intellect to understand people. For the teacher to get the best out of their naturally effusive student they need to:

■ Enjoy the lively banter when it is appropriate to spark new thoughts and ideas; the student learns best this way, but remember there are other students in the classroom.

■ Stick to the point and stay positive; don't nag, as both teacher and student are easily distracted and liable to go off track!

■ Avoid going over old ground.

■ Be calm and clear, otherwise two **E** preferences can talk louder and louder at each other with neither listening.

■ Be aware that you can keep some thoughts to yourself (and you may think of a better way of expressing something, especially criticism, later).

■ Be an enthusiastic and supportive listener; seek to help the student clarify and develop their thinking rather than assert your own.

■ Practise listening skills and encourage the **I** preferences in the class to contribute.

Both teacher and student gather information by seeing the big picture first, using hunches and imagination to infer meaning. The teacher will naturally use their imagination in the classroom and the **N** student will respond well to this, possibly joining in with flights of fancy, anecdotes and stories. A natural affinity between teacher and student is often present because they both look at the world in the same way – with a burning curiosity to understand why things are as they are by exploring patterns, possibilities, ideas and theories. Be careful not to look like you're favouring **N** preference students to the detriment of **S** preference students. Every student needs to be able to contribute in their preferred way. For the teacher to get the best out of their inherently imaginative student they need to:

■ Offer questions/projects that can be explored creatively.

■ Avoid repetitive tasks as they'll quickly lose interest.

■ Encourage the student to become aware of the important contribution of the **S** approach (the value of facts, details, procedure, experiments, applying experience, structure, the step-by-step model).

The teacher is focused first on task and second on people/relationships. The classroom is likely to have a business-like, purposeful atmosphere. Students are given clear guidelines on what is expected in terms of behaviour, homework and so on. At best this means everyone knows where they stand and how to behave. At worst the classroom can resemble a military boot-camp devoid of compassion and fun. Remember the personal relationship you have with this student is key. The Dolphin needs to feel they like their teacher and that the teacher likes them too. If this happens they'll work harder but if they don't they may switch off. This explains why a student can be top of the class one year (with a teacher they like) and show no interest at all in the subject the following year when they change teacher. For the teacher to get the best out of their naturally people-focused student they need to:

■ Offer learning situations that allow for the use of empathy, collaboration and teamworking to counter-balance your natural tendency to focus on task.

■ Give ample and regular praise while offering tactful support to overcome any blind-spots. Feedback can be easily interpreted as criticism so walk on egg-shells when delivering it.

■ Persuade/influence by appealing to the strength of your personal belief in the student (don't let me down, I know you can do it, I like you).

■ Be prepared to compromise occasionally.

The **J** teacher takes pleasure in scheduling their time. They are organised and decisive. They work out a plan and stick to it, often aided by an impressive to-do list. Their classroom is usually very organised. Many Dolphins are reassured by their teacher's organisational zeal. They simply adopt the plan and deliver their side of the bargain, generally completing all tasks on time. Interestingly, some Dolphins will baulk at their teacher's well-intentioned thoroughness. They would like to create their own schedule and work to it rather than adopt someone else's. This is due to the **J**'s desire for control. So two **J**'s together can clash, though at least all their work will be done. Most secondary schools require students to be so organised that two **J**'s are the best combination. For the teacher to get the best out of their fundamentally organised student they need to:

■ Enjoy your shared desire for order, neatness and respecting deadlines.

■ Allow the student independence in planning their work in their own way if they really want to.

■ Be prepared to adjust your own plans if external events interfere with your careful preparations (and encourage the student to also embrace flexibility occasionally).

■ Shake things up now and again to prevent predictability becoming boredom.

■ Avoid making quick decisions about what needs to be done before considering all of the possibilities.

200
Eagle teacher with Teddy Bear student
ENTJ and ESFJ

Eagles and Teddy Bears share two type preferences. Both are energetic, conscientious and natural organisers. Eagles focus their intellect to solve technical problems whereas Teddies concentrate on harmonious relationships; this can lead to clashes. For the teacher to get the best out of their naturally effusive student they need to:

■ Enjoy the lively banter when it is appropriate to spark new thoughts and ideas; the student learns best this way, but remember there are other students in the classroom.

■ Stick to the point and stay positive (don't nag **T** or mother **F** students), as both teacher and student are easily distracted and liable to go off track!

■ Avoid going over old ground.

■ Be calm and clear, otherwise two **E** preferences can talk louder and louder at each other with neither listening.

■ Be aware that you can keep some thoughts to yourself (and you may think of a better way of expressing something, especially criticism, later).

■ Be an enthusiastic and supportive listener; seek to help the student clarify and develop their thinking rather than assert your own.

■ Practise listening skills and encourage the **I** preferences in the class to contribute.

The imaginative teacher can inspire all students, but they do need to respect the need for Teddy Bears to be given clear guidelines, structure, facts, details and procedures; otherwise they can flounder. For the teacher to get the best out of their grounded student they need to:

■ Demonstrate how learning can be applied in the real world.

■ Allow the student opportunities to repeat and practise until satisfied they are competent.

■ Encourage the use of imagination as a useful process (it's not wasting time).

■ Be careful not to look like you're favouring **N** students to the detriment of **S** students. Every student needs to be able to contribute in their preferred style.

The teacher is focused first on task and second on people/relationships. The classroom is likely to have a business-like, purposeful atmosphere. Students are given clear guidelines on what is expected in terms of behaviour, homework and so on. At best this means everyone knows where they stand and how to behave. At worst the classroom can resemble a military boot-camp devoid of fun. Remember the personal relationship you have with this student is key. The Teddy needs to feel they like their teacher and that the teacher likes them too. If this happens they'll work harder but if not they may switch off. This explains why a student can be top of the class one year (with a teacher they like) and show no interest at all in the subject the following year when they change teacher. For the teacher to get the best out of their fundamentally people-focused student they need to:

■ Offer learning situations that allow for the use of empathy, collaboration, and teamworking to counter-balance your natural tendency to focus on task.

■ Give ample and regular praise while offering tactful support to overcome any blind-spots. Feedback can be easily interpreted as criticism so walk on egg-shells when delivering it.

■ Influence by appealing to the strength of your personal belief in the student (don't let me down, I know you can do it, I like you).

■ Be prepared to compromise occasionally.

The Eagle teacher takes pleasure in scheduling their time. They are organised and decisive. They work out a plan and stick to it, often aided by an impressive to-do list. Their classroom is usually very organised. The subject will probably be broken down into lesson-sized chunks and the year

planned out thoroughly. Many Teddies are reassured by their teacher's organisational zeal. They enthusiastically adopt the schedule and deliver their side of the bargain, generally completing all tasks on time. Interestingly, some Teddies will baulk at their teacher's well-intentioned thoroughness. They would like to create their own plan and work to it rather than accept someone else's. This is due to the **J**'s desire for control. So two **J**'s together can clash, though at least all their work will be done. Most secondary schools require students to be so organised that two **J**'s are the best combination. For the teacher to get the best out of their naturally organised student they need to:

■ Enjoy your shared desire for order, neatness and respecting deadlines.

■ Allow the student independence in planning their work in their own way if they really want to.

■ Be prepared to adjust your own plans if external events interfere with your careful preparations (and encourage the student to also embrace flexibility occasionally).

■ Shake things up now and again to prevent predictability becoming boredom.

■ Avoid making quick decisions about what needs to be done before considering all of the options.

201
Eagle teacher with Seahorse student
ENTJ and INFJ

Eagle and Seahorse share two type preferences. Both are intuitive and organised. The teacher needs to resist overpowering the gentle Seahorse if they are to create a harmonious relationship. To help:

■ Slow down and be calm and succinct.

■ Leave plenty of time between question and answer; respect the student's need for time to think and reflect before responding.

■ Allow the student time and space to work on their own; don't stand over their shoulder, waiting to pounce.

■ Avoid trying to fix problems immediately or finish their sentences.

■ Provide written praise (not just verbal).

Both teacher and student gather information by seeing the big picture first, using hunches, inferences and imagination to infer meaning. The teacher will naturally use their imagination in the classroom and the **N** student will respond well to this, possibly joining in with flights of fancy, anecdotes and stories. A natural affinity between teacher and student is often present because they both look at the world in the same way – with a burning curiosity to understand why things are as they are by exploring patterns, possibilities, ideas and theories. Be careful not to look like you're favouring **N** preference students to the detriment of **S** preference students. Every student needs to be able to contribute in their preferred way. For the teacher to get the best out of their naturally imaginative student they need to:

■ Offer questions/projects that can be explored creatively.

■ Avoid repetitive tasks as they'll quickly lose interest.

■ Encourage the student to become aware of the important contribution of the **S** approach (the value of facts, details, procedure, experiments, applying experience, structure, the step-by-step model).

The Eagle is focused first on task and second on people/relationships. The classroom is likely to have a business-like, purposeful atmosphere. Students are given clear guidelines on what is expected in terms of behaviour, homework and so on. At best this means everyone knows where they stand and how to behave. At worst the classroom can resemble a military boot-camp devoid of fun. Remember the personal relationship you have with this student is key. The Seahorse needs to feel they like their teacher and that the teacher likes them too. If this happens they'll work harder but if they don't they may switch off. This explains why a student can be top of the class one year (with a teacher they like) and show no interest at all in the subject the following year when they change teacher. For the teacher to get the best out of their fundamentally people-focused student they need to:

■ Offer learning situations that allow for the use of empathy, collaboration and teamworking to counter-balance your natural tendency to focus on task.

■ Give ample and regular praise while offering tactful support to overcome any blind-spots. Feedback can be easily interpreted as criticism so walk on egg-shells when delivering it.

■ Persuade/influence by appealing to the strength of your personal belief in the student (don't let me down, I know you can do it, I like you).

■ Be prepared to compromise occasionally.

The Eagle teacher takes pleasure in scheduling their time. They are organised and decisive. They work out a plan and stick to it, often aided by an impressive to-do list. Their classroom is usually very organised. The subject will probably be broken down into lesson-sized chunks and the year planned out diligently. Many Seahorse students are reassured by their teacher's organisational zeal. They simply embrace the schedule and deliver their side of the bargain, generally completing all tasks on time. Interestingly, some **J** preferences will baulk at their teacher's well-intentioned thoroughness. They would like to create their own plan and work to it rather than adopt someone else's. This is due to the **J**'s desire for control. So two **J**'s together can clash, though at least all their work will be done. Most secondary schools require students to be so organised that two **J**'s are the best combination. For the teacher to get the best out of their intrinsically organised student they need to:

■ Enjoy your shared desire for order, neatness and respecting deadlines.

■ Allow the student independence in planning their work in their own way if they really want to.

■ Be prepared to adjust your own plans if external events interfere with your careful preparations (and encourage the student to also embrace flexibility occasionally).

■ Shake things up now and again to prevent predictability becoming boredom.

■ Avoid making quick decisions about what needs to be done before considering all possibilities.

202
Eagle teacher with Black Bear student
ENTJ and ESTJ

The Eagle and Black Bear share a desire for control. Both like to be in charge and are comfortable in a leadership role. For the teacher to get the best out of their naturally assertive student they need to:

■ Enjoy the lively banter when it is appropriate to spark new thoughts and ideas; the student learns best this way, but remember there are other students in the classroom.

■ Stick to the point and stay positive (don't nag), as both teacher and student are easily distracted and liable to go off track!

■ Avoid going over old ground.

■ Be calm and clear, otherwise two **E** preferences can talk louder and louder at each other with neither listening.

■ Be aware that you can keep some thoughts to yourself (and you may think of a better way of expressing something, especially criticism, later).

■ Be an enthusiastic and supportive listener; seek to help the student clarify and develop their thinking rather than assert your own.

■ Practise listening skills and encourage the **I** preferences in the class to contribute.

The imaginative Eagle teacher can inspire all students, but they do need to respect the need for Black Bears to be given clear guidelines, structure, facts, details and procedures; otherwise they can flounder. For the teacher to get the best out of their grounded student they need to:

■ Demonstrate how learning can be applied in the real world.

■ Allow the student opportunities to practise until satisfied they are competent.

■ Encourage the use of imagination as a useful process (it's not wasting time).

■ Be careful not to look like you're favouring **N** students to the detriment of **S** students. Every student needs to be able to contribute in their preferred way.

Both teacher and student are task-focused, direct, consistent and honest. The classroom is likely to have a business-like, purposeful atmosphere. Students are given clear guidelines on what is expected in terms of behaviour, homework and so on. If the student challenges the teacher it is likely to be for clarification. At best this means everyone knows where they stand and how to behave. At worst the classroom can be an assembly line of serious learning modules devoid of fun and real engagement. For the teacher to get the best out of their fundamentally task-focused student they need to:

■ Work in ways that test their skill and knowledge competitively (they raise their game for competitions, challenges, quizzes, measuring and beating personal bests).

■ Help them understand that 50% of people are **F** preference and can interpret feedback as criticism.

■ Focus on what the student has achieved and what comes next.

■ Be prepared to compromise occasionally.

■ Avoid trying to fix something without considering potential underlying emotional causes.

The Eagle teacher takes pleasure in scheduling their time. They are organised and decisive. They work out a plan and stick to it, often aided by an impressive to-do list. Their classroom is usually very organised. The subject will probably be broken down into lesson-sized chunks and the year planned out with alacrity. Most Black Bears are reassured by their teacher's organisational zeal. They simply accept the schedule and deliver their side of the bargain, generally completing all tasks on time. Interestingly, some **J** preferences will baulk at their teacher's well-intentioned thoroughness. They would like to create their own plan and work to it rather than adopt someone else's. This is due to the **J**'s desire for control. So two **J**'s together can clash, though at least all their work will be done. Most secondary schools require students to be so organised that two **J**'s are the best combination. For the teacher to get the best out of their naturally organised student they need to:

■ Enjoy your shared desire for order, neatness and respecting deadlines.

■ Allow the student independence in planning their work in their own way if they really want to.

■ Be prepared to adjust your own plans if external events interfere with your careful preparations (and encourage the student to also embrace flexibility occasionally).

■ Shake things up now and again to prevent predictability becoming boredom.

■ Avoid making quick decisions about what needs to be done before considering all of the options.

203
Eagle teacher with Falcon student
ENTJ and ENTP

Eagles and Falcons share three preferences. Both are imaginative, assertive and lively. Clashes are most likely due to their shared desire to be the boss (of ideas), as showcased in *Top Gear*, where the reckless banter and camaraderie can descend into toxic and pointless rants. For the teacher to get the best out of their naturally effusive student they need to:

■ Enjoy the lively banter when it is appropriate to spark new thoughts and ideas; the student learns best this way, but remember there are other students in the classroom.

■ Stick to the point and stay positive (don't nag **T** or mother **F** students), as both teacher and student are easily distracted and liable to go off track!

■ Avoid going over old ground.

Be calm and clear, otherwise two **E** preferences can talk louder and louder at each other with neither listening.

Be aware that you can keep some thoughts to yourself (and you may think of a better way of expressing something, especially criticism, later).

Be an enthusiastic and supportive listener; seek to help the student clarify and develop their thinking rather than assert your own.

Practise listening skills and encourage the **I** preferences in the class to contribute.

Both teacher and student gather information by seeing the big picture first, using hunches, inferences and imagination to infer meaning. The teacher will naturally use their imagination in the classroom and the **N** student will respond well to this, possibly joining in with flights of fancy, anecdotes and stories. A natural affinity between teacher and student is often present because they both look at the world in the same way – with a burning curiosity to understand why things are as they are by exploring patterns, possibilities, ideas and theories. Be careful not to look like you're favouring **N** preference students to the detriment of the 65% of **S** preference students. Every student needs to be able to contribute in their preferred way. For the teacher to get the best out of their inherently imaginative student they need to:

Offer questions/projects that can be explored creatively.

Avoid repetitive tasks as they'll quickly lose interest.

Encourage the student to become aware of the important contribution of the **S** approach (the value of facts, details, procedure, experiments, applying experience, structure, the step-by-step model).

Both Eagle and Falcon are task-focused, direct, consistent and honest. The classroom is likely to have a business-like, purposeful atmosphere. Students are given clear guidelines on what is expected in terms of behaviour, homework and so on. If the student challenges the teacher it is likely to be for clarification. At best this means everyone knows where they stand and how to behave. At worst the classroom can be an assembly line of serious learning modules devoid of fun and real engagement. For the teacher to get the best out of their naturally task-focused student they need to:

Work in ways that test their skill and knowledge competitively (they raise their game for competitions, challenges, quizzes, measuring and beating personal bests).

Help them understand that half of the population are **F** preference and can interpret feedback as criticism.

Focus on what the student has achieved and what comes next.

Be prepared to compromise occasionally.

Avoid trying to fix something without considering potential underlying emotional causes.

The Eagle teacher takes pleasure in scheduling their time. They are organised and decisive. They work out a plan and stick to it, often aided by an impressive to-do list. Their classroom is usually an organised place. The subject will probably be broken down into lesson-sized chunks and the year planned out carefully. The **P** student will either respond:

Positively by accepting your expertise and understanding the long-term benefits they'll reap.

Passively by just accepting your structure/plan for an easy life without really buying into the content or process you are offering.

Negatively by rejecting you, your structure/plan and subject completely (even if they're physically in your room they will not engage and participate).

For the teacher to get the best out of their naturally laid-back student they should note the student doesn't just like options and choice; they need them or they start to itch, squirm and rebel. The secondary school environment is difficult enough for **P** preference students so teachers can help soften the pressure. To help:

Provide as much flexibility as possible (multiple choice homework tasks, choice within the lesson).

Avoid giving out detailed schedules (they'll just lose it anyway!).

Don't be more picky with detail than is absolutely necessary.

Shake things up now and again to prevent predictability becoming boredom. Introduce random surprises and changes.

Help the student identify simple time-management strategies to ensure they can flourish.

204
Eagle teacher with Clownfish student
ENTJ and ENFP

Eagles and Clownfish share two type preferences. Both are lively and imaginative. Clashes are most likely if the teacher leads rather than nurtures the student. For the teacher to get the best out of their naturally effusive student they need to:

Enjoy the lively banter when it is appropriate to spark new thoughts and ideas; the student learns best this way, but remember there are other students in the classroom.

Stick to the point and stay positive (don't nag **T** or mother **F** students), as both teacher and student are easily distracted and liable to go off track!

Avoid going over old ground.

Be calm and clear, otherwise two **E** preferences can talk louder and louder at each other with neither listening.

Be aware that you can keep some thoughts to yourself (and you may think of a better way of expressing something, especially criticism, later).

Be an enthusiastic and supportive listener; seek to help the student clarify and develop their thinking rather than assert your own.

Practise listening skills and encourage the **I** preferences in the class to contribute.

Both teacher and student gather information by seeing the big picture first, using hunches, inferences and imagination to infer meaning. The teacher will naturally use their imagination in the classroom and the **N** student will respond well to this, possibly joining in with flights of fancy, anecdotes and stories. A natural affinity between teacher and student is often present because they both look at the world in the same way – with a burning curiosity to understand why things are as they are by exploring patterns, possibilities, ideas and theories. Be careful not to look like you're favouring **N** preference students to the detriment of **S** preference students. Every student needs to be able to contribute in their preferred way. For the teacher to get the best out of their inherently imaginative student they need to:

Offer questions/projects that can be explored creatively.

Avoid repetitive tasks as they'll quickly lose interest.

Encourage the student to become aware of the important contribution of the **S** approach (the value of facts, details, procedure, experiments, applying experience, structure, the step-by-step model).

The Eagle teacher is focused first on task and second on people/relationships. The classroom is likely to have a business-like, purposeful atmosphere. Students are given clear guidelines on what is expected in terms of behaviour, homework and so on. At best this means everyone knows where they stand and how to behave. At worst the classroom can resemble a military boot-camp devoid of compassion and excitement. Remember the personal relationship you have with this student is key. The Clownfish needs to feel they like their teacher and that the teacher likes them too. If this happens they'll work harder but if they don't they may switch off. This explains why a student can be top of the class one year (with a teacher they like) and show no interest at all in the subject the following year when they change teacher. For the teacher to get the best out of their fundamentally people-focused student they need to:

Offer learning situations that allow for the use of empathy, collaboration and teamworking to counter-balance your natural tendency to focus on task.

Give ample and regular praise while offering tactful support to overcome any blind-spots. Feedback can be easily interpreted as criticism so walk on egg-shells when delivering it.

Persuade/influence by appealing to the strength of your personal belief in the student (don't let me down, I know you can do it, I like you).

Be prepared to compromise occasionally; the Clownfish may go off in a silent huff or a disruptive rant.

The **J** teacher takes pleasure in scheduling their time. They are organised and decisive. They work out a plan and stick to it, often aided by an impressive to-do list. Their classroom is usually an organised place. The subject will probably be broken down into lesson-sized chunks and the year planned out whether or not an Ofsted inspection is looming. The **P** student will either respond:

Positively by accepting your expertise and understanding the long-term benefits they'll reap.

Passively by just accepting your structure/plan for an easy life without really buying into the content or process you are offering.

Negatively by rejecting you, your structure/plan and subject completely (even if they're physically in your room they will not engage and participate).

For the teacher to get the best out of their naturally laid-back student they should note the student doesn't just like options and choice; they need them or they start to itch, squirm and rebel. The secondary school environment is difficult enough for **P** preference students so teachers can help soften the pressure. To help:

■ Provide as much flexibility as possible (multiple choice homework tasks, choice within the lesson).

■ Avoid giving out detailed schedules (they'll just lose it anyway!).

■ Don't be more picky with detail than is absolutely necessary.

■ Shake things up now and again to prevent predictability becoming boredom. Introduce random surprises and changes.

■ Offer simple time-management tips to help the naturally chaotic Clownfish to cope.

205
Eagle teacher with Lion student
ENTJ and ESFP

Eagles and Lions share one type preference. Both are energetic and lively. They direct their energies in such different ways that this is the most likely source of conflict. To get the best out of their naturally sociable student they need to:

■ Enjoy the lively banter when it is appropriate to spark new thoughts and ideas; the student learns best this way, but remember there are other students in the classroom.

■ Stick to the point and stay positive (don't nag), as both teacher and student are easily distracted and liable to go off track!

■ Avoid going over old ground.

■ Be calm and clear, otherwise two **E** preferences can talk louder and louder at each other with neither listening.

■ Be aware that you can keep some thoughts to yourself (and you may think of a better way of expressing something, especially criticism, later).

■ Be an enthusiastic and supportive listener; seek to help the student clarify and develop their thinking rather than assert your own.

■ Practise listening skills and encourage the **I** preferences in the class to contribute.

The imaginative Eagle can inspire all students, but they do need to respect the need for Lions to be given clear guidelines, structure, facts, details and procedures; otherwise they can flounder. For the teacher to get the best out of their grounded student they need to:

■ Demonstrate how learning can be applied in the real world.

■ Allow the student opportunities to repeat and practise until satisfied they are competent.

■ Encourage the use of imagination as a useful process (it's not wasting time).

■ Be careful not to look like you're favouring **N** students to the detriment of **S** students. Every student needs to be able to contribute in their preferred way.

The teacher is focused first on task and second on people/relationships. The classroom is likely to have a business-like, purposeful atmosphere. Students are given clear guidelines on what is expected in terms of behaviour, homework and so on. At best this means everyone knows where they stand and how to behave. At worst the classroom can resemble a military boot-camp devoid of warmth and fun. Remember the personal relationship you have with this student is key. The Lion needs to feel they like their teacher and that the teacher likes them too. If this happens they'll work harder but if they don't they may switch off. This explains why a student can be top of the class one year (with a teacher they like) and show no interest at all in the subject the following year when they change teacher. For the teacher to get the best out of their fundamentally people-focused student they need to:

■ Offer learning situations that allow for the use of empathy, collaboration and teamworking to counter-balance your natural tendency to focus on task.

■ Give ample and regular praise while offering tactful support to overcome any blind-spots. Feedback can be easily interpreted as criticism so walk on egg-shells when delivering it.

■ Persuade/influence by appealing to the strength of your personal belief in the student (don't let me down, I know you can do it, I like you).

■ Be prepared to compromise occasionally, otherwise the Lion may roar or bite.

The Eagle teacher takes pleasure in scheduling their time. They are organised and decisive. They work out a plan and stick to it, usually aided by an impressive to-do list. Their classroom is likely to be an organised place. The subject will probably be broken down into lesson-sized chunks and the year planned vigilantly. The **P** student will either respond:

■ Positively by accepting your expertise and understanding the long-term benefits they'll reap.

■ Passively by just accepting your structure/plan for an easy life without really buying into the content or process you are offering.

■ Negatively by rejecting you, your structure/plan and subject completely (even if they're physically in your room they will not engage and participate).

To get the best out of the naturally laid-back Lion, note that they don't just like options and choice; they need it or they start to itch, squirm and rebel. The secondary school environment is difficult enough for **P** preference students so teachers can help soften the pressure. To help:

■ Provide as much flexibility as possible (multiple choice homework tasks, choice within the lesson).

■ Avoid giving out detailed schedules (they'll just lose it anyway!).

■ Don't be more picky with detail than is absolutely necessary.

■ Shake things up now and again to prevent predictability becoming boredom. Introduce random surprises and changes.

■ Identify simple time-management strategies the Lion can adopt.

206
Eagle teacher with Panther student
ENTJ and ESTP

Eagles and Panthers are both sparky and action-orientated. When the teacher accepts the occasional blips in behaviour they can help the student learn to add calmness and focus to their classroom repertoire. For the Eagle to get the best out of their naturally lively student they need to:

■ Enjoy the lively banter when it is appropriate to spark new thoughts and ideas; the student learns best this way, but remember there are other students in the classroom.

■ Stick to the point and stay positive (don't nag **T** or mother **F** students), as both teacher and student are easily distracted and liable to go off track!

■ Avoid going over old ground.

■ Be calm and clear, otherwise two **E** preferences can talk louder and louder at each other with neither listening.

■ Be aware that you can keep some thoughts to yourself (and you may think of a better way of expressing something, especially criticism, later).

■ Be an enthusiastic and supportive listener; seek to help the student clarify and develop their thinking rather than assert your own.

■ Practise listening skills and encourage the **I** preferences in the class to contribute.

The imaginative teacher can inspire all students, but they do need to respect the need for Panthers to be given clear guidelines, structure, facts, details and procedures; otherwise they can flounder. For the teacher to get the best out of their grounded student they need to:

■ Demonstrate how learning can be applied in the real world.

■ Allow the student opportunities to repeat and practise until satisfied they are competent.

■ Encourage the use of imagination as a useful process (it's not wasting time).

■ Be careful not to look like you're favouring **N** students to the detriment of **S** students. Every student needs to be able to contribute in their preferred way.

Both teacher and student are task-focused, direct, consistent and honest. The classroom is likely to have a business-like, purposeful atmosphere. Students are given clear guidelines on what is expected in terms of behaviour, homework and so on. If the student challenges the teacher it is likely to be for clarification. At best this means everyone knows where they stand and how to behave. At worst the classroom can be an assembly line of serious learning modules devoid of fun and real engagement. For the teacher to get the best out of their fundamentally task-focused student they need to:

■ Work in ways that test their skill and knowledge competitively (they raise their game for competitions, challenges, quizzes, measuring and beating personal bests).

■ Help them understand that 50% of people are **F** preference and can interpret feedback as criticism.

■ Focus on what the student has achieved and what comes next.

■ Be prepared to compromise occasionally.

■ Avoid trying to fix something without considering potential underlying emotional causes.

The Eagle teacher takes pleasure in scheduling their time. They are organised and decisive. They work out a plan and stick to it, often aided by an impressive to-do list. Their classroom is usually an organised place. The subject will probably be broken down into lesson-sized chunks and the year planned out whether or not an Ofsted inspector is due. The **P** student will either respond:

■ Positively by accepting your expertise and understanding the long-term benefits they'll reap.

■ Passively by just accepting your structure/plan for an easy life without really buying into the content or process you are offering.

■ Negatively by rejecting you, your structure/plan and subject completely (even if they're physically in your room they will not engage and participate).

For the teacher to get the best out of their naturally laid-back student they should note the student doesn't just like options and choice; they need them or they start to itch, squirm and rebel. The secondary school environment is difficult enough for **P** preference students so teachers can help soften the pressure. To help:

■ Provide as much flexibility as possible (multiple choice homework tasks, choice within the lesson).

■ Avoid giving out detailed schedules (they'll just lose it anyway!).

■ Don't be more picky with detail than is absolutely necessary.

■ Shake things up now and again to prevent predictability becoming boredom. Introduce random surprises and changes.

■ Identify simple time-management strategies the student can incorporate.

207
Eagle teacher with Tawny Owl student
ENTJ and INTP

Birds share an enquiring and objective mind. Eagles and Tawny Owls are most likely to clash when the student's reserved and independent approach contrasts with the teacher's energetic and organised manner. For the teacher to get the best out of their naturally reserved student they need to:

■ Slow down and be calm and succinct.

■ Leave plenty of time between question and answer; respect the student's need for time to think and reflect before responding.

■ Allow the student time and space to work on their own; don't stand over their shoulder, waiting to pounce.

■ Avoid trying to fix problems immediately or finish their sentences.

■ Provide written praise (not just verbal).

Both teacher and student gather information by seeing the big picture first, using hunches, inferences and imagination to infer meaning. The teacher will naturally use their imagination in the classroom and the **N** student will respond well to this, possibly joining in with flights of fancy, anecdotes and stories. A natural affinity between teacher and student is often present because they both look at the world in the same way – with a burning curiosity to understand why things are as they are by exploring patterns, possibilities, ideas and theories. Be careful not to look like you're favouring **N** preference students to the detriment of **S** preference students. Every student needs to be able to contribute in their preferred way. For the teacher to get the best out of their inherently imaginative student they need to:

■ Offer questions/projects that can be explored creatively.

■ Avoid repetitive tasks as they'll quickly lose interest.

■ Encourage the student to become aware of the important contribution of the **S** approach (the value of facts, details, procedure, experiments, applying experience, structure, the step-by-step model).

Both teacher and student are task-focused, direct, consistent and honest. The classroom is likely to have a business-like, purposeful atmosphere. Students are given clear guidelines on what is expected in terms of behaviour, homework and so on. If the student challenges the teacher it is likely to be for clarification. At best this means everyone knows where they stand and how to behave. At worst the classroom can be an assembly line of serious learning modules devoid of fun and real engagement. For the teacher to get the best out of their naturally task-focused student they need to:

■ Work in ways that test their skill and knowledge competitively (they raise their game for competitions, challenges, quizzes, measuring and beating personal bests).

■ Help them remember that half the population are **F** preference and can interpret feedback as criticism.

■ Focus on what the student has achieved and what comes next.

■ Be prepared to compromise occasionally.

■ Avoid trying to fix something without considering potential underlying emotional causes.

The Eagle takes pleasure in scheduling their time. They are organised and decisive. They work out a plan and stick to it, often aided by an impressive to-do list. Their classroom is usually an organised place. The subject will probably be broken down into lesson-sized chunks and the year planned out whether or not an Ofsted inspector is lurking in the corridor. The **P** student will either respond:

■ Positively by accepting your expertise and understanding the long-term benefits they'll reap.

■ Passively by just accepting your structure/plan for an easy life without really buying into the content or process you are offering.

■ Negatively by rejecting you, your structure/plan and subject completely (even if they're physically in your room they will not engage and participate).

To get the best out of the naturally laid-back student offer options and choice, or they may start to itch, squirm and rebel. The secondary school

environment is difficult enough for **P** preference students so teachers can help soften the pressure. To help:

■ Provide as much flexibility as possible (multiple choice homework tasks, choice within the lesson).

■ Avoid giving out detailed schedules (they'll just lose it anyway!).

■ Don't be more picky with detail than is absolutely necessary.

■ Shake things up now and again to prevent predictability becoming boredom. Introduce random surprises and changes.

■ Identify effective strategies to ensure they can manage their workload successfully.

208
Eagle teacher with Seal student
ENTJ and INFP

Eagles and Seals share one type preference. Both are imaginative and creative. Clashes are likely to result from a difference in style; the in-your-face Eagle and more contemplative and consensual Seal. For the teacher to get the best out of their naturally reserved student they need to:

■ Slow down and be calm and succinct.

■ Leave plenty of time between question and answer; respect the student's need for time to think and reflect before responding.

■ Allow the student time and space to work on their own; don't stand over their shoulder, waiting to pounce.

■ Avoid trying to fix problems immediately or finish their sentences.

■ Provide written praise (not just verbal).

Both teacher and student gather information by seeing the big picture first, using hunches, inferences and imagination to infer meaning. The teacher will naturally use their imagination in the classroom and the **N** student will respond well to this, possibly joining in with flights of fancy, anecdotes and stories. A natural affinity between teacher and student is often present because they both look at the world in the same way – with a burning curiosity to understand why things are as they are by exploring patterns, possibilities, ideas and theories. Be careful not to look like you're favouring **N** preference students to the detriment of the 65% of **S** preference students. Every student needs to be able to contribute in their preferred way. For the teacher to get the best out of their imaginative student they need to:

■ Offer questions/projects that can be explored creatively.

■ Avoid repetitive tasks as they'll quickly lose interest.

■ Encourage the student to become aware of the important contribution of the **S** approach (the value of facts, details, procedure, experiments, applying experience, structure, the step-by-step model).

The teacher is focused first on task and second on people/relationships. The classroom is likely to have a business-like, purposeful atmosphere. Students are given clear guidelines on what is expected in terms of behaviour, homework and so on. At best this means everyone knows where they stand and how to behave. At worst the classroom can resemble a military boot-camp devoid of the compassion the Seal strives for. Remember the personal relationship you have with this student is key. The Seal needs to feel they like their teacher and that the teacher likes them too. If this happens they'll work harder but if they don't they may switch off. This explains why a student can be top of the class one year (with a teacher they like) and show no interest at all in the subject the following year when they change teacher. For the teacher to get the best out of their fundamentally people-focused student they need to:

- Offer learning situations that allow for the use of empathy, collaboration and teamworking to counter-balance your natural tendency to focus on task.

- Give ample and regular praise while offering tactful support to overcome any blind-spots. Feedback can be easily interpreted as criticism so walk on egg-shells when delivering it.

- Persuade/influence by appealing to the strength of your personal belief in the student (don't let me down, I know you can do it, I like you).

- Be prepared to compromise occasionally or the Seal may sulk.

The **J** teacher takes pleasure in scheduling their time. They are organised and decisive. They work out a plan and stick to it, often aided by an impressive to-do list. Their classroom is usually an organised place. The subject will probably be broken down into lesson-sized chunks and the year planned out whether or not an Ofsted inspector is due. The **P** student will either respond:

- Positively by accepting your expertise and understanding the long-term benefits they'll reap.

- Passively by just accepting your structure/plan for an easy life without really buying into the content or process you are offering.

- Negatively by rejecting you, your structure/plan and subject completely (even if they're physically in your room they will not engage and participate).

For the teacher to get the best out of their naturally laid-back student they should note the student doesn't just like options and choice; they need them or they start to itch, squirm and rebel. The secondary school environment is difficult enough for **P** preference students so teachers can help soften the pressure. To help:

- Provide as much flexibility as possible (multiple choice homework tasks, choice within the lesson).

- Avoid giving out detailed schedules (they'll just lose it anyway!).

- Don't be more picky with detail than is absolutely necessary.

- Shake things up now and again to prevent predictability becoming boredom. Introduce random surprises and changes.

- Identify effective strategies to ensure they can manage their workload successfully.

209
Falcon teacher with Falcon student
ENTP and ENTP

The naturally confident and assertive Falcon teacher and student can be a match made in heaven or hell. The equally excitable teacher and student work well together when they focus on learning rather than fun. However, as both are natural entertainers it may be best to share the classroom stage and enjoy each other's wit and charm. As long as the teacher doesn't forget the curriculum or the other students in the class, balance is achieved. For the teacher to get the best out of their naturally effusive student they need to:

- Enjoy the lively banter when it is appropriate to spark new thoughts – the student learns best this way.

- Stick to the point and stay positive (don't nag), as both teacher and student are easily distracted and liable to go off track!

- Avoid going over old ground.

- Be calm and clear, otherwise two **E** preferences can talk louder and louder with neither listening.

- Remember you can keep some thoughts to yourself (and you may think of a better way of expressing something, especially criticism, later).

- Be an enthusiastic and supportive listener; seek to help the student clarify and develop their thinking rather than assert your own opinions.

- Help each other learn to be quiet and encourage the **I** preferences in the class to express themselves.

Both teacher and student gather information by seeing the big picture first, using hunches and imagination to infer meaning. The teacher will naturally use their imagination in the classroom and the **N** student will respond well to this, possibly joining in with your flights of fancy and stories. A natural affinity between teacher and student is often present because they both look at the world in the same way – with a burning curiosity to understand why things are as they are by exploring patterns, possibilities, ideas and theories. Be careful not to look like you're favouring **N** students to the detriment of **S** students. Every student needs to be able to contribute in their preferred way. To get the best out of the imaginative student:

- Offer questions/projects that can be explored creatively.

- Avoid repetitive tasks as they'll quickly lose interest.

- Encourage the student to become aware of the important contribution of the **S** approach (the value of facts, details, procedure, experiments, applying experience, structure, the step-by-step model).

Falcons are task-focused, forthright, consistent and honest. The classroom is likely to have an atmosphere akin to seasoned boxers sparring with each other with ideas and theories. Students are given clear guidelines on what is expected in terms of behaviour, homework and so on. If the student challenges the teacher it is likely to be for

clarification. At best this means everyone knows where they stand and how to behave. At worst the classroom can resemble a court room where justice will be dispensed. For the teacher to get the best out of their naturally task-focused student they need to:

- Work in ways that test their skill and knowledge competitively (they raise their game for competitions, challenges, quizzes, measuring and beating personal bests).

- Help them understand that 50% of people are **F** preference and can interpret feedback as criticism.

- Focus on what the student has achieved and what comes next.

- Be prepared to compromise occasionally.

- Avoid trying to fix something without considering potential underlying emotional causes.

Falcons can be organised and efficient, but they crave anarchy! While enjoying a mutual love of spontaneity, which provides each with relief from the stifling and constraining timetables and deadlines essential in large organisations such as schools, they must also remember to complete any necessary tasks. Although likely to be fun and popular teachers, they also need to focus on the task of preparing the student to succeed socially and academically. Both prefer to start tasks than finish them. Their initial enthusiasm can quickly wane. Both need to ensure they identify and complete the important tasks or the student (or their parents) may eventually ask awkward questions. For the teacher to get the best out of their naturally laid-back student they need to understand the student doesn't just like options and choice; they are essential or they start to itch, squirm and rebel. The secondary school environment is difficult enough for **P** preference students so teachers can help their student achieve by:

- Providing as much flexibility as possible (multiple choice homework tasks, choice within the lesson).

- Avoiding dishing out detailed schedules (they'll just lose it anyway!).

- Mixing things up now and again to prevent predictability becoming boredom.

- Introducing random surprises and changes to keep the Falcon student captivated and on their toes.

210
Falcon teacher with Koala student
ENTP and ISFJ

The Falcon and Koala are opposites on all four preferences. For success they need to appreciate each other's different strengths rather than wish each other would change. The teacher could easily smother or ignore the gentle Koala but this would risk losing out on the ideas and contribution they could make. If the Falcon teacher can pass on some tricks and tips from their armoury of charm and energy, the Koala could gain the assertiveness they generally lack. Praise from a Falcon teacher is rarely dished out without good reason which means it is highly valued by students, especially Koalas and Seahorses. For the teacher to get the best out of their naturally reserved student they need to:

■ Slow down and be calm and succinct.

■ Leave plenty of time between question and answer; respect the student's need for time to think and reflect before responding.

■ Allow the student time and space to work on their own; don't hover over their head, waiting to pounce.

■ Avoid trying to fix problems immediately or finish their sentences.

■ Pair them up with complementary types (Seahorses, Seals, Teddy Bears and Dolphins).

■ Avoid placing them in groups/teams where they are the only **I** preference in a sea of **E** preferences (they'll be smothered).

■ Provide written praise (not just verbal).

The vivid imagination of the Falcon teacher can inspire all students, but they must respect the need for Koalas to be given clear guidelines, structure, facts, details and procedures; otherwise they can flounder. For the teacher to get the best out of their dogged student they need to:

■ Demonstrate how learning can be applied in the real world.

■ Allow the student opportunities to repeat and practise until satisfied they are competent.

■ Encourage the use of imagination as a useful process (it's not wasting time).

■ Be careful not to look like you're favouring **N** students to the detriment of **S** students. Every student needs to be able to contribute in their preferred way.

The teacher is focused first on task and second on people/relationships. The classroom is likely to have a lively and purposeful atmosphere. Students are given clear guidelines on what is expected in terms of behaviour, homework and so on. At best this means everyone knows where they stand and how to behave. At worst the classroom can resemble a military boot-camp full of dispirited and brow-beaten new recruits. A stern atmosphere will be especially distressing to Koalas. Remember the personal relationship you have with this student is key. The Koala needs to feel they like their teacher and that the teacher likes them too. If this happens they'll work harder but if not they may switch off completely. This explains why a student can be top of the class one year (with a teacher they like) and show no interest at all in the subject the following year when they change teacher. To help the naturally people-focused student progress:

■ Offer learning situations that allow for the use of empathy, collaboration and small teamworking to counter-balance your natural tendency to focus on task.

■ Give ample and regular praise while offering tactful support to overcome any blind-spots. Feedback can be easily interpreted as criticism so tread carefully when delivering it.

■ Engage by quietly and regularly stating your personal belief in the student (don't let me down, I know you can do it, I really liked your last piece of work).

■ Be prepared to compromise occasionally to reassure the routine-loving Koala.

The laid-back, flexible and spontaneous teacher with the naturally organised student can be a dream team or a disaster. To create a positive relationship they need to play to each other's strengths. The student can benefit from the teacher's ability to adapt and change plans and

the teacher can benefit from the student's desire to have a plan they can work to and complete. The teacher can also:

■ Encourage and support the student's desire to immerse themselves in order, neatness and respect for deadlines.

■ Allow the student independence in planning their work in their own way if they really want to.

■ Avoid changing plans just for the sake of it; this will only frustrate the student.

■ Encourage the student to embrace flexibility to add excitement to their life.

■ Avoid verbal sparring – loved by Falcons, despised by Koalas!

211
Falcon teacher with Barn Owl student
ENTP and INTJ

The naturally irrepressible Falcon teacher and their reserved Barn Owl student ooze imagination and objectivity. This can be the basis of a strong classroom relationship. To get the best out of their naturally independent student the teacher needs to:

■ Slow down and be calm and succinct.

■ Leave plenty of time between question and answer; respect the student's need for time to think and reflect before responding.

■ Allow the student time and space to work on their own; don't hover over their head, waiting to pounce.

■ Avoid trying to fix problems immediately or finish their sentences.

■ Pair them up with complementary types (Bears and Tawny Owls).

■ Avoid placing them in groups/teams where they are the only **I** preference in a sea of **E** preferences (they'll be smothered).

■ Provide written praise (not just verbal).

Falcon and Barn Owl gather information by seeing the big picture first, using hunches, inferences and imagination to create meaning. The teacher will naturally use their imagination in the classroom and the **N** student will respond well to this, possibly joining in with the sparring, anecdotes and stories. A natural affinity between teacher and student is often present because they both look at the world in the same way – with a burning curiosity to understand why things are as they are by exploring patterns, possibilities, ideas and theories. Be careful not to look like you're favouring **N** students to the detriment of **S** students. Every student needs to be able to contribute in their preferred way. To get the best out of the inherently imaginative student:

■ Offer questions/projects that can be explored creatively.

■ Avoid repetitive tasks as they'll quickly lose interest.

■ Encourage the student to become aware of the important contribution of the **S** approach (the value of facts, details, procedure, experiments, applying experience, structure, the step-by-step model).

Both teacher and student are task-focused, direct, consistent and firm. The classroom is likely to have a business-like, purposeful atmosphere. Students are given clear guidelines on what is expected in terms of behaviour, homework and so on. If the student challenges the teacher it is likely to be for clarification. At best this means everyone knows where they stand and how to behave. At worst the classroom can resemble a military boot-camp full of dispirited and brow-beaten new recruits. For the teacher to get the best out of their naturally task-focused student they need to:

■ Work in ways that test their skill and knowledge competitively (they raise their game for competitions, challenges, quizzes, measuring and beating personal bests).

■ Help them understand that 50% of people are **F** preference and can interpret feedback as criticism.

■ Focus on what the student has achieved and what comes next.

■ Be prepared to compromise occasionally.

■ Avoid trying to fix something without considering potential underlying emotional causes.

When the laid-back, flexible and spontaneous teacher meets the naturally organised student they can complement each other or clash spectacularly. To build a positive relationship they need to play to each other's strengths. The student can benefit from the teacher's ability to adapt and change plans, and the teacher can benefit from the student's desire to have a plan they can work to and complete. The teacher can also:

■ Encourage and support the student's desire for order, neatness and respecting deadlines.

■ Allow the student independence in planning their work in their own way if they really want to.

■ Avoid changing plans just for the sake of it; this will only frustrate the student.

■ Encourage the student to enjoy changing plans now and again.

212
Falcon teacher with Lion student
ENTP and ESFP

The Falcon and Lion combination share a desire for education to be fun, flexible and adventurous. Both are naturally confident, assertive and easily distracted. For the teacher to get the best out of their naturally effusive student they need to:

■ Enjoy the lively sparring when it is appropriate to spark new thoughts and ideas; the student learns best this way, but remember there may be thirty others in the classroom.

■ Stick to the point and stay positive (don't nag), as both teacher and student are easily distracted and liable to go off track!

■ Avoid going over old ground.

■ Be calm and clear, otherwise two **E** preferences can talk louder and louder like PMQs (with neither listening).

- Remember you can keep some thoughts to yourself (and you may think of a better way of expressing something, especially criticism, later).
- Be an enthusiastic and supportive listener; seek to help the student clarify and develop their thinking rather than assert your own.
- Help each other learn to be quiet and encourage the **I** preferences in the class to express themselves.

The imaginative Falcon teacher can inspire all students, but they do need to respect the need for Lions to be given clear guidelines, structure, facts, details and procedures; otherwise they can struggle. To get the best out of the grounded student:

- Demonstrate how learning can be applied in the real world.
- Allow the student opportunities to repeat and practise until satisfied they are competent.
- Encourage the use of imagination as a useful process (it's not wasting time).
- Be careful not to look like you're favouring **N** students to the detriment of **S** students. Every student needs to be able to contribute in their preferred way.

The teacher is focused first on task and second on harmonious relationships. The classroom is likely to have a business-like, purposeful atmosphere. Students are given clear guidelines on what is expected in terms of behaviour, homework and so on. At best this means everyone knows where they stand and how to behave. Remember the personal relationship you have with this student is key. The Lion needs to feel they like their teacher and that the teacher likes them too. If this happens they'll work harder but if not they may switch off completely. This explains why a student can be top of the class one year (with a teacher they like) and show no interest at all in the subject the following year when they change teacher. To get the best out of the fundamentally people-focused student:

- Offer learning situations that allow for the use of empathy, collaboration and teamworking to counter-balance your natural tendency to focus on task.
- Give ample and regular praise while offering tactful support to overcome any blind-spots. Feedback can be easily interpreted as criticism so walk on egg-shells when delivering it.
- Influence by appealing to the strength of your personal belief in the student (don't let me down, I know you can do it, I like you).
- Be prepared to compromise occasionally to avoid pushing the Lion into a huff.

Falcons and Lions can be organised and efficient; it's just such an effort! While enjoying a mutual love of spontaneity, which provides each with relief from the stifling and constraining timetables and deadlines essential in large organisations such as schools, they must also remember to complete any necessary tasks. Although likely to be fun and popular teachers, they also need to focus on the task of preparing the student to succeed socially and academically. Both prefer to start tasks than finish them. Their initial enthusiasm can quickly wane. Both need to ensure they identify and complete the important tasks or the student (or their parents) may eventually ask awkward questions. To help the student progress, understand that the student doesn't just like options and choice; they are essential or they start to itch, squirm and rebel. The secondary school environment is difficult enough for **P** prefer-

ence students so teachers can help their student achieve by:

- Providing as much flexibility as possible (multiple choice homework tasks, choice within the lesson).
- Not offering detailed schedules (they'll just lose it anyway!).
- Shaking things up now and again to prevent predictability becoming boredom. Introduce random surprises and changes.
- Helping the student identify simple time-management strategies to ensure they succeed.

213
Falcon teacher with Seal student
ENTP and INFP

The naturally confident and assertive Falcon teacher and the reserved Seal student share two preferences. Their flexibility and imagination can bind them together. Their differences can be a problem if the quiet and caring student interprets the teacher's energy and analytical zeal as aggressive or cold. For the teacher to get the best out of their naturally intense student they need to:

- Provide written praise (not just verbal).
- Slow down and be calm and succinct.
- Avoid hassling the student for an answer or opinion; respect their need for time to think and reflect before responding.
- Allow the student time and space to work on their own; don't hover over their head.
- Avoid trying to fix problems immediately or finish their sentences.
- Pair them up with complementary types (Seahorses, Teddy Bears and Dolphins).
- Avoid placing them in groups/teams where they are the only **I** preference in a sea of **E** preferences (they'll be smothered).

Both teacher and student gather information by seeing the big picture first, using ingenuity and imagination to infer meaning. The teacher will naturally use their imagination in the classroom and the **N** student will respond well to this, possibly joining in with the crazy anecdotes and stories. A natural affinity between teacher and student is often present because they both look at the world in the same way – with a burning curiosity to understand why things are as they are by exploring patterns, possibilities, ideas and theories. Be careful not to look like you're favouring **N** students to the detriment of **S** students. Every student needs to be able to contribute in their preferred way. For the teacher to get the best out of their inherently imaginative student they need to:

- Offer questions/projects that can be explored creatively.
- Avoid repetitive tasks as they'll quickly lose interest.
- Encourage the student to become aware of the important contribution of the **S** approach (the value of facts, details, procedure, experiments, applying experience, structure, the step-by-step model).

The Falcon is focused first on task and second on people/relationships. The classroom is likely to have a purposeful atmosphere. Students are given clear guidelines on what is expected in terms of behaviour and homework but sometimes Falcons can be inconsistent in executing these guidelines. At worst the classroom can resemble a military boot-camp full of dispirited and browbeaten new recruits. Remember the personal relationship you have with this student is key. The Seal needs to feel they like their teacher and that the teacher likes them too. If this happens they'll work harder but if not they may switch off completely. This explains why a student can be top of the class one year (with a teacher they like) and show no interest at all in the subject the following year when they change teacher. For the teacher to get the best out of their fundamentally people-focused student they need to:

- Create learning situations that allow for the use of empathy, collaboration and teamworking to counter-balance your natural tendency to focus on task.
- Offer ample and regular praise while offering tactful support to overcome any blind-spots. Feedback can be easily interpreted as criticism so walk on egg-shells when delivering it.
- Motivate by appealing to the strength of your personal belief in the student (don't let me down, I know you can do it).
- Be prepared to compromise occasionally or you may find yourself with a sulking Seal.

Falcons and Seals can be organised and efficient; it's just such an effort! While enjoying a mutual love of spontaneity, which provides each with relief from the stifling and constraining timetables and deadlines prevalent in large organisations such as schools, they must also remember to complete any necessary tasks. Although likely to be fun and popular teachers, they also need to focus on the task of preparing the student to succeed socially and academically. Both prefer to start tasks than finish them. Their initial enthusiasm can quickly wane. Both need to ensure they identify and complete the important tasks or the student (or their parents) may eventually ask awkward questions. For the teacher to get the best out of their naturally laid-back student they need to understand the student doesn't just like options and choice; they are essential or they start to itch, squirm and rebel. The secondary school environment is difficult enough for **P** preference students. Teachers can help their student achieve by:

- Providing as much flexibility as possible (multiple choice homework tasks, choice within the lesson).
- Avoiding detailed schedules (they'll just lose it anyway!).
- Shaking things up now and again to prevent predictability becoming boredom. Introduce random surprises and changes.
- Helping the student identify time-management tips to ensure they can succeed in the real world.

214
Falcon teacher with Black Bear student
ENTP and ESTJ

A naturally assertive teacher with an equally forthright student can make for a lively classroom. Mutual respect of each other's competence lies at the heart of a successful relationship. The student can easily admire the sharp wit and creativity of the teacher, while the teacher respects the hard work and dedication offered by the student. For the teacher to get the best out of their naturally confident student they need to:

- Enjoy the lively banter when it is appropriate to spark new thoughts and ideas; the student learns best this way, but remember there may be thirty others in the classroom.
- Stick to the point and stay positive (don't nag), as both teacher and student are easily distracted and liable to go off track!
- Avoid going over old ground.
- Be calm and clear, otherwise two **E** preferences can talk louder and louder with neither listening.
- Remember you can keep some thoughts to yourself (and you may think of a better way of expressing something, especially criticism, later).
- Be an enthusiastic and supportive listener; seek to help the student clarify and develop their thinking rather than assert your own.
- Help each other learn to be quiet and encourage the **I** preferences in the class to express themselves.

The imaginative Falcon can inspire all students, but they do need to respect the need for Black Bears to be given clear guidelines, structure, facts, details and procedures; otherwise they can struggle. For the teacher to get the best out of their grounded student they need to:

- Demonstrate how learning can be applied in the real world.
- Allow the student opportunities to repeat and practise until satisfied they are competent.
- Encourage the use of imagination as a useful process (it's not wasting time).
- Be careful not to look like you're favouring **N** students to the detriment of **S** students. Every student needs to be able to contribute in their preferred way.

Both teacher and student are task-orientated, direct, firm and honest. The classroom is likely to have a business-like, purposeful atmosphere. Students are given clear guidelines on what is expected in terms of behaviour and homework. If the student challenges the teacher it is likely to be for clarification. At best this means everyone knows where they stand and how to behave. At worst the classroom can resemble a military training camp. For the teacher to get the best out of their fundamentally task-focused student they need to:

- Work in ways that test their skill and knowledge competitively (they raise their game for competitions, challenges, quizzes, measuring and beating personal bests).
- Help them understand that 50% of people are **F** preference and usually interpret feedback as criticism.

- Focus on what the student has achieved and what comes next.
- Be prepared to compromise occasionally.
- Avoid trying to fix something without considering potential underlying emotional causes.

The laid-back, flexible and spontaneous Falcon teacher with the naturally organised Black Bear student can be a dream team or a disaster. To create a positive relationship they need to play to each other's strengths. The student can benefit from the teacher's ability to adapt and change plans and the teacher can benefit from the student's desire to have a plan they can work to and complete. The teacher can also:

- Encourage and support the student's desire for order, neatness and meeting deadlines.
- Allow the student independence in planning their work in their own way if they really want to.
- Avoid changing plans just for the sake of it; this will only frustrate the student.
- Encourage the student to embrace flexibility; variety is the spice of life.

215
Falcon teacher with Teddy Bear student
ENTP and ESFJ

This naturally confident and assertive pairing brings energy and enthusiasm into the classroom, although the way they direct their energy can cause conflict. The Teddy is concerned with harmony in relationships and in their work. The more blunt and argumentative Falcon generally mistrusts harmony as boring and will use their imagination to generate alternatives. For the teacher to get the best out of their naturally effusive student they need to:

- Enjoy the gleeful banter when it is appropriate to spark new thoughts and ideas; the student learns best this way, but remember there may be thirty others in the classroom.
- Stick to the point and stay positive (don't nag), as both teacher and student are easily distracted and liable to go off track!
- Avoid going over old ground.
- Be calm and clear, otherwise two **E** preferences can talk louder and louder with neither listening.
- Remember you can keep some thoughts to yourself (and you may think of a better way of expressing something, especially criticism, later).
- Be an enthusiastic and supportive listener; seek to help the student clarify and develop their thinking rather than assert your own.
- Help each other learn to be quiet and encourage the **I** preferences in the class to express themselves.

Falcons can inspire all students using their vivid imagination, but they do need to remember Teddy Bears need to be given clear guidelines, structure, facts, details and procedures; otherwise they can struggle. For the teacher to get the best out of their grounded student they need to:

- Demonstrate how learning can be applied in the real world.
- Allow the student opportunities to repeat and practise until satisfied they are competent.
- Encourage the use of imagination as a useful process (it's not wasting time).
- Be careful not to look like you're favouring **N** students to the detriment of **S** students. Every student needs to be able to contribute in their preferred way.

The teacher is focused first on task and second on people/relationships. The classroom is likely to have a business-like, purposeful atmosphere. Students are given clear guidelines on what is expected in terms of behaviour, homework and so on. At its best this means everyone knows where they stand and how to behave. Remember the personal relationship you have with this student is key. The student needs to feel they like their teacher and that the teacher likes them too. If this happens the Teddy will work harder, but if not they may switch off. This explains why a Teddy student can be top of the class one year (with a teacher they like) and show no interest at all in the subject the following year when they change teacher. For the teacher to get the best out of their people-focused student they need to:

- Offer learning situations that allow for the use of empathy, collaboration and teamworking to counter-balance your natural tendency to focus on task.
- Give ample and regular praise while offering tactful support to overcome any blind-spots. Feedback can be easily interpreted as criticism so walk on egg-shells when delivering it.
- Motivate by appealing to the strength of your personal belief in the student (don't let me down, I know you can do it, I like you).
- Be prepared to compromise occasionally because Teddy Bears can hold a grudge to Olympian standards.

The laid-back, flexible and spontaneous Falcon paired with the naturally organised Teddy can be a dream team or a disaster. To create a positive relationship they need to play to each other's strengths. The student can benefit from the teacher's ability to adapt and change plans and the teacher can benefit from the student's desire to have a plan they can work to and complete. The teacher can also:

- Encourage and support the student's desire for order, neatness and respecting deadlines.
- Allow the student independence in planning their work in their own way if they really want to.
- Avoid changing plans just for the sake of it; this will only frustrate the student.
- Encourage the student to embrace flexibility to broaden their experience.

216
Falcon teacher with Tiger student
ENTP and ISTP

The naturally confident and assertive Falcon teacher and the reserved Tiger student share two preferences. Their objectivity and flexibility can bind them together. Their differences can be a problem if the quiet and fiercely independent student interprets the teacher's energy and analytical zeal as suffocating and over the top. For the teacher to get the best out of their naturally intense student they need to:

◼ Slow down and be calm and succinct.

◼ Avoid hassling the student for an answer or opinion; respect their need for time to think and reflect before responding.

◼ Allow the student time and space to work on their own; don't hover over their head, waiting to pounce.

◼ Avoid trying to fix problems immediately or finish their sentences.

◼ Avoid placing them in groups/teams where they are the only **I** preference in a sea of **E** preferences (they'll be smothered).

◼ Provide written praise (not just verbal).

The vivid imagination of the Falcon can inspire all students, but they do need to respect the need for Tigers to be given clear guidelines, structure, facts, details and procedures; otherwise they can flounder. To get the best out of the grounded student:

◼ Demonstrate how learning can be applied in the real world.

◼ Allow the student opportunities to repeat and practise until satisfied they are competent.

◼ Encourage the use of imagination as a useful process (it's not wasting time).

◼ Be careful not to look like you're favouring **N** students to the detriment of **S** students. Every student needs to be able to contribute in their preferred way.

The teacher is focused first on task and second on people/relationships. The classroom is likely to have a business-like, purposeful atmosphere. Students are given clear guidelines on what is expected in terms of behaviour, homework and so on. At best this means everyone knows where they stand and how to behave. If the student challenges the teacher it is likely to be for clarification. Their relationship is likely to business-like, productive and occasionally superficial. For the teacher to get the best out of their fundamentally task-focused student they need to:

◼ Be prepared to compromise occasionally.

◼ Avoid trying to fix something without considering potential underlying emotional causes.

◼ Work in ways that test their skill and knowledge competitively (they raise their game for competitions, challenges, quizzes, measuring and beating personal bests).

◼ Help them understand that 50% of people are **F** preference and can interpret feedback as criticism.

◼ Focus on what the student has achieved and what comes next.

Falcons and Tigers can be organised and efficient; it's just such an effort! While enjoying a mutual love of spontaneity, which provides each with relief from the stifling and constraining timetables and deadlines essential in large organisations such as schools, they must also remember to complete any necessary tasks. Although likely to be fun and popular teachers, they also need to focus on the task of preparing the student to succeed socially and academically. Both prefer to start tasks than finish them. Their initial enthusiasm can quickly wane. Both need to ensure they identify and complete the important tasks or the student (or their parents) may eventually

ask awkward questions. For the teacher to get the best out of their naturally laid-back student they need to understand the student doesn't just like options and choice; they are essential or they start to squirm, wriggle and rebel. The secondary school environment is difficult enough for **P** preference students so teachers can help their student achieve by:

◼ Providing as much flexibility as possible (multiple choice homework tasks, choice within the lesson).

◼ Avoiding giving out detailed schedules (they'll just lose it anyway!).

◼ Shaking things up now and again to prevent predictability becoming boredom. Introduce random surprises and changes.

◼ Helping the student identify effective time-management strategies to help them succeed.

217
Falcon teacher with Seahorse student
ENTP and INFJ

The naturally confident and assertive Falcon teacher and the reserved Seahorse share one type preference. Both are imaginative and curious which can unite them in the classroom. Their differences can be a problem if the quiet and caring student interprets the teacher's flexibility, energy and analytical zeal as overbearing. For the teacher to get the best out of their naturally intense student they need to:

◼ Slow down and be calm and succinct.

◼ Avoid hassling the student for an answer or opinion; respect their need for time to think and reflect before responding.

◼ Avoid trying to fix problems immediately or finish their sentences.

◼ Pair them up with complementary types (Seals, Teddy Bears and Dolphins).

◼ Avoid placing them in groups/teams where they are the only **I** preference in a sea of **E** preferences (they'll be smothered).

◼ Provide written praise (not just verbal).

Both teacher and student gather information by seeing the big picture first, using ingenuity and imagination to infer meaning. The teacher will naturally use their imagination in the classroom and the **N** student will respond well to this, possibly joining in with flights of fancy, anecdotes and stories. A natural affinity between teacher and student is often present because they both look at the world in the same way – with a burning curiosity to understand why things are as they are by exploring patterns, possibilities, ideas and theories. Be careful not to look like you're favouring **N** students to the detriment of **S** students. Every student needs to be able to contribute in their preferred way. For the teacher to get the best out of their inherently imaginative student they need to:

◼ Offer questions/projects that can be explored creatively.

◼ Avoid repetitive tasks as they'll quickly lose interest.

◼ Encourage the student to become aware of the important contribution of the **S** approach (the value of facts, details, procedure, experiments, applying experience, structure, the step-by-step model).

The teacher is focused first on task and second on people/relationships. The classroom is likely to have a business-like, purposeful atmosphere. Students are given clear guidelines on what is expected in terms of behaviour, homework and so on. At best this means everyone knows where they stand and how to behave. At worst the classroom can resemble a military boot-camp full of dispirited new recruits. The personal relationship you have with this student is the key to reaching them. The Seahorse needs to feel they like their teacher and that the teacher likes them too. If this happens they'll work harder but if not they may switch off. This explains why a student can be top of the class one year (with a teacher they like) and show no interest the following year when they change teacher. For the teacher to get the best out of their naturally people-focused student they need to:

◼ Offer learning situations that allow for the use of empathy, collaboration and teamworking to counter-balance your natural tendency to focus on task.

◼ Give ample and regular praise while offering tactful support to overcome any blind-spots. Feedback can be easily interpreted as criticism so walk on egg-shells when delivering it.

◼ Influence by appealing to the strength of your personal belief in the student (don't let me down, I know you can do it, I like you).

◼ Be prepared to compromise occasionally as Seahorses can quietly stew over a grudge for years!

The laid-back, flexible and spontaneous Falcon teacher with the quietly organised Seahorse can be a dream team or a disaster. To create a positive relationship they need to play to each other's strengths. The student can benefit from the teacher's ability to adapt and change plans and the teacher can benefit from the student's desire to have a plan they can work to and complete. The teacher can also:

◼ Encourage and support the student's desire for order, neatness and respecting deadlines.

◼ Allow the student independence in planning their work in their own way if they really want to.

◼ Avoid changing plans just for the sake of it; this will only frustrate the student.

◼ Encourage the student to embrace flexibility; variety adds spice to life.

218
Falcon teacher with Tawny Owl student
ENTP and INTP

The naturally confident and assertive Falcon teacher and the reserved Tawny Owl student share three preferences. Their flexibility and imagination can bind them together. Their differences can be a problem if the quiet and independent student interprets the teacher's energy and analytical zeal as domineering. For the teacher to get the best out of their naturally intense student they need to:

- Slow down and be calm and succinct.
- Avoid hassling the student for an answer or opinion; respect their need for time to think and reflect before responding.
- Allow the student time and space to work on their own; don't hover over their head, waiting to pounce.
- Avoid trying to fix problems immediately or finish their sentences.
- Avoid placing them in groups/teams where they are the only **I** preference in a sea of **E** preferences (they'll be smothered).
- Provide written praise (not just verbal).

Both teacher and student gather information by seeing the big picture first, using ingenuity, inferences and imagination to generate new meaning. The teacher will naturally use their imagination in the classroom and the **N** student will respond well to this, possibly joining in with flights of fancy, anecdotes and stories. A natural affinity between teacher and student is often present because they both look at the world in the same way – with a burning curiosity to understand why things are as they are by exploring patterns, possibilities, ideas and theories. Be careful not to look like you're favouring **N** students to the detriment of **S** students. Every student needs to be able to contribute in their preferred way. For the teacher to get the best out of their imaginative student they need to:

- Offer questions/projects that can be explored creatively.
- Avoid repetitive tasks as they'll quickly lose interest.
- Encourage the student to become aware of the important contribution of the **S** approach (the value of facts, details, procedure, experiments, applying experience, structure, the step-by-step model).

The teacher is focused first on task and second on people/relationships. The classroom is likely to have a business-like, purposeful atmosphere. Students are given clear guidelines on what is expected in terms of behaviour, homework and so on. At best this means everyone knows where they stand and how to behave. At worst the classroom can resemble a military boot-camp full of dispirited and brow-beaten new recruits. If the student challenges the teacher it is likely to be for clarification. At best both know where they stand. Their relationship is likely to business-like, productive and occasionally superficial. For the teacher to get the best out of their naturally task-focused student they need to:

- Be prepared to compromise occasionally.
- Avoid trying to fix something without considering potential underlying emotional causes.
- Work in ways that test their skill and knowledge competitively (they raise their game for competitions, challenges, quizzes, measuring and beating personal bests).
- Help them understand that 50% of people are **F** preference and can interpret feedback as criticism.
- Focus on what the student has achieved and what comes next.

Falcons and Tawny Owls can be organised and efficient; it's just such an effort! While enjoying a mutual love of spontaneity, which provides each with relief from the stifling and constraining

timetables and deadlines essential in large organisations such as schools, they must also remember to complete any necessary tasks. Although likely to be fun and popular teachers, they also need to focus on the task of preparing the student to succeed socially and academically. Both prefer to start tasks than finish them. Their initial enthusiasm can quickly wane. Both need to ensure they identify and complete the important tasks or the student (or their parents) may eventually ask awkward questions. For the teacher to get the best out of their naturally laid-back student they need to understand the student doesn't just like options and choice; they are essential or they start to squirm, wriggle and rebel. The secondary school environment is difficult enough for **P** preference students so teachers can help their student achieve by:

- Providing as much flexibility as possible (multiple choice homework tasks, choice within the lesson) without giving out detailed schedules (they'll just lose it anyway!).
- Shaking things up now and again to prevent predictability becoming boredom. Introduce random surprises and changes.
- Helping the student adopt time-management techniques to ensure they can flourish.

219
Falcon teacher with Eagle student
ENTP and ENTJ

Two natural leaders can easily clash. To ensure harmony in the classroom they must appreciate that each other's natural ingenuity and vision are delivered using different styles. For the teacher to get the best out of the exuberant Eagle student they need to:

- Enjoy the lively banter when it is appropriate to spark new thoughts and ideas; the student learns best this way, but remember there may be thirty others in the classroom.
- Stick to the point and stay positive (don't nag), as both teacher and student are easily distracted and liable to go off track!
- Be calm and clear, otherwise two **E** preferences can talk louder and louder with neither listening to each other.
- Remember to keep some of your thoughts to yourself (and you may think of a better way of expressing something, especially criticism, later).
- Be an enthusiastic and supportive listener; seek to help the student clarify and develop their thinking rather than assert your own opinions.
- Help each other learn to be quiet and encourage the **I** preferences in the class to express themselves.

As both teacher and student gather information by seeing the big picture first, using hunches and imagination to infer meaning, there is scope for genuine respect and purpose to flourish. The teacher will naturally use their imagination in the classroom and the student will respond well to this, even joining in with flights of fancy, anecdotes and stories. A natural affinity between

teacher and student is often present because they both look at the world in the same way – with a burning curiosity to understand why things are as they are by exploring patterns, possibilities, ideas and theories. Be careful not to look like you're favouring **N** students to the detriment of **S** students. Every student needs to be able to contribute in their preferred way. For the teacher to get the best out of their naturally imaginative student they need to:

- Offer questions/projects that can be explored creatively.
- Avoid repetitive tasks as they'll quickly lose interest.
- Encourage the student to become aware of the important contribution of the **S** approach (the value of facts, details, procedure, experiments, applying experience, structure, the step-by-step model).

Both teacher and student are blunt, direct and consistent. The classroom is likely to have a business-like, purposeful atmosphere. Students are given clear guidelines on what is expected in terms of behaviour, homework and so on. If the student challenges the teacher it is likely to be for clarification. At best both know where they stand. Their relationship is likely to business-like, productive and occasionally superficial. For the teacher to get the best out of their fundamentally task-focused student they need to:

- Be prepared to compromise occasionally.
- Avoid trying to fix something without considering potential underlying emotional causes.
- Work in ways that test their skill and knowledge competitively (they raise their game for competitions, challenges, quizzes, measuring and beating personal bests).
- Help them understand that 50% of people are **F** preference and can interpret feedback as criticism.
- Focus on what the student has achieved and what comes next.

The laid-back, flexible and spontaneous teacher with the naturally organised student can be a dream team or a disaster. To create a positive relationship they need to play to each other's strengths. The student can benefit from the teacher's ability to adapt and change plans and the teacher can benefit from the student's desire to have a plan they can work to and complete. The teacher can also:

- Encourage and support the student's desire for order, neatness and respecting deadlines.
- Allow the student independence in planning their work in their own way if they really want to.
- Avoid changing plans just for the sake of it; this will only frustrate the student.
- Encourage the student to embrace flexibility occasionally as a way to develop new ideas and insights.

220
Falcon teacher with Panther student
ENTP and ESTP

Noel and Liam Gallagher (Falcon and Panther) have been great together and sometimes they clash a little! The naturally confident and assertive Falcon teacher and the equally excitable Panther student share three type preferences. Their hedonistic zeal can bind them together but their shared indomitable energy can become an explosive problem if it gets in the way of learning or pushes aside other students in the class. For the teacher to get the best out of their exuberant student they need to:

■ Enjoy the lively banter when it is appropriate to spark new thoughts and ideas; the student learns best this way, but remember there may be thirty others in the classroom.

■ Stick to the point and stay positive (don't nag), as both teacher and student are easily distracted and liable to go off track!

■ Be calm and clear, otherwise two **E** preferences can talk louder and louder with neither listening.

■ Remember to keep some of your thoughts to yourself (and you may think of a better way of expressing something, especially criticism, later).

■ Be an enthusiastic and supportive listener; seek to help the student clarify and develop their thinking rather than assert your own opinions.

■ Help each other learn to be quiet and encourage the **I** preferences in the class to express themselves.

The vividly imaginative Falcon can inspire all students, but they do need to respect the need for Panthers to be given clear guidelines, structure, facts, details and procedures; otherwise they can head off in the wrong direction. For the teacher to get the best out of their grounded student they need to:

■ Demonstrate how learning can be applied in the real world.

■ Allow the student opportunities to repeat and practise until satisfied they are competent and encourage the use of imagination as a useful process (it's not wasting time).

■ Be careful not to look like you're favouring **N** students to the detriment of **S** students. Every student needs to be able to contribute in their preferred way.

The teacher is focused first on task and second on people/relationships. The classroom is likely to have a business-like, purposeful atmosphere. Students are given clear guidelines on what is expected in terms of behaviour, homework and so on. At best this means everyone knows where they stand and how to behave. If the student challenges the teacher it is likely to be for clarification. Their relationship is liable to be fiery. For the teacher to get the best out of their naturally task-focused student they need to:

■ Be prepared to compromise occasionally.

■ Avoid trying to fix something without considering potential underlying emotional causes.

■ Work in ways that test their skill and knowledge competitively (they raise their game for competitions, challenges, quizzes, measuring and beating personal bests).

■ Help them understand that 50% of people are **F** preference and can interpret feedback as criticism.

■ Focus on what the student has achieved and what comes next.

Falcons and Panthers abhor to-do-lists, schedules and predictability; they rarely reach the status of an acquired taste or a honed skill. While enjoying their mutual love of spontaneity, which provides each with relief from the stifling and constraining timetables and deadlines essential in large organisations such as schools, they must also remember to complete any necessary tasks. Although likely to be fun and popular teachers, they also need to focus on the task of preparing the student to succeed socially and academically. Both prefer to start tasks than finish them. Their initial enthusiasm can quickly wane. Both need to ensure they identify and complete the important tasks or the student (or their parents) may eventually ask awkward questions. For the teacher to get the best out of their naturally laid-back student they need to understand the student doesn't just like options and choice; they are essential or they start to squirm, wriggle and rebel. The secondary school environment is difficult enough for **P** preference students so teachers can help their student achieve by:

■ Providing as much flexibility as possible (multiple choice homework tasks, choice within the lesson).

■ Avoiding giving out detailed schedules (they'll just lose it anyway!).

■ Shaking things up now and again to prevent predictability becoming boredom.

■ Helping the student identify effective time-management strategies.

■ Introducing random surprises and changes; Panthers enjoy surprises.

221
Falcon teacher with Cat student
ENTP and ISFP

The naturally confident and assertive Falcon teacher and the reserved Cat student share only their final letter preference **P**. It is their shared flexible approach that can form the basis of a positive working relationship. Also, when we're presented with someone so different to ourselves it is a great opportunity to learn how effective other approaches can be. For the teacher to get the best out of their naturally reticent Cat student they can:

■ Slow down and be calm and succinct.

■ Leave plenty of time between question and answer; respect the student's need for time to think and reflect before responding.

■ Allow the student time and space to work on their own; don't hover over their head, waiting to pounce.

■ Avoid trying to fix problems immediately or finish their sentences.

■ Pair them up with complementary types (Seals, Teddy Bears and Tigers).

■ Avoid placing them in groups/teams where they are the only **I** preference in a sea of **E** preferences (they'll be smothered).

■ Provide written praise (not just verbal).

The imaginative Falcon can inspire all students, but they do need to respect the need for Cats to be given clear guidelines, structure, facts, details and procedures; otherwise they can struggle. For the teacher to get the best out of their grounded student they need to:

■ Demonstrate how learning can be applied in the real world.

■ Allow the student opportunities to repeat and practise until satisfied they are competent.

■ Encourage the use of imagination as a useful process (it's not wasting time).

■ Be careful not to look like you're favouring **N** students to the detriment of **S** students. Every student needs to be able to contribute in their preferred way.

The Falcon is focused first on task and second on people/relationships. The classroom is likely to have a purposeful atmosphere. Students are given clear guidelines on what is expected in terms of behaviour, homework and so on. At best this means everyone knows where they stand and how to behave. The student needs to feel they can like their teacher and that the teacher likes them too. If this happens they'll work harder but if not they may switch off completely. This explains why a student can be top of the class one year (with a teacher they like) and show no interest at all in the subject the following year when they change teacher. For the teacher to get the best out of their fundamentally people-focused student they need to:

■ Offer learning situations that allow for the use of empathy, collaboration and teamworking to counter-balance your natural tendency to focus on task.

■ Give ample and regular praise while offering tactful support to overcome any blind-spots. Feedback can be easily interpreted as criticism so walk on egg-shells when delivering it.

■ Persuade/influence by appealing to the strength of your personal belief in the student (don't let me down, I know you can do it, I like you).

■ Be prepared to compromise occasionally.

Falcons and Cats can be organised and efficient; it's just such an effort! While enjoying a mutual love of spontaneity, which provides each with relief from the stifling and constraining timetables and deadlines prevalent in large organisations such as schools, they must also remember to complete any necessary tasks. Although likely to be fun and popular teachers, they also need to focus on the task of preparing the student to succeed socially and academically. Both prefer to start tasks than finish them. Their initial enthusiasm can quickly wane. Both need to ensure they identify and complete the important tasks or the student (or their parents) may eventually ask awkward questions. For the teacher to get the best out of their naturally laid-back student they need to understand the student doesn't just like options and choice; they are essential or they start to itch, squirm and rebel. The secondary school environment is difficult enough for **P** preference students so teachers can help their student when they:

◼ Shake things up now and again to prevent predictability becoming boredom. Introduce random surprises and changes.

◼ Encourage the student to identify simple, effective strategies to ensure they can succeed.

◼ Provide as much flexibility as possible (multiple choice homework tasks, choice within the lesson).

◼ Avoid giving out detailed schedules (they'll just lose it anyway!).

222
Falcon teacher with Clownfish student
ENTP and ENFP

This naturally confident and assertive pairing shares a great deal in common. Both are compelled to flaunt their imagination and can often appear on the same wavelength as other students struggle to keep up with their quick observations, anecdotes and verbal sparring. For the teacher to get the best out of their naturally effusive student they need to:

◼ Avoid going over old ground and enjoy the gleeful banter when it is appropriate to spark new thoughts and ideas; the student learns best this way, but remember there may be thirty others in the classroom.

◼ Stick to the point and stay positive (don't nag), as both teacher and student are easily distracted and liable to go off track!

◼ Be calm and clear, otherwise two **E** preferences can talk louder and louder with neither listening.

◼ Remember you can keep some thoughts to yourself (and you may think of a better way of expressing something, especially criticism, later).

◼ Be an enthusiastic and supportive listener; seek to help the student clarify and develop their thinking rather than assert your own.

◼ Help each other learn to be quiet and encourage the **I** preferences in the class to express themselves.

Both teacher and student are driven to gather information by seeing the big picture first, using hunches, inferences and imagination to decipher meaning. The teacher will naturally use their imagination in the classroom and the **N** student will respond well to this, possibly joining in with witty insights and stories. A natural affinity between teacher and student is often present because they both look at the world in the same way – with a burning curiosity to understand why things are as they are by exploring patterns, possibilities, ideas and theories. Be careful not to look like you're favouring **N** students to the detriment of **S** students. Every student needs to be able to contribute in their preferred way. For the teacher to get the best out of their inherently imaginative student they need to:

◼ Offer questions/projects that can be explored creatively.

◼ Avoid repetitive tasks as they'll quickly lose interest.

◼ Encourage the student to become aware of the important contribution of the **S** approach (the value of facts, details, procedure, experiments, applying experience, structure, the step-by-step model).

The teacher is focused first on task and second on people/relationships. The classroom is likely to have a business-like, purposeful atmosphere. Students are given clear guidelines on what is expected in terms of behaviour, homework and so on. At its best this means everyone knows where they stand and how to behave. Remember the personal relationship you have with this student is key. The Clownfish needs to feel they like their teacher and that the teacher likes them too. If this happens the student will work harder, but if not they may switch off. This explains why a Clownfish can be top of the class one year (with a teacher they like) and show no interest at all in the subject the following year when they change teacher. For the teacher to get the best out of their naturally people-focused student they need to:

◼ Offer learning situations that allow for the use of empathy, collaboration and teamworking to counter-balance your natural tendency to focus on task.

◼ Give ample and regular praise while offering tactful support to overcome any blind-spots. Feedback can be easily interpreted as criticism so walk on egg-shells when delivering it.

◼ Persuade/influence by appealing to the strength of your personal belief in the student (don't let me down, I know you can do it, I like you).

◼ Be prepared to compromise occasionally, otherwise the Clownfish can sulk or stomp for ages.

Falcons and Clownfish abhor to-do-lists, schedules and predictability; they rarely reach the status of an acquired taste or a honed skill. While enjoying their mutual love of spontaneity, which provides each with relief from the stifling and constraining timetables and deadlines essential in large organisations such as schools, they must also remember to complete any necessary tasks. Although likely to be fun and popular teachers, they also need to focus on the task of preparing the student to succeed socially and academically. Both prefer to start tasks than finish them. Their initial enthusiasm can quickly wane. Both need to ensure they identify and complete the important tasks or the student (or their parents) may eventually ask awkward questions. For the teacher to get the best out of their naturally laidback student they need to understand the student doesn't just like options and choice; they are essential or they start to itch, squirm and rebel. The secondary school environment is difficult enough for **P** preference students so teachers can help their student achieve by:

◼ Providing as much flexibility as possible (multiple choice homework tasks, choice within the lesson).

◼ Not giving out detailed schedules (they'll just lose it anyway!).

◼ Mixing things up now and again to prevent predictability becoming boredom.

◼ Introducing simple time-management techniques to ensure the Clownfish can prosper.

223
Falcon teacher with Polar Bear student
ENTP and ISTJ

Although not direct opposites the Falcon teacher and Polar Bear student are very different. The student is the most grounded of all types and the teacher the least grounded. If they can respect each other's differences they can both gain from the relationship along with the rest of the class. If they begin to jar and squabble the dissonance can reverberate beyond the classroom. For the teacher to get the best out of their stoical student they need to:

◼ Slow down and be calm and succinct.

◼ Leave plenty of time between question and answer; respect the student's need for time to think and reflect before responding.

◼ Allow the student time and space to work on their own; don't hover over their head, waiting to pounce.

◼ Avoid placing them in groups/teams where they are the only **I** preference in a sea of **E** preferences (they'll be smothered).

◼ Provide written praise (not just verbal).

The imaginative teacher can inspire all students, but they do need to respect the need for Polar Bears to be given clear guidelines, structure, facts, details and procedures; otherwise they can flounder. For the teacher to get the best out of their naturally grounded student they need to:

◼ Demonstrate how learning can be applied in the real world.

◼ Allow the student opportunities to repeat and practise until satisfied they are competent.

◼ Encourage the development of imagination as a useful process (it's not wasting time).

◼ Be careful not to look like you're favouring **N** students to the detriment of **S** students. Every student needs to be able to contribute in their preferred way.

◼ Use the Polar Bear student to check that you are sticking to the correct content – they can be natural auditors.

Both teacher and student are task-focused, direct, forthright and candid. The classroom is likely to have a business-like, purposeful atmosphere. Students are given clear guidelines on what is expected in terms of behaviour, homework and so on. If the student challenges the teacher it is likely to be for clarification. At best this means everyone knows where they stand and how to behave. At worst the classroom can resemble a military boot-camp full of dispirited and browbeaten new recruits. For the teacher to get the best out of their fundamentally task-focused student they need to:

◼ Work in ways that test their skill and knowledge competitively (they raise their game for competitions, challenges, quizzes, measuring and beating personal bests).

◼ Help them understand that 50% of people are **F** preference and can interpret feedback as criticism.

◼ Focus on what the student has achieved and what comes next.

◼ Be prepared to compromise occasionally.

■ Avoid trying to fix something without considering potential underlying emotional causes.

The laid-back, flexible and spontaneous teacher with the naturally organised student can be a dream team or a disaster. To create a positive relationship they need to play to each other's strengths. The student can benefit from the teacher's ability to adapt and change plans and the teacher can benefit from the student's desire to have a plan they can work to and complete. The teacher can also:

■ Avoid changing plans just for the sake of it; this will only frustrate the student.

■ Encourage the student to embrace flexibility occasionally.

■ Encourage and support the student's desire for order, neatness and respecting deadlines.

■ Allow the student independence in planning their work in their own way if they really want to.

224
Falcon teacher with Dolphin student
ENTP and ENFJ

This naturally confident and assertive pairing shares a great deal in common. Both are compelled to flaunt their imagination and can often appear on the same wavelength as other students struggle to keep up with their quick observations, anecdotes and verbal sparring. For the teacher to get the best out of their naturally effusive student they need to:

■ Enjoy the gleeful banter when it is appropriate to spark new thoughts and ideas; the student learns best this way, but remember there may be thirty others in the classroom.

■ Stick to the point and stay positive (don't nag), as both teacher and student are easily distracted and liable to go off track!

■ Avoid going over old ground.

■ Be calm and clear, otherwise two **E** preferences can talk louder and louder with neither listening.

■ Remember you can keep some thoughts to yourself (and you may think of a better way of expressing something, especially criticism, later).

■ Be an enthusiastic and supportive listener; seek to help the student clarify and develop their thinking rather than assert your own.

■ Help each other learn to be quiet and encourage the **I** preferences in the class to express themselves.

Both teacher and student are driven to gather information by seeing the big picture first, using hunches, inferences and imagination to decipher meaning. The teacher will naturally use their imagination in the classroom and the Dolphin student will respond well to this, possibly joining in with witty insights and stories. A natural affinity between teacher and student is often present because they both look at the world in the same way – with a burning curiosity to understand why things are as they are by exploring patterns, possibilities, ideas and theories. Be careful not

to look like you're favouring **N** students to the detriment of **S** students. Every student needs to be able to contribute in their preferred way. For the teacher to get the best out of their inherently imaginative student they need to:

■ Offer questions/projects that can be explored creatively.

■ Avoid repetitive tasks as they'll quickly lose interest.

■ Encourage the student to become aware of the important contribution of the **S** approach (the value of facts, details, procedure, experiments, applying experience, structure, the step-by-step model).

The teacher is focused first on task and second on people/relationships. The classroom is likely to have a business-like, purposeful atmosphere. Students are given clear guidelines on what is expected in terms of behaviour, homework and so on. At its best this means everyone knows where they stand and how to behave. Remember the personal relationship you have with this student is key. The Dolphin needs to feel they like their teacher and that the teacher likes them too. If this happens the student will work harder, but if not they may switch off. This explains why a Dolphin student can be top of the class one year (with a teacher they like) and show no interest at all in the subject the following year when they change teacher. For the teacher to get the best out of their naturally people-focused student they need to:

■ Offer learning situations that allow for the use of empathy, collaboration and teamworking to counter-balance your natural tendency to focus on task.

■ Give ample and regular praise while offering tactful support to overcome any blind-spots. Feedback can be easily interpreted as criticism, so walk on egg-shells when delivering it.

■ Persuade/influence by appealing to the strength of your personal belief in the student (don't let me down, I know you can do it, I like you).

■ Be prepared to compromise occasionally.

The laid-back, flexible and spontaneous teacher with the naturally organised student can be a dream team or a disaster. To create a positive relationship they need to play to each other's strengths. The student can benefit from the teacher's ability to adapt and change plans and the teacher can benefit from the student's desire to have a plan they can work to and complete. The teacher can also:

■ Encourage and support the student's desire for order, neatness and respecting deadlines.

■ Allow the student independence in planning their work in their own way if they really want to.

■ Avoid changing plans just for the sake of it; this will only frustrate the student.

■ Encourage the student to embrace flexibility.

225
Tawny Owl teacher with Black Bear student
INTP and ESTJ

Tawny Owls and Black Bears share one type preference. Both are direct and candid. Conflict is most likely due to the student's desire to discuss and comment regularly which contrasts with the naturally reflective teacher. Remember they can't read your mind. For the teacher to get the best out of their lively student they need to:

■ Listen patiently and enthusiastically to the student as they pour out their thoughts.

■ Stay open to their ideas to see where they lead – the student is thinking out loud and this is how they learn best.

■ Also offer your own thoughts; if you need a timeout ask for one.

■ Encourage the student to think things through before talking otherwise they'll hog the lesson.

■ Steer the student away from controversial subjects/topics, especially in group discussions.

■ Build in plenty of opportunities during lessons for the **E** students to talk things through with other **E** preferences.

The imaginative teacher can inspire all students, but they do need to respect the need for Black Bears to be given clear guidelines, structure, facts, details and procedures; otherwise they can flounder. For the teacher to get the best out of their grounded student they need to:

■ Demonstrate how learning can be applied in the real world.

■ Allow the student opportunities to repeat and practise until satisfied they are competent.

■ Encourage the use of imagination as a useful process (it's not wasting time).

■ Be careful not to look like you're favouring **N** students to the detriment of **S** students. Every student needs to be able to contribute in their preferred way.

Both teacher and student are task-focused, direct, consistent and sometimes blunt. The classroom is likely to have a purposeful atmosphere. Students are given clear guidelines on what is expected in terms of behaviour, homework and so on. If the student challenges the teacher it is likely to be for clarification. At best this means everyone knows where they stand and how to behave. For the teacher to get the best out of their naturally task-orientated student they need to:

■ Focus on what the student has achieved as well as what comes next.

■ Be prepared to compromise occasionally.

■ Avoid trying to fix something without considering potential underlying emotional causes.

■ Work in ways that test their skill and knowledge competitively (they raise their game for competitions, challenges, quizzes, measuring and beating personal bests).

■ Help them understand that half the population are **F** preference and can interpret objective feedback as personal criticism.

The laid-back, flexible and spontaneous Tawny Owl teacher with the naturally organised Black

Bear can be a dream team or a disaster. To create a positive relationship they need to play to each other's strengths. The student can benefit from the teacher's ability to adapt and change plans and the teacher can benefit from the student's desire to have a plan they can work to and complete. The teacher can also:

- Encourage and support the student's desire for order, neatness and respecting deadlines.
- Allow the student independence in planning their work in their own way if they really want to.
- Avoid changing plans just for the sake of it; this will only frustrate the Black Bear.
- Encourage the student to try new approaches and activities.

226
Tawny Owl teacher with Teddy Bear student
INTP and ESFJ

Tawny Owls and Teddy Bears don't share any type preferences. If you can appreciate your differences both will benefit. To best support your student be personal, gentle and diplomatic. Offer compliments and respect their need to socialise. For the teacher to get the best out of their naturally lively student they need to:

- Listen patiently and enthusiastically to the student as they blurt out possibly jumbled thoughts or reminiscences.
- Stay open to apparent wittering to see where it leads – the student is thinking out loud and this is how they learn best.
- Also offer your own thoughts; if you need a timeout ask for one.
- Encourage the student to think things through before talking otherwise they'll hijack the lesson.
- Steer the student away from controversial topics, especially in group discussions.
- Build in plenty of opportunities during lessons for the **E** students to talk things through with other **E** preferences.

The Tawny Owl teacher can inspire all students, but they do need to respect the need for Teddies to be given clear guidelines, structure, facts, details and procedures; otherwise they can flounder. For the teacher to get the best out of their grounded student they need to:

- Demonstrate how learning can be applied in the real world.
- Allow the student opportunities to repeat and practise until satisfied they are competent.
- Encourage the use of imagination as a useful process (it's not wasting time).
- Be careful not to look like you're favouring **N** students to the detriment of **S** students. Every student needs to be able to contribute in their preferred way.

The teacher is focused first on task and second on people/relationships. The classroom is likely to have a purposeful atmosphere. Students are given clear guidelines on what is expected in terms of behaviour, homework and so on. At best this means everyone knows where they stand

and how to behave. At worst the classroom can resemble a mad professor's lab. Remember the personal relationship you have with this student is crucial to the student. The Teddy needs to feel they like their teacher and that the teacher likes them too. If this happens they'll work harder but if not they may switch off. This explains why a student can be top of the class one year (with a teacher they like) and show no interest at all in the subject the following year when they change teacher. For the teacher to get the best out of their fundamentally subjective student they need to:

- Offer learning situations that allow for the use of empathy, collaboration and teamworking to counter-balance your natural tendency to focus on task.
- Give ample and regular praise while offering tactful support to overcome any blind-spots.
- Compromise their occasionally blunt feedback; this can be easily interpreted as criticism so walk on egg-shells when delivering it.
- Emphasise their personal belief in the student (don't let me down, I know you can do it, I like your work).

The laid-back, flexible and spontaneous teacher with the naturally organised student can be a dream team or a disaster. To create a positive relationship they need to play to each other's strengths. The student can benefit from the teacher's ability to improvise and the teacher can benefit from the student's desire to have a plan they can work to and complete. The teacher can also:

- Encourage and support the student's desire for order, neatness and respecting deadlines.
- Allow the student independence in planning their work in their own way if they really want to.
- Avoid changing plans just for the sake of it; this will only frustrate the student.
- Encourage the student to embrace new approaches and activities.

227
Tawny Owl teacher with Dolphin student
INTP and ENFJ

The Tawny Owl and Dolphin share one type preference. They are likely to connect through their vivid enquiring imaginations. Conflict is most likely when the chatty and diplomatic Dolphin annoys the more private and blunt Owl. For the teacher to get the best out of their naturally lively student they need to:

- Listen patiently and enthusiastically to the student as they blurt out possibly jumbled thoughts.
- Stay open to 'silly' ideas to see where they lead – the student is thinking out loud and this is how they learn best.
- Also offer your own thoughts; if you need a timeout ask for one.
- Encourage the student to think things through before talking otherwise they'll hog the lesson.

- Steer the student away from controversial subjects/topics, especially in group discussions.
- Build in plenty of opportunities during lessons for the **E** students to talk things through with other **E** preferences.

Both teacher and student gather information by seeing the big picture first, using hunches, inferences and imagination to infer meaning. The teacher will naturally use their imagination in the classroom and the **N** student will respond well to this, possibly joining in with flights of fancy, anecdotes and stories. A natural affinity between teacher and student is often present because they both look at the world in the same way – with a burning curiosity to understand why things are as they are by exploring patterns, possibilities, ideas and theories. Be careful not to look like you're favouring **N** students to the detriment of **S** students. Every student needs to be able to contribute in their preferred way. For the teacher to get the best out of their inherently imaginative student they need to:

- Offer questions/projects that can be explored creatively.
- Avoid repetitive tasks as they'll quickly lose interest.
- Encourage the student to become aware of the important contribution of the **S** approach (the value of facts, details, procedure, experiments, applying experience, structure, the step-by-step model).

The teacher is focused first on task and second on people/relationships. The classroom is likely to have a business-like, purposeful atmosphere. Students are given clear guidelines on what is expected in terms of behaviour, homework and so on. At best this means everyone knows where they stand and how to behave. At worst the classroom can resemble a military boot-camp full of dispirited and brow-beaten new recruits. Remember the personal relationship you have with this student is crucial to the student. The Dolphin needs to feel they like their teacher and that the teacher likes them too. If this happens they'll work harder but if not they may switch off. This explains why a student can be top of the class one year (with a teacher they like) and show no interest at all in the subject the following year when they change teacher. For the teacher to get the best out of their naturally subjective student they need to:

- Offer learning situations that allow for the use of empathy, collaboration and teamworking to counter-balance your natural tendency to focus on task.
- Give ample and regular praise while offering tactful support to overcome any blind-spots.
- Compromise their occasionally blunt feedback; this can be easily interpreted as criticism so walk on egg-shells when delivering it.
- Emphasise their personal belief in the student (don't let me down, I know you can do it).

The laid-back, flexible and spontaneous teacher with the fundamentally organised student can be a dream team or a disaster. To create a positive relationship they need to play to each other's strengths. The student can benefit from the teacher's ability to adapt and change plans and the teacher can benefit from the student's desire to have a plan they can work to and complete. The teacher can also:

- Avoid changing plans just for the sake of it; this will only frustrate the student.

■ Encourage the student to embrace flexibility occasionally.

■ Allow the student independence in planning their work in their own way if they really want to.

■ Encourage and support the student's desire for order, neatness and respecting deadlines.

228
Tawny Owl teacher with Eagle student
INTP and ENTJ

Tawny Owls and Eagles share two type preferences. Both share a thirst for knowledge and are direct and independent thinkers. As both are natural leaders, the most likely source of conflict is an over-exuberant Eagle student. For the teacher to get the best out of their naturally sprightly student they need to:

■ Listen patiently and enthusiastically to the student as they blurt out possibly jumbled thoughts.

■ Stay open to 'silly' ideas to see where they lead – the student is thinking out loud and this is how they learn best.

■ Also offer your own thoughts; if you need a timeout ask for one.

■ Encourage the student to think things through before talking otherwise they'll hog the lesson.

■ Steer the student away from controversial subjects/topics, especially in group discussions.

■ Build in plenty of opportunities during lessons for the **E** students to talk things through with other **E** preferences.

Both teacher and student gather information by seeing the big picture first, using hunches, inferences and imagination to infer meaning. The teacher will instinctively use their imagination in the classroom and the **N** student will respond well to this, possibly adding their own insights and interpretations. A natural affinity between teacher and student is often present because they both look at the world in the same way – with a burning curiosity to understand why things are as they are by exploring patterns, possibilities, ideas and theories. Be careful not to look like you're favouring **N** students to the detriment of **S** students. Every student needs to be able to contribute in their preferred way. For the teacher to get the best out of their inherently imaginative student they need to:

■ Offer questions/projects that can be explored creatively.

■ Avoid repetitive tasks as they'll quickly lose interest.

■ Encourage the student to become aware of the important contribution of the **S** approach (the value of facts, details, procedure, experiments, applying experience, structure, the step-by-step model).

Both teacher and student are task-focused, direct, consistent and frank. The classroom is likely to have a purposeful atmosphere. Students are given guidelines on what is expected in terms of behaviour, homework and so on. If the student challenges the teacher it is likely to be for clarification. At best this means everyone knows where they stand and how to behave. At worst the culture can resemble a boot-camp. For the teacher to get the best out of their fundamentally strategic student they need to:

■ Focus on what the student has achieved as well as what comes next.

■ Be prepared to compromise occasionally.

■ Avoid trying to fix something without considering potential underlying emotional causes.

■ Work in ways that test their skill and knowledge competitively (they raise their game for competitions, challenges, quizzes, measuring and beating personal bests).

■ Help them understand that 50% of people are **F** preference and can interpret objective feedback as personal criticism.

The laid-back, flexible and spontaneous teacher with the organised student can be a dream team or a disaster. To create a positive relationship they need to play to each other's strengths. The student can benefit from the teacher's ability to improvise and invent and the teacher can benefit from the student's desire to have a plan they can work to and complete. The teacher can also:

■ Encourage and support the student's desire for order, neatness and respecting deadlines.

■ Allow the student independence in planning their work in their own way if they really want to.

■ Avoid changing plans just for the sake of it; this will only frustrate the student.

229
Tawny Owl teacher with Panther student
INTP and ESTP

Tawny Owls and Panthers share two type preferences. Both thrive on autonomy. Conflict is likely if the teacher can't rein in the scattergun and ebullient student. For the teacher to get the best out of their naturally lively student they need to:

■ Listen patiently and enthusiastically to the student as they blurt out possibly jumbled thoughts.

■ Stay open to 'silly' ideas to see where they lead – the student is thinking out loud and this is how they learn best.

■ Also offer your own thoughts; if you need a timeout ask for one.

■ Encourage the student to think things through before talking otherwise they'll hog the lesson.

■ Steer the student away from controversial subjects/topics, especially in group discussions.

■ Build in plenty of opportunities during lessons for the **E** students to talk things through with other **E** preferences.

The imaginative teacher can inspire all students, but they do need to respect the need for Panthers to be given clear guidelines, structure, facts, details and procedures; otherwise they can flounder. For the teacher to get the best out of their excitable student they need to:

■ Demonstrate how learning can be applied in the real world.

■ Allow the student opportunities to repeat and practise until satisfied they are competent.

■ Encourage the focused use of imagination as a useful process (it's not wasting time).

■ Be careful not to look like you're favouring **N** students to the detriment of **S** students. Every student needs to be able to contribute in their preferred way.

Both teacher and student are naturally objective, direct, consistent and blunt. The classroom is likely to have a purposeful atmosphere. Students are given clear guidelines on what is expected in terms of behaviour, homework and so on. If the student challenges the teacher it is likely to be for clarification. At best this means everyone knows where they stand and how to behave. For the teacher to get the best out of their ebullient student they need to:

■ Focus on what the student has achieved as well as what comes next.

■ Be prepared to compromise occasionally.

■ Avoid trying to fix something without considering potential underlying emotional causes.

■ Work in ways that test their skill and knowledge competitively (they raise their game for competitions, challenges, quizzes, measuring and beating personal bests).

■ Help them appreciate that 50% of people are **F** preference and can interpret feedback as personal criticism.

Tawny Owls and Panthers abhor to-do-lists, schedules and predictability; they rarely reach the status of an acquired taste or a honed skill. While enjoying their mutual love of spontaneity, which provides each with relief from the stifling and constraining timetables and deadlines prevalent in large organisations such as schools, they must also remember to complete any necessary tasks. Although likely to be quirky and popular teachers, they also need to focus on the task of preparing the student to succeed socially and academically. Both prefer to start tasks than finish them. Their initial enthusiasm can quickly wane. Both need to ensure they identify and complete priority tasks or the student (or their parents) may ask awkward questions. For the teacher to get the best out of their naturally laid-back student they need to understand the student doesn't just like options and choice; they are essential or they start to wriggle, itch and rebel. The structured, timetabled and routine-laden secondary school environment is difficult for many **P** preferences, especially Panthers. Teachers can help by:

■ Providing as much flexibility as possible (multiple choice homework tasks, choice within the lesson).

■ Avoiding detailed schedules (they'll just lose it anyway!).

■ Shaking things up now and again to prevent predictability becoming boredom. Introduce random surprises and changes.

■ Helping the student identify ways they can organise and manage their time to complete important work without a last-minute rush.

230
Tawny Owl teacher with Lion student
INTP and ESFP

The Tawny Owl and Lion share one type preference. Both are flexible in approach. The teacher needs to focus the attention of the action-loving Lion on the task in hand to prevent conflict from brewing. For the teacher to get the best out of their naturally lively student they need to:

■ Listen patiently and enthusiastically to the student as they blurt out possibly jumbled thoughts.

■ Stay open to anecdotes and stories to see where they lead – the student is thinking out loud and this is how they learn best.

■ Also offer your own thoughts; if you need a timeout ask for one.

■ Encourage the student to think things through before talking otherwise they'll hog the lesson.

■ Steer the student away from controversial subjects/topics, especially in group discussions.

■ Build in plenty of opportunities during lessons for the **E** students to talk things through with other **E** preferences.

The imaginative Tawny Owl teacher can inspire all students, but they do need to respect the need for Lions to be given clear guidelines, structure, facts, details and procedures; otherwise they can struggle. To help their student progress they need to:

■ Demonstrate how learning can be applied in the real world.

■ Allow the student opportunities to repeat and practise until satisfied they are competent.

■ Encourage the use of imagination as a useful process (it's not wasting time).

■ Be careful not to look like you're favouring **N** students to the detriment of **S** students. Every student needs to be able to contribute in their preferred way.

The teacher is focused first on task and second on people and relationships. The classroom is likely to have a purposeful atmosphere. Students are given clear guidelines on what is expected in terms of behaviour, homework and so on. At best this means everyone knows where they stand and how to behave. Remember the personal relationship you have with this student is crucial to the student. The Lion needs to feel they like their teacher and that the teacher likes them too. If this happens they'll work harder but if not they may switch off. This explains why a student can be top of the class one year (with a teacher they like) and show no interest at all in the subject the following year when they change teacher. For the teacher to get the best out of their intrinsically subjective student they need to:

■ Offer learning situations that allow for the use of empathy, collaboration and teamworking to counter-balance your natural tendency to focus on task.

■ Give ample and regular praise while offering tactful support to overcome any blind-spots.

■ Compromise their occasionally blunt feedback; this can be easily interpreted as criticism so walk on egg-shells when delivering it.

■ Emphasise their personal belief in the student (don't let me down, I know you can do it, I like you).

Tawny Owls and Lions can be organised and efficient; it's just such an effort! While enjoying a mutual love of spontaneity, which provides each with relief from the stifling and constraining timetables and deadlines essential in large organisations such as schools, they must also remember to complete any necessary tasks. Although likely to be fun and popular teachers, they also need to focus on the task of preparing the student to succeed socially and academically. Both prefer to start tasks than finish them. Their initial enthusiasm can quickly drain. Both need to ensure they identify and complete priority tasks or the student (or their parents) may ask awkward questions. For the teacher to get the best out of their naturally laid-back student they need to understand the student doesn't just like options and choice; they are essential or they start to itch, squirm and revolt. The structured, timetabled and routine-laden secondary school environment is difficult for many **P** preferences. Teachers can help by:

■ Providing as much flexibility as possible (multiple choice homework tasks, choice within the lesson).

■ Helping the student identify ways they can organise and manage their time to complete important work without a last-minute panic.

■ Avoiding detailed schedules (they'll just lose it anyway!).

■ Shaking things up now and again to prevent predictability becoming boredom.

■ Introducing random surprises and changes.

231
Tawny Owl teacher with Clownfish student
INTP and ENFP

Tawny Owls and Clownfish share two type preferences. Both use their imaginations to bring fun and creativity into the classroom. The most likely source of conflict is when the sociable Clownfish is unable to settle down to work. For the teacher to get the best out of their naturally lively student they need to:

■ Listen patiently and enthusiastically to the student as they blurt out possibly jumbled thoughts.

■ Stay open to 'silly' ideas and stories to see where they lead – the student is thinking out loud and this is how they learn best.

■ Also offer your own thoughts; if you need a timeout ask for one.

■ Encourage the student to think things through before talking otherwise they'll hog the lesson.

■ Steer the student away from controversial subjects/topics, especially in group discussions.

■ Build in plenty of opportunities during lessons for the **E** students to talk things through with other **E** preferences.

Both teacher and student gather information by seeing the big picture first, using hunches, inferences and imagination to infer meaning. The teacher will naturally use their imagination in the classroom and the **N** student will respond well to this, possibly joining in with flights of fancy, anecdotes and stories. An affinity between teacher and student is often present because they both look at the world in the same way – with a burning curiosity to understand why things are as they are by exploring patterns, possibilities, ideas and theories. Be careful not to look like you're favouring **N** students to the detriment of **S** students. Every student needs to be able to contribute in their preferred way. For the teacher to get the best out of their inherently imaginative student they need to:

■ Offer questions/projects that can be explored creatively.

■ Avoid repetitive tasks as they'll quickly lose interest.

■ Encourage the student to become aware of the important contribution of the **S** approach (the value of facts, details, procedure, experiments, applying experience, structure, the step-by-step model).

The teacher is focused first on task and second on people/relationships. The classroom is likely to have a business-like, purposeful atmosphere. Students are given clear guidelines on what is expected in terms of behaviour, homework and so on. At best this means everyone knows where they stand and how to behave. At worst the classroom can resemble a military boot-camp full of dispirited and brow-beaten new recruits. Remember the personal relationship you have with this student is crucial to the student. The Clownfish needs to feel they like their teacher and that the teacher likes them too. If this happens they'll work harder but if not they may switch off. This explains why a student can be top of the class one year (with a teacher they like) and show no interest at all in the subject the following year when they change teacher. For the teacher to get the best out of their intrinsically subjective student they need to:

■ Offer learning situations that allow for the use of empathy, collaboration and teamworking to counter-balance your natural tendency to focus on task.

■ Give ample and regular praise while offering tactful support to overcome any blind-spots.

■ Compromise their occasionally blunt feedback; this can be easily interpreted as criticism so walk on egg-shells when delivering it.

■ Emphasise their personal belief in the student (don't let me down, I know you can do it, I like you, you have great ideas).

Tawny Owls and Clownfish abhor to-do-lists, schedules and predictability; they rarely reach the status of an acquired taste or a honed skill. While enjoying their mutual love of spontaneity, which provides each with relief from the stifling and constraining timetables and deadlines essential in large organisations such as schools, they must also remember to complete any necessary tasks. Although likely to be fun and popular teachers, they also need to focus on the task of preparing the student to succeed socially and academically. Both prefer to start tasks than finish them. Their initial enthusiasm can quickly drain.

Both need to ensure they identify and complete priority tasks or the student (or their parents) may ask awkward questions. For the teacher to get the best out of their naturally laid-back student they need to understand the student doesn't just like options and choice; they are essential or they start to itch, squirm and consider mutiny. The structured, timetabled and routine-laden secondary school environment is difficult for many **P** preferences. Teachers can help by:

- Providing as much flexibility as possible (multiple choice homework tasks, choice within the lesson).
- Avoiding detailed schedules (they'll just lose it anyway!).
- Shaking things up now and again to prevent predictability becoming boredom. Introduce random surprises and changes.
- Helping the student identify ways they can organise and manage their time to complete important work without a last-minute rush.

232
Tawny Owl teacher with Falcon student
INTP and ENTP

Tawny Owls and Falcons share three type preferences. Both use their dazzling imaginations to bring fun and creativity into the classroom. The most likely source of conflict is when the assertive and argumentative Falcon is unable to settle down to work. For the teacher to get the best out of their naturally lively student they need to:

- Listen patiently and enthusiastically to the student as they blurt out possibly jumbled thoughts.
- Stay open to 'silly' ideas to see where they lead – the student is thinking out loud and this is how they learn best.
- Also offer your own thoughts; if you need a timeout ask for one.
- Encourage the student to think things through before talking otherwise they'll hog the lesson.
- Steer the student away from controversial subjects/topics, especially in group discussions.
- Build in plenty of opportunities during lessons for the **E** students to talk things through with other **E** preferences.

Both teacher and student gather information by seeing the big picture first, using hunches, inferences and imagination to infer meaning. The teacher will naturally use their imagination in the classroom and the **N** student will respond well to this, possibly joining in with flights of fancy, anecdotes and stories. A natural affinity between teacher and student is often present because they both look at the world in the same way – with a burning curiosity to understand why things are as they are by exploring patterns, possibilities, ideas and theories. Be careful not to look like you're favouring **N** students to the detriment of **S** students. Every student needs to be able to contribute in their preferred way. For the teacher to get the best out of their inherently imaginative student they need to:

- Offer questions/projects that can be explored creatively.
- Avoid repetitive tasks as they'll quickly lose interest.
- Encourage the student to become aware of the important contribution of the **S** approach (the value of facts, details, procedure, experiments, applying experience, structure, the step-by-step model).

Both teacher and student are direct, consistent and objective. The classroom is likely to have a purposeful atmosphere. Students are given clear guidelines on what is expected in terms of behaviour, homework and so on. If the student challenges the teacher it is likely to be for clarification. At best this means everyone knows where they stand and how to behave. For the teacher to get the best out of their naturally task-focused student they need to:

- Focus on what the student has achieved as well as what comes next.
- Be prepared to compromise occasionally.
- Avoid trying to fix something without considering potential underlying emotional causes.
- Work in ways that test their skill and knowledge competitively (they raise their game for competitions, challenges, quizzes, measuring and beating personal bests).
- Help them understand that 50% of people are **F** preference and can interpret objective feedback as personal criticism.

Tawny Owls and Falcons can be organised and efficient; it's just such an effort! While enjoying a mutual love of spontaneity, which provides each with relief from the stifling and constraining timetables and deadlines that engulf large organisations such as schools, they must also remember to complete essential tasks. Although likely to be quirky and popular teachers, they also need to focus on the task of preparing the student to succeed socially and academically. Both prefer to start tasks than finish them. Their initial enthusiasm can quickly drain. Both need to ensure they identify and complete priority tasks or the student (or their parents) may ask awkward questions. For the teacher to get the best out of their naturally laid-back student they need to understand the student doesn't just like options and choice; they are essential or they start to itch, squirm and rebel. The structured, timetabled and routine-laden secondary school environment is difficult for many **P** preferences. Teachers can help by:

- Providing as much flexibility as possible (multiple choice homework tasks, choice within the lesson).
- Avoiding detailed schedules (they'll just lose it anyway!).
- Shaking things up now and again to prevent predictability becoming boredom. Introduce random surprises and changes.
- Helping the student identify and use simple time-management techniques.

233
Tawny Owl teacher with Tiger student
INTP and ISTP

The Tawny Owl and Tiger share three type preferences. Both like quiet reflection time and prefer to work things out for themselves. Their difference is in the way they absorb information; theoretical Owl teacher versus practical Tiger. For the teacher to get the best out of their naturally reserved student they need to:

- Respect the student's need for privacy and independence.
- Allow the student plenty of time to think through their thoughts.
- Share your ideas and thoughts regularly to ensure you both know what you're doing.
- Take time to clarify your thoughts but don't avoid confrontation; if something needs to be said be calm and direct as you deliver it.
- Use non-verbal communication – smiles and gestures are reassuring to **I** students. You can even use sticky notes/emails to pass on feedback.
- Provide opportunities for the student to see you one-to-one away from the sometimes hectic environment of the classroom.

The imaginative teacher can inspire all students, but they do need to respect the need for around 65% of students to be given clear guidelines, structure, facts, details and procedures; otherwise they can flounder. For the teacher to get the best out of their grounded student they need to:

- Demonstrate how learning can be applied in the real world.
- Allow the student opportunities to repeat and practise until satisfied they are competent.
- Encourage the use of imagination as a useful process (it's not wasting time).
- Be careful not to look like you're favouring **N** students to the detriment of **S** students. Every student needs to be able to contribute in their preferred way.

Both teacher and student are task-focused, direct, consistent and honest. The classroom is likely to have a purposeful atmosphere. Students are given clear guidelines on what is expected in terms of behaviour, homework and so on. If the student challenges the teacher it is likely to be for clarification. At best this means everyone knows where they stand and how to behave. For the teacher to get the best out of their fundamentally task-focused student they need to:

- Focus on what the student has achieved as well as what comes next.
- Be prepared to compromise occasionally.
- Avoid trying to fix something without considering potential underlying emotional causes.
- Work in ways that test their skill and knowledge competitively (they raise their game for competitions, challenges, quizzes, measuring and beating personal bests).
- Help them understand that 50% of people are **F** preference and can interpret objective feedback as personal criticism.

P preferences can be organised and efficient; it's just such an effort! While enjoying a mutual love of spontaneity, which provides each with relief from the stifling and constraining timetables and deadlines essential in large organisations such as schools, they must also remember to complete any necessary tasks. Although likely to be quirky and original teachers, they also need to focus on the task of preparing the student to succeed socially and academically. Both prefer to start tasks than finish them. Their initial enthusiasm can quickly drain. Both need to ensure they identify and complete priority tasks or the student (or their parents) may ask awkward questions. For the teacher to get the best out of their naturally laid-back student they need to understand the student doesn't just like options and choice; they are essential or they start to itch, squirm and rebel. The structured, timetabled and routine-laden secondary school environment is difficult for many **P** preferences. Teachers can help by:

■ Providing as much flexibility as possible (multiple choice homework tasks, choice within the lesson).

■ Avoiding detailed schedules (they'll just lose it anyway!).

■ Shaking things up now and again to prevent predictability becoming boredom. Introduce random surprises and changes.

■ Helping the student identify ways they can organise and manage their work to complete it on time.

234
Tawny Owl teacher with Cat student
INTP and ISFP

Tawny Owls and Cats share two type preferences. Both are observant, reflective and flexible. Conflict is likely to simmer and fester over a period of time rather than suddenly erupt. The teacher needs to check student progress without appearing to interfere to ensure the student flourishes. For the teacher to get the best out of their naturally reserved student they need to:

■ Respect the student's need for privacy and independence.

■ Allow the student plenty of time to think through their thoughts.

■ Share your ideas and thoughts regularly to ensure you both know what you're doing.

■ Take time to clarify your thoughts but don't avoid confrontation; if something needs to be said be calm and direct as you deliver it.

■ Use non-verbal communication – smiles and gestures are reassuring to **I** students. You can even use sticky notes/emails to pass on feedback.

■ Provide opportunities for the student to see you one-to-one away from the sometimes hectic environment of the classroom.

The imaginative Tawny Owl teacher can inspire all students, but they do need to respect the need for Cats to be given clear guidelines, structure, facts, details and procedures; otherwise they can stumble. For the teacher to get the best out of their grounded student they need to:

■ Demonstrate how learning can be applied in the real world.

■ Allow the student opportunities to repeat and practise until satisfied they are competent.

■ Encourage the use of imagination as a useful process (it's not wasting time).

■ Be careful not to look like you're favouring **N** students to the detriment of **S** students. Every student needs to be able to contribute in their preferred way.

The teacher is focused first on task and second on people/relationships. The classroom is likely to have a business-like, purposeful atmosphere. Students are given clear guidelines on what is expected in terms of behaviour, homework and so on. At best this means everyone knows where they stand and how to behave. At worst the classroom can resemble a military boot-camp full of dispirited and brow-beaten new recruits. Remember the personal relationship you have with this student is crucial to the student. The Cat needs to feel they like their teacher and that the teacher likes them too. If this happens they'll work harder but if not they may switch off. This explains why a student can be top of the class one year (with a teacher they like) and show no interest at all in the subject the following year when they change teacher. For the teacher to get the best out of their inherently subjective student they need to:

■ Offer learning situations that allow for the use of empathy, collaboration and teamworking to counter-balance your natural tendency to focus on task.

■ Give ample and regular praise while offering tactful support to overcome any blind-spots.

■ Compromise their occasionally blunt feedback; this can be easily interpreted as criticism so walk on egg-shells when delivering it.

■ Emphasise their personal belief in the student (don't let me down, I know you can do it, I like you).

Tawny Owls and Cats can be organised and efficient; it's just such an effort! While enjoying a mutual love of spontaneity, which provides each with relief from the stifling and constraining timetables and deadlines characteristic in large organisations such as schools, they must also remember to complete any necessary tasks. Although likely to be quirky and innovative teachers, they also need to focus on the task of preparing the student to succeed socially and academically. Both prefer to start tasks than finish them. Their initial enthusiasm can quickly drain. Both need to ensure they identify and complete priority tasks or the student (or their parents) may ask awkward questions. For the teacher to get the best out of their naturally laid-back student they need to understand the student doesn't just like options and choice; they are essential or they start to itch, squirm and rebel. The structured, timetabled and routine-laden secondary school environment is difficult for many **P** preferences. Teachers can help by:

■ Providing as much flexibility as possible (multiple choice homework tasks, choice within the lesson).

■ Avoiding detailed schedules (they'll just lose it anyway!).

■ Shaking things up now and again to prevent predictability becoming boredom. Introduce random surprises and changes.

■ Helping the student identify ways they can organise and manage their time to complete important work without a last-minute rush.

235
Tawny Owl teacher with Seal student
INTP and INFP

Tawny Owls and Seals share three type preferences. Both are independent, reflective and flexible. Conflict is likely to bubble and simmer over a period of time rather than suddenly flare up. The teacher needs to check student progress without appearing to criticise to ensure the Seal blossoms. For the teacher to get the best out of their naturally reserved student they need to:

■ Respect the student's need for privacy and independence.

■ Allow the student plenty of time to think through their thoughts.

■ Share your ideas and thoughts regularly to ensure you both know what you're doing.

■ Take time to clarify your thoughts but don't avoid confrontation; if something needs to be said be calm and direct as you deliver it.

■ Use non-verbal communication – smiles and gestures are reassuring to **I** students. You can even use sticky notes/emails to pass on feedback.

■ Provide opportunities for the student to see you one-to-one away from the sometimes hectic environment of the classroom.

Both teacher and student gather information by seeing the big picture first, using hunches, inferences and imagination to infer meaning. The teacher will naturally use their imagination in the classroom and the **N** student will respond well to this, possibly joining in with flights of fancy, anecdotes and stories. A natural affinity between teacher and student is often present because they both look at the world in the same way – with a burning curiosity to understand why things are as they are by exploring patterns, possibilities, ideas and theories. Be careful not to look like you're favouring **N** students to the detriment of **S** students. Every student needs to be able to contribute in their preferred way. For the teacher to get the best out of their imaginative student they need to:

■ Offer questions/projects that can be explored creatively.

■ Avoid repetitive tasks as they'll quickly lose interest.

■ Encourage the student to become aware of the important contribution of the **S** approach (the value of facts, details, procedure, experiments, applying experience, structure, the step-by-step model).

The teacher is focused first on task and second on people/relationships. The classroom is likely to have a business-like, purposeful atmosphere. Students are given clear guidelines on what is expected in terms of behaviour, homework and so on. At best this means everyone knows where they stand and how to behave. At worst the classroom can resemble a military boot-camp full of dispirited and brow-beaten new recruits. Remember the personal relationship you have with this student is crucial. The Seal needs to feel they like their teacher and that the teacher likes them too. If this happens they'll work harder but if not they may switch off. This explains why a student can be top of the class one year (with a teacher they like) and show no interest at all in the subject the following year when they change teacher. For the teacher to get the best out of their intrinsically subjective student they need to:

■ Offer learning situations that allow for the use of empathy, collaboration and teamworking to counter-balance your natural tendency to focus on task.

■ Give ample and regular praise while offering tactful support to overcome any blind-spots.

■ Compromise their occasionally blunt feedback; this can be easily interpreted as criticism so walk on egg-shells when delivering it.

■ Emphasise their personal belief in the student (don't let me down, I know you can do it).

Tawny Owl and Seal can be organised and efficient; it's just such an effort! While enjoying a mutual love of spontaneity, which provides each with relief from the stifling and constraining timetables and deadlines essential in large organisations such as schools, they must also remember to complete any necessary tasks.. Although likely to be original teachers, they also need to focus on the task of preparing the student to succeed socially and academically. Both prefer to start tasks than finish them. Their initial enthusiasm can quickly drain. Both need to ensure they identify and complete priority tasks or the student (or their parents) may ask awkward questions. For the teacher to get the best out of their naturally laid-back student they need to understand the student doesn't just like options and choice; they are essential or they start to itch, squirm and rebel. The structured, timetabled and routine-laden secondary school environment is difficult for many **P** preferences. Teachers can help by:

■ Providing as much flexibility as possible (multiple choice homework tasks, choice within the lesson).

■ Avoiding detailed schedules (they'll just lose it anyway!).

■ Shaking things up now and again to prevent predictability becoming boredom. Introduce random surprises and changes.

■ Helping identify effective time-management strategies to ensure the Seal can succeed.

236
Tawny Owl teacher with Tawny Owl student
INTP and INTP

Owls share much in common. Both prefer dealing with ideas rather than people. Both are imaginative and curious. Their similarities can be complementary. Clashes are most likely when the independent student fails to seek help when it's needed. To minimise this possibility the teacher needs to:

■ Respect the student's need for privacy and independence.

■ Allow the student plenty of time to think through their thoughts.

■ Share your ideas and thoughts regularly to ensure you both know what you're doing.

■ Take time to clarify your thoughts but don't avoid confrontation; if something needs to be said be calm and direct as you deliver it.

■ Use non-verbal communication – smiles and gestures are reassuring to **I** students. You can even use sticky notes/emails to pass on feedback.

■ Provide opportunities for the student to see you one-to-one away from the sometimes hectic environment of the classroom.

Both teacher and student gather information by seeing the big picture first, using hunches, inferences and imagination to infer meaning. The teacher will naturally use their imagination in the classroom and the **N** student will respond well to this, possibly joining in with flights of fancy, anecdotes and stories. A natural affinity between teacher and student is often present because they both look at the world in the same way – with a burning curiosity to understand why things are as they are by exploring patterns, possibilities, ideas and theories. Be careful not to look like you're favouring **N** students to the detriment of **S** students. Every student needs to be able to contribute in their preferred way. For the teacher to get the best out of their naturally imaginative student they need to:

■ Offer questions/projects that can be explored creatively.

■ Avoid repetitive tasks as they'll quickly lose interest.

■ Encourage the student to become aware of the important contribution of the **S** approach (the value of facts, details, procedure, experiments, applying experience, structure, the step-by-step model).

Both teacher and student are task-focused, direct, consistent and honest. The classroom is likely to have a purposeful atmosphere. Students are given clear guidelines on what is expected in terms of behaviour, homework and so on. If the student challenges the teacher it is likely to be for clarification. At best this means everyone knows where they stand and how to behave. For the teacher to get the best out of their student they need to:

■ Focus on what the student has achieved as well as what comes next.

■ Be prepared to compromise occasionally.

■ Avoid trying to fix something without considering potential underlying emotional causes.

■ Work in ways that test their skill and knowledge competitively (they raise their game for competitions, challenges, quizzes, measuring and beating personal bests).

■ Help them understand that half the population are **F** preference and can interpret objective feedback as personal criticism.

Tawny Owls can be organised and efficient; it's just such an effort! While enjoying a mutual love of spontaneity, which provides each with relief from the stifling and constraining timetables and deadlines essential in large organisations such as schools, they must also remember to complete any necessary tasks. Although likely to be fun and popular teachers, they also need to focus on the task of preparing the student to succeed socially and academically. Both prefer to start tasks than finish them. Their initial enthusiasm can quickly drain. Both need to ensure they identify and complete priority tasks or the student (or their parents) may ask awkward questions. For the teacher to get the best out of their naturally laid-back student they need to understand the

student doesn't just like options and choice; they are essential or they start to itch, squirm and rebel. The structured, timetabled and routine-laden secondary school environment is difficult for many **P** preferences. Teachers can help by:

■ Providing as much flexibility as possible (multiple choice homework tasks, choice within the lesson).

■ Helping the student identify ways they can organise and manage their time to complete important work without a last-minute rush.

■ Avoiding detailed schedules (they'll just lose it anyway!).

■ Shaking things up now and again to prevent predictability becoming boredom.

■ Introducing random surprises and changes.

237
Tawny Owl teacher with Polar Bear student
INTP and ISTJ

Tawny Owls and Polar Bears share two type preferences. Both prefer dealing with ideas rather than people. Both are objective analysers. Their similarities can be complementary. Clashes are most likely when the traditional student fails to connect with the quirky professorial Owl. For the teacher to get the best out of their naturally factual student they need to:

■ Respect the student's need for privacy and independence.

■ Allow the student plenty of time to think through their thoughts.

■ Share your ideas and thoughts regularly to ensure you both know what you're doing.

■ Take time to clarify your thoughts but don't avoid confrontation; if something needs to be said be calm and direct as you deliver it.

■ Use non-verbal communication – smiles and gestures are reassuring to **I** students. You can even use sticky notes/emails to pass on feedback.

The imaginative teacher can inspire all students, but they do need to respect the need for Polar Bears to be given clear guidelines, structure, facts, details and procedures; otherwise they can flounder. They should also:

■ Demonstrate how learning can be applied in the real world.

■ Allow the student opportunities to repeat and practise until satisfied they are competent.

■ Encourage the use of imagination as a useful process (it's not wasting time).

■ Be careful not to look like you're favouring **N** students to the detriment of **S** students. Every student needs to be able to contribute in their preferred way.

Both teacher and student are task-focused, direct, consistent and frank. The classroom is likely to have a purposeful atmosphere. Students are given clear guidelines on what is expected in terms of behaviour, homework and so on. If the student challenges the teacher it is likely to be for clarification. At best this means everyone knows where they stand and how to behave. For the teacher to get the best out of their fundamentally task-focused student they need to:

■ Focus on what the student has achieved as well as what comes next.

■ Be prepared to compromise occasionally.

■ Help them understand that 50% of people are **F** preference and can interpret objective feedback as personal criticism.

■ Avoid trying to fix something without considering potential underlying emotional causes.

■ Work in ways that test their skill and knowledge competitively (they raise their game for competitions, challenges, quizzes, measuring and beating personal bests).

The laid-back, flexible and spontaneous teacher with the naturally organised student can be a dream team or a disaster. To create a positive relationship they need to play to each other's strengths. The student can benefit from the teacher's ability to adapt and change plans and the teacher can benefit from the student's desire to have a plan they can work to and complete. The teacher can also:

■ Encourage and support the student's desire for order, neatness and respecting deadlines.

■ Allow the student independence in planning their work in their own way if they really want to.

■ Avoid changing plans just for the sake of it; this will only frustrate the student.

■ Encourage the student to try novel approaches to prevent staleness.

238
Tawny Owl teacher with Koala student
INTP and ISFJ

The Tawny Owl and Koala share one type preference. Both are reserved and private. The teacher can help develop the flexibility and imagination of their student using a quietly nurturing approach. The Koala needs to be given clear instructions and plans to thrive which can be a challenge for the 'mad professor' style of the teacher. For the teacher to get the best out of their naturally timid student they need to:

■ Respect the student's need for privacy and independence.

■ Allow the student plenty of time to think through their thoughts.

■ Share your ideas and thoughts regularly to ensure you both know what you're doing.

■ Take time to clarify your thoughts but don't avoid confrontation; if something needs to be said be calm and direct as you deliver it.

■ Use non-verbal communication – smiles and gestures are reassuring to **I** students. You can even use sticky notes/emails to pass on feedback.

■ Provide opportunities for the student to see you one-to-one away from the sometimes hectic environment of the classroom.

The imaginative Tawny Owl teacher can inspire all students, but they do need to respect the need for Koalas to be given clear guidelines, structure,

facts, details and procedures; otherwise they can struggle. For the teacher to get the best out of their grounded student they need to:

■ Demonstrate how learning can be applied in the real world.

■ Allow the student opportunities to repeat and practise until satisfied they are competent.

■ Encourage the use of imagination as a useful process (it's not wasting time).

■ Be careful not to look like you're favouring **N** students to the detriment of **S** students. Every student needs to be able to contribute in their preferred way.

The teacher is focused first on task and second on people/relationships. The classroom is likely to have a purposeful atmosphere. Students are given clear guidelines on what is expected in terms of behaviour, homework and so on. At best this means everyone knows where they stand and how to behave. At worst the classroom can resemble a military boot-camp. Remember the personal relationship you have with this student is crucial to the student. The Koala needs to feel they like their teacher and that the teacher likes them too. If this happens they'll work harder but if not they may switch off. This explains why a student can be top of the class one year (with a teacher they like) and show no interest at all in the subject the following year when they change teacher. To nurture the Koala:

■ Offer learning situations that allow for the use of empathy, collaboration and small teamworking to counter-balance your natural tendency to focus on task.

■ Give ample and regular praise while offering tactful support to overcome any blind-spots. Feedback can be easily interpreted as criticism so tread carefully when delivering it.

■ Engage by quietly and regularly stating your personal belief in the student (don't let me down, I know you can do it, I like you).

■ Be prepared to compromise occasionally to reassure the routine-loving Koala.

The laid-back, flexible and spontaneous teacher with the naturally organised student can be a dream team or a disaster. To create a positive relationship they need to play to each other's strengths. The student can benefit from the teacher's ability to adapt and change plans and the teacher can benefit from the student's desire to have a plan they can work to and complete. The teacher can also:

■ Encourage and support the student's desire for order, neatness and respecting deadlines.

■ Allow the student independence in planning their work in their own way if they really want to.

■ Avoid changing plans just for the sake of it; this will only frustrate the student.

■ Encourage the Koala to try new activities and clubs to stretch themselves and get to know more of their peers.

239
Tawny Owl teacher with Seahorse student
INTP and INFJ

Tawny Owls and Seahorses share two type preferences. Both are reserved, curious and private. The teacher can best develop the flexibility and imagination of their student by using a quietly nurturing approach. To thrive the Seahorse needs to be given time to explore their feelings, which can be a challenge for the objective 'mad professor' style of the teacher. To get the best out of their quietly innovative student they need to:

■ Respect the student's need for privacy and independence.

■ Allow the student plenty of time to think through their thoughts.

■ Share your ideas and thoughts regularly to ensure you both know what you're doing.

■ Take time to clarify your thoughts but don't avoid confrontation; if something needs to be said be calm and direct as you deliver it.

■ Use non-verbal communication – smiles and gestures are reassuring to **I** students. You can even use sticky notes/emails to pass on feedback.

Both teacher and student gather information by seeing the big picture first, using hunches, inferences and imagination to infer meaning. The teacher will naturally use their imagination in the classroom and the **N** student will respond well to this, possibly joining in with flights of fancy, anecdotes and stories. A natural affinity between teacher and student is often present because they both look at the world in the same way – with a burning curiosity to understand why things are as they are by exploring patterns, possibilities, ideas and theories. Be careful not to look like you're favouring **N** students to the detriment of **S** students. Every student needs to be able to contribute in their preferred way. For the teacher to get the best out of their naturally imaginative student they need to:

■ Offer questions/projects that can be explored creatively.

■ Avoid repetitive tasks as they'll quickly lose interest.

■ Encourage the student to become aware of the important contribution of the **S** approach (the value of facts, details, procedure, experiments, applying experience, structure, the step-by-step model).

The teacher is focused first on task and second on people/relationships. The classroom is likely to have a business-like, purposeful atmosphere. Students are given clear guidelines on what is expected in terms of behaviour, homework and so on. At best this means everyone knows where they stand and how to behave. At worst the classroom can resemble a military boot-camp full of dispirited and brow-beaten new recruits. Remember the personal relationship you have with this student is crucial to the student. The Seahorse needs to feel they like their teacher and that the teacher likes them too. If this happens they'll work harder but if not they may switch off. This explains why a student can be top of the class one year (with a teacher they like) and show no interest at all in the subject the following year when they change teacher. For the teacher to get the best out of their intrinsically subjective student they need to:

■ Offer learning situations that allow for the use of empathy, collaboration and teamworking to counter-balance your natural tendency to focus on task.

■ Give ample and regular praise while offering tactful support to overcome any blind-spots.

■ Compromise their occasionally blunt feedback; this can be easily interpreted as criticism so walk on egg-shells when delivering it.

■ Emphasise their personal belief in the student (don't let me down, I know you can do it, I like you).

The laid-back, flexible and spontaneous teacher with the naturally organised student can be a dream team or a disaster. To create a positive relationship they need to play to each other's strengths. The student can benefit from the teacher's ability to adapt and change plans and the teacher can benefit from the student's desire to have a plan they can work to and complete. The teacher can also:

■ Encourage and support the student's desire for order, neatness and respecting deadlines.

■ Allow the student independence in planning their work in their own way if they really want to.

■ Avoid changing plans just for the sake of it; this will only frustrate the Seahorse.

240
Tawny Owl teacher with Barn Owl student
INTP and INTJ

Owls share much in common. Both prefer dealing with ideas rather than people. Both are imaginative and curious. Their similarities can be complementary. Clashes are most likely when the independent student fails to seek help when it's needed. To minimise conflict the teacher can:

■ Allow the student plenty of time to think through their thoughts.

■ Share your ideas and thoughts regularly to ensure you both know what you're doing.

■ Respect the student's need for privacy and independence.

■ Take time to clarify your thoughts but don't avoid confrontation; if something needs to be said be calm and direct as you deliver it.

■ Use non-verbal communication – smiles and gestures are reassuring to **I** students. You can even use sticky notes/emails to pass on feedback.

Both teacher and student gather information by seeing the big picture first, using hunches, inferences and imagination to infer meaning. The teacher will naturally use their imagination in the classroom and the **N** student will respond well to this, possibly joining in with new theories and hypotheses. A natural affinity between teacher and student is often present because they both look at the world through the same 'geeky' lens – united by a ferocious curiosity to understand why things are as they are by exploring pat-

terns, possibilities, ideas and theories. Be careful not to look like you're favouring **N** students to the detriment of **S** students. Every student needs to be able to contribute in their preferred way. For the teacher to get the best out of their imaginative student they need to:

■ Offer questions/projects that can be explored creatively.

■ Avoid repetitive tasks as they'll quickly lose interest.

■ Encourage the student to become aware of the important contribution of the **S** approach (the value of facts, details, procedure, experiments, applying experience, structure, the step-by-step model).

Both teacher and student are task-focused, direct, consistent and frank. The classroom is likely to have a purposeful atmosphere. Students are given guidelines on what is expected in terms of behaviour, homework and so on. If the student challenges the teacher it is likely to be for clarification. At best this means everyone knows where they stand and how to behave. At worst the culture can appear stifling. For the teacher to get the best out of their naturally inquisitive student they need to:

■ Focus on what the student has achieved as well as what comes next.

■ Be prepared to compromise occasionally.

■ Avoid trying to fix something without considering potential underlying emotional causes.

■ Work in ways that test their skill and knowledge competitively (they raise their game for competitions, challenges, quizzes, measuring and beating personal bests).

■ Help them understand that 50% of people are **F** preference and can interpret objective feedback as personal criticism.

The laid-back, flexible and spontaneous teacher with the naturally organised student can be a dream team or a disaster. To create a positive relationship they need to play to each other's strengths. The student can benefit from the teacher's ability to adapt and change plans and the teacher can benefit from the student's desire to have a plan they can work to and complete. The teacher can also:

■ Encourage and support the student's desire for order, neatness and closure.

■ Allow the student independence in planning their work in their own way if they really want to.

■ Encourage the student to embrace flexibility

■ Avoid changing plans just for the sake of it; this will only frustrate the Barn Owl.

241
Barn Owl teacher and Polar Bear student
INTJ and ISTJ

Barn Owls and Polar Bears share three type preferences. Both are reserved, objective and conscientious. They differ in the way they make sense of information. The Barn Owl thinks strategically and big picture whereas the Polar Bear is focused on the rational and prudent application of

facts. For the teacher to get the best out of their naturally private student they need to:

■ Respect the student's need for privacy and independence.

■ Allow the student plenty of time to think through their thoughts.

■ Share your ideas and thoughts regularly to ensure you both know what you're doing.

■ Take time to clarify your thoughts but don't avoid confrontation; if something needs to be said be calm and direct as you deliver it.

■ Use non-verbal communication – smiles and gestures are reassuring to **I** students; you can even use sticky notes/emails to pass on feedback.

Barn Owls can inspire all students with their vivid imaginations, but they do need to respect the need for Polar Bear students to be given clear guidelines, structure, facts, details and procedures; otherwise they can flounder. For the teacher to get the best out of their grounded student they need to:

■ Demonstrate how learning can be applied in the real world.

■ Countenance opportunities for the Polar Bear to repeat and practise activities until satisfied of their competence.

■ Encourage the use of imagination as a useful process (it's not wasting time).

■ Be careful not to look like you're favouring **N** students to the detriment of **S** students, every student needs to be able to contribute in their preferred way.

Both teacher and student are task-focused, direct, consistent and honest. The classroom is likely to have a business-like, purposeful atmosphere. Students are given clear guidelines on what is expected in terms of behaviour, homework and so on. If the student challenges the teacher it is likely to be for clarification; though it may come across as pedantic. Ideally this means everyone knows where they stand and how to behave. At worst the classroom can become too mechanistic, humdrum and authoritarian. For the teacher to get the best out of their fundamentally task-focused student they need to:

■ Work in ways that test their skill and knowledge competitively (they raise their game for competitions, challenges, quizzes, measuring and beating personal bests).

■ Help them understand that 50% of people are **F** preference and can interpret feedback as criticism.

■ Focus on what the student has achieved and what comes next.

■ Be prepared to compromise occasionally.

■ Avoid trying to fix something without considering potential underlying emotional causes.

The Barn Owl teacher takes pleasure in scheduling their time. They are organised and decisive. They work out a plan and stick to it, often with an impressive to-do list. Their classroom is usually an organised place. The subject will probably be broken down into lesson-sized chunks and the year planned out, whether or not an Ofsted inspector is due. Many Polar Bears will be reassured by their teacher's organisational zeal. They simply adopt the schedule and deliver their side of the bargain, generally completing all tasks on time. Interestingly, some Polar Bears will baulk at their teacher's well-intentioned thoroughness. They would like to create their own plan and work to it rather than adopt someone else's.

This is due to the **J**'s desire for control. So two **J**'s together can clash, though at least all their work will be done. Most secondary schools require students to be so organised that two **J**'s are the best combination. For the teacher to get the best out of their naturally organised student:

■ Enjoy your shared desire for order, neatness and respecting deadlines.

■ Allow the student independence in planning their work in their own way if they really want to.

■ Be prepared to adjust your own plans if external events interfere with your careful preparations (and encourage the student to also embrace flexibility occasionally).

■ Shake things up now and again to prevent predictability becoming boredom.

■ Avoid making quick decisions about what needs to be done before considering all of the options.

242
Barn Owl teacher and Koala Bear student
INTJ and ISFJ

Barn Owls and Koalas share two type preferences. Both are introspective and conscientious. The coy Koala is more likely to be invisible in the classroom rather than a disruption. For the teacher to get the best out of their naturally reticent student they need to:

■ Respect the student's need for privacy and independence.

■ Allow the student plenty of time to think through their thoughts.

■ Share your ideas and thoughts regularly to ensure you both know what you're doing.

■ Take time to clarify your thoughts but don't avoid confrontation; if something needs to be said be calm and direct as you deliver it.

■ Use non-verbal communication – smiles and gestures are reassuring to **I** students; you can even use sticky notes/emails to pass on feedback.

■ Create opportunities to talk to the student individually or in small groups as this is when they're comfortable and most likely to engage.

The imaginative teacher can inspire all students, but they do need to respect the need for around two thirds of students to be given clear guidelines, structure, facts, details and procedures; otherwise they can struggle. To get the best out of their grounded student:

■ Demonstrate how learning can be applied in the real world.

■ Allow the student opportunities to repeat and practise until satisfied they are competent.

■ Encourage the use of imagination as a useful process (it's not wasting time).

■ Be careful not to look like you're favouring **N** students to the detriment of **S** students; every student needs to be able to contribute in their preferred way.

The teacher is focused first on task and second on people/relationships. The classroom is likely to have a business-like, purposeful atmosphere.

Students are given clear guidelines on what is expected in terms of behaviour, homework and so on. At best this means everyone knows where they stand and how to behave. Remember the personal relationship you have with this student is key. The Koala needs to feel they like their teacher and that the teacher likes them too. If this happens they'll work harder; if not they may switch off. This explains why a student can be top of the class one year (with a teacher they like) and show no interest at all in the subject the following year when they change teacher. To get the most from their naturally people-focused student they need to:

■ Offer learning situations that allow for the use of empathy, collaboration and small teamworking to counter-balance your natural tendency to focus on task.

■ Give ample and regular praise while offering tactful support to overcome any blind-spots. Feedback can be easily interpreted as criticism so tread carefully when delivering it,

■ Engage by quietly and regularly stating your personal belief in the student (don't let me down, I know you can do it, I like you).

■ Be prepared to compromise occasionally to reassure the routine-loving Koala.

The Barn Owl teacher takes pleasure in scheduling their time. They are organised and decisive. They work out a plan and stick to it, often aided by an impressive to-do list. Their classroom is usually an organised place. The subject will probably be broken down into lesson-sized chunks and the year planned out whether or not an Ofsted inspector is lurking in the corridor. Some **J** students will be reassured by their teacher's organisational zeal. They will simply adopt the schedule and deliver their side of the bargain, generally completing all tasks on time. Interestingly, some **J**'s will baulk at their teacher's well-intentioned thoroughness. They would like to create their own plan and work to it rather than adopt someone else's. This is due to the **J**'s desire for control. So two **J**'s together can clash, though at least all their work will be done. Most secondary schools require students to be so organised that two **J**'s are the best combination. To get the best out of the naturally organised student:

■ Be prepared to adjust your own plans if external events interfere with your careful preparations (and encourage the student to also embrace flexibility occasionally).

■ Shake things up now and again to prevent predictability becoming boredom.

■ Avoid making quick decisions about what needs to be done before considering all of the options.

■ Enjoy your shared desire for order, neatness and respecting deadlines.

■ Allow the student independence in planning their work in their own way if they really want to.

243
Barn Owl teacher and Seahorse student
INTJ and INFJ

Barn Owls and Seahorses share three preferences. Both are private, imaginative and organised. They apply their ingenuity in different ways; the Barn Owl coolly detached and the Seahorse smouldering empathy. When the teacher understands their student's need to filter information subjectively their relationship can blossom. To develop their naturally quiet student:

■ Respect their need for privacy and independence.

■ Provide plenty of time for the student to clarify their thoughts.

■ Share your ideas regularly to ensure you both know what you're doing.

■ Use non-verbal communication – smiles and gestures are reassuring to Seahorses.

■ Provide opportunities for the student to see you one-to-one away from the sometimes hectic environment of the lesson.

Both teacher and student gather information by seeing the big picture first, using hunches and imagination to infer meaning. The teacher will naturally use their imagination in the classroom and the **N** student will respond well to this, possibly joining in with flights of fancy, anecdotes and stories. A natural affinity between teacher and student is often present because they both look at the world in the same way – with a burning curiosity to understand why things are as they are by exploring patterns, possibilities, ideas and theories. Be careful not to look like you're favouring **N** students to the detriment of **S** students. Every student needs to be able to contribute in their preferred way. For the teacher to get the best out of their imaginative student they need to:

■ Offer questions/projects that can be explored creatively.

■ Avoid repetitive tasks as they'll quickly lose interest.

■ Encourage the student to become aware of the important contribution of the **S** approach (the value of facts, details, procedure, experiments, applying experience, structure, the step-by-step model).

The student is focused first on people then task, whereas the teacher operates in the opposite way. The classroom is likely to have a business-like, purposeful atmosphere. Students are given clear guidelines on what is expected in terms of behaviour, homework and so on. At best this means everyone knows where they stand and how to behave. At worst the classroom can resemble a military boot-camp full of dispirited and browbeaten new recruits. Remember the personal relationship you have with this student is key. The Seahorse needs to feel they like their teacher and that the teacher likes them too. If this happens they'll work harder; if not they may switch off completely. This explains why a student can be top of the class one year (with a teacher they like) and show no interest at all in the same subject the following year when they change teacher. For the teacher to get the best out of their naturally people-focused student they need to:

- Offer learning situations that allow for the use of empathy, collaboration and teamworking to counter-balance your natural tendency to focus on task.
- Give ample and regular praise while offering tactful support to overcome any blind-spots. Feedback can be easily interpreted as criticism so tread carefully when delivering it.
- Motivate by appealing to the strength of your personal belief in the student (don't let me down, I know you can do it, I like you).
- Be prepared to compromise to avoid divisive stand-offs.

The **J** teacher takes pleasure in scheduling their time. They are organised and decisive. They work out a plan and stick to it, often aided by an impressive to-do list. Their classroom is usually an organised place. The subject will probably be broken down into lesson-sized chunks and the whole year planned out in detail. Many **J** students are reassured by their teacher's organisational zeal. They simply adopt the schedule and deliver their side of the bargain, generally completing all tasks on time. Interestingly, some **J**'s will baulk at their teacher's well-intentioned thoroughness. They would like to create their own plan and work to it rather than adopt someone else's. This is due to the **J**'s desire for control. So two **J**'s together can clash, though at least all their work will be done. Most secondary schools require students to be so organised that two **J**'s are the best combination. For the teacher to get the best out of their fundamentally organised student they need to:

- Enjoy your shared desire for order, neatness and respecting deadlines.
- Allow the student independence in planning their work in their own way if they really want to.
- Be prepared to adjust your own plans if external events interfere with your careful preparations (and encourage the student to also embrace flexibility occasionally).
- Shake things up now and again to prevent predictability becoming boredom.
- Avoid making quick decisions about what needs to be done before considering all of the options.

244
Barn Owl teacher and Barn Owl student
INTJ and INTJ

As both teacher and student share all four preferences they should understand each other even when they don't agree. Good relationships are likely. If there is conflict the likely source is the stubborn streak they share. For the teacher to get the best out of their naturally private student they need to:

- Respect the student's need for quiet and independence.
- Allow the student plenty of time to think through their thoughts.
- Share your ideas and thoughts regularly to ensure you both know what you're doing.

- Take time to clarify your thoughts but don't avoid confrontation; if something needs to be said be calm and direct as you deliver it.
- Use non-verbal communication – smiles and gestures are reassuring to **I** students; you can even use sticky notes/emails to pass on feedback.

Barn Owls gather information by seeing the big picture first, using hunches, inferences and imagination to deduce meaning. The teacher will naturally use their imagination in the classroom and the **N** student will respond well to this, possibly joining in with flights of fancy, anecdotes and stories. A natural affinity between teacher and student is often present because they both look at the world in the same way – with a burning curiosity to understand why things are as they are by exploring patterns, possibilities, ideas and theories. Be careful not to look like you're favouring **N** students to the detriment of **S** students. Every student needs to be able to contribute in their preferred way. To get the best out of the imaginative student:

- Offer questions/projects that can be explored creatively.
- Avoid repetitive tasks as they'll quickly lose interest.
- Encourage the student to become aware of the important contribution of the **S** approach (the value of facts, details, procedure, experiments, applying experience, structure, the step-by-step model).

Barn Owls are task-focused, direct, consistent and candid. The classroom is likely to have a business-like, purposeful atmosphere. Students are given clear guidelines on what is expected in terms of behaviour, homework and so on. If the student challenges the teacher it is likely to be for clarification. At best this means everyone knows what is expected and how to behave. At worst the classroom can resemble a military boot-camp full of dispirited and brow-beaten new recruits. For the teacher to get the best out of their naturally task-focused student they need to:

- Work in ways that test their skill and knowledge competitively (they raise their game for competitions, challenges, quizzes, measuring and beating personal bests).
- Help them understand that 50% of people are **F** preference and can interpret feedback as criticism.
- Focus on what the student has achieved and what comes next.
- Be prepared to compromise occasionally.
- Avoid trying to fix something without considering potential underlying emotional causes.

The Barn Owl teacher takes pleasure in scheduling time. They are organised and decisive. They work out a plan and stick to it, often aided by an impressive to-do list. Their classroom is usually an organised place. The subject will probably be broken down into lesson-sized chunks and the year planned out whether or not an Ofsted inspector is sitting in the corner of the classroom. Many Barn Owl students are reassured by their teacher's organisational zeal. They simply adopt the schedule and deliver their side of the bargain, generally completing all tasks on time. Interestingly, some students will challenge their teacher's well-intentioned thoroughness. They would like to create their own plan and work to it rather than adopt someone else's. This is due to the **J**'s desire for control. So two **J**'s together can clash, though at least all their work will be done. Most

secondary schools require students to be so organised that two **J**'s are the best combination. For the teacher to get the best out of their fundamentally organised student they need to:

- Enjoy your shared desire for order, neatness and respecting deadlines.
- Allow the student independence in planning their work in their own way if they really want to.
- Shake things up now and again to prevent predictability becoming boredom.
- Avoid making quick decisions about what needs to be done before considering all of the options.
- Be prepared to adjust your own plans if external events interfere with your careful preparations (and encourage the student to also embrace flexibility occasionally).

245
Barn Owl teacher and Tiger student
INTJ and ISTP

The student and teacher share half their preferences. The Barn Owl and Tiger are both are naturally quiet, observant, determined and objective. Neither is prone to sentimentality so there is a great deal of common ground on which to build a strong relationship. The main source of conflict is likely to be the Barn Owl's preference for theory and the Tiger's preference for action. For the teacher to get the best out of their naturally reserved student they need to:

- Respect the student's need for privacy and independence.
- Allow the student plenty of time to think through their thoughts.
- Share your ideas and thoughts regularly to ensure you both know what you're doing.
- Take time to clarify your thoughts but don't avoid confrontation; if something needs to be said be calm and direct as you deliver it.
- Use non-verbal communication – smiles and gestures are reassuring to **I** students; you can even use sticky notes/emails to pass on feedback.

Barn Owls can inspire all students with their vivid imaginations, but they do need to respect the need for Tigers to be given clear guidelines, structure, facts, details and procedures, otherwise they can become restless. For the teacher to get the best out of their grounded student they need to:

- Demonstrate how learning can be applied in the real world.
- Allow the student opportunities to repeat and practise until satisfied they are competent.
- Encourage the use of imagination as a useful process (it's not wasting time).
- Be careful not to look like you're favouring **N** students to the detriment of **S** students. Every student needs to be able to contribute in their preferred way.

Both teacher and student are task-focused, direct, consistent and candid. The classroom is likely to have a business-like, purposeful atmosphere.

Personality in the Classroom

Students are given clear guidelines on what is expected in terms of behaviour, homework and so on. If the student challenges the teacher it is likely to be for clarification. At best this means everyone knows where they stand and how to behave. At worst the classroom can resemble a military boot-camp full of muzzled and brow-beaten new recruits. To get the best out of the inherently task-focused student:

- Work in ways that test their skill and knowledge competitively (they raise their game for competitions, challenges, quizzes, measuring and beating personal bests).
- Help them understand that 50% of people are **F** preference and can interpret feedback as criticism.
- Focus on what the student has achieved and what comes next.
- Be prepared to compromise occasionally.
- Avoid trying to fix something without considering potential underlying emotional causes.

The Barn Owl teacher takes pleasure in organising time. They are scrupulous and decisive. They work out a plan and stick to it, often aided by an impressive to-do list. Their classroom is usually an organised place. The subject will probably be broken down into lesson-sized chunks and the year ahead planned. The Tiger student will either respond:

- Positively by accepting your expertise and understanding the long-term benefits they'll reap.
- Passively by just accepting your structure/plan for an easy life without really buying into the content or process you are offering.
- Negatively by rejecting you, your structure/plan and subject completely (even if they're physically in your room they will not engage and participate).

For the teacher to get the best out of their naturally laid-back student they should note the student doesn't just like options and choice; they need them or they start to itch, squirm and rebel. The secondary school environment is difficult enough for **P** preference students so teachers can help soften the pressure. To help:

- Provide as much flexibility as possible (multiple choice homework tasks, choice within the lesson).
- Avoid relying on detailed schedules (they'll probably lose it anyway!).
- Don't be more picky with detail than is absolutely necessary.
- Shake things up now and again to prevent predictability becoming boredom. Introduce random surprises and changes.
- Help the student identify simple effective strategies to ensure they can succeed.
- Tigers love to learn by doing. Like all Cats they can struggle due to the bias in most schools towards students who have **I**, **N** and **J** preferences.

246
Barn Owl teacher and Cat student
INTJ and ISFP

Barn Owls and Cats share one preference. They're both naturally reserved and crave independence. Clashes are unlikely when the teacher allows the student to understand and complete tasks in their own way. For the teacher to get the best out of their naturally quiet student they need to:

- Respect the student's need for privacy and independence
- Allow the student plenty of time to think through their thoughts.
- Share your ideas and thoughts regularly to ensure you both know what you're doing.
- Take time to clarify your thoughts but don't avoid confrontation; if something needs to be said be calm and direct as you deliver it.
- Use non-verbal communication – smiles and gestures are reassuring to **I** students; you can even use sticky notes/emails to pass on feedback.

Barn Owls can inspire all students with their vivid imaginations, but they do need to respect the need for around 65% of students to be given clear guidelines, structure, facts, details and procedures; otherwise they can flounder. To get the best out of the grounded student:

- Demonstrate how learning can be applied in the real world.
- Allow the student opportunities to repeat and practise until satisfied they are competent.
- Encourage the use of imagination as a useful process (it's not wasting time).
- Be careful not to look like you're favouring **N** students to the detriment of **S** students. Every student needs to be able to contribute in their preferred way.

The Barn Owl teacher is focused first on task and second on people and relationships. The classroom is likely to have a business-like, purposeful atmosphere. Students are given clear guidelines on what is expected in terms of behaviour, homework and so on. At best this means everyone knows where they stand and how to behave. At worst the classroom can resemble an austere Victorian schoolroom. Remember the personal relationship you have with this student is key. The Cat needs to feel they like their teacher and that the teacher likes them too. If this happens they'll work harder; if not they may switch off. This explains why a student can be top of the class one year (with a teacher they like) and show no interest at all in the subject the following year when they change teacher. For the teacher to get the best out of their people-focused student they need to:

- Offer learning situations that allow for the use of empathy, collaboration and teamworking to counter-balance your natural tendency to focus on task.
- Give ample and regular praise while offering tactful support to overcome any blind-spots. Feedback can be easily interpreted as criticism so walk on egg-shells when delivering it.
- Inspire by appealing to the strength of your personal belief in the student (don't let me down, I know you can do it, I like you).

- Be prepared to compromise occasionally.

The **J** teacher takes pleasure in scheduling their time. They are organised and decisive. They work out a plan and stick to it, often aided by an impressive to-do list. Their classroom is usually an organised place. The subject will probably be broken down into lesson-sized chunks and the year planned out whether an Ofsted inspector is due or not. The **P** student will either respond:

- Positively by accepting your expertise and understanding the long-term benefits they'll reap.
- Passively by just accepting your structure/plan for an easy life without really buying into the content or process you are offering.
- Negatively by rejecting you, your structure/plan and subject completely (even if they're physically in your room they will not engage and participate).

For the Barn Owl to develop their naturally laid-back student they should note the student doesn't just like options and choice; they need them or they start to fidget, squirm and rebel. The secondary school environment is difficult enough for **P** preference students so teachers can ease the pressure. To help:

- Provide as much flexibility as possible (multiple choice homework tasks, choice within the lesson).
- Avoid giving out detailed schedules (they'll just lose it anyway!).
- Don't be more picky with detail than is absolutely necessary.
- Shake things up now and again to prevent predictability becoming boredom. Introduce random surprises and changes.
- Help the student identify simple effective strategies to ensure they can succeed.
- Cats love to learn by doing. Like other cats they can struggle due to the bias in most schools towards students who have **I**, **N** and **J** preferences.

247
Barn Owl teacher and Seal student
INTJ and INFP

The Barn Owl teacher and Seal student share two preferences. They both enjoy internalising ideas to decipher meaning. Their differences send them in different directions when they decide how to direct and express their conclusions; the teacher objectively and the student personally. The Seal is the biggest daydreamer of all personality types – it can look like they're not interested because they benefit from space to ponder ideas internally. For the teacher to get the best out of their naturally quiet student they need to:

- Respect the student's need for privacy and independence.
- Allow the student plenty of time to think through their thoughts.
- Share your ideas and thoughts regularly to ensure you both know what you're doing.
- Take time to clarify your thoughts but don't avoid confrontation; if something needs to be said be calm and direct as you deliver it.

■ Use non-verbal communication – smiles and gestures are reassuring to **I** students; you can even use sticky notes/emails to pass on feedback.

Both teacher and student gather information by seeing the big picture first, using hunches and imagination to assimilate meaning. The teacher will naturally use their imagination in the classroom and the **N** student will respond well to this, possibly joining in with flights of fancy, anecdotes and stories. A natural affinity between teacher and student is often present because they both look at the world in the same way – with a burning curiosity to understand why things are as they are by exploring patterns, possibilities, ideas and theories. Be careful not to look like you're favouring **N** students to the detriment of **S** students. Every student needs to be able to contribute in their preferred way. To fully develop the inherently imaginative student:

■ Offer questions/projects that can be explored creatively.

■ Avoid repetitive tasks as they'll quickly lose interest.

■ Encourage the student to become aware of the important contribution of the **S** approach (the value of facts, details, procedure, experiments, applying experience, structure, the step-by-step model).

The teacher is focused first on task and second on people/relationships. The classroom is likely to have a business-like, purposeful atmosphere. Students are given clear guidelines on what is expected in terms of behaviour, homework and so on. At best this means everyone knows where they stand and how to behave. At worst the classroom can resemble a military boot-camp full of disgruntled and brow-beaten new recruits. Remember the personal relationship you have with this student is key. The Seal needs to feel they like their teacher and that the teacher likes them too. If this happens they'll work harder; if not they may switch off. This explains why a student can be top of the class one year (with a teacher they like) and show no interest at all in the same subject the following year when they change teacher. For the teacher to get the best out of their naturally people-focused student they need to:

■ Offer ample and regular praise while offering tactful support to overcome any blind-spots. Feedback can be easily interpreted as criticism so walk on egg-shells when delivering it.

■ Motivate by appealing to the strength of your personal belief in the student (don't let me down, I know you can do it, I like you).

■ Be prepared to compromise occasionally.

The **J** teacher takes pleasure in scheduling their time. They are organised and decisive. They work out a plan and stick to it, often aided by an impressive to-do list. Their classroom is usually an organised place. The subject will probably be broken down into lesson-sized chunks and the year planned out whether or not an Ofsted inspection is looming. The **P** student will either respond:

■ Positively by accepting your expertise and understanding the long-term benefits they'll reap.

■ Passively by just accepting your structure/plan for an easy life without really buying into the content or process you are offering.

■ Negatively by rejecting you, your structure/plan and subject completely (even if they're physically in your room they will not engage and participate).

To get the best out of the naturally laid-back student they should note the student doesn't just like options and choice; they need them or they start to itch, squirm and rebel. The secondary school environment is difficult enough for **P** preference students so teachers can help soften the pressure. To help:

■ Provide as much flexibility as possible (multiple choice homework tasks, choice within the lesson).

■ Avoid giving out detailed schedules (they'll just lose it anyway!).

■ Don't be more picky with detail than is absolutely necessary.

■ Shake things up now and again to prevent predictability becoming boredom. Introduce random surprises and changes.

■ Help the student identify simple time-management strategies to ensure they can succeed.

248
Barn Owl teacher and Tawny Owl student
INTJ and INTP

These two Owls have much in common. They are both analytical, objective and enjoy solving problems. This can form the basis of a strong bond which fosters learning and mutual respect. The difference between these Owls is the organisation of the teacher contrasting with the student's more flexible and chaotic approach. For the teacher to help their naturally inventive student they need to:

■ Respect the student's need for privacy and independence.

■ Allow the student plenty of time to think through their thoughts.

■ Share your ideas and thoughts regularly to ensure you both know what you're doing.

■ Take time to clarify your thoughts but don't avoid confrontation; if something needs to be said be calm and direct as you deliver it.

■ Use non-verbal communication – smiles and gestures are reassuring to **I** students; you can even use sticky notes/emails to pass on feedback.

■ Provide opportunities for the student to see you one-to-one away from the sometimes hectic environment of the classroom.

Both teacher and student gather information by seeing the big picture first, using hunches, inferences and imagination to decipher meaning. The teacher will naturally use their imagination in the classroom and the **N** student will respond well to this, possibly joining in with new theories and hypotheses. A natural affinity between teacher and student is often present because they both look at the world through the same 'geeky' lens, united by a ferocious curiosity to understand why things are as they are by exploring patterns, possibilities, ideas and theories. Be careful not to look like you're favouring **N** students to the detriment of **S** students. Every student needs to be able to contribute in their preferred way. For the teacher to get the best out of their intrinsically inquisitive student they need to:

■ Offer questions/projects that can be explored creatively.

■ Avoid repetitive tasks as they'll quickly lose interest.

■ Encourage the student to become aware of the important contribution of the **S** approach (the value of facts, details, procedure, experiments, applying experience, structure, the step-by-step model).

Both teacher and student are task-focused, direct and consistent – seeking the objective truth. The classroom is likely to have a business-like, purposeful atmosphere. Students are given clear guidelines on what is expected in terms of behaviour, homework and so on. If the student challenges the teacher it is likely to be for clarification. At best this means everyone knows where they stand and how to behave. At worst the classroom can resemble a military boot-camp full of dispirited new recruits. For the teacher to get the best out of their naturally task-focused student they can:

■ Work in ways that test their skill and knowledge competitively (they raise their game for competitions, challenges, quizzes, measuring and beating personal bests).

■ Help them understand that 50% of people are **F** preference and can interpret feedback as criticism.

■ Focus on what the student has achieved and what comes next.

■ Be prepared to compromise occasionally.

■ Avoid trying to fix something without considering potential underlying emotional causes.

The Barn Owl teacher takes pleasure in scheduling their time decisively. They work out a plan and stick to it, usually aided by an impressive to-do list. Their classroom runs like clockwork. The subject will probably be broken down into lesson-sized chunks and the year planned out whether or not an Ofsted inspector is due. The Tawny Owl student will either respond:

■ Positively by accepting your expertise and understanding the long-term benefits they'll reap.

■ Passively by just accepting your structure/plan for an easy life without really buying into the content or process you are offering.

■ Negatively by rejecting you, your structure/plan and subject completely (even if they're physically in your room they will not engage and participate).

For the teacher to get the best out of their naturally laid-back student they should note the student doesn't just like options and choice; they need them or they start to itch, squirm and rebel. The secondary school environment is difficult enough for **P** preference students so teachers can help soften the pressure. To help:

■ Provide as much flexibility as possible (multiple choice homework tasks, choice within the lesson).

■ Avoid giving out detailed schedules (they'll just lose it anyway!).

■ Don't be more picky with detail than is absolutely necessary.

■ Shake things up now and again to prevent predictability becoming boredom. Introduce random surprises and changes.

■ Help the student identify effective time-management techniques to ensure they thrive.

249
Barn Owl teacher and Panther student
INTJ and ESTP

The naturally confident and assertive Panther student has to be handled with care. Panther students often have great influence over other class members so it is worth the initial effort to bring these sturdy predators on board. Barn Owls that do so have a valuable ally for years ahead. For the teacher to get the best out of their naturally lively student they need to:

- Listen patiently and enthusiastically to the student's stories/brainstorming/ramblings.
- Stay open to 'silly' ideas to see where they lead – the student is thinking out loud and this is how they learn best.
- Also offer your own thoughts; if you need a timeout ask for one.
- Encourage the student to think things through before talking otherwise they'll hog the lesson.
- Steer the student away from controversial subjects/topics, especially in group discussions. They'll often look for the most controversial thing to say just to add spice to a lesson.
- Build in plenty of opportunities during lessons for **E** students to talk things through with other **E** preferences.

The imaginative Barn Owl teacher can inspire all students, but they do need to respect the need for Panthers to be given clear guidelines and structure. For the teacher to get the best out of their grounded student they need to:

- Demonstrate how learning can be applied in the real world.
- Allow the student opportunities to repeat and practise until satisfied they are competent.
- Encourage the use of imagination as a useful process (it's not wasting time).
- Be careful not to look like you're favouring **N** students to the detriment of **S** students. Every student needs to be able to contribute in their preferred way.

Both teacher and student are task-focused, direct, consistent and honest. The classroom is likely to have a business-like, purposeful atmosphere. Students are given clear guidelines on what is expected in terms of behaviour, homework and so on. If the student challenges the teacher it is likely to be for clarification. At best this means everyone knows where they stand and how to behave. At worst the classroom can resemble a military boot-camp full of restless new recruits, waiting for a chance to mutiny. For the teacher to get the best out of their fundamentally task-focused student they need to:

- Work in ways that test their skill and knowledge competitively (they raise their game for competitions, challenges, quizzes, measuring and beating personal bests).
- Help them understand that 50% of people are **F** preference and can interpret feedback as criticism.
- Focus on what the student has achieved and what comes next.
- Be prepared to compromise occasionally.

- Avoid trying to fix something without considering potential underlying emotional causes.

The **J** teacher takes pleasure in scheduling time. They are organised and decisive. They work out a plan and stick to it, often aided by an impressive to-do list. Their classroom is usually an organised place. The subject will probably be broken down into lesson-sized chunks and the year planned in detail. The **P** student will either respond:

- Positively by accepting your expertise and understanding the long-term benefits they'll reap.
- Passively by just accepting your structure/plan for an easy life without really buying into the content or process you are offering.
- Negatively by rejecting you, your structure/plan and subject completely (even if they're physically in your room they will not engage and participate).

For the teacher to get the best out of their naturally flexible student they should remember the Panther doesn't just crave options and choice; they need them or they start to resist and rebel. The secondary school environment is difficult enough for **P** preference students so teachers can help soften the pressure. To help:

- Shake things up now and again to prevent predictability becoming boredom. Introduce random surprises and changes.
- Help the student identify simple time-management techniques to ensure they can succeed.
- Provide as much flexibility as possible (multiple choice homework tasks, choice within the lesson).
- Avoid giving out detailed schedules (they'll just lose it anyway!).
- Don't be more picky with detail than is absolutely necessary.

250
Barn Owl teacher and Lion student
INTJ and ESFP

Both teacher and student are naturally confident and assertive. They are opposite personality types which can easily lead to misunderstandings. With a little patience they can both learn to enjoy each other's completely different approach to life, learning and school; the Lion breathing fun and flexibility into the organised and driven Barn Owl's classroom. For the teacher to get the best out of their naturally lively student they need to:

- Encourage the student to think things through before talking otherwise they'll hog the lesson.
- Steer the student away from controversial subjects/topics, especially in group discussions.
- Build in plenty of opportunities during lessons for **E** students to talk things through with other **E** preferences.
- Listen patiently and enthusiastically to the student's ideas/brainstorming/ramblings.

- Stay open to 'silly' ideas to see where they lead – the student is thinking out loud and this is how they learn best.
- Also offer your own thoughts; if you need a timeout ask for one.

The imaginative Barn Owl teacher can inspire all students, but they do need to respect the need for Lions to be given clear guidelines, structure, facts, details and procedures, otherwise they can struggle. For the teacher to get the best out of their grounded student they need to:

- Demonstrate how learning can be applied in the real world.
- Allow the student opportunities to repeat and practise until satisfied they are competent.
- Encourage the use of imagination as a useful process (it's not wasting time).
- Be careful not to look like you're favouring **N** students to the detriment of **S** students. Every student needs to be able to contribute in their preferred way.

The teacher is focused first on task and second on people/relationships. The classroom is likely to have a business-like, purposeful atmosphere. Students are given clear guidelines on what is expected in terms of behaviour, homework and so on. At best this means everyone knows where they stand and how to behave. At worst the classroom can resemble a military boot-camp full of dispirited new recruits. Lions benefit most from the opportunity to move around and have a chat with someone to resurrect their enthusiasm and energy. Remember the personal relationship you have with this student is key. The Lion needs to feel they like their teacher and that the teacher likes them too. If this happens they'll work harder; if they don't they may switch off completely. This explains why a student can be top of the class one year (with a teacher they like) and show no interest at all in the subject the following year when they change teacher. For the teacher to get the best out of their intrinsically people-focused student they need to:

- Offer learning situations that allow for the use of empathy, collaboration and teamworking to counter-balance your natural tendency to focus on task.
- Give ample and regular praise while offering tactful support to overcome any blind-spots. Feedback can be easily interpreted as criticism so walk on egg-shells when delivering it.
- Persuade by appealing to the strength of your personal belief in the student (don't let me down, I know you can do it, I like you).
- Be prepared to compromise to prevent a divisive stand-off.

The Barn Owl teacher takes pleasure in scheduling time. They are organised and decisive. They work out a plan and stick to it, often aided by an impressive to-do list. Their classroom is usually an organised place. The subject will probably be broken down into lesson-sized chunks and the year planned out meticulously. The potentially rebellious student will either respond:

- Positively by accepting your expertise and understanding the long-term benefits they'll reap.
- Passively by just accepting your structure/plan for an easy life without really buying into the content or process you are offering.
- Negatively by rejecting you, your structure/plan and subject completely (even if they're physically in your room they will not engage and participate).

For the teacher to get the best out of their naturally laid-back student they should note the student doesn't just like options and choice; they need them or they start to itch, squirm and rebel. The secondary school environment is difficult enough for **P** preference students so teachers can help soften the pressure. To help:

■ Provide as much flexibility as possible (multiple choice homework tasks, choice within the lesson).

■ Avoid giving out detailed schedules (they'll just lose it anyway!).

■ Don't be more picky with detail than is absolutely necessary.

■ Shake things up now and again to prevent predictability becoming boredom. Introduce random surprises and changes.

■ Help the student identify simple time-management techniques to ensure they flourish.

251
Barn Owl teacher and Clownfish student
INTJ and ENFP

Barn Owl teacher and Clownfish student share only one preference **N**, but it is a crucial one. Both endeavour to understand the world by using their active imaginations. At best they will bounce ideas off each other with tenacity and flair. When things go wrong it's usually down to the Clownfish being unable to curb their spontaneity of thought, which can frustrate and disrupt the meticulous planning of the Barn Owl. For the teacher to get the best out of their naturally lively student they need to:

■ Listen patiently and enthusiastically to the student's ideas/brainstorming/ramblings.

■ Steer the student away from controversial subjects/topics, especially in group discussions.

■ Build in plenty of opportunities during lessons for **E** students to talk things through with other **E** preferences.

■ Stay open to 'silly' ideas to see where they lead – the student is thinking out loud and this is how they learn best.

■ Also offer your own thoughts; if you need a timeout ask for one.

■ Encourage the student to think things through before talking otherwise they'll hog the lesson.

Both teacher and student gather information by seeing the big picture first, using hunches, inferences and imagination to generate meaning. The teacher will naturally use their imagination in the classroom and the **N** student will respond well to this, possibly joining in with flights of fancy, anecdotes and stories. A natural affinity between teacher and student is often present because they both look at the world in the same way – with a burning curiosity to understand why things are as they are by exploring patterns, possibilities, ideas and theories. Be careful not to look like you're favouring **N** students to the detriment of **S** students. Every student needs to be able to contribute in their preferred way. For

the teacher to get the best out of their innately imaginative student they need to:

■ Offer questions/projects that can be explored creatively.

■ Avoid repetitive tasks as they'll quickly lose interest.

■ Encourage the student to become aware of the important contribution of the **S** approach (the value of facts, details, procedure, experiments, applying experience, structure, the step-by-step model).

The teacher is focused first on task and second on people/relationships. The classroom is likely to have a business-like, purposeful atmosphere. Students are given clear guidelines on what is expected in terms of behaviour, homework and so on. At its best this means everyone knows where they stand and how to behave. At its worst the classroom can be an oppressive and pernicious prison for the free-spirited Clownfish. Remember the personal relationship you have with this student is key. The Clownfish needs to feel they like their teacher and that the teacher likes them too. If this happens they'll work harder; if not they may switch off completely. This explains why a student can be top of the class one year (with a teacher they like) and show no interest at all in the same subject the following year when they change teacher. For the teacher to get the best out of their naturally people-focused student they need to:

■ Offer learning situations that allow for the use of empathy, collaboration and teamworking to counter-balance your natural tendency to focus on task.

■ Give ample and regular praise while offering tactful support to overcome any blind-spots. Feedback can be easily interpreted as criticism so walk on egg-shells when delivering it.

■ Persuade/influence by appealing to the strength of your personal belief in the student (don't let me down, I know you can do it, I like you).

■ Be prepared to compromise to keep the Clownfish onboard.

The **J** preference Barn Owl takes pleasure in scheduling their time. They are organised and decisive. They work out a plan and stick to it, often aided by an impressive to-do list. Their classroom is usually an organised place. The subject will probably be broken down into lesson-sized chunks and the year planned out whether or not an Ofsted inspection is looming. The **P** preference Clownfish will either respond:

■ Positively by accepting your expertise and understanding the long-term benefits they'll reap.

■ Passively by just accepting your plan for an easy life without really buying into the content or process you are offering.

■ Negatively by rejecting you, your structure/plan and subject completely (even if they're physically in your room they will not engage and participate).

For the teacher to get the best out of their naturally laid-back student they should note the student doesn't just like options and choice; they need them or they start to itch, squirm and rebel. The secondary school environment is difficult enough for **P** preference students so teachers can help soften the pressure. To help:

■ Provide as much flexibility as possible (multiple choice homework tasks, choice within the lesson).

■ Avoid giving out detailed schedules (they'll just lose it anyway!).

■ Don't be more picky with detail than is absolutely necessary.

■ Shake things up now and again to prevent predictability becoming boredom. Introduce random surprises and changes.

■ Offer the student simple time-management tips to ensure they succeed.

252
Barn Owl teacher and Falcon student
INTJ and ENTP

Sherlock Holmes meets Dr Who! The naturally confident and assertive Falcon student has to be handled carefully. Falcon students are often leaders, with their peers ready and eager to follow. It's therefore worth the initial effort to bring these sturdy predators on board. Barn Owls that do so have a charming and witty ally for years ahead. For the teacher to get the best out of their lively student they need to:

■ Listen patiently and enthusiastically to the student's ideas/brainstorming/ramblings.

■ Stay open to 'silly' ideas to see where they lead – the student is thinking out loud and this is how they learn best.

■ Build in plenty of opportunities during lessons for **E** students to talk things through with other **E** preferences.

■ Also offer your own thoughts; if you need a timeout ask for one.

■ Encourage the student to think things through before talking otherwise they'll hog the lesson.

■ Steer the student away from controversial subjects/topics, especially in group discussions.

Both teacher and student gather information by seeing the big picture first, using hunches, inferences and imagination to generate meaning. The teacher will naturally use their imagination in the classroom and the **N** student will respond well to this, possibly joining in with flights of fancy, anecdotes and stories. A natural affinity between teacher and student is often present because they both look at the world in the same way – with a burning curiosity to understand why things are as they are by exploring patterns, possibilities, ideas and theories. Be careful not to look like you're favouring **N** students to the detriment of **S** students. Every student needs to be able to contribute in their preferred way. For the teacher to get the best out of their naturally imaginative student they need to:

■ Offer questions/projects that can be explored creatively.

■ Avoid repetitive tasks as they'll quickly lose interest.

■ Encourage the student to become aware of the important contribution of the **S** approach (the value of facts, details, procedure, experiments, applying experience, structure, the step-by-step model).

Both Barn Owl and Falcon are task-focused, direct, consistent and driven. The classroom is likely to have a business-like, purposeful atmosphere. Students are given clear guidelines on what is expected in terms of behaviour, homework and so on. If the student challenges the teacher it is likely to debate terms! At best this means everyone knows where they stand and how to behave. At worst the classroom can resemble a sanitised production line. For the teacher to get the best out of their fundamentally task-focused student they need to:

■ Work in ways that test their skill and knowledge competitively (they raise their game for competitions, challenges, quizzes, measuring and beating personal bests).

■ Help them understand that 50% of people are **F** preference and can interpret feedback as criticism.

■ Focus on what the student has achieved and what comes next.

■ Be prepared to compromise occasionally.

■ Avoid trying to fix something without considering potential underlying emotional causes.

The Barn Owl teacher takes pleasure in scheduling their time. They are organised and decisive. They work out a plan and stick to it, often aided by an impressive to-do list. Their classroom is usually an organised place. The subject will probably be broken down into lesson-sized chunks and the year planned out with Newtonian precision. The **P** student will either respond:

■ Positively by accepting your expertise and understanding the long-term benefits they'll reap.

■ Passively by just accepting your structure/plan for an easy life without really buying into the content or process you are offering.

■ Negatively by rejecting you, your structure/plan and subject completely (even if they're physically in your room they will not engage and participate).

For the teacher to get the best out of their naturally laid-back student they should note the student doesn't just like options and choice; they need them or they start to itch, squirm and rebel. The secondary school environment is difficult enough for **P** preference students so teachers can help soften the pressure. To help:

■ Provide as much flexibility as possible (multiple choice homework tasks, choice within the lesson).

■ Shake things up now and again to prevent predictability becoming boredom. Introduce random surprises and changes.

■ Help the student identify simple effective strategies to ensure they can succeed.

■ Avoid giving out detailed schedules (they'll just lose it anyway!).

■ Don't be more picky with detail than is absolutely necessary; it will just antagonise and agitate the Falcon.

253
Barn Owl teacher and Black Bear student
INTJ and ESTJ

Barn Owls and Black Bears are both natural leaders. But there can be only one boss in the classroom and the Barn Owl needs to make sure they seize the role. This is best achieved when leading the resolute Black Bear by example. Show the Bear how competent and organised you are and the Bear will concede control. Morsels of appeasement in the form of responsibility will oil the wheels and contribute to a positive relationship. For the teacher to get the best out of their naturally lively student they need to:

■ Listen patiently and enthusiastically to the student's ideas and suggestions.

■ Stay open to 'silly' ideas to see where they lead – the student is thinking out loud and this is how they learn best.

■ Also offer your own thoughts; if you need a timeout ask for one.

■ Encourage the student to think things through before talking otherwise they'll hog the lesson.

■ Steer the student away from controversial subjects/topics, especially in group discussions.

■ Build in plenty of opportunities during lessons for **E** students to talk things through with other **E** preferences.

Barn Owls can inspire all students with their vivid imaginations, but they do need to respect the need for Black Bears to be provided with structure, facts, details and procedures; otherwise they will be lost. For the teacher to get the best out of their grounded student they need to:

■ Demonstrate how learning can be applied in the real world.

■ Allow the student opportunities to repeat and practise until satisfied they are competent.

■ Encourage the use of imagination as a useful process (it's not wasting time).

■ Be careful not to look like you're favouring **N** students to the detriment of **S** students. Every student needs to be able to contribute in their preferred way.

Both teacher and student are task-focused, direct, consistent and objective. The classroom is likely to have a focused atmosphere. Students are given clear guidelines on what is expected in terms of behaviour, homework and so on. If the student challenges the teacher it is likely to be for clarification. At best this means everyone knows where they stand and how to behave. At worst the classroom atmosphere can be stern and stifled. For the teacher to get the best out of their fundamentally task-focused student they need to:

■ Work in ways that test their skill and knowledge competitively (they raise their game for competitions, challenges, quizzes, measuring and beating personal bests).

■ Help them understand that 50% of people are **F** preference and can interpret feedback as criticism.

■ Focus on what the student has achieved and what comes next.

■ Be prepared to compromise occasionally.

■ Avoid trying to fix something without considering potential underlying emotional causes.

The Barn Owl teacher takes pleasure in scheduling their time. They are organised and decisive. They work out a plan and stick to it, often aided by an impressive to-do list. Their classroom is usually an organised place. The subject will probably be broken down into lesson-sized chunks and the year planned out meticulously. Many **J** students are reassured by their teacher's organisational zeal. They simply adopt the schedule and deliver their side of the bargain, generally completing all tasks on time. Interestingly, some **J**'s will baulk at their teacher's well-intentioned thoroughness. They would like to create their own plan and work to it rather than adopt someone else's. This is due to the **J**'s desire for control. So two **J**'s together can spar, though at least all the work will be done. Most secondary schools require students to be so organised that two **J**'s are the best combination. For the teacher to get the best out of their naturally controlled student they need to:

■ Enjoy your shared desire for order, neatness and respecting deadlines.

■ Allow the student independence in planning their work in their own way if they really want to.

■ Be prepared to adjust your own plans if external events interfere with your careful preparations (and encourage the student to also embrace flexibility occasionally).

■ Shake things up now and again to prevent predictability becoming boredom; learning to take things in our stride rather than become flustered is a useful life lesson for both teacher and student.

■ Avoid making quick decisions about what needs to be done before considering all of the options.

254
Barn Owl teacher and Teddy Bear student
INTJ and ESFJ

The Barn Owl teacher can work well with Teddy students. Teddy Bears are keen to please teachers they respect and this can be gained when the teacher uses their shared preference (**J**) for being organised and clear. To get the best out of their naturally lively student the Barn Owl needs to:

■ Listen patiently and enthusiastically to the Teddy's anecdotes and ramblings. They need to socialise before they can settle down to work.

■ Also offer your own thoughts; if you need a timeout ask for one.

■ Encourage the student to think things through before talking otherwise they'll hog the lesson.

■ Steer the student away from controversial subjects/topics, especially in group discussions.

■ Build in plenty of opportunities during lessons for **E** students to talk things through with other **E** preferences.

■ Stay open to 'silly' ideas to see where they lead – the student is thinking out loud and this is how they learn best.

Barn Owls can inspire all students with their vivid imaginations, but they do need to respect the need for Teddy students to be given clear guidelines, structure, facts, details and procedures; otherwise they can flounder. For the teacher to get the best out of their grounded student they need to:

■ Demonstrate how learning can be applied in the real world.

■ Allow the student opportunities to repeat and practise until satisfied they are competent.

■ Encourage the use of imagination as a useful process (it's not wasting time).

■ Be careful not to look like you're favouring **N** students to the detriment of **S** students. Every student needs to be able to contribute in their preferred way.

The teacher is focused first on task and second on people/relationships. The classroom is likely to have a business-like, purposeful atmosphere. Students are given clear guidelines on what is expected in terms of behaviour, homework and so on. At its best this means everyone knows where they stand and how to behave. At its worst the classroom can resemble a military boot-camp full of brow-beaten new recruits. Remember the personal relationship you have with this student is key. The Teddy needs to feel they like their teacher and that the teacher likes them too. If this happens they'll work harder; if not they may switch off. This explains why a student can be top of the class one year (with a teacher they like) and show no interest at all in the subject the following year when they change teacher. For the teacher to get the best out of their fundamentally people-focused student they need to:

■ Offer learning situations that allow for the use of empathy, collaboration and teamworking to counter-balance your natural tendency to focus on task.

■ Give ample and regular praise while offering tactful support to overcome any blind-spots. Feedback can be easily interpreted as criticism so walk on egg-shells when delivering it.

■ Influence by appealing to the strength of your personal belief in the student (don't let me down, I know you can do it, I like you).

■ Be prepared to compromise occasionally.

The **J** teacher takes pleasure in scheduling their time. They are organised and decisive. They work out a plan and stick to it, often aided by an impressive to-do list. Their classroom is usually an organised place. The subject will probably be broken down into lesson-sized chunks and the year planned out in minute detail. Many Teddies are reassured by their teacher's organisational zeal. They simply adopt the schedule and deliver their side of the bargain, generally completing all tasks on time. Interestingly, some **J**'s will baulk at their teacher's well-intentioned thoroughness. They would like to create their own plan and work to it rather than accept someone else's plan. This is due to the **J**'s desire for control. So two **J**'s together can clash, though at least all the work will be done. Most secondary schools require students to be so organised that two **J**'s are the best combination. For the teacher to get the best out of their naturally organised student they need to:

■ Enjoy your shared desire for order, neatness and respecting deadlines.

■ Allow the student independence in planning their work in their own way if they really want to.

■ Be prepared to adjust your own plans if external events interfere with your careful preparations (and encourage the student to also embrace flexibility occasionally).

■ Shake things up now and again to prevent predictability becoming boredom.

■ Avoid making quick decisions about what needs to be done before considering all of the options.

255
Barn Owl teacher and Dolphin student
INTJ and ENFJ

The naturally pleasant Dolphin can gel with all teachers. They share their Barn Owl teacher's imagination and focus on getting the job done. The Dolphin's need to socialise and advocate on behalf of classmates may sometimes create tension, but it's usually well-intentioned and communicated tactfully. For the teacher to get the best out of their naturally enthusiastic student they need to:

■ Listen patiently and enthusiastically to the Dolphin's ideas and stories.

■ Stay open to 'silly' ideas to see where they lead – the student is thinking out loud and this is how they learn best.

■ Also offer your own thoughts; if you need a timeout ask for one.

■ Encourage the student to think things through before talking otherwise they'll hog the lesson.

■ Steer the student away from controversial subjects/topics, especially in group discussions.

■ Build in plenty of opportunities during lessons for **E** students to talk things through with other **E** preferences.

Both teacher and student gather information by immersing themselves in the inner world of their imagination. Both see the big picture first, using hunches, inferences and fantasy to generate meaning. The teacher will naturally use their ingenuity in the classroom and the **N** student will respond well to this, possibly joining in with flights of fancy, anecdotes and stories. A natural affinity between teacher and student is often present because they both look at the world in the same way – with a burning curiosity to understand why things are as they are by exploring patterns, possibilities, ideas and theories. Be careful not to look like you're favouring **N** students to the detriment of **S** students. Every student needs to be able to contribute in their preferred way. For the teacher to get the best out of their inherently imaginative student they need to:

■ Avoid repetitive tasks as they'll quickly lose interest.

■ Encourage the student to become aware of the important contribution of the **S** approach (the value of facts, details, procedure, experiments, applying experience, structure, the step-by-step model).

■ Offering questions and projects that can be explored creatively will also appeal to the student.

The teacher is focused first on task and second on people/relationships. The classroom is likely to have a business-like, purposeful atmosphere. Students are given clear guidelines on what is expected in terms of behaviour, homework and so on. At its best this means everyone knows where they stand and how to behave. Remember, the personal relationship you have with this student is key. The Dolphin needs to feel they like their teacher and that the teacher likes them too. If this happens they'll work harder; if not they may switch off completely. This explains why a student can be top of the class one year (with a teacher they like) and show no interest at all in the same subject the following year when they change teacher. For the teacher to get the best out of their naturally people-focused student they need to:

■ Offer learning situations that allow for the use of empathy, collaboration and teamworking to counter-balance your natural tendency to focus on task.

■ Give ample and regular praise while offering tactful support to overcome any blind-spots. Feedback can be easily interpreted as criticism so walk on egg-shells when delivering it.

■ Persuade by appealing to the strength of your personal belief in the student (don't let me down, I know you can do it, I like you).

■ Be prepared to compromise to avoid unnecessary Dolphin sulks.

The Barn Owl teacher takes pleasure in scheduling their time. They are organised and decisive. They work out a plan and stick to it, often aided by an impressive to-do list. Their classroom is usually an organised place. The subject will probably be broken down into lesson-sized chunks and the year planned out meticulously. Many Dolphin students are reassured by their teacher's organisational fervour. They simply embrace the schedule and deliver their side of the bargain, generally completing all tasks on time. Interestingly, some Dolphins will baulk at their teacher's well-intentioned thoroughness. They would like to create their own plan and work to it rather than adopt someone else's plan. This is due to the **J**'s yearning for control. So two **J**'s together can clash, though at least all their work will be done. Most secondary schools require students to be so organised that two **J**'s are the best combination. For the teacher to get the best out of their intrinsically organised student they need to:

■ Enjoy your shared desire for order, neatness and respecting deadlines.

■ Allow the student independence in planning their work in their own way if they really want to.

■ Be prepared to adjust your own plans if external events interfere with your careful preparations (and encourage the student to also embrace flexibility occasionally).

■ Shake things up now and again to prevent predictability becoming boredom.

■ Avoid making quick decisions about what needs to be done before considering all of the options.

256
Barn Owl teacher and Eagle student
INTJ and ENTJ

The Barn Owl and Eagle are both natural leaders. But there can be only one boss in the classroom and the Barn Owl needs to make sure they capture the role. This is best achieved when leading an Eagle by example. Demonstrate how competent and organised you are and the Eagle will concede control. To get the best out of their innately lively student they can:

■ Listen patiently and enthusiastically to the student's ideas/brainstorming/ramblings.

■ Stay open to 'silly' ideas to see where they lead – the student is thinking out loud and this is how they learn best.

■ Also offer your own thoughts; if you need a timeout ask for one.

■ Encourage the student to think things through before talking otherwise they'll hog the lesson.

■ Steer the student away from controversial subjects/topics, especially in group discussions.

■ Build in plenty of opportunities during lessons for **E** students to talk things through with other **E** preferences.

Both teacher and student gather information by seeing the big picture first, using hunches, inferences and imagination to imbibe meaning. The teacher will naturally use their imagination in the classroom and the **N** student will respond well to this, possibly joining in with flights of fancy, anecdotes and stories. A natural affinity between teacher and student is often present because they both look at the world in the same way – with a burning curiosity to understand why things are as they are by exploring patterns, possibilities, ideas and theories. Be careful not to look like you're favouring **N** students to the detriment of **S** students. Every student needs to be able to contribute in their preferred way. For the teacher to get the best out of their naturally imaginative student they need to:

■ Offer questions/projects that can be explored creatively.

■ Avoid repetitive tasks as they'll quickly lose interest.

■ Encourage the student to become aware of the important contribution of the **S** approach (the value of facts, details, procedure, experiments, applying experience, structure, the step-by-step model).

Both teacher and student are task-focused, direct, firm and honest. The classroom is likely to have a business-like, purposeful atmosphere. Students are given clear guidelines on what is expected in terms of behaviour, homework and so on. If the student challenges the teacher it is likely to be for clarification. At best both know where they stand. At worst the atmosphere can be frosty and resentful. For the teacher to get the best out of their intrinsically task-focused student they need to:

■ Work in ways that test their skill and knowledge competitively (they raise their game for competitions, challenges, quizzes, measuring and beating personal bests).

■ Help them understand that 50% of people are **F** preference and can interpret feedback as criticism.

■ Focus on what the student has achieved and what comes next.

■ Be prepared to compromise to avoid unproductive Eagle strops.

■ Avoid trying to repair something without considering potential underlying emotional causes.

The **J** teacher takes pleasure in scheduling their time. They are organised and decisive. They work out a plan and stick to it, often aided by an impressive to-do-list. Their classroom is usually an organised place. The subject will probably be broken down into lesson-sized chunks and the year planned out whether an Ofsted inspection is due or not. Many Eagles are reassured by their teacher's organisational zeal. They simply adopt the schedule and deliver their side of the bargain, generally completing all tasks on time. Interestingly, some Eagles may reject the well-intentioned thoroughness of their teacher. They would like to create their own plan and work to it rather than adopt someone else's plan. This is due to the Eagle's longing for control. So two **J**'s together can clash, though at least all their work will be done. Most secondary schools require students to be so organised that two **J**'s are the best combination. For the teacher to get the best out of their naturally organised student they need to:

■ Enjoy your shared desire for order, neatness and respecting deadlines.

■ Allow the student independence in planning their work in their own way if they really want to.

■ Be prepared to adjust your own plans if external events interfere with your careful preparations (and encourage the student to also embrace flexibility occasionally).

■ Shake things up now and again to prevent predictability turning to tedium.

■ Avoid making quick decisions about what needs to be done before considering all of the options.

Bibliography

Briggs-Myers, I. (1995) *Gifts Differing: Understanding Personality Type* (Davies-Black).

Bruer, J. T. (1993) *Schools for Thought: A Science of Learning in the Classroom* (MIT Press).

Cotton, K. (1998) *Classroom Questioning* (Northwest Regional Educational Laboratory).

Fuller, C. and Taylor, P. (2008) *A Toolkit of Motivational Skills: Encouraging and Supporting Change in Individuals* (Wiley-Blackwell).

Gilbert, I. (2007) *The Little Book of Thunks: 260 Questions To Make Your Brain Go Ouch!* (Crown House Publishing).

Hammer, A.L. and Kummerow, J.M. (1996) *Strong and MBTI Career Development Guide* (Consulting Psychological Press).

Hicks, B. (2008) *It's Just a Ride.* Available at http://wecanchangetheworld.wordpress.com/2008/03/18/youtube-john-lennon-watching-the-wheels-bill-hicks-its-just-a-ride/ (accessed 13 December 2011).

Higgins, S., Kokotsaki, D. and Coe, R. (2011) *Toolkit of Strategies to Improve Learning: Summary for Schools Spending the Pupil Premium* (Sutton Trust). Available at http://www.suttontrust.com/research/toolkit-of-strategies-to-improve-learning (accessed 22 November 2011).

Hirsh, S. K. and Kise, J. (1996) *Work it Out: Clues for Solving People Problems at Work* (Davies-Black).

Hirsch, S. K. and Kise, J. (2006) *Soul Types: Matching Your Personality and Spiritual Path* (Augsburg Books).

Hodgson, D. (2006) *The Buzz* (Crown House Publishing).

Keirsey, D. (1984) *Please Understand Me: Character and Temperament Types* (Prometheus Nemesis Book Co.).

Kise, J. (2007) *Differentiation through Personality Types: A Framework for Instruction, Assessment, and Classroom Management* (Corwin Press).

Kise, J. and Russell, B. (2008) *Differentiated School Leadership: Effective Collaboration, Communication, and Change through Personality Type* (Corwin Press).

Kise, J., Stark, D. and Hirsch, S. K. (2005) *Discover Who You Are* (Bethany House).

Kline, P. (1991) *Intelligence: The Psychometric View* (Routledge).

Kroegar, O., Thuesen, J. and Rutledge, H. (1998) *Type Talk: The 16 Personality Types that Determine How We Live, Love, and Work* (Tilder Press).

Lawrence, G. (1995) *People Types and Tiger Stripes* (Centre for Applications of Psychological Type).

McKim, R. (1980) *Experiences in Visual Thinking* (Brooks-Cole)

Miller, W. D. and Rollnick, S. (2002) *Motivational Interviewing: Preparing People for Change* (Guildford Press).

Nash, S. (1999) *Turning Team Performance Inside Out* (Davies-Black).

Nash, S. and Bolin, C. (2003) *Teamwork from the Inside Out Fieldbook* (Davies-Black).

O'Connor, J. (2001) *NLP Workbook* (Element).

Robinson, K. (2001) *Out of our Minds: Learning to be Creative* (Capstone).

Rowe, M. B (1986) Wait time: slowing down may be a way of speeding up! *Journal of Teacher Education* 37(1): 43–50.

Royal Society (2011) *Neuroscience: Implications for Education and Lifelong Learning* (Royal Society). Available at http://royalsociety.org/uploadedFiles/Royal_Society_Content/policy/publications/2011/4294975733-With-Appendices.pdf (accessed 22 November 2011).

Russell, M. T. and Karol, D. L. (1994) *16PF5 Administrator's Manual* (NFER-Nelson).

Sivers, D. (2010) *How to Start a Movement.* Available at http://www.ted.com/talks/lang/en/derek_sivers_how_to_start_a_movement.html (accessed 23 November 2011).

Tieger, P. and Barron-Tieger, B. (1997) *Nurture by Nature: Understand Your Child's Personality Type – and Become a Better Parent* (Little, Brown & Co.).

Tieger, P. and Barron-Tieger, B. (1998) *The Art of Speed Reading People: Harness the Power of Personality Type and Create What You Want in Business and in Life* (Little, Brown & Co.).

Tieger, P. and Barron-Tieger, B. (2000) *Just Your Type* (Little, Brown & Co.).

Tieger, P. and Barron-Tieger, B. (2001) *Do What You Are: Discover the Perfect Career for You through the Secrets of Personality Type* (Little, Brown & Co.).

Wiseman, R. (2007) *Quirkology: The Curious Science of Everyday Lives* (Macmillan).

Praise for *Personality in the Classroom*

Personality in the Classroom is another inspirational text from David Hodgson. As a Higher Education and Careers Adviser involved in providing individual guidance, I found Chapter 6 on one-to-one relationships particularly interesting and relevant to my own work with students in a sixth form college.

In this book Hodgson extends the work he started in his first book *The Buzz*, which I use on a daily basis when helping students to choose degree courses and careers. As a Clownfish preference I shall use David's tips when dealing with students of other preferences (we administer the questionnaire with the majority of our students). Knowing their own personality preference is often the first step in helping them make sense of their future path and motivating them towards their goals.

This book encourages teachers to consider their own personality preference in order to understand their pupils. It is a 'must read' for teachers of every age range and I feel that the subtitle describes it in a nutshell: 'Motivating and inspiring every teacher and student'.

**Stella Barnes, Higher Education and Careers Adviser,
Queen Elizabeth Sixth Form College, County Durham**

Personality in the Classroom is a great text for both new and experienced teachers alike. What I found particularly refreshing was the entertaining and often humorous style in which the author's messages are conveyed. Emphasis is placed on the 'how' rather than the 'what' in teaching, which is so important when dealing with today's teenagers if effective teaching is to be achieved.

Hodgson's book encourages both personal and professional development and improvement in a clear and structured way. It positively enforces personal focus and reflection, honing one's awareness of others and the significance of being open-minded and receptive in the classroom.

There is a wealth of fun and interesting activities to utilise in the classroom which will assist teachers in achieving their aims and objectives by using personality types to enhance their teaching outcomes and achieve best practice.

Kam Stylianou, Deputy Headmistress, The Grammar School, Nicosia, Cyprus

Attending David Hodgson's 'Buzz' training was one of the most eye-opening development experiences I've ever had – not just for me, but for the young people I work with who have benefitted from the training indirectly. I regularly refer to *The Little Book of Inspirational Teaching Activities* and *The Buzz Book* on a regular basis, and I intend to make good use of *Personality in the Classroom* to become a more effective educator.

Sam Kalubowila, Widening Participation Coordinator, University of Manchester

David Hodgson's *Personality in the Classroom* has helped me to appraise my own learning preferences. As a direct result I have modified my teaching style to forge stronger relationships with my students. His work has helped explain why some students embrace independent learning tasks whilst others need more support and encouragement to undertake them. Also, why some students crave an opportunity to discuss the topic they are working on whilst others literally groan at the prospect.

I have since modified the teaching activities I use to introduce more role play and I've used a mock trial to add variation and fun. The students were very positive about this. In some instances I have used differentiated learning tasks but with the same core content. Introducing choice can increase cooperation and can have a positive effect on behaviour management, if this is an issue. I have also modified the assessment feedback I give to personalise it as much as possible and to tailor targets to fit the individual. Some students have remarked that they have found this particularly useful.

Finally, I have set up a mentoring group to encourage peer group learning. David comments on how effective peer group learning can be in improving a learner's motivation and achievement. Setting up this group has improved my relationship with the learners. We meet at lunchtimes and the students have a chance to discuss topics more informally and learn from other students nearer their own age.

Lynn Hards, Law Teacher at a sixth form college

David Hodgson's book has helped me understand my own personality type as well as the different personality types of my students and how they interact in the classroom. He explains, with plenty of practical ideas to incorporate in my daily practice, how I can use this understanding to improve my teaching and be able to better respond to all students' needs. He also suggests how one can use the personality type approach to better lead colleagues, whether as a middle leader or head teacher.

**Julia Huber, History Teacher and NQT/PGCE Coordinator,
Southfields Community College, Wandsworth**

I have found reading this book enjoyable and surprisingly quick and easy to relate to. Don't we all love to find out more about ourselves! This is what the first part of the book is about. We then move on to the question of the perfect teacher and then to everyone else. We realise that finding out about ourselves is also about finding out about others.

The best features of this book are the wonderful metaphors and comparisons which make every personality type accessible to the other. We can all relate to someone as an animal – from celebrities to cartoon characters. We can all see, understand and feel where the other is coming from through these comparisons.

This book is not a one-hit wonder; it is a reference book that I will use at all stages of my career. It will be beneficial for NQTs and more experienced classroom teachers as well as senior management teams. I see this book as a quick answer to some complex questions: How do I deal with a student or colleague with a personality type different to mine? How do I teach a group in such as way as to reach successfully as many students as possible? This book provides an almost never-ending wealth of resources and ideas to use in order to become not only the best teacher but also the best human being I can be. It is all too easy to give in to personal learning preferences; it takes more effort to actually understand how others learn and cater for each and every one of them. This book has taught me it is possible.

The most interesting aspect for me is the chapter on playfulness. As adults, play is often considered as childish; however it forms an important part of teaching and learning. The fun activities outlined in Chapter 3 can be used in any subject classroom, but the techniques suggested for developing creative thinking fitted perfectly with teaching students to talk about the world around them in a foreign language. Many of the activities create the perfect learning environment effortlessly and students learn without even noticing they are learning. I have transferred the same techniques used in the classroom into my departmental meetings, and the same thing happened. Instead of being viewed as long and boring they became more fun and everyone gets a chance to shine, whatever their personality type.

In the MFL classroom the Snowman activity was a hit! Not only did students get to write a creative essay as per syllabus but they also found out about themselves and each other. The Story by Numbers activity worked in a similar way. I also found the teacher–student personality type comparison in Chapter 6 extremely helpful. As a quick reference guide on a daily basis or giving feedback to a certain personality type student I found it easy to use and effective.

This book has been an invaluable resource to developing a more personal type of teaching by tailoring my teaching and management style to each and everyone's needs. As a Black Bear myself, prone to offending people around me and also to intolerance (having high standards and expecting everyone else to work to the same standards!) I have learnt to soften some of the harshest features about myself, thus making the most of my relationships.

David simply is a facilitator. He opens our eyes about personality types – making the 'other' less scary and more accessible. We learn about ourselves and each other in an effortless way, thus making us more tolerant of other people and getting the best out of all our relationships. This book does not stop in the classroom. It helps us become tolerant human beings as well. I cannot wait to share it with my students, colleagues, friends and family.

**Malika Power, Head of Modern Foreign Languages, Duke of Kent School, Surrey;
GCSE and A level examiner at a major examination board**

Also by David Hodgson

The Buzz
A practical confidence builder for teenagers

The Buzz is the companion to *Personality in the Classroom* designed for the student and uses NLP and personality type theory to inform and motivate them to make positive life choices.

isbn 978-190442481-9 also available in eBook formats

The Buzz - Audiobook
A practical confidence builder for teenagers

Selected highlights from *The Buzz* narrated by the author.

isbn 978-184590043-4

The Little Book of Inspirational Teaching Activities
Bringing NLP into the Classroom

A collection of activities developed and used with teenagers all over the country that are short, easy to follow and engaging.

isbn 978-184590136-3 also available in eBook formats

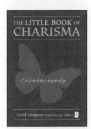

The Little Book of Charisma

The book is a breathless, informative and funny journey through factors contributing to excellence in communication.

isbn 978-184590293-3 also available in eBook formats

Magic of Modern Metaphor
Walking with the Stars

A wonderful collection of stories for teachers, trainers, parents and thinkers sharing ancient wisdom through a modern relationship between grandson and grandad.

isbn 978-184590394-7 also available in eBook formats

With Dave Keeling

Invisible Teaching
101ish ways to create energy, openness and focus in the classroom

A book of new fast, fun activities, requiring little or no set-up, that increase the energy, openness and focus of students (and teachers) and promote a positive and focused classroom atmosphere.

isbn 978-184590685-6 also available in eBook formats

www.crownhouse.co.uk

Personality in the Classroom Events

As well as writing books, David Hodgson delivers inspirational training events across the UK and abroad. He works with schools, colleges and universities to help boost the confidence and achievement of staff and students alike.

Inspiring INSET, conference input, student events and training to:

- Discover and enhance your natural teaching strengths
- Help every student make progress by truly personalising learning
- Improve communication, behaviour, motivation and learning
- Balance the right levels of energy, creativity, resilience and control in each lesson
- Reduce stress and boredom by stretching all students
- Develop your Leadership skills and style

Feedback from conferences, INSET days and student events:

Attending David's training was one of the most eye-opening development experiences I've ever had - not just for me, but the young people I work with.

David was fantastic at the Heads' Conference. The feedback was universally outstanding.

A terrific and inspirational presentation, we felt energised and motivated.

Your presentation was well pitched, mixing humour with a definite message on how Governors' attitudes and beliefs can impact on the positive learning of others

Students and staff were buzzing with talk of brain techniques and personalities.

Thanks again for a brilliant morning affirming the awesome responsibility we have as teachers in getting children to believe in themselves and go for their dreams!

To find out more about David's work or book him for an event contact Independent Thinking Ltd on 08445 890490 or see www.thebuzzbook.co.uk

Quote **'Personality in the Classroom'** and each delegate will qualify for a free personality profiling booklet.